Messina's Federal Budget

Christopher J.A. Messina

ISBN: 979-8-9904951-2-8

This book is dedicated to my children Aiya, Malachi and Hannah and my wife Rebecca, all of whom have endured, er, been treated to many a spontaneous rant, er, calmly considered disquisition about the topics covered in this book.

To my fellow Americans: May our Grand Experimental Republic endure another 248 years.

"No man is really free who is afraid to speak the truth as he knows it, or who is too fearful to take a stand for that which he knows is right. Every man has his Gethsemane."
-       Benjamin Elijah Mays

"The search for happiness is not about looking at life through rose-colored glasses or blinding oneself to the pain and imperfections of the world... It is the purging of mental toxins, such as hatred and obsession, that literally poison the mind."
-       Matthieu Ricard

"The main obstacle to progress is not ignorance but the illusion of knowledge."
-       Ron Graham

"People will forgive you for being wrong, but they will never forgive you for being right – especially if events prove you right while proving them wrong."
-       Thomas Sowell

"If any man is able to convince me and show me that I do not think or act right, I will gladly change; for I seek the truth, by which no man was ever injured. But he is injured who abides in his error and ignorance."
-       Marcus Aurelius

"One of the great mistakes is to judge policies and programs by their intentions rather than their results."
-       Milton Friedman

Contents

The government fails to do dozens of things that people want it to and think it does. The government does thousands of things that normal citizens don't know about, are astonished to discover and feel betrayed by.

The good news is that we as Americans can change all that.

What follows describes how.

Introduction

I started writing this book in the spring of 2009. I did so with the conceit that I was penning something brand new and revolutionary. I wanted to be applauded for creating a brilliant flash of insight, to be packaged eventually in a three-volume set with Adam Smith's *The Wealth of Nations* and Montesquieu's *L'Esprit des Lois*. After the years I have taken to research and write this book, I don't care about that. With the time I have spent reviewing the thoughts, opinions and suggestions of others, I have come to see that what I really have written is a political book. While being praised for crafting a startlingly fresh take on the public fisc might do my ego some good, it would not make this whole effort worthwhile.

I want this book to be effective. I want it to be read, enjoyed, critiqued and most importantly *applied*. I want the ideas presented here to be a focusing point for the incredibly important American public. Each of us is trying his or her best to build something for ourselves, our families and communities. The grand experiment of American republican representative democracy has sputtered along for more than two centuries. We should take the objective lessons learned during this experiment and use those data to course-correct before our current trajectory leaves the American Experiment one more shattered failure on the rocky, indifferent shores of history.

What started as an expression of indignant rage at a shoddy system co-opted by mediocre if cunning parasites, has evolved I hope into a roadmap of reasoned and practicable steps we as a nation can take to fix the main problems which are holding us back. I want this book to be a useful guide for my fellow Americans, so that we may effectively erect and maintain a fair system of clear rules that all of us can abide by on our way to crafting free choices for ourselves.

The work of creating a "more perfect union" is never finished. This book is my attempt to make it simpler for all Americans to participate in that ongoing project.

Plenty of books and articles have been written about the horrid abuses by people who *claim* to be working in "public service." And yet – nothing much seems to be changing. Part of what I as a creator, advisor and manager of enterprises both large and small have always told my employees and colleagues: I don't want to hear about a problem until you've also at least given some thought to what a solution could look like. Many people – me included – have been appalled at one or another outrageous news item concerning the people running "our" government for their own aggrandizement, and thereby our country into the ground.

Part of what any bureaucratic entity's employees *count on* is that the problem appears too big and complicated. When public outrage rears its temporary head, they'll just put on some more magic shows and give out some more goodies, knowing that when the current crisis has passed, Americans will sink bank into their couches to have a beer and watch some TV.

The Caesars called this "bread and circuses," and unfortunately for much of human history, this approach has worked really well. Given the scale of the world crises and the colossal mismanagement of the American Experiment under a bipartisan pack of self-interested, ego-fueled, self-aggrandizing parasites, we are at a moment in time when things are *so stressful* and out of whack, that there is an opportunity for brave individuals to stand up and demand a real change. Not campaign slogan change, but real, fundamental modifications to improve our system of government for the long-term, not a periodic shouting session of competitive lying, er, election cycle.

I have been writing this book for so long that one of the later drafts (circa October 2012) of this introduction contained this line: *Now is the time in this coming election for us to enact a true, sweeping reordering of our government to put the country back onto a truly sustainable trajectory.*

Tragedy Plus Time = Comedy.

What was true in 2012 is – amazingly enough – even *more* true in 2024. Back in 2012, no one would have believed a pack of sociopathic liars could have seized control of 48 State governments and the Executive Branch of the Federal Government to shut down the entire economy and ruin children's lives for no reason whatsoever.

My purpose is not to create yet another laundry list of complaints and criticisms, designed to provide the reader a dopamine rush of temporary outrage. In my desire to create a useful roadmap for fiscal and social strength, I have written a blueprint for *true* change in our Nation's direction. Every idea contained in this book can be questioned, challenged and debated, a debate which I welcome. The *overall framework* represents a true change of direction which is reason for *real* hope, not the vaporware offered by the narcissists who have seized the political stage in the Era of Soundbites. Americans need real, reasoned debate, peppered with civility. That means supposed adult "leaders" *not* tapping 280 snarky characters into their social media accounts, and all of us ignoring, repudiating and denouncing the screaming mobs in the streets that turned the summer of 2020 and January 6th 2021 into a tangible demonstration of the damage caused over the decades by the very ills I diagnose in the following pages.

The great misfortune of America's postwar history has been an unprecedented but illusory "prosperity" based on a level of consumer-product creation and availability. Whether you believe that God created the universe and humanity 6,000 years ago or that all of what you see around you is the product of millions of years of evolution, it seems clear that the burst of economic activity from 1945 to the present has done significant damage to the morale and certainly the physical wellbeing of Americans.

One of the more interesting facets of the human animal is that we thrive under *natural amounts* of adversity and pressure. With no threats and no tension, we lose our edge and begin to decay. There were no 1,000-lbs humans whining about their lives on the African savannah 10,000 years ago.

The citizens of the United States of America today have an excellent opportunity to recommit to a vision of a country which sprang into being as an *idea* of how people can best willingly and freely organize themselves as a society. We can slough off the accretions of two centuries of efforts – some well-intended, others surely not so – to micromanage every aspect of our lives. With a commitment to public sector *restraint* and individual responsibility, we can put ourselves on the best possible footing to provide for the optimal level of individual freedom *and* the optimal level of national cohesion and advancement.

Secondly, in large part I've written this book as a way of cleansing my palate of all the extreme distaste caused by witnessing and studying decades of political arrogance, hubris and ignorance. I am not alone in my disgust; it has been amply echoed for years now. Aristotle was one of the first to point out to us that the reason people go to the theatre (or the movies or binge watch TV dramas) is for an experience of emotional relief. He called it *catharsis*, which is fair enough as he was Greek; I'm calling it *getting it all off my chest.*

Thirdly, I hope what I present here is a clear, concise and robust rebuttal to all of those who are willing to sacrifice *your* freedom for *their* Utopian micro-managed visions of what *everyone else* should do with *your* stolen time, freedom and money.

Lastly, this book should be *actionable and practical.* If you agree with my proposed reorganization of our national budget and governmental structure, you can write "I support Messina's Federal Budget. Vote accordingly or you'll be gone in the next election," on a postcard to your elected representatives. There is a straight line available to you from reading my suggestions to demanding concrete action from your government. No waffling, no wondering "How do I do something about this latest piece of news I just got about corruption and waste." I'm providing the concrete plan; if you agree with it, just demand it be implemented.

If you don't agree *in toto,* I'd love to hear what parts you like, what parts you hate. That's how discussion happens.

Every action starts in part as a reaction to another. In my case, it was in a hotel room in London in September 2008. I was in London for work, and in the space of five minutes, I had two very contrasting pictures of the world.

In the first, as London is five hours ahead of New York, I was on the phone saying good night to my three-year-old daughter who was crying because she didn't understand why Daddy couldn't be home to kiss her good night as I did when I could get home in the evenings. I had to eventually hang up the phone after failing to comfort a despondent child who didn't understand why her father had to be far away in order to earn the money required to feed and house her.

Minutes later, there was Candidate Obama on the TV, excoriating "the rich" and "Wall Street bankers." As I listened to him tell me I was an evil person for working hard to feed my family, I recalled – funnily enough in retrospect – an old episode of *The Cosby Show* in which Dr. Huxtable was telling his son Theo that "You're not rich. Your mother and I are rich. *You* have nothing." He was interrupted by his lawyer wife, who corrected him saying, "We're not rich. 'Rich' is when the money works for you. We work *hard* for the money."

Obama is a typical parasitic politician, the large group who have willfully destroyed our societal goodwill and economic prosperity, all to line their own pockets. The pack of politicians who have driven us towards a financial nightmare are not only fiscally imprudent but downright immoral. *All* freewheeling spenders of other people's money create a false debate between Caring People Who Love the Common Man versus Those Evil Number

Crunchers Who Care More About the Value of The Dollar Than Poor Working People. It's nonsense, designed solely to keep themselves in office and on the taxpayer gravy train.

What those of us who understand the limits of economic activity are trying to tell the American citizenry is that if the government writes a check with its mouth, your ass will end up cashing it. Not just the "rich" guy down the street that may irritate you, or those mean "bankers" in New York. Nope. You, sir, and you, madam, are going to pay for all this insanity. Given the greater mobility of people with a lot of capital, those "rich" folks that Barry Hussein Soetoro Obama, Bernie Sanders, Joe Biden and Hillary Clinton tell you they're going to stick it to are more able to simply up stakes and leave this country for one that will let them keep their assets intact.

Just as one cannot legislate morality, one cannot mandate a financial outcome by wishing it were so or voting it into Law. Just because a politician promises public sector unions that "you can retire after 20 years of work and we'll give you a pension equal to 95% of your last year's salary for the rest of your life" does *not* mean that the hardworking taxpayers who must pay for that government promise 20 or 50 years from now will be able to afford that promise.

When that moment arrives – and it has – and the bill comes due, current taxpayers are sending money straight through the government coffers to retirees not providing any benefit to the citizenry. So *current* students in schools get fewer services, *current* trash does not get picked up as frequently, *current* criminals are not apprehended by the police and in general *current* services are sacrificed because of promises made by politicians long out of office. Every dollar that is taken from immediate tax receipts and shot out the door to a *former* government employee erodes the level of services, safety and quality of life of that community.

Lastly, there is a serious moral and existential cause for us to reorient our thinking about government and society. As Lawrence Lessig points out, "[t]he great threat to our republic today comes not from the hidden bribery of the Gilded Age, when cash was secreted among members of Congress to buy privilege and secure wealth. The great threat today is in plain sight. It is the economy of influence now transparent to all. [...] For the single most salient feature of the government that we have evolved is not that it discriminates in favor of one side and against the other. [I]t discriminates against all sides to favor itself."[1]

Given that we will always have some kind of government, the best way we can refresh the American Experiment to embark on the next 200 years of self-governance is to keep the mental models that have proven their value and to jettison or modify those that seemed useful but whose results have created the problems we now face. Edward O. Wilson wrote a beautiful book, *Consilience: The Unity of Knowledge*, published in 1998, in which he among other things describes how complex biological systems possessed of conscious self-awareness arrange themselves. He contends from his viewpoint of a student of biological systems that humanity has "thought" itself to a current state of problems across societies

---

[1] Lessig, Lawrence, Republic, Lost; How Money Corrupts Congress – and a Plan to Stop It, 2011, p.7

and that the solution to fixing many of the major issues we face at the global level requires humanity to be self-aware enough of the way our mental models bring about outcomes.

Neoclassical economics is what we have today, but there was one more overlapping period, the Era of Model Building, that brought it to fruition. Beginning in the 1930s, theorists added linear programming, game theory and other powerful mathematical and statistical techniques in their efforts to simulate the economic world in ever finer detail. Invigorated by a sense of their own exactitude, they continued to return to the themes of equilibria and perturbations from equilibria. They specified, as faithfully as they could, supply and demand, impulses of firms and consumers, competition, market fluctuations and failures, and the optimal uses of labor and resources.

The cutting edge of economic theory today [1998; in 2020 that is no longer true academically or on Wall Street, but is still true for government, including the Federal Reserve] remains the equilibrium models of neoclassical theory. The emphasis is always on rigor. Analysts heartily agree with Paul Samuelson, one of the most influential economists of the twentieth century, that "economics focuses on concepts that can actually be measured."

Therein lie the strengths and weaknesses of present-day economic theory. Because its strengths have been abundantly celebrated by legions of textbook writers and journalists, let me dwell on the weaknesses. They can be summarized in two labels: Newtonian and hermetic. Newtonian, because economic theorists aspire to find simple, general laws that cover all possible economic arrangements. Universality is a logical and worthy goal, except that the innate traits of human behavior ensure that only a minute set of such arrangements is probable or even possible. Just as the fundamental laws of physics cannot be used alone to build an airplane, the general constrictions of equilibrium theory cannot be used alone to visualize an optimal even stable economic order. The models also fall short because they are hermetic – that is, sealed off the from the complexities of human behavior and the constraints imposed by the environment. As a result, economic theorists, despite the undoubted genius of many, have enjoyed few successes in predicting the economic future, and they have suffered many embarrassing failures.

...

But the theorists cannot answer definitively most of the key macroeconomic questions that concern society, including the optimal amount of fiscal regulation, future income distribution within and between nations, optimal population growth and distribution, long-term financial security of individual citizens, the roles of soil, water, biodiversity and other exhaustible and diminishing resources, and the strength of "externalities" such as the deteriorating global environment. The world economy is a ship speeding through uncharted waters strewn with dangerous shoals. There is no general agreement on how it works. The esteem that economists enjoy arises not so much from their record of successes as from the fact that business and government have nowhere else to turn.[2]

---

[2] Wilson, Edward O., *Consilience*, 1998, pp.214-15

13

Wilson – whose academic and professional focus lies outside of economics and finance – hits if not the bullseye, at least the ring surrounding the bullseye when he identifies the flawed premises on which so many important and very expensive decisions are made. I touch further on in this book the reactions to the overspecification and simplistic mathematics that lie behind neoclassical economics, including why the field of Behavioral Economics has been demonstrated to much more honestly and clearly model actual human behavior. The point that is relevant here is that we have allowed our government to make decisions based on intellectual models of the world which are flawed, which have therefore resulted in suboptimal outcomes for our budget and society. No one set out to make bad policy; in most cases, a lot of thought and hard work went into creating some good first approximations of useful models. Human nature being what it is, those models were then allowed to become the rule rather than just a tool.

In that sense, the entirety of government has become populated by sorcerer's apprentices – invoking from rote memorization old spells and theories as fact instead of the working models and trial ideas they were originally intended to be.

Part of the answer I am hoping to illuminate for my fellow citizens is that government need not rely on outdated economic models to make our collective decisions. We can change course, starting by choosing better models to use for our decision making. Happily for us all, Wilson emphasized the four characteristics by which a model may be judged for its utility in serious problem solving:

1. Parsimony – the fewer the units and processes used to account for the modeled phenomenon, the better.
2. Generality – the greater the range of phenomena covered by the model, the more likely it is to be true.
3. Consilience – units and processes of a discipline that conform with solidly verified knowledge in other disciplines have proven consistently superior in theory and practice to units and processes that do not so conform.
4. Predictiveness – if all three of the above characteristics are adhered to, then this definitive quality by which one judges a model is more likely to be proven by observation and experiment.

It is crucial for our nation's continued positive development that we look critically at the models we use to make decisions about our budget and taxation policies. Throughout this book, I make the case that parsimony and humility in the face of complexity are the rock-solid foundations of an enduring new way to look at funding our government. As it has proven impossible to predict with any accuracy the impacts of various complex interventions in our economy and society, the best thing for us all to do is to chop the Federal Government down to a much smaller set of critical functions, which we can work to make operate well. We must insist that Washington quit doing thousands of other things that the Federal Government has only done and will continue to do poorly.

The serious problem our nation faces right now at all levels of government is that the promises that have been made are outrageous enough that without a *genuine* restructuring and an *honest* appraisal of both the limits and roles of government, those promises will have to be broken. One does not have to look far to see real-life examples of this kind of governmental betrayal of promises. Across the United States, school districts are trying to raise teachers' pay, a wonderful and proper use of taxpayer funds. The horrible thing that thousands of school districts are finding is that even when more money is shoveled at teacher pay, there is very little rise in teacher salaries.

To grab one article at random, from 30 September 2019:

A record number of American public-school teachers have walked off the job over the past two years—and now another strike looms in Chicago. Chief among the teachers' demands is higher pay. They're often right—teacher pay is too low—but for the wrong reasons.

Teachers and their unions typically attribute low salaries to flat or falling state spending on education, with skinflint politicians to blame. But in most places education spending is rising. It isn't showing up in teachers' paychecks because so much of it gets diverted to pay for expensive retirement benefits for former teachers. Politicians' overly generous past promises, sometimes made at the behest of teachers unions, are now coming back to bite the education sector.

The Chicago Public Schools have a pension shortfall of $11 billion. Retirement costs devour more than 25% of the money the system receives from the state. Such costly benefits constrain it and other school systems from offering higher salaries to teachers, increasing support staff, and reducing class sizes. This is the under-the-radar driver of teacher protests in Arizona, West Virginia, Kentucky, Oklahoma, Colorado and North Carolina and cities such as Los Angeles and Denver.

For years, states and school districts didn't save enough money to cover the retirement promises they made to teachers. Now the bills are coming due. They have to be paid; strong contractual protections mean that outside of bankruptcy it is legally impossible to reduce these pensions. It is also morally difficult to cut retiree medical coverage for midcareer employees who have been planning on receiving it.

Today nearly 90% of teachers participate in defined-benefit pension plans. According to a report by the National Council on Teacher Quality, a Washington-based nonprofit, these plans have total estimated unfunded liabilities of more than $500 billion. Consequently most employer contributions aren't saved for future retirees but used to pay off debt. In Arizona 82.7% of the employer contributions to the teacher pension system goes to paying off unfunded liabilities. Chad Alderman of Bellwethers Education Partners, an education policy group, estimates that West Virginia teachers forgo compensation equivalent to more than 20% of their salaries to pay down pension debt.

The cost of providing health insurance for retired teachers has also been rising. By 2016 states and localities were on the hook for about $231 billion in unfunded non-pension benefit liabilities for teachers and other public-education employees. Because the Los Angeles Unified School District covers retirees, its high health-care costs—$2,300 of the $16,000 it spends per pupil—prevent it from offering teachers even higher salaries.[3]

---

[3]   https://www.wsj.com/articles/teachers-want-higher-pay-but-pensions-swallow-up-the-money-11569885425?mod=hp_opin_pos_1

That one issue – the structure of compensation for teachers – demonstrates the problems associated with letting politicians get too cute with how to pay for things. The best way for anyone to pay for anything is with cash on the spot. Anything else turns into a potentially horrible mess of credit defaults and angry people who've been promised something that thirty years later they find out they're not going to get.

The period around 2008 witnessed a lot of personal pain caused by bad government decisions. Greece was a particularly glaring example. Decades of freewheeling spending combined with the harsh dictates of quitting the drachma for the euro meant that after painful fiscal changes were implemented, it resulted in draconian cuts to the purchasing power of Greek pensions. It was heartbreaking to witness the interviews of uneducated Greeks who were promised pensions and were having their power, water and cash turned off as result of demands for fiscal austerity from Germany. But unlike Hollande, Chavez, Obama, Clinton, Trump, Biden and Schumer, millions of rational people understand that just because a politician promises the sun won't come up tomorrow, it doesn't mean it'll be dark forever.

The core thesis of this book is that there exists today in the USA a fundamental mistaken interpretation of the means and ends of government. That fundamental error combined with a deep incomprehension *at the individual citizen's level* of the true meaning of rights and responsibilities has led us towards economic and therefore social ruin. This is not unique to the United States, of course, but other nations' headaches are their own and I do not presume to address them here. This error is not a mistake – it is a deliberate attempt by a small number of people to steal control and power over this nation, a project they've been working on for decades and are close to perfecting.

Lest anyone view this as yet another partisan pamphlet, I want to make something perfectly clear. I am disgusted and appalled equally by almost *all* the political and *most* of the bureaucratic class of this once-rich nation. I don't see the need to split hairs on what is more absurd and awful, Nancy Pelosi's bizarre Bay Area idea that any kind of tax can be "pro-growth," or George W. Bush's insane preoccupation in a post-9/11 world with a *Constitutional Amendment* to ban marriage between two men or two women. Each is an example of both serious stupidity and a deliberate misunderstanding of the role of true *public servants* who should be acting in strict accordance with the Constitution, and not as architects of their version of micromanaged social outcomes.

To take very recent events as of this writing, the massive destruction that all levels of government in true bipartisan fashion foisted on us in their hyper overreaction to the Wuhan Flu Panic of 2020, proves my point that *the entire political class* has proven its worthlessness and its collective willingness to do serious economic, physical, mental and emotional damage to American citizens, if only they can keep their sweaty paws on the levers of power a little bit longer.

Since our elected officials through myriad acts of commission or omission have in the aggregate proved themselves to be less honest and trustworthy *by far* than a Nevada brothel manager, it is the unfortunate civic duty of those of us competent with big budgets and the management of complex systems to step forward and proffer some solutions to our going-rapidly-broke nation.

I have better things to do. When I began this book, I had a business to run, shareholders' interests to look out for, competitors to destroy, employees to lead and a family to raise. On top of all of that, I needed to get to the gym and eat right so the stress of fighting off the various and pointless "regulatory" bullies in Washington and Albany didn't rob my children of their daddy before his time.

During the course of writing this book, through their sweeping collective ignorance and arrogance, combined with powers we the people should never have given them, Chris Dodd, Barney Frank and Barack Obama took away the business I was running, so some of that list changed. Being a resilient person, I stood back up again and moved on to other ventures, but I will tell the story of the value destruction *my shareholders and employees* experienced at the hands of the dumbest law in decades. Multiply my experience by hundreds of thousands of businesses, and you'll understand my contention that the Federal Government in its present form is a destructive tool far more often than a helpful one.

You may be one of those people who say, "I have no interest in politics." That may well be true, but politicians certainly have an interest in *you*. If you feign indifference and don't bother to find out what these clowns are up to and then vote to stop them, then you can be very sure that even while you're sticking your head in the sand because you're "not interested," there's a horde of people who are sticking their hands into your wallet and telling you what color you're allowed to paint "your" house. The only way to ensure your indifference to politics is matched by politics being indifferent to you is to spend the minimal amount of time required to push back at the relentless attacks on your freedom.

Not paying attention and not bothering to vote are akin to living in a plywood shack on a beach in Florida with a Category 5 Hurricane bearing down on you and saying, "I have no interest in the weather."

There is a great passage in Douglas Adams's *The Restaurant at the End of the Universe*. One of the main protagonists of the work, Ford Prefect, is stranded on pre-historic Earth and is seeing how long he can sit quietly while a group of complete morons holds their town meeting. He makes it about twelve seconds, after hearing their completely pointless, idiotic blather. I have felt the same way for years, watching the people who were elected to be useful civil servants preen themselves as if they were rulers, not servants.

I have decided to sacrifice my time and offer my skills and experience in helping my country out of its fiscal mess. This book was started right around the time the Obama budget proposal was floated in late 2010. I needed statins, aspirin, soothing music and a quiet, darkened room just to get through the first paragraph of President Obama's 2011 Budget Proposal without having a stroke. That reading was my inspiration to write this book.

It has taken me a longer time to write – note the other, far more pressing things on my plate mentioned above – than anticipated. I have chosen to focus the specifics of my suggested alternative Federal budget on the 2012 budget, though I dip into the tasty offerings provided in other governmental budgets. The details differ, of course, but the substance of the work does not. My critique of Obama's, Trump's and Biden's budgets lies not in the details but in the fundamentally wrongheaded view of government and the American social contract those budgets represent. While their budgets have been sweeping in their growth of government, they are in keeping with the budgets of the prior twenty years.

I propose here a wholesale reorganization of our governmental structure to offer Americans – perhaps for the first time ever – a truly objective and fairly-administered system of Justice and Fisc that *all* people can rely on as a truly level playing field of opportunity.

Along the way, I have tried my best to listen to and read the opinions of people who define themselves to be squarely opposed to all of what I consider best about America. Some of these people I have known well or slightly over the years and some I don't know personally at all.

I have dipped into the musings of Paul Krugman – who, so far as I can discern, is a committed performance artist of the first water whose tenure at the forefront of saying ridiculously outrageous things with a straight face has by now eclipsed that of Andy Kaufman's impressive run. From his perch on the *New York Times* opinion pages, never mind his role as a professor of economics at Princeton, Krugman has infected more Upper West Side of Manhattan minds than almost anyone else aside from Woody Allen.

I have even with red pen in hand and astonishment splashed across my mien read *Freefall* by Joseph Stiglitz.

Reading Krugman and Stiglitz reminds me of nothing so much as the kinds of doctors referred to in *The King's Speech*.[4] In a scene fairly early in the movie, as the future King, Prince Albert (capably played by Colin Firth) is having his first session with the speech therapist Logue (inspiringly played by Gregory Rush), the Prince lights a cigarette, which Logue tells him to extinguish:

Logue:	I believe sucking smoke into your lungs will kill you.
Duke:	My physicians say it relaxes the throat.
Logue:	They're idiots.
Duke:	They've all been knighted.
Logue:	Makes it official, then.

I try very hard to understand the perspectives offered by those writers, even while assuming (largely based on their own spite-filled utterances and writings) that they would not likely afford me the same courtesy. Without dwelling overmuch on their writing, it will be necessary from time to time to point to examples of their assertions to paint a clear picture of how we as a nation have gotten ourselves into such a mess.

Similarly, I have tried courageously to understand what series of assumptions lie behind the statements from politicians I find baffling. In New York, there is (or was – how fickle the Internet can render one's Fate) a Congressional Representative from Queens named Anthony Weiner. He was on a NY1 political talk show in March 2011 and I found his comments about tax cuts "for the rich" illuminating. It seemed clear from his comments that he doesn't understand that people with large cash flows are sources of *investment,* not simply consumers buying stuff.

He made the case against tax cuts by saying, "Well, if someone at the top end of the income scale gets more money back from the government," – leaving aside the *a priori* mistake about the proper directionality of ownership of wealth creation in this country –

---

[4] *The King's Speech,* directed by Tom Hooper, 2010

18

"that person is not likely to spend that money and contribute to GDP, they're just going to save it."

He literally doesn't get it. One company I co-founded and ran for 3.5 years, for example, was completely funded from private individuals who wrote post-tax checks to fund our operations. In Weiner's world, those private investors creating new jobs just don't exist – the only thing individuals can do is spend money as consumers. Investment in the universe inhabited by Anthony Weiner is done by some vague, impersonal force, *not* by entrepreneurial individuals. Which is funny, because in his response he *almost* shows he understands this. He gets that people save money, but he does not make the next logical step that the saving is in fact capital creation which leads to more investment in new businesses.

Of course, in retrospect, he didn't have time to learn difficult concepts about how the market economy works as he was too busy living off the taxpayers while sending pictures of his crotch to teenage girls. One of the benefits that has accrued to me while writing this book is that it has taken so long to get down on paper, that from the time I wrote the preceding sentence, the aptly named Weiner *decided to run for Mayor of New York City.*

His decision to run for mayor along with his belief that not only should he not be forever ashamed of his appallingly anti-social behavior, but that he by any stretch of the imagination is *qualified* to be mayor of New York City is almost the *perfect example* of everything I point to in this book about the nature of the sociopathic narcissists who run for office in this once-proud nation.

After being exposed[5] – heh, heh – as a continuing phone-sex addict calling himself "Carlos Danger" married to Hillary Clinton's aide-de-camp Huma Abedin, he lost the mayoral Democratic primary, by the way, to Bill de Blasio, a man who supported the Communist killing machine of the *Sandinistas* in Nicaragua in the 1980s, honeymooned in Cuba, and who ran a campaign comprised of vilifying the New York Police Department for supposed and unproven "racism." My fellow citizens went on to make this guy mayor, and as of this writing continue to reap the whirlwind as the hard-won gains of twenty years of work by Mayors Giuliani and Bloomberg unravel daily.

Comedy Minus Time = Tragedy.

I got some of the most astonishing eye-openers from Joseph Stiglitz's book *Freefall: America, Free Markets, and the Sinking of the World Economy,* published in 2010. It is truly breathtaking in its sweep, arrogance and its complete and utter misrepresentation of the causes of the "crisis" of 2007-08. At various points I will touch on Stiglitz's bizarre and unfounded claims and tortured "analyses" which so far as I can tell began with a desired political end in mind and then worked backwards to force selective data to tell an incomplete and ultimately proven empirically to be incorrect view of the causes and effects

---

[5] During the filming of *Weiner,* directed by Josh Kriegman, Elyse Steinberg, 2016, which followed him during his primary run. Get some popcorn and watch it. OMG. Just wowzers.

of the period. He is worth quoting extensively because he is taken so seriously by at least one political faction and therefore ideas like his have contributed mightily to many of the decisions made about fiscal policy both domestically and internationally. His only rival for being both 100% wrong about everything and being appallingly influential to at least one half of the nation is Paul Krugman.[6]

Stiglitz and Krugman – along with many similarly-oriented pundits – remind me as well of *Das Glasperlenspiel* (*The Glass Bead Game*), the final novel published in 1943 by Hermann Hesse. In Hesse's work, the Glass Bead Game is a highly abstract intellectual game played by academic specialists who have learned to manipulate game piece symbols over decades of educational immersion. The Game is very prestigious and there's lots of academic ooohing and aaahing over various combinations of symbols, with "winners" acclaimed by inscrutable criteria. Crucially, for all its prestige and the difficulty smart people face to master the Game, it has absolutely zero relevance to the real world.

I had a wonderful experience back in the mid-1990s. I attended a conference on "development economics" in Washington, D.C. I was in town anyway and since at the time I was living and working in Africa, I was curious to hear what the conference participants had to say.

On stage was Stiglitz. He was Chief Economist at the World Bank at the time. I had never heard of him before, as I lived then as I do now in the real world and always enjoyed arguing with the University of Chicago economists I knew in college. The wonderful part of *just hearing* someone talk without *any context* as to "who" or "what" he is, is that you actually *hear* the words all by themselves. So it was with Stiglitz and I.

As I had no idea who he was or what title he held, I was free to *really hear* what he was saying. And he was saying, quite frankly... nothing. Nothing at all. It was pure and utter nonsense. No content, no connection to the reality of individuals operating in a private sector economy. None of it. I cannot recall what he *did* say (and it does not matter, as I assume it was very much like everything he writes) at that particular conference. But I *do* know that *he made no sense whatsoever.* Whoever this guy up there on stage was, it was perfectly clear to me that *he knew nothing at all about how business works and real decisions get made.*

As I listened to him bloviate, I looked around me in wonderment. I felt like the kid in *The Emperor's New Clothes.* This self-important buffoon up there who so far as I could tell had never had any real business experience, was busy expounding on God only knows what, and everyone around me appeared to be listening reverentially. Some were taking notes. It was truly bizarre. I felt as if I had stumbled by accident into some weird cult, where everyone but me had drunk the Magic Kool-Aid and were hypnotized by the Holy Gibberish emanating from the hieratic priest on the platform. I seem to recall he was wearing Birkenstocks with white socks, but that may be a post-traumatic reconstruction.

---

[6] From an exegetical perspective, I am confirmed in my suspicion that Krugman has dedicated his life to being completely wrong about everything by *The Atlantic*'s Sebastian Mallaby who wrote "Krugman is substantively correct on just about every topic he addresses." Review: Paul Krugman's 'Arguing With Zombies' - The Atlantic. He may as well have written *Creo quia absurdum est.*

I caused a bit of a stir when I decided to save my brain from further assault and stood up to make my way out of the row I was in. As I pushed past people's knees, they looked at me with a mixture of rage – that I was interrupting their view of the clown on stage for a second – and astonishment that I'd be giving up my seat for this magical event when so many people were packed behind us standing, so desperate were they to hear the brilliant nonsense.

One of my favorite half-Americans, Winston Churchill, who spewed quotable verbiage on a near-daily basis, once said that a bad law is one which makes an honest man into a criminal. By that standard, our nation is rife with bad laws which are strangling not only our freedom but – in case you're one of those Americans who doesn't think very much of freedom – also our economy.

Penn Jillette, one of my favorite Vegas headliners, in describing his libertarian convictions put it this way: If you don't want to punish someone who's done nothing wrong, then why do you want to reward someone who hasn't done something right? He put the ends of government through a very American Occam's razor lens: if something is worth forcing people to do with a gun, that is something that the government ought rightly be doing and if not, then the government should not.

The older I get, the more sound become the philosophical assertions of Immanuel Kant. Look him up; he's a rollicking fun read. Boiling his brilliance down, Kant asserts that it's madness to try to make decisions based on a prediction of actions and reactions, as if life is a chess board. As one can never accurately predict what another person's reaction will be, the only way to live a truly moral and philosophically consistent life is to make every decision and take every action based on the moral or logical correctness of that decision or action. Kantian *a priori* principles are the only ones to base a government on, *not* projected outcomes.

Projected outcomes are useful to examine, as a guide to progress, much as private companies compare projections *and assumptions used* as the year unfolds, the better to improve their understanding of what they were right about and what they were wrong about. Governmental budgeting *abhors* such objective self-reflection and analysis – which is why in the private sector, if a manager achieves her goals by year end having spent 20% *less* than was allocated, she is rewarded. Whereas in the government, if a manager gets to the end of the year and still has 20% of the allocated cash yet to spend, *she immediately finds a project to spend that money on.*

This is rational behavior for a public sector bureaucrat. Rather than being praised for achieving the mission under budget, the bureaucrat is punished in the next budget year by a bureaucrat a step or two higher who says "Oh, look, she was able to do everything with 20% less, which means *not* that she is an excellent manager who saved the American people from superfluous expenditure – nope, it means we the All-Seeing Budget Gnomes should not have given her that budget in the first place, so this year we'll chop 20% off her allocation."

Which is a problem because her empire thereby shrinks and maybe, just maybe, this year would have required the full budget. The end result multiplied across hundreds of departments in the government is that costs keep rising every year relentlessly, because the people *spending* our money are not rewarded for efficiency. The bureaucrats in DC are rewarded for wasting money. That is not polemic shrieking – that is simply objectively accurate.

Obama's 2012 budget document offered us $3.8 trillion in spending, which he managed without irony and without moral compunction to offer up as "fiscally responsible." Part of what I loved about the Age of Obama is that there was literally no difference between a headline pulled from *Pravda* a.k.a. *The New York Times* and one pulled on the same topic from *The Onion*. Satirists didn't even need to work anymore; they could simply cut and paste from the regular newspapers. Or vice versa. Little did I expect his VP to pick up that ball so handily four years later.

On a methodological note, I will say that the "post-partisan" President Obama who (as a candidate, mind you) vowed to "broadcast the healthcare debate live on C-SPAN" kept in character by making it really hard to manipulate the data contained in the budget. All the data from Obama's budgets are in Adobe pdf form, though it would have been simple to offer up the budget tables in Excel as well. Later budgets are available in spreadsheet format, which is helpful, but the bureaucrats in charge still do their best to make the "financial statements" of government as impenetrable as possible.

The Trump and Biden budgets were all equally insane. In the course of this book, I have cited one or more of these three Presidents' budgets – the point is not to get bogged down with the horrendous details, but to demonstrate the big picture errors they all make and suggest an alternative far better to taxpayers' interests.

Make government service boring and honorable

A major theme I will come back to repeatedly is that the best way to encourage honorable and diligent attention to the taxpayers' interests is to make all work in the public interest inherently unexciting. Aside from being in the military – which by its nature *is* exciting and therefore draws adrenaline junkies – most of the tasks of government should be like jury duty: important, necessary for a smoothly functioning society, valuable but intrinsically kind of boring.

Alcohol Prohibition, the Drug Wars, making prostitution illegal, the Federal Election Commission – all of these are excellent examples of the fact that laws are no impediment to people seeking to get high in one way or another. Politicians in America are chasing a high – whether that high is for power or popularity or anything else does not matter. The only way to stop people turning into politicians is to remove the high that comes with public service.

Water follows gravity around any obstacle. So too will reward-seeking politicians chase power, no matter the obstacles thrown in their paths. The only way to "clean up" politics is to remove the gravitational attractors. Remove the possibility for power, wealth and fame and the people interested in those things will have to find another avenue to get their fix.

As a wise friend of mine with deep experience in Florida State politics once said: "Ethics laws are designed to apply to people without any ethics." She gave as an example term limits in Florida – when finally enacted, one old crocodile in the legislature finally had to give up his seat. *The very next day* my friend walked into another State Senator's office, and there was the term-limited former legislator sitting in the anteroom, having been hired on as some kind of "senior advisor staffer." Think of a Wal-Mart Greeter, but for $180,000 per year paid by the good citizens of Florida.

Another major theme in this book is that ideas matter. Tragically, history shows us that bad ideas matter more than good ones. Bad ideas and good ideas both may be expressed simply or with great complexity. The results of both take time to bear fruit. Bad ideas have lots of defenders, for whom admission of having had a bad idea can lead to unpleasant consequences, including loss of income, status and power. They will fight tooth and nail to defend the monster that gives them those tasty goodies.

Whereas champions of good ideas see good things happening and therefore lose interest in the good idea as a Daily Cause. You never hear of the right to vote or the change in medical policy for surgeons to scrub between patients being a "permanent revolution," do you? It is obvious why. The good brought about is clear to all and no longer needs cheerleaders or - given the ominous proclivities of all perpetual revolutionaries - enforcers.

Our nation began with some really good ideas and kept a few bad ones around for a range of historical accidents. Over time, we improved the net balance of more good ideas over bad ones. We are at a point now where some of the Old Bad Ideas are long vanquished, and the ones that survived are being augmented by a crop of New Bad Ideas are creeping, insidious ones that do not blare loudly, but are quietly and persistently corrosive.

The Old Bad Ideas are pretty obvious: Slavery, Prohibition, the New Deal.

The New Bad Ideas are awful but come cloaked in pretty clothing: Universal Basic Income, Healthcare or Housing as a Right, Progressive Taxation, Agricultural Subsidies, Occupational Licensure, Drug Prohibition and – in a nod to one of the greatest value destroyers in American history – a *Green* New Deal.

During the long journey this book has taken me, I have on occasion lost hope in its purpose. But then I get the occasional jolt of encouragement. One such shot in the arm was Bernard Connolly's masterpiece from 1995, *The Rotten Heart of Europe: The Dirty War for Europe's Money,* which was so impactful it got him fired from his job as Senior Economist at the European Commission. And just a few years after I read his clear exposé of the EU's totalitarian, anti-democratic, unaccountable project to control all of Europe, along came Brexit! So there is hope even in the darkest of times.

Even when I have wobbled, I have carried on writing this book with the aim of it becoming a practical tool for honest Americans who want to perfect this fine American Union, this grand experiment, this wholly new thing in human history. We can be the city on the hill through our actions, not our words. Our words are what empower us to shape the future course of our experiment, so I hope mine assist us in this rollicking ride.

The Plan of the Book, or What You Can Expect from Here

This is the section where you're expecting me to wring my hands over the lack of civic engagement of the citizenry and join the chorus of the self-appointed "smart people" bemoaning the petty desires of everyday folks who want to watch "reality TV" rather than parse the nuances of *The Anti-Federalist Papers.*

I'm not going to do that. People have more amusing things to do than delve into 18th century debates on the nature of constitutional governance. I respect that.

If deep reading into the historical and philosophical background to various bits of our governmental structure or cultural life is your thing, by all means go for it. What I am saying *here* is that the problem is *not* as one wag put it that the government has lost its faith in the people – which it has. No – the problem is that most Americans are reasonably good, reasonably honest people who are working hard to make a life for themselves and hopefully their loved ones. We all have little time free to first *discover* what horrible things "our" government gets up to and then – having uncovered the cesspool – gin up the energy to collect *other* people to come together to do something about it.

This problem exists because while we – the normal people – were busy running our lives, a whole class of parasites steadily burrowed themselves into our pocketbooks *and our lives* and have tried as hard as they can to remain stuck into both like ticks.

We need to apply hot metal to the ticks so they release their blood-sucking grip on our bodies politic. Once they've been forced from power, we can chuck them onto the bonfire of history.

This book sketches the problem in just enough detail so we can all speak the same language. It's designed to make the headaches concrete *and clear* so there is no more "Look over here!" and "These are not the budget detail drones you're looking for!" sleight of hand distractions our political class has gotten so good at.

Having provided the structural engineering diagram – if you'll permit me the very stretched simile – I then show where to cut away the bad parts to leave us with a much sounder, secure and future-focused economy, government and society.

Figure 1: Washington, DC is besieged by powerful negative influences

A very important lesson for us all to learn, relearn and live by is that individuals make decisions, whereas groups make nothing except possibly mayhem.

In the context of the massive waste and absurdity that characterizes "our" government, it is crucial to bear in mind that *at every step of the way,* someone, somewhere has through a decision or failure to act caused each and every dollar wasted to be flushed down a bottomless rabbit hole. Once we start forcing *individual* accountability on civil servants and politicians, we'll be delighted and amazed at how quickly fiscal order and spending restraint become the normal state of affairs.

Make no mistake: There are legions of these parasites who will do all in their power to tell you that what is described in the pages that follow is wrong. They won't give you any rational arguments for *why* what I'm laying out is wrong – because they can't. That does not mean they won't scream and yell about it – if ignoring it doesn't work. (I'm talking to you, Paul Krugman and 90% of the Media Industry of 2020-23.)

You – and I – will know this book is a success when its author is called "racist" in the media. (Note to future generations, who are reading the 18th revised version 3D printed in immersive holographic gold ink: There existed at the time of writing a group of Americans who believed in a totalitarian thought control doctrine called "Political Correctness" or "being woke" in nonsensical shorthand. Any time anyone said *anything* these petulant mini-fascists did not like, they immediately called that person "racist," irrespective of whether the topic under examination had anything remotely to do with "race." Another group of Americans – let's call them "rational" – were delighted to be so labeled because the label highlighted the intellectual bankruptcy of their accusers.)

Enjoy.

Chapter 1: Messina's Guiding Principles

Simple is always better. Simplicity is easy to understand, easy to analyze and easy to operate. When it comes to government, simplicity is every American's best friend. The *only* Americans who hate simple government are the people who make their living off the problems created by overly complex and usually useless laws and rules. Make no mistake: everyone who lives off the taxpayer dime *loves* complexity. The politicians and government contractors building 20,000 square foot mansions around DC *rely* on things being so complex that it's hard for an average citizen to begin to understand how it all works.

Kurt Vonnegut put this phenomenon better than I ever could in *The Sirens of Titan*. In that majestic work of "fiction," he describes how a bright young graduate of Harvard Business School named Ransom K. Fern talked himself into a job as President of Magnum Opus, Incorporated, "a marvelous engine for doing violence to the spirit of thousands of laws without actually running afoul of so much as a city ordinance." He made his pitch to the soon-to-be Chairman and sole owner of Magnum Opus, Noel Constant in the latter's squalid Hotel Wilburhampton room 223. He explained how layers of complexity would transform the IRS's current clear vision into Constant's revenue streams into an impenetrable fog of confusion.

> "Mr. Constant, sir," said young Fern, "right now you're as easy for the Bureau of Internal Revenue to watch as a man on a street corner selling apples and pears. But just imagine how hard you would be to watch if you had a whole office building jammed to the rafters with industrial bureaucrats – men who lose things use the wrong forms and create new forms and demand everything in quintuplicate, and who understand perhaps a third of what is said to them; who habitually give misleading answers in order to gain time in which to think, who make decisions only when forced to, and who then cover their tracks; who make perfectly honest mistakes in addition and subtraction, who call meetings whenever they feel lonely, who write memos whenever they feel unloved; men who never throw anything away unless they think it could get them fired. A single industrial bureaucrat, if he is sufficiently vital and nervous, should be able to create a ton of meaningless papers a year for the Bureau of Internal Revenue to examine. In the Magnum Opus Building, we will have thousands of them! And you and I can have the top two stories, and you can go on keeping track of what's really going on the way you do now."

Kurt was writing from the point of view of a man who had witnessed the firebombing of Dresden during WW2 and had perhaps even fewer illusions about the workings of institutions both public and private than even Joseph Heller or Machiavelli. What matters for our discussion here is that if you replace the term "Magnum Opus" with "the Federal Government" and the "Bureau of Internal Revenue" with "the American taxpayer," you have a crystal-clear understanding of the current state of our Republic.

Kurt and I are both semi-trained anthropologists from the University of Chicago. The path we followed reminds me of the Pralite monks, described by that fine documentarian Douglas Adams in Book One[7] of his five-book trilogy. Pralite monks are adherents to a religious order that undergo extreme mental training as part of their preparation for full monkhood. The mismatch between their excellent mental training and the rewards to be gleaned from applying that training to the field whence it sprung leads to fairly predictable results, as described by Mr Adams:

> The galaxy is littered with ex-Pralite monks, all on the make, because the mental control techniques the Order have evolved as a form of devotional discipline are, frankly, sensational - and extraordinary numbers of monks leave the Order just after they have finished their devotional training and just before they take their final vows to stay locked in small metal boxes for the rest of their lives.

Time will tell whether the University of Chicago Anthropology Department is as proud of this prodigal son as they became of Kurt over time. Lest the fine faculty who imparted their wisdom to me get the wrong end of the stick, I am *not* suggesting that the life of an academic anthropologist is akin to living trapped in a small metal box. I am saying that the valuable intellectual tools and analytical frameworks they exposed me to have vast applicability outside the halls of academe.

My approach to a comprehensive Federal Budget follows. There are a few very clear, *simple* guiding principles, and each specific example of implementation is a replication of the pattern determined by those few principles. It is simple because the only way we can slay the dragon of the cancerous Federal Government is to ignore its fierce defenders who will throw sparkly confetti in our eyes to blind us to how very simple it is to dismantle the massive beast we've allowed to grow into a cancer bent on consuming our entire nation right before our eyes.

Complexity is a given in the world, whether in biological or social systems. What matters is *how* we understand complexity and whether we give it the proper respect. We can never "fix" complex problems with a multitude of patches here and there, but *only* by first finding and then fixing the simple root cause. If you're trying to stop massive oil pollution in a river and combat huge fires sparked from the same oil, all of which is spewing from a leaky oil pipeline, you focus on closing the leak in the pipe, not fighting the fires and trying to mop up the oil from the river. Fix the leak and the other problems vanish. The same principle applies to fixing the destructive horrors spewing from the DC Swamp.

Complexity will always occur. The deepest flaws at the heart of what I can only assume are well-intentioned efforts to micro-manage social outcomes are philosophical flaws. The fundamental flaw at the core of the social-engineering attempts of people like FDR Roosevelt, the Clintons, Bushes, Obamas, Stalins, Chavezes, Bidens and Carters is believing that one can "manage" such a wildly complex system as our nation for subjectively desirable *outcomes* rather than simply setting fair initial conditions.

To take a social phenomenon at random: At any given point in time, the statistical observation of who has less money and who has more is an empirical observation of the

---

[7] Adams, Douglas (b. 1952, Cambridge, England, d. 2001, Santa Barbara, California), *The Hitchhiker's Guide to the Galaxy*, 1979.

emergent properties of a complex system. That snapshot in time is merely an objective description of a moment in time. This is important, because at the heart of so many horrible or just plain poorly-defined feats of social engineering – er, legislation – lies a fundamental misunderstanding of the nature of "reality."

Every time politicians or bureaucrats see a snapshot of society they don't like, they immediately attack the symptom they dislike – whether it's that Ms. X has "too much" money, or "Corporation Y" has made "excess profits." Since it's easier by far to rail against the personal target of the day – whether Congress hauling Samuel Insull back from Turkey for trial or Bernie Sanders screaming about Mark Zuckerberg[8] – to whip up political fury than to lay out dispassionate, clear and objective rules that *everyone* has to follow, the temptation of egomaniacal politicians – redundant, I know – is to rail rather than propose solutions.

When governments get into trouble, meaning when politicians promise the undeliverable to constituents and then panic because they cannot pay for it, the only smart thing to be done is to slash the costs of government. Raising taxes on the productive private sector to pay for deadweight transfer payments is immoral, unjust, a breach of the rule of law and – worst of all – ineffective.[9]

Since that is the smart thing to do in the face of unfunded promises, that is of course exactly what politicians *don't* do. Heck, no – that'll get them thrown out of office. So, they either raise taxes and fees and set up dense thickets of regulations to pour more cash into the public treasury – at least until they run out of somebody else's money – or they set about devaluing the unit of account (otherwise known as inflation, when your dollar suddenly buys a lot less than it did). I will touch on the nature of money in the section on the Federal Reserve, but briefly here, indebted governments and kings throughout history have *loved* to cheapen the currency. Inflation makes things cost "more" in current unit terms – for example, an apple that cost $1 last year and now costs $2 this year demonstrates price inflation of 100%.

But that does *not* mean that the *value* of that apple has increased at all. When a king borrowed $1,000 from one of his subject bankers, and the loan was priced in dollars, if 100% inflation occurred between the time period he borrowed the $1,000, he was really paying back only half of what he had borrowed to begin with. Inflation is another tax on *you,* the taxpayer. Don't worry about the details of that for now – just bear it in mind.

---

[8] Samuel Insull (1859 – 1938), British American founder of major electric utilities in the Midwest brought cheap ubiquitous power to Americans, for which he was excoriated following the Crash of 1929. Mark Zuckerberg is an American college dropout who runs an Internet platform dedicated to monetizing through targeted advertising people's oversharing and startling, voluntary privacy violations.
[9] Biggs, Hassett & Jensen, "A Guide for Deficit Reduction in the United States Based on Historical Consolidations that Worked," American Enterprise Institute Economic Policy Working Paper 2010-04, December 27, 2010.

Of course, in late 2023, that concept became a lot more tangible for many Americans than when I began writing this book. The Biden Inflation is atrocious and working Americans are feeling the pinch at the gas pump and the supermarket on a daily basis.

The main principle that lies behind this entire book is that when it comes to government, less is more. Rather than a massive sprawling government that does millions of things badly, we should be paying for a government that does a few strictly defined things, with governance guiderails in place that ensure the very few civil servants do their jobs well. So far as we the people should be concerned, every single item in the Federal Budget should meet four equally binding tests:

1. Is this a standalone proper use of the taxpayers' limited resources?

2. Does the expenditure meet the "Is this logical?" standard of fiduciary responsibility?

3. Does this expenditure unfairly benefit one American over another one? If so, don't spend the money.

4. Can a given goal be achieved by *not* spending the dollar more effectively than by spending it?

All great systems have at their core simple, easy-to-explain organizing principles. My organizing principle is that each extra step between a private individual's resources and a bureaucrat's spending introduces opportunities for fraud, waste and corruption. The best - and *least expensive* - way to manage the risks associated with big pools of cash sloshing around is that *in every single case* the steps between taxation of the populace and government expenditure ought always be the least number possible. It is always cheaper *not* to spend a dollar in the first place, so before we even commit to minimizing the steps between the taxpayer's wallet and some bureaucrat's checkbook, we need first to be sure that it might not be better to *not* spend the dollar in the first place.

The great truth which makes every centralizing, control-freak technocrat bleed fresh ulcers of frustration is that *local is better.* You'd think this would be a welcome idea. Great numbers of Americans both in and out of government extol the virtues of local agricultural produce and local production of various goods to save on carbon-emitting shipping. But the irony is that while many bureaucrats and politicians are huge fans of local *production,* they secretly *hate* local *decisions.* They're way keen to have local farmers produce organic onions, but only if those locals have been "certified" by some distant, urban-office-suited, definitely not-for-profit association or organization or something like that, staffed by eager beaver liberal arts majors whose parents are wondering why *they* sacrificed so much so their kids could turn out to be such obnoxious, useless flakes who spend their days interfering in other people's lives.

Local decisions are dangerous, you see, because local decisions are made by strange people far away from the halls of political power who - gasp! - might not even know what the current crop of self-anointed "elites" thinks is best for each and every locality. Local, transparently made decisions are the best protection against corruption and waste in both public and private finances.

Locals create wealth. Locals create equity, jobs and strong communities.

Distant bureaucrats serve themselves, far removed from whatever original intention went into the creation of their particular jobs.

Nothing is perfect. No system or rule is "absolutely better" in achieving optimal fiscal results. Local decisions to work well require a muscular and intellectual *engagement* by citizens to bring about good outcomes. The possible flaws in "local is better" as an absolute rule were brought home to me by friends in a town on Long Island, New York. The details are only of interest to the parties involved, but I am sure we can all find things to relate to in this tale.

To set the scene, there was an increase in traffic on a previously quiet residential street, as it connects a railroad station to a light industrial area a few miles away. Over time, as both commuters *and* industrial activity increased, the quiet street experienced a great deal of traffic, which was both annoying to residents and a potential danger to kids playing in the street.

Residents asked the town council to erect a barrier, effectively turning the street into two cul-de-sacs or dead ends. The town council reviewed the relevant local, county and State laws and determined that this particular street could not legally be blocked off. Enraged residents on that street got active and at the next election, voted in a whole slate of Close the Street candidates, who upon taking office, promptly hired a contractor to build a barrier across the street.

The county, joined by the owners of the industrial park, immediately sued the town. Six months and $700,000 in legal fees paid by the town (and therefore the taxpayers) later, the county sent a demolition crew to take down the barrier and repave the section of street, all at an additional cost of $250,000. So, *local*, motivated knuckleheads cost their neighbors *and themselves* a pointless near million dollars, just to have a busy street outside their front doors again.

I suppose my point about local decisions meaning enhanced accountability rings true here. If you're one of the normal people in town who had nothing to do with this insanity and only really paid attention when you were hit with a "special assessment" of $5,500 to pay for this stupidity, you could wander over to the idiots on the town council who voted for this and, I dunno, toss a bucket of warm beer on them, something that would be impossible to do had the same road-closing been authorized by the stroke of an anonymous pen in an office somewhere in DC.

Start Simple: Let's Make Sure We're All Counting the Same Way

As you cannot manage what you cannot measure, there is one crucial condition which all Americans should insist on: that the fantasy of the government's accounting be jettisoned in favor of GAAP or IFRS or whatever accounting standard the rest of the world must live with. Just as there should not be two Rules of Law, only one, so too should there not be one set of accounting rules for the private sector and another, utterly arbitrary set for the political class.

The Ancient Greeks had it spot on. When they chose democratically to spend the public treasure on construction of the Acropolis, the public accounts were chiseled in stone and updated for everyone to see. In similar fashion, Americans should demand that the federal budget and all governmental accounting be transparently and immediately depicted for all to see, including *all* obligations incurred. That last point is perhaps the most critical of all as politicians – ever wily in their evasion of accountability and honesty – try various ways to steal taxpayer cash to fund pet projects via vaguely-defined guarantees that somehow never end up on the nation's balance sheet. That must end.

Once there is an apples-to-apples comparison, everyone can have a clear view of how resources are being used in pursuit of the country's benefit.

A budget that year after year meets those criteria would make us once more a country with a strong economy, a sound currency and stable prospects. More importantly, perhaps, it would make us a nation whose actions *finally* live up to its ostensible principles.

This is not just a practical consideration. It is also a moral one. Songsters across the political spectrum sing about how much they care about people. The best way for us as a country to provide in a stable fashion the best possible socioeconomic outcomes for both current and future citizens is to have a *simple, clear and objective* rule of law that *everyone* follows.

Clear, transparent budgeting and accounting will permit any educated, interested citizen to examine the degree to which government operations are living up to the expectations set them. There is some good news here – after lots of hardworking civil servants over the years have created various systems of accountability, there is already a culture of expenditure tracking and analysis throughout the government. Ask any grant-receiving college professor whose work is based on government research grants how hard it has become to divert cash allocated for, say, mass spectrometer equipment purchases to Ferrari leasing and Champagne getaways to the mountains.

We don't have to reinvent the wheel here – we can adopt the best practices already in place. What we are looking to modify is the sprawl and mission creep that every bureaucracy is prone to. In Chapter 30 on optimizing tax policy, I go into more depth about the need for harmonizing accounting principles between the public and private sector. For now, just keep in mind that simplicity and transparency are the taxpayers' friend and the current complexity the government hides behind is to our detriment.

Also, let's keep this in mind. There are only four ways to spend money.

Type 1 – you spend your own money on yourself. You take reasonable care to get value for money and consider your purchases carefully. PJ O'Rourke once said this is the kind of spending middle-aged men do at sportscar dealerships.

Type 2 – you spend someone else's money on yourself. The inimitable PJ said this is the kind of spending the middle-aged man's young girlfriend does at Bergdorf Goodman.

Type 3 – you spend your own money on someone else. Think of gifts – you spend enough time for it to matter, depending on the goal. Again, PJ said this is the kind of spending the middle-aged man does at Tiffany.

Type 4 – you spend someone else's money on someone else. This is how government bureaucrats spend money. In PJ's phrasing, who cares how it gets spent?

Proposed Budget Summary

Rather than keep you in suspense, here is the overall summary view of the budget I propose which will restore balance to the nation, trim the sails of an arrogant Administrative State and prepare us for the next two hundred years in far better form that the previous decade has indicated we are doomed to endure. You'll notice quite a few changes from the status quo.

Currently 90% of annual federal spending is on autopilot, meaning Congress only has 10% to argue about theatrically before forcing our unborn grandchildren to borrow from foreigners. My budget assumes a number of things, one of which is an aggressive privatization asset sale, with all proceeds going firstly to pay down borrowed money to reduce the deadweight of interest payments and secondly to funding private retirement accounts if needed actuarially as we turn off the stupidity of Social Security and put retirement fund control where it belongs – in each citizen's private hands.

Table 1: Summary of my budget proposal for 2024 onwards, compared to 2023 Biden budget

Budget Line Item	Biden 2023	Messina 2024	Messina 2025	Messina 2026
Education	90,000,000,000	25,000,000	-	-
Housing & Urban Development	47,900,000,000	25,000,000		-
Labor Dept	42,000,000,000	10,000,000	2,000,000	
Homeland Security	97,300,000,000	-	-	-
Customs / Border Control	17,000,000,000	55,000,000,000	120,000,000,000	120,000,000,000
Immigration & Citizenship	8,300,000,000	15,000,000,000	20,000,000,000	15,000,000,000
US Coast Guard	13,800,000,000	15,000,000,000	25,000,000,000	30,000,000,000
FEMA	29,500,000,000	25,000,000	-	
Social Security	10,100,000,000	250,000,000	25,000,000	-
US Post Office	290,300,000,000	150,000,000,000	40,000,000,000	20,000,000,000
PBGC	8,200,000,000	125,000,000	10,000,000	
Amtrak	3,300,000,000	3,000,000,000	250,000,000	200,000,000
Agriculture	210,000,000,000	180,000,000,000	170,000,000,000	30,000,000,000
Commerce	16,300,000,000	4,000,000,000	3,000,000,000	2,500,000,000
Small Business Administration	50,000,000,000	20,000,000	-	
War Department	816,000,000,000	900,000,000,000	1,000,000,000,000	1,100,000,000,000
Veterans Affairs	301,400,000,000	325,000,000,000	350,000,000,000	375,000,000,000
Energy	48,200,000,000	20,000,000,000	15,000,000,000	10,000,000,000
EPA	11,880,000,000	750,000,000	750,000,000	750,000,000
Federal Aviation Administration	18,600,000,000	20,000,000,000	22,000,000,000	25,000,000,000
Directorate of Intelligence	100,000,000,000	50,000,000,000	50,000,000,000	50,000,000,000
Health & Human Services	242,100,000,000	100,000,000	25,000,000	-
Medicare	846,000,000,000	120,000,000	-	-
Medicaid	536,000,000,000	120,000,000	-	-
Centers for Disease Control	11,000,000,000	2,000,000,000	10,000,000	-
Admin Children & Families	73,800,000,000	150,000,000	25,000,000	-
Food & Drug Administration	8,400,000,000	4,000,000,000	4,000,000,000	4,000,000,000
Interior	17,600,000,000	17,600,000,000	19,000,000,000	19,000,000,000
Justice	37,700,000,000	200,000,000	20,000,000	-
Drug Enforcement Agency	3,100,000,000	120,000,000	-	-
State Department	60,400,000,000	50,000,000,000	45,000,000,000	40,000,000,000
Treasury Department	20,530,000,000	10,000,000,000	10,000,000,000	10,000,000,000
Alcohol, Tobacco & Firearms	1,700,000,000	30,000,000	-	-
FDIC	2,400,000,000	2,000,000,000	1,900,000,000	1,800,000,000
SEC/CFTC	2,500,000,000	2,400,000,000	5,000,000,000	5,000,000,000
National Science Foundation	9,000,000,000	9,000,000,000	10,000,000,000	10,000,000,000
Smithsonian	2,000,000,000	2,200,000,000	2,300,000,000	2,400,000,000
NASA	27,400,000,000	27,400,000,000	35,000,000,000	40,000,000,000
Federal Election Commission	81,700,000	-	-	-
United Nations Dues	20,000,000,000	10,000,000	-	-
Development Finance Corp	1,000,000,000	5,000,000	1,000,000	-
Block Transfers to States	3,000,000,000,000	-	-	-
Interest on Federal Debt	659,000,000,000	395,400,000,000	237,240,000,000	142,344,000,000
Annual Total	7,687,891,700,000	2,261,085,000,000	2,185,558,000,000	2,052,994,000,000

It is a solid overview. Don't get buried in the details as there is some overlap in categories; commentary follows. In general, the $7.7 trillion cost for 2023 is correct. My budgetary suggestions for 2024 and 2025 are how I suggest we right-size Leviathan.

What about the people?

Change will undoubtedly be hard. It always is. Along with a streamlined Federal Government will come stiffer competition for fewer, higher-paying public sector jobs. I will discuss that in more depth, but in general, competitive markets always make better decisions than constrained, unionized, controlled markets like current Federal employment practices. Core to my proposals will be to replace current, stifling and insider-protective employment practices with open-market competitive pricing for talent. Coupled with a much, much smaller bureaucracy, higher pay will drive far better personnel selection for those people who work hard enough to qualify for the privilege of serving the American taxpayer.

In addition to the core value of providing remuneration competitive to private sector alternatives, to ensure the taxpayer will be getting value for hard-earned money, there will be some new rules for employment by any level of government:

1. As an entry-level bureaucrat, you need at least 10 years of private sector experience. For a higher-level job, at least 15 years, 3 of which need to be as a direct P&L manager.
2. A two-term limit for *every single elected job* at any level of government. No more permanent parasites like Chuck "Assemblyman Soundbite" Schumer doing nothing with his life but stroking his ego by standing in front of microphones and spending other people's money.
3. No more public sector unions permitted. Do away with the raft of insane rules and regulations which stymie effective hiring *today* never mind in the blissful future state this proposed restructured budget defines.
4. No more public sector defined benefit pensions.

There is nothing wrong with creating rules for Federal employment – there are already plenty of rules in place. We just need to simplify the great mass of those rules and use the *Federal Register* as biomass inputs to retro-fitted, coal-burning utility plants. Based on some quick, back of the envelope estimates, I'm betting that will provide at least twenty years of fuel to run a dozen old coal plants.

Wherever there are layoffs to be made, all the people affected by these layoffs should be given an option on the way out the door. They can accept either a two-month severance package *or* the ability to join the military for two years, if they can pass the physical and other exams.

Through many discussions across government, one of the biggest themes of frustration I have heard is around the hiring and firing of personnel. The unions which have become entrenched in the government, along with sets of rules which have settled upon the previous ones like so many layers in sedimentary rocks almost guarantee mediocre outcomes for the American taxpayer.

I have tried hard to let the original sources of my analysis shine through without interference from me. While there are dozens of examples of conversations I have had over the years with people at all levels of various Federal bureaucracies concerning the truly illogical "processes" put in place to in practice hinder excellence in team building, I'm quoting here from David Shulkin's excellent account of his time as the Secretary of the Veterans Administration, spanning the end of the Obama Administration into the beginning of the Trump Administration. Tellingly, the title of his book is *It Shouldn't Be this Hard to Serve Your Country.*[10]

Here follows the start of Chapter 9, Moving and Shaking, which describes his first steps of running the VA after his confirmation by the Senate.

> Back in Washington, I needed to build an entirely new management team, but VA positions do not offer competitive salaries, and the agency's overall low morale didn't help recruitment. The hiring process itself was too long and complicated, which often weeded out the best candidates. Perversely, I wasn't allowed to see résumés, which were instead filtered by the human resources professionals and then sent to a committee of three Senior Executive Service (SES) employees. This panel would then review the already-filtered group of candidates and apply specific criteria to make a final determination. Included in these criteria were prior government experience, veteran status, and a number of other factors that were never quite clear to me. Someone with exactly the qualifications I was looking for could very easily slip through this many cracks.
>
> The first candidate sent over to me was someone who worked for the Federal Aviation Authority (FAA) and had spent a long time in government but had absolutely no health care experience. When I asked to see the résumés of other candidates, I was told *no*. So I rejected the candidate from the FAA, and the process of reposting for the position began again. Time and time again, I referred experienced health care executives who had worked with me in previous positions to apply for open VA hospital jobs, but they never made it through the screening.

Shulkin captures the essence of the problem in two paragraphs. A seasoned executive from the private sector takes a serious pay cut to serve his country in an important role. The *basic* thing any CEO takes for granted – the ability to hand select the management team to execute his or her mandate – is denied to a "CEO" in the Federal Government.

Everything about the insanity he describes is almost guaranteed to deliver negative outcomes. Straight out of the gate he cites the long and complicated process required to hire someone. In competitive employment markets, where the best candidate for a role will have multiple job offers, speed of employment is crucial. Time is money and if a qualified candidate with a mortgage and dependents is told she'll have to spend 120 days on paperwork before taking a job with the VA for $90,000 versus a job in the private sector for $110,000 and can start next Monday, the taxpayer is already losing the battle for talent.

The very idea that I as a manager *cannot see the resume* of the job candidate is so crazed that even Kafka would have crossed that out of his manuscript as being too farfetched to be plausible.

The scenario Shulkin cites of personally referring experienced executives into the black hole of the hiring process is one I've heard time and time again. In the private sector, the CEO is in charge of everything – that's the point, that the buck stops on his or her desk. If the CEO of a private company referred an executive for an open role, whether or not the

---

[10] Hachette Book Group, 2019

referred person got the job, there would be immediate follow up and in the case of the candidate *not* being hired, the explanations provided as to *why* would be delivered to the CEO in person by the hiring manager if requested. The idea that the head of the VA could recommend experienced people for jobs in the organization he is the supposed leader of, and just have those people rejected by an unelected bureaucracy is precisely one of the horrendously damaging symptoms my proposed restructuring is designed to eradicate.

Decentralization

In my budget, simplicity is next to holiness. Right next door to simplicity is another great friend to the American people: decentralization.

I am not the first to float this idea, but I'm going to pound it home with vigor. *Many* of our problems as a nation result *not* from the "rotating door" between the private sector and various public bureaucracies. Quite frankly, from what I have seen up close, the American people largely benefit from having someone in a public role regulating, say, the auto industry who, y'know, *comes* from that industry and therefore knows something. The taxpayers should very much be able to tap the experience of the private sector to solve serious problems or set limits on the government's ability to meddle in lots of things.

No – the problem lies both in the unfortunate proliferation of the government and in the centralizing collection of all these various government agencies in one place: Washington, DC.

As tempting as the jokes about fetid swamps may be, I'm going to move on to why it is in all our interests to disperse what will be left of the government across the 50 states. There are five main reasons why the Republic will be stronger as we disperse Federal operations across the country.

1. National Security. It's harder to attack our leadership if it's not in one place.
2. Accountability. Let's have the *leaders* of each agency live right amidst real communities, which are predominantly private sector.
3. Transparency and citizen engagement.
4. Economic integration.
5. Demystification of and familiarization with the functions of government.

Decentralization is not only a great way to disseminate skills and familiarity with the operations of the (remaining) few things the Federal Government ought to do. There is a deeply moral side to distributed network systems, the lessons of which our children will absorb as they watch "the government" operate, not as some distant thing in Washington, but as part and parcel of governance in a representative republic.

Consider these two systems of organizing emergency water supplies for a small city of 100,000 people. In this case, the scenario calls for public safety and human health to mean that each person needs access to one week's worth of fresh water, calculated to be 50 gallons.

In a centralized system, 50 gallons x 100,000 people = 5,000,000 gallons of water are held in central warehouse or warehouses, with each person entitled to draw 50 gallons from the warehouse in time of need. When disaster strikes, all kinds of things from basic road and communication interruption to actual physical damage of the warehouse facilities can mean severe delays in, say, a family of 4 getting their 200 gallons in a timely – read: *before we die or get sick* – fashion.

In a distributed system, each family or small community grouping – say an HOA of 100 homes – maintains 50 gallons per person in or near people's homes. When disaster strikes, the people in the distributed system have immediate, direct access to the necessary water, without waiting on bureaucrats to show up, open warehouse doors, form distribution queues, fill out forms, check no one is abusing the system by taking more than they're entitled to, along with any and all other potential problems which can arise in a crisis. And all of that assumes that there are bureaucrats on hand to perform those tasks, or that they are willing to do so.

Americans watched in horror and disgust in January 2020 as Puerto Ricans who were suffering for years from a series of natural disasters compounded by official incompetence discovered a warehouse full of disaster aid supplies.[11] The cots, water, medical supplies and food had been stored in the warehouse *since September 2017* as a result of donations provided not only by government but by individual citizens and people around the world in reaction to Hurricane Maria.

Carlos Acevedo, who was the *director of the island's emergency management agency* was fired, but the damage was done. Such rank incompetence in the face of human misery should be a capital offense, or at least an offense whose punishment permits solid citizens to pelt one with rotten soft fruit in the stocks, but we can leave that fun debate for another time. Leaving that aside, *even if* Carlos had the best of intentions, the fact is that humans make mistakes. I don't pretend to know what mix of incompetence and corruption went into the warehouse full of life-saving goods sitting idle in Ponce while people starved, shivered and lacked bedding, but my point remains. Even in cases of human error – maybe the guy with the manifest for the warehouse gets cholera or the flu, or a family home is destroyed, or two people in charge each assumes the other one is on the case – the result is the same: a centralized system of emergency assistance is vulnerable to single points of failure.

In the early part of 2020, everyone got a lesson in the power of resiliency based on *individual* responsibility and distributed networks. As the coronavirus Wuhan Flu spread across the world, along with an arguably more virulent panic over the virus, suddenly normal supply chains for toilet paper – oddly – and basic foodstuffs stopped working. People panicked and began to hoard items, instantly turning a nation of 350 million into preppers in need of one year of food.

The resiliency of a distributed system independent of central control is also one of the reasons why there is such vociferous debate about the *meaning* of the Second Amendment. People who want to restrict individual access to firearms constantly point to the bit about "a well-regulated militia," and take it to mean that only a given State has the

---

[11]   https://www.chicagotribune.com/nation-world/ct-nw-puerto-rico-diasaster-supplies-20200119-eso3eivojvdajoxgpma47ox234-story.html 18 January 2020

right to regulate a militia, and therefore only the centralized State government or other political unit can control the guns. Presumably, under such a model, in time of crisis, the State would mobilize the militia into action and each individual would go to some central armory to get a weapon distributed to him or her.

From a preparedness standpoint, that is pure folly, as we see from the water and food supplies example above. Seas of electronic and physical ink have been spilled on this topic, so I'm not going to delve into it further here, but in keeping with my "repeating patterns," simple is better theme, the more things left in the hands of the individual, the stronger Americans and our nation are. In 1961 South Africa, Nelson Mandela during apartheid understood this principle well when he founded Umkhonto we Sizwe – the "Spear of the Nation" in Xhosa – as the armed wing of the ANC (African National Congress). MK deliberately lacked centralized structure and command – by design, the various cells of MK operated independently of one another so that when the South African police or army caught any of them, the damage to the movement was contained.

With scary prescience, that marvelous Frenchman, Alexis de Tocqueville in 1833 described the basis for Americans' freedom from government micromanagement and oppression in his eighth chapter entitled "What Tempers the Tyranny of the Majority in the United States." You know what that great thing was? *"Absence of Administrative Centralization."*

I have previously made the distinction between two types of centralization, calling one governmental and one administrative.

Only the first exists in America, the second being almost unknown.

If the directing power in American societies had both these means of government at its disposal and combined the right to command with the faculty and habit to perform everything itself, if having established the general principles of the government, it entered into the details of their application, and having regulated the great interest of the country, it came down to consider even individual interests, then freedom would soon be banished from the New World.

But in the United States, the majority, even though it often has a despot's tastes and instincts, still lacks the most improved instruments of tyranny.

In all the American republics the central government is only occupied with a small number of matters important enough to attract its attention. It does not undertake to regulate society's secondary concerns, and there is no indication that it has even conceived the desire to do so. The majority, though ever increasingly absolute, has not enlarged the prerogatives of the central authority; it has only mode it omnipotent within its own sphere. Thus despotism, though very oppressive on one point, cannot cover all.

Besides, however far the national majority may be carried away by its passions in its ardor for new projects, it cannot make all the citizens everywhere bow to its will in the same way and at the same time. The sovereign commands of its representative, the central government, have to be carried out by agents who often do not depend upon it and cannot be give directions every minute. Municipal bodies and county administrations are like so many hidden reefs retarding or dividing the flood of the popular will. If the law were oppressive, liberty would still find some shelter from the way the law is carried into execution, and the majority would not know how to enter into the details and, if I dare call them so, the puerilities of administrative tyranny. Indeed it does not even imagine that it could do so, for it is not entirely conscious of its own power. It is only aware of its natural strength, ignorant of how art might increase its scope.

It is worth thinking about this point. If ever a democratic republic similar to that of the United States came to be established in a country in which earlier a single man's power had introduced administrative centralization and had made it something accepted by custom and by law, I have no hesitation in saying that in such a republic despotism would become more intolerable than in any of the absolute monarchies of Europe. One would have to go over into Asia to find anything with which to compare it.[12]

Well, it has all come to pass, hasn't it? The "most improved instruments of tyranny" are firmly in the grasps of the government. NSA and private companies manage massive supercomputers collecting data on everyone, "your" health insurance provider turned into an arm of the IRS, "public safety" CCTV cameras blanketing the nation... Fascist mayors and governors sent police to arrest a man alone sitting on a beach (Gov. Phil Murphy, Democrat-NJ), a Dad playing t-ball in an *empty park* (Gov. Jared Polis, Democrat-CO), and a judge who demanded a working mother apologize for having "wrong thoughts" for daring to operate a clean hair salon in the face of panicked, unconstitutional, fascist edicts (Judge Eric Moyé in Texas) whose Governor rapidly had to revise Texas's idiotic draconian economic destruction, but not before she had to spend a night in jail.[13]

The various levels of American government had proven definitively by May 2020 to have most assuredly "conceived the desire to regulate society's secondary concerns." With the advent of the Biden Unity Government[14] and thousands of National Guard troops garrisoned in the US Capital against a wholly imaginary "insurrectionist conspiracy" composed of "white supremacists" and libertarians among other horrors, to weaponizing the judiciary against political foes, the current 2021-2024 trend in government is towards a warm embrace of total social control.

Frighteningly, in a misnamed article which would make George Orwell blush, "Saving Democracy," Jason Kelly interviewed two University of Chicago law professors, Tom Ginsburg and Aziz Huq, who were spruiking their book *How to Save a Constitutional Democracy* (University of Chicago Press, 2018).[15] For those sentient Americans alive during the Trump and Biden Administrations, it is impossible to avoid sensing a certain ingrained opinion about the 44th President in some media and academic quarters.

The gist of their comments – and feel free to refer in true Chicago fashion by going to the original text – is that an unelected professional technocratic class provides continuity and some degree of stability in managing governmental affairs, which is true and a fairly bland observation; further, that said technocratic class *should* control and determine, not

---

[12] Alexis de Tocqueville, *Democracy in America,* trans. George Lawrence, Anchor Books, 1969, pp.262-3

[13]   https://www.newsweek.com/texas-judge-orders-jail-sentence-hair-salon-owner-who-kept-business-open-despite-stay-home-order-1502164

[14] Copyright, Christopher Messina, 2020

[15] University of Chicago magazine, Spring 2019

just manage the policies which give rise to those affairs, which is most assuredly *not true* in a representative republic.

How insane is *that*? Here are a couple of *law professors* stating that true freedom in a representative republic comes from maintaining a stable of unaccountable bureaucrats who are *immune* to control – they call it "interference" – by the elected representatives and their appointed officials the American people have seen to vote into office.

Ponder that for a while. Roll it around on your mental tongue. That the two professors in question teach at the same law school that Barry Hussein Soetoro Obama was an adjunct instructor at should sadly come as no surprise.

Justice Clarence Thomas, having grown up in the Jim Crow South, having been denied the use of "white" water fountains and the right to cross a "white" public park, is highly sensitive to the idea that unelected, unaccountable administrative state bureaucrats, along with enabling judges, can flout the clear written laws which Congress creates. In a 2015 opinion,[16] he excoriates the Supreme Court for aiding and abetting this non-democratic destruction of the rule of law, writing that they "have overseen and sanctioned the growth of an administrative system that concentrates the power to make laws and the power to enforce them in the hands of a vast and unaccountable administrative apparatus that finds no comfortable home in our constitutional structure."

We need to massively trim down the administrative state so that – as in de Tocqueville's time – the government once more is "only occupied with a small number of matters important enough to attract its attention."

Milton Friedman rightly observed years ago that "Hell hath no fury like a bureaucrat scorned." Those people who feather their own beds by increasing the complexity of government and its intrusion in our lives will fight intensely to keep their privileges.

This important job, that of trimming the Federal Government back to its proper size, my dear fellow citizens, falls to us. That is as the Founders intended. They understood that a self-interested class would try to create a protective bubble for themselves using *our money* by convincing us that *they know better than we do.*

Ronald Reagan said many brilliant things. You don't need to take my word for it; you know that is true, because every single centralizing power-hungry politician and media babbling head parrots the "fact" that he was "dumb." Reagan warned us that if we sink back a bit further into our couches and hide our heads hunched over watching a tiny slice of the population scream at each other on social media, that we will ultimately deserve the position of slavery we are being asked to accept. "To sit back hoping that someday, someway, someone will make things right is to go on feeding the crocodile, hoping he will eat you last--but eat you he will."

You've seen on the cover of this book how I deal with feisty lizards.

----

[16] Justice Clarence Thomas, Department of Transportation v. Association of American Railroads, 2015

Itinerant Bureaucracy

I would take the idea of decentralized government even further by setting up a system of rotating office locations. A rolling stone gathers no moss, and as anyone who has ever moved house can attest, there is nothing quite like having to pack up and move things to inspire lean living. Every time I've moved, I have not only shed unused possessions, but the knowledge that I may move again makes me pause to consider any new purchase very carefully. If I don't like something enough to want to pack it up and move it again, then clearly, I don't really need or want it.

Monarchs throughout history knew the best way to keep the nobles and military officers (in our world, sadly, the bureaucrats) in line and from getting above themselves, was to impose costs on them and move them around a lot. It's hard to build a base constituency of personal loyalty when you are administering a new city or region every five years.

By coupling radical budgetary transparency, a "jury duty"-like view of civil service and frequent headquarters relocations, the American taxpayer would not only develop a much firmer sense of national pride and unified purpose, but we'd get far better value for money from our bureaucracy.

Budget and Impoundment Control Act of 1974

Wherever possible, existing mechanisms of government should be modified to suit the refreshed, invigorated new dispensation I propose. We've got a lot of work to do to hack Leviathan back to a much smaller version of its current cancerous state.

The Congressional Budget and Impoundment Control Act of 1974 was signed into law creating the House Budget Committee on this date. The bill overhauled the Budget and Accounting Act of 1921, which had been intended to assist Congress in its appropriations role by requiring the President to submit an annual budget. As the process grew more institutionalized, Presidents sought to exert greater control over federal spending. Frustrated with President Richard M. Nixon's impoundment of congressionally appropriated funds, Congress reasserted its budget authority. By shifting the federal government's fiscal year from July 1 to October 1, Congress gained the time to respond to the President's annual budget message and properly legislate federal spending. The act created both the House and Senate Budget Committees and the Congressional Budget Office (CBO). The CBO was charged with gathering data and estimates and supplying the committees with proper information to assist the federal budget process. The House Budget Committee became a standing committee on July 12, 1974, in the 93rd Congress (1973–1975), but it did not organize until August 14, 1974. Albert Ullman of Oregon served as the first chairman of the committee.[17]

---

[17]https://history.house.gov/Historical-Highlights/1951-2000/Congressional-Budget-and-

Starting with those processes and organs which already exist, we must insist that our elected Representatives get to work on creating transparent budgets based on clear principles, all debated in the bright sunshine of public review. Entities like the CBO can be enhanced by including new, rotating temporary members from the general public, kind of like grand jury duty.

Also, be very wary of all entities which project into the future. There is nothing wrong with financial modeling and creating *pro forma* financial predictions. It is very important not to let those models supplant reality and first principles. The CBO staff are diligent folks but they are not perfect, as hearings on how their predictions were off by $1,000,000,000,000 demonstrate.[18]

In the coming chapters, we will dive into the granular details of the current state of the Federal Budget, along with my recommendations for change. Bear in mind my organizing principles of simplicity and the four equally binding tests of relevance for each piece of our vast Federal machinery. Keeping that lens focused will make the road to reform and reinvigoration of our splendid experiment in self-governance clear and achievable.

Thank you for coming on this journey with me into a very rough neighborhood. Dante Alighieri and Joseph Conrad would be proud of your fortitude!

Comparison of Messina's Budget v. Current Budget

It's always best to lay things out at the start. The folks in DC sure can shovel cash out the door, can't they? "Mandatory" expenditures are on autopilot, absent significant changes in the law, "Interest" *must be paid* and does not provide a single service to taxpayers. Therefore the "Discretionary" column is the slice of spending that people in Congress theoretically "debate" – HAH! – the merits of during every budget preparation. My budget is 100% discretionary, meaning it must be affirmed and voted on every year.

Impoundment-Control-Act-of-1974/
[18] Rep. Smucker Questions CBO Processes in Wake of $1 Trillion Deficit Projection Error (youtube.com)

43

Figure 2: Federal Expenditures 2007-2021

Year	Mandatory	Discretionary	Interest*	Total
2007	2,019,000,000,000	1,279,000,000,000	237,000,000,000	3,535,000,000,000
2008	1,610,000,000,000	1,120,000,000,000	253,000,000,000	2,983,000,000,000
2009	2,112,000,000,000	1,219,000,000,000	187,000,000,000	3,518,000,000,000
2010	1,954,000,000,000	1,370,000,000,000	196,000,000,000	3,520,000,000,000
2011	2,073,000,000,000	1,300,000,000,000	230,000,000,000	3,603,000,000,000
2012	2,032,000,000,000	1,285,000,000,000	220,000,000,000	3,537,000,000,000
2013	2,086,000,000,000	1,147,000,000,000	221,000,000,000	3,454,000,000,000
2014	2,400,000,000,000	1,100,000,000,000	229,000,000,000	3,729,000,000,000
2015	2,612,000,000,000	1,100,000,000,000	223,000,000,000	3,935,000,000,000
2016	2,427,000,000,000	1,086,000,000,000	240,000,000,000	3,753,000,000,000
2017	2,500,000,000,000	1,219,100,000,000	263,000,000,000	3,982,100,000,000
2018	2,522,000,000,000	1,278,000,000,000	325,000,000,000	4,125,000,000,000
2019	2,777,000,000,000	1,359,000,000,000	393,000,000,000	4,529,000,000,000
2020	2,975,000,000,000	1,438,000,000,000	479,000,000,000	4,892,000,000,000
2021	2,966,000,000,000	1,485,000,000,000	378,000,000,000	4,829,000,000,000

* Interest on debt for 2020 (which is 1 Oct 2019 - 30 September 2020) was calculated *before* the insane Wuhan Panic Borrowing Splurge. Same for projections for fiscal 2021, based on budget planning which preceded the Insane Fiscal Blowout due to Wuhan Panic. Estimates as of February 2021 show total Federal spending for 2021 to be between $7,500,000,000,000 and $9,000,000,000,000.

Missing is a line item for bulk transfers to States, which is a significant chunk of cash. I have not even bothered to add the $2,600,000,000,000 that Congress recklessly added to 2020-2021 expenditures and debt issuance all because of irrational panic over a slightly worse seasonal coronavirus. 2020 expenditures may well have been closer to $7 trillion, in addition to the appalling economic damage done by governors and mayors which have destroyed businesses and lives, all in a fruitless attempt to combat a virus which spread virulently anyway. The total money spent in 2023 was nearer to $7.5 trillion.[19]

Next up is a breakdown of how revenues relate to all this sea of cash being squandered by the mandarins in Washington, DC. For fun, go check out the U.S. National Debt Clock : Real Time[20] which combines the glittering distraction of a pachinko parlor with the looming sense of dread one feels while approaching a brick wall at 120 mph with no brakes. As is clear from Figure 3, the Federal Government has lost the ability to constrain spending to what the American taxpayers can afford.

---

[19] Financial Report of the United States Government - Financial Statements of the United States Government for the Fiscal Years Ended September 30, 2023, and 2022 (treasury.gov)
[20] https://usdebtclock.org

Year	Revenue	Annual Deficit	National Debt
2007	2,568,000,000,000	(967,000,000,000)	9,008,000,000,000
2008	2,524,000,000,000	(459,000,000,000)	10,025,000,000,000
2009	2,105,000,000,000	(1,413,000,000,000)	11,910,000,000,000
2010	2,165,000,000,000	(1,355,000,000,000)	13,562,000,000,000
2011	2,303,000,000,000	(1,300,000,000,000)	14,790,000,000,000
2012	2,450,000,000,000	(1,087,000,000,000)	16,066,000,000,000
2013	2,775,000,000,000	(679,000,000,000)	16,738,000,000,000
2014	3,020,000,000,000	(709,000,000,000)	17,824,000,000,000
2015	3,250,000,000,000	(685,000,000,000)	18,151,000,000,000
2016	3,270,000,000,000	(483,000,000,000)	19,573,000,000,000
2017	3,320,000,000,000	(662,100,000,000)	20,245,000,000,000
2018	3,330,000,000,000	(795,000,000,000)	21,516,000,000,000
2019	3,464,000,000,000	(1,065,000,000,000)	22,719,000,000,000
2020	3,710,000,000,000	(1,182,000,000,000)	28,000,000,000,000
2021	3,860,000,000,000	(969,000,000,000)	

While the blend of tax revenue changes slightly from year to year, the breakdown of estimated revenue by type is shown in Figure 4. Productive taxpayers are by far the largest source of tax revenue. That is history. The chapters that follow provide insight into why I propose such a drastic reorganization of our Federal government's priorities.

Figure 4: Estimated Sources of Tax Revenue Fiscal Year 2021

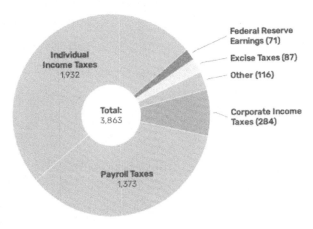

Federal Tax Revenue FY2021 Estimate in USD Billions

Individual Income Taxes 1,932

Federal Reserve Earnings (71)

Excise Taxes (87)

Other (116)

Total: 3,863

Corporate Income Taxes (284)

Payroll Taxes 1,373

Chart: The Balance • Source: The Office of Management and Budget

Given that I work from first principles and am not trying to perform the mathematical gymnastics of, say, the Congressional Budget Office, the line items to be kept and the line items to be jettisoned are laid out clearly. What cannot be predicted is national income and the taxes derived, which form the revenue side of the government's income statement. I have laid out two years' worth of projections based on my revised budgetary model. This is to give the reader a sense of the value of restrained, right-sized government. The myriad complexities are the same as they are in the private sector. For example, I assume *a priori* that it is more efficient to hire workers one needs and let go those one does not, just as in the private sector, so abolishing public sector unions will have an instantly beneficial effect on government finances, the proper function of the few things we want government to do and on overall societal wellbeing.

Starting with the next chapter, we will have a romp through the Federal Bureaucracy. Bring a friend – it's not a safe neighborhood. I've divided the entire Federal edifice into two buckets – those things we the taxpayers need to toss on the garbage heap of history and those things we the taxpayers should continue to fund, with some suggested improvements where applicable.

Lastly, I've included some overall thoughts on proper policy going forward, in the hopes that if we can make these changes, that we can also set up barriers to another crop of hyper-motivated parasites to try to recreate the oppressive administrative state we're currently suffering under.

Let's get started, shall we? First up are the Departments that either have outlived their utility or were bad, stupid ideas to begin with.

Onwards!

Figure 5: The Memorial to the Federal Budget B.M. (Before Messina) I hope to see erected on the National Mall after this book's suggested changes have been adopted.

Chapter 2: Department of Education

Year Founded	1979
Founded under President	Jimmy Carter
Funding Budget 2023	$88,300,000,000
Insane "COVID Relief" Additional Cash 2021	$81,900,000,000
Messina's 2024 Budget Proposal	$25,000,000
Messina's 2025 Budget Proposal	$0
Degree to which Messina's Plan is Better	Infinitely
Should a Federal Dept of Education exist?	No

Is this a standalone proper use of the taxpayers' limited resources?	No
Does this expenditure unfairly benefit one American over another one?	Yes
Does the expenditure meet the "Is this logical?" standard of fiduciary responsibility?	No
Can the goals be achieved by *not* spending the dollar more effectively than by spending it?	Yes

First to go is one of the dumbest ideas our governing class has ever come up with. Jimmy Carter signed this into being in 1979. That alone is sufficient argument to make this ridiculous waste of taxpayer money and abuse of the nation's children go away immediately.

Scrap it *in toto*. Wipe roughly $90 billion off the budget instantly. (I wish I were smart enough to read the budget figures to understand *even generally* how much this parasitic enterprise puts us on the hook for, but that is the headline number.) In conception, creation and operation this is an utterly ridiculous waste of taxpayer money and human time. It was insane enough in January 2021 that $73 billion was being tossed at this beast, but then the Biden Administration for no *rational* reason – meaning, one that would benefit children – added another $82 billion on top of that in the name of a virus whose impact on children is zero. All so the teachers' unions and Department of Education could *close the schools indefinitely* so "teachers" could day drink and kids could have their lives and proper development ruined.

This beast is so obviously awful that Ronald Reagan beat Jimmy Carter in 1980 with *abolishing the Department of Education* a key plank in his platform. He tried again in 1982, after the Democrat Tip O'Neill managed to saddle Reagan with more spending, giving hefty weight in his State of the Union talk about the horrific damage this ridiculous department was doing and would continue to do to America. The GOP for whatever stupid reason quietly dropped the rational dismantling of this bad idea in 1984 when Reagan won 49 out of 50 States for reelection. That is easily one of the dumbest mistakes in the history of American politics. This bureaucratic beast should never have lasted a year.

Billions of dollars every year pay for salaries and benefits to unelected, unionized bureaucrats who do nothing but bolster the strength of teachers' unions. Nothing done by the Department of Education has *anything* to do with educating a single child. Contrast that with the approximately $5 *million* of private money that is spent specifically on promulgating the teaching of American History in "our" schools.[21]

In Obama's 2012 budget, there was plenty of opportunity for astonishment, but this snippet would have Orwell rolling on the floor with breathless laughter and Goebbels crowing with delight at the ironic twist of delivering The Big Lie. The Big Lie in this instance is that such a thing as a Federal bureaucracy tasked with any kind of involvement in educating our young should even exist in the first place.

> **Helps States and Districts Do More with Less by Evaluating What Works and Paying for Success.** Now more than ever we cannot waste taxpayer dollars on programs that do not work. That is why the Budget includes significant resources to continue the Department's efforts to evaluate investments launched under the Recovery Act and to initiate several new evaluations of interventions in adult and postsecondary education. In addition, the Budget contains $100 million to help States and districts provide important information to principals and teachers about their progress in meeting their reform goals and improving outcomes for students. As we learn what works, we also should reward those who are able to get extraordinary results from the dollars they spend. The Administration is launching a series of low-cost incentive programs including "pay for success bonds" that provide funding only after results are achieved; prioritizing cost-saving initiatives within Race to the Top and Investing in Innovation; and creating a prize for State and local grantees with the greatest cost savings.

It's a marvel of poetic insanity. "Now more than ever we cannot waste taxpayer dollars on programs that do not work." So let's blow $100 million of money we've made our grandchildren borrow from the Chinese by off-shoring our own manufacturing sector on wildly ill-defined busywork dreamt up by unaccountable bureaucrats. And when those bureaucrats are done pestering teachers and principals – thereby keeping them from doing anything related to actual teaching – when some "rise to the top," as statistics says they inevitably will, we'll hand out cash prizes and plaques.

It's complete madness. We need to eliminate this entire beast immediately. The education of the young is a job for local communities, and at *worst* could require State involvement.

Devolving control of primary and secondary education back where it belongs will encourage true involvement from local communities. Having been as heavily involved in my children's education as possible, I have seen firsthand how teachers and parents who find some things ridiculous often find ourselves shrugging and accepting some insane dictate from the State or Federal government. The alternative is to home school your children – which is a step increasing numbers of parents have taken, largely because of the parents'

---

[21] Further proof that private markets will deliver services people want are the number of organizations dedicated to teaching History to high schoolers. Here is an interview I did with the Executive Director of one of those not-for-profits bringing historical awareness to children: https://youtu.be/cVoK4hixzCw

inability to swallow one more offense against their beliefs by the secular "Education" Authorities.

If you want to allow your local school to shape your child's future by teaching them that the universe is 6,000 years old, with trips to museums showing cavemen riding dinosaurs, then go right ahead. Alternatively, if you want your community's schools to offer a curriculum emphasizing a vibrant education based on computer science and engineering, then that is what your local schools should offer. The market for education will become a robust one as families realize there are options available between what "Dinosaur Riding Cavemen School" offers versus what a kid can expect to learn at the "Computer Science, Rigorous Math and Other Things Needed to Compete Globally School."

Every community must be involved closely in the education their children receive. There is plenty of room in that statement for communities large and small to request guidance and advice from anyone claiming to be a teacher or educational expert. The crucial difference between local communities overseeing education policy, curriculum and practice and being dictated to by a faceless Federal government is that local schools teach independence of thought.

Are you, dear reader, sensing a pattern? Federal bureaucrats demand the authority to teach your child what *the bureaucrats* have decided is worth learning. Other Federal bureaucrats run things like the Federal Election Commission which upon pain of imprisonment or stiff monetary fines tell you what you can and cannot *say* during an election. Both are serious assaults on your rights under the First Amendment and both are blatant attempts at thought control.

My 2024 Budget is $25 million, which is enough to hire some wind-down professionals to fire everyone in the department and to find competent real estate brokers to start selling off any assets the Department of Education has.

By 2025, if all goes well, the cost to taxpayers at the federal level will be a big fat zero, which accords nicely with the value delivered by the Department of Education since 1979. As a reminder to future generations, I propose an architectural contest to create an enduring monument to this disastrous abuse of power. To kick things off, here is my contribution, which can be erected as if it were an entrance to the former building in Washington, now turned into condos or something else of actual use.

Figure 6: Proposed memorial "entrance" to the defunct Department of Education building

Professional Politicians Fear *Nothing* as Much as an Educated Populace

Education of a thoughtful, responsible citizenry is *far* too important to be entrusted to government. Government should be – and will become, if we all pull together – a smoothly-functioning utility sticking to a very few, carefully defined and delineated tasks.

The only way that will occur and *continue* as the new status quo is for a robust citizenry composed of thoughtful, truly educated *individuals.*

Why do I aver that today's professional politicians – versus my hoped-for future of part-time, reluctant politicians drafted like jury duty – *hate* educated people? Because it's really hard to lie to smart people who are paying attention and have trained themselves to spot nonsense from a mile off on a foggy day. On a practical level, Niall Ferguson cites dozens of studies showing the lack of financial literacy prevalent in American society:

It is a well-established fact, after all, that a substantial proportion of the general public in the English-speaking world is ignorant of finance. According to one 2007 survey, four in ten American credit card holders do not pay the full amount due every month on the card they use most often, despite the punitively high interest rates charged by credit card companies. Nearly a third (29 percent) said they had no idea what the interest rate on their card was. Another 30 percent claimed that it was well below 10 percent when in reality the overwhelming majority of card companies charge substantially in excess of 10 percent. More than half of the respondents said they had learned 'not very much' or 'nothing at all' about financial issues at school. A 2008 survey revealed that two thirds of Americans did not understand how compound interest worked. In one survey conducted by researchers at the University of Buffalo's School of Management, a typical group of high school seniors scored just 52 percent in response to a set of questions about personal finance and economics. Only 14 percent understood that stocks would tend to generate a higher return over eighteen years than a US government bond. Less [sic; sorry, Niall, you meant "fewer" here] than23 percent knew that income tax is charged on the interest earned from a savings account if the account holder's income is high enough. Fully 59 percent did not know the difference between a company pension, Social Security and a 401(k) plan.[22]

So. Politicians and public sector unions have been in charge of "education" for fifty years, managing in that time to fill kids' heads with a range of dubious propagandistic assertions about nonexistent things like "systemic racism" and "gender fluidity" while dumbing down "unimportant" subjects like, oh, grammar, mathematical reasoning, analytical logic, *American History* and financial literacy. During the same period of time, we've spawned a nation of credit-card-indebted video junkies unable to discern insane fiscal decisions from basic financial prudence. I leave it to you to decide whether the Political Class *intended* that result or if they're merely delighted at its occurrence. I am constantly reminded that it is usually smarter to attribute insane outcomes to ignorance and laziness rather than coordinated conspiracies, which after all take effort and are nearly impossible to keep hidden.

Let's turn for inspiration back to the benefits of truly educated, motivated citizens. At the *very least*, an educated voting public would understand the sweeping lies peddled by egomaniacs pushing their favorite new pet projects. I am not here to provide historical glory to fools, but current readers (2024) will know about whom I am writing when I talk about a relative child who auditioned for a role as a US Congressional Representative in a district with the *fewest* actual voters of all 435 districts in the nation, who trotted out one ridiculously dumb idea after another about brand new "New Deals" involving, for example, *retrofitting every single building in the entire United States* as a way to "save money" on energy.

---

[22] Ferguson, Niall, *The Ascent of Money; A Financial History of the World*, 2008, pp10-11. Go read Niall's book for the references and more importantly his sound layman's explication of monetary developments.

The horror about this goofball's act is *not* that she promulgated these truly ridiculous totalitarian fantasies, but that 100% of people did *not* automatically laugh at her idiocy and move on to more pressing matters, like what to have for lunch or whether to scrape old gum from the sidewalk. Other fools in her political party who *really* should know better – including *the Senators* from her State – gleefully jumped in front of microphones to echo this nonsense. Presumably, they would not have done so had most of their constituents known how appallingly insane, stupid and value-destructive implementation of even a portion of her giggling idiocy would prove to be.

In between proposing the stupidest ideas ever to emerge from Congress, she took time to do social media videos about applying her makeup before heading to the floor of the House of Representatives. Really. I couldn't make that up if I tried.

The strongest defense against poor decision making is a well-educated populace. The education of strong-minded, clear-thinking citizens cannot be the result of a centralized power structure controlled by groupthink ideologues. To take a prominent example at random, Stanford University has promulgated *speech codes* to "protect" fragile snowflakes from "harmful language."[23] To fuel your outrage, astonishment or sense of bemusement, feel free to browse their insane offering. Hint: "American" is an offensive adjective. Stanford receives tens of billions of dollars from *American* taxpayers every year. *American* taxpayer largesse and appallingly expensive tuition support 2,888 teaching faculty and 15,750 non-teaching administrative staff who "serve" 16,937 students.

Perhaps *Americans* should send those dollars to someone not offended by our very existence. Perhaps parents paying Stanford tuition should wonder why they are paying 5.5 times as many salaried workers than actual *teachers.* Mayhap tuition and fees would be vastly *lower* if there were, say, 250 administrators and 500 buildings and maintenance staff.

Qualitative problems are not solved by quantitative means

We used to have a country that was honest about the relative skills, aptitudes and drives of individuals. In 1940, someone who *achieved* a high school diploma had *studied* hard and learned difficult material. Such graduates could – shocker! – deploy correct grammar in formulating letters and essays of various kinds, could use mathematical reasoning in their business affairs and had a fair grasp on the broad sweep of history. Whether that history could have been expanded to include a broader cast of characters, versus the "standard model" of rich European white folk is a different discussion – the students having learnt the history being taught enabled them to place events in some kind of context. At least with a grounding in actual history, students would *have* a foundation upon which *to add* a broader cast of characters, nations and causes.

For a wide range of reasons, we've backed ourselves into a corner on education, which is *not* an assembly-line process of defining "inputs" like "class size," "teacher salary"

---

[23] stanfordlanguage.pdf (wsj.net) /
https://s.wsj.net/public/resources/documents/stanfordlanguage.pdf

and so on to produce "outcomes," defined even more poorly as regards to things like "grades" or "skills." As with so many things in life, the most valuable are hardest to create, infuriatingly difficult to define and evaporate under too much scrutiny.

As Jay Greene, a "professor of education reform" – whatever on earth that might be in practice, though I support the idea in principle – at the University of Arkansas wrote recently[24] about the current candidates for president both crowing about the great idea of "hiring more teachers" as the "solution" to myriad problems, up to and including the national macroeconomic picture.

For decades we have tried to boost academic outcomes by hiring more teachers, and we have essentially nothing to show for it. In 1970, public schools employed 2.06 million teachers, or one for every 22.3 students, according to the U.S. Department of Education's Digest of Education Statistics. In 2012, we have 3.27 million teachers, one for every 15.2 students.

Yet math and reading scores for 17-year-olds have remained virtually unchanged since 1970, according to the U.S. Department of Education's National Assessment of Educational Progress. The federal estimate of high-school graduation rates also shows no progress (with about 75% of students completing high school then and now). Unless the next teacher-hiring binge produces something that the last several couldn't, there is no reason to expect it to contribute to student outcomes.

Here is not the place to rehash the arguments on all sides – some good, some silly – about the state of education in America. What is relevant here is that the Federal Government should get completely and utterly out of the way. The insanity of taxpayers in, say, Ohio sending money to Washington and then asking Ohio senators and congressmen to get that money sent *back* to Ohio for schools is self-evident. What is at stake here is both containing the size and cost of the national government *and* pushing back at the relentlessly moving, inch-by-inch strain of totalitarianism in American political life that goes back to the 1920s. It went from claiming inches to grabbing yards and miles under Obama. Under Trump and the flimsy excuse of the Wuhan Virus Panic, those miles of totalitarian ground suddenly expanded exponentially to complete home imprisonment of hundreds of millions of formerly-free Americans. Biden came into office demonstrating immense Fellow Traveler Silliness by simultaneously getting a vaccine *but continuing to wear a face mask* which is so dumb in medical terms that my brain keeps throbbing in agony at the sheer illogic of it all.

I am not so worried about the ridiculous people who desperately love the Administrative State taking over every aspect of every American life – the fellow travelers of Bill Ayers and Jane Fonda well know who they are and rely on everyone else believing their clear motives don't exist. If we as Americans take back the power Washington has grabbed unto itself and starve the massive bureaucratic beast of its oxygen (our hard-earned cash and wide open credit card), we'll see improved schools under local control and the angry Lefties can go back to crying in their fantasy-lands about what a shame it is the *lumpen proletariat* don't understand *why* Oliver Stone and Noam Chomsky know what's "better" for us....

———————————————

[24] Greene, Jay, *The Imaginary Teacher Shortage*, Wall Street Journal Opinion, 8 October 2012

Better-educated, more discriminating students who are taught locally in ways that work rather than ways that hew to demands made by an unaccountable "Department of Education" will end up providing a stronger set of *individuals* better suited to the rigorous demands of life and competition. Clear-thinking citizens educated to reason, debate and form intelligent decisions are what the founders of our nation had in mind when they embarked on this unique project in self-governance.

There are so many examples of wasted taxpayer dollars to choose from. To grab an outsized example of pure waste, let us return to those heady days of yesteryear, 2010. Not satisfied with the normal, annual, run-of-the-mill massive taxpayer boondoggle, in 2010 the Obama Department of Education got to blow $97,400,000,000 (that's $97.4 BILLION dollars not including the ongoing interest payments on that borrowed cash) in special "Recovery Act" money.

> As of September 30, 2010, the Department of Education's entire $97.4 billion in Recovery Act appropriation has been awarded. Grant recipients reported that approximately 275,000 education jobs, such as teachers, principals, librarians, and counselors, were saved or created with this funding during the most recent quarter. ED administers 21 programs under the Recovery Act. Read the ED Recovery Plan [PDF, 901K] to learn about the purpose, benefits, cost, evaluation, and more for each program.[25]

Why on earth did a single penny have to be allocated so that "Education" could "Recover" from a mortgage market catastrophe caused by decades of Federal housing policy? That bad policy only accelerated and got worse under Bill Clinton and his colossal moron of a HUD Secretary, Andrew Cuomo, who later as Governor of New York went on to kill tens of thousands of elderly New Yorkers by jamming them into nursing homes instead of sending them to empty Naval Hospital Ships sitting in New York Harbor to assist them. Oh, and he wrote a book about how great a Governor he was while many women came forward to describe how he sexually assaulted them. But I digress — somehow all the damage Clinton and Cuomo did by destroying the housing market meant that Obama's pals in Congress got to shovel *Ninety-Seven and a Half BILLION dollars* at the Department of "Education."

It only gets worse when it comes to higher education. No matter the set of outrageous statistics one chooses, the *moral* of this story is clear — throwing piles of dollars at a centralized education bureaucracy has not resulted in an excellently-educated, rational citizenry.

We need to stop throwing money at "more" and start figuring out — locally, mind you, locally — how to get the kinds of results we got 90 years ago in the reality of tight financial times. And when — G-d willing — each community has learnt those lessons and set their educational ship aright, then I hope they can maintain that cost and educational discipline when better times come along. Given that all educational expenditures and

---

[25] IDEA Special Education Grants to States Recovery Plan

decisions will be locally controlled, my faith in better cost management is strong under local control.

During this transition period, when the heavy hand of Propagandist Leviathan still sits oppressively on the shoulders of teachers, parents and children across our fair land, we must make sure to enhance the experience of that oppression as uniformly and possibly, all to drive awareness of its scourge and increase appetite for its destruction.

Once again, I apply the same, simple, consistent guiding principles, which in this case means *that every rule created by the government must be adhered to by the politicians and bureaucrats who are in office when passed.* Regarding the Department of Education, this means that the Common Core standards and *mandated* state-level testing *must* be given to *every* child in America – including all the kids of, oh, I don't know, the President and Senators whose children at Sidley Friends in DC *didn't have to sit through the boring standardized tests that my children in Florida and New York did.*

I am not a fan of centralized control of anything, so I am not saying that private school students overall should have to take these tests. No – I am saying that the *children* of all politicians and government employees in those schools must.

On test day, when kids across the nation have to endure standardized tests in public schools, the Long Arm of the Department of Education must reach into private schools across the nation and specifically take the children of the Political Class to a separate room to endure the same exams.

The fun of that mild torture aside, none of my proposed craziness and micromanagement of kids who have already suffered enough by having a politician as a parent is worth our tax dollars *or* more importantly a just and proper use of scarce economic and social resources.

Does your community want to teach that the world is 5,600 years old and that dinosaurs roamed the earth with cavemen and that all things like the half-life of Carbon-14 are simply elegant "tricks" played by G-d to test your faith? Go right ahead. Have at it.

It cannot be any sillier than teaching kids that humans are inherently good, that diagramming sentences undermines creativity, that there are "better ways" to teach math than what worked for 2,500 years, and that everything Americans do in the world is wrong while everything everyone else does must be put in context as a reaction to American unbridled – and unique, mind you – "evil" intent. *That* narrative has been dominant in primary, secondary and tertiary education ever since Vietnam-era education deferments gave us The Draft Dodger Generation's self-appointed infestation of the educational machine.

To improve our society and increase children's faith in this nation as a unique beacon of light in a dark world, we must restore educational themes which reinvigorate pride in our nation's past while continuing efforts to improve how we all live together and treat one another. Since going forward, education will be locally controlled, time will tell how students raised in, say, the Great State of Florida, will differ in their opinions from children taught by lemon-sucking perpetual America-haters on the Upper Left Side of Manhattan. In the battle of ideas for the soul of the nation, I sure hope one faction wins over the other.

A High School Diploma Used to Be Evidence of Actual Accomplishment

As the nation readjusts its priorities and *each community* decides how best to set educational priorities and curricula for its children, a magical thing will happen. Excellence will once more become a competitive priority, as parents demand the best for their children. Once common (circa 1920) high school topics like Classical Greek, Latin and *actual* History and Geography will come back into fashion.

How excellent will it be when a young woman or man can say proudly – without a hint of irony or defensiveness – "I finished my junior year of high school, took my aircraft mechanic or water treatment proficiency certificate and have entered a professional apprenticeship program." With parents beaming proudly. Or another student saying, "I decided to stay for my fourth year and am graduating with a full high school diploma; I am a member of the National Greek Honor Society and am heading to University next year to continue my studies." Likewise, with parents beaming proudly.

When education meets local needs, when students feel pride in their communities and nation and experience a sense of purpose in their progression from school to a productive working life, Americans will have once more course-corrected and made full use of our ongoing experiment in self-governance.

Decentralization Protects Society from Propaganda

Isn't amazing how a simple guiding principle can be so effective? Keeping it simple and making sure most decisions are local also applies with great benefit to the nation's educational system. Centralization allows infection or contamination spread far and wide. Using my example above – whether one agrees with my characterization or not – should the fine citizens of the Upper West Side of Manhattan vote *locally* to appoint school administrators to oversee a curriculum of continuing Western culture self-hatred, then no one in Central Florida, Northern Montana or the Upper *East* Side of Manhattan should have any say in their pedagogical choices.

The transformation of American "education" under people like Bill Ayers[26] was no accident. He and his band of fellow ideologues were if nothing else good students of history. (I invite you to savor the irony of *that* fact...) They looked at effective educational efforts of the past, for example the Jesuits in the Roman Catholic Church. Bill realized that the way to change America was to grab young minds and spend decades drumming leftist ideological nonsense into their heads.

As of early 2024, their plan has worked a treat. You've got idiot children on college campuses physically attacking *speakers* who say things the poor snowflakes don't like. When we were kids, we were all taught to chant "Sticks and stones may break my bones, but

---

[26] Commie flake that Barack Obama looked to for guidance. He was a cofounder and leader of The Weather Underground responsible for bombing US government buildings. Later spent his career as an "elementary education theorist," rather than dangling from a rope as a traitor and terrorist.

words will never hurt me!" in response to bullies and loudmouths. It was a sound doctrine. Some chunk of today's children have been taught to believe that *words* are themselves violence.

It's ridiculous; there are few things I dismiss out of hand without debate, but this whole "intersectionality," perpetual victimhood snowflake nonsense is one of those few things. I read *The Emperor's New Clothes*; from the time I was five, I knew that it was right to shout out "He's naked!" when confronted with such stupidity. As a nation, we have real things to worry about. Some coddled snowflake's fainting spell over a guest speaker who makes mean claims about the value of personal effort and the content of one's character rather than the color of one's skin are not among those things.

The ideological drift leftward in American indoctrination, er, education, is no accident and has been pursued with vigor and purpose by Leftists. The best defense against this nonsense creeping into *your* community's school is to make sure all educational decisions are made locally, so no Commie moron like Ayers or Obama can disseminate nonsense from a fantasy-factory making up lies about American history all the way from Washington, DC to your child's desk in Pasadena, Dallas, Anchorage or Indialantic.

In the universities, the Leftist Struggle Committees have only grown bolder in the last decade. Whimsical dreams of sociology professors who desperately wanted to fire tenured colleagues in the Economics department who not only dared suggest that free markets were not the root of all evil but might actually perform socially beneficial purposes remained dreams for decades. Until the Obama Education Department mandarins began to strip away due process on college campuses and began to reward the oppressive tools of censorship that Commies everywhere have always loved so dearly.

A Mole Hunt for Diversity 'Bias' at Villanova
An atmosphere of fear-imposed silence makes it impossible to achieve a real liberal-arts education.

By Colleen A. Sheehan and James Matthew Wilson
March 29, 2019 6:26 p.m. ET, *Wall Street Journal Opinion*

Like many colleges in the U.S., Villanova University has launched an effort to monitor its faculty for signs of "bias" in the classroom. As Villanova professors, we believe this mole hunt for bias undercuts our ability to provide students with a liberal education.

Last fall we were notified by the Villanova administration that new "diversity and inclusion" questions would be added to the course and teaching evaluations that students fill out each semester. In addition to the standard questions about the intellectual worth of the course and the quality of instruction, students are now being asked heavily politicized questions such as whether the instructor has demonstrated "cultural awareness" or created an "environment free of bias based on individual differences or social identities."

In short, students are being asked to rate professors according to their perceived agreement with progressive political opinion on bias and identity. Students are also invited to "comment on the instructor's sensitivity to the diversity of the students in the class." Professors are rated on their "sensitivity" to a student's "biological sex, disability, gender identity, national origin, political viewpoint, race/ethnicity, religious beliefs, sexual orientation, socio-economic status, etc." The "etc." in particular seems like an ominous catchall, as if the sole principle of sound teaching has become "that no student shall be offended."

However well-intentioned, the new assessment of faculty "sensitivity" and "bias" will harm Villanova's mission to provide a liberal education. Professors will now have a powerful incentive to avoid discussion of anything that might be deemed offensive or insensitive to the various social identities and political viewpoints listed (or not listed, by grace of that "etc.").

A biology professor may avoid teaching about sexual dimorphism for fear of being labeled "insensitive" to "gender identity." Professors of political philosophy, history or literature may avoid introducing the texts of John C. Calhoun, Abraham Lincoln, Mark Twain, Harriet Beecher Stowe, Frederick Douglass or Flannery O'Connor, for fear their sometimes racially charged language may be interpreted as "insensitivity." Catholic teaching prizes philosophical reasoning, but one cannot reason with others if the mere posing of an argument could be deemed an act of "bias."

And what about sensitivity to social identities, given Villanova's Catholic character? Those who teach courses about Catholic doctrine on marriage and the family may now live in fear that their own university will treat such views, and those who teach about them, as insensitive or worse. In fact, the "sensitivity" questions appear almost perfectly designed to stifle Catholic moral teaching in the classroom.

The larger implications are even more disturbing. The new evaluations will allow a professor's professional performance to be recast as a human resources or even a legal problem. Think about it: You can't fire a professor for being conservative, but you certainly can fire him for creating a "hostile work environment." At a minimum, all charges of insensitivity, injustice and bigotry will become part of the faculty's permanent record. How long will it be before professors cease to challenge their students for fear of losing their careers and livelihoods?

For many decades, Villanova's mission as a Catholic university has been to initiate students into the life of the mind, encouraging them to seek the good, the true and the beautiful even as they are challenged beyond our walls to pursue justice and the common good in the service of "charity in truth." The adoption of the new dogma of mandatory "diversity and inclusion" places that entire undertaking in danger. As professors dedicated to liberal education, we consider it essential to challenge our students to subject their ideas as well as the predominant opinions of our time to critical examination—however difficult and uncomfortable this may be. We urge our own university as well as other liberal-arts institutions to reject such ideological policing and recommit themselves to the principles of liberal education.

This cannot be achieved in an atmosphere of fear-imposed silence. We professors—and our students—must be free to think and question and debate. Surely respecting diversity must also allow for diversity of thought.

Ms. Sheehan is a professor of political science at Villanova and a co-director of its Matthew J. Ryan Center for the Study of Free Institutions and the Public Good. Mr. Wilson is a professor of religion and literature.

These professors paint a picture of Maoist Struggle Committees that is kind of hard to believe exists in America. How many more hysterical leftwing movies does Hollywood need to make to tell Americans that Joe McCarthy was crazy to insist that Communism is an existential threat to American freedom? What *else* could this kind of insane persecution of individuals *based on points of view or even simple expression of ideas in debate* be but a fundamental threat to freedom?

Americans used to understand the difference between policing thought versus policing actions. Certain segments of the country – some knowingly, some thoughtlessly with what they think are good intentions – have turned thought itself into a crime. This may be startling news to recent graduates of our Snowflake Factories: *It is not a crime for someone to believe green people are inferior, or that people attracted to inanimate objects are insane. It is not even a crime to express those opinions verbally or in print. It is, however, a crime for you to attack physically a green person trying to marry a toaster.*

See the difference?

The more I have delved into the educational policies in the nation, the more disgusted I have gotten. We must all pay attention to the biases we bring to any topic, and I most assuredly am no exception to that rule.

My background in finance and entrepreneurship made me fertile ground to hear a message about "results," and "accountability" and all the other happy catch phrases that *for-profit* education businesses that call themselves "schools" promulgate to win public approval.

The claims made by Teach for America distract the nation from the hard work of truly reforming the education profession. Instead of building a profession that attracts well-qualified candidates to make a career of working in the nation's classrooms, our leaders are pouring large sums of money into a richly endowed organization that supplies temporary teachers. If we were serious about improving teacher quality, we would encourage all future teachers to get a solid education and preparation for teaching, and we would expect districts and states to construct a support system to help them get better every year. Instead of expending so much energy on whom to fire, we would focus energy on making teaching a prestigious profession in which classroom teachers have considerable professional autonomy over what and how they teach.

By its design, TFA exacerbates teacher turnover, or "churn." No other profession would admire and reward a program that replenished its ranks with untrained people who expected to move on to a new career in a few years. Our schools already have too much churn. Too many teachers leave the classroom with the first five years, especially in high-poverty schools. These schools need stability and experience, not churn. Few members of TFA stay in the classroom as long as five years. Researchers have found that experience matters; the weakest teachers are in their first two years of teaching, which is understandable because they are learning how to teach and manage their classes. Researchers have also found that staff stability matters. The more that teachers come and go, the worse it is for the schools and their students.[27]

There were many "Ah ha!" moments when reading *Reign of Error*, but this one was the gut punch. To look at analogues in the two industries I know best – finance and technology – there is *nothing* so valued as long, deep experience. Sure, the press loves to talk about the $20 million in venture capital raised by a 22-year-old, but the reality is that all the capital and tech that go into whether a venture survives or not is always due to the accumulated decades of gray-hair experience. In finance, for sure age and experience count for a huge amount – that is what stands between the "obviously brilliant" new product idea shining out from a 23-year-old analyst's Excel sheets from turning into toxic waste in investors' portfolios. Or the proper guidance through a complicated merger transaction which only gets done right and to everyone's satisfaction because someone with 20 years of experience doing 150 deals is leading the effort.

Part of all this is the mistaken attempt to apply industrial-type standards to something as impossible to quantify as education. Many of our worst government policies start with the best of intentions; testing is strongly among them. The ideas in the 1990s focused on testing and "accountability," which meant firing teachers whose students did not do well on tests and closing "failing" schools. In 1989 under President Bush, a panel was convened, and six ambitious national goals were announced for the year 2000.

President Clinton enthusiastically supported the national goals (he had drafted the language for them at the Bush summit) and added two more for good measure. In 1997, Clinton asked Congress to authorize voluntary national testing in reading and mathematics for students in fourth and eighth grades, but Congress – controlled by Republicans – refused. Clinton's proposed national tests disappeared and so did the national goals. None of the goals that had been proclaimed to much fanfare in 1990 was reached by the year 200, and the Goals Panel quietly vanished.

---

[27] Ravitch, Diane, *Reign of Error; the Hoax of the Privatization Movement and the Danger to America's Public Schools*, Knopf, 2013, pp.143-144

61

Undaunted, the second President Bush persuaded a willing Congress to pass his No Child Left Behind legislation in 2001. Democrats and Republicans alike agreed on the importance of accountability for teachers, principals and schools, especially if their students were not achieving. The administration and Congress agreed that testing would spur school improvement. Unlike the first President Bush's six national goals or Clinton's eight national goals, NCLB contained one goal: All children would be "proficient" in reading and mathematics by 2014. This time, however, the goal was not merely a devout desired wish, but a federal mandate, with real consequences for schools whose students did not meet it.

NCLB opened a new era of testing and accountability in American public schools. Educators and parents who objected to the new emphasis on testing were outraged. They railed against the tests, they filed lawsuits, they protested, all to no avail. Politicians dismissed them as anti-testing fanatics, and the courts rejected their lawsuits.

The anti-testing forces lashed out against the wrong target. Testing was not the problem. Tests can be designed and used well or badly. The problem was the misuse of testing for high-stakes purposes, the belief that tests could identify with certainty which students should be held back, which teachers and principals should be fired or rewarded, and which schools should be closed – and the idea that these changes would inevitably produce better education. Policy decisions that were momentous for students and educators came down from elected officials who did not understand the limitations of testing.[28]

In sum, I am punting on the obligation to cover inadequately in a very a few pages what others cover comprehensively in thousands. The only reason I include this section at all is to reiterate my aversion to the over-centralization of American society. Dismantle the Department of Education entirely. If we decide there is any value in continuing centralized testing, turn it over to another department, like the National Science Foundation, or leave all testing decisions to the States.

Federal Money and Law Cause Massive Social Damage to Communities

While most normal Americans want the same things for their children – safe and effective schools providing a valuable education to prepare them for the rigors of life in a competitive world – all too often the bizarre preoccupations of increasingly strange fringe groups drive policy in schools. Abolishing the Department of Education will let free Americans once more choose *locally* how best to educate their offspring.

Sports for example are clearly one excellent part of an education. Exercise is good for the body, mind and spirit. Teamwork teaches discipline and how to work with others. Good sportsmanship is a trait that used to be universally valued in America and still is in some places. Competition in a strenuous environment of continuous improvement is a valuable way to teach preparedness and focused thinking.

---

[28] Ravitch, Diane, The Death and Life of the Great American School System; How Testing and Choice Are Undermining Education, Basic Books, 2010, pp149-150

All great things.

Just count on maniacs in Washington, DC to destroy the healthy, wonderful effects of sports in our schools.

A group of congressional Democrats signed a letter in June 2020 demanding that the Department of Education allow males to participate in girls' sports. Connecticut Senator Richard Blumenthal and 27 other Democratic members of Congress signed the letter, which stated that the department's order "discriminates against transgender youth" by ruling that it is a violation of women's access to education and athletics for public schools to allow biological males who identify as female to participate in female sports.

"The decision of the Department of Education to issue a determination targeting transgender student athletes on the eve of Pride Month is not coincidental. It is a transparent example of their campaign against the rights and dignity of LGBTQ+ children," said lead signer Connecticut Representative Jahana Hayes in a statement.

The Education Department's ruling, issued on May 15, provoked backlash from Democrats and transgender rights advocates, who called it "another attack from the Trump administration on transgender students."

In March, the Justice Department filed a statement of interest in a federal case against the Connecticut Interscholastic Athletic Conference's policy requiring males to compete against females. Three female high-school students and their families filed a federal lawsuit seeking to block transgender athletes from competing in girls' sports in Connecticut. The female athletes argued that they have been personally harmed by a policy allowing biological males to compete against them in their running events, missing their chances at championship titles, state records, and scholarship opportunities. The girls also filed a complaint last year with the Department of Education.

One of the girls, Chelsea Mitchell, who attended Canton High School, missed out on achieving the title of state champion four times because she was competing against transgender athletes. Another, Alanna Smith, who went to Danbury High School and is the daughter of former MLB pitcher Lee Smith, has placed close behind transgender competitors as well.[29]

Now, if the people of Connecticut want to let girls lose to boys in competitive sports, they – or, rather, each individual school district – are free to make that stupid decision. But why on earth Senator Blumenthal thinks it's *right* or *just* for him to shove his oar in to tell parents in the other 49 States how their school athletic programs should be run is exactly what is wrong with this nation's government and provides a glaring example of why we need to fix it.

I am not going to wade into the current (2018-2024) cultural insanity over the apparently sweeping "epidemic" of "transgender" *children* in this nation. Well, I guess I just did. I feel *enormous* empathy for *anyone* who suffers from an illness or mental disease. I cannot imagine how painful it must be to be convinced of anything as disturbing as believing that one has been born into the wrong gender. What I find very hard to accept as objective

---

[29] Mcardle, Mairead, "Congressional Dems Sign Letter Demanding Education Dept. Allow Males in Girls Sports," *National Review Online*, 19 June 2020

reality is that we have a sudden epidemic of children who suffer from a genuine gender dysphoric disorder. Or if we do, then we as a nation need to fund a comprehensive study into our food chain, environmental and other factors to see *why* suddenly hordes of children are being born into the "wrong" bodies. But we don't likely have a physical oversupply of boys who should be girls in a medically objective sense, so it's more likely one more cultural enthusiasm pushed by ideologues on the constant hunt for *anything* to divide us.

A brilliant woman, Abigail Shrier, has been investigating this cultural phenomenon. She has summarized her findings in a trenchant and timely critique, *Irreversible Damage: The Transgender Craze Seducing Our Daughters.* Her main point is that one of the newest attempts for teenage girls to grapple with the mental, emotional and physical changes wrought by puberty is to jump on a trendy train which seeks to explain that normal discomfort with a radical and largely insane idea, that the "real reason" for this teenage angst is that they should actually have been born with a penis. If I had a better imagination or were writing fiction, it'd be hard to top that notion.

Whatever the *biological or psychological basis* for this sudden rash of "transgender" kids, this lunatic focus on letting biological males compete in girls' sporting events is ridiculous. If a given school district wants to vote to let Jimmy run 100-meter sprints against Sally, Priya and Aisha, then they can do so – and parents in that school district can then choose whether to stay in that district. Wow – what a difference freedom of choice makes.

But not in the totalitarian dreams of Biden[30], Blumenthal et alia, who want to force rational people to adopt highly debatable propositions, all of which have as the article points out, real world damage potential for the girls suddenly put at a disadvantage. Not "just" fair play and sportsmanship is at stake; very often next steps in athletic and academic achievement depend upon winning at one's chosen sport.

All of these crucial issues regarding our children are far too important to let a damned politician have any say in them, and certainly not a Federal politician. These are town council level debates, if indeed they are to be held at all. I feel deeply for any family who is grappling with a teenager so disturbed from equilibrium as to believe the "only" solution to feeling such emotional pain is to undergo complicated, dangerous gender reassignment surgery. I feel just as much for anyone who is genuinely gender dysphoric. There has always been a tiny percentage of the population that experiences this issue and it must be very difficult to grapple with.

Whatever the situation of those families, one thing I am sure of is that *no one involved* is helped in any way by the Federal Department of Education. There is no need to discriminate for or against them beyond the general American ideal that everyone should be treated fairly. On an individual level, we all experience setbacks which we may or may not perceive as fair; that does not mean a biological teenage boy should be able to enter into physical competition with a biological teenage girl if the sport in question is defined as being for females exclusively.

---

[30] One of President Biden's first acts as President was to sign on 20 January 2021 <u>Executive Order on Preventing and Combating Discrimination on the Basis of Gender Identity or Sexual Orientation | The White House</u>

Federal Money and Law Cause Higher Education Costs

Make no mistake. Any time the government "subsidizes" something, the cost for the thing subsidized rises.

When it comes to doling out cash to students for higher education, the impact is the same whenever a distant bureaucracy hands out cash "subsidies." The price of the good or service rises immediately to equal the price beforehand plus the subsidy.

Combine decades of cost-inflation from politicians giving out the goodies with the insane laws that prohibit private sector employers from giving prospective employees intelligence and aptitude tests, and you get the overpriced and pointless phenomenon of hundreds of colleges that on their own would never be called into existence.

There is a great Dilbert cartoon where Dilbert yells at the Pointy-Haired Boss "You're fixing the wrong problem!"

One of the most self-serving "ideas" the Political Class came up with was not only to inflate tuition with subsidies, but to then *forgive* the debt incurred if the student chooses to go "into public service." How good is that? *Hey, kid! The cost of college is absolutely insane, mainly because of our meddling in the education market. How's this for a deal? You go rack up $300,000 worth of debt loaned to you by the sheeple, er, taxpayers and then – wait for it! – instead of following your dream of being an entrepreneur or embarking on an exciting private sector career, you take a public sector union job. That way, you get above-market pay, complete job security for life, a taxpayer-funded pension that pays you a crazy amount of cash you'd struggle to accumulate via private savings – especially after we change the rules on IRA inheritability – with zero health care costs (to you, of course, not the stupid sheeple) and – best part! – you get all these crazy goodies and we **erase** your college debt! You in, kid?*

The idea that it's "morally superior" to take a job with the Parks Department versus a job in, say, customer support at Microsoft, and therefore the taxpayers should write off the educational debt owed us is insane. Rather than continuing to pick winners and losers in this dumb game, let's eliminate it entirely *or* make the debt the joint responsibility of the university and the student. Let's see how excited Harvard is take a real risk on a student completing all four years and turning productive enough afterwards to pay off their debt if Harvard is on the hook for it should the darling snowflake default because said snowflake bought the lie that they should "follow their bliss" instead of taking a cold, hard objective look at the world, their own talents and limitations and finding a way to be a productive, contributing member of society.

That used to be called being a responsible adult by the deeply moral people who used to organize our society, whereas "following one's bliss" was what the useless town junkie did.

College kids and young adults were drawn like iron filings to an electromagnet to both Comrade Bernie Sanders and Fellow Traveler Elizabeth Warren during the 2019-2020 Democratic primaries because both were promising to wipe away all student loan debt. FDR would be proud – even the Socialist in a Wheelchair wouldn't have been so brazen in buying votes, and he invented the practice.

To be fair, the kids are right about one thing – the cost of a college education has soared beyond all rationality. In a free market where such things are determined, by the time Harvard, say, or the University of Chicago (which in a rational world would have a 20x value premium over the former institution) had continued to raise their prices over and above the combined growth of GDP and inflation, fewer and fewer people would have seen any reason to pay ginormous amounts of money to send their precious ducklings to get learned up bigly.

In summer of 2021, the Biden Administration "decided" to just "forgive" student loans for up to $20,000 per deadbeat borrower. Absolute madness and as fine a demonstration of the irresponsible arrogance of the Political Class as one could conceive of. Roughly 65+% of Americans never go to college in the first place, and many of those either pay for their education outright or subsequently paid off whatever loans they took out. As one outraged father said to Senator Elizabeth Warren – in an encounter caught on video – "I worked hard and saved and paid for my daughter's education. Do I get a check from the government, too?" She *laughed* in what she probably thought was a disarming way and said, "Of course not!"

Liz, read a room! Her laughter and dismissive answer clearly made the father's blood pressure skyrocket. He kept after her, saying, "I worked double shifts. We didn't take big vacations. I didn't buy a new car. I saved so she could go to college. My neighbor did none of those things, went on expensive vacations, always had a new car and now you're going to give him $20,000 to pay off his kid's loans?! How is that fair?" She was trying to get away from him and brush him off, but he wasn't having any of it.

"So you're going to pay for people who didn't save any money and those of us who did the right thing get screwed?" he said. She made some mumbling response about should we not have started Social Security because it was not available just before it was enacted? Of course that is a stupid statement and not even remotely analogous – the Biden Administration wants randomly to give $1,000,000,000,000 to people who happen to carry student debt right now, without any considerations of fairness or rationality. The courts, thank God, put a stop to this (October 2022), as the Constitution grants the power to spend money to Congress, not to the Executive Branch.

But Biden charged on anyway, ignoring the Supreme Court. As of 21 February 2024, the Biden-Harris Administration gave $138,000,000,0000 away to deadbeats who decided not to pay their student loans.[31]

To be clear, I lay a great deal of the blame for that massive debt load at the feet of the same Federal idiots now trying to "fix it." When Biden was VP under Obama, Obama's brilliant plan was to take student loans away from banks, who have a business model based on credit risk and collections, and just "save money" by having the government lend the money directly. He claimed the taxpayer would turn a profit. As with everything to do with free markets, of course he was exactly wrong. Not only did this genius move *not* turn a profit, it's turned into a massive loans explosion, feeding the skyrocketing costs of college.

---

[31] FACT SHEET: President Biden Cancels Student Debt for more than 150,000 Student Loan Borrowers Ahead of Schedule | The White House

Note I didn't say "education," as it is impossible to correlate many of the Leftist indoctrination camps with anything a classical scholar would call "education."

If the public policy point for Biden's massive cash giveaway attempt is - and it's the only good one I've heard yet - that an 18-year-old with uneducated parents did not know what they were signing when they incurred these loans, then *maybe* some "fix" is appropriate. But nothing about fixing that problem means the taxpayer should be on the hook for a dime.

When fixing financial market problems, it's always best to lay the responsibility closest to where the blame is. So by all means, let's convene a commission to examine the entire ecosystem, including front and center the fat universities who have tax exempt endowments. Let's lay it all out, gather data about the range of types of loans, sizes of loans and distribution of terms. Our analysis should include benchmarking 'fair loan terms' and comparing outliers. Then we can as a society say, "All right. There is $1.2 trillion of money here that we are judging to be an unfair albatross around borrowers' necks because universities lied to them and the government lied to them about the absolute value of "going to college," without reference to major, quality of school and a host of other real-world conditions.

"Here's what's gonna happen. $400 billion of that was interest to scumbag lenders with unfair clauses. The lenders are going to eat that cost and it will be wiped off the borrowers' balance sheets. $700 billion of that will come from universities writing a check to cover that amount of debt still owed by borrowers. The remaining $100 billion will be cleared up by taking all "out of benchmark loans" and turning them into benchmarked loans, thereby resetting repayment terms for those impacted borrowers.

"Going forward, all educational loans will be dual obligations of the college or university and the student. Everyone involved should have an incentive to place properly prepared students in courses of study that will lead – on average – to a career with earnings to repay any loans. Irritate us again with this nonsense and we'll revoke endowment tax-benefited status."

First, convert *all* Federal student loans into dual-obligation loans with the mutual borrowers being the student *and* the university receiving the funds. Just watch loan delinquency and non-payment rates plummet as universities are suddenly incentivized to make sure their former students pay taxpayers back.

Second, kill the whole Federal loan scheme going forward.

Third, force universities to publish the kinds of metrics other not-for-profits publish so prospective students understand in dollar terms the potential likely cost-benefit decisions to be made.

Done. Not a penny required from the taxpayers.

Federal Regulation Created the Artificial "Need" for a College Education

I hope you, dear reader, can take a moment to understand how much money I spent on aspirin during the research I did to write this book. I hope the toll on my liver will on balance prove to have been less than if I'd chugged a highball instead of popping a couple of aspirin every time I came across something so pointless and insane that I needed *something* to prevent my head exploding.

So many of the laws, rules and regulations we are drowning under can be swept away by simply tracing their root causes. If you are patient enough, you will find the "keystone" of the entire edifice, which when removed, will render all the insane tangle of laws built upon it obsolete.

In the case of the American "education" system, it is accurate to say that hundreds of billions – if not trillions – of dollars have been wasted solely because the Supreme Court ruled in its 1971 decision *Duke v. Griggs* that it was illegal for a company looking for employees to require job applicants to take a test to prove their proficiency in relevant skills. That seems strange, you might think. If a company needs someone to, say, file hundreds of folders about customers daily, it would be good to know which applicant is not only fluent in the alphabet, but how quickly each applicant can apply that alphabetical knowledge to taking a pile of folders and putting them in the right place in filing cabinets.[32]

If I need someone to measure a length of wood and cut it to size, I'd like to know if that person understands units of measure, how to apply a ruler to a piece of wood, how to mark the wood with a pencil and then how to deploy a saw to cut the wood to a desired length. The Supreme Court *made it illegal for me to give a potential worker any kind of test to see if that potential worker could perform those tasks.* Why, a reasonable person should ask, would a judge rule that an employer be *prohibited* from finding out whether a job applicant can, you know, *do the job?*

If you, dear reader, have any good answers to that question, I look forward to hearing them! Especially since the vetting process a potential Justice goes through while the Senate performs its "advise and consent" role in judicial appointments means that the Justices who were on the side of this stupid ruling *themselves* had to pass a battery of tests to qualify for their jobs.

Oh, where would our Governmental Solons be without hypocrisy and an utter lack of irony as their constant familiars?

Companies responded to this insane ruling. Companies *still* want to know whether the person they hire can perform the tasks required, so they looked for other ways to test for competency. When one is trying to solve a problem, and one is unable to directly test for information about that problem, the next best thing is to look for analogues or proxies for that thing. In this case, to keep with our same example, an employer is now *banned* by law from giving three candidates a 20-minute quiz to test spelling and alphabetical aptitude. So how can that employer discern the same desired information? *Well, she might reason, I know that it's impossible to graduate from high school without passing a range of tests, and it's reasonable to assume that one couldn't pass written exams without a minimum degree of capability with letters and words. Therefore, I'm going to assume that anyone with a high school degree is qualified to do this job.*

---

[32] Those fans of Ignatius P. Reilly, familiar with his office career will understand the desirability of competency tests. Reading *A Confederacy of Dunces* will help you understand my book more deeply.

So far so good. If one of the three candidates has a high school diploma, that person gets the filing job.

But hold on. What if all three candidates possess a high school diploma? If the employer is still permitted under the Labor Laws, then she can ask to see each of their high school transcripts.

Hey! One of the three failed English Composition twice and got a C+ in senior year. Okay – I can count him out. Each of the other two both got A's in their English and writing-related classes. So do I give the job to the taller one, because some of our filing cabinets are really high? Or the more attractive one who will have to bend over frequently because all our filing cabinets are only two drawers high? Or maybe the quiet one because I really cannot handle one more stream of inanity from the administrative staff.

In the end, artificially interfering in the labor market does no one a service – not employers who need jobs done well, nor employees who should find work in which they can succeed. Just as water flows around obstacles, people will always try to find the information they need.

One of my favorite stories in this vein comes from a friend who – years ago, well past any statute of limitations and for a company that no longer exists, for all the hungry class action lawyers out there – ran the shipping department for a cosmetics company. During the holiday season from Thanksgiving to Christmas, they were always three times as busy as normal times, so the company would hire seasonal workers to work packing gift boxes.

Because of the industry and the schedule, the main applicants happened to be women who were the secondary breadwinner in a household. Now – if you're running a shipping department, you want to be sure that the people you hire to pack boxes for you show up on time reliably and focus during the 4-9 hours per day they are scheduled to work. What you *don't want* is someone who will suddenly call out sick or leave early.

The main cause of sudden absence is usually small children. They get sick on a dime and unlike teenagers, when they get sick, they cannot be told to go home on their own; they need to be picked up from school, often with no notice.

Under Labor Laws in the United States, it is illegal to ask an applicant any personal information. You're not allowed to ask, "Are you married?" or "Do you intend to get pregnant?" or any of a host of related questions, the point of these laws being that it's "discriminatory" to screen out people who might, you know, not be able to do the job required. I am *not* making a value judgment; it's just a fact. If I need to hire someone for an assembly line job, I don't want to invest months in training that person, only to be told he or she will be out for 6 months on maternity or paternity leave. While it may be "fair" to the new parent, and while in theory I may be able to replace that person with a temporary worker, it is not discriminatory to say that from an operations perspective, it'd be a whole lot simpler to *not hire* someone likely to be taking half a year off in the foreseeable future.

Back to the gift box packing position. An employer is not permitted to ask about family topics, *but nothing prevents an applicant from offering information*. So this executive kept pictures of young children on her desk, facing the job applicant. Often in a bid to build rapport during an interview, the applicant would see the pictures of the kids and say things like, "Oh, I remember that age. Mine are already in college – how old are yours?" Or, perhaps, "That's a coincidence – are those recent pictures? I've got three at home between 6 and 10; we got portraits done at the mall last year just like those…"

69

The first person would get the job. The second would not.

Another colleague – again, years ago – worked in a temporary staffing agency. They did all the interviewing and hiring for temporary workers. They handled office jobs mainly, people who had to answer phones and do basic administrative tasks. On the whole, the staffing agency really did match the letter of the law to the spirit of the law; they did not discriminate on race or sex or age of disability.

But... one of their clients was a big-time fashion house or something like that. The point was the client who hired the temp agency only needed front desk staff when they needed anyone at all. And it was always on very short notice, so they paid really well. The catch was the hiring manager – in person, not in writing or over the phone – made it crystal clear that this contract was based on the agency only sending over very physically attractive temps to sit at the front desk.

So as to not leave a paper trail that could get any of them in legal hot water, they had a shorthand code to single out those candidates who would qualify for Front Desk Hottie work. Every interview was conducted, and notes were taken. A choice few candidates had meeting notes that started with "Interview was conducted in meeting room B." That note was factually true, but what it really meant was "don't send this one to the front desk job."

As this relates to the Department of Education, this whole idea of diplomas, certificates and degrees has been distorted past the "simple" idea of giving one a credential for mastering a course of study. When real money is on the line, people will game any system presented to them, and the more the government tries to make things "fair," all that happens is that connected, clever people use those silly rules to their advantage while other qualified people lose out.

Tax University Investment Funds and Quit Giving Taxpayer Dollars to Universities

If you can stand the immediate migraine, take some time to listen to politicians speak about taxes. A certain chunk of them intone a religious mantra with a few variants, but *all* of their statements include something about someone (else, of course), "paying their fair share." You want to know which massive group of wildly rich corporations are *not* paying *anything,* never mind "a fair share" in any definition of the word? The propaganda factories called "universities."

Simplicity is the taxpayer's friend. It is hard to hide massive waste of money in a simple system. It is beyond ridiculous that university endowments operate free of taxation and then hit up the American taxpayer for cash to fund operations. So not only are Americans *not* getting taxes paid by the endowment funds for investment performance, but those same hardworking, overtaxed Americans (that'd be *you,* dear reader) are then asked to cough up crazy amounts of cash so Harvard and Yale can charge $95,000 per year to drill goofy nonsense into impressionable minds, all propaganda delivered by the same ageing cohort of selfish Draft Dodging Baby Boomers.

Are you sensing a pattern yet? If you haven't, you should schedule an appointment with your neurologist.

President Trump's Administration made a step in the correct direction when new rules ordering university endowments to pay an annual tax when the endowment had at least $500,000 per student. In an environment of insanely rising costs for "higher" education, costs which are often borne by the American taxpayer, it makes sense that if universities are sitting on so much cash instead of, say, helping struggling families pay for tuition, then the American taxpayer should demand to be compensated in some way.

I would add different tests, like no more than 10% of the people on the payroll of a university can be non-professors. But that's just creating new conditions to game, which is not the point of simplicity and true equality.

In the name of real fairness, universities should pay taxes on their endowment returns and no Federal dollars should go to higher education.

Local taxes must be allocated to students' families, not union-controlled school districts

The biggest change which will reinvigorate American public education is to strip the spending power from teachers' unions. Students and their families should be the economic voice which shapes education in their communities. Schools must compete to offer their educational services. Good schools with excellent teachers will attract students and thereby the funding which comes along with student choice.

Currently government bureaucrats send money to school districts, which then send the money to individual schools, whose principals then manage those budgets to hire teachers and perform all the other operational requirements of a functioning school. Having sat for a decade on various PTOs and School Advisory Committees in Brevard County, Florida, two things have jumped out at me.

1. Our school district is populated by a majority of caring professionals who are dedicated to education.
2. The bureaucracy created to handle taking dollars in from the State, County and Federal coffers is unwieldy, too large and unresponsive to the parents of the county.

I don't blame anyone for that, not as individuals, anyway. Bureaucratic systems are their own organisms. The current funding structure means the system is geared towards pleasing the source of funds, not necessarily the real constituents which are the parents and children of the district.

Under my rational reorganization, the dollars flow to each family as a spending credit (not as cash). The entire service model would change to be responsive to the customers who can vote on a yearly basis – or perhaps in special circumstances, more frequently – with their education spending credits.

Schools can choose to pay their teachers more – or less – depending on skill, performance, results delivered. You know, how people are judged in the free market, which is the *only* system which has ever delivered consistently higher quality for ever-lower costs, and the only one which has ever tried to. All without any "expert" bureaucrat trying to micromanage anything.

Requiem for a failed experiment

The examples of the damage wrought by this pestilential abuse of power would fill 600,000 pages at least. Feel free to do some research on your own. The Department of Education must be abolished immediately for the vast improvement of the nation.

R.I.P., Department of Education.

We save an annual $90,000,000,000 immediately by putting an end to a failed social engineering experiment, and that's just the budget for the silly department, not including the insanity of the losses from loans which should never have been made in the first place, or all of the societal rot that is inevitable whenever a centralized unaccountable power is giving free reign to promulgate whatever goofy nonsense happens to be popular with the Ruling Class at the time. Hopefully we as a nation have learnt something about wasting trillions of dollars letting Washington bureaucrats pester America's schoolteachers, and that we won't let *that* craziness happen again.

A man can dream. But millions of thoughtful, focused individuals can change bad policy.

The multiple horrors of the DC Swamp and the overwhelming complexity of the bureaucratic beast we've allowed to grow means that even the politicians supposedly "in charge" of all this have no clue how any of it works. You can each call, write and email your representatives to tell them you are bringing them good news! They just have to vote to abolish this parasitic waste of taxpayer dollars once and never be bothered about the distortion and ruination of good education again.

Find your Representative with this helpful link:
https://www.congress.gov/members/find-your-member

They work for you. Remind them of that.

Figure 7: Winner of the "Requiem for the Department of Education" Memorial Sculpture Competition

Chapter 3: Department of Housing & Urban Development

Year Founded:	1965
Founded by President	Lyndon Johnson
Funding Budget 2021	$71,900,000,000
Messina's 2024 Budget Proposal	$25,000,000
Messina's 2025 Budget Proposal	$0
Degree to which Messina's Plan is Better	Completely
Should a Federal HUD exist?	No, no, no, no, no, no. **NO**.

Is this a standalone proper use of the taxpayers' limited resources?	No
Does this expenditure unfairly benefit one American over another one?	Yes
Does the expenditure meet the "Is this logical?" standard of fiduciary responsibility?	No
Can the goals be achieved by *not* spending the dollar more effectively than by spending it?	Hell Yes

This abusive waste of your tax dollars is a holdover from President Johnson's Great Society zaniness. He announced this vast spending spree during a commencement speech at the University of Michigan on 22 May 1964.

HUD should be instantly defunded. Any stray holdover obligations of the department are to be immediately handed off to the states and municipalities in which they are resident. Better yet, all HUD assets should be auctioned to private bidders.

There are multiple reasons why this galloping beast of bureaucratic whimsy and politicians' dirty dreams should be taken out back behind the barn for a shot behind the ears. It may not be new, but it's still true and maybe especially so in the Age of Obama-Trump-Biden: listening to politicians speak is a thorough exercise in seeing what life is like once you step – or, more aptly, get shoved – Through the Looking Glass.

In *Politikspeke,* actions and policies that damage the economy and restrict freedom are declared to do precisely the opposite, received with much hypnotic nodding and murmured agreement from some segments of the population.

I went to my favorite search engine and typed in "What does HUD do." In response, I was provided a link:

What does HUD do?

The Department of Housing and Urban Development (HUD) is the Federal agency responsible for national policy and programs that address America's housing needs, improve and develop the Nation's communities and enforce fair housing laws. HUD's business is helping to create a decent home and suitable living environment for all Americans, and it has given America's cities a strong national voice at the Cabinet level. HUD's programs include:

- Providing mortgage insurance to help individuals and families become homeowners;
- Development, rehabilitation and modernization of the nation's public and Indian housing stock;
- Development of HUD-insured multifamily housing;
- Development, improvement and revitalization of America's urban centers and neighborhoods;
- Providing rental subsidies to lower-income families to help them obtain affordable housing; and,
- Enforcement of Federal Fair Housing laws.

HUD is assisted in carrying these various programs and in managing its own operations by a variety of independent contractors and vendors.[33]

Let's take it step by step to see just how impracticable and often downright insane is this described mandate.

Table 2: Department of Housing & Urban Development task breakdown

Task	Should Fed Govt do this?	*Can* Fed Govt do this?	Is this patently insane?	Should *HUD* do this?
Create "national policy" to "address America's housing needs"	Probably Not	Highly Doubtful	Quite Possibly	No
"Improve and develop the Nation's communities"	No	No	Yes	No
Enforce fair housing laws	No	Yes*	Yes	No
Create "a decent home and suitable living environment for all Americans"	No	No	Yes	No

The sharp-eyed will note I score "improve and develop the Nation's communities" as patently insane. It is indeed insane to believe this can be done, but it's more nuanced than that. To call it insane is to shift attention away from its true nature. This kind of bureaucratic beast has nothing to do with helping a single person, never mind something as ridiculous and big-picture fluffy as "developing" *the entire Nation's* "communities."

Nope, this is traditional Progressive *Diktatorspeke* for "we're going to control every aspect of your lives and fine you and put you in jail if you don't like it."

You'll notice I score the bit about "enforce fair housing laws" with an asterisk. "Fair housing" for those of you who are not aware, is the Orwellian euphemism which describes forcing *you* (via FDIC-insured bank deposits) to make loans to people who cannot afford to repay them. Which is another way of saying "fair lending laws" steal money from

---

[33] http://portal.hud.gov/hudportal/HUD?src=/program_offices/sub/guide/general

hardworking, frugal people who save their money only to give it to deadbeats who will take that cash and never, ever repay the person who saved that money from a combination of hard work and personal sacrifice. These laws grew out of a fantasy that for a range of statistical distortions conflated skin color with creditworthiness, claiming that – even once such pernicious *and governmentally-approved* practices as redlining were revoked – the primary cause for Person X failing to get a mortgage was her skin color.

This fantasy *is the root cause* of the 2007-08 financial crisis. When I note that the Feds can enforce these crazy laws, it's important to realize that strictly speaking the German government in 1939-1945 was enforcing the laws and from 1948-1993 the South African apartheid government was enforcing the laws, but that does not mean that the laws in question were good, rational or moral ones.

The bad ideas, negative impacts and trillions of wasted dollars stemming from HUD's very existence is like the biggest, wildest, fastest growing metastasized cancer ever. Here's a snippet grabbed at random from Obama's 2010 budget:

> **Improves the Way Federal Dollars are Spent**
> **Assists Cities in Using Their Funds More Effectively to Support Job Creation.** The Budget supports the launch of an interagency effort led by HUD and the Department of Commerce's Economic Development Administration (EDA) to help communities to better employ the Federal investments they already receive, promote high-impact strategies, and build the local capacity needed to execute those strategies in economically distressed areas. This effort will enable these communities to create more effective partnerships with businesses and non-profits that will attract critical private investments to promote job creation. With leveraged support from HUD, other Federal agencies, and the philanthropic community, the Federal Government offers targeted EDA funds, technical assistance, and a National Resource Bank—a "one-stop shop" of experts that communities can draw upon for a full range of services, including fiscal reforms, re-purposing land use, and business cluster and job market analysis. (p.95)

This is beyond laughable. The only thing more useless, slow-moving, and detrimental to the public purse than one federal agency is anything involving "an interagency effort." This insanity summarized above is *WishfulSpeke* for "if lots of unaccountable bureaucrats get to waste more time and money preparing PowerPoint presentations for other useless parasites, then somehow 'effective partnerships' with non-profits and businesses are going to 'promote job creation.'"

Frankly, I'd prefer if the author of this section were more honest, for example by saying, *"We will open up the breast of the red-feathered rooster on the third toll of the bell past midnight on Midsummer's Eve and shall do as the entrails spilled into the moonlight instruct. Jobs shall thereby be created. Bippity-boppity-boo."*

In a series of annual documents chock full of ridiculous entries, this one comes near to topping the list. A "National Resource Bank" which will be a "'one-stop shop' of experts" that "communities" can "draw upon for a full range of services, including fiscal reforms, re-purposing land use, and business cluster and job market analysis."

You know when something is not for real? When there is no such thing being done in the private sector. "Business cluster analysis" — I read that a few times and still have no clue what is meant by this, and how doing what I presume is an exercise involved in taking a map of a given location and then marking on the map where and what kinds of businesses are "clustered" has anything to do with what *individual decisions* free actors in a market economy would thereby take. I understand *fully* what would happen in a command-and-control, centralized Soviet-style economy. Based on "the clusters," some bureaucrat would then decide "what the right next business" should be to — I'm betting, and betting hard — *diversify* the cluster's composition.

Whether individual, free market consumers of business services and products would therefore make better free use of this newly diversified cluster is wide open to debate.

More crucially, if individual business owners, local Chambers of Commerce or even local governments choose to embark on such analyses, then that's fine. It's just an utterly pointless waste of US taxpayer dollars to presume that "experts" in a Washington-based bureaucracy can help "communities" thousands of miles away with a laughably broad "full range of services."

Aside from "fiscal reforms," which would mean putting a red line through this entire farcical exercise, *none* of the quoted section about the "National Resource Bank" means anything practicable. *What on earth does any of that mean?*

Sorry. I know *exactly* what it means.

Allow me to translate: We'll create another unaccountable bureaucracy with an impossible mission, give it a really fancy, important-sounding name, immediately give it an acronym (NRB), then arm twist some Member of Congress into giving support for a totally ludicrous amount of cash, say $800 million to start, then with that in hand, let the jockeying for political payola begin. That means who gets an unreasonably-large salary and a fancy title that implies they *run* the NRB, or better yet — to limit potential accountability and derailment of future title-hopping adventures — implies they *have oversight of* the NRB.

For the actual "work" the NRB shall do, we'll get a pack of eager 22-year-olds (preferably impressionable, attractive and *willing to please their Congressman*), all sparkly-eyed about a job in The Capital, who will dash about feeling important, writing long-winded papers an assistant professor at a decent college would write "C-" with some withering remarks across the top of, but in D.C. will get nods of approval on the way to a pay grade increase, in part because a concrete pile of paper is seriously-justifiable "work product" when some nosy pest from the CBO Ombudsman shows up wondering where $800 million of the taxpayer cash has been flushed away to this time, but largely because, as I am sure Chris Dodd or Teddy Kennedy told every cute intern who ran into him five whiskeys into happy hour on a Tuesday, *Who really cares? The "poor" we're here to "help?" Sheesh, they'll never read it, and if they did and cared, all it would tell them is that the gravy train is making a stop on their doorstep, so they'd best nod and say "yes, please" to whatever bag of cash is coming their way. Where'd you say you were from again, honey? Wisconsin? Really? You know something? I've always loved cheese. Beautiful state. I'll bet you grew up on a farm; you've got that healthy, rosy complexion...*

Just to keep this current, when I tried to *find* this "National Resource Bank" on the HUD website in August 2021, it was nowhere to be found. I'd be glad to hear it, but that does not mean that the Obama Administration gave it a try, found out it was stupidly pointless and then defunded it. Heavens, no! The bureaucrats who were hired to implement this thing – whether it ever got any traction I leave it to someone else to discover – merely remained on the taxpayer dole, er, payroll, and got shuffled to some other parasitic, value-destructive, freedom-sucking cubicle farm.

HUD Section 8

One particularly horrible and horrifying waste of taxpayer money has been HUD Section 8 vouchers, the application of which has degraded and destroyed communities across the nation.

The entire problem can be summed up as *People do not value what they do not work for and achieve for themselves.* Beyond and superseding that in importance when it comes to any justification for taking tax dollars from a productive citizen in order to just give that money to someone else who has not worked for that wealth, there is no legal or moral justification for taking a dollar from person X's children and giving it to person Y's children in the form of rent subsidies.

But then, legal, moral or equitable considerations simply don't figure into the calculations that create and drive something like HUD. The whole purpose of evil nonsense like HUD rests on the perpetual delusions of the Draft Dodger Generation, that there is some kind of woolly-headed altar of "goodness" at which any amount of *your* – certainly not *their* – dollars are to be thrown.

Defund it all immediately. If individual communities would like to keep subsidizing the rents of some of their residents, then they can vote at the local – or better yet, personal – level to do so. A list of all HUD rent subsidy recipients can be provided immediately to the mayors of the towns they are in. Perhaps – and this is just a suggestion – all the *landlords* who have been busy sucking at the Federal HUD Section 8 teat for all these years could be first in line to personally subsidize the continuation of deadbeats inhabiting their rental properties. Let's see how quickly that idea is taken up.

Here is how this community- and personal responsibility-destroying disincentive-to-work and unjust-wealth-redistribution scandal is described in Obama's Budget:

> Provides Housing Opportunities
> **Preserves Affordable Rental Opportunities.** The President's Budget requests $19.2 billion for the Housing Choice Voucher program to help more than two million extremely low- to low-income families with rental assistance to live in decent housing in neighborhoods of their choice. The Budget funds all existing mainstream vouchers and provides new vouchers targeted to homeless veterans, families, and the chronically homeless. The Administration remains committed to working with the Congress to improve the management and budgeting for the Housing Choice Voucher program, including reducing inefficiencies, and re-allocating Public Housing Authority reserves based on need and performance. The Budget also provides $9.4 billion for Project-Based Rental Assistance to preserve approximately 1.3 million affordable units through increased funding for contracts with private owners of multifamily properties. This critical investment will help extremely low- to low-income households obtain, or retain, decent, safe and sanitary housing.

How great is that? Where is there any notion of local community (never mind individual, which is anathema to the collectivist mind) responsibility for ensuring safe neighborhoods or for private markets meeting a private need?

I *love* the language. Orwell could not have done better: "...rental assistance to live in decent housing in neighborhoods of their choice." After reading that, I realized something. I choose to live in a 25,000 square foot mansion beachfront property in Newport on at least four acres of manicured parkland, as I believe it would improve my mood and give my children some space to stretch out in, which in turn would put them into the proper frame of mind to excel in school and sports, thereby increasing their chances of a successful life. I cannot afford the $85,000 per month in rent for decent housing in my neighborhood of choice, so *you*, the American taxpayer have to top up the roughly $1,500 per month I can afford.

In practice, Section 8 has meant that Working Taxpayers A, B and C work hard to provide for their families and buy nice homes in a neighborhood that *they* are constantly creating and maintaining. Then the Federal Government decides that Loyal Democratic Party Voters D, E, and F who don't like what they can afford *don't* have to work as a community to make life as pleasant as possible where they are. No! The Federal Government gives them cash *taken* from A, B and C and moves them in right next door to A, B and C.

Of course, D, E and F don't value what they have not worked for, so *at best* A, B and C can expect a natural deterioration in maintenance of physical structures, attractiveness of yards, etc. Empirically, Section 8 has caused far more damage than that, when G, H and J, who are the Dangerous Dope-Slinging Pals of D, E and F decide to hang around or move in.

As a result of this mad abuse of the public, the value of the homes owned by A, B and C decline, which sucks for them, because the Federal Government is not going to compensate them for the lost equity in their homes, nor do anything about the increasingly unsafe and violent neighborhood their kids can no longer play in. All because the Government has decided to *give* goodies to some people that other people have to work hard for.

You don't believe that narrative? Go ask the long-term residents of Glen Cove, Long Island, or of Slavic Village in Cleveland.

It needs to stop immediately.

In any event, from a fundamental fairness perspective, the Federal Government has *no business* being involved in community composition micromanagement. Lest the legions of auto-screeching chattering classes take time to put down their *New York Pravda* Arts & Leisure section long enough to argue about the way I characterize the Abstractions A through J above, the fundamental point is that even if D through J are lovely people who tend their rent-subsidized lawns and apartments, *there is no justification for the government to force some Americans to give money to other Americans.*

That is what is at issue here. I have strayed into the classic collectivist error of arguing about *outcomes,* however empirically supported they are, when the issue here is *not* what "happens" because of Section 8 vouchers interfering in what should be private housing markets. The point is that governmental distortion is *in and of itself* an *a priori* evil phenomenon, without Constitutional justification and guaranteed to decay the bonds of a strong civil society.

HUD and its abusive micromanagement of our lives has nothing to do with making life better for anyone. You don't have to take my word for it. Just look at the people who *support* Section 8 vouchers – they claim *right there in the language describing the purpose of the vouchers* that the vouchers exist to improve poor people's lives *by giving them a choice of where to live.* And yet... the very same politicians and political groups *hate* school vouchers, which give poor people the right to *choose* which school their child attends, rather than being confined to the geographical "school district" they happen to live in.

Now why would that be? If "choice" of where to live is so important that politicians are willing to steal from hardworking taxpayers so that non-taxpayers can live in better places, why wouldn't the same logic apply to school choice? Surely a child's education is far more important for her long-term success as a thinking, reasoning, actively employed citizen than where she happens to live. So, for former HUD Secretary Andrew Cuomo who was subsequently now Governor of New York, "choice" when it means ruining property values for hardworking taxpayers is a great thing, but "choice" when it means letting poor families escape failing public schools dominated by teachers' unions who vote 99.99% Democrat is bad. Oh, wait, I think I just discovered a possible reason...

If there were massive "landlords unions" who funneled all their campaign contributions to Democrat politicians, then Section 8 would end immediately. No more choice – you are to live in the neighborhood you are zoned for and get services from a public sector union employee! Just as teachers' unions hate parents choosing where to send their children, if landlords were public sector employees rather than entrepreneurs, they, too, would be against choice.

I would add that if for whatever reason we as a country decide to continue Section 8 vouchers, then the proponents of this plan – including every member of Congress who votes for it, every bureaucrat who administers it, and every landlord who gets paid by it – must have their *personal* homes ringed by recipients of the Section 8 program. That's right – all the houses surrounding Bill and Hillary Clinton's place in Chappaqua *must* be rented to HUD Section 8 recipients. Ditto for Cuomo, Schumer and all the rest of them. And the *opponents* of the program get to choose *which* Section 8 recipients get to call Bill and Hillary neighbor.

Let's see how long this insane abuse of the public trust and taxpayer fisc endures under *those* conditions.

The Housing Crisis

As for the Federal Government doing anything productive about "the housing crisis" which was in the main *caused* by decades of Federal distortion to the housing mortgage market, that is beyond crazy.

There are plenty of private-sector solutions to this national nightmare. As I was writing this, I saw an announcement from the Alaska Permanent Fund Corporation that the Fund is investigating investing $400 million to a company dedicated to buying houses in the lower 48 to turn into rental properties.

> MAY 25, 2010 - The Alaska Permanent Fund Corporation Board of Trustees approved continued investigation into a $400 million commitment to a single-family homes strategy...

Under the single-family homes strategy, a company would purchase packages of vacant homes in the lower 48, manage those homes as rental properties. The Fund would not purchase or directly own the properties, but subject to further negotiation would provide up to a $400 million investment to American Homes 4 Rent LLC, which already owns 1,000 single family homes.

"The reported shift in consumer interest from owning homes to renting, combined with the surplus of single-family homes in many markets has created this unique opportunity," said Board Chair Bill Moran. "When we created the allocation to Special Opportunities, the purpose was to create room within the Fund where we could take advantage of unexpected investment opportunities such as this single-family homes strategy."

Ironically, one of the good ideas I have read about dealing with the destruction of equity value in individual homes and its link to societal decay was buried amidst the sea of egregious errors in Stiglitz's otherwise nonsensical tome. I don't know what came over him, but he suggested a way to deal with the "housing crisis" without tossing people out in the street by letting banks become equity partners with deadbeats. I am sure he phrased it differently, but the basic idea was to let the person behind on mortgage payments to enter into more of a "partnership" with the lender, providing opportunity for the markets to calm down and eventually enable both the borrower and the bank to stabilize their finances. Unlike Stiglitz and Krugman, I will admit a good idea when I see one, even when it emanates from a source that is usually wrong. A broken mechanical clock is right once or twice a day.

No solution is ever perfect, even free market solutions. Many pools of professional capital realized the excellent returns to be had from owning portfolios of single-family homes as permanent rental properties. Combine the weight of billions of dollars with the ability to close on a purchase quickly and big data analytics which allow someone sitting comfortably in a cubicle in San Francisco or New York to qualify, value and bid on a property in Des Moines, New Orleans or Santa Fe within seconds, that means increased competition for real families looking to get a foot onto the property ladder in those local communities.

But it's better than Big Government trying to mismanage it.

Human beings are survival machines. Darwin taught us that, and even clear subspecies – for example, say, politicians – are fighters when their food source is threatened. That core part of the human animal, the lizard brain ready to kill rather than be killed, explains the frenzied, desperate and still-not-ending quest for politicians and their watercarriers in the media to frantically point the finger of blame for the financial crisis at every possible person or entity, except themselves.

Jesse Jackson and Bill Clinton's crusade to *force* bankers to "lend" *your* deposited hard-earned money to people who could not afford to repay those loans is the main cause of the crash of 2007. Oddly enough, *some* of the people who supported the CRA did so in reaction to *another* stupid abuse of Federal power created under Democrats, this time the Sainted Socialist in a Wheelchair. The Housing Act of 1937 made the Veterans Administration and the Federal Housing Administration mainly lend money to white applicants, one strong cause of inequality in opportunity to development home ownership equity and therefore wealth in minority communities. In 1968, the same pack of interfering big government politicians passed the Fair Housing Act largely – though they'd never admit this, the factual record be damned! – to remedy the problems caused by their original 1937 foray into distorting the housing market.

By shoveling Federal support to mortgages, but only in *some* neighborhoods, not others, the government did indeed put its foot on the scales of not only economic outcomes but – because of the way redlining was applied – for deplorable societal inequities. Under the New Deal's fun new Home Owners Loan Corporation, the Federal government shoveled cash into working class neighborhoods, so people would not lose their homes. So far, so good as intentions go, but here's where the odd mix of policy and prudence come together to create suboptimal outcomes: Instead of just saying to *everyone* with a mortgage or who wanted a mortgage, *"Here's a bucket of cash courtesy of your Uncle Sam at a low fixed rate,"* the concerned bureaucrats who were actually looking out for the interests of the taxpayer said, *"Hey, if you live in an area with a lower statistical likelihood of foreclosure, then you can have this loan."*

In practice, during that time period, those fault lines between neighborhoods that were a good credit risk or a bad credit risk – relatively speaking, because the New Deal was *designed* to help folks in financial trouble – were mainly defined by ethnicity. So predominantly "white" neighborhoods got New Deal mortgage cash whereas mixed or black neighborhoods did not. This was a terrible injustice and underlay the development of "redlining" which was *created by the Federal Government by Democrats, by the way,* and not a product of "racist" bankers. The only reason I point out the origins of this horrific, unjust and worst of all economically destructive practice is because current myths spun by decades of teachers, professors and talking heads on TV have made it "common knowledge" that mean-spirited "white Republican racist bankers" created the redlining that made credit more expensive or simply unavailable to black Americans trying to buy a home. Nope – New Deal Democrats did it.

The policies of redlining were abhorrent, ignorant and destructive. That is true. Ending discrimination of any kind *aside from financial* is the best path forward for this country. To the extent cynical politicians try to feather their own nests by spreading lies about the *origins* and original champions of these policies, it is important to keep the factual record straight. FDR's New Deal champions in the Democrat Party created redlining. Whatever it takes for more Americans to throw the Myth of FDR's Greatness on the trash heap of history, the better.

Housing is Unaffordable *Because* of Government Subsidies

While the three main drivers of price increases in housing markets are (1) fiat currency, (2) the existence of Federally-guaranteed mortgage markets and (3) insane "fair lending" laws which force thrifty Americans to *give* free houses to deadbeats, I will focus here on the simplest force to understand – the mortgage markets backed by Fannie Mae and Freddie Mac.

If you are an American struggling hard to save enough money for a down payment to afford a home while price increases around you surpass your earning increase every year, putting home ownership forever out of reach, pay close attention and get ready to call, write and berate "your" legislative representatives to fix this nonsense.

I am not going to reinvent the wheel. In 2014, the American Enterprise Institute published a great piece[34] by Edward Pinto entitled "From the American dream... to bailout

America." As part of that 22-page work which I urge you to read, he abstracted a timeline of the most critical events that made the financial crisis inevitable. As he so pithily summarizes this slow-motion trainwreck: "From 1992 onward, 'skin in the game' was progressively eliminated from housing finance. And it worked – Fannie's supporters in and outside Congress successfully protected Fannie's (and Freddie's) charter privileges against all comers – until the American Dream became Bailout America."

TIMELINE

1991 HUD Commission complains "Fannie Mae and Freddie Mac's underwriting standards are oriented towards 'plain vanilla' mortgage"

1991 Lenders will respond to the most conservative standards unless [Fannie Mae and Freddie Mac] are aggressive and convincing in their efforts to expand historically narrow underwriting

1992 Countrywide and Fannie Mae join forces to originate "flexibly underwritten loans"

1992 Congress passes the inaptly named "Federal Housing Enterprises Financial Safety and Soundness Act." Rather than protecting taxpayers from having to bailout Fannie and Freddie, affordable housing mandates planted the seeds leading to future bailout

1993 Fannie approves ACORN's loan program, allowing for "down payments of the lesser of $1000 or 3%."

1994 Fannie Mae commits to transform housing finance system and plans $1T in lending to low and moderate income borrowers

1994 Fannie's Trillion Dollar Giveaway

1994 Fannie proceeds with 3% down loans over objection of chief credit officer.

1995 HUD's National Homeownership Strategy commits lending industry to weakened underwriting standards, including further reductions in down payments

1996 Fannie and Freddie are creating mega-liabilities with miniscule capital to support it.

1997 HUD study complains Fannie and Freddie's credit guidelines are more likely to disqualify borrowers with low incomes, limited wealth, and poor credit histories

1998 Flexible underwriting standards are nothing more than standards that lead to bad loans

1999 Fannie eases credit to increase lending; increases risk of taxpayer bailout

2000 FHA leads the way with looser lending standards

---

34   https://www.aei.org/wp-content/uploads/2014/10/pinto-bailout-america-timeline-government-mortgage-complex_1305029805.pdf

2000 Fannie's CEO, Franklin Raines, announces new $2 trillion "American Dream Commitment" on top of earlier $1 trillion commitment

2000 HUD imposes massive increases in Fannie and Freddie's affordable housing mandates, calls for deeper push into subprime

2000 Franklin Raines, Fannie's CEO, calls for "bending financial markets to serve the families buying [newly built] homes"

2001 Easy credit creating bull market in housing

2002 CEO of government sponsored Fannie Mae cites government agency FHA as its only competitor for public funding of housing

2003 Countrywide's Mozilo calls for the elimination of down payments, announces expansion of its "House America" commitment to $600 billion

2004 Having met $3 trillion in previous commitments, Fannie's CEO, Franklin Raines, announces plans to renew and expand —American Dream Commitment

2004 HUD trumpets "revolution in affordable lending"

2004 HUD rulemaking imposes massive increases in Fannie and Freddie's affordable housing mandates, calls for Fannie & Freddie to "reach deeper into the subprime market"

2004 Fannie's Franklin Raines tells national lender group: "We have to push products and opportunities to people who have lesser credit quality"

2004 By the end of 2005 there could be a perfect storm of delinquencies

2006 National Association of Realtors reports 46% and 19% of first-time buyers and repeat buyers respectively nationwide put down no money. NAR President Thomas Stevens isn't worried

2010 HUD finds "the sharp rise on mortgage delinquencies and foreclosures the result of rapid growth in loans with high risk of default"

2010 Financial Crisis Inquiry Commission ignores the government's efforts to promote flexible underwriting standards throughout the mortgage industry. During the boom low delinquency rates reduce losses, making loans appear less risky to investors. The government's encouragement of weakened loan standards promoted a race to the bottom and led to the origination of unprecedented quantities of risky loans.

All this insanity is directly attributable to the government-driven campaign to force banks to *give away money* to people who could never pay it back. This madness was called "fair lending." As an aside, I *roared* with laughter when I first heard that phrase. I was in DC in 2009, at a dinner party and was talking about this whole financial mess being caused by Federal intervention in the housing markets. One of the guests – a classic DC liberal but otherwise a nice guy – was listening to me closely and interjected to say, "Are you talking about the Fair Lending Laws?"

Thank heavens I was not chewing at the time as I may have choked to death. When I finally regained my composure from my laughing fit, I spluttered, "WHAT? *That's* what forcing banks to lend to deadbeats is called?" It was a magical moment which did not increase my circle of friends by one more, but it was delightfully clarifying in its own way.

I know you, dear reader, are sensing recurring patterns. Here is another one. Government bureaucrats had already gathered data about home ownership and bank lending and in the course of so doing, had identified people with lower credit. At that point, a *logical* and societally productive response would have been, *"OK. Let's fund an outreach program through banks or local governments to hold free seminars on household finances. Let's walk people through the fundamentals of living within one's means, including proper budgeting, ideas like emergency funds and the like. Let's be explicit that we want to enable more Americans to be able to afford a home to own and let's educate individuals to develop the tools necessary to climb the economic ladder."*

That kind of educational approach rooted in fostering individual freedom and responsibility always bears fruit when it is offered. But the "downside" to that approach would be no galloping growth Fannie and Freddie offering fat salaries to politically connected insiders while leaving the rest of the country with the whopping big bill upon their collapse.

Big Government exists to grow more Big Government – *not* to fix the "problems" they may identify. The chief risk every person manages is personal career risk. If a bureaucrat starts a *career* in "helping the poor," the last thing that person wants is for the poor to help themselves so there are no longer any poor people to "help."

In the midst of a government-caused depression due to a hyper overreaction to the Wuhan Virus in the first half of 2020, economic observers were noting the economic burden on people over 60 years of age who still had very large mortgages.

If the US had a monetary policy grounded in reality, not the fantasies spun by the Federal Reserve and our goofy fiat currency, that coupled with an absence of political meddling in mortgage markets would mean house prices *couldn't* have risen to these absurd heights in the first place. One of the best things about a grounded currency, based in real value, is that it places strict limits on spending. If you can't just print more dollars, *everyone* must make *real* decisions about priorities.

New York City Housing Authority

NYCHA deserves a special shout-out because it is a perfect illustration of everything that is absolutely bound to happen when we encounter a Type 4 expenditure. Remember our four types of spending? Type 4 is the one where you spend someone else's money on someone else.

The NYCHA is such a horrendous disaster because while politicians *love* to trumpet how much they are "helping" [insert constituency here], they *hate* to let the taxpayers know *how much* this grand "help" actually costs. You know there is a real problem when a *Democrat* names and shames a *Democrat* mayor for failures so vast they just can't be hidden anymore.

NYCHA owns and operates 174,000 housing units. Public Advocate Letitia James – we'll revisit the rationale for such a publicly-funded position later – in 2018 put NYCHA on the "landlord shame list." As of this writing, instead of making life better for poor New Yorkers, she was as Attorney General blowing millions of taxpayer dollars on a pointless, civil suit against President Donald Trump for a supposed "fraud" the Trump Organization against Deutsche Bank, which it should be noted, is not a complainant to this suit and has no idea why she claims Trump "defrauded" a sophisticated bank.

Anyway, back to her possibly useful actions in 2018.

> The list was created in 2010 to shame the private landlords whose buildings had the most housing violations and infractions. Ms. James said she included the city's Housing Authority to shine a light on the long-troubled agency.
>
> The 2018 list included NYCHA and 100 private landlords.
>
> "For too long, the most glaring example of this ill treatment has been at the hands of the City itself—and this year, we are finally putting NYCHA on notice," Ms. James said in a statement.
>
> Mayor Bill de Blasio, who launched the worst-landlord list when he was public advocate in 2010, said on Wednesday that NYCHA shouldn't be included on the list because the city doesn't need to be shamed into fixing apartments.
>
> "Why that watch list matters is to push a lot of landlords who would try to do nothing but for the attention. We're in the polar opposite situation," he said. "We don't need to be pushed."
>
> The city's public-housing authority is currently under threat of a federal takeover because of poor conditions at its buildings, including rampant mold inside apartments, heating problems and malfunctioning elevators.
>
> On Tuesday, Mr. de Blasio met with U.S. Housing and Urban Development Secretary Ben Carson to discuss a plan that would keep the authority under local control.
>
> A judge rejected an earlier settlement agreement between NYCHA and federal prosecutors following an investigation into health and safety violations at the apartment buildings.
>
> The city and the federal government have until the end of January to establish a plan for nearly $32 billion in repairs to NYCHA apartments.
>
> According to the public advocate office's data, there are more than 240,000 open work orders at NYCHA developments, which have about 400,000 residents.[35]

There is poetry in this, especially for a New Yorker who left the city for Florida and referred to my birth city as The People's Republic of DeBlasiostan for the long eight-year miserable slog of his horrendous term as mayor.

But why – you, the reasonable reader may ask – am I making such fun if illustrative hay out of what is surely a problem for the New York City (or maybe State) taxpayer to solve? Because it's magically the problem of *all* American taxpayers. I've quoted this gem *in toto* from a recent email from my former "Representative" Jerrold Nadler:

Fighting the Public Housing Crisis in NYC & Nationwide
In New York City, federal disinvestment in public housing has led to crumbling buildings and unnecessary hardship for tenants. In my view, individuals in New York

---

[35] https://www.wsj.com/articles/new-york-city-housing-authority-ranks-no-1-on-worst-landlord-list-11545265029

City Housing Authority (NYCHA) face immoral conditions- collapsing ceilings, years-long leaks, and broken elevators- that would have resulted in any private landlord having their property seized. This is a crisis that can no longer go ignored. That is why I joined Congresswoman Nydia Velázquez to author the *Public Housing Emergency Response Act,* which would allocate $70 billion for public housing repairs nationwide. Under our proposal, $32 billion would go to NYCHA to ensure our residents have access to affordable housing that won't jeopardize their health. Safe, affordable housing is a basic right for every American, and I believe it is past time for the federal government to step up to the plate and ensure quality housing for all. To read more about the Public Housing Emergency Response Act, please click here.[36]

This was the second section of a longer email which began with heaps of predictable nonsense about how more government restrictions to Second Amendment rights will magically cure the nation of evil morons who like to kill lots of people at once.

Just check out the breathless tone – and not just because his physician probably suggests that Jerry could say "no" to a second helping of pie every once and awhile. According to Jerry, it's been perfectly fine for him to ignore the "crisis" of New Yorkers *in his Congressional district* who have lived with rats, mold, leaks and broken elevators for years. Apparently, October 19th, 2019 will be his Pearl Harbor – this is the day he can finally no longer ignore those problems. *What happened, Jerry? Did the homeless woman who accosted Comrade Mayor De Blasio in his gym to ask him about public housing[37] drum up some gumption and find your office in Raeburn?*

Instead of drawing the correct conclusion – that centralized bureaucracies can *never* be responsive to local concerns and therefore Federal support for public housing should be abolished – Jerry draws the only conclusion he can, the one that continues to fluff his ego and centralize power in DC for no justifiable reason.

"Safe, affordable housing" most assuredly cannot be a "basic right for every American," as the muddle-headed Upper Left Side of Manhattan Congressman contends. The fact that he can write it, that most if not all of his constituents will read it and nod in the affirmative, is one more condemnation of the propaganda factories our schools have become. "Rights" are things that exist by the absence of constraints – "life, liberty and the pursuit of happiness" spring to mind.

Note that none of those things cost anything or require anyone *else* to do anything at all. So long as I don't kill you or lock you up, I've already acknowledged your rights to the first two. I'm not sure how I'd interrupt your pursuit of happiness, but you get the picture.

Rights can *never* be things that someone else must pay to give you. Certainly nothing like "healthcare" or a house to live in.

---

[36] **From:** Congressman Jerry Nadler <CongressmanNadler@mail.house.gov> **Sent:** Friday, October 18, 2019 4:28 PM **To:** Christopher Messina **Subject:** Enough Is Enough: We Must End the Gun Violence Epidemic

[37] Entertain yourself by searching the web for videos of the Mayor of New York running from a woman who interrupted His Lordship's Holy Morning Workout.

Had Jerry written the following, he'd be on surer Constitutional ground. "Safe, affordable housing for every American is an honorable goal for this nation to strive for. I for one am proud to serve my fellow citizens in slashing meaningless Federal regulation and in slashing taxes and regulations so that I am not robbing honest people of the ability to afford their own homes. For those few who due to ill health, mental incapacity or random misfortunate find themselves in lack of a safe place to lay their head at night, I offer firstly *my personal money and hours of labor* to help out those of my neighbors in need. I urge you, my fellow, caring American, to consider what *you* can do with your community to insist that parasites like me pay attention to the very few things government can do, and when you've slapped my capacious rear end back into my box, continue to live lives of purpose and joy."

Had he written that, I'd have had no problems with it.

He didn't. The reasons he didn't are why I wrote this book and why you're reading it.

Figure 8: The new "entrance" for the shuttered Department of Housing and Urban Development

Chapter 4: Department of Labor

Year Founded:	1913
Founded by President	William Howard Taft
Funding Budget 2021	$41,700,000,000
Messina's 2024 Budget Proposal	$10,000,000
Messina's 2025 Budget Proposal	$0
Degree to which Messina's Plan is Better	Completely
Should a Federal Labor Department exist?	No

Is this a standalone proper use of the taxpayers' limited resources?	No
Does this expenditure unfairly benefit one American over another one?	Yes
Does the expenditure meet the "Is this logical?" standard of fiduciary responsibility?	No
Can the goals be achieved by *not* spending the dollar more effectively than by spending it?	Yes

This is something to be done away with instantly. What could it possibly be *for?* That is disingenuous hyperbole. The correct question is: What in the context of the proper use of *everyone's* tax dollars could this entire army of federal workers, coupled to a shifting cast of political appointees *possibly be for?* If your answer is to deal with violations of labor law, then the (revamped) Department of Justice or more appropriately state and local officials should deal with legal violations or labor laws.

This beast was created in the waning hours of Taft's presidency, so took its first formative steps under President Woodrow Wilson.

This is one of those great instances that we all (should have) learned about as children when reading *The Emperor's New Clothes.* To paraphrase a Congressman who was grilling Jon Corzine at the MF Global hearings held on 8 December 2011, as the former CEO of both Goldman Sachs and MF Global, not to mention a former Governor and Senator kept answering negatively to every question about his actual duties as CEO of MF Global, the Congressman in mock exasperation asked "What is it that you *do*…?"

The magic of the Internet is that I searched for that very question and got this helpful tidbit straight from the Department of Labor's website:

Question: What does the Department of Labor do?

Answer: The Department of Labor (DOL) fosters and promotes the welfare of the job seekers, wage earners, and retirees of the United States by improving their working conditions, advancing their opportunities for profitable employment, protecting their retirement and health care benefits, helping employers find workers, strengthening free collective bargaining, and tracking changes in employment, prices, and other national economic measurements. In carrying out this mission, the Department administers a variety of Federal labor laws including those that guarantee workers' rights to safe and healthful working conditions; a minimum hourly wage and overtime pay; freedom from employment discrimination; unemployment insurance; and other income support.

Wow. That's quite a mandate.

In business, I have often found it helpful to summarize such complexity into tables or charts to aid in comprehension and analysis. I have taken the text above and taken the literal grammatical construction, including clausal relations, to be my guide in creating the following summary table.

I feel free to do this because Washington is chockfull of lawyers who presumably received training in both logic and grammar. Therefore, where there are some obviously insane logical relations in the text, I have had to assume that the bureaucrats in charge of drafting the language *meant* this insanity. It is either that or their grammar is as poor as their efficacy, and they are reinforcing my contention that they would better serve their country by picking up a shovel and clearing a city street of post-storm runoff muck.

Browse through the table below. Take your time. Maybe get a cup of tea and some cookies to munch thoughtfully.

Table 3: Department of Labor task breakdown

Task	Should Fed Govt Do This?	*Can* Fed Govt Do This?	Is this patently insane?
fosters the welfare of job seekers	No	No	Yes
fosters the welfare of wage earners	Maybe	No	Maybe
fosters the welfare of retirees	Maybe	No	Yes
promotes the welfare of job seekers	No	No	Yes
promotes the welfare of wage earners	No	Maybe	Yes
promotes the welfare of retirees	No	Maybe	Yes
Improving working conditions of job seekers*	*	*	Yes
Improving working conditions of wage earners	No	No	No
Improving working conditions of retirees*	*	*	Yes
Help employers find workers	Maybe	Maybe	No
Advancing opportunities for profitable employment for job seekers	Maybe	No	No
Advancing opportunities for profitable employment for wage earners	No	No	Yes
Advancing opportunities for profitable employment for retirees	*	*	Yes
strengthening free collective bargaining	No	Yes	No

tracking changes in employment, prices, and other national economic measurements	Yes	Yes	No
Enforce Federal laws that guarantee workers' rights to safe and healthful working conditions	Yes	Maybe	No
Enforce Federal laws concerning a minimum hourly wage and overtime pay	Yes	Maybe	No
Enforce Federal laws concerning freedom from employment discrimination	Maybe	Maybe	Maybe
Enforce Federal laws concerning unemployment insurance	Maybe	Maybe	Maybe
Enforce Federal laws concerning other income support	No	Yes	Yes

 * I had to highlight these two pieces. What would constitute "the working conditions" of someone *seeking* a job or someone who is *retired*? By definition, that person *does not have a place to work, therefore cannot be subject to working conditions.*

My favorite part of institutionalized unfairness lies in the phrase about enforcing Federal laws regarding minimum wage laws. One of the biggest, most glaring asymmetries of opportunity exists in the context of "internships," which is just a low-level job with access to high-level people and industries. Across this great land of ours, the children of parents who can afford to subsidize their room and board are able to get dressed up nice and go to work in, say, Hollywood studios, art galleries, the White House, major corporations and financial firms. These young people get access to relationships and work experience that are simply denied to the children of poorer parents (or to people who rightly believe that they should be paid, oh, I don't know, the *minimum wage* to do a job in a for-profit enterprise).

Leaving aside my admittedly dogged objection to the "intern" workaround to paying people a basic wage, we come to the absolutely most offensive part of what the Department of Labor actually *does* day to day. Going by the core guiding principle that *anything* the taxpayer dollars pay for should be of equal benefit to all Americans, the very idea that taxpayer dollars are used to pay for "strengthening" one side or the other in a private (i.e. employee-employer) negotiation is *a priori* insane and an inappropriate use of public funds.

No publicly funded agency should be involved in "strengthening free collective bargaining," whatever on earth that could be taken to mean. Unions who wish to make a pitch to employees that they are a better way for individuals to earn income should not be prevented from making that pitch and laying out their case, but the Federal (or any) government should do *nothing* in relation to such arrangements other than uphold laws designed to give everyone equal protection under the law.

You'll notice that I don't score this piece of the DOL's "mandate" as insane. It is not insane. It is, however, patently unjust and an abuse of governmental power to throw the weight of the government in favor of one private interest over another private interest. Where applicable, the government – preferably at a much more local level – should absolutely stand ready to defend the rights of employees enshrined in law, as the government should in all cases.

But we must put an immediate end to this lopsided, poorly conceived, and atrociously executed department driven by a political agenda which asserts the *interests* of some segments of Americans as opposed to defending the *rights* of all Americans.

Have there been times in this nation's history when working people were subjected to dangerous and even slave-like conditions? Yes. Have the battles that changed those conditions been long won? Yes. In those instances where companies are not complying with labor laws, the Department of Justice or – better by far – State or local government officials can enforce change.

So that is the overall mission statement of the Department of Labor. Let's grab a year at random and see what specific mischief a motivated President and/or Congress can get up to by making use of this army of bureaucrats.

To illustrate what I am banging on about in this book, I grabbed a section somewhat at random from a budget. Here is the summary of Labor's budgetary rationale from 2012. I've added a column to provide you a line by line judgment.

Funding Highlights: Comments

• Provides $12.8 billion, a 5 percent reduction from the 2010 enacted level. This reflects a shift in investments to a new Workforce Innovation Fund and increases for worker protection and mine safety programs. The Budget achieves savings through a reduction in funding for the Senior Community Service Employment Program, and transfers it to the Department of Health and Human Services to improve coordination with other programs for seniors. The Budget also includes a 25 percent reduction in the Job Corps construction budget.	"We shifted some cash around."
• Invests almost $380 million in the Departments of Labor and Education for a competitive "Workforce Innovation Fund" that will allow States and regions to compete for funds by demonstrating their commitment to transforming their workforce systems, including breaking down program silos and paying programs for success.	Nonsense. Utter nonsense. Not that such a fund focused on innovation in work is bad, but the idea of it being a *federal* program instead of a State or county-wide program is ludicrous. Not a cent of that will help any of the "workforce" supposedly targeted.
• Supports reform of the Workforce Investment Act to match unemployed workers with jobs and to give workers a chance to upgrade their skills to compete in the global economy.	Gibberish. Pure gibberish. Again – not a bad idea for local communities to enact, but idiotic and impracticable from The Swamp.
• Provides short-term relief for businesses in States with indebted Unemployment Insurance systems, coupled with opportunities for States to improve the long-term solvency of these systems	Great abuse of the taxpayer. "So, some States cannot even handle sending checks to people who are not working, so we're going to take *your* hard earned

so that they can pay back their debts and provide adequate benefits when they are needed.	money to pay off cash another State borrowed to pay someone not working." Crazy.
• Expands the use of work-sharing, allowing firms to retain workers by reducing employees' weekly hours instead of having to lay them off and giving workers a partial unemployment check to supplement their reduced paycheck.	"We are going to pay unproductive people to keep doing jobs they are no good at, rather than letting them find something they are value-additive at doing." More insanity.
• Safeguards workers' pensions by encouraging companies to fully fund their employees' promised pension benefits and assuring the long-term solvency of the Federal pension insurance system.	"First, we are going to 'encourage' companies to set aside retirement cash, then when that fails, we're going to toss more money down a black hole of defined benefit boondoggles."
• Increases support for agencies that protect workers' wages, benefits, and health and safety and reduces the inappropriate misclassification of employees as independent contractors.	Aside from the Leftist ideological obsession to remove all personal choice from work arrangements... No, that's all there is to this idiocy.
• Assists families who need to take time off to care for a child or other loved one by helping States launch paid leave programs.	"States may or may not offer family leave but we're going to go pester them about it. They love that."
• Creates new opportunities to save for retirement by establishing a system of automatic workplace pensions and doubling the small employer pension plan start-up credit.	"We're going to send a pack of 23-year-old know-nothings to bug companies and States about financial matters these kids don't understand, for zero productive purpose."

There! That was a refreshing refutation in nine boxes of the entire *raison d'être* of the parasitic, damaging, deadweight waste of space, time and money known as the Labor Department. I can end right there – and so can you – but I've got a few more choice bits of pointlessness to hammer home, so you're well-armed when someone asks you, "But *why* don't we need a Department of Labor?"

Unemployment "Insurance" Boondoggle

If individual States want to maintain systems of unemployment benefits, they can go right ahead. I would strongly urge them to change how those benefits are funded, but that is a topic for my gripping nine-volume sequel, *The History of Americans Scamming Whatever System Presents Itself.* The Federal Government should have nothing whatsoever to do with State or local unemployment benefits.

Since we'll be dissolving the Department of Labor, this pointless interference in people's lives will evaporate in the wind.

Arguably, all our society would be better off if everyone took personal responsibility for the sudden emergencies and downturns like periods of joblessness. We'll once more develop more resilient individuals who don't blow money they don't have on products they don't need, assuming that if their income dries up suddenly that some faceless governmental body will shower them with weekly wealth.

On the extreme scale, we witnessed in the effects in 2020-21 of the idiotic policies emanating the Wuhan Panic. First, multiple States shuttered their economies for no reason at all, then the Federal Government began printing money so fast it'd make the Weimar Republic central bank blush. By April 2021, the $600 *per week additional cash* piled on top of State unemployment rates meant that companies with many open positions couldn't find workers. If you were a busboy or waiter before the Fake Wuhan Pandemic arrived, making $500 per week, why on earth would you quit the comfy lifestyle that $800+ per week affords, when all you need to do is smoke pot and drink beer while hanging out doing nothing? And if you happened to be "lucky" enough to live in a State or city whose idiot tyrants declared that no one has to pay rent "because of" a seasonal virus, then Bingo-Squared! *Fire up that bong and let's play some Fortnite!*

There are a dozen reasons why we need to abolish the misnamed "unemployment insurance," but that is a long topic to be addressed elsewhere. Just ponder this: Do you expect everyone else around you to pay for *your* car or house insurance? No, you don't. Policies exist for individuals to buy things like accidental disability compensation. People should be free to buy those policies and insurance companies should be free to sell those policies. No government involvement is required.

These Petty Tyrants Waded into Micromanaging Your Investments

If only the ever-grasping hand of the Administrative State would stop at the boundaries laid out for it in law. But nope!

Obama Labor Secretary Tom Perez issued an insane set of regulations in 2016, declaring that the Department of Labor – not, mind you, the SEC, the Treasury, the Fed or anyone else who could potentially lay claim to financial markets expertise, however fleetingly – knows better than you and an entire industry how to manage your retirement funds. I am not going to waste space here, but you can plunge down this rabbit hole if you wish by starting at the Labor Department website.[38]

Of course, the "argument" for all this top-down control of *your* financial decisions stems from the paternalistic view that Americans are too stupid to make their own retirement decisions. You know how we fix that? By destroying the Department of Education and letting individual communities decide what to teach their children. Here in Florida, the State has mandated every high school student pass a semester long class on personal and business finance and economics. Imagine that! Students being taught to make sound financial decisions.

This is not new – it used to be called Home Economics and was a standard class taught even when I was in high school in the 1980s. I encourage every school to offer such a

---

[38]   https://www.dol.gov/sites/dolgov/files/legacy-files/ebsa/temporary-postings/savings-arrangements-final-rule.pdf

class. There are plenty of resources available to help parents in those schools choose what kind of curriculum should be in place. They don't need "help" from a bureaucrat in Washington.

National Labor Relations Board (NLRB)

This $325 million abuse factory needs to be shuttered instantly. Whatever the original intent behind its creation, the NLRB has turned into one more political hammer used to distort the proper functioning of markets and to rape any pretense of the rights to due process of some Americans over the "rights" to extort economic rents by whoever happens to have spent the most on lobbyists or the most recent Presidential election.

Its abuses are myriad. Picking somewhat at random, in 2011 the NLRB was linked in a *quid pro quo* a decision to stop harassing an American firm (Boeing) with abusive lawsuits at the behest of the Obama Administration with the *same-day* successful forced capitulation by Boeing to a machinist union's demand for legal commitment to build 737s in Washington, a union state. In New York, we call this "paying protection money to gangsters," the prosecution of which happens under the RICO act. In Washington, this is called (in private) "punishing our enemies" or (in front of the teleprompter) "fair."

On 26 June 2014, the Supreme Court ruled that the NLRB "recess appointments" made by Barack Obama were invalid, and therefore the commissioners so appointed were not valid members of the NLRB. So, you would assume the affected individuals were immediately out of work and looking for new jobs, right?

Au contraire. Welcome to Chavez's, er, Obama's Permanent Revolution. After the Supreme Court ruled that their appointments were invalid, they were still going to work and collecting a paycheck from you, the American taxpayer. They simply kept working and getting paid for months on end! On your dime! How good can it get? Next time your boss fires you, don't bother handing in your card key and employee ID. No, no, no – you'll be back at your desk on Monday, still doing your job and payroll will keep putting cash into your checking account every two weeks, just like before. You'll be Melvin[39] in *Office Space*, hopefully without the acne and stapler obsession.

Feel free to do some research into how long that madness went on, and if in fact the Supreme Court's ruling was obeyed. You've by now gotten the sense that the outrages of government are infinite, so I have to choose when to stop digging in what will prove to be a bottomless hole of bad behavior.

On a bigger picture level than "just" the NLRB, I have always found baffling Americans' willingness to put up with occasional lopsided application of The Law. If you support the NLRB, I can assure you that is due to the insanely naïve viewpoint that one is always going to be on the winning side of that asymmetry.

---

[39] Played to hilarious effect by actor Stephen Root. 1999, directed by Mike Judge.

Trust me on this one. By the law of averages, some day *you will be* on the unfriendly end of the sharpened stick. So be careful about to whom you give the rights of sharp stick deployment.

Equal Opportunity Employment Commission (EEOC)

I never knew that the proper spelling of "boondoggle" was "E – E – O – C." I am glad that has been cleared up for me. This colossal waste of money and endless source of bureaucratic torture was created in 1964 to combat discrimination in the workplace. That may well have been an imperative then; it is certainly not any longer. But bureaucracies don't dissolve themselves when their mission is done and that is definitely true here.

Table 4: EEOC Budget and Staffing History 1980 to Present[40]

Funding ($000) In Millions			Staffing (FTE)		
Fiscal Year	President's Request	Enacted	Approved Ceiling	Actual End of Fiscal Year	
1980	$130,622	$124,562	3,527	3,390	
1981	$147,647	$144,610	3,696	3,358	
1982	$145,239	$144,739	3,740	3,166	
1983	$149,598	$147,421	3,327	3,084	
1984	$157,940	$154,039	3,125	3,044	
1985	$164,055	$163,655	3,125	3,097	
1986	$158,825	$165,000	2,976	3,017	
1987	$172,220	$169,529	3,125	2,941	
1988	$193,457	$179,812	3,198	3,168	
1989	$194,624	$180,712	3,198	2,970	

[40] http://www.eeoc.gov/eeoc/plan/budgetandstaffing.cfm scraped 7 June 2013

1990	$188,700	$184,926	3,050	2,853
1991	$195,867	$201,930	3,050	2,796
1992	$211,271	$211,271	2,871	2,791
1993	$245,341	$222,000	3,071	2,831
1994	$234,845	$230,000	3,000	2,832
1995	$244,562	$233,000	3,020	2,813
1996	$268,000	$233,000	3,219	2,676
1997	$268,000	$239,740	3,022	2,586
1998	$246,000	$242,000	2,680	2,544
1999	$279,000	$279,000	2,839	2,593
2000	$312,000	280,928	2,946	2,852
2001	$322,000	$303,195	3,055	2,704
2002	$310,406	$310,406	3,055	2,783
2003	$323,516	$321,815	2,800	2,617
2004	$334,754	$324,944	2,765	2,462
2005	$350,754	$326,804	2,640	2,441
2006	$332,228	$326,883	2,381	2,246
2007	$322,807	$328,745	2,381	2,158
2008	$327,748	$329,300	2,381	2,176
2009	$341,900	$343,925	2,556	2,192
2010	$367,303	$367,303	2,556	2,385
2011	$385,303	$366,568*	2,470	2,505
2012	$385,520	$360,000	2,571	2,346

2013	$373,711	$370,000**	2,354	2,147
2014	$372,923	$364,000	2,250	2,202
2015	$365,531	$364,000	2,347	2,191
2016	$373,112	$364,000	2,250***	2,202
2017	$376,646	$364,000	2,347	2,082
2018	$363,807	$379,500	2,347	1,968
2019	$363,807	$379,500	2,347	2,061
2020	$355,800	$389,500	2,347	1,939
2021	$362,481	$404,490	2,347	1,927
2022	$445,933	$420,000	2,347	
2023	$464,650	TBD	2,347	

*Includes fiscal year 2011 rescission of $734,606 (PL-112-10)

**The continuing resolution (CR) passed by Congress on March 21, 2013, provided an annualized level of $370 million. However, that amount was subject to a mandatory 1.877 percent across the board rescission (equal to $6.9 million) and a 0.2 percent across the board rescission (equal to $726,000), in addition to the 5 percent reduction (equal to $18.1 million) required under sequestration. EEOC's final funding is $344.2 million.

*** This was the revised actual in the FY 2016 Enacted Budget. 2,347 is the Commission's target.

Imagine how quickly we can save $450,000,000 *every year!* How good is that? All it takes is the simple dissolution of this completely ridiculous organ of state abuse. Below is a sampling of the tidbits on offer for what this *Federal* parasite sticks its fingers into. All employment issues must be handled at the most local level possible. It is madness for some pack of bureaucrats in DC to get involved in any potential employer-employee disputes in, say, a small town in South Dakota.

EEOC Initiatives

E-RACE The E-RACE Initiative is designed to improve EEOC's efforts to ensure workplaces are free of race and color discrimination. Specifically, the EEOC will identify issues, criteria and barriers that contribute to race and color discrimination, explore strategies to improve the administrative processing and the litigation of race and color discrimination claims, and enhance public awareness of race and color discrimination in employment.
LEAD (Leadership for the Employment of Americans with Disabilities) is the EEOC's initiative to address the declining number of employees with

targeted disabilities in the federal workforce. The goal for this initiative is to significantly increase the population of individuals with severe disabilities employed by the federal government.

The **Youth@Work** initiative is a national education and outreach campaign to promote equal employment opportunity for America's next generation of workers.

Unfortunately, what started as a potentially needed remedy to a few sorry instances of social discrimination has taken on a life of its own. It is almost unheard of for a corporation or individual or union to put itself out of business, and this EEOC is as fine an example of a corporate body striving to feed itself, whether any actual need for it exists. All these projects with fancy names are make-work justifications to keep paying thousands of people who are not doing anything of value.

I am not naive. Do some people across a rainbow of hues and a swath of ethnicities or religious persuasions choose to feel that other people not similarly colored or similarly persuaded are inferior in some way? Sure they do. Always have, always will. What is amazing about the ideals of the American Project are that we as a nation are pretty much the only people that have committed to ameliorating the impacts of the darker sides of human nature.

Does that mean that *as a country* we are infected with a disease of discrimination that needs perpetual rooting out by the Federal Government? No.

This boondoggle costing $400,000,000+ per year employs thousands of people *who have every incentive to find "discrimination" whether it exists or not*. It is a "solution" chasing a problem which automatically creates serious headaches for us. In the private sector, if a company creates a product or service to meet a market need, the company may find out that the need they built their business on either does not exist or does not exist in sufficient amounts for the company to make a product.

In the real world of private business, the company then goes bankrupt because there was no real need for what they were selling.

In the Federal Government, success in properly identifying a real – not imaginary or ideological – need *has nothing to do with getting hundreds of millions of dollars in funding every year*. Whether the EEOC was ever needed, it most assuredly is not now. Billboards on interstates are full of lawyers who will sue the pants off any company acting in a discriminatory way.

In the Information Age, with instant connectivity everywhere and knowledge dissemination never easier, employment-related issues can and must be dealt with at the local level. At the most extreme, a State Government may get involved, but there is never a reason for the DC Swamp to send its Creatures out into the nation, pestering locals and grinding them into bankruptcy by sheer weight of the oppressive Administrative State.

End this nonsense immediately.

Democrats want to strip you of more freedom of choice

The idiots in California passed a law AB5 which effectively bans an individual from choosing to work for him or herself. The "gig" economy is characterized by jobs like Uber drivers and has long been a mainstay of how truckers make a living. Democrats hate lacking control over people, so they want to turn independent contractors into employees, claiming in some weird way that more bureaucracy and less freedom is better for you, no matter how stupid you are to like living your life the way you want.

The Mercatus Center did a study[41] of the impacts of this asinine law and found significant harm.

> Institute senior fellow Liya Palagashvili, Seton Hall University assistant professor of economics Paola A. Suarez, and Mercatus fellows Christopher M. Kaiser and Vitor Melo examine through empirical means how AB5 affected the labor market. The researchers took a period from January 2011 to September of 2023, four years after the 2019 law was signed, and focused on overall employment and labor force participation, traditional employment, and self-employment.

> Here are some of the key takeaways:
> Despite AB5 proponents' claims that the law would increase full-time employment and offer benefits and protections, the researchers found "robust evidence that AB5 is significantly associated with a decline in self-employment and a decline *in overall employment*."

> ➤ AB5 reduced the level of self-employment by 6.7 percentage points to 28%.
> ➤ AB5 reduced the level of overall employment by 7.3 percentage points to 14%.
> ➤ The researchers did not find significant evidence that AB5 increased W-2 employment.

Only in the mind of a control freak Progressive Democrat can taking away an individual's freedom of choice in how to make a living be a positive thing. Odd, because they seem to love choice when it comes to abortion, but hey, that's just a fetus. When it comes to a living person who wants to do what she or he wants for a living, well, *we can't have that, sheeple slave.*

Not content with ruining lives and damaging the economy in California, the Democrats want to bring this nightmare to every American. Here in the Biden Administration's Labor Budget overview is the Orwellian language they use when talking about stripping you of your rights to choose how to work:

> The misclassification of workers as independent contractors robs them of their rightful wages, benefits, and protections. To address this, the FY 2023 Budget increases funding to the Wage and Hour Division (WHD) by more than $61 million over the FY 2021 enacted level. This funding increase will enable WHD to aggressively combat worker misclassification. It will also fund WHD's effort to protect essential workers by 4 safeguarding their pay and recovering back wages, with particular emphasis on the workers most vulnerable to wage violations and

---

[41] New Research Quantifies Harms to Independent Contractors of California's AB5 | Independent Women's Forum (iwf.org)

exploitive labor conditions. WHD will also be able to fully enforce the other areas under its purview like prevailing wages and family and medical leave.

There is no "misclassification of workers," in their magical Governmentese. What Democrats mean by misclassification of workers is "Anuja runs a one-person LLC providing coding services to a range of businesses large and small. She prefers the flexibility this provides her. Democrats don't like that Anuja is free because she might start to vote Republican, if she already doesn't. They want to demand she pick *one* of her clients and become an employee of that one client. It makes taking money from her paycheck easier and also hopefully Anuja will hate her job so much that another grift called a union will show up – with Democrat encouragement – to tell her they can get her better working conditions – maybe even like the ones she had before it became illegal for her to run her own business."

Who says independent contractors are "being robbed of their rightful wages, benefits and protections?" What on earth does any of that stupidity mean? How many independent contractors called the California Legislature begging to have their economic freedom taken away?

I am not for or against private sector unions. I am against the government forcing people to do things they don't want to do.

"The Wage and Hour Division" of the Department of Labor. That phrase alone is justification for demolishing this absurdity.

Figure 9: Department of Labor Memorial Frieze. Maybe we could get fancy and find the Latin for "It sure sucked while it lasted." Certo suxit dum duravit, perhaps.

Chapter 5: Department of Homeland Security

Year Founded:	2002
Founded by President	George W. Bush
Funding Budget 2023	$97,290,726,000
Messina's 2024 Budget Proposal	0*
Degree to which Messina's Plan is Better	Completely
Should a Federal DHS exist?	No*

Is this a standalone proper use of the taxpayers' limited resources?	No
Does this expenditure unfairly benefit one American over another one?	Yes
Does the expenditure meet the "Is this logical?" standard of fiduciary responsibility?	No
Can the goals be achieved by *not* spending the dollar more effectively than by spending it?	Yes

* Components like Customs and Border Control will remain – you know, the useful bits, but shuffled off to another Department or sit on their own. DHS itself serves no purpose.

This bellwether of Bush II's administration needs to be wrapped up immediately, its remaining functions like Customs & Border Control set free, and its catchy logo abolished to the Federal Archives Bizarre History Section. No one ever made clear to any of us why it was so important to create an entirely new bureaucracy for national security, when part of the problems with the *then-current* national security was the proliferation of siloed bureaucracies each fighting for its own slice of the pie.

As someone who lived through and with the aftermath of the downtown New York attacks of 11 September 2001, I greeted several of President Bush's subsequent pronouncements with utter bafflement. Elsewhere I discuss the kabuki theatre known as the USA PATRIOT Act. Here, I aver with equal assurance that this particular wellspring of perpetual cost and little positive effect can be done away with instantly. We and our wallets will be the safer for it.

This is the third largest department by budget allocation in the entire Federal government. Can it immediately and set the few good components free to operate their missions on their own.

The critical error at the heart of the creation of DHS is that one can spend any amount of time and money on "full alert" for unknown terrors. Surprises come. The best thing we as a nation can do is to accept that 99.9% of the things we worry about will never come to pass and the world-changing events both positive and negative that change the course of history are always unanticipated.

The best thing to do to "prepare" for the next major disaster is to maintain a vibrant, wealthy and resilient society composed of individuals who take their civic duty seriously. When towers fall or viruses appear, we can rally to respond.

Unlike Operation Warp Speed, say, which had a definite goal – create a vaccine – the bureaucratic beast of DHS lumbers onward from its original goal of "fighting Islamic terrorism."

One of the aftereffects of the September 11th attacks and the creation of DHS is the existence of 78 state-level "fusion centers." The idea for them came from a positive place, but the very nature of terrorist threat-detection and prevention renders their operation problematic and – as memories of actual attacks dim – vulnerable to budget-cutting. It is impossible to remain in a state of high alert; as weeks bleed into months and into years, whatever initial crisis created these fusion centers, the urgency is lost, the mission wanders and it becomes one more ever-expanding line item on the budget.

While our domestic security forces must always be prepared to deal with an unexpected surprise, it is impossible for anyone to remain on a heightened alert footing for any period of time. President Washington in his farewell address highlighted the dangers of a standing army. Many American thinkers throughout history have been wary of the mindset that a constant state of military "preparedness" has on our way of thinking and our way of life.

Chillingly, as of June 2022 when I was doing a fresh revision of this book, the US Capitol was ringed with chain link fencing and surrounded by National Guardsmen. The Supreme Court had similarly been fenced in because rational debate has disappeared in this country. More specifically, in a horrific breach of protocol, someone for the first time ever leaked a preliminary draft of a pending decision that could overturn the poorly reasoned *Roe v. Wade.* The American Left's immediate reaction to anything they don't like is a childish temper tantrum, but one in which people get hurt or killed by mob violence. That combined with an embarrassment to New York State called Chuck Schumer, who as a sitting Senator stood on the Supreme Court steps and threatened Justices Kavanaugh and Gorsuch by name, resulted in morons "protesting" outside Justice Kavanaugh's home *and* the police arresting on 8 June 2022 a man who drove from California with the express intention of murdering him in his home.

Instead of condemning publicly anyone who would try to murder a Supreme Court Justice, *that very same day* President Biden flew to California to be a guest on a late-night comedy show. I'm not going to provide the host any more press – if you care who it is, look it up. What matters is that instead of saying he'd instructed the Attorney General to enforce Federal law by arresting every green-haired moron with a tambourine who showed up to pester Justice Kavanaugh's family, he went on weird rants about how "evil" and full of "white supremacy" the Republican Party has become (in his mind.) Wow, thanks for "bringing down the temperature and eliminating the harsh rhetoric" to bring us all together as you promised to do from your basement bunker during the Wuhan Freakout. Good job, Joe.

Kumbaya.

Even *more* chillingly, the highest officials in the Pentagon and the U.S. Secretary of Homeland Security Alejandro Mayorkas embarked at the outset of Biden's Presidency upon a purge designed to locate and root out "white supremacy" in the ranks of our armed services. No one has provided *any* evidence that, in the words of Mayorkas, "Domestic violent extremism poses the most lethal and persistent terrorism-related threat to our country today." At least not in the way he means it, as a threat coming from "the right."

Piling on, during his first major speech as the nation's top law enforcement officer early in April 2021, Biden's Attorney General Merrick Garland pledged that the Justice Department was treating domestic terrorism as a top priority. In his words, "The Department of Justice is pouring its resources into stopping domestic violent extremists before they can attack, prosecuting those who do and battling the spread of the kind of hate that leads to tragedies like the one we mark here today," without providing any evidence of this supposedly dire threat other than the alleged presence of some active duty service members at the Capitol Building on 6 January 2021 when some overenthusiastic Trump supporters decided to express their First Amendment rights via property damage. Those citizens were encouraged to do so no doubt by more than six months of such behavior in the summer of 2020 from "protestors" across the country who did billions of dollars in property damage and murdered many honest citizens, while the press and one political party described the psychotic violence as "mostly peaceful protests."

In the first two years of the Biden Administration the Pentagon, the Department of Justice and the Department of Homeland Security were *all* focused on ferreting out a thing which does not exist. They're going to hold "investigations" until they find some white people to arrest.

That sounds a whole lot like Communist governments throughout the Cold War – as well as North Korea, Cuba, Michigan, California, Canada and Venezuela today – who were holding constant "investigations" to discern who was still loyal to the Communist plan, amazingly enough resulting in officials close to Stalin or other leaders getting executed because of never-defined "subversion."

As you, dear reader, will no doubt realize by now, when "important" people's reputations and careers are on the line, *results will be provided.* Defense Secretary Lloyd Austin, Attorney General Garland and DHS Secretary Mayorkas have *declared* that "white supremacist domestic terrorists" are the *single most dangerous threat to America* that exists today.[42] While the fervent investigations petered out, the lasting damage includes drastically reduced recruitment numbers for a military that tells its candidates that it's chock full of white supremacists.

This is the same Mayorkas who has declared repeatedly from April and May of 2021 that there was "no crisis" at the southern border, despite record numbers of illegal border-jumpers pouring into the country, a lie he continued to spout even coming into the November 2022 midterm elections, despite the millions of illegal border jumpers. Hey, if he's wildly and utterly wrong about one thing, why wouldn't he be wildly and utterly wrong about other things? To be fair to these functionary heads of departments, they are echoing what their boss, President Joe Biden said in his speech before (a limited selection of) Congress on 28 April 2021 after making some noises about Al Qaeda: "And, we won't ignore what our own intelligence agencies have determined – the most lethal terrorist threat to the homeland today is from white supremacist terrorism."

If the first part of his sentence is true, I would like to modify my comments on funding the US Intelligence Community to recommend all such funding be pulled. If our Intelligence Community has "determined" that "white supremacists" are the biggest threat facing the nation, we are clearly not getting value for money and we should fire the lot of them. What is the second biggest threat? Salmonella? Musical theatre?

---

[42] DHS to undergo internal review to root out 'extremism' (nypost.com) 27 April 2021

I am not even going to opine on whether Merrick Garland may in some small way be looking for payback against Republicans who denied him a hearing to become a Supreme Court Justice during Obama's last year in office. An honest judge or prosecutor would recuse him- or herself from any investigations which most assuredly are politically tainted; I'd be willing to bet a large amount of my net worth that AG Garland is not sending out investigators to peer into the affairs of Democrats during his search for "white supremacists," no matter how pale their skin may be nor how much that party was the backbone of the KKK.

When the "investigations" roll on, what are the odds that normal, rational, intelligent people under their authority are going to come back after 60, 30 or heck, 2 days to say *"Um, OK, boss, this is gonna be hard to hear, because you've made all these grand statements to the press and all, and I get that your boss, President-in-Waiting Harris has built her career on racially-divisive nonsense like this, but, um, well, we searched through millions of soldiers and DHS employees and found, like, 4 or 5 knuckleheads who were dumb enough to hang a Confederate flag in their lockers and a chick who likes to make Hitler jokes for shock value. But there is no grand 'white supremacist' threat. As for 'domestic terrorists,' the only people hurling Molotov cocktails and attacking Federal buildings in Portland and Minneapolis are all self-described left-wing anarchists and the like who are being egged on by Congressional Representative Maxine Waters who may be many things, but 'white supremacist' isn't one of them. So, well, ummm... I know you'd have preferred some show trials and a parade of central casting white dudes with a couple of tattooed ink tears and maybe even swastikas shaved into their buzzcuts, but there's no evidence of any of that. Sorry. It's all in the report I'll leave on your desk. I'll see myself out."*

Wake up, America. This nonsense has to end. Idle hands are the Devil's plaything and an *entire* department based on the premise of constant paranoiac vigilance will inevitably tend towards totalitarian thinking and repression. I hope over time, this particular episode becomes an historical footnote that the nation shivers to remember how close we came this time to insanity. In the heat of the moment, the Biden Administration's handmaidens in the media are dutifully pouring out reams of content about this lurking "white supremacist" threat. They're providing no concrete examples, but I suppose that doesn't matter – we're just to trust that they're on the case and that there's no way that they'd manufacture falsehoods out of thin air just to drive ratings through fear of a big conspiracy now that their daily bread Donald Trump isn't around to give them their hourly dose of dopamine outrage.

I don't know why I am hopeful. We are still taking our shoes off while going through pre-flight security, all because one idiot tried to blow up his sneakers in 2001 on a flight from Paris to Miami. He hadn't even gone through *American* pre-flight security, so there is no evidence that he *would* have evaded security in, say, New York had he tried to wear a foot bomb through the checkpoint. One ugly, evil moron who was too incompetent to even get the small amount of explosives in his sneakers to go off, as he fumbled with matches seated in coach while people around him were yelling "What are you doing?!" Hundreds of millions of people performing kabuki theatre because of this idiot; if his goal was to inconvenience hundreds of millions of travelers, we've let him win.

It's a wonder I can even get out of bed in the morning.

Customs & Border Control

Year Founded:	July 31, 1789
Founded by President	George Washington
Year Subsumed by DHS	2003
Funding Budget 2023	$17,500,000,000
Messina's 2024 Budget Proposal	$55,000,000,000
Messina's 2025 Budget Proposal	$120,000,000,000
Degree to which Messina's Plan is Better	Completely
Should a Federal Customs & Border Control exist?	Yes

Is this a standalone proper use of the taxpayers' limited resources?	Yes
Does this expenditure unfairly benefit one American over another one?	No
Does the expenditure meet the "Is this logical?" standard of fiduciary responsibility?	Yes
Can the goals be achieved by *not* spending the dollar more effectively than by spending it?	No

This is the entity that has been securing our borders for centuries. It is now a part of the Department of Homeland Security. It needs to be a standalone department once again, with increased funding to control the flows of people and goods into and out of our nation's borders.

Great folks doing a very important job. Not only should the folks who perform their jobs well at Customs get paid well, but wherever possible, solid Americans should bake cookies and cupcakes for them. Or bring fresh veggie plates for those wary of gluten or bulging waistlines. The CBP website has a great summary of the roles and responsibilities CBP has assumed over the years:

> On March 1, 2003, U.S. Customs and Border Protection became the nation's first comprehensive border security agency with a focus on maintaining the integrity of the nation's boundaries and ports of entry.
>
> Before CBP, security, compliance and facilitation of international travel and trade were conducted by multiple organizations. The consolidation of these roles and responsibilities allowed CBP to develop seamless security procedures while ensuring compliance with the nation's immigration, health, and international trade laws and regulations.
>
> In establishing CBP, its leadership ensured that the best traditions of its legacy agencies continued from:
> - U.S. Customs Service, which traced its original functions to July 31, 1789, and noted its role as the progenitor of numerous federal bureaus and agencies. The Customs Service closed with the dawn of CBP, but its commissioner became the leader of CBP and the majority of its staff and responsibilities came to CBP.

- Immigration inspectors, who traced their responsibilities to the establishment of the Office of the Superintendent of Immigration on <u>March 3, 1891</u>.
- Agriculture inspectors, who traced their roles to the passage of the Plant Quarantine Act on <u>Aug. 20, 1912</u>.
- Border Patrol agents, who brought their responsibility for maintaining the integrity of the U.S. borders as they have done since Congress authorized the hiring of Border Patrol personnel on <u>May 28, 1924</u>.
- In addition to this core of specialties and responsibilities present at CBP's founding, CBP also developed an air and marine monitoring capability with the formation of its third uniformed division, the Office of Air and Marine on <u>Jan. 17, 2006</u>.

The uniformed ranks are only a portion of CBP's specialized corps. They are joined by forensic scientists, international trade specialists, public affairs officers and cadres of other specialists and employees who work together to make CBP's processes more secure, cost effective and efficient.

Because of the work of the people of CBP, the nation's borders and the American communities around them have never been more secure. But there is much more to be done. As CBP progresses into its second decade, the nation will see a fully integrated approach to international security, trade and travel that makes the world safer, facilitates international travel and trade, and drives the continuous improvement of CBP's operations.[43]

There are myriad reasons for supplying robust funding to Customs. One of the most crucial is in preventing the introduction of invasive species to the United States. The one great thing the Aussies have gotten right – aside from diaphanous summer party dresses, Balmain bugs, Hunter Valley Semillon and cool, breathable cotton shirts for Sydney evenings on the beach – is a strict set of controls around invasive species.

Here in the United States, bad decisions around "exotic pets" have wrought insanely expensive havoc across the country. The Florida Everglades are chock full of pythons and anacondas from Asia and South America. The voracious lionfish has destroyed fish populations across the coral reefs and shores of Florida. With no natural predators, humans have resorted to spearfishing competitions to control the population. That is not working, by the way.

Related to this is one of the few areas of private life for which I *do* support robust, overlord-micro-control. Newsflash: You don't need a tiger or a crocodile or an Asian snake as a pet. If you really, really, really *need* that kind of interaction, volunteer at a zoo or move to the country where the animal is native. We need to institute a nationwide ban on this zaniness for the same reason it's illegal to have a "hobby" collection of smallpox virus in your "carefully controlled" spare bedroom in your Chicago apartment. We don't allow the latter and should not allow the former because the escape of the animal and its subsequent danger to the general public is an unacceptable and unnecessary risk for all Americans to bear.

---

[43] https://www.cbp.gov/about/history

Immigration and Customs Enforcement (ICE)

ICE is usually lumped together with CBP for obvious operational reasons. Should someone be in the country illegally, they are not likely to be hanging out on the border, waiting for a CBP agent to find them. So ICE agents enforce the laws throughout the country.

This is a very important arm of law enforcement and one we need to fund robustly and support fully. ICE needs the resources to grab lawbreakers and deport them instantly. Given the millions of people who broke the law by wandering across our southern border in the last few years, ICE may need a special appropriation of double, triple or quadruple their budget to fire "immigration enforcement temps" to locate, capture and deport up to 10 million (maybe more) people in this country illegally.

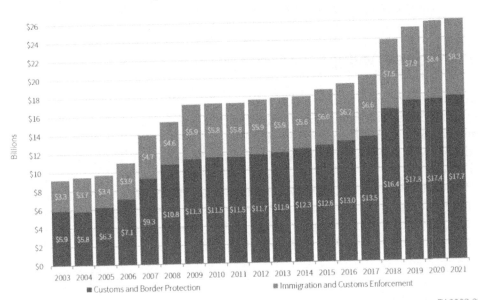

Figure 2: CBP & ICE Annual Budgets, FY 2003-2021

Source: Congressional budgets, gross budget authority as provided in Conference Reports, FY 2003-2021.

U.S. Citizenship and Immigration Services

Year Founded:	1891 in Treasury Department
Founded by President	Benjamin Harrison
Year Subsumed by DHS	2003
Funding Budget 2023	$8,300,000,000
Messina's 2024 Budget Proposal	$10,000,000,000
Messina's 2025 Budget Proposal	$25,000,000,000

Degree to which Messina's Plan is Better	Marginally
Should a Federal USCIS exist?	Yes

The USCIS[44] serves a valuable and appropriate role in dealing properly with immigration to the United States. In terms of function and fiscal impact, it's also one of those rare things in a bureaucracy: an agency that pretty much pays for itself. US citizenship or even work visas are – or have been historically – a valuable thing which people prove by their willingness to pay for it.

It's also already spread throughout the nation geographically, which means the transition to the new, distributed model of Federal governance I propose will not change their operations one bit. USCIS employees are already embedded in towns and cities throughout our fair and delightful land.

Keep up the good work, folks! We need legal immigration to build a younger workforce to replace or inspire the lazy dropouts native born. We are going to at least double this agency's budget, to make sure we have the bandwidth of qualified people willing to help honest immigrants navigate the system on the way to full citizenship.

Immediate Emergency Funding to Fix Broken Border

Because of the insanity of the last few years of basically open borders, this entity needs a serious increase in funding and clarification of mission. The entirety of Customs and Border Control along with ICE and Immigration needs many multiples of current funding. We must locate every single person of the millions who have flowed across the border since Biden took office.

Thank God for excellent civil servants who are telling Americans about the insanity on our southern border. I cannot for the life of me discern how the Biden Administration policy of letting unvetted people stream across our southern border is in any conceivable universe supposed to benefit the United States of America.

---

[44] Our History | USCIS / https://www.uscis.gov/about-us/our-history

NEW: Internal CBP data provided & confirmed by CBP sources reveals thousands of "special interest aliens" from mostly Middle Eastern countries have been apprehended by Border Patrol while crossing into U.S. illegally over last 2 years.

Syria: 538
Yemen: 139
Iran: 659
Iraq: 123
Afghanistan: 6,386
Lebanon: 164
Egypt: 3,153
Pakistan: 1,613
Mauritania: 15,594
Uzbekistan: 13,624
Turkey: 30,830

Date range 10/1/2021 - 10/4/2023

These are Border Patrol apprehensions between ports of entry only, this data does not include CBP encounters at ports of entry.

Some or many of these military aged men could just be people in search of a better life. But we know Hezbollah and Hamas have operations in Latin America, for example, and it is unfortunately a high probability there are now dormant terror cells waiting quietly both within our borders and in Mexico. As the war which Iran and Hamas began in Israel on 7 October 2023 expands, it is likely that Americans are going to experience a true home front battle front – if not dozens at once – launched by these men who crossed our border unhindered, unchecked and unvetted.

Even if every single border jumper is a nice person looking for a better life, we cannot have a constant state of chaos in our nation. We claim to be a nation of laws. The longer we allow lawlessness to prevail, the less respect people have for the idea of following the law. Remember, we want a government that focuses on a very few things, staffed by qualified, well-compensated, non-unionized patriots. Getting our house in order with respect to our borders is a top priority.

All-2024

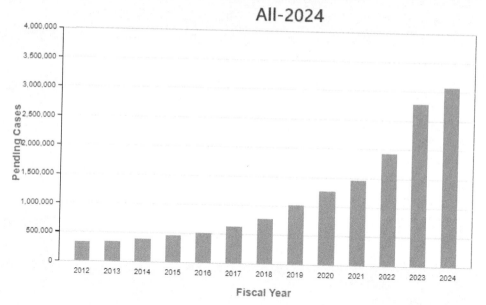

We need to commit real dollars to finding and arresting every single illegal entrant who violated our laws and borders. They need to be expelled from the country and those who make a serious claim for asylum need to be held in detention until that hearing happens. Similarly, no more screwing around with years long back logs. We will set up fully functional asylum courts to hear the volume of cases in a swift fashion.

All that costs money which we would rather not spend. But part of what I am making the case for with this book is that acceptance of the objective reality of our fiscal and operational situation is critical, followed swiftly by effective application of resources dedicated to fixing the problem at hand.

Not filtered through the lens of ridiculous union regulations. Let's get our border under control and our house in order. No more insane waits for a court date far in the future.

Figure 10: The official new entrance portal to every immigration courthouse. Welcome to America.

Transportation Security Administration

Year Founded:	1 March 2003
Founded by President	George W. Bush
Year Subsumed by DHS	2003
Funding Budget 2023	$8,300,000,000
Messina's 2024 Budget Proposal	$10,000,000,000
Messina's 2025 Budget Proposal	$11,000,000,000
Degree to which Messina's Plan is Better	Marginally
Should a Federal USCIS exist?	Yes

We do require security at airports and the TSA does a reasonable job of accomplishing that. I say "reasonable," because no one is ever going to be perfect at a job which the public views as an inconvenience at best. It's repetitive and people rarely thank TSA agents for their work. As a frequent traveler, I always try to say something positive to them. That said, there is always room for process improvement, which we need to create the proper incentives to achieve.

A lot of that improvement will come simply from stripping away damaging union protections. A lot more will come from the rotating, jury-duty-like governing Boards of Directors we will be mandating for the few government departments that remain.

I know it gives them a thrill, but do TSA Agents need to X-ray my crotch?

Quite a few things happened after the World Trade Center and Pentagon attacks. One of those is the typical bureaucrat striving to grab more power, aided and abetted by lobbyists and salesmen flogging fancy new kit. A lot of that new kit has been insanely invasive of normal people's privacy. Metal detectors and X-ray machines for luggage are just fine. The ridiculous "assume the position" body scanners are both rude and pointless. Then again, no planes have fallen out of the sky or slammed into buildings since they were implemented.

Causation or coincidence? Hard to know. But I'm not averse to someone checking to be sure I'm not going to be the next victim of a Libyan Lockerbie attack, finding myself suddenly plummeting to the earth from 30,000 feet without a parachute after my plane got blown in two.

Air Marshal Service

This line item needs to be either eliminated or *sharply* curtailed, with *any* continuance of the program set up on entirely new lines. For example, if we want to continue to randomly place an "Air Marshal" on commercial airlines, perhaps this is "rotating duty" for members of the military Special Operations Forces, who arguably are far better trained to handle serious in-air disturbances than another Federal civil servant trained in law enforcement and given a sidearm.

The TSA website describes their function:
Federal Air Marshals serve as the primary law enforcement entity within TSA. We deploy on flights around the world and in the United States. While our primary mission of protecting air passengers and crew has not changed much over the years, Federal Air Marshals have an ever-expanding role in homeland security and work closely with other law enforcement agencies to accomplish their mission. The men and women who make up the Federal Air Marshal Service are dedicated, well trained law enforcement professionals, each equipped with the knowledge, skills, and abilities necessary to keep our aviation system safe and secure.

The Air Marshal program is another fine example of good intentions run amok (charitably) or misguided legislating done in the heat of passionate hysteria (more likely). In 2009, taxpayers spent $200 million *per arrest* made by the Air Marshals Service.

Duncan Blasts "Useless" Air Marshal Service
June 19, 2009 12:00 PM

Washington, DC -- Mr. DUNCAN: Madam Speaker, probably the most needless, useless agency in the entire Federal Government is the Air Marshal Service.
In the Homeland Security Appropriations bill we will take up next week, we will appropriate $860 million for this needless, useless agency. This money is a total waste: $860 million for people to sit on airplanes and simply fly back and forth, back and forth. What a cushy, easy job.
And listen to this paragraph from a front-page story in the USA Today last November: "Since 9/11, more than three dozen Federal air marshals have been charged with crimes, and hundreds more have been accused of misconduct. Cases range from drunken driving and domestic violence to aiding a human-trafficking ring and trying to smuggle explosives from Afghanistan."
Actually, there have been many more arrests of Federal air marshals than that story reported, quite a few for felony offenses. In fact, more air marshals have been arrested than the number of people arrested by air marshals.
We now have approximately 4,000 in the Federal Air Marshals Service, yet they have made an average of just 4.2 arrests a year since 2001. This comes out to an average of about one arrest a year per 1,000 employees.
Now, let me make that clear. Their thousands of employees are not making one arrest per year each. They are averaging slightly over four arrests each year by the entire agency. In other words, we are spending approximately $200 million per arrest. Let me repeat that: we are spending approximately $200 million per arrest.
Professor Ian Lustick of the University of Pennsylvania wrote last year about the money feeding frenzy of the war on terror. And he wrote this: "Nearly 7 years after September 11, 2001," he wrote this last year, "what accounts for the vast discrepancy between the terrorist threat facing America and the scale of our response? Why, absent any evidence of a serious terror threat, is a war to on terror so enormous, so all-encompassing, and still expanding? The fundamental answer is

that al Qaeda's most important accomplishment was not to hijack our planes but to hijack our political system."

"For a multitude of politicians, interest groups and professional associations, corporations, media organizations, universities, local and State governments and Federal agency officials, the war on terror is now a major profit center, a funding bonanza, and a set of slogans and sound bites to be inserted into budget, grant, and contract proposals."

And finally, Professor Lustick wrote: "For the country as a whole, however, it has become maelstrom of waste." And there is no agency for which those words are more applicable than the Federal Air Marshal Service.

In case anyone is wondering, the Air Marshal Service has done nothing to me, and I know none of its employees. But I do know with absolute certainty that this $860 million we are about to give them could be better spent on thousands of other things.

As far as I'm concerned, it is just money going down a drain for the little good it will do. When we are so many trillions of dollars in debt, a national debt of over $13 trillion, we simply cannot afford to waste money in this way.[45]

As this Congressman so eloquently demonstrates, the culture of Washington and the Untouchable Political Class has become such a horrible, turgid wasteland of immorality and complete abrogation of basic fiduciary duty that it needs to be revamped wholesale. Air Marshals are a good idea in theory. In practice, it has been a spectacular waste of money, with more Air Marshals being arrested and convicted of crimes than their having made arrests.

If that is not enough, this pointless make-work bureaucracy is composed of people who feel discriminated against at work! As recently as February 2020, the GAO was issuing reports and recommendations to deal with complaints by the Air Marshals service! Apparently, the poor dears don't like their work schedules and family time at home.

> From fiscal years 2016 through 2018, FAMS employees filed 230 discrimination complaints with TSA's Civil Rights Division, though employees may have reported additional discrimination complaints through other means. In 2012, FAMS adopted an action plan to address discrimination and has taken some steps called for in the plan, such as sustaining a FAMS Ombudsman position. However, due to a loss of management focus on the plan, FAMS has not fully implemented other planned efforts, such as holding diversity focus groups. Taking steps to reaffirm its efforts to prevent discrimination would demonstrate leadership commitment to reducing concerns of discrimination within FAMS.[46]

---

[45] http://duncan.house.gov/2009/06/22062009.shtml

[46] Federal Air Marshal Service Has Taken Steps to Address Workforce Issues, but Additional Actions Needed GAO-20-125: Published: Feb 12, 2020. Publicly Released: Feb 12, 2020.

Biden's 2023 budget has requested $843,334,000 for this ongoing stupidity. Eliminate it immediately. One cannot be discriminated against if one is not employed. Same thing with work-life balance. Problems solved.

U.S. Coast Guard

Year Founded:	1 March 2003
Founded by President	George Washington
Year Subsumed by DHS	2003
Funding Budget 2023	$13,800,000,000
Messina's 2024 Budget Proposal	$15,000,000,000
Messina's 2025 Budget Proposal	$25,000,000,000
Degree to which Messina's Plan is Better	Marginally
Should a Federal Coast Guard exist?	Yes

This is a military organization and needs to stand on its own. It certainly does not belong under the DHS umbrella. Our coastlines and shipping lanes require improved security.

The 2023 budget has a line item for $2,044,414,000 for "Retired Pay." All of these incurred defined benefit obligations are going to be sunset and no new ones created. Anyone receiving a defined pension payout as a retiree will be offered a one-time payout into a tax-equivalent privately-owned fund or can choose to remain on the plan they are on now. Depending on the private-sector commission pulled together to examine the timing and amount of payments, with *lots* of input from actuaries, it may even be feasible to make the choice an annual thing, so people who are more nervous about transitioning to a private fund system can observe how it goes for early adopters. None of my ideas for improving the relationship of government to citizens are focused on punishing or hurting anyone. Whether or not a given job or even entire department is to remain after our massive house-cleaning, those people already retired who made their decisions based on certain promises will not be stripped arbitrarily of what they worked for.

For now, all these general obligations incurred to retirees must be tracked carefully and dealt with cleanly, until there are no more retirees collecting cash directly from the government coffers.

Disinformation Governance Board

Year Founded:	May 2022
Founded by President	Joe Biden
Funding Budget 2023	Any amount is too much
Messina's 2024 Budget Proposal	-$500,000*

Degree to which Messina's Plan is Better	Completely
Should a Federal Ministry of Truth exist?	No

* President Biden, VP Harris and Secretary Mayorkas should be fined *personally* for even proposing this atrocity. I know that is a dream, but on principle, any President or VP who suggests such an insane attack on fundamental rights should be punished in some way. This madness never passed any rational sniff test.

Clearly the Biden Administration *wants* this book to be a runaway bestseller. This is so ludicrous it can only be a thumb in the eye of the American people. *See? We can get away with whatever we want. We're even going to create an official Ministry of Truth to dictate what you're allowed to believe is fact. We're going to put a completely flaky lunatic in charge of this appalling affront to the First Amendment, a woman who in recent years has declared blatant lies to be true. Suck it, America. We're in charge and you, the lumpen peasantry had best get in line.*

At the most optimistic end of the spectrum, the "idea" behind this appalling affront to the First Amendment was that some people are giving other people "dangerous" information. In yet one more moment of utter absurdity in government, the woman put in charge of this madness has a rock-solid track record of doing nothing *but* peddling lies to the American people as if they were fact.

Here is a bizarre snippet of conversation in which Nina Jankowicz gives a clear sense of how little she trusts the average person to think critically. In the picture below, she's the smug nutcase in the upper right-hand corner.

The Post Millennial ✔
@TPostMillennial

Biden's "Ministry of Truth" director says she wants "verified people" like her to be able to edit people's tweets so they can "add context to certain tweets"

12:12 PM · May 11, 2022 · Twitter Web App

This is the transcript of her talk. I should get hazard pay for having had to listen closely to this offensive world salad:

"And I am eligible for – because I'm verified. But there are a lot of people who shouldn't be verified who aren't, you know, legit, in my opinion. I mean they are real people but they're not trustworthy. Anyway, verified people can, um, essentially start to 'edit' [air quotes] Twitter, the same sort of way Wikipedia is, so they can add context to certain Tweets. Ummmmm... So, just as an easy example, not from any political standpoint, if President Trump were still on Twitter, and tweeted a claim about voter fraud, someone could add context from one of the sixty lawsuits, uh, that went through the court [sic] or, uh, something that an election official in one of the States said, perhaps your own Secretary of State [laughs while bearded dude nods] and his news conference something like that. Adding context so that people have a fuller picture rather than just an individual claim on a Tweet."

Don't be fooled by her "random" example of Donald Trump. Her example was absolutely not from any political standpoint. Yup. She's "legit," right? You can tell from her perfect command of English as demonstrated by her grammatical perfection and clear delivery of a cogent set of thoughts. I frankly would expect more from a Bryn Mawrtyr, but such is the decadent age in which we live.

She delivered this perky pep talk[47] to the eleven other True Believers nodding along in sheer agreement at her brilliance. They were all so excited by the prospect of her protecting us all from dangerous ideas. Cuz, y'know, like, other Americans who maybe – the HORROR! – vote, like Republican or something equally extremist and hate-filled, can, like say stuff, but it's not "legit" stuff, so we need to be sure to censor them and, like, hound their employers to fire them and stuff, until every last one is silenced.

Her very exciting proposal is that some wonderful, "verified" idiot who managed to get a blue check from Twitter could come upon something *you,* poor, benighted, probably dumb slob felt fit to post online – and proceed to *change what you wrote.* I have no idea *why* you were posting something to the Leftist Indoctrination Swamp, but let's say you did. In her happy world, if someone *she* agrees with comes across your stupid comment, that special "legit" person can change what you wrote. In many instances, who could care? In some very specific instances, in this bizarre cancel culture where people lose their real-world jobs because an online pack of losers decides to scream about a joke they don't find funny, someone modifying *your* words could get you fired if the words were changed in a certain way.

That is leaving aside the very appalling idea in the first place that someone thinks he or she has made a comment or contributed to an online debate – perhaps in good faith, but that does not matter to free speech – only to find out (or never find out) that the entire

---

[47] If you can bear the agony: The Post Millennial on Twitter: "Biden's "Ministry of Truth" director says she wants "verified people" like her to be able to edit people's tweets so they can "add context to certain tweets" https://t.co/KgMxUn3HsG" / Twitter

intent of what he or she wrote has been changed by some nasty busybody that Biden's Czarina of Ultimate Truth has deemed "legit."

Mind you, this appalling gibberish was *not* coming from a random Comparative [Insert Stupid Non-Academic Topic] Studies major at the Yale Comintern. No, this was coming from the putative *Head* of a Federal Agency. Does it never occur to people like her how condescending, obnoxious and just plain *rude* is her belief that we dumb idiots couldn't go get additional contexts or points of view on our own? Oh, no! We're too stupid for that, so after taking in a 128-character assertion from someone, we'd all just say, "Yup! That's gotsta be all there is to this matter, thems is the facts, yup."

It is therefore clearly up to some other set of total geniuses – we know this because they got blue checks from Twitter as a verified account, but then again, even some of them aren't "legit" in her mind – to guide us poor dumb dumbs on the Path to Correct Thought by editing someone else's writing to add context.

Just remember, this is how these obnoxious, self-appointed overlords think; she was just foolish enough to say it out loud for everyone to hear. They are superior to us – in ways that remain baffling to us but are apparently evident to themselves – so they should be able to wade into something as basic as your social media feed to alter what you say. For your own good, you see, to combat "disinformation," you see.

Tangentially, I *loved* her reference to Wikipedia which is one of the most error-prone, ridiculous non-sources of non-information imaginable. For fun, when I was reading the Wikipedia entry on "National Merit Scholarship," I noticed that my name was not listed among those who won that award. I corrected that error, by adding my name to the list. Thankfully, I have never been cited elsewhere on the site. A few days later, I got a notification telling me someone had edited my entry.

The Nina Jankowicz Truth Determination Improv Crew hard at work editing your social media posts

I looked and some guy had "pointed" via hyperlink my name in the Merit Scholarship entry to Chris Messina, an actor a few years younger than I am who as it happens is not a Merit Scholar. He's a funny actor, also from Long Island, but he and I are different people. I corrected that misattribution. A day later, the erroneous link was reinstated, and so it remains, I assume until someone who cares more than I do forces the correct academic distinction between me and the movie actor.

The point is not about that particular entry. The point is that an open source of "information" with no standards, lacking "final say" editorial control is not very valuable. The budding Mistress of Truth was clearly enthusiastic about an online army of correct-thinking hordes who would go forth to amend, edit, delete and "add context to" millions of people's writings. She was so enthusiastic because she clearly believed all of those doing the editing would take *her* word for what is "true" as final. Irony, much?

During Congressional hearings about this madness, Secretary Mayorkas looked like what he was – a man ordered to defend the indefensible. When pressed on whether the Steele Dossier, which was a completely manufactured pack of lies about Trump's supposed relationship with the Russians paid for by Hillary Clinton's campaign in 2016, was "disinformation," Mayorkas dodged and weaved and kept babbling about Latin American cartels "spreading disinformation" to poor people in Central America and how this great new Board would combat or rebut that disinformation. Senator Josh Hawley kept pressing him, saying – reasonably enough – "you and I cannot even agree on what constitutes 'disinformation' so how is the government of which you and I are each a part going to deal with something, if we cannot even agree on what it is?"

The answer of course is that the Biden Administration – in line with many before it – has demonstrated a super heroic ability to be appallingly tone deaf, even more than most political entities. The people running the show have so badly drunk the Kool Aid that they *really believe* that there is a mortal danger to their power (yes, that's true) and American health (nope, not at all) should anyone be allowed to hear things like "a mask made of a t-shirt does nothing to prevent viral transmission."

Logic and the American people got a win on this particular bit of abusive idiocy. By 18 May 2022, the outcry was so huge, from so many segments of society, the Biden DHS beat a hasty retreat. Well, a minor retreat. The Administration said the initiative was "on pause," which is not the same thing as canceling it entirely.

I guess now we'll all suffer from a tidal wave of misinformation, without Nina to protect us.

I wonder how much of this book she would have redlined, with my zany assertions of unaccountable bureaucrats making rules for us all, often with penalty of imprisonment? Crazy stuff – I must be a conspiracy theorist, reporting facts like that.

Federal Emergency Management Agency (FEMA)

Year Founded:	1 April 1979
Founded by President	Jimmy Carter
Funding Budget 2023	$29,500,000,000 (includes $19.4 billion for the Disaster Relief Fund)
Messina's 2024 Budget Proposal	$25,000,000
Messina's 2025 Budget Proposal	0
Degree to which Messina's Plan is Better	Completely
Should a Federal FEMA exist?	No

Where to begin describing how utterly pointless this boondoggle is?

So many bad ideas wrapped up in one set of phenomenally good intentions. Not to beat a battered tin drum, but this sure is in keeping with my assertion that if we just reversed *everything* Jimmy Carter ever did, the nation would thereby be improved immensely. The idea that there should be Federal-level coordination for disaster response is perhaps not completely ridiculous. Big, sweeping events which impact multiple states at one time can probably do with some coordination of response on a large geographic scale. There may even have been a stronger justification in 1979 for maintaining an entire bureaucracy "on standby" against such emergencies when the Internet did not exist and no one had mobile phones.

With the advent of distributed networks and real-time image transmission, while a possible need for emergency coordination could arise to organize materials and people for hurricane aftermath relief, that coordination could just as easily be handled on an ad hoc basis by officials in the Department of the Interior and the Department of Defense. Corporations have multiple contingency plans for unexpected emergencies as they arise; they do not keep entire teams of employees sitting around getting paid to *maybe* deal with a crisis once every few years. There is no reason that the Federal Government cannot do the same thing; heck, it's precisely how State and local governments deal with unexpected crises.

If you're having trouble sleeping, you can have a read[48] of "Publication 1," delightful Soviet nomenclature for their "capstone doctrine," and I am not making that terminology up. It is page after page of organizational existential justification leavened with a hearty dose of wildly boring allusions to how downright dangerous nature can be.

FEMA in Publication 1 provides some helpful highlights of their accomplishments over the years. As you read through each of the tasks they highlight, it may well occur to you to ponder, as I have, whether another government entity would have performed the same task if FEMA didn't exist.

---

[48] https://www.fema.gov/sites/default/files/2020-03/publication-one_english_2019.pdf

Unique Response Coordination Efforts in Our History

Cuban Refugee Crisis – 1980: FEMA was tasked to help process more than 100,000 refugees arriving on Florida's shores.

Space Shuttle Columbia Disaster – 2003: FEMA coordinated the collection of debris from the shuttle accident across Texas and Louisiana.

Bam, Iran Earthquake – 2003: At the request of the Iranian Government, FEMA sent two International Medical Surgical Response Teams to set up a temporary field hospital.

Haiti Earthquake – 2010: Supporting USAID, FEMA established a Joint Information Center on the island. FEMA also sent search and rescue teams, communications equipment, and staff from the Mobile Emergency Response Support system.

Increase in Arrivals of Unaccompanied Children – 2014: FEMA coordinated a government-wide response to address the needs of an influx of unaccompanied children crossing into the U.S. along the southwest border. Over 57,000 children crossed the border, many in need of food, water, shelter, and social and medical services.

Ebola Virus – 2014: FEMA collaborated with over a dozen Federal agencies, states, the private sector, and other nations in combatting the spread of Ebola domestically and overseas.

Figure 11: FEMA Highlights, taken from Publication 1

None of these items required FEMA as an entity to exist. Picking up Space Shuttle debris? How about NASA coordinating with the National Guard and the legion of active soldiers, sailors and airmen stationed in the Southeast?

Dealing with refugees? Don't we have Customs and Border Control within ICE? Why is FEMA dealing with this?

Setting up a "Joint Information Center" in Haiti after an earthquake? That requires a massive Federal bureaucracy costing $9,000,000,000 per year, not including $20-40 billion for the Disaster Relief Fund? Two Silicon Valley interns on loan to the government for the duration of our assistance in Haiti could set up and run a resilient "Joint Information Center" and they'd get to tell awesome stories of being serious humanitarians in a disaster zone in the Caribbean when they were back in Mountain View, flirting with Stanford summer interns on team-building sailing excursions out of Sausalito.

We could even have cool T-shirts made for them, featuring local artists from the impacted disaster area. Printed on sustainably sourced cotton handwoven in refugee camps at $60 a pop, putting cash in the hands of the actual folks displaced by the earthquake. That's some economic development we should all get behind.

None of these highlighted tasks are necessarily bad uses of taxpayer money. Equally, none of them required that FEMA exist to have them accomplished.

Flood insurance – poor folks subsidizing rich folks' beach houses. At its best, this is a waste of taxpayer money that encourages people to build houses in risky, flood-prone areas. Now, I'm all for freedom and if you decide to spend $150,000 building the house of your dreams in a flood plain prone to 50-year floods, go for it. Just don't ask the rest of us to pay for it.

Feel free to troll through the 2023 budget. It's online.[49] Especially look through the budget tables starting on page 97. Under the Cybersecurity line items, you can ponder as I do what "Stakeholder Engagement" means and why it costs $26,000,000 to accomplish. I gather that is a travel and fancy snacks budget for DC bureaucrats to go speak with corporations to tell them – surprise! – there is a risk of a cyber-attack happening to them.

Or $138,000,000 for "management and business activities."

It's a boondoggle and waste of money.

---

[49] FY 2023 budget in Brief FINAL with Cover (dhs.gov)

Chapter 6: Social Security Administration

***"The greatest Ponzi game ever invented"* according to a Nobel Laureate Economist who was speaking _in favor_ of it!**

Year Founded:	August 14, 1935
Founded by President	Franklin D. Roosevelt
Number of employees	60,000
Funding Budget 2023	$10,100,000,000
Messina's 2024 Budget Proposal	$250,000,000*
Messina's 2025 Budget Proposal	$0
Degree to which Messina's Plan is Better	Completely
Should a Federal SSA exist?	No

Is this a standalone proper use of the taxpayers' limited resources?	No
Does this expenditure unfairly benefit one American over another one?	Yes
Does the expenditure meet the "Is this logical?" standard of fiduciary responsibility?	No
Can the goals be achieved by *not* spending the dollar more effectively than by spending it?	Yes

* Wind down funding. Very generous, but within 12 months, all individually controlled accounts will be set up and a funding mechanism put in place.

When it comes to marijuana, we got to – in the wise words of Bob Marley – legalize it. When it comes to the Social Security Administration, we got to privatize it and abolish payroll taxes. Leaving the money that belongs to hundreds of millions of people in the centralized hands of government bureaucrats is folly of the most obvious type.

Thankfully for us all, there is a very simple, direct way to remove this albatross from around the necks of American taxpayers which I lay out below. I am going to bury the lede here by first laying out the whole insane story behind "Social Security," so that my fine fellow Americans who have been too busy to peel back the stinking layers of lies they've been told since FDR, can get a firm grip on why this particular pack of lies emanating from the Swamp has been and will continue to be so horrible for *all* Americans.

The sins, errors, good intentions and flat-out lies behind the creation and ongoing corrosion of "Social Security" all emerge from the same eternal font whence all demagoguery emanates, or at least at which all political howling stops by for a drink or two. Behind *every* single future promise of a cash payment for which no *real investment* is made, lies the same pack of lies:

1. That *anyone* can know the state of the economy of the future that will need to bear the costs of that liability,
2. That non-risk-taking, public sector *bureaucrats* and politicians are mythical, perfect capitalist beings who can therefore *guarantee* financial results for a century, and

3. As a result, the government can always be relied upon to provide income in retirement to every single American citizen.

I had enormous fun - if that is the right word - reading Eric Laursen's *The People's Pension* which he at least has the courage to write as a committed Communist who refers to friends as "comrade," so we don't need to wonder about his point of view.

I often wonder: was there ever a time in American history when *Americans* rather than "Democrats," "Republicans," "Whigs," "Tories," and "Morons" tried to understand one another's viewpoints and have a rational discussion about public policy? Has the advent of 24/7 news blather and instant Internet nonsense just *created* a sense of bigger discord than existed previously?

I am not so sure. Laursen for example in his Prologue about the dynamics of how Social Security dollars get sucked from productive uses and funneled through bureaucratic channels discusses one of the federal government's multiple accounting fictions. He rightly points out that Social Security funds have bought Treasury bonds for years, thereby masking a chunk of the federal budget deficit. Even that fun will come to an end in 2036 or so:

> That [shell game of SSA trust fund buying Treasury debt] was projected to end in 2036, by which date some 70 million baby boomers would have retired, nearly doubling the elderly population and draining the trust funds. Since, by law, Social Security isn't allowed to borrow money, it would then have to get by on just what its payroll tax collections brought in each year. Congress could make up the difference, but only if it wanted to. If not, the Social Security Administration (SSA) estimated the program could continue paying only a little less than 80% of normal benefits.
>
> That would certainly be a problem, progressives argued, but not as serious a one as the program's critics claimed. The ratio of workers to retirees was expected to decline from 3-to-1 to 2-to-1 by 1990. It had already dropped from 18-to-1 in 1950 to 4-to-1 in 1965 without precipitating a disaster - even though government spending on education, social services, and the Cold War was expanding fast at the same time. That's because worker productivity, and average wages, continued to go up - increasing the payroll tax revenues that support Social Security.[50]

These two paragraphs are like a public policy haiku of the mistaken assumptions and bizarre beliefs of totalitarian statists, who have taken to calling themselves "Progressives" because it sounds so much less threatening. After all, who doesn't like progress?

To begin with, in Laursen's world, a payroll tax that started at 2% and is now 15.3%, including Medicare, sucking cash out of the private economy to pay for transfer payments with ever-increasing numbers of beneficiaries and ever-decreasing numbers of workers to pay for it, while driving the country to bankruptcy is not "precipitating a disaster." Hmmm. I am curious to learn what *would* constitute a fiscal disaster in his worldview....

---

[50] Laursen, p.9

To continue unpacking his statements, he then goes on to explain that this "non-disaster" was such a good result, *not* because spending was kept in line with the original 2% tax. No – he fails to mention the expansion of this tax from 3% in 1950 to 7% in 1965. Instead, he tells the reader a not-so-subtle lie by saying there was no disaster "because worker productivity, and average wages continued to go up - increasing the payroll tax revenues that support Social Security."

There is no other adjective for that statement. It is as complete a lie due to its omission of the reality of increased *rates* of wage confiscation as if he never mentioned rising wages. If "worker productivity" – never mind more efficient capital employment, and the labor-saving inventions those risk-taking capital investors enabled, both of which are for him *a priori* evils – had gone up sufficiently to pay for all this social engineering, the Social Security payroll tax would have still been at its 1965 rate of 2%.

But it didn't and it wasn't.

As of 2018, that Social Security tax rate had risen to 12.4%. So much for "worker productivity" naturally generating sufficient growth to allow steady-rate tax theft by the Feds to shovel cash at retirees.

David Stockman rightly points out in his magisterial work *The Great Deformation; The Corruption of Capitalism in America* that the current (2017) drag on the working man was then a roughly 16% deadweight drag when one takes into account all components of the payroll tax, including unemployment "insurance." After the legislated benefits increases, the loss of means-testing, the Medicare addition in 1965, Nixon's insane double-indexing caper and the Carter and Reagan payroll tax increases, we are no closer to a solvent system, far from it.

Accordingly, Federal and state payroll taxes for social insurance generate $1.2 trillion per year in revenue – **four times more than the corporate income tax**. So with the highest labor costs in the world, the U.S. now imposes punishing levies on payrolls. It thus remains hostage to a political happenstance – that is, the destructive bargain struck eight decades ago when high tariff walls, not containerships loaded with cheap goods made from cheap foreign labor, surrounded its harbors.

Yet there is more to the story, and it is worse. The current punishing payroll tax is actually way too low – that is, it drastically underfunds future benefits owing to positively fictional rates of economic growth assumed in the 75-year actuarial projections. As a result, the benefit structure grinds forward on automatic pilot facing no political opposition whatsoever. In the meanwhile, our fast-approaching day of reckoning is thinly disguised by trust fund accounting fictions.

In truth, the trust funds are both meaningless and broke. Annual benefit payouts already exceed tax receipts by upward of $50 billion annually, while the so-called trust fund reserves - $3 trillion of fictional treasury bonds accumulated in earlier decades – are mere promises to use the general taxing powers of the US government to make good in the rising tide of benefits.

The New Deal social insurance mythology of "earned" annuities on "paid-in" premiums that have been accumulated as trust fund "reserves" is thus an unadulterated fiscal scam. Social Security is really just an intergenerational transfer payment system.[51]

The fact that Social Security is just a way of shooting money straight out the door to current retirees from current workers is undisputed. What is even more magical – in a gallows-humor kind of way – is that much like Jonathan Graber *lying* to the American people about ObamaCare to get it passed, but *unlike* Graber in that he *put the truth in writing*, the (oddly) revered economist Nobel Laureate Paul Samuelson wrote in 1967, from his delusional Keynesian perch in the Johnson Administration, that there was nothing to worry about because GDP would definitely grow at 5% forever.

Are you beginning to sense a pattern here?

> The beauty of social insurance is that it is *actuarially* unsound. Everyone who reaches retirement age is given benefit privileges that far exceed anything he has paid in. And exceed his payments by more than ten times (or five times counting employer payments)!
>
> How is it possible? It stems from the fact that the national product is growing at a compound interest rate and can be expected to do so for as far ahead as the eye cannot see. Always there are more youths than old folks in a growing population. More important, with real income going up at 3% per year, the taxable base on which benefits rest is always much greater than the taxes paid historically by the generation now retired...
>
> Social Security is squarely based on what has been called the eighth wonder of the world — compound interest. A growing nation is the greatest Ponzi game ever contrived. And that is a fact, not a paradox.[52]

Here's a fun idea for you: Call your auto insurer and tell them that the $8,700 per year they are charging you as a family of 4 drivers, two of them teenagers, should only cost you $45 per year. When they balk at that idea, soothe their nerves by telling them that the "beauty" of your proposed payment plan versus theirs is that it is "actuarially unsound." Remind them that the entire Federal and State governments of the US operate on that principle, so they should be delighted to experience the same "beauty" for themselves. Give me a call and let me know how long your coverage lasts.

Samuelson's whole premise rested on two predictions which he mistakenly labeled "facts." One, that economic growth would continue at 3% on a real basis (which is 4-6% on a nominal basis depending on long-run inflation patterns and under Biden in mid-2022 is closer to 16%) "as far ahead as the eye cannot see," and two, that economic growth *necessarily* results in a growing population as well, both suppositions which did not turn out to be true. Hence, the deep trouble we're in.

> When 5 percent growth turned out to be a Keynesian illusion and output growth decayed to 1-2 percent annual rate at the turn of the century, the actuarial foundation of Samuelson's Ponzi game came crashing down. It is now evident that

---

[51] Stockman, p174
[52] Samuelson, Paul, *Newsweek*, November 13, 1967

Washington cannot shrink, or even brake, the fiscal doomsday machine that lies underneath.

The fiscal catastrophe embedded in the New Deal social insurance scheme was not inevitable. A means-tested retirement program funded with general revenues was explicitly recommended by the analytically proficient experts commissioned by the Roosevelt White House in 1935. But FDR's cabal of social work reformers led by Labor Secretary Frances Perkins[53] thought a means-test was demeaning, having no clue that a means-test is the only real defense available to the public purse in a welfare state democracy.

When the American economy was riding high in 1960, Paul Samuelson's Ponzi was extracting payroll tax revenue amounting to about 2.8 percent of GDP. A half century later, after a devastating flight of jobs to East Asia and other emerging economies, the payroll tax extracts two-and-one-half times more, taking in early 6.5 percent of GDP. So the remarkable thing is not that wooly-eyed idealists who drafted the 1935 act succumbed to social insurance's Faustian bargain at the time. The puzzling thing is that 75 years later – with all the terrible facts fully known – the doctrinaire conviction abides on the Left that social insurance is the New Deal's crowning achievement. In fact, it is its costliest mistake.[54]

David Stockman takes a more charitable view of humanity than I do. I don't find it puzzling at all that fiscally-illiterate, innumerate liberal arts majors who vote with what they think is their hearts don't understand that this stupid abuse of the public fisc is a disaster. It's not (entirely) their fault: The halls of Academe are 90% filled with the dregs of the Draft Dodger Generation, the most selfish bunch of brats ever to poison the well of domestic comity and strong individual civic responsibility this nation has produced. Those brats – who made sure to get tenure and therefore pensions and benefits to rival those of, say, a Congressman's – have done their all to deform the thinking of American students, to further garner unto their parasitic selves the wealth of the grandchildren that all other generations believe should be helped rather than harmed by one's actions.

After that refreshing detour to visit someone with real-world comprehension of fiscal realities, not barmy Socialist feel-good bromides, let's go back to Comrade Laursen. What is most terrifying to me as an *American* is the completely crazy views he cites *in support of* "social insurance" programs. He agrees with "European anarchists and revolutionaries" like I.M. Rubinow who opined in 1935 that the ills bred by "capitalist society" and not racist evil nonsense was at the root of the rise of Nazism in Germany. In Laursen's view, "...Social Security, national health care and unemployment insurance were never just methods for paying for and delivering services. They were the key to unlocking reserves of human potential and neutralizing the racial and other group hatreds that the modern world had unleashed."[55]

---

[53] For more on the long-run damage this idiot did to America, see Chapter 4 Dept of Labor
[54] Stockman, p.175
[55] Laursen, p.23

Wow, that is some incredible news scoop. So, the "modern world" with its "capitalism" *was the origin point* for ethnic hatred. Because groups self-identifying and then hating other groups and, I don't know, occasionally attacking each other, had never before happened in human history. I'm going to make a note to ring up the Anthropology Department at the University of Chicago which did its level best to educate me to let them know that everything they have to say about human social organization needs to be tossed out. All their fancy books, theses and lectures are pointless because *all* human strife and group hatreds only began after the Industrial Revolution. Some clown in 1935 said so, so they'd best get in line. I'm sure they'll be pleased to down pens and quit squatting amidst various communities around the world for years on end doing fieldwork. No need – Rubinow's rendered it moot.

I am terrified by the fact that this fool Laursen presumably got an education somewhere and he can write this claptrap *and have it edited and published and possibly taken seriously* by other people who presumably got an education of some kind somewhere in this fair land of ours.

He carries on in the usual vein of all people who have never actually created something, who have never actually *worked* for something. They all just assume that there exists a pile of cash *a priori*.

> Crucially, Bismarck's system of social insurance required a person to work and earn the money - that is, the right - to participate. This was quite different from the anarchist conception of mutual aid, which extended to everyone who belonged to a particular community by virtue of their humanity.[56]

Oh, the horror! How *dare* society require someone to *work* to earn money! How unfair, capitalistic, and downright *alienating* is that!

This whole thing about "a particular community" is the heart of not only Laursen's problem, but Obama's and the Clintons' and all their fellow travelers. The *crucial error* and sweeping dishonesty of their approach to the world is to take a *voluntary* form of cooperation, like a guild or a mutual aid society and then *force* that mutual community support model into a bureaucratic, *involuntary model* of social control. In a mutual aid society, I can *choose* whether to contribute money to a common pool from which someday I may be required to draw. In the draconian, Federal, centralized form, *there is nothing voluntary* about the State taking my cash whether I think they will be prudent stewards of my money or have any chance of using it in ways that I find of socioeconomic value.

There is nothing *cooperative* about government bureaucrats taking my cash without my willingly giving it to them, and my facing the threat of punishment both financial and criminal should I not "cooperate." That right there is *precisely* what Hayek meant when he said that all Socialist programs taken to their logical implementation are authoritarian dictatorships.

While not alone in this respect, Obama excelled at this type of constant lie. Every time he talked about his fun new plans to tax the stuffing out of everyone, he *always* said in

---

[56] Laursen, p/22

131

his best reasonable-yet-young-grandpa voice as if he were saying something so obvious he couldn't believe he had to say it, "We're gonna ask some folks to pay some more..." Funny – when I "ask" someone for something, she might either give it to me or she might not. But when the Federal Government "asks" me for money, if I choose to say no, they come after me with fines and penalties in addition to the original "request," and if that doesn't work, they send heavily armed people who will put me in handcuffs and lock me in a little cement and steel box that I'm not allowed to leave.

Gosh, Obama and his ilk sure do have a different definition of the word "ask," don't they? Maybe I shouldn't be surprised – after all, they belong to a political party whose leaders are unsure of what the meaning of "is" is and cannot determine which restroom to use by taking a quick peek down their shorts.

Let's dip back into a fresh helping of Zany Nobel Laureate Krugman's comments on Social Security, shall we? You can go search through his verbiage for all the articles but in essence his argument boils down to two things: Treasury bonds will always yield a superior return to a mixed-asset model including equities, *despite that being the core investment allocation model* followed by all professional asset managers and there's no problem anyway because Social Security is part of the overall Federal budget and, well, if there's a budgetary crisis, then, well, it's not only a Social Security crisis, so, well, anyway, it won't be a problem somehow.

That was a more coherent explication of his "thoughts" on Social Security than how he presents them.[57]

Once more, this man whose only private sector job was advising Enron[58] completely missed the boat on the ever innovative and competitive market in wealth management.

One of the glories of all the research I did for this book – you're welcome, my fellow Americans, for sparing you the brain ache of wading through so much tripe – is that I got a serious appreciation for the genius of folks like Krugman. Reading so many of his pieces calls to mind the comments of one of my true American heroes – Ed Ricketts – who was a fellow alumnus of The College at The University of Chicago, ran a biological laboratory in Monterrey, CA and co-starred in John Steinbeck's *The Log from the Sea of Cortez*. In the book, Ed describes to his great friend John the life trajectory of his father:

> Ed regarded his father with affection. "He has one quality of genius," Ed would say. "He is always wrong. If a man makes a million decisions and judgments at random, it is perhaps mathematically tenable to suppose he will be right half the time and wrong half the time. But you take my father – he is wrong all of the time about everything. That is a matter not of luck but of section. That requires genius."[59]

---

[57] Confusions about Social Security

[58] For my younger readers in 2023 and those picking up the gold-printed Centenary Edition, Enron was an energy trading company in Houston whose CFO and CEO committed fraud on such a breathtaking scale that not only did company executives go to prison, and the company go bankrupt, but the event collapsed a massive accounting firm *and* gave us more stupid, value destroying laws in the form of Sarbanes-Oxley.

[59] Steinbeck, John, *The Log from the Sea of Cortez*

I can only assume that what lies at the heart of the assumptions of the Laursens, Graebers, Krugmans, Stieglitzes, Chavezes, Bidens, Pelosis and Obamas of the world is a deep, abiding ignorance of *where* wealth comes from, of *how* an economy creates bounty as an emergent property of millions of *individual* decisions. All their pronouncements on *how* a pile of money "should be divided" *assume* that the pile exists in the first place. In the fine authoritarian tradition, having come upon a pile that others have created, they feel utterly free to command the confiscation and redistribution of that wealth as they see fit, with jail time and censure for those who dare argue.

Nancy Pelosi understands how to create wealth safely: via insider trading on sure things which she has done for decades as a Washington insider not subject to insider-trading rules as the rest of the poor unwashed (that would be *you,* by the way, dear reader, unless you're a member of Congress or a staffer thereto). She and her husband make a habit of buying real estate and then steering Federal funds for construction projects that will benefit the value of that real estate. Or in taking shares in the Visa IPO *while presiding over legislation that will impact Visa's ability to make profits.*

And then, when some uppity reporter[60] had *the audacity* to insist in a press conference that she answer some basic questions about a possible conflict of interest in her both overseeing credit card company legislation *while* being in on the Visa IPO slush fund, she refused to answer his very reasonable question and went off on an incoherent tirade about how she has long been one of the fiercest fighters against "the credit card companies." A good follow up question should have been, "Why are you as a public servant choosing to 'fight' a company that legally provides financial services that Americans can choose to do business with or not? What are you 'fighting' them about?"

Clearly, since she steals from the trough willy-nilly, she assumes that anyone who has made a profit by risking capital to create a product or service that others *willingly* buy, has come by that wealth dishonestly. After all, she and her husband certainly have made money in ways that would put them in jail if she were not a member of Congress, so why shouldn't she vote to tax folks some more? The Pelosis came by their money dishonestly so perhaps she cannot conceive of the possibility of others getting rich honestly.

Get Governmental Paws off *Your* Retirement Funds

I could go on in this vein for thousands of pages, but my point has been made. A decentralized system is always more resilient *and honest* than a centralized, Statist control system can ever be. That very guiding principle is behind Bitcoin, other cryptocurrencies and the entire technical model of the blockchain. By distributing databases over hundreds of independently-owned servers, it is *impossible* for one entity – say, the government – to control information. The majority of those databases have to agree that, for example,

---

[60] Steve Kroft, one of a few journalists I will call "heroic."

"Person A bought Car B from Person C at a cost of D and it happened at this particular time on this particular date." Any rogue database that claims otherwise, that Person G actually owns Car B, will be ignored. Transparency promotes honesty. A file stamped "Top Secret" gives its owner wide, wide latitude to act well or poorly – who can know? Reading a "Top Secret" file when you're not allowed to results in going to jail. Quite a different idea than the blockchain or distributed government.

While the *goal* of the State providing a safety net for all Americans is a good one, the *method* by which that goal is reached needs to change. Doing so, thankfully, is easier than ever before due to advances in technology, including machine learning and artificial intelligence systems, which can provide the sort of real-time monitoring and fraud-detection that even 10 years ago relied upon masses of human experts to perform.

Yet again, the evolution of a free society and technology has done what capitalism always does: it takes a luxury product (in this case, expert financial advice) that at first only the very rich could afford and makes it available to everyone for pennies. Given the advancements in distributed data management and portfolio theory, there is no need for government bureaucrats to hold on to the money you earned, so they can dole it out to you as they see fit decades from now.

The steps to Social Security *true reform* are:

1. Perform an audit of current obligations to retirees and those nearing retirement. The cutoff period should be 20 years before retirement. While the Ponzi scheme structure is a bad one, we as a nation are not going to suddenly revoke a program that people currently depend on. Give those beneficiaries a choice between staying with the Social Security plan or switching to their own retirement account controlled by them.
2. Set up a structure of private retirement savings accounts, like Australia's Superannuation program or in line with the privatization of retirement accounts in Chile, including learning about the pros and cons of both those systems after 35+ years of empirical data along with much more data from private sector asset management best practices. All new workers will be enrolled in this privately-controlled retirement fund market.
3. In yet-another tax-related move, introduce the franking credits from Australia's system. It is high time that equity owners of businesses are not taxed twice on the same income. Dividends paid to shareholders are post-tax, and therefore should not be taxed again at the individual level.
4. Over a scaled five-year period, continue to levy payroll taxes on the following schedule, with the proceeds going directly into the new individual private savings accounts:

Year	Total rate
1	15%
2	12%
3	9%
4	6%

5	3%
6	0%

5. In Year Six – ideally the calendar year 2030 – shut the doors on this stupid experiment, having returned worker's wealth to its point of origin under the individual control of the worker, and auction off all the real estate infested by the Social Security Occupation Forces. The net proceeds from those real estate sales are to be distributed pro rata to each private retirement account. From that point onwards, levy a compulsory proportion of a worker's actual *earnings*, not deadweight payroll taxes, into their personally controlled private retirement account.

The goal here is dual: to invigorate current and future citizens in their careers, by giving them a much clearer picture of what their efforts are yielding and how the investment choices made in their superannuation retirement accounts impact their capital base over time.

Under this restructuring of retirement finances, we achieve myriad wonderful benefits:

1. Removal of governmental paws from the fruits of citizens' labor.
2. Foster a stronger sense of individual responsibility, ownership and *understanding* of how the system of savings and investment works.
3. Remove one of the biggest blocks of "autopilot" spending which has brought the USA to bankruptcy.

Figure 12: The new entrance to the former Social Security Administration Building, now middle-class condominiums, designed to remind all that enter here how close to Hell they are.

Too many Americans have fallen into a state of childish dependency on government. This is not an accident – as I have demonstrated repeatedly through my research, the Political and Bureaucratic Classes need powerless dependents to keep themselves in power. Every American starting in grade school needs to understand the core principles of how our economic system works, where jobs come from, where the *capital* comes from to create those jobs and how *everyone* can and should play an active role in our society.

Giving every worker a monthly superannuation retirement fund statement showing what they themselves earned for their retirement goes a very long way to inoculating people from the stupid Marxist, defeatist nonsense far too many people make a living peddling to our fellow citizens.

It is *long* past time for Americans to call Paul Samuelson's Ponzi scheme the criminal fraud it is, just as the Madoff and other schemes were.

Chapter 7: U.S. Postal Service

Founded	26 July 1775
Founded by Second Continental Congress	King George
Funding Budget 2023	$290,300,000,000
Messina's 2024 Budget Proposal	$150,000,000,000
Messina's 2025 Budget Proposal	$40,000,000,000
Degree to which Messina's Plan is Better	Completely
Should a Federal Post Office exist?	No

Is this a standalone proper use of the taxpayers' limited resources?	No
Does this expenditure unfairly benefit one American over another one?	Yes
Does the expenditure meet the "Is this logical?" standard of fiduciary responsibility?	No
Can the goals be achieved by *not* spending the dollar more effectively than by spending it?	Yes

This is amongst the most complex arms of Leviathan. Much has been studied and written about how best to (or whether to) continue this entity into the 21st century. The BLUF is that the US Postal Service in my opinion should continue to exist. It is a valuable part of our history, has played some roles well, has had some setbacks and could use some improvement. It differs little from many private sector companies in that respect. Many improvements, right-sizing and simplification would benefit the Postal System, some of which have already been started.

When I began to research in earnest for this book, I already came to the subject of the Post Office with some hearty concerns. Way back in the dark ages, when dinosaurs roamed the earth and the first dotcom crash had yet to occur – we're talking early 2000 – a colleague of mine in Silicon Valley worked for one of the major consulting firms.[61] Her firm had been retained by the US Postal Service to help them find cost savings and corporate improvements to, you know, make the Post Office at least *break even* for the American taxpayer, rather than continue as a massive sinkhole of endless costs.

She relayed to me with gallows humor how the first kick-off project meeting went. For those not in the consultancy business, that meeting is the one where the consulting team meets with the executives of the business client – in this case, the US Post Office – to go over the plan of research, timing of interviews, and the usual things one would think of when designing a research plan designed to firstly discover the condition of the business, in

---

[61] Feel free to do some Independent Research to discover what the firm's name is. For the point I am making here, it's irrelevant to provide a name, because many other firms have done the same kind of work repeatedly for various organs of the government, all to no benefit to the US taxpayer.

the hopes of course of providing after exhaustive analysis a plan for the business to improve its operations, cut its costs and thereby improve its profitability.

At that meeting, the officials from the Post Office start off by saying, "We are so glad you are here to help us in improving this fine American institution founded by Ben Franklin and part of the growth of the United States. Before you get started on your plan of action, it is important that you know that the contract signed with the Postal Workers Union has a few limitations on what we're allowed to change. Here is a brief list summarizing the things you *cannot suggest we do* to change the Post Office." The list was three pages long, single-spaced in small font. It included things like the beginning five items:

1. You cannot suggest we close *any* Post Office locations.
2. You cannot suggest we lay off or reduce hiring of any employees.
3. You cannot suggest we restructure pay and benefits for any employees.
4. You cannot suggest we change the services offered by the Post Office.
5. You cannot suggest we change the price of stamps or any other service.

There were three more pages *after* those five constraints. Even people who are not involved in business decision making know that the four main things which impact a business's ability to make a profit are the costs of people, real estate, the price of services offered and the number of goods or services offered. In fact, everything *aside* from those core concerns is quite literally peripheral.

What has made me curious for all these years, frankly, is *what else* came after those five restrictions. My friend was true to the NDA she signed, so she wouldn't show me the actual document, and try as I might strain my creative faculties, I cannot really add much more. The point is those restrictions were spelled out by the *public sector union contract* the Post Office had signed with their employees. That union contract – which should not be legal in the first place – binds the hands of American taxpayers who are forced to subsidize billions of dollars per year in pay and benefits to support operating losses for an entity that with the advent of email is just one more competitor to UPS and FedEx.

You, the taxpayer, can take this away from my little vignette: On top of already wasting billions of your dollars every year, the management of the Post Office then engaged a private consulting firm for probably $800,000 - $2,000,000, all to perform a "study" whose *only professional recommendations* could possibly include "Buy slightly cheaper staples and off-brand cleaning supplies."

And those were year 2000 dollars, which may well prove to be equivalent to $700,000,000,000,000 in 2023's Biden Weimar-lite Wuhan Panic Inflation Dollars.

I have only one suggestion for the Post Office, aside from the blanket suggestion that we abolish all public sector unions and defined benefit pension plans. Privatize it while preserving some parts of its public mission. Brilliant innovations occur in specific places and times and under specific conditions. What that means for the Post Office is that when it was founded and for a good 200 years afterwards, it was one of the great institutions which knit a growing country together, which enabled long-distance communication and commerce – think the Sears Roebuck Catalog – and was a truly worthy institution. It still plays a valuable role in American society, but its years of billion-dollar losses and the absurdity of our subsidizing $0.60 stamps for letters in an age of email – which kids under 25 already think is "for old people" because of texting – bears careful reexamination.

Every old-timesy "historical town" across the country has a general goods mercantile. In the back of such establishments is the US Post Office. The local postal official was just one part of someone's business, unless you were in a really big city. The idea that the taxpayers maintain 31,247 standalone post office buildings[62] across the country is absurd. There are ten post offices within a 15-minute drive radius from my home in Florida; that is pure insanity.

On a purely economic basis, the USPS should be subjected to the same kind of existential competition as its private sector alternatives. I am open to the idea and robust, rational debate, that there are some valuable civic roles the Post Office plays, which give it a special role in American life.

As 2021 unfolded, it proved itself to be the Year of Infinite Gifts. Until as recently as, say, July of 2020, Americans of all kinds would have agreed with the proposition of the bipartisan commission on voting *co-chaired by Jimmy Carter,*[63] that "noted among its many findings and recommendations that because it takes place outside the regulated environment of local polling locations, voting by mail creates increased logistical challenges and the potential for **vote fraud**, especially if safeguards are lacking or when candidates or political party activists are allowed to handle mail-in or absentee ballots."[64]

That quote about the obviously higher risks of fraud associated with voting by mail rather than by showing up to a physical location is taken from a statement issued *by The Carter Center,* lest my partisan friends scream that I'm quoting FOX News. The history of American voting has often been one of continuous attempts to improve the integrity of the franchise – fancy talk for making the vote an honest accounting of votes cast. In the words of the 1970s cigarette commercials for Virginia Slims, we've come a long way, baby.

By August 14th of 2020 according to Nancy "Insider Trading is How I Got Rich and I Don't Even Have to Pretend Otherwise Because I'm in Congress" Pelosi, the only thing standing between the American citizenry and a totalitarian takeover replete with ballot boxes stuffed the way Joe Kennedy paid Mayor Daley to do in 1968 for his son Jack was the holy US Post Office. So important is this bulwark against despotism that she called the House of Representatives back from vacation to "save" this vital American institution.

Why, later generations may wonder, did this suddenly matter so much? Well, as I am sure you'll read in your American History courses at Hillsdale College or the University of Chicago, but not at Yale or UC Berkeley, the American Left hated Donald Trump so much that after years of ridiculous investigations and then a disgusting cheapening of the Impeachment Clause, they were so fevered in their hatred of the man that they then destroyed the US economy over a virus whose mortality statistics were within the standard deviation norms of a really bad seasonal flu. Because the nanny state tinpot dictators

---

[62] https://facts.usps.com/size-and-scope/

[63] 2005 Commission on Federal Election Reform, co-chaired by former U.S. President Jimmy Carter and former Secretary of State James A. Baker III,

[64] https://cartercenter.org/news/pr/2020/united-states-050620.html

wanted to see how far they could push the American sheeple, they demanded everyone stay locked in their homes and tried to prevent schools or businesses from opening. One consequence of this national insanity was to then say, "Well, if it's not safe for a person sitting alone on a beach reading a book,"[65] then it surely cannot be safe for people to vote in person, so we're going to send out hundreds of millions of ballots whether a given voter requested one or not, and to ballot rolls which have been *proven* to be rife with erroneous or outdated entries, with only a few months' warning, despite all logic in the face of abundant empirical evidence *from an election in New Jersey in 2020* that massive fraud will result.

When President Trump in his inimitable fashion wrote something to that effect on the Internet, the Democrats immediately became the Champions of All That is Good and Holy in American Life, the institution formerly known as the Post Office. Charles Bukowski, among many other long-time employees of that august institution, might have a few choice words to say about that description. Taking reluctant historical leave of the Muse-like role the Post Office played in the art of Mr. Bukowski, in the performance art present (2020-2024) of American political theatre, the irrational hysteria whipped up by a set of politicians who clearly believed massive mail-in voting would improve their chances in the upcoming election had gone from insanity to farce. I'm not saying *which party* believes mail-in ballots will improve their chances.

I will note that the postal letter carriers' union endorsed Joe Biden for President on 21 August 2020.

Two Congressmen, including Democratic Caucus Chairman Hakeem Jeffries, wrote to the FBI on Monday to urge, if you can believe it, a criminal investigation of Postmaster General Louis DeJoy.

"This conspiracy theory is the most far-flung thing I think I've ever heard," says Stephen Kearney, who worked at the USPS for 33 years, including as treasurer and a senior vice president. "DeJoy was not appointed by President Trump," but by the USPS's bipartisan governors. (Who, as it happens, selected him unanimously.)

"You can find valid operational reasons for the actions taken by the Postal Service so far," says Mike Plunkett, another longtime USPS executive who now leads the Association for Postal Commerce. "In no way do I detect any criminality behind them, and I'm at a loss as to how one would reach that conclusion."

The Democratic letter to the FBI cites news reports that the USPS is decommissioning hundreds of mail-sorting machines. But the context is that overall mail volume has fallen 33% since 2006. "They've been taking machines out of service for years now, and I've been encouraging them to do it more aggressively," says Hamilton Davison, the president of the American Catalog Mailers Association. "I think that's a good thing for America, because we don't want to pay for stuff that we don't need."[66]

---

[65] New Jersey Governor Tim Murphy had police arrest a man alone on beach reading because his being outside violated the unconstitutional home imprisonment edicts to "fight the spread of Wuhan Flu."

[66] "Nancy Pelosi Goes Politically Postal; Congress ought to be embarrassed by this evidence-free

In the midst of 50 million unemployed Americans, with politicians and the media doing everything they could to whip people into a state of unjustified panic, instead of calmly assessing the policies that brought the United States to complete and utter bankruptcy, we were treated to the appalling spectacle of the House of Representatives *spending more time "legislating"* rather than staying on vacation, passing this ridiculous $25 billion cash infusion to the Post Office *which was already funded well into 2021*, and continuing our spiraling descent into a banana republic where politicians spend all of their time launching "investigations" and criminal prosecutions of their rivals.

The $25 billion was not only unnecessary, but the entire episode was a manufactured farce designed to help Joe Biden possibly win the 2020 Presidential Election. The Senate refused to vote on this idiocy, and even if they did, President Trump would not have signed it, which if you'll recall from watching your Saturday morning Schoolhouse Rock video on how a bill becomes a law means this whole farce — travel expenses and staff overtime paid by *you*, the taxpayer — was not a proper use of Congress's time, but a partisan exercise designed for political gain.

That means you, the American taxpayer, have been forced to pay for political advertising benefiting one party over another. I keep listening for the "campaign finance" crowd to scream about this, but yet, I hear crickets. I wonder why that could be?

Lastly, I would like to thank the fine folks at the Department of Homeland Security for striking two blows in endorsing my budget plan. In the snippet below[67] from the Office of Inspector General, we get this gibberish:

> The U.S. Department of Homeland Security considers the Postal Service to be a national critical infrastructure because of its ability to reach all U.S. citizens in a crisis. With the onset of COVID-19, mail mix and volumes changed dramatically as consumers increasingly turned to online shopping for their retail needs. While it is unclear whether this will be a permanent shift, the Postal Service is serving an important role in supporting Americans during this historic event. Additionally, the Postal Service's role in processing election and political mail has become an important service for many voters, further illustrating the unique role the organization plays in our country. With so much at stake, postal operations and employees must be held to the highest standards.

A "crisis" is a point in time, not a two-year, government-manufactured fake emergency based on lies and a deliberate misreading of objective data. In a real crisis, people need to be contacted electronically or in person. What the hell is a mail delivery service going to do in a real crisis? It's ridiculous. It does make me wonder, however, if there is *any* wasteful expenditure in Washington these clowns *can't* claim is "necessary" because of the Wuhan Virus?

---

conspiracy theory." Op-Ed, Wall Street Journal, 14 August 2020

[67] United States Postal Service Office of Inspector General - Congressional Budget Justification - Fiscal Year 2022. (uspsoig.gov)

As illustrative as these snapshots of Postal History are, what matters going forward is whether we the American taxpayer continue to spend billions of dollars every year to subsidize operating losses. I suggest we strike a balance, starting with ripping up the public sector union agreement.

As with so much else throughout the tangled spiderweb of our Federal leviathan's nervous system, much of the drag on Federal finances – that'd be a drag on *you*, dear taxpayer – is caused by insane defined benefit pension fund packages. As those obligations will be turned into individually owned assets for each former Postal employee, there will be a one-time hit to the governmental balance sheet, but then no further costs going forward.

Congress already has taken a step towards forcing fiscal sanity on the Post Office by forcing it to prefund future health benefits for employees.

Let's permit the USPS to compete with other mail and package delivery services. One immediate cost-cutting measure is to go back in time to a quainter, more practical era when rural post offices were assigned to an official who operated out of a storefront in town. People came to pick up packages from the post office, rather than having everything delivered to them; on a *local basis* which is how decisions should be made, the *local* postal official will know that, say, Mrs. Patel had surgery last week and will not be mobile for awhile, so provision can be made to deliver her mail directly if no one can pick it up for her. Given the prevalence of thieves roaming suburbia stealing packages from front porches, this method of centralized package collection is already a market-driven choice made by consumers.

We can also put a truly independent committee in charge of disposing of the extensive real estate collection around the country. There are some beautiful old buildings which can find new life as residential or business facilities, many of which will prove to be really cool historical buildings.

The civic roles played by the USPS are also perhaps worthy of maintaining, again in a more stripped-down form. Plus, I dig stamp collecting.

Figure 13: The New Benjamin Franklin Memorial Rave Post Office Entrance in D.C.

Chapter 8: Pension Benefit Guaranty Corporation

Founded	September 2, 1974
Founded under President	Gerald Ford
Funding Budget 2023	$8,200,000,000
Messina's 2024 Budget Proposal	$125,000,000*
Messina's 2025 Budget Proposal	$10,000,000**
Degree to which Messina's Plan is Better	Completely
Should a Federal PBGC exist?	No

Is this a standalone proper use of the taxpayers' limited resources?	No
Does this expenditure unfairly benefit one American over another one?	Yes
Does the expenditure meet the "Is this logical?" standard of fiduciary responsibility?	No
Can the goals be achieved by *not* spending the dollar more effectively than by spending it?	Yes

* Wind down costs to sell off insurance policies to private sector reinsurers, sell real assets and lay off {BGC employees.

** In case some asset dispositions or policy sales would have been adversely affected by an arbitrary one-year deadline.

In a government awash in Really Stupid Ideas, this is a viable contender for Dumbest Thing Ever. Its whole existence captures the essence of Poor Governance in one terrible entity. The reason for its creation is the *same reason lurking behind every idiotic policy, law or department* we are suffering from. That idea is that humankind can *completely eliminate* Risk rather than just managing bad events as they occur.

Please take a moment to ponder that statement. It's kind of like a Zen *koan* which summarizes in a few baffling, brain-twisting syllables this entire book. As a nation, we waste more time and money on this fantasy than all other fantasies combined.

We must move swiftly to privatize the obligations of this ridiculous experimental policy mistake immediately. There is no grace period, no transition period. Sell the assets and liabilities in a clear, public process and get this nonsense off the Federal balance sheet, preferably within 90 days, or as soon as is reasonable so that the market does not think it is a hard deadline forced sale.

It was a bad idea from the outset and does nothing but steal money from hardworking Americans who made good financial decisions to give that stolen money to Americans who made poor financial decisions and now want to be bailed out of their stupidity.

Kids used to read a story about an industrious ant who worked all summer and saved for winter and his pal the goof off grasshopper who spent the summer hopping around singing carelessly. Come winter, the ant had food to feed his family while the grasshopper starved to death in the cold. I am sure the "progressive" fools who hijacked the "Education" department in this country have either banned that story or modified Aesop's brilliant telling to make the government come along to redistribute the ant's store of food to the grasshopper in the name of "social justice."

I digress. It's so hard not to.

There are at least four major problems with the existence of the PBGC.

Their website says it perfectly:

- Q: What is the Pension Benefit Guaranty Corporation (PBGC)?

A: PBGC is a federal agency created by the Employee Retirement Income Security Act of 1974 (ERISA) **to protect pension benefits in private-sector defined benefit plans** - the kind that **typically** pay a set monthly amount at retirement. If your plan ends (this is called "plan termination") without sufficient money to pay all benefits, PBGC's insurance program will pay you the benefit provided by your pension plan up to the limits set by law. (Most people receive the full benefit they had earned before the plan terminated.) Our financing comes from insurance premiums paid by companies whose plans we protect, from our investments, from the assets of pension plans that we take over as trustee, and from recoveries from the companies formerly responsible for the plans, but not from taxes. Your plan is insured even if your employer fails to pay the required premiums.[68]

Here is another beast created by politicians to stop the functioning of rational adults in a risk-filled world. The *whole* purpose of this *public sector entity* is to guarantee payments from private sector companies to private sector employees. That is it. You are forgiven it you are wondering why on earth the government should guarantee any financial agreements between private parties.

Beyond the *a priori* bad idea of putting all Americans on the hook to pay off a *privately negotiated* financial promise between a company and its employees, Congress of course cannot stop at simple bad fiscal choices. No, no, not when there is additional irresponsible havoc to be wrought by piling more bad ideas on top of an original, colossally stupid one.

Because Congress *cannot keep its hands off anyone's money,* they *don't* leave the capital in the PBGC to protect workers. No, no – why do that? They count PBGC premium income ***as general government revenues*** in the year received! So when Congress spends $400,000,000 more than they promised, they literally *raid* the PBGC fund by demanding increases in per-person contributions from private sector pension plans.

Yup – so millions of workers – not, mind, you, evil bloodsucking 1% Wall Streeters – have more cash taken from them so that Congress can claim that there was no additional $400,000,000 in spending! *Nope, nothing to see here – we may have incurred some additional costs but look at this Magic Cash Machine called the PBGC – it gave us the exact amount of cash, so there was no increase in spending!*

That's called a Ponzi scheme in the real world – because that money will not be available to meet PGBC obligations that may come due later. Lest you succumb to someone nitpicking who says, "but the worker doesn't pay that extra premium – the company does," please remind yourself and the nitpicker that by definition those extra dollars are coming

---

[68] http://pbgc.gov/about/faq/pg/general-faqs-about-pbgc.html

145

from somewhere. I don't have to be Elizabeth Warren's fellow traveler to know that the likely first source of that extra cash is going to be money *not* given to the workers it is designed to pay benefits for. And in the case of a pension fund run by a company that goes out of business, the government has become the source of the cash to pay off the obligations.

Hint: that's *you* the taxpayer.

How insane is that? You, perhaps, have lived a prudent life, never spending beyond your means. You have managed your retirement funds in self-directed, conservative investment products. You paid off your mortgage. The PBGC is taking money from *you* to cover retirement promises someone *else* made to another person you have nothing to do with. And this is being done to you by politicians who spend all their time scolding you, shaking their head at how selfish you are.

Even with the magical money and influence machine, politicians who know nothing about finance, insurance, investing or actuarial mathematics insist on meddling for political gain.

One of the most disgraceful examples of this was the treatment of Charles Millard,[69] who was PBGC Director from 2007 to 2009. Under his leadership, the agency's deficit shrank from $18.9 billion to $11.2 billion. In February 2008, a new proposal about how to allocate the PBGC's funds was put forward, in keeping with best practices of financial portfolio management. For purely political reasons, Mr. Millard was attacked. He had had the unmitigated *gall* to speak directly and at length with the hedge funds that were managing pension money. He and his staff did so to understand as well as possible the managers who would be looking after pension recipients' money.

A core responsibility of the people that manage pension funds is what is known as "due diligence." Due diligence means that you do everything you practically can to get to know the fund manager, understand how s/he makes investment decisions, whether they are of sound character, etc. Due diligence performed properly is what kept hundreds of people from investing with Bernie Madoff.

But according to the innumerate idiots at the *New York Times* editorial page and his Democrat political opponents, Mr. Millard spoke to hedge fund managers "too much."

His case is a microcosm of what is wrong with our political system. His firing had nothing to do with his performance on the job, which saw a vast improvement in the PBGC's financial position. It was a purely political attack. I'll bet a stack of gold coins that not one single person who attacked him could tell you what the "right" or "appropriate" or "unsuspicious" amount of discussion would be. Is nine hours of meetings over six months just right for due diligence, whereas seven hours would be irresponsibly shirking one's fiscal duty to pensioners? Would eleven hours mean corrupt collusion between the pension fund allocators and the investment firm?

---

[69] http://charlesmillard.com/

Figure 14: The PBGC Wind-Up Committee handling its duties with actuarial care and aplomb

It's ridiculous. The more politicians create political problems for people trying to do a good job, the fewer qualified people will step forward to help solve the nation's problems. Even without the threat of political evisceration preventing more qualified candidates to step up to run this thing, there is no rational reason for this beast to exist.

The only solution is to scrap publicly funded defined benefits pensions, so there is no chance of corruption or the appearance thereof. Then Americans will have to think carefully about whether they'd prefer to keep leaving their financial futures in the hands of a company which may not exist in a decade, or have their financial affairs in their own privately-owned separate accounts.

The only money allocated to this in my budget is to hire an investment bank to run a process selling off the assets to the private sector.

Chapter 9: Amtrak

Founded	May 1, 1971
Founded under President	Richard Nixon
Funding Budget 2023 (approx. grant subsidy)	$3,300,000,000
Messina's 2024 Budget Proposal	$3,000,000,000*
Messina's 2025 Budget Proposal	$250,000,000**
Degree to which Messina's Plan is Better	Completely
Should a Federal Amtrak exist?	No

Is this a standalone proper use of the taxpayers' limited resources?	No
Does this expenditure unfairly benefit one American over another one?	Yes
Does the expenditure meet the "Is this logical?" standard of fiduciary responsibility?	No
Can the goals be achieved by *not* spending the dollar more effectively than by spending it?	Yes

* Care, maintenance and payroll support while privatization goes forward. It is short-sighted to defer needed maintenance and capital improvements while the assets are being sold. Defined benefit pensions will face the same sunsetting as all other public section defined benefit pensions.
** In case some assets take longer than a year to sell. After 24 months, there should be nothing left and Amtrak can be shuttered.

The time is long past for privatizing Amtrak. The very fact that many Americans call it "Amcrash" should give you a sense of why. I am not immune to sentiment and am also practical enough to know having installed rail miles and other capital goods, it would be better to find uses for those than just ripping them up. The national rail service has a fascinating history which I urge you to dive into.[70]

Amtrak is a tricky beast. Some portions of the system run profitably, whereas others do not. On an overall basis, it's been a money-loser for decades. In terms of rail service, a certain sort of American swoons over the European rail network, and wishes those crass Americans would eschew their isolating, polluting and – GASP! – greenhouse gas emitting gas guzzling SUVs and massive land yachts for the communal delights of traveling via scheduled rail travel.

Don't get me wrong. It's really hard to meet cute Australian backpackers by chance if you're driving between Midwestern cities or even between European cities, and it's tough to quaff chilled Beaujolais Nouveau to complement your warm, crusty baguettes and cheese plate while shifting gears, so rail travel definitely contains some upsides.

Rail is very well suited to the densely packed European continent, and works well along the US's Eastern corridor, but passenger rail gets less efficient the farther West one gets in the States. It's not impossible to travel by rail across the States. Kind of like flying between remote airports, you still need someone in a car or bus to get you to your final

---

[70] Historic Timeline — Amtrak: History of America's Railroad

destination. When one factors in the long time periods and inflexible schedules, for most Americans, it just makes more sense to get in a car instead.

That said, many people enjoy traveling by rail and rail certainly moves a lot of freight in a far more fuel-efficient manner than trucks ever could. There is a huge amount of installed capital expenditure that has gone into the nation's rail infrastructure, so presumably when Amtrak is parceled out for privatization, there will be buyers for those assets. For those concerned about the loss of rail service to remote locations, that is always a risk, but the government can put – a very few – conditions of sale on some assets to ensure some service remains.

As with any asset sale, the more constraints the seller puts on the new owners, the lower the price to be paid, but let's let the free market decide what each of Amtrak's miles of assets are worth.

I've got some good news! In keeping with simplicity, and in reducing the number of inflexible costs associated with running any rail service, once we abolish all defined benefit pension plans from public life, private capital can step in to make decisions about which pieces of the vast Amtrak rail network they'd like to buyout and operate. As with many other financial headaches, a large part of Amtrak's financial problems stem from defined benefit pension plans.

There are a few very simple steps to getting this yoke off the taxpayers' neck. Firstly, we run a privatization bidding process. Let all proposals be put forward – if we are lucky, everyone will agree on the proper division of the various assets. Or maybe we'll be luckier if multiple parties see different benefits and therefore different assets go into a bidding war, which will mean investors pay the Treasury more for the assets than expected. Either way, the ongoing liability for this nonsense will cease.

As for the Amtrak employees, they can choose to go along with their new private owners, if they are offered employment or they can choose to take a one-time buyout of their pension. We will immediately calculate the current value of all the pension obligations owed to Amtrak employees. In return for their renunciation of public union status, each worker will be given ownership and control of their new superannuation fund. No new defined benefit obligations can ever again be created by Amtrak.

Chapter 10: Department of Agriculture

Year Founded	May 15, 1862
Founded by President	Abraham Lincoln
Funding Budget 2023	$210,000,000,000
Messina's 2024 Budget Proposal	$120,000,000,000
Messina's 2025 Budget Proposal	$100,000,000,000
Degree to which Messina's Plan is Better	Completely
Should a Federal Dept of Agriculture exist?	Yes

Is this a standalone proper use of the taxpayers' limited resources?	Yes
Does this expenditure unfairly benefit one American over another one?	Not my version
Does the expenditure meet the "Is this logical?" standard of fiduciary responsibility?	Yes
Can the goals be achieved by *not* spending the dollar more effectively than by spending it?	Partially

The USDA plays an important role in American life, mainly in providing oversight and security over our food supply chain. In addition, a strong argument could be made to hand responsibility for some wild species management to the USDA. The very dedicated, valuable people who fill those roles need to be applauded and funded properly. Two years after he signed it into law, during his final address to Congress, Honest Abe called the USDA "The People's Department." At that time, 50% of Americans lived on farms, compared to 2% today.

Sadly, the USDA has over time expanded its remit into areas which have little if anything to do with agriculture as a reasonable person would understand the term. The whole range of market-, social- and health-distortive subsidies to our agricultural producers must be sharply curtailed.

The only topics anyone at the USDA should be focused on relate to food quality, food supply safety and optimizing the value of agriculture in American life.

Here is the funding summary copied from Obama Budget 2012 to provide you a sense of how far afield from agricultural pursuits the USDA has drifted:

Funding Highlights:

• Provides $23.9 billion in discretionary funding, a decrease of $3.2 billion. Consistent with Administration priorities, investments are made in renewable energy and key research areas. Savings are created by reducing direct payments to high-income farmers, refocusing USDA's homeownership programs, and targeting USDA conservation programs.

• Invests $6.5 billion in renewable and clean energy to spur the creation of high-value jobs, make America more energy independent, and drive global competitiveness in the sector.

- Increases funding for the Agriculture and Food Research Initiative to $325 million and targets increases for research in areas that are key to American leadership: human nutrition and obesity reduction, food safety, sustainable bioenergy, global food security, and climate change.

- Refocuses rural housing assistance to programs that work better, providing 170,000 new homeownership opportunities, of which at least 30,000 are expected to go to low income rural borrowers.

- Maximizes efficiency and effectiveness of forest restoration efforts to improve forest health and resiliency by combining and streamlining multiple programs.

- Funds for the Wetlands Reserve Program and the Environmental Quality Incentives Program to restore and protect 271,158 acres of wetlands and provide over $1.4 billion for conservation assistance.

- Provides $7.4 billion to support supplemental nutrition assistance available to low-income and nutritionally at-risk pregnant and post-partum women, infants and children up to age 5.

- Provides $35 million for the Healthy Food Financing Initiative to bring grocery stores and other healthy food retailers to underserved communities.

Table 5: Highlights of USDA Misappropriations

Highlight	Agriculture related?	Comment
Invests $6.5 billion in renewable and clean energy	No	Whether stealing from productive citizens to "invest" in other citizens' enterprises is a good idea aside, this has nothing to do with agriculture.
spur the creation of high-value jobs in energy	No	
make America more energy independent,	No	Dept of the Interior and private energy companies do this.
Refocuses rural housing assistance to programs that work better	No	USDA should have zero to do with housing.
Funds for the Wetlands Reserve Program and the Environmental Quality Incentives Program	Tangentially	Splendid, but USDA should have zero to do with this.
Provides $35 million for the Healthy Food Financing Initiative to bring grocery stores and other healthy food retailers to underserved communities	Tangentially	If underserved communities provided real demand for "healthy food retailers," those stores would exist. $35 million purely wasted.

The summary line items in the budget say it all. "Invests $6.5 billion in renewable and clean energy to spur the creation of high-value jobs, make America more energy independent, and drive global competitiveness in the sector." The never-abandoned conceit of the Political Class is that the public sector ever "invests" in anything.

Government *by definition* is a tax and a cost on actual productivity. Government is necessary for some very narrowly defined functions, and that cost is worth bearing. But when government strays into areas far better left to private investment, all we get is

151

financial destruction and lost opportunities for American individuals to increase national wealth and wellbeing.

Jumping ahead to 2023, we get the expansion of the USDA's remit far beyond anything to do with agriculture. Taken from the Biden 2023 budget, here are the stated "strategic goals" of the USDA:

STRATEGIC GOAL 1: COMBAT CLIMATE CHANGE TO SUPPORT AMERICA'S WORKING LANDS, NATURAL RESOURCES, AND COMMUNITIES

"Climate change poses a significant risk to agriculture, forests, and grasslands across the United States and the communities that support and depend on them. Now is the time to act. Our agricultural lands, National forests, and private working lands require conservation and restoration efforts to strengthen their resilience to drought, invasive species, and wildfire. The Department must lead with investments in science, research, and climate-smart solutions. These investments will mitigate the impacts of climate change, increase adaptation to climate change, generate new income opportunities, and build generational wealth in disadvantaged communities. Agriculture can lead the fight on climate using climate-smart agriculture, forestry, and renewable energy practices that sequester carbon, reduce emissions, improve adaptation, and increase market opportunities for all producers. USDA is working to develop and implement a comprehensive climate-smart strategy that is centered on voluntary incentives and meeting the needs of our diverse producers, landowners, and communities. Our approach includes significant investments in resources for all producers and landowners. Additionally, it provides a host of new tools to deploy important conservation practices and the research essential to inform them."[71]

This one straight out of the gate is ridiculous. Period. Global cooling was going to kills us all in the 1960s, from human-driven "excess" carbon in the atmosphere. Then it was global warming that was going to kill us, *from the very same causes.* Then when the inconvenient data failed to show warming, they switched to "climate change" which is kind of indisputable. Oh, but that is a crisis, too.

To "fix" this, we are supposed to believe that giving DC bureaucrats a slush fund of $1.5+ billion will somehow magically translate into electric utilities increasing carbon sequestration, and uh, other stuff. Go read the fairy tale if you want more details.

STRATEGIC GOAL 2: ENSURE AMERICA'S AGRICULTURAL SYSTEM IS EQUITABLE, RESILIENT, AND PROSPEROUS

There is a great deal of room for debate about the continued relevance of the programs under this heading. A few of them are highlighted here, and all are about the US taxpayer providing a "risk cushion" for commodity prices. Given the broader macro view of maintaining food security in North America, these programs made some kind of sense a

---

[71] https://www.usda.gov/sites/default/files/documents/2023-usda-budget-summary.pdf

century ago. With modern markets and modern, real-time data collection and analysis, I am not so sure the private sector is not doing a better job now.

Commodity Programs
The Budget provides $9.1 billion for commodity program payments to maintain an effective farm safety net. Commodity programs are critical components of the farm safety net, serving to provide risk management and financial tools to farmers and ranchers. Approximately 1.8 million farms are enrolled in the Agriculture Risk Coverage (ARC) and Price Loss Coverage (PLC) programs, which are helping cushion the financial strain felt by producers due to continued low prices for many commodities.

Federal Crop Insurance Program
The Budget provides $13.2 billion for the Federal crop insurance program, enough to provide crop insurance coverage for $151 billion in crop value. Crop insurance provides farmers and ranchers a means to effectively manage their risk through difficult periods, helping to maintain America's safe and affordable food supply.

Farm Loans
The Budget includes funding to fully support the estimated $10.7 billion demand for farm loans, providing loans to over 33,000 farmers and ranchers to finance operating expenses, refinance debt, or acquire a farm. In addition, the Budget provides $61 million for the Heir's Relending Program, authorized in the 2018 Farm Bill, to resolve ownership and succession of farmland.

STRATEGIC GOAL 3: FOSTER AN EQUITABLE AND COMPETITIVE MARKETPLACE FOR ALL AGRICULTURAL PRODUCERS

A good deal of money is spent on promoting market exports for American agricultural products and for inspection services. The details are worth deep discussion for the impacted industries, which they actively do. This is a good use of tax dollars.

STRATEGIC GOAL 4: MAKE SAFE, NUTRITIOUS FOOD AVAILABLE TO ALL AMERICANS

Number 4 is not a bad goal. Food chain safety is one of the great successes of industrial society and we want to continue this. Elsewhere I touch on how this positive food inspection regime can be taken too far and become an abusive tool of state oppression when dealing with small local farms with direct customers. For all major food processors, we the taxpayer want diligent inspectors doing a good job.

"The Budget includes $1.2 billion to fully fund the costs necessary to support nearly 8,600 FSIS personnel who ensure the safety of meat, poultry, and egg products at over 6,600 processing, slaughter, and import establishments in the U.S. Nearly 90 percent of these personnel act as frontline inspectors and investigators and provide surveillance to protect the Nation's food supply."

Included here is the massive line item for food stamps or what are now called SNAP (Supplemental Nutrition Assistance Plan) vouchers. It comes to nearly $150 billion out of a $210 billion budget. There have to be better, preferably local, solutions to providing healthier food to people who need it. I do not address it here beyond saying Federal food

153

stamp programs have to come under strict scrutiny and civic debate, with this idea being phased down to States and local governments by 2030. We're not going to leave low-income single moms and their kids high and dry instantly, so these programs should continue while a better system is worked out.

STRATEGIC GOAL 5: EXPAND OPPORTUNITIES FOR ECONOMIC DEVELOPMENT AND IMPROVE QUALITY OF LIFE IN RURAL AND TRIBAL COMMUNITIES

There are billions in this bucket about rural broadband and housing assistance – neither of which the Department of *Agriculture* should have anything to do with. Read the details if you like. Everything in this bucket is pure make work hogwash that President Lincoln would be astonished by.

As an example, here is something to cut instantly:

Partners with Rural Leaders to Grow Rural Economies and Tackle Rural Poverty
The Budget provides $39 million for a renewed and expanded initiative to leverage USDA's extensive network of offices to help people in high poverty communities, including energy communities, tap into Federal resources, referred to as the Rural Partners Network initiative. USDA will coordinate with other Federal agencies on an all of Government approach to connect rural stakeholders with Federal programs and resources.

Nonsense, nothing but nonsense. Take that $39 million – if we *must waste it* – and *give it to the people in high poverty communities*. The appalling conceit of hiring bureaucrats on lovely salaries, benefits and retirement plans to go talk to poor people, saying, "Hey, here is a brochure of Federal programs that could help you," is offensive and ridiculous at the same time. We live in a world awash in information; community leaders who are looking for resources can find them. Whenever you read "an all of Government approach," that means that *no one is ultimately responsible for a given outcome.* It's pure crap. Can it.

There has been a line item like this in the last 12+ budgets. Clearly after hundreds of millions of dollars spent in "partnering with rural leaders," they are no good at eliminating rural poverty.

STRATEGIC GOAL 6: ATTRACT, INSPIRE, AND RETAIN AN ENGAGED AND MOTIVATED WORKFORCE THAT'S PROUD TO REPRESENT USDA

Getting and keeping employees is *not* a strategic goal. It is the basic thing required by any organization. This being the Federal Government, of course, this section of the budget waffles on for pages about diversity and inclusiveness and in a paean to the ongoing madness about the Wuhan Panic which absurdity's "reality" is a core tenet of Democrat religious belief, we get treated to some nonsense about whether it might be like, OK, for, like, people getting paid by the taxpayer to actually go to work.

"As the landscape of talent continues to evolve, it is imperative that USDA seek to continuously find ways to attract talent that represents the diversity of America. The COVID-19 pandemic has also catapulted leaders to rethink and reimagine where and how we work. In the coming years, we will build on best practices for a hybrid work environment and continue to evaluate the future of work at USDA."

154

Florida, Sweden, Texas, South Dakota and the rest of the rational world ignored the crazed nonsense around the Wuhan Panic, with statistically similar Wuhan Flu-related results to States and nations which destroyed their kids' lives. But in Washington, DC, the absurd crying and screaming over a seasonal respiratory virus has become a religious pillar of belief. And why wouldn't it? It was a two-year vacation from going to the office. If I were a DC bureaucrat, I'd keep screaming about masks and vaccine cards and other nonsense in my pajamas from my backyard.

Here we find that the "pandemic" – whatever that might have been aside from a man-mad freakout fest ruining children's normal development – has "catapulted" leaders to "rethink and reimagine how and where we work." For a second, I was encouraged. I thought we had "catapulted leaders" somewhere physical. Perhaps towards Canada or into the ocean, then I realized that "leaders" had not been launched into the air using medieval war machines, but the catapulting in question was metaphorical.

Oh, well.

Anyway, the damned Wuhan Fakedemic is over, however sad that makes slacker Swamp emplpyees. We the people are reimagining a vastly shrunk Federal workforce, so those "leaders" with their reimagining can focus each one's imagination personally on where he or she will be working when his or her cushy Federal gravy train job ceases to exist.

What the USDA *should* be doing

Agriculture is a complex, wide-ranging field of practice and study. Given the necessity – right after breathable air and potable water – of food to keep the human animal upright and functioning, research and education is a wonderful use of taxpayer funds. Much as pruning an olive tree back to its roots enhances its productivity, taking an axe to the USDA will yield stunning productivity as it moves forward on its new, clarified, focused path. The USDA should abandon all activities extraneous to agriculture and focus solely on these five key areas:

1. Secure the agricultural supply chain,
2. Foster distributed networks for resiliency,
3. Provide farmers with research focused on improving the *quality* of the foods produced to optimally nourish a free, educated citizenry,
4. Enforce best practices for humane animal husbandry, and
5. Research and enforce best practices for managing, mitigating and minimizing the externalized costs to the environment and society from agricultural activities.

The transformation of agriculture into agribusiness has been disastrous for the United States, across so many dimensions it is hard to imagine that we have permitted the change to occur. Starting with the insane prevalence in our society of constant chronic medical conditions which did not exist pre-1945 such as Type 2 diabetes (which used to be called "adult-onset diabetes" until too many overweight teenagers raised on fast food developed it), huge distortions to *our bodies and minds* have occurred as the consequence of centralized power and "authority" over nutrition guidance. I touch on that in a bit more detail below, but for now, ponder the fact that billions of dollars in corporate interests have been funneled into *government propaganda posted in schools about "proper" nutrition which bears no relation whatsoever to what our bodies were evolved – or designed – to thrive on.*

As with so much else in our exploded, pointless and parasitic government, there are many things the USDA has done which may have started with good intentions, but have ended up as a train wreck. Let's look unflinchingly at the carnage, take a deep breath and resolve to fix the mess we've allowed some people to create. With the lessons learnt, we the people can press the USDA to make some much-needed improvements.

Enforce best practices for humane animal husbandry

Ardent, moral carnivores and hunters – myself included – should be ashamed that American law permits the mistreatment of animals raised for meat and animal products like eggs and milk.

The United States should immediately ban the use of confinement barns for "producing" animal protein. Confining cows, sheep, pigs and birds indoors *for their entire lives* on cement is morally abhorrent *and* results in a meat product inferior in flavor, deficient in nutritional value, dangerous to humans because of antibiotic resistance and horrendous for the environment that bears the brunt of hundreds of millions of gallons of concentrated animal waste pumped into the air, land and water by the likes of Smithfield.

Oscar Wilde said a lot of great things, among them he pre-stole my assertion that bad artists borrow while good artists steal. In his spirit, when it comes to best practices in animal husbandry, I defer to Temple Grandin who has deep experience in and asymmetric understanding of how animals experience the world and particularly in how humans can best manage the process of killing animals as the necessary part of meat production.

If it turns out that the only way to raise animals responsibly is on myriad small farms and not in massive factories, then so be it. Diversity of supply means resiliency should one farm operation experience a bout of sickness, for example, and also means economic resiliency among farming communities .

Don't be fascists

Milton Friedman said famously that "Hell hath no fury like a bureaucrat scorned." We live in an age of galloping scientific knowledge. That is fine. It is also fine for scientists at the USDA, say, or I dunno, the FDA or CDC, to do research and *make recommendations* to Americans about food science. I am even open to the idea of broad standards applied to massive food producing conglomerates as a way of standardizing best safety practices. Americans used to experience far more outbreaks of food poisoning and the like.

Because of the desirability of food safety nationally, I do not advocate a return to laissez-faire conditions which led Upton Sinclair to write *The Jungle* in 1906. Most Americans were fed Sinclair's Socialist lies during junior high when they read his work of complete fiction, which he described as "muckraking" reportage of actual conditions in the meatpacking industry.

The meatpackers of the day were *already* asking for Federal inspections of meat because the added costs would be a barrier to entry for smaller competitors and European nations were demanding proof of quality from a government sources, so the wild lies Sinclair told – complete with the usual nonsense about industrialists being evil people cutting every cost they could – bore little relation to reality. But when did a motivated Socialist ever let facts get in the way of a good story?

Sinclair's wild lies aside, there was definitely room for improvement in hygiene and processing in 1906. A great deal of improvement was made and American food supplies are some of the safest in the world, largely as a result of the hard work of USDA scientists and food inspectors.

That said, in modern day America, there are plenty of experienced producers of food who use centuries-old traditional practices to eschew chemicals on the food they grow, or an absence of any fossil-fuel based energy inputs. The Amish famously spring to mind.

Back to Milton Friedman, who could have been writing about the USDA attacking an Amish farmer 150 miles from Washington, DC. Amos Miller's farm has been in business for 30 years. No one has ever alleged getting ill from eating his products and – crucially from my point of view – he is selling only to private food club members how have been apprised of how he grows his products. That is even leaving aside the attacks on his religious freedom, which are integral to who and why he manages his farm.

> The farm supplies everything from grass-fed beef and cheese, to raw milk and organic eggs, to dairy from grass-fed water buffalo and all types of produce, all to roughly 4,000 private food club members who pay top dollar for high quality whole food.
>
> The private food club members appreciate their freedom to get food from an independent farmer that isn't processing his meat and dairy at U.S. Department of Agriculture facilities, which mandates that food be prepared in ways that Miller's Organic Farm believe make it less nutritious.
>
> Amos Miller, the farm's owner, contends that he's preparing food the way God intended — but the U.S. government *doesn't see things that way*.
>
> They recently sent armed federal agents to the farm and demanded he cease operations. The government is also looking to issue more than $300,000 in fines — a request so steep, it would put the farm out of business.
>
> This is an attack on Amish religious freedom just 150 miles from Washington D.C.[72]

---

[72] https://thewashingtonstandard.com/amish-farm-under-threat-from-feds-for-refusing-to-abandon-traditional-farming-practices-video/

The USDA and its counterparts at the Pennsylvania Department of Agriculture apparently didn't like the way a religious organic farmer was raising food that 4,000 "free" Americans voluntarily buy, so it sent *armed Federal agents* to an Amish farm.[73] Kind of like how heavily armed agents stormed Gibson Guitars in 2011 for using Indian rosewood, while *not* similarly raiding Martin Guitars who also used Indian rosewood in their luthier process.[74]

The inexplicable raid nearly two years ago on a guitar maker for using allegedly illegal wood that its competitors also used was another targeting by this administration of its political enemies.

Interestingly, one of Gibson's leading competitors is C.F. Martin & Co. According to C.F. Martin's catalog, several of their guitars contain "East Indian Rosewood," which is the exact same wood in at least 10 of Gibson's guitars. So why were they not also raided and their inventory of foreign wood seized?

Grossly underreported at the time was the fact that Gibson's chief executive, Henry Juszkiewicz, contributed to Republican politicians. Recent donations have included $2,000 to Rep. Marsha Blackburn, R-Tenn., and $1,500 to Sen. Lamar Alexander, R-Tenn.

By contrast, Chris Martin IV, the Martin & Co. CEO, is a long-time Democratic supporter, with $35,400 in contributions to Democratic candidates and the Democratic National Committee over the past couple of election cycles.

The Gibson Guitar raid, the IRS intimidation of Tea Party groups and the fraudulently obtained warrant naming Fox News reporter James Rosen as an "aider, abettor, co-conspirator" in stealing government secrets are but a few examples of the abuse of power by the Obama Administration to intimidate those on its enemies list.[75]

I digress. The Feds showing up at peaceful places — an Amish farm, say, or a quiet guitar-making artisan shop — armed as if they're taking down a Mexican drug cartel is bad enough. The stress they have imposed on honest Americans with their weaponized Gestapo shock tactics are an affront to decency and those horrendous actions *alone* should see the people involved stripped of their badges and sent to the corner to have a long think about what they've done.

But doing so to enforce arcane rules inaccessible to common sense makes it all the more appalling.

You can find the complete saga yourself online. I paste here the Legal Update from Miller's website (https://www.millersorganicfarm.com/Legal-Update_ep_77.html):

Date: 2021-07-27
Dear Members,

---

[73] https://open.substack.com/pub/christophermessina/p/pennsylvania-taxpayers-foot-the-bill?r=erlb4&utm_campaign=post&utm_medium=web&showWelcomeOnShare=true

[74] https://www.aei.org/carpe-diem/now-the-gibson-guitar-raids-make-sense-it-was-on-the-political-enemies-list/

[75] Investors Business Daily, 26 May 2013

First of all, let's not forget to give thanks to God our Creator for all things good. In this life we will have trials and tribulations, but let's not forget that God will win and be with us to the end if we trust and believe in Him.

As many of our members are aware, there was a teleconference court hearing that took place on Monday, July 19th, with Judge Smith. Although the final ruling was not made that day, we just received a note the end of last week that the Judge ruled in favor of USDA. This will certainly be a difficult time for us here at the farm and very likely for you as a member of the farm. We will keep you posted with more details as to what may become of this situation.

From Amos Miller's Organic Farm & Staff

For full story: https://www.foodsafetynews.com/2021/07/judge-orders-amos-miller-to-pay-250000-fine-within-30-days-or-risk-jail/

You can download the judgment here.

To people who are willing to help, all members and prospective members of our private Association, Miller's Organic Farm (www.MillersOrganicFarm.com is a century-old Amish family farm in Bird-in-Hand, Pennsylvania - serving its Private Member Association. The farm raises its animals and other pure foods the way nature intended and we are proud to be entirely chemical, cruelty and GMO-free. The animals are born and raised without antibiotics or hormones and they spend their entire lives naturally and stress-free out on pasture. All of the farm's food is traceable, pure, and grown on nutrient-dense soil, under traditional time-honored methods.

The farm is now under attack by the USDA about non-conforming practices, the practices which pre-date the USDA. They are suing the farm to comply with USDA laws, concerning the way the farm animals are processed and how our food is labeled. The farm and its members believe that we have the right to free assembly and the right to choose how our food is processed and consumed without the USDA dictating to the farm.

Our Farmer, Amos Miller, needs your help to preserve traditional farming the way God intended. In order to defend the way, the farm has produced its pure foods for more than 100 years to preserve this time-honored way of traditional farming practices.

Amos and his family know that how the food is grown, raised, and processed has a direct connection to the health of the people who consume it. We oppose cruelty in any shape or form. The farm's focus is to grow real nutrient-dense, chemical-free foods, taking care that NO harm is done to neither the animals, the environment, or the people who consume our foods. We are what we eat and this is clearly an undeniable fact.

The ever-increasing environmental toxins from the overuse of synthetic chemicals make modern farming very questionable. The ethical part, consuming animal foods, leaves doubts in the minds of many. Members of our community have joined us because they have chemical sensitivities and only started to heal and thrive once they began consuming REAL nutrient-dense foods. They depend on our farm foods.

Our members trust our Amish farmer and his integrity is priceless.

Thank you!

Are you aware your tax dollars are spent terrorizing a religious man producing food for willing, knowledgeable consumers? Are you a fan of this governmental abuse of this man, his business, his family, his religious freedom and his community? I'm not.

159

If trimming the USDA budget removes their ability to do this to other people, that is yet another great reason for slashing the Federal Leviathan down to a nub.

I recall with great fondness a tremendous meal I had in Piraeus a few years ago. I was visiting a Greek shipowner client and he asked if I'd like to go to his favorite restaurant in all of Europe. How could anyone say "no" to that? Given the man's extreme wealth from decades of owning ships, he could have been talking about a Michelin 3-star restaurant that only billionaires could line-jump on short notice. Instead, his favorite restaurant turned out to be a storefront taverna overlooking the water with plastic tables and an owner who cooked and brought everything out. It was delicious.

One particularly amazing kebob was composed of spiced sheep intestines wrapped around vegetables, cooked over a slow fire. The chef was particularly proud that his taverna was famous for this dish, a Greek delicacy going back centuries, because the obnoxious busybodies in Brussels at the European Union Food Fascism Directorate (not sure if that's the accurate name) had made a point of "outlawing" it throughout Europe.

He even ducked behind the counter to show me a handful of citations condemning him, fining him and demanding he stop cooking this delicacy. We roared with laughter together over the feckless fools in Brussels.

That is the only proper response Americans should have to the USDA torturing Amos Miller.

USDA must stick to its knitting

Here's another good one: "Refocuses rural housing assistance to programs that work better, providing 170,000 new homeownership opportunities, of which at least 30,000 are expected to go to low income rural borrowers." This is something the *federal government* should have nothing whatsoever to do with. If on a town, county or state basis, the elected officials have made the case to those non-federal taxpayers that the government should somehow be involved in providing housing, then so be it.

But *why* the federal government in general and the Department of *Agriculture* should be involved is one more excellent example of unaccountable bureaucracy run amok. Kill this silliness. The irony here is that non-creative thinking has led to the weird idea of the USDA getting involved in "building houses."

The majority of Americans lived in rural areas on farms or in farming communities up until World War II. As more opportunities for cash-compensated work opened up in factories and cities, that coincided with the mechanization of agriculture into "agribusiness" to create volatility in stable housing situations for millions of people. After the supreme idiocy of the Clinton Administration letting the Chinese Communists into the World Trade Organization at the same time as heavy-handed unions drove American manufacturing jobs to Mexico and beyond, the US economy experienced a massive shift from producing things to producing pampered whiners at the top end of the salary scale and a huge number of disaffected young male drug addicts at the bottom end.

We can ameliorate many of these headaches at the local level by permitting old-fashioned work in return for room and board type of arrangements. Hell, we let pampered upper middle class kids work for free as "interns," so why can't anyone up and down the chain get to choose a working arrangement that gives them a start or a leg up in the world?

The democratization of information continues apace; one of the most inspiring people I've seen in terms of living a solution out of a problem is a guy named Aaron who has an interesting YouTube channel and website (123homefree) describing his journey from being homeless to being "homefree." He is not a burden on society in any way. He travels with his goats in his little goat-pulled wagon. He trades his goats' mowing services for the right to camp on small farmers' land, makes his own goat butter, is an expert forager and in general, provides lots of creative services and products, often on a swap basis with his local community. He himself talks about his lifestyle as a solution to the epidemic of homelessness.

I raise the example of Aaron and his goats as further proof that societal resiliency and creativity originate at the individual and local level. The communities in which Aaron lives his peripatetic lifestyle are comfortable with his presence and value what he has to offer. I hesitate to even point him out because some officious bureaucrat may watch his videos and decide to hunt him down to fine him for not having a "food license" of some kind.

There is no bureaucracy in human imagination that would have a cubicle dweller in DC say, "I know! Rather than send food stamps to unhappy people without purpose who will trade the stamps for drugs or buy crap food with no nutritional value, why don't we spend $1,000 per person in central California to equip them each with a tiny mobile shelter and four goats?" There is of course a (small, temporary) place for emergency assistance to needy families for food stamps at the non-Federal level, but the larger point here is that minimum wage laws and the potential liability for a small farmer all conspire to prevent such mutually beneficial arrangements from occurring.

It is a balancing act which requires judgment. We don't want industrial farmers who hire migrant labor to say, "Hey, these 50 people who come up here from Mexico every harvest season are actually entrepreneurs so I can screw them out of fair pay," but if we as a society approach these issues locally and transparently, many people currently begging on the streets of our cities would welcome the opportunity to swap their labor in the fresh air and beautiful countryside scenery for a hut or lean-to on a farm. Not all these things need to be permanent. Rich and middle-class folks voluntarily spend weeks camping out in the wilderness; why not let folks down on their luck take a few steps back towards self-sufficiency and pride in trading work for room and board for a while?

Taking a break from solutions, let's get back to the Nightmare, shall we?

In keeping with the Obama Administration's desire to punt downfield any spending *cuts,* we got this waste of ink and paper:

> **Decreases Long-Term Agricultural Spending.** The Budget includes a decrease in agricultural spending of $2.5 billion over 10 years. The Administration proposes that farm policy target payments to only those who really need them. The savings would be generated by reducing payments to wealthy farmers.

These three sentences precisely say nothing about the real details of a "decrease in agricultural spending of $2.5 billion." It also curiously mute on how mechanically, accounting-wise or any other way, how such hypothetical reductions which are "over 10 years" can be included in a one-year budget. But it does manage to include a campaign sop to the Democrat base by alluding to "wealthy farmers."

161

Under the ironic general heading of *"Improves the Way Federal Dollars are Spent"* we get treated to this nugget:

Redirects Aid to Needy Rural Americans. Agriculture, when compared to other sectors of the economy, has weathered these tough economic times relatively well. For instance, net farm income is forecast to be $79 billion in 2010, an increase of $16.8 billion—or 27 percent—from 2009, and the third largest level of income earned in the history of U.S. farming. Further, the top five years for farm earnings have occurred since 2004, attesting to the profitability of farming this decade. Finally, in every year since 1996, average income of farm households has exceeded average U.S. non-farm household income. However, the economic situation in some non-farm rural communities is very different. Over a third of non-metropolitan counties lost at least 10 percent of their population from 1988 to 2008. Population loss tends to reduce property values, increase tax burdens, reduce the supply and demand for local goods and services, and result in the loss of young, highly-skilled workers. Given the unique needs of rural farm and non-farm communities, the President's Budget proposes to refocus and reprioritize assistance to rural America to more appropriately address these needs.

So... The core of rural economies – farms – are doing better on average than non-farm households, but because one *result* of myriad other factors including mobility based on *individual*, personal preferences has been an erosion in population in some rural areas, somehow the US taxpayers as a group need to write checks to rural counties.

It is astonishing to me that I need to point out the insanity of any federal bureaucracy claiming to analyze the needs of *thousands* of "rural communities," sifting cause from effect and in some magical way choosing which rural areas "deserve" taxpayer cash and which should be left to muddle along on their own steam. Visual aides are a wonderful thing. Here's a picture of the United States, with each county color-coded into urban, suburban and rural.

Majority of U.S. counties are rural, especially in the Midwest

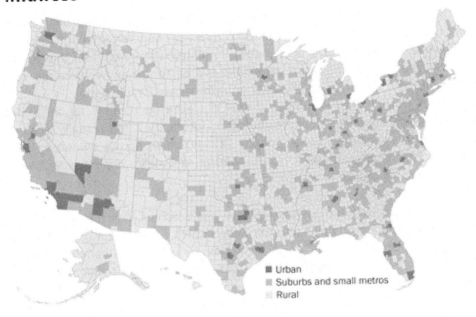

Source: Pew Research Center analysis of National Center for Health Statistics Urban-Rural Classification Scheme for Counties.
"What Unites and Divides Urban, Suburban and Rural Communities"

PEW RESEARCH CENTER

I invite you to ponder what superhuman skills and judgment it would take for any set of government employees – no matter how well-intentioned – to examine objectively every single community in each of the rural counties on this map. Mind you, doing an objective, observational assessment is just the *first step* in any kind of "analysis" which must include accounting for dozens of future-state scenarios involving hundreds of independent and dependent factors. In short, it's a fool's errand and arrogant bureaucratic folly to believe that this is a task a distant centralized bureaucracy can accomplish.

If it can't be done, it shouldn't have our grandchildren's borrowed money thrown at it. To go back to Penn Jillette's guiding wisdom: is this the sort of analysis that should be done looking down the barrel of a gun?

Refocuses Rural Housing Assistance to Programs that Work Better. The Administration proposes to refocus USDA's single-family housing assistance programs to improve effectiveness. USDA has effectively used the guaranteed single-family housing loan program to provide homeownership assistance to low to moderate income rural borrowers. The Administration proposes to provide single family housing mortgage assistance primarily through the guaranteed program and includes a $24 billion loan level with roughly $4 billion in loans expected to be made to low-income rural borrowers. Overall, this loan level is expected to provide as many as 170,000 new homeownership opportunities for rural Americans.

I think the American people deserve to know which of the cast of wet-behind-the-ears kids proficient in Excel came up with this magical "170,000" number. Why not 184,576? Or 92,560? If I were to present a woolly, unsubstantiated statement like this to my investors, I'd be laughed out of the room before they voted to fire and replace me with someone more competent, say a sleepy 4th grader or an intoxicated, rabid gerbil.

Looking back from 2024, I'm curious if it would even be possible for the USDA bureaucrats to tell us how many "new homeownership opportunities" this actually created? Note the weasel word language – it does *not* say "170,000 new homes owned by rural Americans." Nope! That kind of thing is measurable! It says new *"opportunities"* were created, which is almost impossible to measure.

I wonder if the government has managed to ban teaching kids the story of *The Emperor's New Clothes*. The more I delve into the details of what churns out of the Beltway swamp, I can only presume that all "our" government mandarins have read and internalized Joseph Goebbels's belief in The Big Lie. One of the enduring legacies of telling people that the government is a source of wellbeing rather than a boring administrative organ that paves roads is that we have apparently allowed generations of people to become thoroughly useless.

An excellent example of this Conditioned Uselessness in the population is the creation of the problem of "food deserts." Ever since I heard the term "food deserts," I have had my jaw slack in wonderment. The idea behind this phrase is that there are some places in America which – for a range of reasons both apparent and probably hidden, like much of the Invisible Hand – it is difficult for people to procure life-nurturing foodstuffs. Beyond that, the idea that *retail outlets for farm products* are the natural way for people to get food confirms for all time the loud yelling into the void that Wendell Berry and other writers have been doing for decades. Governmental decisions since Earl "Rusty" Butz was the Secretary of Agriculture[76] have fostered dependency and lopsidedness to the agricultural / urban balance of American society.

Supports Efforts to Combat Food Deserts. The Administration supports expanding access to healthy foods for low-income Americans in rural and urban food deserts by providing $35 million in the Office of the Secretary. In addition, other funds of Rural Development and the Agricultural Marketing Service will be available to support USDA's portion of the Healthy Food Financing Initiative. The funding will provide grants, loans, loan guarantees, and other assistance to expand retail outlets for farm products in food deserts.

---

[76] 1971-1976, he focused on mechanization and chemicalization of industrial farming at the expense of smallholding family farms. Butz was forced to resign after telling one of the worst jokes in the history of American racist ribaldry to John Dean and Pat Boone. That is a seriously high bar to clear.

Leaving aside the *vast* discussion of why "food deserts" exist in certain places – e.g. consumers in those places have chosen not to buy healthy foods in question, thereby causing food retailers to destock those perishable items rather than continue to lose money – the idea that a $35 million unaccountable slush fund should be handed to the Secretary of Agriculture to, you know, kinda, like, well, when she's got a second, choose how to allocate that cash to *individual* store owners in *fifty* states is pure insanity of the first water.

What it really means is that $35 million will be distributed in big chunks to whatever large supermarket conglomerates can afford permanent lobbying staffs and be first to fill out the Byzantine paperwork required to get this cash, without *any possibility* of the outcomes ever being audited to the benefit of the US taxpayer. It's more crony capitalist theft, pure and simple.

Or maybe I am not giving the Department of Agriculture credit. Perhaps they have a secret weapon. Perhaps they have a Divination Department, with a full time Accredited Diviner-Seer who uses her specialized tools along with her assistants from the netherworld to "see" with her fifth eye the vast complexity of the nation's food supply to identify which food deserts should get a chunk of that $35 million.

Perhaps.

Perhaps not.

In keeping with my rock-solid core guiding principle that it is always better to *leave the capital and skills at the most local level* when trying to solve these problems, anything that is done in this regard should be educational – and *local* – in nature. For example, how on earth any of these "food desert" communities can exist in rural areas is a testament solely to the failure of individuals and local communities to grow produce for direct consumption. In busy downtown New York City, there are community gardens where people grow fresh fruits and vegetables. So how on earth are there "food deserts" in the rural areas of this country where there is far more open land surface and sunlight? Turning over soil with seeds, watering, weeding and harvesting are *individual* activities requiring *individual* initiative, and therefore anathema to the Centralizing Progressives' dream of Total State Control Over Our (But Not Their) Lives.

Figure 15: The Special Divination Assistant to the Secretary of Agriculture Apportioning Food Desert Relief Funds

Americans are Less Healthy Because of Industrial Food

Something fascinating happened on the way to Economic Development. Americans from 1945 to, say, 1985, enjoyed an impressive improvement in quality of life. There were some hiccups in there on the fiscal and policy fronts, but as we think about our food supply, huge advances in food safety were made. The improvement in quality control and safety along with advances in preventive medicine and public health did wonders for reducing infant mortality and decreasing preventable diseases and conditions. I will leave it to historians, sociologists, anthropologists and medical historians – among others – to debate happily the relative weights to be given to vaccinations, food security and a booming post-war economy.

Post-1985, I would argue that the trajectory of our food supply improvement reversed. Instead of increasing food quality, we embarked upon the era of Industrial Food. It is no surprise that fresh, "whole" foods are better for the human body than highly processed, chemical preservation-laden "edible products" which can sit on a supermarket shelf for weeks without spoiling. What is undisputable is the existence of myriad horrific diseases and conditions which have plagued our population since the 1990s.

Huge numbers of Americans suffer from chronic conditions.

CHRONIC DISEASES IN AMERICA

 1 IN **2** Adults in the US has a **chronic disease** & **1** IN **4** Adults in the US has **two or more**

THE LEADING CAUSES OF DEATH AND DISABILITY
and Leading Drivers of the Nation's **$2.7 Trillion** in Annual Health Care Costs

HEART DISEASE	CANCER	CHRONIC LUNG DISEASE	STROKE	ALZHEIMER'S DISEASE	TYPE 2 DIABETES	CHRONIC KIDNEY DISEASE

The most appalling and indefensible transformation in American society in the last 60 years has been the insane increase in obesity in our population. While we can have long debates around the relative impacts of sedentary lifestyles of a "service" economy versus a physical labor force, there is *no* excuse for the startling rise in childhood obesity. Kids have crazy energy and should run around constantly, burning fuel as they do so.

As the data show, clearly America's children have been packing on the pounds. I am more willing to believe that highly processed foods and oversized sugary drinks full of empty calories are to blame for the change in the population, rather than our children suddenly refusing to move their bodies.

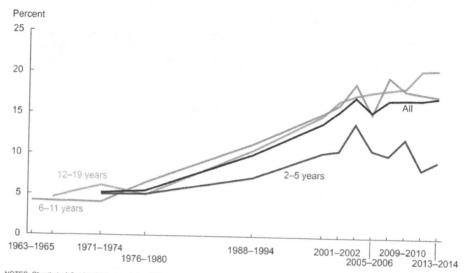

Trends in obesity among children and adolescents aged 2–19 years, by age: United States, 1963–1965 through 2013–2014

NOTES: Obesity is defined as body mass index (BMI) greater than or equal to the 95th percentile from the sex-specific BMI-for-age 2000 CDC Growth Charts.
SOURCES: NCHS, National Health Examination Surveys II (ages 6–11) and III (ages 12–17); and National Health and Nutrition Examination Surveys (NHANES) I–III, and NHANES 1999–2000, 2001–2002, 2003–2004, 2005–2006, 2007–2008, 2009–2010, 2011–2012, and 2013–2014.

As we can see from the chart below, in a mere 18-year period, the number of Americans considered to be "obese" rose from 30.5% - which is already horrifying – to 42.4%.

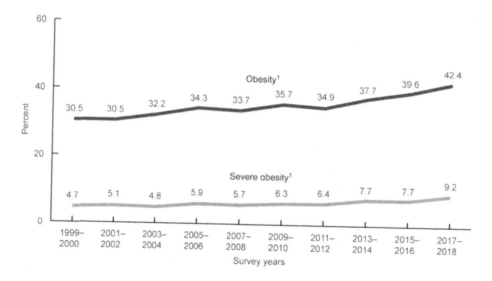

Lots of things contribute to these results, but the big one which everyone cites is a transition from hard farm labor or hard manual labor had already been made by the mid-1980s. So why suddenly did Americans sitting at desks and commuting in cars become a great deal unhealthier?

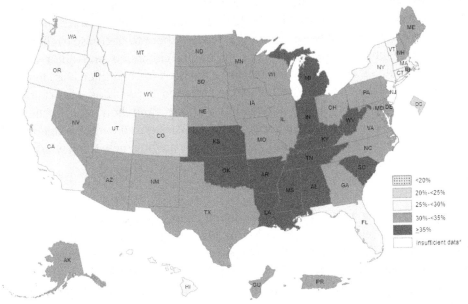

Figure 16: Prevalence† of Self-Reported Obesity Among U.S. Adults by State and Territory, BRFSS, 2019

Lest we be sidetracked by the ongoing Magical Attention Distraction Show that is Washington, let's also be clear about something. The financial incentives for farmers are so skewed by the Federal Government that they are *penalized* for choosing to grow things like fresh fruits and vegetables.

Specialty Crops

The USDA refers to fresh fruits and vegetables as "specialty crops." Specialty crops do not receive subsidies. In fact, farmers who participate in commodity subsidy programs are generally prohibited from growing fruits and vegetables on the so-called "base acres" of land for which they receive subsidies. This provision, enacted in 1996, restricts the ability of both small and large commodity farmers from diversifying their crops and including fruits and vegetables as part of their production.

If Americans increased their consumption of fruits and vegetables to levels recommended by federal dietary guidelines, production of these crops would require an additional 13 million acres of land.[77]

Yes, you are reading that correctly. If Americans ate the vegetables and fruits *the Government's own dietary guidelines suggest*, by the simple law of supply and demand, those life-nurturing foodstuffs would be *even more expensive* than they already are, because farmers on the government cash dole are prevented from producing them.

---

[77] http://www.pcrm.org/health/reports/agriculture-and-health-policies-unhealthful-foods, The Physicians' Committee, 5100 Wisconsin Ave., N.W., Ste.400, Washington DC, 20016

Arguably, the lack of fresh foods in "food deserts" is due to the relatively high cost of fresh, perishable foods. So people on tight budgets buy less fresh food, which then spoils and cost grocery store owners cash in lost inventory, leading them to decrease availability of fresh foods in poor neighborhoods, leading to increasing childhood and adult obesity, leading to Michelle Obama's admirable Let's Move! campaign for healthier kids, leading – insanely enough in our crazy society – to her being criticized by weirdos who claim that being obese is not an objective medical liability but a *"right"* somehow, and further that when a *medical doctor* advises an obese person on the dangers posed by being significantly overweight, that such advice is no longer medical advice. It's a whole new thing which never existed before 21st Century America called "fat shaming."[78]

I digress.

One really interesting area where the pendulum of social policy swings in long, slow arcs is in the area of wild game meats. Back in the 1700s and 1800s, hunters fanned out across the States to provide deer, boar and game birds to meat stores in our urban centers.

Current rules around slaughtering – which are one of the *best things* our government has ever done and continues to do well – require that animals be inspected before and after death. This makes sense when domesticated animals are reared and delivered to a USDA-monitored slaughterhouse. However, it's hard to persuade a white-tailed deer to let a government inspector poke and prod it for a minute before a hunter shoots it. The result is a complete lack of wild game meats being readily available to consumers. Which is a bummer because venison is tasty, lean protein.

Currently, this problem is "solved" in part for feral hogs. Ranchers set live traps and then must deal with getting a dangerous animal from the trap to a slaughterhouse so that it can be processed in accordance with USDA regulations. If you've ever had the joy of hunting wild pigs, you'll know that transferring a seriously angry feral pig or wild boar from a trap to a slaughterhouse is a significantly dangerous activity.

Providing a mechanism for wild game to be managed and brought into the commercial food supply would also do wonders for other problems we have. Invasive species are a major disruptor to our natural ecosystems. Here is a perfect example of local not only being better but being required. Local townships or maybe counties at the largest unit should make all rules relating to wild game harvested meats. On a basic level, if a hunter is willing to eat the venison from the deer she shot, then local butchers should be able to sell cuts from that same animal.

I would like to see a few hundred thousand "Amos Miller hunters" across the land, thinning out the invasive wild boars and other animals who do huge damage to both human agriculture and native wild ecosystems. I'd buy braces of quail, dove and pheasant from local hunters every damned day if I could.

The formerly free American citizenry have shown themselves to be willing to become sheeple in many areas of life. There is a fine balancing act between coming together

---

[78] Millions of citations I refuse to endorse here. Go warm up your Internet search engine and prepare to be astonished.

to vote for people who create clearly-beneficial rules to improve public health, say around the licenses required to operate a water treatment facility, and permitting an out of control, unaccountable, anonymous Administrative State to create burdensome rules with no logic. American adults are reasonable enough to be entrusted to choose whether to buy the meat shot by a local hunter – just as they are reasonable enough to go for lunch at a seafood or sushi restaurant, read the warnings about raw oysters or raw food in general, and decide whether to order a meal.

Chapter 11: Department of Commerce

Year Founded	February 14, 1903
Founded under President	William Taft
Funding Budget 2023	$16,300,000,000
Messina's 2024 Budget Proposal	$4,000,000,000
Messina's 2025 Budget Proposal	$3,000,000,000
Degree to which Messina's Plan is Better	Completely
Should a Federal Commerce Dept exist?	Yes

Is this a standalone proper use of the taxpayers' limited resources?	Yes
Does this expenditure unfairly benefit one American over another one?	No
Does the expenditure meet the "Is this logical?" standard of fiduciary responsibility?	Yes
Can the goals be achieved by *not* spending the dollar more effectively than by spending it?	No

President Taft's Valentine's Day gift to the nation was originally the Department of Commerce and Labor. Not content to limit its meddling in the economy to one department, Congress in 1913 split Labor into its own abusive bureaucracy. That is great news, because we only need to get rid of one Department rather than attempting to carve out the cancer from this one.

While private enterprise tends to look after the needs of the economy, in a complex world where political economy still matters, this government bureaucracy can be of assistance to the private sector, from data aggregation and statistics dissemination to representing American business interests in other nations.

All of the tasks associated with data collection, aggregation and provision for use by Americans should be maintained and possibly expanded. Everything else the Department does in the areas relating to "helping" American business should be subject to examination.

Data collection, aggregation and analysis are big topics, with lots of room for smart, capable Americans to contribute their skills to project-based efforts. Here is one more fabulous area for *voluntary* "jury duty like" public service. Some of the best things our government currently does involves public-private partnership projects of a few months' duration.

The current vision for Commerce's existence is miles away conceptually from a core service related to data management. This was taken from their website on 16 March 2024:

> The Department of Commerce's mission is to create the conditions for economic growth and opportunity for all communities. The Department's Fiscal Year 2025 Budget maintains funding for essential programs and activities and makes prudent investments to position our workers and businesses for success in the 21st-century. Specifically, the Budget invests in driving U.S. innovation and global competitiveness, fostering inclusive capitalism and equitable economic

growth, addressing the climate crisis, expanding opportunity and discovery through data, and providing 21st-century service to deliver on the Department's mission.

The Budget proposes $11.4 billion in discretionary funding and $4 billion in mandatory funding. This funding will complement investments in high-speed Internet access and climate resilience provided by the Bipartisan Infrastructure Law, the Inflation Reduction Act, and the Infrastructure Investment and Jobs Act, as well as investments to revitalize the domestic semiconductor industry provided by the CHIPS and Science Act.[79]

If I tried, I could not come up with a bigger pile of stupidity. I am going to whip through this quickly. You can play your own version of "pick the most absurd phrase" at your leisure.

When did a bureaucracy in the Swamp develop the conceit that it *can* "create the conditions for economic growth and opportunity for all communities?" Leaving aside the madness inherent in believing that it *should* do something so vague and sweeping in the first place, *how* is this bureaucracy supposed to achieve this weird goal? Who defines what is a "community?" Is it geographically defined? Diversity defined? Religiously defined? I don't see how even the first step is possible.

How is a DC bureaucracy going to make "prudent investments to position our workers and businesses for success?" What the heck does that even mean? Investments in *what?* Real professional investors who allocate private capital to businesses make these complex judgments every day *for a single business or maybe an industry sector.* And they often get it wrong. Remember, private investors are performing either Type 2 or Type 3 expenditures. Government bureaucrats are performing Type 4 activities which is like throwing someone else's cash at someone else. How careful do you think they are in that process, never mind whether it is remotely possible they could be effective?

How is Commerce going to "drive U.S. innovation and global competitiveness" when I personally have witnessed them ignore investing in businesses *which the rest of the government including Defense and State have identified as critical to American economic and military security?* It's absurdity.

On to the really fun gobbledygook. What is "inclusive capitalism" and how is the Commerce Department going to "foster" it? So far as I understand, free markets are all inclusive already. No one is stopping anyone in America from working hard to create something from nothing. So how does the current market we have differ from "inclusive capitalism?" It's nonsense.

Similarly, what on earth is "equitable economic growth?" Really. I am not being snarky. Can someone who speaks Leftist reach out and tell me what that might mean?

The Commerce Department is going to "address the climate crisis." First off, there is no "climate crisis" to address, so that must be a relief. Secondly, all this jargon is code for "we're going to throw your tax dollars at our donors for free cash into their businesses, so long as they mouth the religious incantations about 'carbon' and 'climate change' and 'the energy transition.'" It's ridiculous. If private sector investors are panicked about the

---

[79] Budget and performance | U.S. Department of Commerce

173

weather, they are free to put their money on the line. DC bureaucrats have no business performing pseudo-religious sacrifices with scarce taxpayer dollars.

Finally, we come to something that makes a modicum of sense, although in context, I am sure it was a mistake. They are going to "expand opportunity and discovery through data." Wonderful, I think Commerce should do nothing but gather empirical data and process it in various ways for Americans to make use of. Somehow, I don't think that is what the author meant, but let's take the win and move on.

Census Bureau

There are three kinds of lies: lies, damned lies and statistics. Mark Twain made that popular, and it's tough for a phrase in search of a publicist to find a better one.

Whilst the Census is incredibly important in that it determines things like number of Congressional Representatives – and Electors – per State, it is a task that I believe reasonable people can accomplish without too much distortion of either process or outcomes.

One would think that an agency devoted to collecting statistics – basically, counting things and people – would not be subject to any biases. Numbers are numbers, right? At least that was what I was told in grammar school; newer approaches to mathematics as "reimagined" by non-mathematician "education professionals" have apparently changed the "facts" of math into subjective feelings, much like gender identity.

As tempting as it is to go off on that tangent, I'll leave it for the TED Talk I won't be asked to give.

What I will cover is how completely subjective, often arbitrary, and usually political are the *choices* bureaucrats make about what numbers to count and *how* to summarize them distort our understanding of basic facts.

A perfect example of this process is the statistical definition of income distribution. This is a fairly straightforward idea. Let's say you've got 100 people who all earn an income. To understand how much money each of them make in relation to the others, let's assume 20 of them earn between $1,000 and $2,000 dollars, 20 earn between $2,001 and $3,000 and so on, with equal numbers of people falling into five "buckets" of earnings. The bar chart graph one could use to summarize those data looks like this:

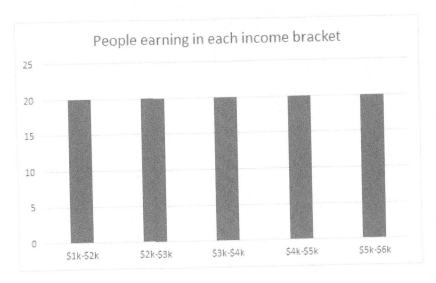

People earning in each income bracket

Phil Gramm and John Early highlighted the serious problem that such arbitrary choices by unelected bureaucrats have.

> The Census Bureau also fails to count $1.9 trillion in annual public transfer payments to American households. The bureau ignores transfer payments from some 95 federal programs such as Medicare, Medicaid and food stamps, which make up more than 40% of federal spending, along with dozens of state and local programs. Government transfers provide 89% of all resources available to the bottom income quintile of households and more than half of the total resources available to the second quintile.
>
> In all, leaving out taxes and most transfers overstates inequality by more than 300%, as measured by the ratio of the top quintile's income to the bottom quintile's. More than 80% of all taxes are paid by the top two quintiles, and more than 70% of all government transfer payments go to the bottom two quintiles.
>
> America's system of data collection is among the most sophisticated in the world, but the Census Bureau's decision not to count taxes as lost income and transfers as gained income grossly distorts its measure of the income distribution. As a result, the raging national debate over income inequality, the outcome of which could alter the foundations of our economic and political system, is based on faulty information.[80]

---

[80] https://www.wsj.com/articles/the-truth-about-income-inequality-11572813786?mod=hp_opin_pos_1   By Phil Gramm and John F. Early, 3 November 2019

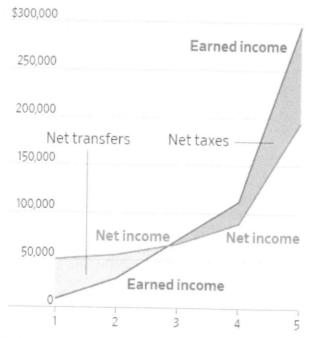

How Redistribution Works

Average earned and net income by quintile,
2017

$300,000

250,000

200,000

Net transfers   Net taxes

150,000

Earned income

100,000

Net income   Net income

50,000

Earned income

0

1   2   3   4   5

Figure 17: Adjusting income statistics to account for taxes and transfer payments

The reality of how much cash each quintile of the population has to spend on supporting their families, saving for the future and investment and the like is accurately depicted in Figure 17.

Why, the alert reader may ask, do my undergarments appear bunched about this very dry topic? Because real decisions regarding the misallocation of *our* tax dollars are made based on numbers like these. As Gramm and Early point out in their excellent essay, if people are told *by the Commerce Department statisticians* that there is rampant income inequality which is *not already being addressed through myriad transfer programs*, then the American people may well turn from their tugged heart strings to empower the Government to *take more from productive people* to give to others.

As I touch on in multiple places, there is always a place for a rich nation to make accommodation for safety nets and support for those who fall on hard times. What we need to do is *be honest* about the accounting for that safety net and understand whether the *Federal* government has any role to play in funding it.

At the very least, we should be able to expect that the statistics provided to us by the people we pay are accurate representations of reality.

Small Business Administration (SBA)

Year Founded	July 30, 1953
Founded under President	Dwight D. Eisenhower
Funding/Financing Budget 2023	$50,000,000,000
Messina's 2024 Budget Proposal	$20,000,000
Messina's 2024 Budget Proposal	$0
Degree to which Messina's Plan is Better	Completely
Should a Federal SBA exist?	No

Is this a standalone proper use of the taxpayers' limited resources?	No
Does this expenditure unfairly benefit one American over another one?	Yes
Does the expenditure meet the "Is this logical?" standard of fiduciary responsibility?	No
Can the goals be achieved by *not* spending the dollar more effectively than by spending it?	Hell Yes

Straight into the dustbin of history with this nonsense. The United States of America has the biggest, deepest pools of entrepreneurial investment capital in the world. The *private sector* provides all the investment capital required for business creation, growth and development. Aside from dollars, because of the Internet, there is no shortage of business-related advice for potential entrepreneurs to access. I don't need to debate whether this was a good idea in 1953, as opposed to a DC bureaucracy at its predecessor agencies, Small Defense Plants Administration[81] and the Reconstruction Finance Corporation[82], looking for a way to keep their salaries and benefits intact, so they pivoted away from wartime spending priorities to claim the peacetime economy could also benefit from their advice and guidance.

Once more the Federal bureaucracy provides hilarity without comedic writers required. *The very idea* that a government bureaucracy can assist entrepreneurs in building successful businesses is absurd from the get-go. Yet that is the *entire premise* behind the appalling waste of money and time known as the "Small Business Administration." The very name is a great example of the irony I am talking about; only a government bureaucrat would name something involved in the very dynamic, unpredictable and exciting activity that is entrepreneurial business development as "administrative" in nature.

Here is their mission statement:

------

[81] On July 31, 1951, the Small Defense Plants Administration (SDPA) was created by an amendment to P.L. 81-774, the Defense Production Act of 1950, and was given "primary responsibility in the field of channeling defense contracts to small producers." As hostilities with Korea subsided, so did the perceived need for the SDPA.

[82] https://www.federalreservehistory.org/essays/reconstruction-finance-corporation President Hoover signed the Reconstruction Finance Corporation Act on January 22, 1932, establishing the Reconstruction Finance Corporation (RFC).

Mission Statement

Maintain and strengthen the nation's economy by enabling the establishment and vitality of small businesses and by assisting in the economic recovery of communities after disasters.

Goal 1

Ensure equitable and customer-centric design and delivery of programs to support small businesses and innovative startups

Goal 2

Build resilient businesses and a sustainable economy

Goal 3

Implement strong stewardship of resources for greater impact

1.1 Ensure all entrepreneurs have access to capital to start and grow their business

1.2 Build a thriving national innovation ecosystem that promotes investments in all small business communities

1.3 Grow exporting opportunities to help small businesses across the country expand into new markets

1.4 Build back an inclusive and proficient small business contracting base ready to compete for all federal procurement opportunities

1.5 Build an equitable entrepreneurial ecosystem through tailored training and counseling

2.1 Help small businesses recover from the pandemic and become more resilient

2.2 Prepare small businesses and rebuild communities affected by natural disasters

3.1 Strategically manage resources by integrating quality data, evidence, and risk in decision-making processes

3.2 Build an inclusive and high performing workforce

3.3 Develop and deploy technology-driven solutions to enhance mission delivery

You'll notice the trendy gobbleydegook around "inclusive and proficient small business contracting base" ready to suck cash from the taxpayers (1.4) and *all* of the nonsense in Goal 3. You know how it's gobbleydegook? Because real businesses don't write crap like this. Have fun pondering each ridiculous bullet point. Enjoy.

Anyway, once a bureaucrat had this fantasy of the government "advising" businesses, it became the job of Congress to flatter themselves even further that they were 'doing something' by foisting this insane economic drag on us all. Never mind all the details of how the SBA actually "works" as outlined in incredible detail regarding the SBA's providing the fuel for the fraudulent activities of a politically-connected, Washington, DC-based company called Allied Capital in *Fooling Some of the People All of the Time* by David Einhorn.

I cite Einhorn's book here in order to urge you to read it. I get nothing personally from the recommendation and indeed he himself has committed all the proceeds from the book's sales to charity. I urge you to read it because it lays out in clinical and horrifying detail how dysfunctional, corrupt and money-wasting *in practice* something that sounds so good *in theory* can be. The SBA exists to perpetuate itself as a bureaucratic entity. Its employees and managerial team have consistently aided and abetted fraud *against you, the American taxpayer* for years, have lied, denied and obfuscated the truth about their incompetence even in the face of Freedom of Information Act requests as their own Office of Inspector General (OIG) found when their audit report on BLX (Allied Capital) was basically fully "blacked out" when shown to the public.[83]

---

[83] www.sba.gov/ig/7-28.pdf

In November 2008, Patrick Harrington – who features heavily in Einhorn's discussion of Allied Capital – was sentenced to ten years in federal prison[84] for defrauding the American taxpayer of $76,900,000 via his lax oversight of the SBA. Below is a press release dated 2 February 2010 from Rep. Nydia Velazquez who for years was a recipient of campaign donations from Patrick Harrington and the other executives at Allied Capital.[85]

Velazquez Comments on Small Business Administration Budget for Fiscal Year 2011 [86]

WASHINGTON, Feb. 2 /PRNewswire-USNewswire/ -- Rep. Nydia M. Velazquez (D-NY), the Chairwoman of the House Committee on Small Business, released the following statement regarding the Administration's Fiscal Year (FY) 2011 budget for the Small Business Administration (SBA):

"In last week's State of the Union address, President Obama made clear the importance of small businesses to our economic recovery. Given the pivotal role small businesses play in job creation, it is important that the President's FY 2011 budget reflect the priorities of our nation's small firms.

"The Small Business Administration is the sole agency tasked specifically with meeting small business needs and it must have adequate resources to assist entrepreneurs. Whether it be advising businesses weathering difficult economic conditions or assisting those starting a venture, the SBA must ensure demand for technical services are met. Studies repeatedly demonstrate that the agency's programs not only help create jobs, but also generate revenues that reduce the deficit in the long term.

"Given the ongoing credit crunch, the budget should also help make loans more affordable and available for entrepreneurs. The SBA is responsible for providing small businesses with over $28 billion in capital, annually. Traditionally, these initiatives offer small businesses additional financing options when banks stop lending. While I am pleased that the President has made small business access to capital a priority, we must ensure the FY 2011 budget does not increase costs for small business borrowers. I look forward to working with the Administration to address that issue.

"In light of current fiscal restraints, the President has also advocated eliminating ineffective and wasteful programs. American families are making tough decisions during these difficult economic times and the SBA should do the same, prioritizing programs that have a proven track record of supporting small business job growth. The President's budget offers an important blueprint for getting our economy back on track. In coming weeks, Congress will be examining it carefully and looking at all options for strengthening and improving the SBA."

The press release of Nydia Velazquez is a fine example of parody issued without irony as fact. The idea that bureaucrats without skin in the game – people who are *by definition* risk-averse civil servants – are going to be of *any* real assistance to an

---

[84] Former Business Loan Express Executive Gets 10 Years (Update2), Bloomberg, 13 November 2008
[85] Einhorn, David, *Fooling Some of the People all of the Time*, 2008, John Wiley & Sons, Chap.26
[86] www.prnewswire.com/news-releases/velazquez-comments-on-small-business-administration-budget-for-fiscal-year-2011-83362972.html

entrepreneur is just insane. As she writes, the SBA "is the sole agency tasked specifically with meeting small business needs." To that I say heartily, "Thank heavens; amazingly enough we only have one pointless waste of money to disassemble." The US has one of the most robust capital markets in the world. Businesses are funded every day by new capital, whether equity or loans or other relationships. The government has *no* fit purpose interfering in the private sector from an investment standpoint.

Kill the SBA, and give all their employees the option of working for 12 months on road crews filling in potholes around our cities. Pick up a shovel, be useful and get some much-needed exercise, or be out of a job. That sounds like a real set of incentives to me. The fresh air and exposure to the vagaries of weather might spark fresh thoughts and initiative in their currently-dead-end bureaucratic lives.

All these grandstanding politicians claiming they want to help "small business" give me heartburn. If these people honestly wanted to help businesspeople (without regard to size), they would just fire their own staffs, turn the thermostats in the Capitol Building down five degrees and *leave us all alone.*

I love listening to these self-serving parasites lie to the American people. While daily vilifying "Big Business," they in the same message intone about the virtues of "small business," without understanding that *most if not all* "small" business owners want to grow their business into a big business. For politicians, however, once some magical line of private sector growth is crossed, a businessperson goes from being the beneficial, somewhat folksy, preferably-small-town source of all employment bounty into being an evil, soul-sucking Capitalist to be demonized and taxed to death.

Oh, and by the way, if the small business owner happens to make any *profits* from her enterprise, then that small business owner is vilified as "the wealthy" upon whom more taxes ought to be levied so they "pay their fair share." In the Land of DC, jobs are excellent things, but job creators are evil. Unless of course those job creators pony up election cash for political coffers, in which case they are solid citizens looking to increase the impact of Beltway interference in supposedly private enterprise.

Transitional Department of Blockage Elimination

Core to my budget approach – even though it may get obfuscated a bit – is that there are many self-driven individuals who believe genuinely in public service. I am not averse to a one-year wind-down period for SBA employees. A *real* one-year wind-down period – as in the buildings in which they sit will be sold or have new private sector leases beginning in 365 days, and the cash for their salaries will sit in a sequestered bank account that only draws cash down and cannot be replenished.

Those folks can spend a year ferreting out business-killing rules and regulations across this fair land. They will be paid on a success basis, kind of like how "bug bounty" programs work in cyber security. In the interests of strengthening the nation's resilience and security one citizen at a time, let's give these people soon-to-be-released into the free market competitive wild a lesson in private sector incentives; a possible one-year contract would have terms like the following:

1. Salary equivalent to 65% of previous year's base salary,
2. Monthly rule kill target of 10 business-constraining rules,
3. Failure to meet monthly target results in immediate termination,
4. Success in meeting monthly target results in a bonus of $500 per rule eliminated,
5. For each rule over 10 killed per month, a $750 bonus,
6. No carryovers; 10 rule target resets every first of the month.

If, say, an SBA employee who had made $80,000 per year performs well in identifying and eliminating bad rules, we as Americans should be delighted to find after twelve months that we have paid out:

Base salary = .65 x 80,000 =	52,000
Month 1, 10 rules squelched =	5,000
Month 2, 20 rules squelched =	12,500
Months 3-12, 20 rules squelched =	125,000
Total cash compensation =	$194,500

What a great way to wrap up a career formerly spent in lackluster paper-pushing! How splendid to offer a truly experiential transition to the private sector.

Figure 18: SBA Memorial Monument - Requiem for bureaucratic meddling in the free market

We can even get the nation's children involved in cheering them on. We can hold art contests for the best slogan and design. I can see hundreds of thousands of poster boards across the nation (and posted to social media) of variations on "I'm a Rule Bounty Hunter!" splashed across t-shirts, hats and beer cozies. "Don't Worry America! When I Find Another Rule Destroying Freedom, I *CANCEL* It!"

Get the SBA out of Financing Anything

On the loan and loan guarantee side, during that same 12-month wind-down period, a portfolio manager will be assigned to sell off the entire portfolio to the private sector. Let rational market participants price what these loans and loan guarantees are worth in the free market.

Chapter 12: Department of War ~~Defense~~

Year Founded	1789 (as War Department)
Founded under President	George Washington
Year Founded as Department of Defense	1949
Founded under President	Harry S Truman
Funding Budget 2023	$816,000,000,000
Messina's 2024 Budget Proposal*	$900,000,000,000
Messina's 2025 Budget Proposal	$1,000,000,000,000
Degree to which Messina's Plan is Better	Completely
Should a Federal Dept of Defense exist?	Hoo-Rah!

Is this a standalone proper use of the taxpayers' limited resources?	Yes
Does this expenditure unfairly benefit one American over another one?	No
Does the expenditure meet the "Is this logical?" standard of fiduciary responsibility?	Yes
Can the goals be achieved by *not* spending the dollar more effectively than by spending it?	No

* Under the managerial reforms described below.

At last, something the Federal Government is in the business of doing. America's security relies on our ability to kill people that need dying. It's Whack-An-Evil-Mole out there and our enemies multiply almost faster than we can obliterate them.

First off, language matters. This reactive whiny nonsense about our military being for "defense" has got to go. We need a damned *War* Department, because sadly the optimists who thought history ended when World War II ended were deluded and flat out wrong. The threats to the USA have grown exponentially since then and require a far more forceful physical rebuttal than they have been getting recently.

One of the few true functions of the Federal Government, and one if not the only thing standing between us and complete chaos, the Department of War requires ample funding,[87] funding which every American should be happy to contribute to. That said, in true Beltway fashion, there is a vast heaping of nonessential expenditure contained in the DoD budget that can be shaved forthwith. That rational reevaluation of priorities must come with a wholesale managerial shake-up, taking advantage of the excellent experience and managerial skills of the private sector.

In a dangerous word, it is beyond irresponsible to leave the management of non-warfighting aspects of the War Department to military personnel. Just as our military is the most effective in the world *because it is under civilians' ultimate control,* so too do we need to create a more effective "blend" of private sector expertise so that we can provide the tip of the spear the best support possible. All of us owe it to the brave men and women who

---

[87] Refer to www.comptroller.defense.gov for current and previous budget details.

are the actual warfighters to make sure we equip, train and support them properly in their missions.

Part of that managerial shake up is tied to many of the issues plaguing Leviathan more generally. More effective development and deployment of both our warfighter and support functions have nothing to do with dollar amounts, but with insanely restrictive hire-and-fire rules created by the Federal bureaucracy. Currently, if the head of a Command, say SOUTHCOM, identifies a need for a civilian role involving cyber research with a given set of linguistic skills, the Command cannot simply find a qualified person and hire him or her. No, this is the Federal government, so all kinds of job classification codes and seniority need to be taken into account.

Unsurprisingly, this leads to severely suboptimal staffing. Long, tortured hiring processes in the real world mean negative selection. Qualified candidates with in-demand skills have options for employment, so if the Federal bureaucracy requires six months to make a job offer to someone who can get a job offer from a private company in one day, what do you think happens to the overall quality of the Federal employee pool?

Funding Highlights:

- Provides $553 billion for the base budget, an increase of $22 billion above the 2010 appropriation. This reflects continued investment in national security priorities such as cybersecurity, satellites, and nuclear security. The Budget also includes a series of management and acquisition reforms that will produce a net of $78 billion in savings through 2016.

- Maintains ready forces and continues efforts to rebalance military forces to focus on both today's wars as well as potential future conflicts.

- Enhances the Administration's commitment to maintaining a reliable nuclear deterrent by increasing investments in the nuclear weapons complex and in weapon delivery technologies, and to nonproliferation by preventing the spread of nuclear materials around the world.

- Supports the Administration's goal to provide the Nation's military with the most effective and modern equipment possible in a cost-efficient manner. Departmental priorities include improving business practices, such as developing and purchasing weapons consistent with improved acquisition policy.

- Continues strong support for servicemembers and military families.

- Supports access to medical care for over 9.6 million servicemembers, retirees, and their families. This includes ongoing support for wounded warrior transition units and centers of excellence in vision, hearing, traumatic brain injury, and other areas to continuously improve the care provided to wounded, ill, and injured servicemembers.

- Reinvests $100 billion of expected savings in high-priority areas such as the development or purchase of unmanned intelligence, surveillance, and reconnaissance assets; more ships; a new ground combat vehicle; the Advanced Extremely High Frequency satellite; and the stealthy F-35 Joint Strike Fighter.

- Continues the reform agenda to achieve more efficient business operations.

- Invests in long-term scientific and technological innovation to ensure that the Nation has access to the best defense systems available in the world.

- Invests in new and on-going cybersecurity research and development and improvements to existing cybersecurity capabilities.

Close and dear to my heart are the myriad problems associated with defending and promoting the USA's interests in a difficult and increasingly connected world. Having lived through the attacks on downtown New York on 11 September 2001, and been involved in various ways ever since then in contributing my efforts to improving national security, I know there are millions of patriotic Americans who love this country and will do anything they can to protect it.

National Defense Strategy Commission

There is little value in my spilling more ink on this topic. There are vast numbers of resources for you to avail yourself of regarding our military and its relative state of preparedness. I would suggest you start with things like this Commission.[88]

I would also suggest if you are one of the 93% of Americans who have no personal contact with the military, that you change that.

What's in a Name?

With all due respect to the Swan of Avon, human memory and therefore understanding are dependent upon words. While a rose called "ratcrapknockweed" might indeed carry the same sweet odor, its renaming might begin to change what flowers go into lovers' bouquets at the corner flower shop. We need to be clear and firm in the words our society depends on. Mothers are *not* "birthing persons," for example – to call them that is not only ridiculous but part of a subversive plan to drive a wedge between Americans' understanding of the world and objective reality. The further a certain strain of the political class gets in achieving their desire to separate reality from political decisions, the more power they get and the faster our Republic will dissolve into a totalitarian dictatorship.

We need to get rid of the weak-kneed semantic innovations of the recent past and remind our enemies and ourselves what our military capability is for. This department needs to be immediately renamed The War Department. No more of this wishy-washy nonsense that says our military preparedness is only to be used *defensively*. That makes it sound as if we are reactive to world affairs and threats to our nation and our citizens.

We make *war* upon those who would molest us. The local Y and various community centers offer classes in self-defense and pottery on alternate Thursdays.

See the difference?

---

[88] About Us - Ndscommission (senate.gov)

Fund our warfighter fully. Rebuild our Navy and Air Force. Restock the Arsenal of Democracy. Implement private sector volunteer oversight boards for all financial decisions. You really will not like what happens if we fail.

Chapter 13: Department of Veterans Affairs

Year Founded	March 3, 1865
Founded under President	Abraham Lincoln
Funding Budget 2023	$301,400,000,000
Messina's 2023 Budget Proposal	$325,000,000,000
Messina's 2024 Budget Proposal	$350,000,000,000
Degree to which Messina's Plan is Better	An improvement, hopefully
Should a Federal VA exist?	Yes

Is this a standalone proper use of the taxpayers' limited resources?	Yes
Does this expenditure *unfairly* benefit one American over another one?	No
Does the expenditure meet the "Is this logical?" standard of fiduciary responsibility?	Yes
Can the goals be achieved by *not* spending the dollar more effectively than by spending it?	Maybe

This is a serious line item in our budget, and one that requires strengthening in some areas and improving in a few others. Many of our nation's problems historically have matched every other nation's problems with veterans: they're a pain in the ass expense no one wants to bear. I am not being crude here – heck, the ageing soldier's poverty and stress is the stuff of art. Everyone from Van Dyck to Picasso have used the image of the wounded soldier's impoverished family as an artistic theme. At least the United States has *tried* to look after the wounded men and women who have lain their lives on the line to protect this nation.

By taking a very careful look at the *total costs* in dollars and lives that war incurs, we will not only increase our respect for those who put their lives on the line for this country, but also as a citizenry greet with careful skepticism any politician's heated enthusiasm for going to war in the first place. When we only count the current day, cash on the spot costs for deploying our armed forces overseas, we lie to ourselves and future generations about the true expense of military action.

President Hoover under General MacArthur's guidance in 1932 sent tanks into a veterans' encampment across the Anacostia River, arguably giving us FDR's disastrous Presidency. The Bonus Expeditionary Force was composed of World War I veterans who in the depths of the Depression wanted the inflation-compensation bonus that was given to civilians but not the military during the Great War. Sending tanks and soldiers to burn down a veterans' encampment turned out to be the gift the Socialist in a Wheelchair was looking for in terms of beating President Hoover at the next election.

The night before Thanksgiving 2018, I was out walking with my wife in New Orleans. We encountered a young man sitting in a doorway asking for money. There are lots of homeless in New Orleans, begging from the tourists. This guy called me "sir" in a way I've only heard on military bases. We talked a bit. He was looking for another $20 to get a room for the night. It was Thanksgiving and I was already in a grateful mood enjoying a fun vacation with my family in New Orleans; I handed him $40. Was he lying? I don't know. Did he need that money? I am quite sure he did – whether as advertised for a place to sleep out of the weather or for chasing the dragon, I'll never know.

What I *do* know is that there is a completely unacceptable level of human damage endured on our nation's behalf by our veterans. Even beyond the physical scars of war, suicide rates, drug and alcohol abuse and the myriad familial dysfunctions borne by veterans' families are a national disgrace. I remain a firm believer in individual responsibility which is in no way contradicted by a belief that to those who have borne the battle we owe not only honor but all the assistance that can reasonably be provided to help those who continue to suffer.

I have the honor of being a Board Member of the Combat Control Foundation[89], which is the fundraising arm for the Air Force Special Operations community. In that capacity, I have heard a lot of stories about active combat deployment for US Special Operators. I will breach no confidences, but I will note there is a strong reason why for all the money spent and data gathered, military leaders and psychiatrists are completely unable to predict how a given deployment will impact a given service member. Americans have *zero idea* of what we ask these – mainly – young men to do in service of their country. All combat is difficult and can be scarring, but the up close and personal nature of Special Operations is a whole different human experience than, say, a drone operator sitting in air conditioning while piloting a UAV shooting missiles from two miles in the sky.[90]

In those close combat situations, there is no predicting how any individual will react. Ten men can witness the same situation as part of the same mission. Five might be bothered by it somewhat, two might shrug it off entirely, two might experience some enduring Post Traumatic Stress and one may be driven to suicide ten years later. Which reaction any one of them might have is unpredictable before deployment. The young men themselves who volunteer for these dangerous roles also don't really know what it's going to be like when they are deployed. They have no idea of the horrors they will see or the evil they will encounter.

Americans *owe* it to these men – and all service members – to provide the best care possible to those who – in President Lincoln's words – have borne the battle.

In the beginning of this book, I referred to David Shulkin's experience as Head of the VA. Here is a man who tried hard to improve the services offered to our veterans and faced a blizzard of institutional obstacles from unelected, unionized public sector employees. In keeping with the general guidance in this book, once we dismantle the public sector unions, the new leadership at the VA can fire useless people and hire good people at will, the way the real world does.

There is a massive book called CFR. This book has an enormous list of every possible condition that a veteran can experience.[91] Tied to each line item is a code and in theory when a VA physician or other worker examines a veteran, a complete, fully accurate and

---

[89] https://www.combatcontrolfoundation.org
[90] For more detailed longitudinal studies on the types of combat and the impact on those who fight for us, I recommend reading *On Killing – The Psychological Cost of Learning to Kill in War and Society*, Lt. Col. Dave Grossman, 1995, Little Brown & Company
[91] https://www.benefits.va.gov/warms/bookc.asp

proper evaluation translates into a status which then determines the quantity and quality of services the veteran shall receive.

I have come to get a glimpse into how that theoretical process works in practice. In 2022, I was privileged to join the Board of Directors for the Combat Control Foundation. I have gotten to know some of the airmen who served as Combat Controllers and have heard numerous stories about how the VA fails or succeeds in its mission.

No one is perfect and no system is perfect, especially one with rigid hierarchical processes for diagnosing a veteran's range of possible "disabilities," including things like Subpart B.4.55 *Principles of Combined Ratings for Muscle Injuries* all of which are then taken into consideration with another range of things like "unemployability" to come up with dollar figures and hours of treatment.

I propose below a Commission to examine the VA to determine optimal service delivery. No matter what the outcome, I suggest strengthening the VA budget in coming years. Under the new way of evaluating all government service delivery, that does *not* automatically mean it will get spent; it does mean that we make sure there are resources available to deliver services in the most direct, distributed and efficient way possible. Many of the services that veterans' organizations provide from private donations could in a better operating model be delivered from the VA itself; it is incumbent upon us all to examine which of those services can be handled under a better operating model within the VA system.

Separate medical care from services evaluation

American taxpayers owe a clear debt to every person who commits to military service. Should that person be injured in the course of duty, there is no ambiguity about our obligation to pay for any and all care required to treat and assist our veterans. Not for nothing, having a clear vision of the inevitable costs that decades of treatment require is a good idea when Congress is debating initiating hostilities in the first place. Everything has a cost, even the finest cause of defending life and liberty.

Going forward, actuaries in an ideal world should be engaged to provide cost estimates not just for the coming year's budgeted outlays for military action, but what that military action is likely to mean in the years afterward. There are real, long-tailed costs associated with military action. While nothing can be predicated precisely in advance, there are commonly accepted and fairly accurate ranges of estimation that data scientists, traders and actuaries perform all the time.

I know I am likely dreaming on this idea. Military action is often if not always undertaken for non-financial reasons, so debating the percentage of wounded requiring care 20 years from now when deciding whether to help a NATO member kick an aggressor from their territory is probably not a useful thing to do. No one can predict the next October 7th, when an evil terrorist death cult decides to attack Americans or our allies. Our military exists to destroy those who would do evil in this world. That is a crucially important moral and occasionally existential mandate which we must support.

In the spirit of complete transparency of public finances, these are analyses worth performing, so we know how to allocate funds appropriately. Private companies constantly analyze future contingencies for capital reserve planning. How wonderful it will be for the US government to do the same thing.

Time for Evaluation and Reform

The VA health care system has grown from 54 hospitals in 1930, to include 150 hospitals, 800 community-based outpatient clinics, 126 nursing home care units and 35 domiciliary units. It receives decidedly mixed reviews from those people who depend on its services. We owe the absolute best in care to our veterans.

At this stage in its development, I think a Commission need be created composed of military veterans and volunteers from the private sector to examine the history, current state of affairs all with an eye towards making recommendations for improvements. Let no stone be unturned, no cow be sacred and certainly no government public sector unions be involved.

I spent a long time during writing this book examining each aspect and department of our Federal government. Some of the things needed cutting are obvious – Department of Education, HUD – but many of the things which warrant retention are too complex for one person to make sweeping, definitive statements on.

The VA in theory is a critical obligation we all owe to the men and women who have borne personally the brunt of our wars, along with their families. There is room for improvement in *how* we deliver services to those in need. As sunlight is always the best disinfectant, let's create this VA Analysis and Improvement Commission with all due haste. With such a glaring need, there is no excuse to avoid making this commitment now, whoever happens to be in the White House or Congress.

Chapter 14: Department of Energy

Year Founded	4 August 1977
Founded under President	Jimmy Carter
Funding Budget 2023	$48,200,000,000
Messina's 2024 Budget Proposal	$20,000,000,000
Messina's 2025 Budget Proposal	$10,000,000,000
Degree to which Messina's Plan is Better	Completely
Should a Federal DOE exist?	Yes*

Is this a standalone proper use of the taxpayers' limited resources?	Yes*
Does this expenditure unfairly benefit one American over another one?	Yes
Does the expenditure meet the "Is this logical?" standard of fiduciary responsibility?	Yes*
Can the goals be achieved by *not* spending the dollar more effectively than by spending it?	Maybe

* Only in the sharply modified form described here.

Jimmy Carter's signature on the enabling legislation is reason enough to cancel this agency. The importance of energy to society, however, persuaded me to look more carefully at whether this beast benefits the taxpayer. The bulk of its current spending does not meet the test for whether taxpayers should continue to fund its operations.

Current roles: Throwing taxpayer cash at cronies of incumbent politicians
Proposed roles: Data collection, maintenance and dissemination
                   Big checks written for pure R&D

I have nothing against *some* kind of Federal agency involved in dealing with national and international energy issues. What needs to be pared back sharply is the range of inappropriate intrusions into the private sector that has become second nature to a big chunk of this unaccountable bureaucracy.

I have grabbed a few summary examples from three recent Administrations, one from Obama (2011), Trump (2018) and Biden[92] (2023), along with quick annotations placed against each line item. A pattern emerges which is worth acknowledging and fixing.

Below is a snapshot of Obama's 2011 budget, with my commentary appended on a line-by-line basis.

2011 **Funding Highlights:**

Provides $29.5 billion, a 12 percent increase over the 2010 enacted level. This reflects increases for priority areas such as clean energy, nuclear security, and research and development. Savings are achieved through cuts to inefficient fossil energy programs.	More Climate Hysteria Apocalypse Church religious incantations.
• Doubles the number of Energy Innovation Hubs, adding three areas of research to focus on critical materials including rare earth materials, battery and energy storage, and new grid technologies and systems to help Smart Grid and improve energy transmission efficiency.	Excellent use of taxpayer dollars into fundamental and applied research.
• Positions the United States to lead in the clean energy economy by providing $5.4 billion for long-term research and development at the Office of Science and $550 million for the Advanced Research Projects Agency–Energy.	All research projects need to be examined carefully by bipartisan and public-private committees. Federal research needs to be sharply curtailed.
• Makes a significant commitment to U.S. energy technology leadership, more than doubling energy efficiency research, development, and deployment and increasing renewable energy investments by over 70 percent.	Nonsense.
• Initiates a public-private effort to reduce energy usage in our Nation's commercial buildings by 20 percent by 2020. The Department of Energy's programs include a "Race to Green" grant competition and a pilot program to provide retrofit loan guarantees that will focus on universities and hospitals. These programs complement an expanded and redesigned tax incentive for commercial building upgrades.	More nonsense.
• Helps reach the goal of one million advanced technology vehicles on the road by 2015 through more than $580 million to assist in research and development, a competitive grant program to support deployment in communities across the country, and enhancements to the existing electric vehicle tax incentive.	Read: We made Elon Musk a billionaire for no good reason at all.
• Increases the percentage of electricity produced by clean energy sources by encouraging early commercial deployment of innovative clean energy technologies with additional loan guarantee support for nuclear power plants and innovative energy efficiency and renewable energy projects. This financing support complements tax incentives (e.g.,	Yawn. Scrap all these focused "tax incentives" which do nothing but distort markets and enrich crony capitalists willing to spend millions on lobbyists.

Section 1603 grants and Section 48c credits) for renewable energy generation and manufacturing.	
• Eliminates inefficient fossil fuel subsidies that impede investment in clean energy sources and undermine efforts to address the threat of climate change.	Whew! Ah, nostalgia! Back in 2011, climate change was a mere "threat," before it became a "crisis."
• Includes $7.6 billion to maintain a safe, secure, and effective nuclear weapons stockpile in support of the planned decrease in deployed U.S. and Russian weapons under the New Strategic Arms Reduction Treaty approved by the Senate.	Keep the nukes safe. Amen.
• Strengthens national security through funding for the detection, elimination, and securing of nuclear and radiological material worldwide.	A fine idea. Is Energy the right group to tackle this?
• Continues the Nation's efforts to reduce environmental risks and safely manage nuclear materials.	Sounds vague and fuzzy. Can we get some specifics?

Whatever the good intentions, the US taxpayer cannot afford all this bureaucracy. Private sector energy producers and distributors are better placed to improve and grow the grid without too much interference from above.

A hallmark of the Central Planning Mindset is that they can *change the metric of an emergent property*. More accurately, their folly is that they can change outcomes *in the precise way they desire*. A good Progressive believes that the All-Seeing, Omniscient Government of Keynes's Fantasy can aggregate statistics on, say, the electricity consumption of the nation and then choose to engineer a change in the next set of statistics, with little to no understanding of what drives the inputs that give rise to the aggregated figures.

Reduces Buildings' Energy Use by 20 Percent by 2020. The 80 billion square feet of non-residential building space in the United States present an opportunity to realize large gains in energy efficiency. In 2010, commercial buildings consumed roughly 20 percent of all energy in the U.S. economy. The President's Better Buildings Initiative will, over the next 10 years, seek to make non-residential buildings 20 percent more energy efficient by catalyzing private sector investment through a series of incentives to upgrade offices, stores, universities, schools, hospitals and other commercial buildings. The Budget proposes to make American businesses more energy efficient through three new initiatives: re-designing the current tax deduction for commercial buildings and upgrades by changing it to a credit and increasing the program by $1 billion; launching two new pilot projects that focus on increasing financing opportunities for universities, schools, and hospitals by providing loan guarantees; and creating a $100 million "Race to Green" competition for State and municipal governments to implement innovative approaches to building codes, standards, and performance measurements so that commercial building efficiency will become the norm. These programs build on the Administration's commitment to retrofitting residential and government buildings, particularly through the Recovery Act investments and the Administration's proposed Homestar program. The Administration continues to call on the Congress to pass the Homestar bill, which would create jobs by encouraging Americans to invest in energy saving home improvements. (p.75, 2011 budget)

Peter Schweizer's book *Throw Them All Out* is both a refreshing litany of the sleazy abuses of crony capitalism *and* a depressing reminder that despite all the evidence of this nasty behavior being in plain view, politicians and the parasites sucking cash off the backs of hardworking Americans go about their lives with impunity. Peter wrote his book, some people got a nice sense of righteous indignation, other people blithely ignored it because they are too busy trying to survive in the Socialist People's Republic of Beltwayistan and... nothing happened.

No one got fired, not one got sued, no one lost a job or (private) money, though the American people lost hundreds of millions of dollars wagering on *someone else's* potential rich payoff.

The table below is copied from Schweizer's book. Retyping it was an excellent exercise in drilling home to my how irritating and irresponsible this sleazy behavior is. I hope you, dear reader, get a feeling for how outrageous an abuse of the public trust this sort of thing is.

The metric that is relevant is the ratio of dollars raised for the 2008 Obama campaign by his Finance Committee members to the *Federal* (read: YOUR) dollars that were shoveled at the companies controlled by these same Finance Committee members.

That ratio is 1:24,783. Yup, let me repeat that: If I raised ONE DOLLAR for Obama's campaign, my company got $24,783 from you, the American sucker, er, citizen. And I got it basically free of charge, meaning if my company used that $24,783 to create a product that made *me* millions of dollars, I got to keep all the millions I made and you, the American sucker, er, citizen, *maybe* got the original $24,783 back. Quite possibly, you got nothing back at all, even if I did well; there was sure to be some Senator or President saying "well, look at all the money in payroll and income taxes this company generates. Why bother asking for the original $24,783 back?..."

And if I failed? If, say, I was George Kaiser, the owner of Solyndra who sucked up $528,000,000 of *your* taxpayer-funded cash in loan guarantees? Well, you the taxpayer took it on the chin, buddy - complete loss. And *not* just the $528,000,000, either! Nope, because *that* money was borrowed! So you are *still paying interest* on that cash, and the total bill if, say, it was funded with 10-year Treasury bonds will be $528,000,000 (1+3.48%)^10 = $743,358,177.

So, if George Kaiser, the billionaire Oklahoman who owned Solyndra *raised* $19,489.17 for Obama's campaign, his company put *you and me* on the hook for $743,000,000, to *no* benefit to you and me whatsoever. $19,489.17 is the price of a new Honda Civic, or it was when I was midway through writing this book, well before the Biden Inflation kicked in. So next time you decide to buy a new midsize Japanese sedan, just think that if you were smart and connected enough to give that money to the next President, instead of a car that depreciates by 20% the moment you drive it off the dealer lot that you'll replace in 5-12 years, you could instead take $528,000,000 from the American sucker, buy a professional football team, and have cash left over to spend the rest of your life dining at 3-star Michelin Guide restaurants for breakfast, lunch and dinner.

194

Would you like more foie gras with your Champagne-poached quail eggs and baked-in-Paris-flown-in-this-morning-to-Washington croissants, sir? May I freshen up your coffee with some gold dust? Oh, and the President called to see if you'll be joining him for his weekly fundraising dinner tomorrow night. Yes, of course, the taxpayer is paying for the Secret Service to drive you there. The American people are so grateful to you for you being you that they even requested via a White House snap poll that you be provided with a half-dozen escorts to keep you company for the night. What? Oh, yes, sir that kind of escort. Yes, sir, the whole night. Yes, sir, including breakfast in bed the following day. And yes, after last month's unfortunate incident, we've made sure none of the young ladies have a whipped cream allergy.

Table 5: Department of Energy grant and loan recipients from the Obama campaign's National Finance Committee

Name	Company	Amount from Taxpayers (US$)	State	Amount contributed to Obama
Bruce Heyman (Goldman Sachs)	Cogentrix	$90,000,000	Colorado	$76,167 $65,600
David Heller (Goldman Sachs)				
Bruce Heyman (Goldman Sachs)	First Solar	$4,700,000	California	
David Heller (Goldman Sachs)				
Ian Cumming	Leucadia Energy	$260,000,000	Louisiana	
Ian Cumming	Leucadia Energy	$1,600,000,000	Indiana	
Ian Cumming	Leucadia Energy	$1,600,000,000	Illinois	
Frank M. Clark		$200,00,000	Pennsylvania	$75,100
John Rogers Jr.				$193,598
Daniel Weiss	Powerspan	$100,000,000	North Dakota	$20,857
Zeb Rice				$12,712
Bob Nelson	Sapphire Energy	$135,000,000	New Mexico	$13,300
Louis Susman	Solar Trust of America	$2,100,000,000	California	
Steve Westly	Tesla, Edeniq, Recyclebank, Amyris Biotechnologies	$465,000,000	California	$500
Bruce Heyman (Goldman Sachs)	U.S. Geothermal	$96,800,000	Oregon	
David Heller (Goldman Sachs)				

Total		$11,346,800,000		$457,834

Source: Schweizer, Peter

The case of First Solar is such an egregious rape of decency and the rule of law that it alone could prove the hypothesis that the Obama Administration's approach to governance was based entirely on Goebbels's Big Lie. As the snippet from the Washington Examiner shows, the US taxpayer gave free cash to a company *to sell its production to itself.*

Firm Sells Solar Panels, Taxpayers Pay

A heavily subsidized solar company received a U.S. taxpayer loan guarantee to sell solar panels to itself, says the Washington Examiner.

First Solar is the company and the subsidy came from the Export-Import Bank (Ex-Im). Here's the road of subsidies these solar panels followed from Perrysburg, Ohio, to St. Clair, Ontario.

- First Solar is an Arizona-based manufacturer of solar panels.
- In 2010, the Obama administration awarded the company $16.3 million to expand its factory in Ohio.
- In 2010, then-Ohio governor Ted Strickland announced more than a million dollars in job training grants to First Solar.
- The Ohio Department of Development also lent First Solar $5 million, and the state's Air Quality Development Authority gave the company an additional $10 million loan.

After First Solar pocketed this $17.3 million in government grants and $15 million in government loans, Ex-Im entered the scene.

In September 2011, Ex-Im approved $455.7 million in loan guarantees to subsidize the sale of solar panels to two wind farms in Canada.

That means if the wind farm ever defaults, the taxpayers pick up the tab, ensuring First Solar gets paid.

But the buyer, in this case, was First Solar. A small corporation called St. Clair Solar owned the wind farm and was the Canadian company buying First Solar's panels. But St. Clair Solar was a wholly owned subsidiary of First Solar. So, basically, First Solar was shipping its own solar panels from Ohio to a solar farm it owned in Canada, and the U.S. taxpayers were subsidizing this "export."

This subsidy undermines the arguments for Ex-Im's existence. Ex-Im, whose authorization expires May 31, is supposed to be a job creator, helping U.S. manufacturers beat foreign manufacturers by having U.S. taxpayers backstop the financing.[93]

The Government cannot get away from attempts at micromanagement, this time of the auto industry.

Helps Put One Million Advanced Technology Vehicles on the Road by 2015. To reach this goal and become the first in the world to do so, the Budget

---

[93] Timothy P. Carney, "Firm Sells Solar Panels -- to Itself, Taxpayers Pay," *Washington Examiner,* 19 March 2012

proposes new efforts to support electric vehicle manufacturing and adoption in the United States. The Budget transforms the existing $7,500 tax credit for electric vehicles into a rebate that will be available to all consumers immediately at the point of sale, and advances innovative technologies through new R&D investments, building on the Recovery Act investments. In addition, the Budget proposes an investment of $588 million for vehicle technologies—an increase of 88 percent above current funding levels, including a new effort to reward communities that invest in electric vehicles and infrastructure and remove regulatory barriers through a $200 million grant program, modeled after the Race to the Top program.

Why should the Government *borrow* $588,000,000 to "invest" in R&D for "vehicle technologies?" If there is an expected consumer demand for these features, the private sector will provide the funding. If not, then the R&D ought not to be spent. Never mind the insanity of *some* Americans giving *another* American $7,500 each time that *other* American decides to buy a car. How is that a positive thing for the country?

Why does Washington need to "reward communities" that invest in electric vehicles and infrastructure? Leaving aside the sweeping, Mao-esque tone (how precisely does one define the corporate entity that is to be rewarded; more prosaically: to whom is the check made out?), by what metrics are such awards to be judged? And by whom?

In kind terms, the whole thing is insane. In objective terms, it is an evil breach of the public sector's fiduciary duty to *all* Americans, not just the few that wrote campaign checks.

And in practice, it made Elon Musk a billionaire by *you* the taxpayer handing over cash subsidies to anyone who bought a Tesla.

Biden's 2023 budget for Energy leads off with his heading:

Investing in Domestic Clean Energy Manufacturing; Advancing Environmental Justice; Tackling the Climate Crisis; and Modernizing and Ensuring the Safety and Security of the Nuclear Stockpile

---

It is enough to make a brave man cry. There are five priorities captured in that headline. Let's go through them one by one, shall we?

1. **Investing in Domestic Clean Energy Manufacturing.** Nonsense and idiocy. If there were a real market for "clean energy," investors would be pouring cash into it. Energy Department bureaucrats have no expertise or mandate from the taxpayer to throw cash at fairy tales. This is classic Type 4 spending all over again; no one allocating this cash will earn a dollar more in their paycheck should all these "investments" work out well, nor will they lose their jobs or a dollar should they fail. Solyndra, anyone?
   The idiocy is compounded by both political meddling and the cultural whims of the moment. Even if we think it is a good idea to hand a massive checkbook to bureaucrats, those bureaucrats are already constrained in what they are allowed to invest in. For example, Energy can hand out billions to companies who are, say, processing rare earth magnets in a factory in the US, but they cannot make an investment in the *mine* from which the raw materials will come.

2. **Advancing Environmental Justice.** I have no words. I have zero idea what that might even be supposed to mean. Since I cannot get past that wall of

incomprehension, I cannot begin to imagine *how* Energy bureaucrats would accomplish such "advancing."

3. **Tackling the Climate Crisis.** There is no such thing. Climate changes. Humans adapt. We will continue to adapt. "Climate Crisis" in Democrat, globalist, COP-never-ending and World Economic Forum code means "Let's tax the crap out of the little people for daring to use gasoline powered cars while we the self-anointed elites fly our private jets to gabfests around the world to yap about how evil carbon is." Ridiculous and pointless. They've been screaming "crisis" at us for decades. Yawn.

4. **Modernizing our Nuclear Stockpile.** Finally, something the department should be doing. Great. Let them get after it.

5. **Ensuring the Safety and Security of our Nuclear Stockpile.** Great. Bang on. Quick question, though — why is this not the responsibility of the War Department? Whoever is in charge, keep it up.

The budget justification goes on for another 120 pages after that. Feel free to browse at your leisure.[94]

I am grabbing one nugget, which is all my doctors have told me my blood pressure can handle before stroking out:

> The Request provides $727 million for the new office of State and Community Energy Programs, which includes $502 million to weatherize at least 50,000 homes through the Weatherization Assistance Program, including $30 million for the Weatherization Readiness Fund to support health and safety upgrades necessary for weatherization and efficiency retrofits and $100 million for the Low Income Home Energy Assistance Program (LIHEAP) Advantage pilot to retrofit and decarbonize low-income households through energy efficient electric appliances and systems that reduce energy bills.

Does *anyone* believe this insanity? So 50,000 homes will be "weatherized" at a cost of $10,040 each. That will cost $502 million. Why not $500 million? I always tell students or employees to be on the look out for "arbitrary specificity." It is a sure sign of lies or the piles of pre-fertilizer horses produce.

That weatherization will do *what*, precisely? The US average for annual electricity costs range between $960 - $1,728, with an average of $1,404.[95]

In what rational economic universe would a private homeowner chunk down cash equivalent to 5.8 – 10.5 years of electricity costs, without knowing how much money that may end up saving off monthly bills? "In no rational universe," is the answer.

---

[94] doe-fy2023-budget-in-brief-v6.pdf (energy.gov)
[95] Average Electric Bill per Month [2024]: National + by State (ipropertymanagement.com)

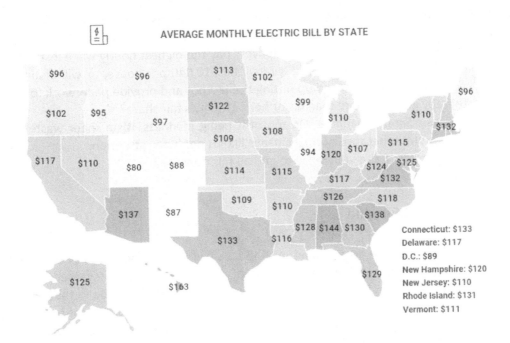

$96 $96 $113 $102 $96

$102 $95 $122 $99 $110 $110 $132

$97 $108 $109

$117 $110 $80 $88 $114 $115 $94 $120 $107 $115 $124 $125

$117 $132

$137 $87 $109 $110 $126 $118

$138

$133 $116 $128 $144 $130

$125 $163 $129

Connecticut: $133
Delaware: $117
D.C.: $89
New Hampshire: $120
New Jersey: $110
Rhode Island: $131
Vermont: $111

Then there is more cash to "retrofit and decarbonize low-income households through energy efficient electric appliances and systems that reduce energy bills." What are they smoking in the Biden White House? Would those be the annoying "energy efficient" appliances that use 9% less electricity but do such a poor job that I run them twice now instead of once?

There is nothing wrong with making housing stock better. There may even be an argument for a local utility to offer projects like this to their customers. But there is *no* way on earth the Federal Energy Department should have anything to do with it.

I have not even touched on the extra juice in that one ridiculous line item. "The Request provides $727 million for the new office of State and Community Energy Programs." So there is a *whole new boondoggle, er, bureaucracy* called into existence with ($727 million - $502 million=) $225 million worth of *overhead* to presumably send twentysomethings out into the 50 States to pester people about energy efficiency. How much carbon will all that travel emit?

I am sorry, but this is such a bottomless pit of infinite gifts, I cannot stop. *What is the procedure* for choosing *which* 50,000 homes will get this absurd weatherization upgrade? There are approximately 144,000,000 houses in the United States. That is 0.035% of houses. Who chooses? Is it a lottery? Do people volunteer or is this like being drafted, where your house is getting weatherized whether you like it or not?

Will each State get an allocation of homes? Is it a straight-line allocation with each of 50 States getting 1,000 houses weatherized? Or will it be census-weighted? Will it be granular to the county level? Will income levels be yet another filter applied? Given the DEI obsessions of this crowd, will the selection process be further racially weighted? Who wins the contracts to do each weatherization? Is it one contracting firm per State for efficiency? Or will it be further broken up? Do Energy bureaucrats decide that or does it go to each

State? Will a Democrat-run Energy Department allocate funds to a right-to-work State that does not unfairly tilt the playing field towards unionized workers? Will the insanity of "prevailing wage rules" which demand taxpayers pay the highest hourly wage instead of the most competitive be part of this? Will it *really* be $10,040 per house, or will bidding rules mean a given contractor could end up hitting the jackpot and provide paperwork for 5x that amount, thereby getting "more than his or her or thingy's fair share?"

Madness. Simple madness. On top of it being madness, it's a sheer waste of *your* money. This continues because normal citizens like us don't pay attention.

Pay attention. Raise your voice to end all this nonsense.

Loan Guarantees Must End

Could anything be crazier than putting taxpayers on the hook to pay off bad debts incurred by risky companies? The world is full of risk-takers who get rewarded when their investments work out and lose when they don't. The DOE should *not* be in the business of doling out loan guarantees like a parent of a high-school kid with a credit card. At the very least, *if* we the taxpayer continue to fund private-sector enterprises – and there are some good arguments to be made for doing so – then we the taxpayer should at least get the most preferential returns available, *not* dole out loan guarantees for pennies.

This is the summary description of Section 1703 which allows the DOE to spend your money willy-nilly on nifty new projects staff members like:

> The US DOE's Loan Program Office can provide Section 1703 loan guarantees. **Section 1703 of Title XVII of the Energy Policy Act of 2005** authorizes the U.S. Department of Energy to support innovative clean energy technologies that are typically unable to obtain conventional private financing due to high technology risks. In addition, the technologies must avoid, reduce, or sequester air pollutants or anthropogenic emissions of greenhouse gases. Technologies we will consider include: biomass, hydrogen, solar, wind/hydropower, nuclear, advanced fossil energy coal, carbon sequestration practices/technologies, electricity delivery and energy reliability, alternative fuel vehicles, industrial energy efficiency projects, and pollution control equipment. Technologies with more than three implementations that have been active for more than five years are excluded. Title XVII specifies that the Energy Department must receive either an appropriation for the Credit Subsidy Cost (CSC) – the expected long-term liability to the Federal Government in issuing the loan guarantee – or payment of that cost by the borrower. Under Section 1703, borrowers pay the CSC directly. In some cases, however, 1703 projects may also be eligible under 1705, thereby qualifying them for appropriated CSC.

Solyndra is one Obama and the Federal apparatus wish people would forget about – a $528,000,000 to $750,000,000 hole in the Federal balance sheet incurred by the pen of an *unelected bureaucrat* with no former experience in structuring venture capital investments nor in managing a loan portfolio of any size. By summer 2016, the Obama Administration's wish had largely come true. It is one more outrageous breach of fiduciary duty; most

Americans who are too busy leading their lives to pay close attention to the corruption in DC have completely forgotten about this abuse of the public trust.

As the bureaucrats in Washington *count on* our collective ignorance and plain old exhaustion to hide their misuse of taxpayer money, I'm trying hard to make it really, really clear just what they do. For those people who are not fluent in finance, and whose eyes glaze whenever someone starts talking about "equity versus debt" and preferred debentures and loan guarantees, here is a table showing what *we the taxpayer* could have received from our guaranteeing Solyndra's debt versus the other kinds of options available for providing them capital.

Table 6: Comparison of risk and return profiles of various options to finance Solyndra

Financing Option	Possible Best Return*	Possible Worst Return**
Equity investment	Infinite	($528,000,000)
10-year loan at 5% interest	$264,000,000	($528,000,000)
Loan guarantee on 10-year loan	$ 15,840,000	($528,000,000)

* I have kept this *really* simple, which will drive finance types crazy, because it's not a Net Present Value, taking into account the time value of money, inflation, etc. It's a simple sum of 10 years of straight, non-compounding interest payments in return for the loan at a non-market rate of interest. My point is to show that a loan paid back in full is not such a great deal for the taxpayer, under the best of circumstances.

** In keeping with the simplicity, I have not even accounted for the interest accrued by the taxpayers *borrowing* the $528,000,000 in the first place.

Solyndra was not alone in taking advantage of no-strings-attached taxpayer-funded largesse. The more one plumbs the depths of the Obama Administration's squandering of national treasure, the worse the stories get. While these sorts of expenditures exploded under Obama, his Administration was by no means unique in its abuse of the public treasury.

There are many groups keeping an eye on the machinations of the Federal Leviathan. FactCheck.org has provided some color on this fiasco:

> There are two loan guarantee programs for renewable energy companies. The first was created under section 1703 of Title XVII of the Energy Policy Act of 2005. It was designed to help support U.S. companies developing "a new or significantly improved technology that is NOT a commercial technology," according to the Energy Department's description of the program. It was a self-pay credit subsidy program, meaning the companies receiving the loan would have to pay the government a fee "equal to the present value of estimated payments the government would make in the event of a default."
>
> The second program was created with the passage of the American Recovery and Reinvestment Act of 2009, more commonly known as the stimulus law. The recovery act amended the Energy Policy Act of 2005 to create section 1705 for "commercially available technologies," as the Energy Department explains on page 12 of a 2009 report on stimulus funding. The stimulus provided more funding for the loan guarantee programs. The loans under the new program also came with no credit subsidy fees, making them more attractive and less expensive than those

under the program signed into law by President Bush. It was under this program that Solyndra was able to get financing, although the company initially applied under the section 1703 program.

In a March 2009 press release announcing a $535 million loan guarantee for Solyndra, the Energy Department said: "This loan guarantee will be supported through the President's American Recovery and Reinvestment Act, which provides tens of billions of dollars in loan guarantee authority to build a new green energy economy." Damien LaVera, an Energy Department spokesman, confirmed that Solyndra's funding came solely from section 1705.

Solyndra was the first company to receive a loan guarantee under either program. Since then, the program has helped nearly 40 projects at a cost of about $36 billion — mostly under section 1705. Jonathan Silver — the former director of the Energy Department's loan office who recently resigned — testified that the section 1703 program did not generate much interest perhaps because start-up companies found "the potential self-pay credit subsidy cost to be prohibitive."[96]

It is worth bearing in mind that today's horror shows began with yesterday's attempts at micromanagement. We have the DOE in large part because President F.D. Roosevelt did not want Wendell Willkie's shareholders to profit after they risked their capital to build the electric grid. The Tennessee Valley Authority was created mainly out of personal spite on behalf of the Socialist in a Wheelchair.

We get this wonderful glimpse into the past as David Lilienthal captured his memory of a dinner held on 31 April 1940 at which he spoke to the National Industrial Conference Board:

> I met a good many outsize brass hats. Floyd Carlisle [banker and board Chairman of the Consolidated Edison Company of New York] was very cordial, as he always is, and took pains to plant himself beside me and introduce me to a good many obviously curious bigwigs, who looked me over with that intense expression that you would use if someone introduced you to a notorious but nevertheless redoubtable person like Jesse James.
>
> [....]
>
> Floyd Carlisle said an amusing thing. Presenting me to a group of men, while we were having drinks before dinner, he said with a great grin, of course, as he always does when he is serious, "Fifty years from now, when this country is completely Socialist, people will say that the first great administrator of a Socialist venture in this country, who broke the ice and made all the rest of the developments possible was David Lilienthal; *or*" (long pause) "they will be cussing your name plenty."[97]

As there are many cusses being aimed at the vast Regulatory and Administrative Law Juggernaut that even Lilienthal's mentor FDR could not have imagined in his wildest class warrior dreams, I thought I'd do my fellow Americans a bit of a solid in terms of giving

---

[96] http://www.factcheck.org/2011/10/obamas-solyndra-problem/
[97] Lilienthal, David, The Journals of David E. Lilienthal, The TVA Years: 1939-1945, p.160

them – a la Barney Frank's demands for *NAMES!* – a NAME they can put to the origins of the insane mess we find ourselves in.

Pointless, Damaging, Growth-Destroying Gummint Meddling: Thy name is Lilienthal. More to the point, given the current (2024) writing, in his very own diaries, FDR's champion Lilienthal was referring to his own projects as making the country into a "completely Socialist" nation. Back then, before the horrors of the Soviet Union, Cuba and Venezuela were documented, the American Progressive Left did not shirk from their true intention, which was to turn the USA into a Socialist Workers' Paradise.

The Government Wants to Ban Your Lightbulbs and Keep Your Clothes Dirty

The totalitarian mindset will not allow anyone to make a free choice. The litany of stupid, destructive and *expensive* rules an aggressive minority have forced on American citizens is appalling.

> ➤ Federal rules mandated changes in power usage by your dishwasher and clothes washing machines.
> ➤ Federal rules were proposed to ban incandescent light bulbs, so that only more expensive LED bulbs were allowed to be sold in American stores.

If you noticed after the 1990s that your top loading clothes washing machine began to do its job a lot less effectively than before, you're not going crazy. By 2007, the energy efficiency mandates delivered to us from the Department of Energy made sure that *not a single* machine tested by Consumer Reports could be labeled "excellent" or even "very good." In 1996 before the Dept of Energy began to micromanage how you wash your socks, of the 18 top loading machines tested by Consumer Reports, 13 were "excellent" and 5 were "very good."

Politicians and their unelected bureaucratic handmaidens have basically ruined a perfectly good and useful product, all because of their fevered dreams about how much energy one "should" use in getting one's clothes and bedding clean. This particular idiocy has at least three immediate consequences:

1. Americans have to deal with dirtier clothes.
2. Americans addressed this issue by running the washing machine another cycle.
3. That extra cycle meant all "energy savings" thus disappeared.

So we get dirtier clothes, higher water usage by running our machines more than once, and that entire chain of events means the original purpose of the government sneaking into your home to tell you what to do – saving energy – failed.

On the indoor lighting front, society has come a long way since we risked burning ourselves to death – or asphyxiation – using candles or kerosene lanterns to turn night into day. Much like the washing machine example above, micromanagers in government want to tell each of us *what kind* of light we're going to be "allowed" to enjoy in our homes.

Environmental groups led by the Natural Resources Defense Council sued the Trump administration on Tuesday over its decision to keep energy-efficiency requirements for household incandescent lightbulbs at their current level.

With their lawsuit, advocacy groups asked a panel of federal judges to review the U.S. Energy Department's decision in December not to raise energy-efficiency standards, a move that could have phased out incandescent bulbs and steered consumers to longer-lasting, but slightly costlier, LED bulbs that consume less energy. Raising the standards, the advocacy groups said, would save money on consumers' monthly electric bills and prevent carbon-dioxide pollution that has driven climate change.

An energy conservation law signed by President George Bush in December 2007 set a Jan. 1, 2020, deadline for energy officials to start a rule-making process to determine whether energy standards for incandescent lightbulbs should be changed.

"The Department of Energy seems dead-set on keeping energy-wasting incandescent and halogen bulbs on the market despite the fact that many countries around the world have already decided to phase them out," said Noah Horowitz, director of NRDC's Center for Energy Efficiency Standards.[98]

Note the entire collectivist enterprise in this lawsuit. I am going to leave aside the very real consumer preferences in the *type* of light one enjoys – many people hate fluorescent lighting or prefer incandescent to LED because of the kind of light those different bulbs emit. A rational nation with free choices in a free market would let competition for consumer dollars determine the range of bulbs on offer.

But the Orwellian-named "Natural Resources Defense Council" has determined that *in aggregate,* one type of bulb – LED – will *collectively* consume less electricity over time than another, so therefore in true collectivist, Progressive, totalitarian control fashion, we are to ignore individual rights and choices in favor of the holy collective.

Their entire lie above motivations is exposed in their claim that mandating LED bulbs – which are more expensive to buy but cheaper to power – will save consumers money on their monthly electricity bills. Well, maybe overall, but definitely not on an individual level. The comparison between bulbs depends on the given consumer using the different types of bulbs in the same socket *for the entire life of the light bulb.* I don't know what percentage of users that it, but it's definitely not 100%.

LED bulbs can last seven years. That's great news if you know for sure you will be living in the same place for seven years. What about the college student with two years left to go on her degree, who goes shopping for replacement bulbs for her off-campus apartment she's renting? What about *any* renter, whose average stay in a given rental home is under seven years? Should that person be forced to buy a more expensive light bulb three months before their lease is up because the NRDC wants lower electricity bills *collectively?*

Is the NRDC raising a "Renter Compensation Fund," to which any one of tens of millions of Americans can apply for compensation for having been forced to buy a $6 light

[98]   https://www.wsj.com/articles/environmental-groups-sue-u-s-over-lightbulb-energy-standards-11582671309?mod=hp_listb_pos4

bulb when a perfectly excellent incandescent version used to be available for $1.20? Somehow I doubt it.

To be doubly extra special sure that we dumb people understand how *crucial* it is that we be denied yet another consumer choice in a formerly-free market, they are sure to add on that "bad" choices in terms of what kind of light bulb you use make you guilty of contributing to "climate change."

Enough of *all* this micromanaging of product characteristics, from light bulbs to dishwashers to automobiles to semi-automatic rifles.

Federal Energy Regulatory Commission (FERC)

Year Founded	1 October 1977
Founded under President	Jimmy Carter
Funding Budget 2023	$508,400,000
Messina's 2024 Budget Proposal	$75,000,000*
Messina's 2025 Budget Proposal	$0
Degree to which Messina's Plan is Better	Completely & Utterly
Should FERC exist?	No.

* Wind down budget to lay everyone off while a bipartisan, public-private Committee is pulled together to decide what should take its place to perform a very few tasks like pipeline inspections, which could well be handled in a small, focused area within the Dept of Energy.

These people need to be reined in immediately. Jimmy Carter's signature is like the Mark of Cain – it alone suffices to determine decisive action.

The Federal Energy Regulatory Commission, or FERC, is an independent agency that regulates the interstate transmission of natural gas, oil, and electricity. FERC also regulates natural gas and hydropower projects. Sounds bland, huh?

FERC has the amazing skill of angering everybody across the political spectrum. The environmental Left – broadly speaking – along with the acolytes of the Climate Hysteria Apocalypse Church scream, yell and sue FERC for the grave sin of helping companies transmit natural gas and electricity around the nation for people to use.

Rational market participants trading in energy markets loathe FERC for using its fake Administrative Courts to enforce poorly worded rules to slap $500 million fines on companies for participating in supposedly free energy markets in the US.

It's got to go. It serves no useful purpose, aside – potentially – from some civil engineering tasks associated with the examination of pipeline infrastructure and the like. But all their nonsense associated with their ham-handed "regulation" of electricity trading markets is a dead weight drag on the economy and serves no useful purpose. If someone can find a reason for such regulation, it should be turned over to the revamped, merged SEC and CFTC.

As with many of the examples of Terrible Ideas which morphed into Permanent Leeches on the Body Politic, this sprang from the New Deal.

We have here a quote from the personal diary of the first leader of the Tennessee Valley Authority – the model of destroying private energy markets – from 5 June 1940:

> Reread Brooks Adams' *The Theory of Social Revolutions* this afternoon, sitting in our car on the overlook above Norris Dam. The last time I read it I was a sophomore or junior in college, more than twenty years ago. What a different meaning and content the very same words can have! I ought to read it again twenty years hence. Administrative experience and the intensity of thinking about the issue of governmental action versus "free enterprise" make the book stimulating and give me a considerable feeling of confidence that the force of events is on "my" side.

Lest the dear reader think I am quoting at random, rest assured I am trying to demonstrate that ideas matter. Specifically, bad ideas matter, because the longer they go unchallenged, the more they appear normal and people stop questioning them.

Governmental bureaucrats have become the modern priesthood. They are *utterly convinced* they are on the side of the Light and the Good – in large measure because of self-interested government propaganda going all the way back to FDR, who had it pumped out incessantly, in between seedy car rides with his mistress cousin.

In the "market" for electricity, the tradition of Socialist control of assets is long and deep, stretching back to the TVA. In an example taken at random of the attitude of government bureaucrats to their lofty position, I heard an almost perfect statement made in Washington, DC in [July 2014, I think] by Colette D. Honorable, who became a FERC Commissioner for the term 5 January 2015 – 30 June 2017. At the time I heard her, she was the Chairman of the Arkansas Public Service Commission, and in that role was giving a talk at the annual NARUC (National Association of Regulatory Utility Commissioners) convention.

The speaker just prior to her on the podium whose name I cannot recall made some comments about wasteful government expenditures, highlighting in particular what many Americans came to know as "ObamaPhone" due to one of the best videos ever uploaded to YouTube during the 2014 Presidential election – the policy of shoveling taxpayer cash[99] at some Americans for the "right" to have a mobile phone. Ms. Honorable got up after him and responded to his comments by saying basically that she'd talk to him offline later about this, and that he'd have a different view *if he knew how much good the "free" phone program was doing.*

That right there is the almost perfect example of the original sin of Tax-and-Spend Socialists – focusing *solely* on the benefits to the recipient, without balancing that judgment by examining whether the *cost* to others is justified. It is *obvious* that the person getting a "free" phone derives great benefit from having the phone. What is far less obvious is that everyone else should be paying for it.

An even better example came in my own hometown. I was delighted to be invited to the celebratory dinner at the Empire State Building, to mark the retrofitting of that landmark in partnership with the Rocky Mountain Institute.

As I was wandering around the pre-event cocktail hour, mingling with the other guests, I came upon a man standing alone near an exhibit and introduced myself. He was

---

[99] Some persnickety commentators have tried to "correct" lying, mean-spirited commentators like me by claiming that this program – officially called SafeLink Wireless – is not paid for with tax dollars, which is supposed to make us back off criticisms of this terrible abuse of governmental power. While technically true in that the cash does not come from government tax receipts, it does come from Americans who are forced to pay a "universal service fee," which is tacked onto your phone bill, the cash from which is funneled to *yet another* governmental beast – the Universal Service Administrative Company set up by the Federal Communications Commission. So, it's a tax – it's a fee you are forced to pay, layered on top of your mobile phone service, the cash from which fattens bureaucrats' pensions and then gives free mobile phone service to other people who don't have to pay for it. The mobile carriers are happy to collude in this theft, as a portion of the cash they collect comes right back to them when they provide phone service to the SafeLink Wireless program recipients.

not wearing a name tag and I found it a little strange that he did not proffer his name in response to my own, but in the course of a lifetime of cocktail parties, I have developed the skills necessary to plow on with the social niceties even when my counterpart drops the conversational ball.

As the evening was in honor of Amory Lovins, the founder of RMI, I asked my interlocutor how he was involved with the organization. He responded enthusiastically, by saying he'd been involved with Mr. Lovins and RMI for decades, ever since they had helped him sue to stop a coal power plant then being proposed in Arizona. I, naturally enough, followed up this line of conversation in true Dale Carnegie fashion, by saying, "Oh, so you're from Arizona?"

To which, he gave me a very strange look and said, "No, I'm from Washington." As I was struggling to find something to say in response to this, the man's very nice wife appeared and introduced herself. As I was telling her my name, I said to her husband that I was sorry but I hadn't caught his name and what company he was with, because it was so loud in here (it wasn't).

It turns out that the man with whom I was having this odd conversation was the Chairman of FERC, Jon Wellinghof, who clearly had been laboring under the idea that I knew who he was, which was why he was not wearing a nametag and why he did not offer his name in reply to my introduction.

I tell this story *not* as a personal criticism of Mr. Wellinghof's social graces; he seemed like a nice guy, nor those of his wife who was a very engaging conversationalist. Once I knew who he was, his previously odd behavior made all the sense in the world. As Chairman of FERC, he was used to being approached for a range of self-interested reasons. In a roomful of energy-related executives, it was reasonable of him to expect that I was just another person looking to curry favor with FERC.

I of course was not trying to get something from him; I was just wandering around the room saying hello to people who were not engaged in a conversation – and the reason he was not has a lot to do with our insane system of government. As a colleague from Duke Energy – who overheard the whole conversation and couldn't stop laughing – told me later, if an energy company executive has a conversation – no matter how benign and even in a cocktail party context – with a FERC commissioner, that executive must file a whole pile of paperwork about it as soon as (s)he gets back into the office. So, it's easier on the whole *not* to say hello to the FERC Chairman at an event like that, which probably explains why he was standing alone in the first place.

What I *do* find objectionable, what I *am* criticizing Wellinghof for – and largely what this whole book is about – is the conceit of someone living in Washington, who recruits someone else in Colorado to collaborate on an effort to stop construction of an electricity generation plant in Arizona, all based on an ideological hatred of coal, an immensely useful mineral of great importance economically to millions of Americans. It was especially objectionable once I knew that the man telling me of his decades-long opposition to coal was the head of FERC, an agency which *should* be ideologically-neutral in its approach to its mission which is *supposed to be* to act as "an independent agency that regulates the interstate transmission of electricity, natural gas and oil."[100]

His policy leanings mean that he was in a position to impose serious economic burdens on all American taxpayers, 98% of whom don't even know his role exists. By eschewing coal or oil-fired plants for, say, wind and solar energy, financial distortions are placed between energy consumers and their – now restricted by arbitrary policy fiat – producers. Such "policy choices" are a burdensome, retrogressive tax which disproportionately hurts households who make less income than others.

[T]he most destructive consequence of wind and solar power result from periods of oversupply.

Coal and gas generating plants have to be kept on standby and ramped up to cover the shortfall resulting from still air and darkness. That forces them to operate less efficiently and pushes their costs up. During periods of low demand, wind and solar can produce too much electricity, creating gluts and driving wholesale prices negative, meaning grid operators have to pay consumers to burn unwanted energy. That makes nuclear, coal and gas generators unprofitable, necessitating extra subsidies to save the power stations needed to keep the lights on.

These costs fall on everyone sharing that grid, as Europe's experience shows. In 2016, Germany paid €1 billion (about $1.13 billion) for discarded renewable output. Each year Germany dumps 50,000 of the 85,000 gigawatt-hours of wind power it produces on neighboring countries at low cost. "Poland and the Czech Republic see Germany as an aggressor, overproducing electricity and dumping it across the border," the Journal reported in 2017. Poland is installing phase shifters on its western border to repel current from the German side. A spokeswoman for the Czech national grid called the energy dumping "collateral damage of a purely political decision of the German government."
Similar conflicts have arisen between U.S. states. Surplus California electricity plays havoc with wholesale prices in Arizona and is a factor behind the planned closure of the Grand Canyon State's Navajo Generating Station.

One answer is for states to institute capacity markets, which pay power stations for merely remaining operational rather than for the electricity they supply. That is, consumers must pay for both unwanted renewable energy and underused gas and coal plants. In Germany, Europe's wealthiest country, 1 in 6 people is threatened with fuel poverty, defined as energy bills eating up more than 10% of household income.[101]

There are details galore to dive into regarding the grid in our nation. The more we allow free market forces to develop solutions, the better off we will all be. I have not even touched on modular nuclear power which should be the Holy Grail for those who fear carbon and "greenhouse gases." A nation full of fusion reactors serving decentralized locations will be an energy-rich place without the bane of long-distance transmission lines and the like.

---

[100] http://www.ferc.gov/about/ferc-does.asp
[101] https://www.wsj.com/articles/when-theres-too-much-sun-and-wind-11552245478

Energy is a huge topic. Dive in. Get involved. What I know for sure is that the current form of the Department of Energy is not serving American taxpayers well for what it costs. Let's fix it.

Chapter 15: Environmental Protection Agency

Year Founded:	2 December 1970
Founded by President	Richard Nixon
Funding Budget 2023	$11,880,000,000
Messina's 2024 Budget Proposal	$750,000,000*
Messina's 2025 Budget Proposal	$750,000,000
Degree to which Messina's Plan is Better	Completely
Should a Federal EPA exist?	Yes

Is this a standalone proper use of the taxpayers' limited resources?	Yes (my version)
Does this expenditure unfairly benefit one American over another one?	Not my version
Does the expenditure meet the "Is this logical?" standard of fiduciary responsibility?	Yes (my version)
Can the goals be achieved by *not* spending the dollar more effectively than by spending it?	Sometimes

* No more lawyers, only scientists

This is an agency that needs to be reined in drastically and repurposed. What began as a good idea has turned into a cancerous scourge on society. Rather than performing the excellent and socially-valuable tasks of, say, utilizing science and evidence in the cause of furthering public health by striking a reasonable balance between human activity and the broader environment, the EPA has turned into yet another machine of social control dominated by an ideologically rabid crew of social engineers totally convinced – but unable to prove to you and me, Joe Dumbhead Public – of how much more smarterer and betterer than us they are at running everything that impacts our lives.

Administrator Ruckelshaus was confirmed by the Senate on December 2, 1970, which is the traditional date we use as the birth of the agency.

Five months earlier, in July 1970, President Nixon had signed Reorganization Plan No. 3 calling for the establishment of EPA in July 1970.

Two days after his confirmation, on December 4, Ruckelshaus took the oath of office and the initial organization of the agency was drawn up in EPA Order 1110.2.

That brilliant visionary leader Richard Milhous Nixon created the EPA, may his name and memory be forever a blessing amongst the nations. The EPA website has a good history[102] summary:

The American conversation about protecting the environment began in the 1960s. Rachel Carson had published her attack on the indiscriminate use of pesticides, *Silent Spring*, in 1962. Concern about air and water pollution had spread in the wake of disasters. An offshore oil rig in California fouled beaches with millions of gallons of spilled oil. Near Cleveland, Ohio, the Cuyahoga River, choking with chemical contaminants, had spontaneously burst into flames. Astronauts had begun photographing the Earth from space, heightening awareness that the Earth's resources are finite.

In early 1970, as a result of heightened public concerns about deteriorating city air, natural areas littered with debris, and urban water supplies contaminated with dangerous impurities, President Richard Nixon presented the House and Senate a groundbreaking 37-point message on the environment. These points included:

- requesting four billion dollars for the improvement of water treatment facilities;
- asking for national air quality standards and stringent guidelines to lower motor vehicle emissions;
- launching federally-funded research to reduce automobile pollution;
- ordering a clean-up of federal facilities that had fouled air and water;
- seeking legislation to end the dumping of wastes into the Great Lakes;
- proposing a tax on lead additives in gasoline;
- forwarding to Congress a plan to tighten safeguards on the seaborne transportation of oil; and
- approving a National Contingency Plan for the treatment of oil spills.

Around the same time, President Nixon also created a council in part to consider how to organize federal government programs designed to reduce pollution, so that those programs could efficiently address the goals laid out in his message on the environment.

Following the council's recommendations, the president sent to Congress a plan to consolidate many environmental responsibilities of the federal government under one agency, a new Environmental Protection Agency. This reorganization would permit response to environmental problems in a manner beyond the previous capability of government pollution control programs:

- The EPA would have the capacity to do research on important pollutants irrespective of the media in which they appear, and on the impact of these pollutants on the total environment.
- Both by itself and together with other agencies, the EPA would monitor the condition of the environment--biological as well as physical.
- With these data, the EPA would be able to establish quantitative "environmental baselines"--critical for efforts to measure adequately the success or failure of pollution abatement efforts.
- The EPA would be able--in concert with the states--to set and enforce standards for air and water quality and for individual pollutants.

- Industries seeking to minimize the adverse impact of their activities on the environment would be assured of consistent standards covering the full range of their waste disposal problems.
- As states developed and expanded their own pollution control programs, they would be able to look to one agency to support their efforts with financial and technical assistance and training.

After conducting hearings during that summer, the House and Senate approved the proposal. The agency's first Administrator, William Ruckelshaus, took the oath of office on December 4, 1970.

Over the years, the EPA has done some wonderful work to improve the health of our environment and of our citizens. Sadly, it has gone off track a bit into partisan la-la land and needs to be brought to heel. We need and want an EPA chock full of talented scientists. We do not need one more agency staffed by lawyers whose only solution to any problem real or imagined is to sue and prosecute.

Obama's first head of the EPA was a woman named Lisa Jackson who, simply put, did not do her job as head of the New Jersey EPA before jumping at the chance to have a larger bully pulpit to pester hardworking Americans for little to no valid reason.

The *first time* I'd heard of this woman I was sitting in traffic along a highly, ahem, scenic stretch of River Road in Edgewater, NJ, stopped at a red light on the way to Mitsuwa, the Japanese specialty foods market. *Right outside my car window* was an untreated Superfund site between the roadway and the Hudson River. This Superfund site had been sitting there for the duration of Lisa Jackson's tenure at the New Jersey EPA and she had done nothing about it. On the radio was a news broadcast with this very woman intoning smugly about how she was going to work for Obama by cleaning up America's environment.

If irony could be bottled, that moment would have been a fine vintage.

While it's important to ground this work in examples of actions taken or opportunities missed, I've tried hard to make this a useful, readable book no matter which Administration is in office. If I could ask for *one* thing to come from publishing this book to justify all the time and expense incurred in researching and writing it, it would be to leave my fellow citizens with a handy guide against which to judge the claims of whichever cast of folks is sitting with fancy titles throughout our (ever-shrinking, G-d willing) government. As I write this, I have kept near to hand Walter Bagehot's *The English Constitution*. While an enormously erudite and enlightening book, it's also a bit too historically grounded, a bit of "wise chat" that depends upon one's understanding the context and characters about which he is writing.

For those who do not love constant footnote references, I have tried mightily when introducing the *dramatis personae* to always provide a summary of who they are and why they were so lucky to grace these pages. I'm providing them immortality, so they should be delighted to be so included. I make no claims whatsoever about Lisa Jackson as a human being; as one my former employees, I grade her performance at the EPA as a solid F.

As ever, there are countless anecdotes from which to choose when highlighting how abusive governmental agencies run roughshod over decent American citizens. I chose to print this one *in toto* because it provides such a perfect picture of the horrendous abuses inflicted on good Americans by an overreaching, all-powerful, unaccountable, *unelected* bureaucratic state. Here thankfully the Supreme Court does the right thing and rules against the evil, mean-spirited officials at the EPA who apparently get great delight out of abusing viciously a taxpaying couple who *thought* they were "free" to buy a piece of land and build a house on it. Silly fools – don't they know they're just puppets of the Administrative State and should bow and scrape and beg before their bureaucratic "superiors?"

Have a read for yourself:

Court backs Idaho couple in battle with EPA

By Valerie Richardson
The Washington Times Wednesday, March 21, 2012

An Idaho couple facing ruinous fines for attempting to build a home on private property that the federal government considered protected wetlands may challenge an order from the Environmental Protection Agency, the Supreme Court ruled Wednesday in a unanimous decision.

The case was considered the most significant property rights case on the high court's docket this year, with the potential to change the balance of power between landowners and the EPA in disputes over land use, development and the enforcement of environmental regulations.

Critics called the EPA action a clear example of overreach, as the property in question was a small vacant lot in the middle of an established residential subdivision in the Idaho Panhandle. The government argued that allowing EPA compliance orders to be challenged in court could severely delay actions needed to prevent imminent ecological disasters.

Justice Antonin Scalia, writing for the court, said that Michael and Chantell Sackett are entitled to appeal the EPA order, rejecting the agency's argument that allowing landowners timely challenges to its decisions would undermine its ability to protect sensitive wetlands.

"The [law's] presumption of judicial review is a repudiation of the principle that efficiency of regulation conquers all," Mr. Scalia said in the decision. "And there is no reason to think that the Clean Water Act was uniquely designed to enable the strong-arming of regulated parties into 'voluntary compliance' without the opportunity for judicial review - even judicial review of the question whether the regulated party is within the EPA's jurisdiction."

The EPA issues nearly 3,000 administrative compliance orders a year that call on suspected violators of environmental laws to stop what they're doing and repair the harm they've caused. Major business groups, homebuilders, road builders and agricultural interests all came out against the EPA in the case.

Mr. Sackett said the Supreme Court ruling affirmed his belief that "the EPA is not a law unto itself."

"The EPA used bullying and threats of terrifying fines, and has made our life hell for the past five years," Mr. Sackett said in a statement. "As this nightmare went on, we rubbed our eyes and started to wonder if we were living in some totalitarian country. Now the Supreme Court has come to our rescue and reminded the EPA - and everyone - that this is still America."

Congressional Republicans, who had rallied to the Sacketts' cause, called the Supreme Court ruling a clear rebuke to President Obama and his environmental agenda.

"This decision delivers a devastating blow to the Obama administration's 'War on Western Jobs,'" said Sen. John Barrasso, Wyoming Republican and chairman of the Senate Western Caucus. "This victory by one Western couple against a massive Washington bureaucracy will inspire others to challenge this administration's regulatory overreach."

Building on a 'wetland'

The case stemmed from the couple's purchase of a 0.63-acre lot for $23,000 near Priest Lake, Idaho, in 2005. The Sacketts had begun to lay gravel on the land, located in a residential neighborhood, when they were hit by an EPA compliance order informing them that the property had been designated a wetland under the Clean Water Act.

The Sacketts were ordered to stop grading their property and were told that they would face fines of up to $75,000 per day if they did not return the parcel to its original state. When the Sacketts attempted to contest the order, the agency denied their request for a hearing.

Justice Scalia noted that the Sacketts' property bore little resemblance to any popular conception of a wetland, protected or not.

Reading a summary of his opinion in court, he noted that the Sacketts have never "seen a ship or other vessel cross their yard."

The 9th U.S. Circuit Court of Appeals, which rejected the couple's appeal in September, said the Sacketts had other avenues of relief, such as undergoing a wetlands permitting process - the cost of which would be as much as 12 times the value   of   the   land.

The government also argued that couple had the option of engaging in "informal discussion of the terms and requirements" of the EPA order, including "any allegations - believe[d] to be inaccurate."

Such an option hardly constitutes adequate recourse, Justice Scalia wrote.

"The mere possibility that an agency might reconsider in light of 'informal discussion' and invited contentions of inaccuracy does not suffice to make an otherwise final agency action nonfinal," he wrote in his 16-page opinion.

The Pacific Legal Foundation in Sacramento, which represented the Sacketts without charge, called it "a precedent-setting victory for the rights of all property owners."

"This is a great day for Mike and Chantell Sackett, because it confirms that EPA can't deny them access to justice," said the foundation's principal attorney, Damien Schiff, who represented the couple in court. "EPA can't repeal the Sacketts' fundamental right to their day in court."

The Supreme Court's ruling makes it clear that "EPA bureaucrats are answerable to the law and the courts just like the rest of us," Mr. Schiff said in a statement.

Green fears

Several environmental groups opposed the Sacketts' challenge, arguing that a ruling in the couple's favor would make it more difficult to protect wetlands and noting that the lawsuit was supported by industry groups such as the American Petroleum Institute.

Larry Levine, senior attorney with for the Natural Resources Defense Council, said in a January blog post that a ruling in favor of the Sacketts would

215

"make it harder for the EPA to take action to promptly correct ongoing environmental harms."

The EPA will be "bogged down in court, using limited resources to fight lawsuits instead of enforcing the Clean Water Act," Mr. Levine predicted. "Or, more likely, EPA will cut down on the use of such orders to avoid getting bogged down in court."

Justice Samuel Anthony Alito Jr. added in a concurring opinion that Congress needs to clarify confusion over the scope of the Clean Water Act. He said the opinion issued Wednesday is "better than nothing, but only clarification of the reach of the Clean Water Act can rectify the underlying problem."

While agreeing with the decision, Justice Ruth Bader Ginsburg said in her own opinion that she agreed only with the narrower finding that the Sacketts have the right to contest the EPA finding that their property is subject to the Clean Water Act. The court did not decide larger issues, Justice Ginsburg said.

Rep. Raul R. Labrador, the Idaho Republican who represents the Priest Lake area, congratulated the Sacketts for their "unwavering courage and selfless sacrifice."

"The federal government is an intimidating force against ordinary citizens, and standing up to its bureaucracy requires extraordinary bravery," Mr. Labrador said in a statement. "The EPA is one of the many federal government agencies whose overreach jeopardizes our civil liberties and obstructs our pursuit of prosperity."

I thought this was a compelling article to cite in its entirety. An unelected bureaucrat at the EPA told the Sacketts who bought a piece of real estate for $23,000 that if they did not remove gravel to return the 0.63 acres to its "natural state," that the Sacketts would be fined $75,000 *per day* until such pristine state of nature was achieved.

Barney Frank in 2009 famously demanded thunderously the **_NAMES_** of individual executives at AIG during the hysteria of the (government-caused) financial crisis. How about we Americans demand the **_NAMES_** of the individual EPA morons who abused this couple? One of them we already know: Lisa Jackson. But how about the colossal idiot who threatened two law-abiding Americans with an annual fine of $27,375,000 over a piece of *private property* worth $23,000? Why hasn't this person been fired, arrested and imprisoned for harassment?

Or how about publishing the **_NAMES_** and **_ADDRESSES_** of the judges on the 9th U.S. Circuit Court of Appeals who suggested the Sacketts pay *twelve times* the value of the property to challenge its wetlands designation?

Anytime someone threatens another person knowing that there is *practically no personal risk* to doing so, that is called bullying. The EPA and the 9th U.S. Circuit Court of Appeals are bullies in this instance – make no mistake about it. I bet the EPA bureaucrats and 9th Circuit judges would not be so quick to recommend someone spend $276,000 for a *piece of paper* saying their 0.63 acres worth $23,000 is or is not a wetland if another court – or better yet, a voluntarily-convened panel of five average citizens – could find the bureaucrats and judges *personally liable* for that $276,000 plus damages should their ruling be overturned.

Oh, and let's not forget the $27,375,000 *per year* in fines for not removing gravel from a piece of land that prior to the Sacketts' purchase was just another residential lot in just another residential area somewhere in the United States. Let's put their honors and the

EPA staff on a payment plan – unless they've all got massive trust funds, they're gonna take a while to pay that off...

Oh, the dreams I have.

Even *more* appalling, subsequent to the Supreme Court's *unanimous ruling* against the EPA in this ridiculousness, the EPA kept at haranguing this fine couple, leading to Judge Edward Lodge in the U.S. District Court in Idaho to *continue the EPA's harassment.*[103]

Yup, you read that right. Most Americans believe that if the Supreme Court rules on something, that, well, the word "supreme" in the title should put the matter to rest. Nope! Not for hyperaggressive bureaucrats who want to torture a couple who poured some gravel into puddles on a piece of land separated from Priest Lake by a road. That's because their tiny piece of land is on what *used to be* the Kalispell Bay Fen which fed into said Lake.

Guess how many millions of Americans have homes on what *used to be* soggy bits of ground which are now covered by asphalt, lawns and, you know, houses to live in?

A notice on the Pacific Legal Foundation's website as of 30 March 2020[104] said the EPA had *after 13+ years of harassment* "formally withdrawn its administrative complaint against the Sacketts." How nice of them. I want you as a bit of thought experiment homework to try to work out *how many millions of taxpayer dollars* were blown on this pointless nonsense. Think of the hundreds if not thousands of hours of EPA employees' time, then the hours spent taking the Sacketts to court, *then* preparing to fight for the government's right to abuse two people over 0.63 acres of suburban land *all the way to the Supreme Court,* then going *back* to the District court in Idaho *after being rebuked 100% by the Supreme Court's Justices.*

The mind boggles. Then after it gets done boggling, it gets angry. We have real issues in this nation – child trafficking, fentanyl overdosing, elected officials remaining in office – to deal with. Tax dollars into the many millions were spent harassing two law-abiding citizens over a random 0.63 acre parcel of land. Everyone involved should be identified, fired and stripped of their pensions.

In other news, some busybodies at the EPA unleashed a torrent of poisoned water into the streams of Colorado in the summer of 2015.

Wonderfully, a concerned citizen in Colorado had published a letter in the *Silverton Standard* less than a week prior to the accident.

From a letter to the editor in the Silverton (Colo.) Standard published July 30 regarding an Environmental Protection Agency plan to plug a leaking mine in the area; on Aug. 5 the EPA, trying to stop a leak at the nearby Gold King mine, accidentally released three million gallons of toxic wastewater into Cement Creek, which feeds into the Animas River, turning it bright yellow:

> Based on my 47 years of experience as a professional geologist, it appears to me that the EPA is setting your town and the area up for a possible Superfund blitzkrieg. . . .
> Here's the scenario that will occur based on my experience:

---

[103] Case No. 2:08-cv-00185-EJL

[104] https://pacificlegal.org/press-release/epa-withdraws-compliance-order-against-sacketts/

Following the plugging, the exfiltrating water will be retained behind the bulkheads, accumulating at a rate of approximately 500 gallons per minute. As the water backs up, it will begin filling all connected mine workings and bedrock voids and fractures. As the water level inside the workings continues to rise, it will accumulate head pressure at a rate of 1 PSI per each 2.31 feet of vertical rise. As the water continues to migrate through and fill interconnected workings, the pressure will increase. Eventually, without a doubt. The water will find a way out and will exfiltrate uncontrollably through connected abandoned shafts, drifts, raises, factures and possibly talus on the hillsides. Initially it will appear that the miracle fix is working.

"Hallelujah!"

But make no mistake, within seven to 120 days all of the 500 gpm flow will return to Cement Creek. Contamination may actually increase due to the disturbance and flushing action within the workings.

The "grand experiment" in my opinion will fail. And guess what [the EPA] will say then?

Gee, "Plan A" didn't work so I guess we will have to build a treatment plant at a cost to taxpayers of $100 million to $500 million (who knows). . . .

God bless America! God bless Silverton, Colorado. And God protect us from the EPA.

—Dave Taylor, Farmington

Awesome. Just awesome. If a *private* company had caused this accident, oh the lawsuits and cries for criminal prosecution emanating from the frenzied press release mills at the Sierra Club on up to the Obama White House and – of course – EPA! But because the *Environmental Protection Agency* did it – and failed to tell *anyone* for 24 hours! – I with my keen ears heard... crickets. Or I would have heard crickets if the EPA hadn't just killed them all by releasing a torrent of poison into the environment.

Orwell was a dreamy-eyed optimist.

218

Congressional Science Committee "Oversees" the EPA

My Congressional representative[105] on 5 November 2015 was holding a virtual town hall and responded to a resident's question about the EPA. He calls the EPA arrogant and obnoxious – to *all* questions the Congress asks the EPA, the EPA claims that everything they do is "based on science," but when the Congress asks – logically enough – to read and review the science underlying all their rules, the EPA just stonewalls and refuses to provide anything.

This is a particular pattern of "science as religious totem" worship that Americans get subjected to *constantly* by the Political and Chattering Classes. The EPA's obnoxious refusal to provide the *evidence* they claim underpins their often abusive rulings is its own argument for dismantling the entirety of the Administrative State. Outside of the EPA, throughout 2020 rational Americans who wondered why on earth the nation's *schools and economy* should be completely shut down were screeched at by the media and the Democrats that we should "follow the science."

What they meant in that instance was to shut up and do what we were told. It had nothing to do with "science" anymore than the EPA's appalling abuse of the Sacketts in Idaho had anything to do with "science." In the Case of the Manufactured Wuhan Panic of 2020, of course the "issue" was not public health or safety which many States and Nations managed without draconian, arbitrary and illegal shutdowns and home imprisonment-without-trial orders. The "issue" at stake was psychotic Democrats destroying the nation as their last-ditch attempt to get Donald Trump out of office.

I heap scorn in this book where it is deserved. Republicans come in for as much opprobrium in these pages as do Democrats, but in this particular instance, Trump Derangement Syndrome so badly mangled the mental faculties and whatever moral faculties Democrat leaders may have had that they pushed Democrat-run States right off the economic and educational ledge, all so they could – in some weird way only they perceive – blame their actions on Donald Trump.

I digress here only to point out the pattern of some politicians or bureaucrats of intoning about some abstract sacred "science" to attempt to shame their opponents into silence – after all, who wants to be "anti-science?" – but when actually challenged to *present* the data and conclusions of this supposed "science," they demur, run away from the cameras and if pressed, lash out at their questioners, usually calling their opponents "racist" on the way out the door.

Back to the EPA's refusal to hand over objective scientific evidence to Congressional overseers. That is fairly simple; if your boss asks you for something and you don't deliver it, you're fired.

So now we've got a clearer sense of the problems with the EPA. Now, how do we as Americans reassert control over what *should* and *could* be of great environmental benefit to us all?

---

[105] The Honorable Bill Posey, representing the 8th District of the Great State of Florida

Firstly, *all* employees of the EPA aside from administrative staff need to be educationally qualified scientists and/or practicing naturalists, not lawyers. No more lawyers at the EPA. Period. If there is legal action to be taken as a result of EPA *scientific* – fully-disclosed in a peer-reviewed fashion – concerns, then should the issue involved be confined to one State, that State's Attorney General can assign a lawyer to the case. In instances where the problem is not confined to one State, then the (revamped) Department of Justice can provide legal support as necessary.

As part and parcel of their pernicious participation in the evils of the Administrative State, any and all rules promulgated by the EPA since its inception are to be stripped of all penalties and fines and punishments. The revised EPA scientists are free to draw up that list and bring it to Congress, saying, "Unelected, unaccountable bureaucrats drew up these rules – including insane fines like $75,000 per day to normal American homeowners over a 0.63 acre lot worth $23,000 – and since they are all void under the Constitution, we'd like to ask you to go over this list and draft valid laws to replace these illegal takings based on Chevron deference."

In Homage to FDR

Here is a tremendous way to derive enormous social benefit from the personnel line items in the vast Federal leviathan. As I am suggesting winding down wholesale departments of the overreaching Federal government, that wind down must be accompanied by a process to shrink the beast with as little near-term disruption as possible.

There *are* some things which can be better handled under a larger-picture view of the country. One of those things is the management and eradication of ecologically damaging invasive species. Let's honor the Socialist in a Wheelchair and offer the vast number of soon-to-be-non-civil-service employees a retraining package involving a fresh perspective, lots of healthy outdoor exercise coupled with a chance for *real* public service.

Much as eradicating smallpox was a big picture, global goal which could only be achieved by person-by-person, individual efforts, so too can we unleash a literal army of workers to eradicate invasive species. Michele Obama got great plaudits for her campaign to get sedentary schoolkids moving physically, as exercise is good for you. Let's take a page from her playbook and offer impacted, soon-to-be-laid-off federal workers the choice to reaffirm their commitment to national service by working as python hunters, fire ant eradication ground troops or wild hog trappers for a period of time as they transition to new jobs and careers.

Think of the fresh perspective a DC swamp denizen will get tramping around in hip waders in Florida swamps, dodging alligators and mosquitoes while eliminating 20-foot invasive pythons from our national waters! Win-win-win.

Some people get a gold watch when they leave a job. We're going to give these folks a suntan, hearty exercise and a fresh perspective.

National Environmental Policy Act

The road to hell is paved with good intentions. A single road to Denver… took 13 years of "study" to relieve congestion. This law from 1970 was designed to balance the process of human development with regard for the environment.

In reality, of course, it became a ridiculous tool for anti-development crusaders to prevent infrastructure development for the whole population.

We need to create a framework based on reasonable time limits. No more endless reviews and calls for study. Whether it is a road in Denver or a nickel mine in Michigan, taxpayers deserve swift, efficient decision-making. As opposed to this endless round of nonsense where anyone can bring a fresh objection – "My dog Wiff-Wiff will get insomnia from the trucks rumbling by to the mine site!" – which restarts the review clock, we need a conclusive, time-limited system to make decisions.

Such a system must in effect state, "OK, this mining company or this road builder has assembled the gazillion pages of social and environmental review, engineering plans and studies and whatever other bureaucratic hurdles busybodies have put in the path of progress. Those documents are publicly available. The 180-day review and whine, er, discussion period has started. At the end of 180 days, the Decision Committee will render its judgment. Wiff-Wiff will have to get over himself."

Chapter 16: Federal Aviation Agency

Year Founded:	August 23, 1958
Founded by President	Dwight D. Eisenhower
Funding Budget 2023	$18,600,000,000
Messina's 2024 Budget Proposal	$20,000,000,000
Messina's 2025 Budget Proposal	$22,000,000,000
Degree to which Messina's Plan is Better	Completely
Should a Federal FAA exist?	Yes

Is this a standalone proper use of the taxpayers' limited resources?	Yes
Does this expenditure unfairly benefit one American over another one?	No
Does the expenditure meet the "Is this logical?" standard of fiduciary responsibility?	Yes
Can the goals be achieved by *not* spending the dollar more effectively than by spending it?	No

Created as the successor agency to the Civil Aeronautics Administration, this is an excellent use of taxpayer dollars. Flight paths are mostly across State borders, and the coordinated security of airline passengers is a fine example of good civil servants doing great work for their nation. Safe, efficient and reliable air travel for both people and cargo is directly in the national interest, and an agency devoted to assuring proper levels of maintenance, training and oversight is an excellent national resource.

This is the kind of utility that our tax dollars *should* support robustly.

There need to be *more*, better trained and well-equipped teams of inspectors.

There are mind-numbing details galore in any well-run organization focused on logistics, which are not worth going into here. One particular program is worth highlighting as a guidepost to the *kinds* of processes and professionals the FAA should maintain. The Known Shippers program was based on an El Al system, where basically security officers said, "I'm not allowing anything on this plane unless it comes from someone I know personally."

Inertia destroys innovation – or why you can't fly LA-NY in 90 minutes

However, even when an agency's purpose and mandate are in line with the taxpayers' interests, that does not mean everything works perfectly. That is the nature of any organization, and part of what I argue here is that more skills and best practices experience from the private sector be applied rigorously in the public sector. The same problems which plague other government entities also exist within the FAA, to our great detriment. Few things in this world are harder to kill than a governmental program. The reasons are familiar: the vast majority of the country would look at a failing program and say reasonably enough, "Oh, that didn't work. Let's try something else," then go back to their daily lives.

Whereas the people who are *staffing* the failure will dedicate their entire days to keeping the beast afloat.

The cultural changes that must come in the FAA are the same that will come from destroying the pernicious impact of public sector unions and freeing up roles for market based employment.

Let's leave that cultural reorganization to aerospace industry professionals. Let's be sure to fund it well and demand they deliver safe skies and encourage innovation.

Figure 19: Ebullient celebration prevails at the FAA upon hearing of the salutary operational changes wrought

Chapter 17: Directorate of National Intelligence

Year Founded:	2005

Founded by President	George W. Bush
Funding Budget 2023	$100,000,000,000
Messina's 2024 Budget Proposal	$50,000,000,000
Messina's 2025 Budget Proposal	$50,000,000,000
Degree to which Messina's Plan is Better	Classified
Should a Federal Intelligence Service exist?	Who wants to know?

Is this a standalone proper use of the taxpayers' limited resources?	Yes
Does this expenditure unfairly benefit one American over another one?	No
Does the expenditure meet the "Is this logical?" standard of fiduciary responsibility?	Yes
Can the goals be achieved by *not* spending the dollar more effectively than by spending it?	Yes

A number of direct budget line items are tied to "national security." As with pornography, it's hard to define the limits of what *is* relevant to national security versus what is not, but "I know it when I see it."

One reason it is hard to know how much "intelligence" costs annually or how that money is spent is because Americans firstly cannot agree amongst ourselves about what is and is not crucial to national security. Secondly, because other nation-state and powerful forces that we – like it or not – compete with on the global stage have very different understandings of their own national security interests. Like it or not, we do not live in a vacuum and for existential reasons, often need to react to aggression by others. Pearl Harbor comes to mind as do the terrorist attacks of 11 September 2001.

Concretely, for example, most Western democracies long ago gave up on the zero-sum mercantilist assumptions that underlay international commerce back when Adam Smith was writing about the Wealth of Nations. American children all spend lots of time in school learning about the Triangle trade, or at least they did before the Commie idiots grabbed ahold of the Department of Education to replace education with propaganda. Either way, for a long time, when one studied what now looks like "economics," one was studying the relative strengths of various nations trading with / against each other.

In the West, post WW2, most countries adopted freer markets and freer trade. With the fall of the Berlin Wall, many formerly Communist bloc nations decided that the West was onto something and began to indulge in some free trade themselves. Nothing is ever static in human relations, but at the time, many people who should have known better got swept up in the optimism and declared that history was at an end and we're all just steps away from living in *Star Trek* where people work for virtue, not to feed themselves.

But the emergent Chinese Communist Party is decidedly and clearly mercantilist in its outlook. While the dumb, fat, dreamy West floated along in a fantasy that China once "integrated" into the "international community" – a thing that the Chinese and many other countries simply do not believe exists – would be a nice player in the world so that all boats would rise, the Chinese Communists embarked on a 100-year marathon[106] to dominate the planet. Huawei is a national champion[107] in China, a category which has no direct corollary in the United States. Huawei is a telecommunications equipment supplier with annual sales topping $100 billion. It began life with heavy subsidies from the Chinese government. As Steve Mosher wrote in December 2018, commenting on the arrest in Canada of Meng Wanzhou on 6 December 2018 on suspicion of espionage:

> These various state subsidies continue, giving Huawei a huge and unfair advantage over its free market competitors.
> Huawei stands in the same relationship to the Chinese Communist Party as German steelmaker Alfried Krupp did to Germany's National Socialists in the days leading up to WWII.
> Just as Germany's leading supplier of armaments basically became an arm of the Nazi machine after war broke out, so is China's leading hi-tech company an essential element of the party's cold war plan to dominate the world of the future.
> As far as "Princess" Meng is concerned, I expect that she will be found guilty of committing bank fraud, ordered to pay a fine, and then released. Even a billion dollar fine would be chump change for a seventy-five-billion-dollar corporation like Huawei.
> The real payoff of her arrest lies elsewhere. It has exposed the massive campaign of espionage that Huawei is carrying out around the world at the behest of the Party. It has revealed how that Party dreams of a new world order in which China, not America, is dominant.
> The two Chinese characters that make up Huawei's name literally mean, "To Serve China." That's clear enough, isn't it?

You may have heard of or read the phrase "China Inc." It denotes a very real thing – that there is no such thing as an independent, private company in China. All companies exist in one way or another to serve the interests of the Chinese Communist Party. Here in the US, CNN and most of the media exist to serve the interests of the Democrat Party, so there is nothing new about private enterprise supporting political interests. What is different is that in the USA, Ted Turner made a conscious choice to turn his innovative 24 hour news channel into the Communist News Network as a platform for the Left wing of the Democrat Party. Presumably, he made that decision because he thought it would pay more cash dividends to him than just researching and delivering objective news reporting. He could in theory switch it to the Conservative News Network tomorrow morning if he wanted to. In China, the difference is that he would not have the choice to make that change.

Combine the differences in respect for history and its lessons between Chinese and American societies, and you get serious conflict. That is just one example of a nation whose worldview and interests collide with those of the USA. I highlight it because China is a very large potential competitor as well as potential collaborator, but there are always going to be nations which spy on us and on whom we spy. It is inevitable. What is up to us by choice is

---

[106] With all due respect to Michael Pillsbury, author of a book with that title
[107] Mosher, Steven W, *Bully of Asia: Why China's Dream is the New Threat to World Order"*

how we choose to pursue espionage and how much we should spend of our limited resource on it.

National Intelligence Program

While there is a huge need for adequate intelligence about the outside world, its threats and conditions and some ability to process raw data into potentially useful analytical material, it is a never-ending problem for a democracy to do this effectively. I don't have some magic formula for making this onerous task easier. I *do* however suggest strongly that we reduce the 22 different branches of the Federal government tasked with "intelligence" down to a handful. Not one – because nothing is as healthy as competition, even when that competition can on occasion turn collaborative.

And there are still very different tasks required, which would not make sense to sit in one department.

Linguistic skills and the associated understanding that can only come from direct knowledge and experience of a language, for example, should be the province of a rejuvenated Foreign Broadcast Information Service which became after the Cold War "ended" the first time the Open Source Enterprise. This is one *excellent* use of taxpayer funds – providing not only direct language training to civil servants and military professionals, but also as a supportive source of materials and training throughout the nation from grammar schools through adult education.

We live in an international, interconnected world and the more Americans attain and practice language skills, the more broadly disseminated through the nation will such skills be.

Given the very nature of the activities of intelligence gathering, it is perfect for dramatic treatment. In fact, a good chunk of the *structure* of modern intelligence organizations in the West was dreamt up by an author of fiction.[108]

Ever since then, intelligence-themed movies, shows and novels have poured forth. Don't get me wrong. I've been a fan of Piper Perabo ever since her astonishingly frank, fascinating, redefining-the-edges-of-the-thespian-envelope turn in *Lost and Delirious*.[109] So watching her run around every week on TV as a tight-skirt CIA agent badass is refreshing mental Doritos, and not the second-rate, Cool Ranch flavor either. But it's got precious little to do with national intelligence.

There is no line item in the budget for this. Fascinating.

The National Intelligence Program (NIP) funds intelligence activities in several Federal departments and the Central Intelligence Agency (CIA). NIP's work is critical to not only protecting American citizens, but also safeguarding our economy from outside threats to foster continued economic growth.[110]

---

[108] Ian Fleming
[109] 2001, directed by Léa Pool

Laudable goals, yes. Achievable? Maybe. Achievable the way the government goes about things? Hit-or-miss / random. That's not just some snarky commentary. It's an important way for all educated Americans – which should be *all* Americans – to think about the trade-offs involved in spending money on a set of murky activities which by their nature cannot be discussed in the full light of day without diminishing or eliminating their efficacy. Ever since George Washington used spies to gather information during the War for Independence, there has been a certain queasiness with "underhanded" methods of warfare.

There are 22 separate "intelligence" agencies in the Federal Government, which collectively cost somewhere around $52,000,000,000 - $160,000,000,000 per year. The NSA which was started on 4 November 1952 as a code-breaking unit now employs 55,000-120,000 people[111] with a budget around $10,000,000,000 per year, some big chunk of that dedicated to big data gathering and surveillance. In 2013, a low-level contractor violated his oath and contractual duties to steal a lot of classified information related to this, likely with the help of Russia, where is now in hiding. I'm not wading into the debate of whether this guy deserves a Presidential pardon and a ticker tape parade or a fair trial ending in his swinging from a rope by the neck until dead. There may even be some intermediary opinions one could form on his appropriate fate. I am not going to increase this traitor's fame by adding his name to this immortal work, but the one takeaway I think is clear is that a much smaller group of better-vetted intelligence professionals, combined with a much more focused mission would result in a probabilistically lower chance of such security breaches happening in future.

The Office of the Director of National Intelligence (DNI) was set up in the frenzy post-September 11th, 2001, with a startling lack of focused purpose, "acquired a staff of protocol officers to attend to visiting foreign liaison officials. The DNI's office would balloon to more than three thousand staff members and contractors, most of them looking for a mission."[112] Grandmothers in America used to say that idle hands are the Devil's playground. Grandfathers agreed and therefore made sure to provide as much idle time as possible, often with helpful suggestions. As generations of parents will agree, that's pretty accurate. Just ponder what happens if you give highly-educated idle hands lots of fun, invasive tools to play with.

Americans need to demand of their Congressional Representatives and the Executive that *all* intelligence agencies be collapsed into four – two civilian and two military – and all unnecessary redundancy is eliminated. This needs to be done for both national security as well as fiscal reasons. We never want just one intelligence agency. Every corporate body is subject to groupthink, a natural outgrowth of the way humans interact with one another. One tends to hire and promote people with whom one agrees and vice versa. We'll never entirely solve the problem of groupthink, but by keeping some

---

[110] 2011 Budget, p. 65
[111] Secret Squirrels *love* keeping data like this classified. Whatever the number, it's too many.
[112] Crumpton, Henry A., The Art of Intelligence; Lessons from a Life in the CIA's Clandestine Service, Penguin, 2012, p.7

competition in intelligence gather and analysis, the taxpayers will get the optimal mix of competition between agencies, crucial results-checking and rational fiscal policy.

This need for a solid reexamination of the US's national intelligence capabilities is stronger than ever before, I would argue. The intertwined issues of security and privacy have always existed, but technology has already reached a point that makes an objective reevaluation a valuable exercise. I would urge all my readers to be very careful about how they think about the relative need for security and intelligence services to protect American interests, with how much (or indeed, at all) permission should be granted the government for domestic surveillance activities. Be especially careful because *most* people who express an opinion about this have a horse in the race and are *not* giving you an objective view of the topic. Bruce Schneier has been working and writing about security from an objective point of view for a very long time and I'd be hard pressed to improve upon his framing of the debate. In his book *Data and Goliath,* he puts it this way:

> Often the debate is characterized as "security versus privacy." This simplistic view requires us to make some kind of fundamental trade-off between the two: in order to become secure, we must sacrifice our privacy and subject ourselves to surveillance. And it we want some level of privacy, we must recognize that we must sacrifice some security in order to get it.
>
> It's a false trade-off. First, some security measures require people to give up privacy, but others don't impinge on privacy at all: door locks, tall fences, guards, reinforced cockpit doors on airplanes. And second, privacy and security are fundamentally aligned. When we have no privacy, we feel exposed and vulnerable; we feel less secure.

You will of course form your own opinion, but as Americans we have historically been *highly suspicious* whenever a government claims that our freedoms are optional and that someone knows better than each of us acting as informed individuals. (I originally wrote those words sometime in 2018 or so – how very apropos and timely they became during the Wuhan Panic of 2020 when dozens if not thousands of government officials suddenly decided they liked wielding arbitrary, illegal, baseless, tinpot dictator totalitarian controls of the entire US population, all "necessary" because of a manufactured fear about a virus whose survival rate for anyone infected under 70 years of age was around 99.98% as of November 2020.)

A group of which I have been a member, Business Executives for National Security, did a study. The results were published and are available here: www.bens.org/ Have a read of it and form your own thoughts. My conclusions are already stated – we don't need a bloated workforce and $100+ billion to have a good sense of what is happening in the world. Less is more.

> Much of the current surveillance debate in the US is over the NSA's authority, and whether limiting the NSA somehow empowers others. That's the wrong debate. We don't get to choose a world in which the Chinese, Russians and Israelis will stop spying if the NDA does. What we have to decide is whether we want to develop an information infrastructure that is vulnerable to all attackers, or one that is secure for all users.

Since its formation in 1952, the NSA has been entrusted with dual missions. First, signals intelligence, or SIGINT, involved intercepting the communications of America's enemies. Second, communications security, or COMSEC, involved protecting American military – and some government – communications from interception. It made sense to combine these two missions, because knowledge about how to eavesdrop is necessary to protect yourself from eavesdropping, and vice versa.

The two missions were complementary because different countries used different communications systems, and military personnel and civilians used different ones as well. ...[T]hat world is gone. Today, the NSA's two missions are in conflict.

Laws might determine what methods of surveillance are legal, but technologies determine which are possible. When we consider what security technologies we should implement, we can't just look at our own countries. We have to look at the world.

We cannot simultaneously weaken the enemy's networks while still protecting our own. The same vulnerabilities used by intelligence agencies to spy on each other are used by criminals to steal your financial passwords. Because we all use the same products, technologies, protocols and standards, we either make it easier for everyone to spy on everyone, or harder for anyone to spy on anyone.[113]

As Schneier makes clear, change usually if not always renders obsolete the original *purpose* of most bureaucratic entities. But one thing is *always certain.* A bureaucracy is a living, breathing entity and will fight viciously until its last dying breath rather than admit that it has become irrelevant and therefore should no longer exist. Tragically for us all, many individual humans continue to commit suicide; it would be awesome if our bloated, irrelevant and damaging governmental entities occasionally chose to do the same.

Cybersecurity is National Security

Wherever I am traveling, when I get the chance, I ask Americans to tell me about their thoughts regarding the OPM Breach. 95% of the time, I get blank stares. 4.95% of the time, I get something like, "Wasn't that the Russians hacking the CIA or something like that?" Sadly, only 0.05% of the time – and usually in Washington or New York – do I get the appropriate level of basic *awareness* of the event happening in the first place.

Their own website has this under What Happened:[114]

In 2015, OPM announced two separate but related cybersecurity incidents that have impacted the data of Federal government employees, contractors, and others:

---

[113] Schneier, Bruce, *Data and Goliath,* W.W. Norton, NY, 2015, pp.164-165
[114] https://www.opm.gov/cybersecurity/cybersecurity-incidents/

In June 2015, OPM discovered that the background investigation records of current, former, and prospective Federal employees and contractors had been stolen. OPM and the interagency incident response team have concluded with high confidence that sensitive information, including the Social Security Numbers (SSNs) of 21.5 million individuals, was stolen from the background investigation databases. This includes 19.7 million individuals that applied for a background investigation, and 1.8 million non-applicants, primarily spouses or co-habitants of applicants. Some records also include findings from interviews conducted by background investigators and approximately 5.6 million include fingerprints. Usernames and passwords that background investigation applicants used to fill out their background investigation forms were also stolen.

While background investigation records do contain some information regarding mental health and financial history provided by applicants and people contacted during the background investigation, there is no evidence that health, financial, payroll and retirement records of Federal personnel or those who have applied for a Federal job were impacted by this incident (for example, annuity rolls, retirement records, USA JOBS, Employee Express).

Earlier in 2015, OPM discovered that the personnel data of 4.2 million current and former Federal government employees had been stolen. This means information such as full name, birth date, home address and Social Security Numbers were affected.

You read that right. Millions of people who *underwent Federal background checks* for secure roles or any role in our government had some or all of their detailed data stolen. That is a massive security risk to the nation – in impact and long-term consequences, the damage done to our national security is many times worse than Pearl Harbor was.

Since it was invisible, no one outside those directly impacted noticed.

We face formidable adversaries in the world. All of them have discovered that it's a whole lot better to attack our commercial and governmental networks from the comfort of an air-conditioned cubicle in Moscow, Beijing or, frankly, anywhere, than it is to pick up a gun and try to shoot American soldiers somewhere.

China in particular is very effective at stealing American secrets, both public sector and valuable private sector intellectual property. This is a *massive* topic so the only thing I am going to say here is that money spent on improving American industrial resilience, on improving the skills of our computer science graduates, our coders and, frankly, everyone's better understanding of how computers and networks operate, is money well spent.

I have been actively involved with many public-private partnership committees focused on cyber security. All of the times I was compelled to bang my head against the wall in frustration centered on the total mismatch of incentives provided by the Federal Government.

The main problems with the government's approach to operations is arrogance and unaccountability. When the bureaucracy is empowered to disdain their *true* employers – the American taxpayers – you get seething resentment and create masses of otherwise honest people who decide it's logical and moral to ignore the laws and regulations put forth by the government. The SEC was hacked in 2016 and the officials there dithered.

Some SEC officials were aware of the breach in 2016 but initially failed to connect it to possible illicit trading. After the incident, stock exchanges cited the Edgar hack as they pushed the SEC to pare back information they are required to report about customers' orders.

"Publicly traded companies know that, if they were hacked, litigation would be flying and the SEC could be investigating," said Joseph Grundfest, a law and business professor at Stanford University who was previously an SEC commissioner. "But when the SEC is hacked, nothing bad happens to anyone at the commission, and all the fingers instead point to the hackers."[115]

This is massively true when it comes to companies who get hacked. Law enforcement like the FBI encourage companies who have been hacked to come forward, so the Feds can assist. The problem with that is that sometime *later,* another part of the government will stroll along to *fine* the company who has violated Federal law by "allowing itself" to be hacked. No joke.

Talk about blaming the victim. Would *you* as the CEO of a company that got hacked voluntarily disclose that to the Feds? Arguably, you would be in breach of your fiduciary duty to your shareholders by exposing them to punitive fines from the government.

So basic nonsense like that must be fixed. Either the Feds want to understand incoming threats to America or they don't. In the real world which this book is designed to force them into, one must choose.

Lastly, and reinforcing *everything* I am trying to accomplish with this book, the best way to reduce our nation's cyber risk is to reduce the threat surface. Companies understand this clearly: If there are millions of open, unprotected ports and IP addresses facing the Internet, each one of those attack vectors into one's systems is a risk. Smart companies restrict the number of contact points from the internal network to the wild global internet.

In some ways, wildly complex issues can be boiled down to basics. For example, our entire electric grid was built and worked *before* the Internet existed. There is no reason for *any* utility or power station to be connected to the Internet. Air gap everything. Make the Chinese and Russians physically break into each building one by one to get access to the controls. Quit putting them online behind vulnerable firewalls so a talented hacker who would run from a physical fight can break into our critical infrastructure from the safety of his beige office cubicle somewhere in another country.

This is a huge topic. I've brushed across it here. Get involved. Demand your legislators take appropriate action.

---

[115] https://www.wsj.com/articles/overseas-trader-network-charged-with-hacking-secs-corporate-filing-trove-11547562262?mod=hp_lead_pos6

Figure 20: Proposed new entrance for Intelligence HQ to, you know, stay quietly hidden

Chapter 18: Department of Health & Human Services

Year Founded:	April 11, 1953 / May 4, 1980
Founded by President	Dwight Eisenhower
Funding Budget 2023	$242,100,000,000
Messina's 2024 Budget Proposal	$100,000,000
Messina's 2025 Budget Proposal	$25,000,000
Degree to which Messina's Plan is Better	Completely
Should a Federal HHS exist?	Yes*

Is this a standalone proper use of the taxpayers' limited resources?	Yes*
Does this expenditure unfairly benefit one American over another one?	No*
Does the expenditure meet the "Is this logical?" standard of fiduciary responsibility?	No*
Can the goals be achieved by *not* spending the dollar more effectively than by spending it?	No

* In the modified form presented here, not in the current form.

Here is one more bureaucratic entity that in some cases is one of the finest developments of civilization. In other areas, I would opine that the things it attempts to do are best done at a local level or not done at all by the government. There is nothing wrong *per se* with some publicly funded scientific research and possibly some capital expenditures made in pursuit of a healthier population. What has gone wrong with *how* this bureaucracy operates is what needs serious fixing.

Time after time we have seen evidence that some functions of human wellbeing are best delivered communally. Publicly funded sewers and waste treatment plants are two splendid examples of collective action that have made all our lives better.

Beyond the stench of the Thames in 19th century London, the rampant waterborne diseases which swept through the population periodically were pushing the population to the breaking point. More specifically, the newly built Houses of Parliament abutted the Thames and by June 1858 the "Great Stink" coming off the Thames was so awful that on 15 July, the Leader of the House of Commons Benjamin Disraeli put forward a new bill to accelerate the work being done by Joseph Bazalgette who'd been working on a sewage and draining plan for the metropolis under the original 1855 Metropolitan Local Management Bill.

Bazalgette, flush with new funds and possessed of a strong mandate, came up with a solution to remove all waste from London, to be flushed away from the city.

Bazalgette replaced 165 miles of old sewers as well as constructing 1100 miles of new ones. It required the excavation of 3.5 million cubic yards of earth by hand – there were no mechanical diggers at the time. The construction consumed 318 million bricks and demand was such that it forced up the price of them in London by about 50%.

The need for more bricklayers meant that wages had to be increased from 5 shillings (25 pence) per day to 6 shillings (30 pence) or more. It consumed nearly a million cubic yards of concrete. A special mill was built at Crossness to produce this, together with a railway to distribute it.

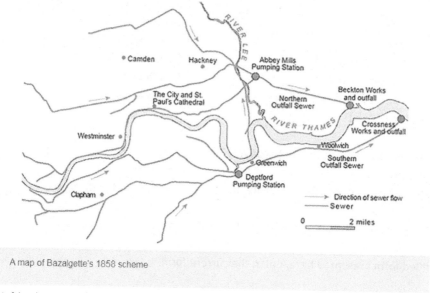

A map of Bazalgette's 1858 scheme

Most of the scheme was very carefully designed to flow by gravity, but at critical points, all of the sewage would have to be pumped to a higher level using huge steam pumps. Those installed at Deptford in 1864 were at the time the largest ever built.

The project made pioneering use of Portland cement, which was water resistant, rather than conventional lime mortar. Because its manufacturing process was so new, Bazalgette insisted on a draconian regime of quality control, with every batch being tested before it was used.

The southern drainage scheme was completed in 1865 and the northern one in 1868. Most of the pumping stations were opened by Royalty, and some of the enormous sewage pumps were even named after members of the royal family. Joseph Bazalgette was knighted for his considerable services to London in 1874 and retired in 1889, dying in Wimbledon two years later.[116]

The details of urban water and waste management can and do fill thousands of volumes. For our purposes here, this kind of public works is the very essence of what government *should* be doing for us. Public health is very much what tax dollars should be used for, whereas individual medical services are not an efficient use of tax dollars.

I provide some details below, because this area of the economy and government has so much ink spilled about it. I want my readers to understand my critiques and why I propose the changes that I do. Should all I propose come to pass, HHS as it exists will fade away to a tiny fraction of what it is today, and that fraction will mainly be a data-collection group. I propose a Memorial Statue where its offices once were:

---

[116]   https://www.open.edu/openlearn/science-maths-technology/engineering-technology/how-london-got-its-victorian-sewers

235

See if you can guess what all the things in red and blood red have in common in the chart below.

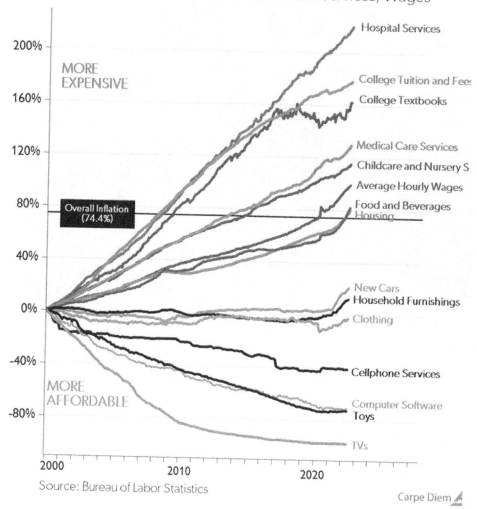

Price Changes: January 2000 to June 2022
Selected US Consumer Goods and Services, Wages

Source: Bureau of Labor Statistics

Carpe Diem

If you guessed that all those things are heavily regulated and subsidized by every level of government bureaucracy, you'd be right! The overwhelming effect that government has on *anything* is to decrease quality and increase cost. Amazingly, the free market does exactly the opposite. Every stupid thing – which is to say, everything – the government has done to "lower costs" for medical care has had exactly the opposite impact.

Beyond grasping that simple fact, every American needs to understand the crucial difference between "medicine" and "public health." In keeping with my overarching theme that local is better, personal decisions are better than bureaucratic dictates, a dollar saved is better by far than a dollar spent, and simple rules are always better than complex, here is *my* submission to the Health Care Wars.

When you think about these proposals, I am confident you will come to see the logic of the system I've suggested. Every complexity and annoyance that you face when dealing with the American "healthcare system" stems from pointless bureaucracy created by stupid rules dreamt up by politicians and "experts" who have never learned that the market always delivers better results than any pack of clever people, no matter how well-intentioned, ever has.

Six Simple Rules to Fix American Health Care:

1. All doctors, hospitals, pharmaceutical company products and any medical service or device at all must be priced transparently *before* services are rendered.

2. No discounting is allowed; no more "in-network" versus "out-of-network" nonsense. The mess we are in is because companies have been able to "blend" their overall effective price by negotiating low prices for some and then sticking others with a massive bill so it all averages out. That is fundamentally at odds with the *moral imperatives* of a rational, *wealthy* society to provide good healthcare for all. In *any other area* of the economy, politicians would howl about "discrimination" if a service cost one person more than another, based not on the service, but the characteristics and group affiliation of the customer. The posted price is to be the price for the service rendered.

3. Insurance company policies must describe precisely what coverage is included and at what prices. An average consumer must be able to compare lists of medical costs against lists of reimbursement rates from a possible insurance plan.

4. The government will be the "insurer of last resort," providing cost coverage for catastrophic medical events when they occur to a citizen. To prevent this line item become one more galloping price hike, the same free market for care will exist, with hospitals laying out their transparent costs for services.

5. One can only sue a doctor *in the actual county* in which the alleged malpractice occurred. No forum shopping for friendly judges likely to slap huge awards for no reason.

6. Due to the specialized nature of medicine and science, all medical malpractice lawsuits must first be reviewed by a "medical grand jury" composed of randomly selected physicians *and* non-physicians, to ensure only true malpractice suits get brought to trial.

Wow. Isn't it amazing? In six rules, I just created the conditions for an effective *free market* in healthcare.

Let's have a quiz! Grammar school kids do this with ease with little to no notice, so I am betting you can, too!

First, examine this chart, which lays out the costs of care for a few common procedures and office visits at two local hospitals, alongside three – imagine that, *three!* – health insurance plan options offered.

Figure 21: An Example of a Transparent Market for Health Care Services

Procedure	Hospital_A Cost	Hospital_B Cost	Insurer_1 Covers	Insurer_2 Covers	Insurer_3 Covers
Skin cancer biopsy	$1,750	$2,000	$800	$475	$1,900
Setting a broken arm	$2,250	$1,950	$750	$600	$1,400
Baby delivery + 2 nights stay	$6,000	$8,000	$7,000	$3,500	$9,000

The different insurance plans cost:

Insurer_1 $150 per month
Insurer_2 $250 per month
Insurer_3 $475 per month

Quiz: Which plan would you take?

In this example, the answer is pretty clear, even though some thought is required. If you are a woman of pregnancy age, you might look closely at the costs of delivery a baby whereas if you are a 22-year-old unmarried man who is hypervigilant about birth control, the broken arm line item might draw your attention. In the real world, there are more variables, including how much is the monthly cost for each of the insurance plans, are there deductibles, etc. Hospital A may be a mile from your home and Hospital B twenty miles away. If you live in Florida, you may be more focused on coverage for skin cancer-related costs than if you live in North Dakota, where you may be more focused on winter diseases. But the beauty of a free market with *transparent prices* is that you can make a decision.

We *assume* the existence of online tools that pull together all the hotel room prices in, say, downtown Detroit five months from now, so we can compare prices, location and relative levels of service before booking our vacation stay. And yet we have allowed politicians and corrupt business executives to completely destroy our ability to intelligently select services for the most valuable thing we each own – our own bodies. Our world is awash in the tools and insights of "big data" and the wonders of the free flow of information, yet in 2019, insurance companies and hospital administrators stated publicly with a straight face and an apparent absence of shame that "we can't figure out the price for services ahead of time...."

Demand that your elected officials vote to dismantle the bureaucracy which has ruined what should be the jewel of the world's medical systems.

As you will see below, President Trump issued an Executive Order to require exactly that, and yet the insurance and medical industries have resisted doing what *every other business in the country does* – telling you what a service will cost before you commit to buying it.

Outlaw Certificates of Need

Here is one of those party pieces you can deploy – at least until everyone in your circle has read this book – to annoying effect at lighthearted social gatherings: "A free beverage to the first person who can tell me what a 'Certificate of Need' is!"

It is one more glaring example of hypocrisy coupled with social damage, all dressed up in fancy language declaring that this horribly stupid practice is in fact *the opposite* of what it is. Politicians claim they want better quality healthcare at a lower cost for American citizens. The *only way* to lower costs while increasing quality is through competition. If there is *one* liquor store in town, do you think the price of a case of beer will be higher or lower than in a liquor store in another town of the same size that has four supermarkets, five liquor stores and a dozen corner bodegas all selling beer?

What is true for beer is true for medical services. Why should politicians restrict private capital from offering competitive services by building all the "extra" hospitals they want? In a true market with hands-off (from the government) rules, politicians should *want* more private capital to take the risk of providing excellent services to any given population. If that capital to build a hospital, attract staff and offer needed services at a lower price than currently exists in a given place, why would any politician acting logically try to block private investors from deploying their investment capital?

Yet that is *exactly* what a "Certificate of Need" does. If you and I are doctors and decide that Town B in State C is both growing in population and whose local hospital is poorly run, and therefore decide to build a new hospital, we must *first ask permission of the current local hospital.* How great is that for the extant local hospital?

To keep it consistent, let's say you own the only liquor store in a town of 4,000 people. A group of people comes to you. They represent the supermarket that is currently prohibited by law from selling alcohol as well as a group of investors who show you a presentation about a fancy new upmarket-style liquor store which will be the 87th they operate in a tristate area. The artist's rendering of the new liquor store makes your heart sink – it's a whole lot nicer and well laid out than your rundown establishment. You make a seriously comfortable living flogging booze in a place where the next place to buy alcohol is a 30-minute drive to Town D. These people ask you to sign a Certificate saying "Town B sure does need more diversity in alcohol sales venues, therefore I, the current monopolistic price-controller of all the brain-fuzzing liquids within 25 miles give permission to these two new competitors who are *sure* to take money from my pocket. Sure – you guys go right ahead and good luck to you!"

Would you sign that piece of paper?

ObamaCare – Decades of Bad Ideas Bundled into One Opportunistic Garbage Heap

"ObamaCare" is a catchall for every stupid intervention into the market between a patient and those who stand ready to provide care to that patient. It is also a glaring example of the political class's ongoing presumptive overreach of what I am preaching for here: a resumption of their *deliberately* limited mandate. And finally, as if that was not sufficient, the law is as sterling an example of the pernicious influence of for-profit lobbying as you or I are likely to see in our lifetimes.

During the fifteen years of my writing, various lawsuits *brought by multiple States* as well as the U.S. House of Representatives plowed or are plowing their way through the courts, with decidedly mixed results.[117] As an exercise in participatory democracy, I urge my readers to go research on their own each of these legal actions – I suggest you focus first on the ones in your State as that gives you a starting point should you want to add you efforts to reform begun by others.

Thank heavens for proactive defenders of liberty, I say, but I also bemoan the fact that States and individuals are forced to waste time and money fighting back against a government that seems to want nothing so much as to perpetuate its existence and increase its reach. All bureaucracies are cancerous if not kept under strict control.

I remember watching the entire "debate" in the House of Representatives, including the roll call vote. It was a parade of Democrats who each walked up to the microphone and made some noises about "supporting this historic legislation," and Republicans who gave impassioned speeches about all the great ideas the GOP had for improving the medical marketplace, but whose squawking rang a little hollow as they never bothered to introduce all these great policy ideas when they could have actually been passed. The GOP had also at times previous had control of Congress and the Presidential pen – but they hadn't passed any of the very good ideas I heard that day on the floor of the House of Representatives.

I'll give this to the Democrats on this issue: while every idea they have is wrong, have been proven wrong in terms of skyrocketing costs and plummeting quality of care, when they *got their moment* with Pelosi as Speaker, Obama with the Executive pen and Harry Reid doing everything possible to maintain order in the Senate, *they seized the moment* to ram through one of the most horribly destructive pieces of legislation in the nation's history.

Subsequent to seeing one of the most insane things I hope anyone ever gets to see again – though I know that is wishful thinking – I sent a rather strident email expressing my astonishment to a few people I've known a long time and whom I respect across a range of dimensions.

What I got back told me why bad policy happens. To my (by no means lone) predictions that the law as described was a colossal disaster which could *never work* as The Glib One – *You can keep your doctor. You can keep your insurance if you like it. More*

---

[117] 'Breathtaking in its Expansive Scope', ObamaCare's individual mandate loses again, this time in the 11th Circuit. Wall Street Journal REVIEW & OUTLOOK AUGUST 13, 2011

government interference with expanded mandatory coverages will LOWER costs. – claimed, I got back impassioned responses which had *nothing* to do with the objective "merits" of the law. No, in a very painful exchange, I got back *personal* stories of financial pain forced on families by illness.

It was a difficult exchange on a personal level. But it highlighted the appalling fact that politicians whip up people's subjective passions to support initiatives with *no basis* in objective facts.

As I listened to the frightening litany of stupid comments of each Democrat Congressional Representative get up to the mike to be read into the historical record as "supporting this historical legislation," all I heard was a parade of idiots parroting their party's line and striving to make their mark on the historical record as being in favor of something they clearly did not understand the mechanics of but which *sounded* so gosh-darned great when the Dear Leader intoned about it at His impressive press podium. What my email correspondent heard was a righting of personal wrongs, experienced as a close family member suffering from cancer at the end of a life which included service in the Merchant Marine, as he made hard choices between pain medication and leaving some money for his wife to use after his death.

Lost in that impassioned *hope* that ObamaCare would at least prevent that kind of thing happening to other Americans was the *fact* that ObamaCare as written would *do nothing* to alleviate that kind of suffering, would in fact make medical care *more expensive* and push the country – and patients – towards bankruptcy faster.

Politics is always about emotion, not reason. That fact alone makes this book relevant and my work in writing it worthwhile. In the cold light of day, outside the frenzy and emotional energy of election season, I want clear-thinking Americans to have the time and space to really think about the means and purposes of the government we all pay for.

What has proven most exasperating is the extent to which those of us who opposed this Nanny State insanity predicted how expensive and pointless (read: governmental) this would prove. Take for example the "crisis" of the uninsured.[118] A rallying cry of those supporters of State Expansion was this huge shadowy "national disgrace" of the "uninsured." When the ObamaCare rollout occurred, Obama's minions assured us that by November 2010, 325,000 Americans so devoid of health insurance would have grabbed the government-designed health insurance policy lifeline thrown them by The All-Caring Nanny State.

The actual number thus "saved" from this supposed "crisis?" 8,011.

Seas of electronic ink have been spilled on this topic. I will add no more than to echo the legislation sucked, it was sold on a lie, based on manipulation of data, fraudulent assumptions and driven solely by a desire for centralized power, having nothing to do "health" or "medicine."

If we follow my recommendations, it will be washed away as a matter of course. Everyone but insurance executives, hospital administrations and ambulance chasing lawyers will be delighted.

---

[118] *The 8,011-Person Crisis*, WSJ Editorial, 12 November 2010

Extreme Cyber Risk, er, Electronic Health Records

One of the "best" parts of this crazy law fits firmly all three of the criteria I laid out above. Based on the unproven fantasy that more data electronically available is a better thing for most if not all doctor-patient interactions, the law *required* hospitals and doctors to "invest" (read: "spend cash on nonessential items which do not relate directly to patient care") what some estimated[119] will come to $1,000,000,000,000 (Gosh, $1 trillion looks a lot more impressive when you write it out) in payments to software companies and IT consultants.

When you get an ear infection or your child gets chicken pox, do you call IBM and Accenture for medical advice? How about the august law firm of Dewey, Cheatem & Howe, LLP,[120] who presumably will be getting your call later when your drunk neighbors convince you that you should sue the doctor who tried to help you when you were sick?

Let's have a reading direct from the holy text of ObamaCare, shall we?

> "A typical 500-bed hospital will be eligible starting next year to receive $6 million for implementing digital health records, according to a June report by PricewaterhouseCoopers. But if the hospital doesn't act by 2017, it would lose as much as $3.2 million a year in Medicare funding."[121]

Something that many rational people do not want to happen, the electronic capture of their intimate health records, has now become a bludgeon by which the federal government *forces* hospitals to take serious risks with Americans' personal security. Given the overwhelming personal, societal and economic risks from breaches of cybersecurity, it is beyond insane to *require* everyone's personal medical information to be stored in readily hackable form.

Long before the advent of the Internet, and the ability to store medical records electronically, organized crime in the New York area (and probably elsewhere) hit upon an excellent way to boost their blackmail revenue. These racketeers who have always known the value of blackmail hired young women with secretarial degrees to become temporary office workers in Manhattan, mainly at temp firms specializing in doctors' offices. They would rotate through their assignments, until a vacancy appeared at a psychiatrist's office.

That is when they would begin to deliver to their real employers, the organized crime bosses who steered them into this line of work. They made copies of the doctors'

---

[119] "The Economics of Health Information Technology in Medication Management: A Systematic Review of Economic Evaluations," Daria O'Reilly, McMaster University, June 2012

[120] With all due respect to the Car Guys, who have had this firm as House Counsel for years.

[121] *Qualms Arise Over Outsourcing Of Electronic Medical Records*, WSJ HEALTH INDUSTRY NOVEMBER 1, 2010, By AMOL SHARMA in New Delhi and BEN WORTHEN in San Francisco

treatment notes of famous or prominent people – bank CEOs, corporate board directors, actors and the like – in order for the mob to them blackmail those individuals.

Now imagine how much easier it is – and how much wider the net – to hire a hacker to probe security weaknesses in online medical records.

Even *if* it is a good idea to have comprehensive electronic records, it does not necessarily follow that those records need to be centrally stored out of a patient's personal control. A patient could carry around their own records on, say, their handheld smartphone or a memory stick which they could then share with doctors as they choose. Given that a person is most concerned with his or her health, that solution surely is preferable to vast data lakes managed by indifferent bureaucrats. The very fact that the ObamaCare drafters defaulted to a centrally controlled solution versus personal control tells you all you need to know about that kind of Administrative Statist mindset.

The Medical Industry Manufactured a "Need" for Professional Healthcare

Often, it helps to step backwards a bit on any topic, to see whether the shiny ball being shaken in front of you matters at all. First of all, probably 99.9% of all humanity was born, lived and died without ever speaking with a doctor in the Western sense. Further, for hundreds of years, many of those doctors were concerned with balancing "the four humors" and other grasping-in-the-fog attempts to provide cures in the face of invisible things they didn't understand, like viruses and bacteria.

As recently as 1860, *most doctors* and the Head of the American Medical Association *laughed* at Dr. Ignaz Semmelweiss's idea that it was, you know, a good idea to wash your hands and tools of the blood from your last surgical patient before plunging those hands and tools into your next surgical patient. He had been insisting obstetricians wash their hands in chlorinated solution between examining each patient since 1847 with demonstrable benefit in Vienna, but for the next two decades, the majority of medical "professionals" thought this whole idea of washing one's hands between surgical or other procedures was ridiculous.

Now, there are tests galore for a range of ailments. In any event, the idea that humanity *needs* modern medical care is a dubious one at best. Can it be useful? Sure and when it is, it is a delightful service to procure. Kind of like an automated ice maker, but no one insists the Federal Government get involved in providing "automated ice as a right."

I am not unique in this world in having at one point been told that there was an indication I would need some tests, the outcome of which would point to either a rapid and miserable death or a normal lifespan. The few weeks it took to do the tests required to (thankfully) bring me out on the more favorable side of that binary outcome were agony. With three children under 5 years of age, it was all I could do to focus on work and maintain a smile for my family while wondering if instead of me they'd be relying on my life insurance payout in 6 months.

Am I glad such testing was available? Yes, and if it had been a bad diagnosis, would I have been glad a potential cure existed? Also, yes. Nowhere in that chain of reasoning did I require governmental legislation.

When looking for a spokesperson for ObamaCare, there are so many to choose from, but I'm going to stick with Paul Krugman, because, well, he's just so damned *wrong* about almost everything he opines on, that it's hard not to choose him. One evening, my feeling of equipoise was disturbed. I – while fumbling around in the couch pillows for the remote – was unable to avoid seeing him interviewed during the Obama Administration on *Charlie Rose* where he was busy extolling the virtues of The One. It would seem that The One for the first time in history (which, as I recall, we were waiting for, or He was waiting for us or we were all on a metaphorical beach waiting for the oceans to recede before each other to become history... I get confused....) *gave Americans the right to healthcare.*

At least Krugman is true to the authoritarian tradition. He made that assertion without irony or awareness that in a free society, *something some other person must provide cannot be a "right."*

How about this little thought experiment analogue? Sociological studies show that men between 16 and 42 are 87% less likely to get in drunken fights, miss work and mouth off to police officers when they get an effective, deep tissue massage at least four times per week. I know that would be a surprising empirical result, but let's just say those studies showed it to be true.

Based on those findings, Obama, Pelosi and Reid enlist "experts" like Grubman and Krugman to help sell Congress on a new law. Let's say the law is given a really fun name by its legislative sponsors, say the Holistic And Palpable Percussive Yet Entirely Noteworthy Demonstrably Intensive Naturopathy Grounding Act. That law gets passed and says that for the overall *collective* benefit of society, any man between those ages has *the right* to get a massage four times per week. *What*, you exclaim in surprise? There may not be a massage therapist available to massage a particular man at a particular time, or may in fact not want to accept new patients. Perhaps the man in question refuses to bathe for weeks on end and the person providing said deep tissue massage cannot get near him without gagging. Or any one of thousands of possible reasons – go on, have a stab at writing down as many as you can.

Too bad, sayeth the Krugmans of the world; we passed a law, based on solid sociological studies, that says in effect that a person's time and skills are not his or her own when his or her massage services happen to be demanded by a man within that age bracket. He has the "right" to be relieved of muscular stress, so "society" is 87% safer from his actions.

But wait! How will this work? What happens when current and prospective massage therapists decide to do something else with their careers? What happens *when – not if –* the stupidity of this means that the Feds start paying $9 per hour for a Medicare-funded massage, versus the free market rate of $70-250? What happens if there are insufficient numbers of massage therapists to meet the aggregate need? What if there are "too many" in, say, lower Manhattan and "not enough" in, say, Amarillo, Texas? Will the Federal Government start "busing" therapists from Manhattan to Amarillo? This is starting to sound like Soviet collective farms under Stalin...

Too bad, sayeth the Krugmans of this world. Sociological studies – from "experts," no doubt, who got "certificates" from a limited number of schools – show the *collective society* will be more peaceful if men between 16 and 42 can get an hour-long massage whenever they get the urge. So – in some way to be determined – any given massage

244

therapist will be *compelled* to provide stress relief. *That* like it or not is what it means when you make it a "right" to have something another person must provide.

For simplicity's sake, I am leaving out the ACLU's certain lawsuits about the discrimination inherent in not permitting women between 16 and 42 to have those same rights, and the fun we'd all have watching Krugman, Stiglitz and the Clintons saying there's not enough data yet to support the idea that women between 16 and 42 aren't as stressed in a musculoskeletal fashion, so until that data comes in, women should "put some ice on it" if they should be so stressed.

And, as always, take it as a given that the above hypothetical in no way diminishes the value to our society of those fine folks who do not identify as "male" or "female." Can a person born a woman who identifies as a man have the "Krugmanian right" to a deep tissue massage four times per week? Does (s)he need to drop trousers to prove male status? Or are we to take him/her at its word that deep down inside where it counts, (s)he experiences stress as a man and therefore needs some muscular rubbing? What about when a biological male shows up for his massage appointment and during his massage tells his massage therapist that deep down inside, where it counts, he really identifies as a woman? Should "he" be kicked off the table mid-rub to make way for the next appointment? Should the session be completed and subsequent appointments be cancelled? So many questions...

Something another person provides can never be a right.

The Centralizing Politician Power Grab Myths About "Health Care" Costs

There are a few people who benefit from the insane rats' nest of stupid rules and regulations standing between you, the American citizen and a person, say, a doctor, from whom you would like to receive, I dunno, let's call it health care. You and your doctor are not among them.

The toady apologists for the centralizing totalitarian Statists like Paul Krugman tell us that emergent properties of our terrible system are not things that can be fixed, but are somehow fixed in place by the Hand of God Almighty. Things like insurance companies standing between patients and doctors. Things like "pharmaceutical formularies" which are massive bureaucracies adding a layer of costs between drug manufacturers and insurance companies.

Krugman will tell you that we "need" insurance companies because medical costs rise over time.

Did you catch the core error? He posits as *a given* that costs will rise. But he does not say why or how that price inflation occurs.

His very description of "why" health insurance is "necessary" to pay for medical costs is wrong. He posits that "because" costs are so high, the only way to pay for them is via complicated insurance run by the government either in whole or in part via regulation. But to take a similar example, it's like saying "because" someone might get into a catastrophic car crash, the "only way" to pay for maintaining and running a car is via "insurance." Can you imagine how much more cumbersome and expensive it would be to fill up your gas tank or get your oil changed if you had to present a "car insurance" card to the gas station before services?

245

Automobile insurance exists to protect against extreme events, not to pay for your weekly gas or oil filter change. There are numerous competitive options if you want to shop around for the best price/quality combination for brake realignment or minor repairs.

Similarly, there is no "need" for insurance for maintaining one's car day to day. That is true for *everything else in a free market economy.* Yet Krugman and his pals – "health economists" – insist that somehow healthcare is *sui generis* a wholly different thing, immune to the salutary effects of price transparency and competitive markets.

He's wrong. It's better to pay for things out of pocket, with complete price transparency *before* a doctor pokes you in the ribs and suggests an MRI, CAT scan and a full blood panel. As part of being an operating business in America, every doctor, hospital and everyone else in health care must post the price for their services or products *so a customer can make an informed choice before committing to a legally binding commercial relationship.*

Crazy, huh? They should do what everyone else is required to do.

Trump Demanded Price Transparency – The Swamp Waited Him Out

I make a lot of noise, so it's quite possible President Trump heard this brilliant idea and decided to do something about it. I mean, this wacky idea of presenting prices to patients before they commit to services certainly would not have come up within the confines of Washington, DC. He may have heard it from someone else who had the equally brilliant insight.

No matter the cause, 24 June 2019, he signed Executive Order 13877, with the heady title **Improving Price and Quality Transparency in American Healthcare To Put Patients First**, demanding just that.[122] The hospitals and insurers bitched and moaned and cried about how "impossible" it would be to come up with such price lists, which is odd because they are certainly able to charge people $90 for a Tylenol tablet after the pill has been swallowed. Given their ability to slap me with wildly exorbitant bills after discharge, I had assumed they could just, y'know, grab the prices from somewhere and print them up before I entered the operating theatre.

Maybe I am being unfair. Perhaps hospital bills are a quantum phenomenon. They exist in a perpetual state of indeterminacy along a probability distribution which gets perturbed the more one tries to fix it in time and space, but the moment a sucker, er, patient is legally committed to pay the fee, the bill's infinite potentiality field collapses into a single reified state which then causes the patient to faint in shock.

That sounds about right.

---

[122] Executive Order 13877—Improving Price and Quality Transparency in American Healthcare To Put Patients First | The American Presidency Project (ucsb.edu)

Fast forward to January 2024. Just think about all the times you have encountered a pre-service price list from The Health Care Industry since President Trump signed that Order into effect. Oh, right, you haven't because they continue to flout the law.

Once again, if you work in an industry favored by a powerful political constituency, then feel free to ignore pesky things like laws and legal executive orders. But if you, insane prepper conspiracy theorist, don't trust banks and prefer to keep $10,001 in legal tender in your home, the police and FBI can come seize it under "civil forfeiture" laws created under the Biden-sponsored Comprehensive Forfeiture Act of 1984, even if you are never even charged with a crime.

"Medicare for All" is Social Control, not Medicine

At its heart, ObamaCare was never about medicine, healthcare or insurance at all. It is about completing totalitarian state control over every aspect of *your* life, dear reader.

In the United Kingdom, the stories of tragic wait times and poor hospital conditions are legion. But the main *fundamental* flaw in the UK system – which the ObamaCare trainwreck is *designed* to bring us in the form of single payer, one government health care system – is that it *literally strips away an individual's right over her body.*

Given how much noise the chattering classes and the pro-choice Left make about "a woman's right to choose," you'd think those same people would be natural enemies of a system which strips *in toto* the right of an individual to make his or her own healthcare choices. But in the bizarre, dropped backwards through the Looking Glass world of Democrat Party politics, the *only* "freedom to choose" any citizen should have is discriminatory – only half the population is allowed to choose to have an abortion. All other medical procedures are *not* to enjoy the same privilege of freedom of choice and control over one's body.

The very logic of a single-payer, collectivist healthcare system means that *your* healthcare, fitness, choice to exercise or smoke are *not* yours at all – they're *ours* in a very real, economically-binding way. Once "healthcare" is fully socialized, the real result is that "you" no longer exist. You are simply a number merged into a group, with no rights at all.

In fact, under single-payer systems, you don't even have the right to try an experimental drug or treatment. In the US currently, if you have a horrible, terminal illness which is a near-term death sentence, you can sign a liability waiver to get into an early-stage drug trial, which you are willing to do on the chance that it may be the cure you're praying for. In the United Kingdom, *you are not allowed to sign up for an experimental drug.* The reason why is bone-chilling: because if you, say, have three months to live and you take this experimental drug, that drug may extend your life 20 years, but may have severe side effects that render you, say, paraplegic and therefore *make you a burden on the socialized medicine system,* a burden which you *would not have been had you just died quietly, politely and in a collectively-minded way in three months.*

This kind of medical care rationing is not – and cannot be, under a centralized system – limited to only experimental procedures or medicines. As of 6 April 2019, the *Times of London* reported that a full two years after being told to stop withholding cataract surgery, the National Health Service was still doing so. In a headline startling in its clarity, the paper reports that "Elderly go blind as NHS ignores eye surgery rationing advice."[123] The Royal College of Ophthalmologists is appalled that because of cost cutting, the NHS wants to wait until elderly patients die before they become eligible for surgery to prevent or alleviate blindness.

Canada under the Trudeau government is busy encouraging citizens to commit suicide if they're feeling a little down and cannot pay their rent. The supposedly humane law was started to allow serious 7th standard deviation edge cases – two months to live, excruciating pain from late-stage liver cancer kind of situations – but in a terrifyingly short period of time has expanded to allow teenagers whose brains are not fully formed to call this life quits with government help if, you know, they're not feeling so positive about thing just now. It saves the taxpayer money rather than treating the patient.

This is the sort of cold, brutal, centralized bureaucratic decision which Americans can come to expect if ObamaCare grinds to its logical conclusion of destroying the private market for medical care and insurance. The Democrats have spent and continue to spend along with their dimwitted media allies huge amounts of money and time pooh-poohing the "fake" bogeyman of "death panels." They rightly understand that death panels issuing the very kinds of rulings which currently prevail in the UK for experimental medicines are precisely what central, single payer, socialized medicine demands. Paul Krugman – rabid ObamaCare fan along with any other Socialist program proposed by anyone ever and my favorite, self-cleaning Socratic foil – in a rare moment of candor stated:

> Eventually we do have a problem. That the population is getting older, health care costs are rising... there is this question of how we're going to pay for the programs. The year 2025, the year 2030, something is going to have to give... we're going to need more revenue.... Surely it will require some sort of middle class taxes as well. We won't be able to pay for the kind of government the society will want without some increase in taxes... on the middle class, maybe a value-added tax. And we're also going to have to make decisions about health care that has no demonstrated medical benefits. So the snarky version, which I shouldn't even say because it will get me in trouble, is death panels and sales taxes is how we do this.[124]

There are so many things wrong with this brief statement, to unpack its every assumption and implication is like appreciating the infinite depth and layers of nuance to the most perfectly inspired haiku. Just how much significant meaning can one consistently wrong wingnut "economist" pack into 134 words? Let's have a stab at it, shall we?

_____

[123] https://www.thetimes.co.uk/article/elderly-go-blind-as-nhs-ignores-eye-surgery-rationing-advice-bp5x77t0g
[124] https://www.washingtonexaminer.com/red-alert-politics/krugman-death-panels-and-sales-taxes-is-how-we-do-this

Paul's Fun Statement	Messina's Translation and Commentary
Eventually we do have a problem.	*We sure, do, Paul, in the main because folks like you can't leave well enough alone.* I am betting very heavily that *Paul's* intention with this very clumsy, *almost* grammatical sentence fragment is to make some Solomonic observation about an objective state of affairs which he believes cannot be altered, but merely addressed through the very expensive advice of a pack of folks who studied the same outdated equilibrium models of economics promulgated from Samuelson onwards. We *do* have a problem, but not in the way Paul thinks. The problem *is* the way Paul thinks because far too many horrible policies and decisions are forced on Americans because – thus far – we've permitted clowns like this to be in positions of authority. For those Americans who have been too busy to care, it's worth recalling that *the only private company* that ever hired Paul Krugman for his advice was Enron.
the population is getting older	Well, for now, that appears to be the trajectory, but changes in migration patterns, birth rates or repeated influxes of, say, innovative coronaviruses from Chinese biohazard labs, could alter the demographic trends. On the positive side, once Americans wake up, shake their heads free of the bad ideas forced on us by FDR onwards, adopt the rational path forward described helpfully in this book, then young Americans who can once more pay for a year of college with the cash earned during the previous summer's job, might start feeling optimistic about the future and start acting like busy little bunnies again, in the way the Greatest Generation did when war-weary men came home after being feted by Gigi in Paris and Beth in London for a few sweet weeks in 1945. But if the current population distribution trajectory continues, then, yes, the population in the US will skew older until the Boomers leave us all in peace. But leaving *all of those complexities aside,* the age distribution of the population is *not* an ironclad condition which *predetermines* whether the cost of anything – mobile phone service, sustainable bamboo flooring, frozen pizzas or "healthcare" – will rise, fall or stay constant over time. It is important to keep that firmly in mind, because this whole "folks are getting older" mantra is one of the linguistic tools our political and chattering classes use to form the subconscious impression that there is some solid,

	irrefutable relationship between ageing people and rising medical costs.
health care costs are rising	That most assuredly need not be true, which is what Paul wants you to believe. It is true now, given decades of stupid government policy and Americans' delight in parasitic lawyers and the voters' tolerance to date of completely value-destructive and cost-additive "insurance" and "benefits" bureaucracies.
there is this question of how we're going to pay for the programs.	Fascinating. Nothing in here about quality of life, the dedication and self-sacrifice of years of study it takes to become a doctor, or the dedication to purpose of the nurses that care for patients. No mention of the fact that for millions of years, human beings were born, lived and died without ever seeing a doctor. No mention of the myriad personal choices – to smoke or not, to drink heavily or not, to exercise or not, to have unprotected sex or not – that go into every individual's state of health. No mention of *any* of the things that normal people consider when thinking of healthcare. No mention of the fact that for every single *elective,* out-of-pocket medical procedure not covered by insurance, prices come down while quality rises in sharp contrast to all "covered" procedures whose prices do nothing but rise, rise, rise. No mention of fixing the tax code and solving the nation's addiction to unlimited credit, to leave more hard dollars in people's pockets with which they can make their own medical decisions. Nope! None of that, because all of those ideas diminish the authority of tinpot authoritarian nanny state brats. All that exists in the minds of centralizing control freaks is how "we" are going to pay for the collective "programs" which replace all individual choice with bureaucratic dictates. You've had about a decade of ObamaCare thus far – how are you enjoying your "health care" delivered by the same pack of fools who mismanage the DMV? Costs have been *skyrocketing* every year since Obama jammed through his awful, lie-based takeover of 1/6th of the economy. To which his apologists and the *liars who are on record declaring their whole argument for ObamaCare was based on fraud and lying to the American people* say, "Wow – but costs would have been *higher* without our passing this important legislation, that was so important that Nancy Pelosi wanted to "deem" it passed without making her Democrat

	Congressclowns go on record as voting for it, and further was so excited to force it into law because everyone would get to find out what was in it."[125]
The year 2025, the year 2030, something is going to have to give	Notice that none of these meddling clowns ever addresses *current* problems, which might actually have a solution. (See, for example, this entire book.) No – that's tough, you see, because you'll get judged in real time as to how well your prescribed solutions work! When you say in 2013 that things will be tough 12 years from now, well, that's just dandy. Beyond the long-dated, reputation-protecting mechanism, you'll note that *should* some "crisis" occur between 2025-2030, in the minds of Fellow Travelers, the "something" that has "to give" can only mean higher taxes and lower quality of care. Implicit in Paul's very being is that *government* control and heavy taxation are the only solution to everything, which would be an odd trait to observe in an "economist" if one didn't understand that one of the three core defining characteristics of centralizing statists is a lack of irony. The other legs to their ideological stool consist of appallingly unjustified arrogance and a breathtaking amount of hypocrisy. Logically, even if one supposes some "giving point" in 2025, what could "give" could turn out to be the entire, insane, bureaucratic micromanaging morass that does not deliver any actual medical care and just lines the pockets of societal parasites. We could actually have the system I propose here – which is great for us dumb working stiff Americans because it's easy to understand and based on free choice, without the controlling oversight of our elite superiors.
we're going to need more revenue	Ah ha! There it is! The poisoned, decaying heart of the Progressive's terrible belief system. With all these complex moving parts – age-related infirmities, innovations in medicine, innovations perhaps in philosophical approaches to ageing, bad policy *causing* costs to rise – the default answer to every "problem" a Good Progressive perceives is to tax the living bejesus out of everyone they can focus the

---

[125] She made this absurd statement while trying to tell us all how great tighter micromanagement of our personal medical care was going to be.

IRS on.

But there is nothing in the Constitution or anywhere else that says "We the People" must pay collectively for individual health care. That has been the operating assumption and therefore the ongoing destruction of quality healthcare in America since the late 1960s, a dumb reality we can put the brakes on *whenever we want to.* So while the Krugmans of the world see aggregate statistics about the "healthcare costs" of 350+ million people, comprising each $42 per pill aspirin administered in the hospital, or each ridiculous $275 "therapeutic massage" scammed out of the taxpayer by stupid laws in the People's Republic of NewYorkistan, or crystal chakra realignment in the Bay Area at $385 a pop, or the *hundreds of billions of dollars* stolen by Medicare and Medicaid fraud because the government cannot be bothered to check that an invoice is *genuine* before paying it, rational people see a bloated, waste-filled, fraud-riddled system – and that's before the parasitic trial bar ambulance chasers who form a core Democratic Party donor class levy an annual tax on *every single doctor* in the form of malpractice insurance premiums which costs then trickle down to each one of us who reluctantly goes for a doctor visit – which we don't *need* to pay for at all.

We can tear down the entire stupid bloated edifice, so that the *proven* magic of free choice in a free-market economy can do what it has done in *every single other area of human endeavor* – raise quality while reducing costs. So even if from a policy perspective one wants to keep track of aggregate expenditures on health care, under a truly free system permitting Americans true *choice* – and not just in abortions, the only area of medical treatment the American Left sees as holy – in medical services, those healthcare costs will *decline*, not rise. But all of that is irrelevant – because no matter what happens to the statistics of healthcare costs, those costs – with a very few exceptions – will be paid for the way people pay for everything else, at the individual level.

Also, pay close attention to the political class's constant insistence on mislabeling "government tax receipts" as "revenue." Words matter, as we all discovered in 1Q20 when the Chinese Communist Government strong-armed the misnamed World Health Organization (WHO) into

252

taking massive time and effort to *insist* that the whole world stop calling the Wuhan Virus which appeared in Wuhan, Hubei Province, Communist People's Republic of China by its proper name – the Wuhan Virus which causes the Wuhan Flu – and start calling it some nonsensical thing like "COVID-19" instead. The American Left (and therefore the Media, which is mostly the same thing) in true Leninist Useful Idiot[126] mode, immediately – during what they thought was a scary pandemic, with real people dying, mind you – started scolding everyone that to call something by its proper name was somehow – wait for it.... wait for it... you guessed it! – "racist." The Useful Idiots even got a Legislative Champion in the form of the junior Senator from California – of course – Kamala Harris, who *introduced a resolution on the Senate floor* condemning the use of "Wuhan Virus" as "racist," this bit of theatre pandering to the already-convinced dingbat base happening *while across the way, her Fellow Traveler Insider Trader and House Speaker Nancy Pelosi was forcing the House of Representatives to repudiate 230 years of requiring in-person voting on national legislation.*[127]

I digress. I told you Krugman's utterances are like a multi-layered onion of rotten ideas. Anyway, calling the productivity-draining cash stolen by the government "revenue" makes it sound like something productive. It's not. It's a tax and a cost of keeping the country running. Certain well-defined and *constrained* areas of communal concern are worth paying taxes for – healthcare ain't one of them – but make no mistake. There is nothing productive about government expenditures.

Surely it will require some sort of middle-class taxes as well.	To be fair, this phrase could be shoved into *anything* Paul and his ilk write. There is nothing – *Climate! Water! Poverty! Propaganda, er, "Education," Shoelaces!* – that falls within the purview of the average American liberal for which the answer is *not* a slew of new taxes on the middle

---

[126] Fun fact: While Vladimir Lenin called for the creation of a Comintern – Communist International – which would sow propaganda in (initially, in his plans) non-Communist countries, the fools who were to set about forging their own iron chains in the midst of freedom were actually named by Ludwig von Mises.

[127] *'The founders would be ashamed': Kevin McCarthy slams new remote Congress rules,* Susan Ferrechio, New York Post, 15 May 2020. Kevin McCarthy (R-CA, 23rd District) at the time was House Minority Leader.

	class. To be fair, they always lie and say all the new taxes will fall on "THE RICH!" who already pay 60% of the nation's taxes, are adept at skirting new ones and therefore every new tax aimed at THE RICH *always* ends up soaking the middle class because in the words of Willie Horton, that's where the money is.
We won't be able to pay for the kind of government the society will want	Oh, my! Is it just the Boomer in him that makes him say things like this on a continuous basis? Wow, the hubris! Have you, dear reader, yet noticed the so very subtle linguistic legerdemain *all* these freedom thieves deploy daily from the opinion pages of *New York Pravda* (where Krugman spews nonsense week in, week out) to the billions of hours of constant howling on cable "newsfotainment" propaganda factories to the legions of armchair social justice warriors whining behind their keyboards or dumbphone screens? "The society" does not have the agency capability for active, transitive verbs. "The society" cannot "want" anything. "The society" as an emergent property of actual individual actors may *be* composed of mindless sheep or it may prove to *be* composed of active, freedom-loving individual citizens who prize the words of the Declaration of Independence over the current whiny plank of some pandering politician's Gimme Everything For Free While I Suck My Thumb Helplessly platform. Because if active citizens vote for and demand the "kind of government" that I lay out in these pages, then not only can We The People pay for *that* kind of government, but we'll have a rising cash balance in the Treasury for years to come — a true rainy day fund to deal with those consistently-appearing "rare events," be they hurricanes, viruses or the emergency cash required to sharpen the citizenry's sticks against the next Socialist huckster that shows up. In this particular instance, Paul is waffling on about the healthcare market as distinct from the practice of medicine, though he stupidly conflates the two concepts. Paul posits that the individuals who constitute our society — I know, he hates individuality, but I'm trying hard to translate his totalitarian nonsense into real world terms my rational readers can apprehend — *want* a comprehensive Nanny State who slaps their bottoms when they're born,

coddles them literally throughout life and then decides via death panel when to quit giving them healthcare lacking in demonstrated medical benefits. That slew of constant hands-on interference would indeed cost a vast amount of cash, so if the "society" wants such insane restriction of personal freedom and collective existence, there's not enough money in the world to "pay" for that insanity. Why he believes that the little people – not him, you can bet your ass – would *want* to be taxed at 95% and dictated to is kind of baffling, but then again, this kind of muddy thinking is par the Krugmanian course.

I leave it to you, dear reader, to ponder the myriad philosophical difficulties presented by the idea that some faceless bureaucracy will make all these decisions for you, because you are clearly not qualified to make important medical decisions. Who, then, is this magically qualified class of special Americans who *are* capable of making medical decisions for you? Do *you* get to turn around and make *their* medical decisions for them? I think you know the answer to that rhetorical question.

| And we're also going to have to make decisions about health care that has no demonstrated medical benefits. | Typical. Just typical. Krugman and his ilk get all hot and bothered about "healthcare" because it's one of the areas that politicians have stupidly *allowed* useless parasites like him to meddle in. Rest assured, he'd love to make across the board decisions about *everything* in your life – from which type of light bulb you're allowed to buy, how much fuel your car must consume, to which fabrics are permitted – all based on whether said product or service has "demonstrated benefits" to you, the poor sap who thought you lived in a free country. |

"No demonstrated medical benefits." That's a fairly bland way of saying, "Oh, so you've got a horrible wasting disease and there's a treatment which will extend your life another six months so you can spend more time with your family, but it's really expensive and 'we' don't want to pay for it, and if you think about it, is another 180 days *really* a demonstrable medical benefit? 'We' don't think so; so no, you can die on time, please."

In a free country the *individual* – GASP! Can you hear the liberals fainting and panting at the *gall* of people in post-woke America to actually use the outdated term "individual" in a non-pejorative or ironic way? – makes the choice about what risks to take and which health care choices present the possibility of a benefit to his or her life and wellbeing. The United States was once a nation of free individuals and will be again one way or another. A good start is for each of us to reassert the fundamental truth that a free society is one that prizes the rights and responsibilities of *individuals* instead of groups based on race, amorous predilection or any other artificial construct designed – ironically – to separate us from one another, rather than – as the squealing social justice warriors would have it – bring us together as a nation.

Here's a fun thought experiment. Paul and his cronies want to make medicine a *collective* concern, meaning the individual has no meaning beyond a unit of expenditure and no rights at all beyond the right to pay crazy high taxes to be told to wait in line, hopefully long enough so that "we" don't have to pay for any healthcare at all. Logically therefore he should be *happy* to have the collective make all his healthcare decisions. *Collectively,* the nation would be better off if we were spared his incessant, narcissistic bloviations so if Paul were, say, to come down with migraines which prevented his writing further damaging articles, while his painful migraines could be cured with caffeine and aspirin, should his agony be alleviated, society would once more be afflicted by his utterances. So "we" believe that a $0.85 course of treatment has "no demonstrated medical benefit." *No aspirin and caffeine for you, Paul!* Not quite a death panel, but it sure would be fun to deliver him the news. Loudly. In a brightly lit room.

So the snarky version, which I shouldn't even say because it will get me in trouble, is death panels and sales taxes is how we do this.	I can't improve on this at all. I'll let it stand as is. Soak it in, kids. This is the kind of rank stupidity, immorality and appalling arrogance that gets one a fake Nobel Prize in Economics. (I say fake because Alfred Nobel did *not* create a prize for what he thought was no more useful than reading pig's entrails by the full moon, and certainly never considered a real intellectual discipline in any way.)

I've saved this bit for dessert. You know *where* Krugman made these remarks in favor of a government deciding who gets to live and who gets to die based on cost-benefit analysis? He publicly endorsed the American government operate death panels in February 2013 at the Sixth & I Historic Synagogue in Washington, D.C. Yup, that's not a typo; in a *Jewish house of worship* in the Capital of a nation that sacrificed blood and treasure to put an end to Nazi Germany – a government that *excelled at death panels* – Paul Krugman extolled the virtues of the central government deciding who lives and who dies, based on the money available from sales taxes.

Leaving aside the spectacular tastelessness demonstrated in his choice of venue for these awful remarks, the weirdest part of Krugman's sudden moment of candor is that *for every other good or service in a free market economy,* "death"/rationing panels and increased taxes are not required to improve quality and decrease costs. Quite the contrary. Part of what I find utterly baffling about the pure idiocy which seems to be part of everyone (or everyone who's had an impact thus far) who approaches "healthcare" is leaving basic economic principles at the entranceway to the debate stage, without ever referring to those core ideas ever again.

But because the busybodies never tire of tinkering with a terrible system that is only getting worse with every attempt they make to "improve" it, they never want to state the logical conclusion which is a self-appointed group of elites who get to decide who lives and dies. Although it is an *obvious* logical outcome to a system of centralized cost controls, no politician wants to admit they're electing themselves to the panel which decides your grandmother dies while theirs lives. Therefore they are at great pains to *lie to you* to convince you that – for some vague reasons they never get around to presenting – this would not happen in America.

Maybe if Presidential Candidate and perpetual Communist Gadfly from Vermont Bernie Sanders could take a break from praising Chavez and Maduro's Bolivarian Revolution in Venezuela to, you know, check out the pesky details of the supposedly wonderful British NHS, his passion for universal government-run medical "care" in the US might be dimmed. Probably not. Facts have never been much of a concern for self-proclaimed Leftists. Bernie's got four houses and is a millionaire, after a lifetime in "public service," and as a Senator, he's got awesome health insurance, so why should he care how awful healthcare becomes for the lumpen proletariat? Heck, true to form, like Marx, he considers rural dwellers to be "sacks of potatoes" not even worthy to be included in the supposed great Class Struggle being waged – in a theoretical universe far, far away – between Capital and Labor.

A man I had the great pleasure to meet, Les Halpin, was diagnosed with ALS (Lou Gehrig's Disease). In fighting his disease, he did a great deal of research into any and all promising, emerging treatments. In the course of his highly-motivated research, he came across some promising potential treatments which may have proven valuable and effective in treating if not curing ALS.

He lobbied for the right to try experimental medicines, and to allow *all other Britons* the same right. He set up a foundation so that other very sick people would be able to lobby the British government to *try anything* that might extend or improve their lives.

On the whole, with the exception of brave people fighting to restore individuality to medicine, far too many governments love the idea of complete cradle to grave control over your body. Americans have been conditioned to live in this bizarre universe.

That's your future, unless we rational adults modify the course we are on.

A Rich Nation Should and Can Provide Emergency Aid

The centralizing Statists will tug on your heart strings about "caring for the least of us." They are lying because none of their proposals help the poor. We *can* as a nation agree that we'll never let a citizen be refused service if they need it. We already do that *now* with catastrophic results by demanding emergency rooms take patients who cannot pay their bills – but then torture them for exorbitant payment. Let's keep the former idea and ditch the latter part.

I'm for single-payer backstop - meaning, we as a nation agree to cover catastrophic care for one of our citizens who needs it. Combine *that* with competitive market pricing for medical services, allow insurance companies to compete based on their service offerings, force ambulance chasing lawyers to do something productive for a living by abolishing medical malpractice lawsuits, set the annual deductible for healthcare at $15,000 per person or something, and just watch healthcare costs plummet to the bottom.

Maybe Americans will start, I dunno, saving for their own care again. Whether they do or not, we will have affordable medical care again in this country.

To highlight the absurdity we have allowed the government and massive lobbyists to saddle us with, I offer this vignette:

The Real Reason Healthcare in America is a Mess

By David Von Drehle Columnist September 23 at 5:05 PM

The late Neal Patterson often told the story of trudging from one doctor's office to the next in one hospital after another with his cancer-stricken wife, with her heavy medical files in two shopping bags. His point: the utter lack of communication and coordination in the health-care sector. It was an especially powerful story because Patterson was the billionaire founder of one of the world's leading health-care IT firms, Cerner Corp. If that was his experience, imagine what it's like for Joe Average. I watched something similar recently. After the Food and Drug Administration approved a new treatment to slow multiple sclerosis, a loved one asked her neurologist to prescribe the medicine. That seemingly straightforward process set off a several-months-long marathon of countless phone calls, hours on hold and heaps of paperwork. She had to pin down her insurance company on its rules for approval and relay those to her prescribing doctor. She had to negotiate a discount from the pharmaceutical company and relay the new price to the insurance company. She had to convey their eventual agreement to the pharmacy benefit manager at precisely the right time to have the medicine arrive at the hospital for infusion at a pre-scheduled appointment.

A patient needs the endurance of Shackleton, the determination of Tubman and the organizational skills of Eisenhower planning D-Day.[128]

---

[128] https://www.washingtonpost.com/opinions/the-real-reason-health-care-in-america-is-a-mess/2017/09/23/28e8f7cc-9f97-11e7-8ea1-ed975285475e_story.html?hpid=hp_no-name_opinion-card-d%3Ahomepage%2Fstory

Consumer-driven outcomes work best. People spend cash out of their pockets every day in the name of health. We need to remove all these massively expensive middlemen, permit free competition, demand pre-service price transparency and destroy the ambulance chaser lawsuit industry. It is a massive lie that insurance companies are needed for everyday healthcare.

Compare numbers spent every year on all manner of "nutraceuticals" and vitamins. Whether those products are a scam or not, people shell out for them. Ponder how better education and rational competition in medicine would divert those dollars to real medicines and real doctors. There is an entire multibillion dollar industry which arguably should not exist. Amazingly, while Congress is busy dictating the exact percentages of cashflows that must be spent on care versus administration, and demanding any new drug face years of trials, they completely punted on the snake oil business, er, vitamins business.

In comparison, women – mainly – in America spend $52,000,000,000 per year on *cosmetics*.

Florida is Full of Ambulance Chaser Billboards

There is one *major* cause of skyrocketing healthcare costs that ObamaCare most assuredly does *nothing* to stop – and that is TORT REFORM. For those unfamiliar with the term "tort," in this instance it refers to the bizarre American tradition of suing doctors and hospitals every single time life doesn't go your way.

I'm not saying there is occasionally cause to bring legal action for medical negligence. But the rules need to be tightened up – no forum shopping, for example. You get hurt in County X, you sue in County X. And if you're suing, you need to post 20% of your claimed damages to begin proceedings, that fund is forfeit if you lose. Right now, all of us are being gouged to pay for the occasional plaintiff who "wins" $25 million settlement for a mistake in surgery.

That nonsense has to end. $57 billion is a big annual deadweight loss on the system. Remove it.

Medicare

Year Founded:	July 30, 1965
Founded by President	Lyndon Johnson
Funding Budget 2023	$846,000,000,000
Messina's 2024 Budget Proposal	$120,000,000
Messina's 2025 Budget Proposal	$0
Degree to which Messina's Plan is Better	Completely
Should a Federal Medicare exist?	In sharply limited form, if at all

Medicare is born out of a valuable intention, but given how the intention has turned into practice, we need to radically reform this entire system. Remember that it is always easier to simply not spend a dollar to achieve an end. If we replace Medicare with an obligation for doctors and hospitals to serve Americans in need, in return for removing the threat of medical lawsuits and the massive costs of insurance to guard against those lawsuits, we have the beginnings of truly collaborative social system.

The best thing that the unleashing of the free market economy has shown is that millions of free people making free choices results in that most wondrous of things: A Price. Letting dynamic markets develop prices out of the hurly-burly of human interaction is the biggest and most wonderful that could happen to the ordering of human affairs.

Applying this to medical care in this country would have outcomes far better than those currently on offer, which are subject to enormous price and service distortions. Wresting control of patient care from bureaucrats[129] is the first step in helping alleviate the yawning crevasse which is the insane future costs of Medicare.

Solving the problem of health costs will *never* be accomplished from the central government. The *only* solutions that work are local ones. This is and has always been a nation of volunteers. Across the nation, people dedicate their time to helping others less fortunate. We need to institute two years of national service *for everyone.* Starting with doctors. Many will find their role in the armed forces; many others will pick up a shovel and clear brush and garbage from our highways. And some of them will volunteer their medical expertise. Many already do; it's past time we made this a much more publicly-valued part of American life.

Medicaid

Year Founded:	July 30, 1965
Founded by President	Lyndon Johnson
Funding Budget 2023	$536,000,000,000

---

[129] Three Simple Ways Medicare Can Save Money, John C. Goodman, WSJ 11 August 2011

Messina's 2024 Budget Proposal	$120,000,000
Messina's 2025 Budget Proposal	$0
Degree to which Messina's Plan is Better	Completely
Should a Federal Medicare exist?	In sharply limited form, if at all

As this is another suppose third rail of American politics, let's be clear. When citizens who are struggling with inflation, a distorted economy based on ridiculous economic shutdowns over a seasonal flu and all the other things they are struggling to afford hear that Medicaid will be "expanded" or "contracted," they react. Health care is a terrifying looming threat – accidents and sudden illness can destroy a family's finances in an instant – under the current stupid "system." So when pollsters ask people about Medicaid, unsurprisingly, people with middle class jobs and relatively good corporate health insurance see another drain on their paycheck and say "no!" to more Medicaid and people in less secure jobs with no healthcare say "yes!" to the *idea* of government covering their health care bills.

But when you pause and consider those responses, you realize that what *all Americans* really want is good healthcare at a reasonable cost. There are myriad reasons – mostly dumb and all of which could have followed a different path, the path, ahem, that I am laying out here – why "healthcare" is so ridiculously mispriced, but the good news is that when we *fix* the underlying structural flaws, health care will improve patient outcomes while retail prices to Americans come down.

American doctors fought a long, *cultural* battle for respect and high incomes. In the 19th century, there were no real medical schools as we would think of them, there were plenty of snake oil salesmen – who were always itinerant, which should tell you something if your "doctor" wants to get out of town quickly after selling you his patent medicine – and doctors on the whole struggled to make living. I refer you to Maggie Mahar's fabulous book *Money-Driven Medicine: The Real Reason Health Care Costs So Much* (Harper/Collins 2006) for an in-depth discussion of the development of the doctor's role in American life. Suffice it to say that doctors strove for professional respectability *and* a sort of guild system designed to restrict their numbers in order to increase their economic power.

That worked quite well until the 1980s when they got outflanked by MBA management types and the trial lawyer-insurance company ecosystem, whose members spend *all* their time on figuring out commercial monopolies, rather than just *some* of their time as the doctors had done. That was about when rising insurance premia, a systematized medical malpractice lawsuit industry and the rise of "health insurance" rackets began to tell doctors that *"You can keep your comfy lifestyle, but with all these new sharks in the water, why don't you slice a little off the top for protection?"* Sounds familiar doesn't it, like the central casting thug who controls a few blocks of a city: *"Nice little grocery store you got here – sure would be a shame if someone burned it down…"*

Application of Private Sector Best Practices in Risk Management

Newt Gingrich in a debate with Herman Cain in Texas on 5 November 2011, highlighted that folks like American Express lose 0.03% per year to fraudsters, while Medicare and Medicaid experience annual losses due to fraud around 10%. Gingrich recounted the story of Sam Palmisano, the CEO of IBM, visitingPresident Obama and offering up a real solution to slash Medicare fraud starting in 60 days.

Palmisano described his interactions with the Obama White House briefly during a recorded interview with the *Wall Street Journal* Viewpoints Executive Breakfast Series on 14 September 2010. The interviewer kept asking him why the Administration did not take IBM up on the offer to implement currently-available solutions to save $200 billion in fraud (that is $200,000,000,000), which would enable them to pay for their expansion of health insurance coverage. To his enormous credit, Palmisano's only repeated answer was: "You'll have to ask them."

So why not outsource payables to a consortium of Amex, MasterCard, Visa and IBM? Within 180 days, the American people will have a system up and running that ferrets out most of the fraud in the system and ensures that only real bills are paid. The Federal Government already pays private contractors for many services, so why is this one not a prime candidate for privatization? Nancy Pelosi should love this one, as she got sweetheart Visa IPO allocations while fighting valiantly against legislation in the Congress that would have *simply provided competition* for point-of-sale credit card fees from merchants.

The obvious and long-running nature of Medicare fraud is so pervasive it became a literary device to advance the plot of a fictional Florida murder investigation. Carl Hiaasen's excellent crime-fighting screw-up Andrew Yancy discovers during questioning an addicted, alcoholic doctor the Medicare fraud he helped perpetuate.

> "Then at least clue me in on how the scam worked. Where did Nick get all those Medicare numbers?"
>
> "He bought a list of, like, ten thousand names," the doctor said. "Some clerk that worked at one of the hospitals. Mount Sinai or Baptist, I don't remember."
>
> As Yancy had suspected, Midwest Mobile Medical was a ghost-patient operation, billing comical sums to Medicare for electric power chairs, stair lifts, walkers and other durable home-care items that would never be delivered. The senior citizens whose IDs had been hijacked remained in the dark because the government checks were mailed directly to Midwest Mobile.
>
> Such fraud was epidemic throughout South Florida and practically risk-free, thanks to Medicare's stupendously idiotic policy of paying out claims before asking questions. By the time the FBI zeroed in on a brazen cheat such as Nicholas Stripling, he would have already shut down his operation, banked a few million and scurried on. Had he not been killed, he by now would have resurfaced with a new storefront and a new company logo, working the same easy swindle.[130]

The ongoing failure of *multiple* Administrations to *simply fix this flaw* is just an additional supporting pillar to Americans' justifiable disgust with "our" government.

---

[130] Hiaasen, Carl, *Bad Monkey*, Alfred A. Knopf, New York, 2013, p.90

Something so basic a Floridian journalist-turned-novelist (whose *oeuvre* I love, by the way, and about whose work P.J. O'Rourke once rightly said "it's better than literature") can see it just doesn't get done.

What Can You Do About This Madness?

First off, make sure you are framing the issue properly, so you can demand rational actions from your legislative representatives. Would you go buy a car and wait 30 days for some third party to tell you what it costs? No, that is ridiculous. So why do you accept it when you pay for medical services?

People as - GASP! Oh, the Progressive Pain of it all! – *individuals* need to start taking responsibility for their own health.

They manage to find money to buy new iPhones / Xboxes / cars / cigarettes just fine. How about they start prioritizing their expenditures and start - GASP! The Progressives *hate* individual free will and responsibility – saving money instead of spending it, because some day they may get sick?

I know, crazy dreamer, crazy dreamer. Plenty of medical clinic businesses in Florida, for example, already offer monthly subscriptions to people who need it. Watch the market work its magic. For working class, often Hispanic immigrant families who work in the cash economy, a local storefront medical office subscription service *is* perfectly excellent "medical insurance."

The market will always find a solution if it's not messed with.

Every single thing the government touches becomes more expensive, not less. Prices in competitive medical markets - think Lasik or plastic surgery - have declined not risen, while quality has risen, not declined. Any medical procedure that a person needs to pay for improves in quality and declines in price over time. That is the wonderful beauty of free markets – turning unimaginable luxuries into commonly-afforded goods.

When the geniuses in Washington tried to get around a hurdle *of their own creation* and allowed medical benefits to be non-taxed during WW2, that started this whole train of craziness in motion. Wrap your brain around *that* fun fact. It's not as if Congress looked at out of control medical costs and said, "We need to help people afford medical care!" Nope! *First* they created insanely high punitive income tax rates on people during wartime, and *then* because the nation's war machine required factory workers who were not able to be paid more cash (because of those stupid high tax rates), instead of just *repealing* the stupid high tax rates, they allowed companies to offer "benefits" with a dollar value, but permitted workers to receive those valuable non-cash benefits on an untaxed basis.

All stupid, value-destroying roads lead right back to the same damned source: Congress and its never-ending desire to steal every dollar it can from you.

Fight the power. You'll feel better and prices will come down while quality goes up.

Food and Drug Administration

Year Founded:	June 30, 1906
Founded by President	Theodore Roosevelt
Funding Budget 2023	$8,400,000,000
Messina's 2024 Budget Proposal	$4,000,000,000
Messina's 2025 Budget Proposal	$4,000,000,000
Degree to which Messina's Plan is Better	Completely
Should a Federal Drug Administration exist?	In sharply limited form

Is this a standalone proper use of the taxpayers' limited resources?	Yes*
Does this expenditure unfairly benefit one American over another one?	No
Does the expenditure meet the "Is this logical?" standard of fiduciary responsibility?	No
Can the goals be achieved by *not* spending the dollar more effectively than by spending it?	Sometimes

* This gets a "Yes" only under my revamped FDA, *not* under the current structure which spends 45,876 words defining "lettuce" for American farmers.

Before we get stuck in, let's see what the helpful folks who write copy for government websites have to tell us about the FDA.

FDA Mission

The Food and Drug Administration is responsible for protecting the public health by ensuring the safety, efficacy, and security of human and veterinary drugs, biological products, and medical devices; and by ensuring the safety of our nation's food supply, cosmetics, and products that emit radiation.

FDA also has responsibility for regulating the manufacturing, marketing, and distribution of tobacco products to protect the public health and to reduce tobacco use by minors.

FDA is responsible for advancing the public health by helping to speed innovations that make medical products more effective, safer, and more affordable and by helping the public get the accurate, science-based information they need to use medical products and foods to maintain and improve their health.

FDA also plays a significant role in the Nation's counterterrorism capability. FDA fulfills this responsibility by ensuring the security of the food supply and by fostering development of medical products to respond to deliberate and naturally emerging public health threats.[131]

Whew! There are a whole lot of good ideas packed into one organization. If the FDA in its current form were part of a for-profit corporation, it would have long ago gone through a reorganization or two. There are serious, critical and indeed existential issues at

---

[131] https://www.fda.gov/about-fda/what-we-do

stake that a revamped and refocused Drug & Medical Device Administration could play a serious role in addressing. No one has a sound argument for suggesting the nation *not* get the benefit of that list of mission headings.

One thing which is *a priori* insane is the FDA having anything to do with tobacco products. When that idea was proposed – maybe under Clinton? – doctors and scientists unanimously protested. The FDA exists to ensure safe products. There is no way to consider tobacco products safe for human consumption, so why bother with this idiotic farce of the FDA checking tobacco for... what, precisely? Nonsense; scrap the piece of the portfolio tomorrow morning.

Do we want some third-party, hopefully objective set of eyes validating the safety of our food chain? Absolutely. Is this actually a good use of taxpayer dollars? Absolutely. Should this be a federal expense versus a local? Absolutely, as the American food supply system is so complex and cross-State borders that in this instance, it is a glaringly excellent and appropriate application of the Constitution's insistence that cross-border trade be regulated. So the "food" portion of the FDA's responsibility needs to be separated into a different entity. Maybe one that already exists, like the USDA. Just a thought.

We need to recognize the historical context in which the FDA was created, to see why two apparently different things - "food" and "drugs" - were conflated in one regulatory mandate. Secondly, we need to ask whether that is still a compellingly logical way to organize this institution. Thirdly, we need to ask whether the empirical evidence of the FDA's various actions over the years justifies the perpetuation of their methods now and into the future, or whether better alternatives are available.

Arguably, all of the food safety issues should be turned over to the USDA, but I am more than willing to open this up to debate, because of the weird conceptual space that "supplements" occupy in our system. For real food – not "supplements" – *all* of the FDA's activities should be either turned over to the USDA, devolved down to the States when the issue involves commerce or activity within a single State's borders and abolished entirely.

In keeping with the structure of the book, first on the docket for discussion is a topic near and dear to sleazebags and shysters across the sweep of American history. Every Western movie usually has a stock character of some fast-talking itinerant salesman calling himself "doctor" and flogging "patent medicines," usually based on heroin or cocaine or something equally fun and useful for curing disease. Once the cocaine and heroin industries began to be taxed by the government in the form of the DEA and the prison-industrial complex, new products moved into the space left by people desperate to buy their way to good health without going to see a real doctor.

Vitamins and Supplements – Snake Oil for the 21st Century

One area the FDA has utterly abrogated responsibility is the multibillion-dollar snake oil factory, er, supplements business. It is appalling that supermarket aisles, "health food" and any number of websites flog a whole range of mostly useless, occasionally useful and often downright harmful "supplements" whose sellers make outrageous claims about. If you watch any slick TV ad, it's just the modern version of the 19th century traveling snake oil salesman who wandered town to town selling outlandish concoctions, tinctures and unguents, all of which could cure any ill or improve any life. The TV ads now come with a *tiny print quick talking* disclaimer at the end that the FDA has not evaluated these beneficial claims, nor has the substance under concern been lab tested in any way.

The subtlety to the new snake oil business is one part grain of truth and nine parts implicit societal trust of "government."

> The modern supplement era began in 1994, when Congress passed the Dietary Supplement and Health Education Act, or DSHEA. In the decades before, the supplements industry was overwhelmingly focused on vitamins and minerals. Much of the regulation centered on recommended daily allowances of products like vitamin C, iron or calcium.
> DSHEA established the first broad framework for regulating supplements. It also gave supplements a legal definition: as substances intended to "supplement the diet," containing "dietary ingredients" such as herbs, botanicals or vitamins.
> At the same time, however, the law sharply curtailed FDA's power. Companies were not required to notify FDA provided the dietary ingredients had a history of use before the law was passed. For the first time, DSHEA allowed them to make claims on the label suggesting supplements affected the structure or function of the body – for example, by boosting the immune system or protecting prostate health. And DSHEA codified a loose arrangement: Under the law, as FDA notes on its website, "unlike drug products that must be proven safe and effective for their intended use before marketing, there are no provisions in the law for FDA to 'approve' dietary supplements... before they reach the consumer." The agency can act only after a supplement is on the market and evidence shows it's unsafe.[132]

There you have it – the bizarre nature of intrusive micromanagement of every aspect of your life from one department of government, coupled with a complete abrogation of responsibility from another. To be clear, FDA scientists and the medical community are *appalled* that this carve-out for snake oil charlatans was made available. It is *ridiculous* that we are bombarded with ads which make ridiculous claims about supposed health-boosting benefits from products with *no scientific* data to support those claims.

People spend billions of after-tax dollars on this nonsense, when all they need to do is eat a balanced diet and get sufficient exercise and sleep. You'll note they don't expect an insurance company to pay for their multivitamin.

Remove the FDA from this absurdity.

For-profit drug discovery is the global engine of medical advances

One thing which causes lots of real anguish is the cost of prescription drugs. Right now, Americans are basically subsidizing the costs of medicines around the world to European countries (who *could* afford to spend more on drugs if they weren't so busy

---

[132] Jennifer Couzin-Frankel, "The Supplement Sleuth: Some dietary supplements are spiked with drugs. Pieter Cohen is out to expose the hazards," *Science*, 21 August 2015, Vol 349, issue 6250, pp.781-2

writing resolutions bashing Israel at the United Nations) and plenty of emerging economies whose citizens cannot truly afford some medicines.

Medical research set free will solve medical problems for humanity. Let me clarify that statement: when parasitic sleaze are prohibited from trying to steal money from companies searching for cures, we will all be better off.

The laboratories of this world are chock full of smart people pursuing valuable medical research.

I wrote this book to simplify complex problems. The parasites who drain our nation of its productivity *love* complexity. They thrive on it. Simple things can be identified and fixed. Complex things are like Whack-A-Mole.

One of the massive burdens on our national innovation machine – you know, the system that creates medicines, vaccines and treatments for the things that make us sick, sad and dead – is the overwhelming threat of legal action from scumbag class action lawsuit parasites. (After a dozen revisions, that was the most accurate and most polite term my editors and I could agree on.) In 2016:

- 27 securities class actions were filed against pharmaceutical companies, up from 19 lawsuits in 2015 and 15 in 2014.
- Those 27 lawsuits more than doubled the 1997-2015 average of 12 lawsuits per year.
- 80 lawsuits were filed against overall health care sector companies, an 86% increase from 2015 and the fifth consecutive year of such increased securities litigation.[133]

Please note that these are *not* medical malpractice lawsuits, where someone claims injury and wants redress. No – these are law firms who take 33-40% of total class action awards, leaving pennies for the huge "class" of claimants. One simple fix for this particular headache is to fix the law to say that the law firm "representing" the class of allegedly damaged claimants can only get paid at most 35% *of the amount the smallest claimant beneficiary receives.*

The difference in payout means, for example, in a class action suit for 3 million people "injured" by a drug, where each claimant receives a gross amount at trial of $10, under current rules, a law firm gets paid this: 3,000,000 x $10 x 35% = $10,500,000.

Under my proposed rule, making the law firm's "reward" for gumming up the legal system to line their own pockets at the expense of society, for the same case and same ruling, the law firm would get paid this: $10 x 35% = $3.50.

Note to Bernie Sanders and all the people screaming about the costs of drugs and how pharmaceutical companies are "ripping us off:" Companies exist to make a profit. These insane "anti-lottery" jackpot anti-justice rip-offs are another form of tax or cost on drug

---

[133] Cornerstone Research and the Stanford Law School Securities Class Action Clearinghouse, "Securities Class Action Filings – 2016 Year in Review"

companies. Those costs – despite every Socialist's fervent dream and intention – are never borne by drug company executives; they are passed on to consumers.

By removing the double taxation of corporations and their owners (that'd be you, the shareholders, who are more likely to be a blue collar or service worker with a pension or 401(k) than you are to be a caricature of a Wall Street Fat Cat from Depression era cartoons) *and* reforming class action lawsuits, pharmaceutical companies will have more incentive to invest in new treatments *and* have reduced costs which will drive consumer costs down for pharmaceuticals.

In addition, one thing the might of the American Government *should* be used for is to demand intellectual property protection for American pharmaceutical companies. On average, it takes a new drug twelve years to be approved by the FDA, all at a per drug cost of $2.4 billion, not including the drugs that fail to gain eventual approval. Since patent protection on drugs lasts 20 years, that means a pharmaceutical company has a scant eight years to reap the financial fruits of its massive investment. Once patent protection runs out, any company can make "generic" copies of the drug at vastly lower prices.

Americans bear the major brunt of these costs because foreign governments demand a much lower price for the drugs made by American companies. The not so secret threat is that if the drugs can't be bought cheaply, then the foreign nation will just permit one of their domestic chemical companies to copy it. Faced with making some money on foreign sales versus none, most companies cave in. The American Government should get involved in these discussions and threaten massive retaliation to any country that permits intellectual property theft in its borders.

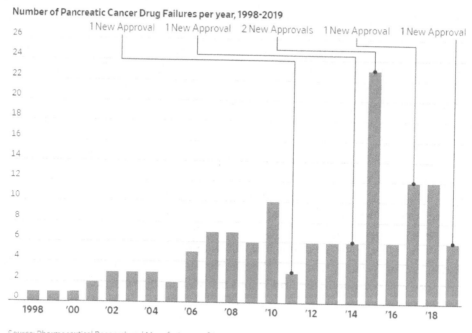

Number of Pancreatic Cancer Drug Failures per year, 1998-2019

Drug development is a complex, very expensive proposition, with the odds of success being far lower than spending billions of dollars on research and trials which end up going nowhere. *Anything* that discourages investment in pharmaceutical research and development is bad for the improvement of health care for Americans.

Over a delightful breakfast one morning in St. Simon's, Georgia, I read with great interest a newspaper article on insulin costs for Americans.[134] It is tough to get angry in the Golden Isles on a Sunday morning over eggs and biscuits, but I managed it.

There is an entire category of company which most Americans know nothing about – carrying the Orwellian label "pharmacy benefits manager" – that stand between drug manufacturers and the public. They negotiate kickbacks, er, rebates, for *their own financial benefit* as a condition of getting a drug onto a given insurance company's "formulary" list. Nowhere in the medical treatment value chain from physician to patient did anyone ever say before, *"Hey! Wait a minute! The doctor diagnosed my shoulder pain and prescribed an anti-inflammatory and a steroid for a two-week course of treatment. The pharmacist in town studied hard to have his profession and he's ready to disburse my prescriptions when I get over there. The drug companies that make each compound have a ready supply for the pharmacist to call on. I can pick up my prescriptions later today. Something is missing here... what can it be...? Oh, I know! How about a massive corporation be set up with thousands of non-medical bureaucrats who take it upon themselves to sit between the pharmacist and the drug companies to "negotiate" a price for those drugs and take a cut for themselves. I sure would like to see that happen. I won't feel better until that's how the medical system works for me!"*

Back to the insulin article which ruined my Golden Isles breakfast. Even when the *inventor* of something wanted it to be cheap, cheap, cheap to save lives, bureaucrats and their pals in Congress managed to make it expensive.

Canadian scientists discovered insulin in 1921, treated the first diabetic patient in 1922 and sold the patent to the University of Toronto for 3 Canadian dollars. The university did not charge royalties to drug companies that wanted to make the medicine.

The price of modern versions of a drug that more than 7 million Americans need to live nearly tripled from 2002 to 2013, according to one study. Type 1 diabetics paid an average of $5,705 for insulin in 2016 – nearly double what they paid in 2012, according to the Health Care Cost Institute.

How did something invented in 1921 and made basically free by its original patent owner come to cost so much, one might ask? In a truly free market, insulin would likely be a "give away" to diabetes patients to earn their customer loyalty so they buy more deodorant and toothpaste at CVS or Publix. There have been developments of the basic drug over the years, along with improvements in delivery mechanisms and the like. Sadly, this has let to higher costs, but those higher costs have not yet had the desired effect of bringing more producers into the market to bring costs down again.

Let's see what goodies the 2023 budget has for us.

---

[134] Altucker, Ken, "Insulin cost has diabetics desperate," USA Today Weekend 22-24 March, 2019

Pandemic Preparedness

The FY 2023 budget makes a transformative investment of $81.7 billion in pandemic preparedness and biodefense across the Department of Health and Human Services (HHS) to enable an agile, coordinated, and comprehensive public health response to future threats and protect American lives, families, and the economy.

$1.6 billion of this mandatory funding will support preparedness activities within FDA, allowing FDA to expand and modernize regulatory capacity, information technology, and laboratory infrastructure to respond rapidly and effectively to any future pandemic or high consequence biological threat. With these investments, FDA aims to strengthen the personal protective equipment supply chain by building analytics and creating predictive modeling capabilities. FDA would also use these new resources to speed development of diagnostics, as well as support efforts with international partners to strengthen foreign inspections, harmonize premarket review of therapeutics and diagnostics, and reduce zoonotic pathogen spillover.

Right after the Holy Apocalyptic Climate Hysteria Church, the brand spanking new religion of "Pandemic Preparedness" has devoted adherents among some people of a certain political party. If you can manage to fit *both* "Pandemic Preparedness" *and* "Climate Mitigation" into one sentence, from a funding standpoint it's not 2+2=4, you're looking at 2+2=500. And that's not even in the New Math.

$81,700,000,000 allocated to HHS to slosh around, all because one party used a bad seasonal flu to ruin people's lives and oust a President they didn't like. As Milton Friedman said, *there is nothing in this world nearly as permanent as a temporary government program.*

No one can prepare for a pandemic. It is nonsense. Leaving aside the objective, statistical *fact* that the government-manufactured Wuhan Hysteria *itself* may be labeled a pandemic, while the seasonal coronavirus on which the edifice of lies was built was most certainly *not* a pandemic, there is no point in our interconnected world in blowing billions of dollars every year "preparing" for one.

Resiliency and flexibility in distributed systems are the preconditions for effective spontaneous response to surprises, which is what an emergency is. This includes "pandemics," hurricanes, snowstorms, and earthquakes. Is it useful for local governments and military units to study past emergencies to learn lessons from those, with the goal of being able to respond more effectively to the next crisis? Yes. Should this be a multi-billion boondoggle every year with permanent staff who do nothing but "prepare" for the unexpected? Absolutely not.

Centers for Disease Control

Year Founded:	1 July 1946
Founded by President	Harry S Truman
Funding Budget 2023	$10,675,000,000
Messina's 2024 Budget Proposal	$2,000,000,000
Messina's 2025 Budget Proposal	$0
Degree to which Messina's Plan is Better	Completely
Should a Federal CDC exist?	No.

Abolish this nonsense. Whatever credibility this crew had, they lost completely during the insane Wuhan Hysteria, rendering them untrustworthy. Prior to the advent of the global internet, there were often good reasons for centralizing resources and knowledge.

The CDC (Centers for Disease Control and Prevention) *should have been* an excellent use of taxpayer money. There are myriad serious threats to health that can only be perceived on a massive scale. In statistics, the larger the number of observable events, the more reliably can one draw conclusions. The *idea* for entities like the CDC was based in that undisputable characteristic of statistics-based public health measures.

Throughout the writing of this book, I have been nothing but a fan of the great work that dedicated doctors and scientists do on behalf of public health for not only Americans, but humanity on a global scale. That said, I have been *appalled* by the insane politicization of what *should have been* a rational, science and fact-based department into a propaganda wing of an oppressive regime.

I am finishing this version in December 2023. Earlier this year, the CDC was still suing to return idiotic and pointless mask mandates for people in airports and on airplanes.

My proposed budget for 2024 is about $2 billion, mostly focused on winding down scientific responsibilities, disposing of real estate and to finish up or transition any important data-related and research efforts, all of which should be completed by December 2024, so the complete shut down of the CFD is effective 1 January 2025.

During the Wuhan Manufactured Hysteria (roughly February 2020 – May 2022, although some morons have tried to keep it going and going in perpetuity), I have developed a sharpened appreciation for the value of scientific investigation and mitigation of infectious disease outbreaks. It is also an excellent lesson in how *bad government spending* necessarily crowds out *good government spending.* In the midst of the Wuhan Virus Hysteria Pandemic, politics played a hugely outsized role, which no amount of spending on public health could have altered. What did happen during the fear mongering over this coronavirus is that the CDC and Federal and (some) State Governments traded rational science for political convictions. A huge chunk of American society turned on public health officials who were spouting clear nonsense about a seasonal flu and destroying the economy and – far more importantly – children's lives as part of their irrational dictates.

Since 2010, spending on state public health departments has dropped 16 percent per capita and the amount devoted to local health departments has fallen 18 percent, according to a KHN and AP analysis. At least 38,000 state and local public health jobs have disappeared since the 2008 recession, leaving a skeletal workforce for what was once viewed as one of the world's top public health systems.[135]

When public faith in institutions erode, myriad problems arise. Not only have more and more Americans started just ignoring what the CDC and others have to say, but resentment over forced masking and being faced with losing your job or taking a vaccine which has not proven to do anything (at best) and has shown to cause complications (sadly) arouses justifiable anger in rational people. Public health officials were inundated with hate mail and calls to such a degree that many quit out of exhaustion and fear. Now add on the weight of evidence which proves that forced vaccination was actually *harmful* and there is no excuse for this entity to remain in existence.

I argue that the very fact of so much government waste that average citizens see every day leads us to lump valuable, hardworking civil servants into a big mass of perceived waste. Add to this the outsized role the American media played in turning a virus into a political issue – by July 2020, 94% of Democrats believed the economy should remain shut until a vaccine was created while 98% of Republicans believed shutdowns were pure economic theatre designed to made Trump look bad – and it became a focal point for bitter disagreements about almost everything happening in the society as a whole. Those figures pretty much have not changed.

Vaccination research, production and dissemination is a perfectly wonderful use of taxpayer money. For example, yellow fever has recently been making an outbreak in Angola, stretching the resources of the four factories globally that manufacture the yellow fever vaccine.[136] Those things need to continue, but not with Federal funding.

As a society, we will get more robust, dependable outcomes from a network of independently funded mini-CDCs, at universities, hospitals and private foundations. Americans already donate billions of dollars to medical and social wellbeing related causes every year. Now that their taxes will be lowered dramatically, they'll be able to dig even deeper to support locally-governed and driven initiatives.

In keeping with the long, proud American tradition of erecting public art memorials to significant events, people and institutions in our history, here is my contribution as a suggested symbolic "memorial entrance" to the shuttered CDC, as a warning to us all about slipping into over-centralization in scientific pursuits.

---

[135] https://apnews.com/e28724a125a127f650a9b6f48f7bb938
[136] Kai Kupeferschmidt, "Yellow fever outbreak triggers vaccine alarm," *Science*, 8 April 2016

Figure 22: Proposed new "entrance" to the former CDC building in Washington, DC

Ridiculous. Scrap in toto. We save billions immediately. As a colleague put it succinctly: All these regulations are great for lawyers, consulting firms and some technology companies, and the government loves it, but it's bad for society.

One the most awful parts of a thoroughly awful law – ObamaCare – is the technocrats' insistence that inserting massive amount of IT spending in the space between doctor and patient is a good idea.

To the extent that big data and all kinds of smart diagnostic and treatment tools exist or are developed, people will pay for them. In 2017, Americans were estimated to spend $30,000,000,000 on "alternative medicine[137]," which is another way of saying people will absolutely spend their own dollars on treatments they believe will make them healthier.

Beyond that – and I am going to give some policymakers the benefit of the doubt – when the idea for electronic records was floated as part of the ObamaCare massive societal makeover, many of the motivations were positive. Frontline medical staff and their patients do indeed have better outcomes with complete data. If you're allergic to certain medications, you wear a bracelet so that if you're incapacitated, hospital staff know not to inject you with something that could harm you.

Following from that, the "best" or easiest idea for disseminating that data was through centralized databases, which patients, doctors and – of course – insurance companies could interact with in the cloud. Despite the myriad cybersecurity risks associated with the idea of multiple logins accessing one massive data pool, that was the best idea the drafters of the law could conceive of.

Well, in the interim, a wonderful technology called "blockchain" developed thousands of new use cases. Without diving too deeply into the subject, what it means for this particular issue is that every individual patient – or family – can now have a personalized, privately-controlled medical history *that they own and control access to*. In practice this means that a person can carry their medical records on a chip on jewelry, or as a file on their phone and give access to doctors when requested.

Individually controlled medical files means there is no longer a need for massive IT expenditures by hospitals and doctors' offices. Distributed data controlled by individuals empowers each citizen to own and control their own medical information.

There are dozens of research pieces available to search for.[138] Go poke around the Internet searching for, say, "blockchain solutions for controlling one's healthcare data" and see what you find. The free market creates solutions to meet needs; that is as true in medicine as in anything else.

Public Health

---

[137] Americans Spend $30 Billion a Year Out-of-Pocket on Complementary Health Approaches | NCCIH (nih.gov)
[138] https://hbr.org/2020/06/what-blockchain-could-mean-for-your-health-data

One of the strangest things happened on the way to the forum. Somehow, "public health" got confused with "health care" in this country, to the vast detriment of both. Public health is the area of expertise involved with – oddly – the overall "health" of the population. This is different than just "adding up" the individual "health" of every person. Statistics about how many people get cancer, how many of those happen to live near toxic waste dumps are all a *part* of both medical care and public health, but the actual things people do and actions taken are very different.

In medicine, a doctor or set of medical professionals treats one person at a time. In public health, we benefit from trained professionals supported by the public interest and tax dollars to create and operate programs which benefit everyone.

US cities, states and the federal government did incredible things from the late 1800s to improve overall conditions for citizens. From improved waste management, water treatment and sewage systems to broad-based vaccinations and public health facilities, huge strides were made. Public health is one of the great, wonderful and *appropriate* things that we pool our money via taxes for.

The great thing about public health expenditures is that they really do tick all the boxes I set forth at the beginning of this book. I promised you simplicity and clarity, didn't I? I'm keeping promises, which means I'd be an utter failure as a politician.

One of the most enduring headaches our society faces is the pain, suffering and loss that results from drug and alcohol abuse. Drug policies around criminalization and punishment cost billions of dollars per year, with arguably nothing to show for it.

Public health expenditures on addressing the *social causes* of drug addiction get a lot less attention and far less consistent funding. This is not an indictment of the political will of the American people at all. Almost *all of us* prefer to "do something" about a problem, and the most immediate thing "to do" about drug problems is to focus on dealing with the stoned criminal, the truant pot-smoking 16-year-old.

Cops, politicians and all kinds of well-intentioned politicians can point to solid statistics about arrests made, prison sentences served, etc.

So why am I harping on pedantically about the difference between "public health" and "healthcare?" Because – and some of you filling up your Messina Budget Bingo Card surely have foreseen this – politicians *misuse* the general public's misunderstanding of that difference to throw cash at a range of things that will *never* see a positive return. Citing "public health" in order to invest $6,000,000,000 in cancer treatments *sounds* so great and compassionate, but it's a lie. Now – don't get me wrong. Should society vote to allocate $6,000,000,000 to medical research to improve cancer treatments because we believe in advancing *medicine* (what "healthcare" used to be called), then that's fine.

It's just not public health.

The *entire edifice* of the lies on which not only ObamaCare but *all* its Socialist predecessors and successors were built was that "public health" statistics justify the complete government micromanagement of the pediatric wellness visit you take your 5-year-old to every year – or did, until government interference in the healthcare market made it prohibitively expensive to do so.

Pay very close attention to whatever promises politicians are making. Always ask yourself, "Is this clown talking about medical care or public health?"

Reopen Mental Health Centers

Of all the things government spends time and money doing, one of the arguably *best* things the government used to do was operate centralized hospitals and asylums for the mentally ill. The maintenance of safe places for the care, treatment and occasional confinement for public safety of the mentally ill is a sound application of public financing. Protecting the general public from possible harm from dangerous people suffering delusions, hallucinations, paranoia and a wide panoply of mental afflictions is one of the few areas where individual healthcare shares conceptual space with public health.

The Federal Government got out of the asylum business during the Carter and Reagan years. I am not going to simplify a very complex issue – many of the facilities were funded inadequately and operated poorly, but the decades since the closure of centers for involuntary commitment have shown the dangers of the mentally unwell left to their own devices, oftentimes ending up homeless.

As with much of this book, when it comes to a moral imperative, I'm making the case for a policy. Letting the mentally and emotionally unstable wander the streets without supervision has proven to be a failure for all concerned. Instead of locking up insane people in prisons for crimes, we need to divert those dollars back to asylums. The details will need to be sorted included the division of responsibility between local, State and Federal governments.

Under the current lack of a system, we are getting the worst of both worlds. We're spending a fortune to arrest and incarcerate people who have committed a crime because they're not mentally well. In prison, they are *not* getting the right kind of care to optimize chances for recovery. What landed them in prison may well have been a fatal shove onto subway tracks or a random assault. I am not saying every unwell person is violent, but many are, which is why there are victims of assault and their attackers are locked up in prison.

On this front, given the pervasive issue of mental illness-caused homelessness, this is one area in which the Federal Government *could* and *should* be of great use to society. One of our toughest issues is mental health treatment. During the last 200 years, the country has gone through a series of changes to how we deal with mental illness, only to arrive at this awful point.

Until WW2, any efforts to deal with people in the population who exhibited signs of what came to be called mental illness were all local. During WW2, alarming statistics arose regarding the prevalence of serious mental illnesses in the population. "Among all men rejected for induction during the war, 18% had been rejected because of 'mental illness,' 14% more because of mental retardation, and 5% because of neurological diseases. Once in uniform, among all men discharged for disability, 38% 'were due to mental disease.'"[139]

---

[139] Torrey, E. Fuller, M.D., American Psychosis; How the Federal Government Destroyed the Mental Illness Treatment System, Oxford University Press, 2014, p.22

Dr. Robert H. Felix was the driving bureaucratic force behind starting federal direct involvement in mental illness patient treatment. He championed the bill that President Truman signed on 3 July 1946 to create the National Institute of Mental Health (NIMH.) As an aside, one of my favorite books as a child was *Mrs. Frisby and the Rats of NIMH,* which I advise anyone of any age to read.

There were few voices of dissent raised at the time regarding this radical change in the federal government's role. The two people who objected were both Republicans from Ohio, Senator Robert A. Taft and Representative Clarence J. Brown. Prior to his stint in Congress, Brown had been the Ohio state statistician – which I think every State should have today, if they don't – secretary of state of lieutenant governor. His comment were trenchantly prescient:

> I agree with everything that has been said as to the necessity for research and study of this problem, but it seems to me that we must always draw the line somewhere or build a fence to define the field of activity in which the federal government can participate and the field in which the responsibility rests with the local and state governments and with the individual citizens themselves. I believe the federal government should lead the way in research, in furnishing information and advice to the people of their states and their local subdivisions, but I don't think the federal government should take the responsibility of administering aid to the individual all the way through.
>
> [I am also concerned that states will stop funding mental healthcare]... because a lot of our citizens are very short-sighted and don't seem to realize that when the federal government spends the money it comes them just as much, if not a little more, as when the local government spends the money, and they have to pay for it in the end anyhow.[140]

Short-sighted citizens looking to "Washington" to fund local things? No way! Gosh, how times have changed!

If you are wondering why thousands of insane people wander the streets of our cities, you can point to Dr. Felix and his co-conspirators, er, co-creators of the NIMH legislation, whose secret goal was to shut down all the mental hospitals in favor of a fuzzy headed notion of community mental health treatment. Drs Jack Ewalt, William Menninger and Francis Braceland helped Felix write the original plan for the federal legislation and their propaganda efforts were helped by a journalist Mike Gorman.[141] Gorman was a Communist and with the backing of a rich woman, Mary Lasker, became one of the most effective lobbyists in DC history. His Communist convictions drove his passion for centralizing control of mental health treatment into federal hands.

For a detailed history of this Fearsome Fivesome's role in the 1950s in creating the horrific conditions in our streets today, I urge you to read Dr. Torrey's book, *American Psychosis.* Suffice to say, their desire to shut down the mental hospitals in favor of having

---

[140] Torrey, p.25

[141] Aside from a slew of articles on the horrible conditions in mental hospitals, he published a book on the topic in 1948, *Oklahoma Attacks Its Snake Pits.*

the insane wander amongst us, hopefully getting treatment as required from a dozen different sources, worked out as planned and all of it is paid for by the federal government.

Communities and States need to start caring for the crazy in controlled settings again, for the benefit of the mentally ill and the safety of the public.

Welfare – Helping the Weakest, Expanding Opportunity for the Weaker and Booting the Scam Artists out the Door

One of my favorite half-Americans once said that you can judge the quality of a society by how it treats its weakest members. Or at least lots of people claim Winston Churchill said this. In any event, finding the right balance between helping struggling victims of circumstance (e.g. children born into impoverished or crime-ridden families) while making sure that scarce taxpayer dollars do not allow otherwise able-bodied adults to lounge around stoned all day is one of the hardest things to do, human nature being what it is. As a nation, Americans used to value hard work and be morally *ashamed* of being unable to provide for one's family. That *inner drive* to support one's community by first and foremost supporting one's family has been sapped unfortunately in many areas of the country after decades of governmental handouts.

It is most assuredly to our credit as a nation that we have conceived of and implemented a safety net to assist those most truly in need of a helping hand. It is equally correct to note our moral failings in structuring and mismanaging a program based in good intentions, so that it has a corrosive rather than beneficial effect on our fellow citizens. We can create programs which ennoble while they assist. Our social assistance dollars and programs need to give people access to the dignity work provides which is as crucial as the dollar to feed one's children. Pride in one's work, a sense of structure and (hopefully) purpose in one's life do more to enhance social harmony than any handout ever can. A program based on helping people get into productive patterns also avoids the unnecessary tensions between false categories of "givers" and "takers."

I have quoted at length one of the most fascinating, succinct descriptions of the difficulties surrounding the proper function and structure of any welfare plan. In a land of plenty, those who suffer *despite their best attempts to survive* can be provided with the necessities of life in a way that benefits *everyone* involved. This caution about our current, terrible system of public assistance comes from Mary Douglas in her 1990 Foreword to the English translation of Marcel Mauss's *The Gift: Form and Reason for Exchange in Archaic Societies*.[142]

Charity is meant to be a free gift, a voluntary, unrequited surrender of resources. Though we laud charity as a Christian virtue we know that it wounds. I

---

[142] Mauss, Marcel, *The Gift: Form and Reason for Exchange in Archaic Societies,* trans. W.D. Halls, 1990, Norton, New York; original *Essai sur le Don,* 1950, Presses Universitaires de France

worked for some years in a charitable foundation that annually was required to give away large sums as the condition of tax exemption. Newcomers to the office quickly learnt that the recipient does not like the giver, however cheerful he be. This book explains the lack of gratitude by saying that the foundations should not confuse their donations with gifts. It is not merely that there are no free gifts in a particular place, Melanesia or Chicago, for instance; it is that the whole idea of a free gift is based on a misunderstanding. There should not be any free gifts. What is wrong with the so-called free gift is the donor's intention to be exempt from return gifts coming from the recipient. Refusing requital puts the act of giving outside of any mutual ties. Once given, the free gift entails no further claims from the recipient. The public is not deceived by free gift vouchers. For all the ongoing commitment the free-gift gesture has created, it might just as well never have happened. According to Marcel Mauss, that is what is wrong with the free gift. A gift that does nothing to enhance solidarity is a contradiction.[143]

Mauss's work and Douglas's foreword are of interest to us here because of what his extensive body of research says about the necessity for *social* obligations to be *tied* to monetary or other social-goods exchanges. The absence of those non-monetary ties are wildly destructive of society's health and people's public-space relationships.

To put that another way: each *individual* is healthier and happier when he or she needs to *work* for or in some other way be obligated to the person or group that provides economic help. Society as a whole is better off when each individual is respected and valued. Part of feeling valued is feeling obligated and responsible, *not* being the upward-gazing recipient of charity, however well-intentioned and however desperately-needed.

Douglas spends a good deal of effort in her foreword discussing the intellectual history of Mauss's research and the sociological and anthropological data behind his analyses. The reason the analysis of gift exchanges across cultures matters crucially to Americans today is because of what *illuminating* the human drive behind social wealth distribution can tell us about *how* to manage and maintain such mechanisms.

> [Mauss]... discovered a mechanism by which individual interests combine to make a social system, without engaging in market exchange. ...The gift cycle echoes Adam Smith's invisible hand: gift complements market in so far as it operates where the latter is absent. Like the market it supplies each individual with personal incentives for collaborating in the pattern of exchanges. Gifts are given in the context of public drama, with nothing secret about them. In being more directly cued to public esteem, the distribution of honour, and the sanctions of religion, the gift economy is more visible than the market. Just by being visible, the resultant distribution of goods and services is more readily subject to public scrutiny and judgments of fairness than are the results of market exchange. (p.xiv)

This echoes our current socio-political experience directly. How many politicians are sitting in their taxpayer-funded seats *precisely* because of their playing the role in the public theatre of the Great Savior of the Downtrodden, or the Fairest Arbiter of Economic

---

[143] Mauss, p.vii

Injustice? In 2008, Candidate Obama hit a nerve *on all sides of this debate* with his off-the-cuff remark to a man who quickly was dubbed "Joe the Plumber" about "spreading the wealth around." Those prone to believe the free market economy is a way to shaft some segment of the population heard a man who was on their side. Those who have worked hard to pull together some assets out of nothing but their own efforts and sacrifice heard a man who was denying their hard work and who wanted nothing more than to take the fruits of their labor to hand it over to deadbeat losers who'd rather steal than lift a finger.

This book is decidedly *not* the forum to rehash the entire 19th and 20th century argument between Anglo-Saxon utilitarianism and its French critics who can broadly be labeled various flavors of collectivist-socialists. However, it *is* important for us to face squarely that there are always going to be competing pushes and pulls between strictly individual rewards to encourage individual effort and the social value of a society providing *the appropriate level* of socialized insurance. Despite the caricatures so prevalent during an election cycle of heated rhetoric, there is not a single American voter or politician of sound mind who is blind, say, to the horror of a small child going to sleep homeless and hungry through no fault of her own, just because she happened to be born to parents who are financial failures for any of a range of reasons, whether temporarily or permanently.

How we as a society choose to strike that balance and *to maintain* that balance as our economy and society evolves lies at the heart of what will either permit the American Republic to endure and thrive or see it atrophy and wither into second-class status, vulnerable to assaults from without and within. Douglas explicitly expressed Mauss's failure to carry his analysis of "archaic" forms of reciprocal gift exchange into an operating model for "social democracy," the late 19th century French term for what we would understand as the warm-blanket, womb-to-tomb welfare state.

> The problem now [written in 1990] is the same as it was for Mauss when it comes to applying his insights to contemporary, industrial society. Yet this is what he wanted to see done. ...[H]is own attempt to use the theory of the gift to underpin social democracy is very weak. Social security and health insurance are an expression of solidarity, to be sure, but so are a lot of other things, and there the likeness ends. Social democracy's redistributions are legislated for in elected bodies and the sums are drawn from tax revenues. They utterly lack any power mutually to obligate persons in a contest of honour. ...If we persist in thinking that gifts ought to be free and pure, we will always fail to recognize our own grand cycles of exchanges, which categories get to be included and which excluded from our hospitality. More profound insights into the nature of solidarity and trust can be expected from applying the theory of the gift to ourselves.   (p.xv)

As an anthropologist by inclination and (decidedly incomplete) training and an investment banker by trade, I am always concerned with seeing problems and suggesting solutions in a context of optimizing both value and equity. What many – in my experience – finance people take for granted, which is that Economics can be a holistic framework through which to make rational and equitable decisions about how to permit the social allocation of resources, is often a source of outrage to people who have a different view of what the proper *ends* of production of goods and services should be.

Without elaboration, the most useless comment on that social argument is the anodyne "they're both partly wrong and partly right." With elaboration, what I mean is that

Economics when blinded to the truth of human decision-making *outside* the "rational expectations" model – which is to say 99.9% if not 100% of human decision-making – can push policy-makers and voters down lines of reasoning which are as absolute in the undesirability of social outcomes as those which lead from a strict Communist program of the myth of centralized planning. The prosperity or poverty – both economic and otherwise – of a society is a delicate, emergent property of a wildly complex system of individual interactions motivated sometimes by greed, sometimes by charitable impulse, and most commonly some blend of both. *It is the boundaries of permitted behaviors that determine what set of outcomes are possible and therefore likely to emerge.*

We cannot legislate outcomes in such a complex, dynamic, and ever-changing system. We can however do our best to ensure consistency of rules and predictability of rights and responsibilities, so that people can make the best decisions possible about what to do with their next 5 seconds, 10 minutes or 50 years. We can also ensure chaos and despotism by refusing to set clear, simple and realistic boundaries for *everyone* to follow.

When it comes to whether or how we permit the persistence of institutionalized social insurance policies like nationalized healthcare or Social Security, what centuries of both experience and theory show us is that the ongoing obligation to American society and each individual citizen is that we keep such structures to an absolute minimum *and* ensure that they are funded and managed transparently and at a level as close to the smallest community as possible.

Ted Koppel writes about this close connection between community, charity and the right way to help people in need. He describes the way local Mormon communities have structured assistance to individuals in need.

> Anything that comes doesn't have to be a disaster on the scale of Katrina, or indeed any kind of collective emergency. Where a family is no longer able to deal with its own setbacks, whether that be a lingering illness, a sudden death, or perhaps the loss of a job, it is still expected to turn to its ward bishop. It is through a bishop's "recommend" that a ward member can be granted access to what is variously referred to as a "bishop's storehouse" or "Lord's storehouse."
>
> A recommend, which can be bestowed or withdrawn, is an incredibly powerful tool for influencing behavior. To a ward member experiencing hard times, the bishop's storehouse can be an indispensable resource. "It's like a grocery store," [Bishop] Caussé explained, "but you don't have to pay. You know, there is no cashier and you cannot pay at the end. You choose to come with your recommendation of the bishop and you will take whatever food you need for your family." A recommend is not an open-ended license to load up a shopping cart, but it is a generous extension of charity for the time that the bishop determines it will take a family to become self-reliant again. Those availing themselves of the bishop's storehouse are expected to volunteer their own time to work at the storehouse for a few hours each week. Several of my hosts stressed the high priority that the church places on volunteering, both as a means to strengthen the fabric of the community and as a way for those receiving help to restore their own self-esteem.
>
> I saw this effort to treat everyone as useful and functional firsthand during my visit to a bishop's storehouse. I was struck there by the presence of a young staffer who was clearly challenged. His nametag identified him as a church elder. He was, it was explained to me, incapable of fulfilling the duties of a missionary overseas, but with supervision he could assist with simple tasks at the storehouse

to fulfill his obligation. It would be the first of several instances in which I witnessed a determination not to consider or treat any member of the community as anything other than productive.[144]

The real tragedy of taking charity and social support networks out of the hands of the immediate community is that once "someone else" is responsible for your neighbor's wellbeing when he stumbles, then you are immediately absolved from doing anything about it. Prior to the vast Federal and State bureaucracies of professional do-gooders, individual communities had mutual aid societies, religious institutions and informal word-of-mouth assistance systems in place.

Dag Hammarskjold said once that "[i]t is more noble to give yourself completely to one individual than to labor diligently for the salvation of the masses." He was expressing in fresh wrapping a truth which many societies have evolved independently. As far back as Moses, whom G-d chose because he was the shepherd who walked into the wilderness to save a single, lost sheep, the Judeo-Christian-Islamic tradition has emphasized personal, individual responsibility as the cornerstone of a sound society.

G-d did not choose as his mouthpiece the shepherd who said to himself, "Ah, the two hundred sheep I have not lost are doing fine, night is coming, and there is a chance that the lost one has already been eaten by wolves, so *for the good of the herd overall,* I am going to abandon the one who needs me the most." G-d chose the shepherd who risked life and limb to find the *one* lost sheep, scared and alone in the wilderness.

Jack Kennedy using the words of an effective speechwriter exhorted a generation of Americans to ask not what their country could do for them, but what they could do for their country. I submit to my fellow Americans today that asking what a bankrupt Treasury and an entrenched bureaucracy we need to fire as a matter of fiscal reality can do for you is pointless; you should be asking what you can do for your neighbor and the people you see around you every day, while denying that lying, self-interested, self-insulated and *self-appointed* elites have anything but scorn, derision, harm, pain and financial devastation to offer you.

---

[144] Koppel, Ted, *Lights Out,* Crown Publishing, 2015, pp192-193

Administration for Children and Families (ACF)

Year Founded:	April 15, 1991
Founded by President	George H.W. Bush
Funding Budget 2023	$73,800,000,000
Messina's 2024 Budget Proposal	$150,000,000
Messina's 2025 Budget Proposal	$0
Degree to which Messina's Plan is Better	Completely
Should a Federal ACF exist?	No

This is one more terrible Federal experiment which needs to end. Once politicians start waving around pictures of scared runaway teens and abused children, everyone runs for the exits. No one wants to be caught on camera with a tightly edited soundbite on the evening news as voting against helping children in danger. One of the reasons we find ourselves staring in wonder at the nightly news as our society unravels before our eyes is *because* everyone is terrified of being made to look bad by the media. I had it happen over a statewide debate in Florida about schools reopening in August of 2020 while the media was busy whipping the nation into a panic over the Wuhan Virus.

Wary of the media, I requested final edit on the story. I didn't get it and when the segment aired on the evening news, I could see why I should have insisted or declined the interview. The actual interview was about twenty minutes long, during which I calmly expounded on the need for children to be in a physical school, how the American Academy of Pediatrics was recommending strongly kids go back to school, how many children in troubled homes need school as a refuge, and a whole lot more. The *one sentence* they edited those twenty minutes down to was the comment I made (in a broader context about freedom of choice and how adults in schools need to weigh their relative health risks) to the effect that if teachers didn't want to do their jobs, they should quit.

Ouch.

What is required is *not* more cowardly tossing away billions of dollars on good intentions, but a focus at the *local community* level or if required the county level for funding and administration of services for the most vulnerable in our society. States and local communities should be in charge of this. Make every ACF employee available to local governments to hire or not.

Close it.

Office of Head Start

Year Founded:	1965
Founded by President	Lyndon Johnson
Funding Budget 2020	$12,400,000,000

Messina's 2024 Budget Proposal	$0
Messina's 2025 Budget Proposal	$0
Degree to which Messina's Plan is Better	Completely
Should a Federal Head Start exist?	No

"There is nothing in the world nearly so permanent as a temporary government program." Milton Friedman. Head Start began as an eight-week experimental program in the summers of 1965 and 1966.

Their own website says it clearly:

> Established in 1965, Head Start promotes school readiness for children in low-income families by offering educational, nutritional, health, social, and other services. Since its inception, Head Start has served more than 36 million children, birth to age 5, and their families. In 2018, Head Start was funded to serve nearly 1 million children and pregnant women in centers, family homes, and in family child care homes in urban, suburban, and rural communities throughout the nation.[145]

Whilst the goal of providing assistance to struggling young families who lack the means for whatever reason to make sound choices for their infants and toddlers is a noble one, the idea that anyone other than *local* government and – even better! – *local communities* should be organizing and providing these services is ridiculous. The 2021 Budget contained this snippet.

> **Continues Strong Support for High-Quality Early Childhood Programs.** Because effective investment in early childhood is so critical to children's ability to reach their full potential and the Nation's future economic health, the Budget includes $8.1 billion for Head Start and Early Head Start to serve approximately 968,000 children and families, maintaining the historic expansion undertaken with Recovery Act funds. (pp. 84-85)

We must put an end to this insane idea that "effective investment in early childhood" equals dollars lumped into a centralized, national pot, distributed by an unaccountable bureaucracy to Poverty Industry Professionals dancing and begging for the right to spend the money supporting their own career choices.

If States or better yet local communities want to fund programs that are similar to Head Start, they are more than welcome to do so. An *annual* $8,100,000,000 *principal loan amount* that our grandchildren will have to pay off *not including accrued interest* is entirely ridiculous.

Local is better. It may take a village to raise a child, but it does not take a Federal government.

---

[145] https://eclkc.ohs.acf.hhs.gov/about-us/article/head-start-program-facts-fiscal-year-2019

Chapter 19: Department of the Interior

Year Founded:	3 March 1849
Founded by President	Zachary Taylor
Funding Budget 2023	$17,600,000,000
Messina's 2024 Budget Proposal	$17,600,000,000
Messina's 2025 Budget Proposal	$19,000,000,000
Degree to which Messina's Plan is Better	Completely
Should a Federal Dept of Interior exist?	Yes

Is this a standalone proper use of the taxpayers' limited resources?	Yes
Does this expenditure unfairly benefit one American over another one?	No
Does the expenditure meet the "Is this logical?" standard of fiduciary responsibility?	Yes
Can the goals be achieved by *not* spending the dollar more effectively than by spending it?	Yes

The Department of the Interior does a wonderful job in some instances. For example, it oversees the National Parks system, which provides Americans and visitors alike with the ability to experience both the natural beauty of America as well as many historical sites of importance to our nation.

Running the national parks, keeping a good accounting of the nation's natural assets is a valuable service. Another highly appropriate role les in overseeing permitting and licensing for extractive businesses to ensure that the American taxpayer is compensated appropriately by anyone wishing to make a profit by mining, oil & gas or agricultural on public lands.

Anything extraneous to that must be slashed immediately.

Bureau of Indian Affairs: $2.7 billion, 8,343 FTEs

This insane holdover of paternalism-married-to-bureaucratic-survival must be eliminated instantly. It's ridiculous.

http://www.doi.gov/tribes/

The U.S. Department of the Interior places a high priority on respecting the government-to-government relationship between the federal government and the federally recognized American Indian and Alaska Native tribes. We are committed to their prosperity by partnering with them to address challenges in the areas of economic development, education and law enforcement as well as other issues they are concerned about. Our work supports Indian self-determination because it helps to ensure that the tribes have a strong voice in shaping the federal policies that directly impact their ability to govern themselves and to provide for the safety, education and economic security of their citizens. We provide services directly, or through contracts, grants or compacts, to 564 federally recognized tribes with a combined service population of approximately 1.9 million American Indians and Alaska Natives.

The budget for the BIA is $2.7 billion with 8,343 full-time employees. That turns out to be $1,241 per Native American. Why don't we cut them each that check and move on? More importantly, why don't we get over the fiction that public sector bureaucrats have a single clue about how to grow a risk-capital-based business? As a thought experiment, what if instead of paying 8,343 unionized bureaucrats, we paid for full-time college, trade school or graduate school costs for 8,343 Native Americans every year?

Enough with this insane paternalism – here is one line item that can be immediately eliminated.

Office of Special Trustee for American Indians: $518 million, 710 FTEs

In FY 2011, the Department will maintain its emphasis on providing services to the beneficiaries of the Indian trust. The Office of the Special Trustee for American Indians (OST) will continue its role in the oversight and operations of the fiduciary responsibility by daily monitoring trust reform in accordance with the Comprehensive Trust Management Plan (CTM). All proposed funding supports the Department's Indian Fiduciary Trust Responsibilities.

The United States Congress has designated the Secretary as the trustee delegate with the responsibility for approximately 55 million surface acres of land, 57 million acres of subsurface minerals estate of land and $3.6 billion that is held in trust by the Federal Government on behalf of American Indians, Alaska Natives and federally recognized Indian Tribes. Trust Management of these assets includes conserving, maintaining, accounting, investing, disbursing, and reporting to individual Indians and federally recognized tribes on asset transactions generated from sales, leasing and other commercial activities on these lands. Through implementation of the CTM, appropriate trust administration for trust beneficiary services, ownership information, management of trust fund assets, and tribal self-determination/self-governance activities, the Department's goal of Fulfilling Indian Fiduciary Trust Responsibilities, will be realized." – page OST-1, 2011 Budget Justifications

There are 710 people spending $518 million in overhead to manage maybe $20 billion in assets? Why? A hedge fund or private equity fund manages many multiples of this amount of assets, usually with a staff between 15-30 people. Even if we choose to pay a staff of 30 to run this and pay them *handsomely* to do so, managing these assets should cost nearer $100 million per annum.

More importantly, it is time for the country to say that we have all had quite enough of this insane paternalism. All evidence points to the fact that the tribes involved can stand up and sort out their financial largesse on their own. Judging from the Native Americans I have met (including the executives of some of their tribal wealth funds), I have not a shred of doubt that they can manage their own affairs just fine, thank you.

A true test of whether the current crop of BIA bureaucrats adds any value will be whether any Native American tribes choose to hire one or more of them after the BIA is dissolved.

Figure 23: Proposed "entrance" for the shuttered Bureau of Indian Affairs building

US Fish and Wildlife Service

Finally! A government agency with an excellent purpose, and a wholly justified use of public funds! Lest you think my endorsement of its purpose means I believe it should remain a *federal* organization, trust me when I say it does not.

It is a complex thing to regulate – the nation's fisheries and game stocks. That's a big picture job, and yet most impacts to USFW are local, as are most of the employees. Having local officials manage Federally owned hunting and fishing resources is an excellent personal connection between the Federal Government and local communities.

288

The services and conservation management the USFW provide are also a great example of sustainable government. Hunters and fisherwomen pay annual licenses and often pay day use fees for hunting on public land, making outdoor sports an immediate and quantifiable vote on the value of these resources to Americans across the nation.

National Park Service

Year Founded	1916
Founded by President	Woodrow Wilson
Funding Budget 2023	$3,600,000,000
Messina's Budget 2024	$4,000,000,000
Messina's Budget 2025	$4,500,000,000
Degree to which Messina's Plan is Better	N/A
Should a Federal National Park Service exist?	Yes

Founded seven years after Teddy Roosevelt left office, the Park Service inherited 230 million acres of public land which he created during his Presidency. "After becoming president in 1901, Roosevelt used his authority to protect wildlife and public lands by creating the United States Forest Service (USFS) and establishing 150 national forests, 51 federal bird reserves, 4 national game preserves, 5 national parks, and 18 national monuments by enabling the 1906 American Antiquities Act."[146]

One of the absolute best things to ever come out of the legislative sausage factory is our system of National Parks and Monuments. From Edwin Muir who pushed mightily in the 1800s for the protection of our great natural spaces to President Roosevelt – the good one that shot bears, not the Socialist in a wheelchair – who created many of the first National Parks, down to the present day, it is a wonderful part of the United States and something all Americans should be proud of and use frequently.

The problems with National Parks are similar to all other problems in government. It's exciting to announce *new* parks and attractions. It's an excellent reelection campaign phot op to cut the ribbon the great new historical building or awesome new network of waterfall hiking trails. But it's a lot less thrilling to provide continual maintenance funding for the operations and upkeep of extant parks and monuments.

Delayed maintenance and other capital expenditures added up to a $12 billion backlog by summer of 2020, just as the Wuhan Virus Panic was hitting the economy hard.

In keeping with our newly refreshed adherence to the U.S. Constitution, all the National Parks should be turned over to a non-governmental perpetual trust or returned to the individual States in which they are found. I suggest continuation of funding for the next few years to improve capital maintenance and get the Parks ready for State control.

---

[146] https://www.nps.gov/thro/learn/historyculture/theodore-roosevelt-and-conservation.htm

Bureau of Land Management

If you are wondering with the BLM does, they've helpfully spelled it out clearly on the home page of their website: "The Bureau of Land Management's mission is to sustain the health, diversity, and productivity of public lands for the use and enjoyment of present and future generations."

Well, that's nice. Certainly it is a better mission than the horrendously parasitical propaganda factory known as "the Department of Education" or "Housing and Urban Development," whose employees seem to find no shame the fact that America's cities have deteriorated rapidly since HUD was created.

I digress.

Nowhere in the Constitution is there a provision which allows this metastasizing cancer of Leviathan to exist.

The federal government today claims to own or control the following percentages of the western states: Nevada – 86%, Arizona – 75%, Utah – 75%, Oregon – 75%, Idaho – 75%, Alaska – 71%, Wyoming – 65%, New Mexico – 60%, California – 55%, Colorado – 50%, Montana – 45%, Washington – 40%.

As part of paying off the insane National Debt and funding individual retirement accounts to replace the Social Security Ponzi Scheme, we will need a process to privatize vast amounts of those Federally owned lands.

Figure 24: The Federal Government is in violation of the Constitution; it owns far too much land, especially in Western States. We are way past time for that land to be sold out of their hands.

290

Article I Section 8 Clause 17:

> To exercise exclusive Legislation in all Cases whatsoever, over such District (not exceeding ten Miles square) as may, by Cession of particular States, and the Acceptance of Congress, become the Seat of Government of the United States, and to exercise like Authority over all Places purchased by the Consent of the Legislature of the State in which the Same shall be, for the Erection of Forts, Magazines, Arsenals, dock-Yards, and other needful Buildings;

The intent was that the federal government would have to **ask** existing states or new states created for specific parcels of land **only** for the above stated purposes. This was to head off the historical tendency of governments to seek more power and control by grabbing up everything including land.

Figure 25: David Wolosik's essay about how the Feds illegally seized millions of acres of land, despite having no Constitutional authority to do so.

Agencies were created with absolute national authority over resources that were to be managed at the state and local level. Without regard for the Constitution and with total disdain for Americans at the state and local level who will have to live with and/or suffer under their decisions, these entities were conjured out of thin air.

- U.S. Department of Interior - March 3, 1849
- U.S. Fish and Wildlife Service - February 9, 1871
- U.S. Forest Service - 1905
- National Park Service - August 25, 1916
- Tennessee Valley Authority - May 18, 1933
- Bureau of Land Management – 1946

As with all large, unaccountable bureaucracies, great mischief and damage can be done if captured by ideologically driven idiots. A fine, publicly motivated citizen I follow on Substack, David Wolosik writes powerfully about the myriad abuses of the Federal Government. He is particularly scathing and accurate about the massive amount of land owned in violation of the Constitution by the Federal Beast. Here is a snippet from a recent piece[147] he wrote on this topic.

---

[147]   https://open.substack.com/pub/wholeamericancatalog/p/biden-thinks-he-can-shut-down-wyoming?r=erlb4&utm_campaign=post&utm_medium=web

Back when we lived in Pennsylvania, I believe it was on *America's Voice News,* we saw a secretly recorded video of a *Sierra Club* meeting where they were desperately trying to come up with an animal to use as the reason to shut down logging in the Northwest. They came up with the Spotted Owl.

- It was declared endangered in 1990.
- U.S. Forest Service, BLM and outrageously, private land logging was shut down on millions of acres since supposedly the owl needed "old growth forest" to survive.
- When it was spotted nesting in Kmart signs, fence posts, etc., that was said to be an anomaly.
- The Forest Service admitted it was discovered that actually the larger and more aggressive Barred Owl are decimating the Spotted Owl. However, logging was still on hold, too bad.
- Meanwhile, generations of loggers were forced out of business and lost their homes. Whole vibrant towns supported by logging dried up and died. We saw these towns when we were coming west. All over a clever scam.

I am old enough to remember this madness. So there you have it – a perfect example of the massive damage a one "small" lie can do to American prosperity. A bunch of enviro-nutters at the Sierra Club colluded with bureaucrats to manufacture and perpetuate a lie about the Spotted Owl which destroyed communities and ruined an industry. The same limousine liberals who backed this lie most assuredly never stopped buying furniture and home fittings made of wood products. They just wanted to stop logging done by Americans in a sustainable way, instead offshoring those jobs and sourcing that lumber from other countries.

Leviathan is not just annoying – it is destructive of human liberty, prosperity, freedom and community.

22,000,000 acres for a solar farm, but no permit for 10 acres for an antimony mine

The Biden Administration's Interior Department is pushing forward with the idea of blanketing millions of acres of Western land with solar panels, all in the name of "clean energy" and "net zero" carbon emissions.

David Blackmon wrote some perfect commentary[148] about the ridiculously transparent, hypocritical crony capitalist climate religion driving these sorts of insane proposals.

---

[148] Monday's Energy Absurdity: Biden's 22 Million-Acre Solar Farm Is His Worst Idea Yet (substack.com)

DOI has spent decades fighting against oil and gas development on designated regions of federal lands in the West that supposedly present prime breeding ground for sage grouse, birds that exist in the millions all over the Intermountain Western United States. These birds are so plentiful that Wyoming has an open hunting season on them. These 22 million acres represent a geographic space far larger than the designated critical sage grouse habitat.

What about all the millions of migratory birds that fly over these vast spaces each and every year? Do Roth and Haaland believe none of them will be killed or otherwise impacted by these vast solar arrays that span dozens of miles? How many permits for "takes" of these and other animals are Roth and Haaland willing to issue to the developers of these projects, knowing full well of the carnage that is about to happen? 1,000? 1 million? 10 million? More than that, all in the name of mounting the biggest crony capitalist scheme in the history of the world?

What about all the "endangered" plants these arrays will destroy? DOI has spent a decade holding up a proposed antimony mining operation in Nevada on the canard that it would somehow threaten 10 acres of a subspecies of buckwheat - that's right: buckwheat. How many acres of this same buckwheat and other supposedly critical plant species would be destroyed across 22 million acres of solar development?

These people are so insane, if you tried to make this up for a fictional plot, your editor would scribble red ink across it as being completely implausible. How does one become such a destructive busybody in the first place? What kid grows up to become an adult in DC who even thinks such nonsense? *"Hey! Carbon's like really bad, like you know? John Kerry and this guy Podesta said so, so I believe it. How about we blanket a crazily large chunk of land with solar panels manufactured by China using massive amounts of mined material - which we hate, so we have to get from 3rd world nations out of sight of our liberal donors - and huge amounts of carbon-emitting fossil fuels, all to destroy millions of acres of habitat. Because carbon."*

These folks cannot be shown the door fast enough.

Chapter 20: Department of Justice

Year Founded:	July 1, 1870*
Founded by President	Lyndon Johnson
Funding Budget 2023	$37,700,000,000
Messina's 2024 Budget Proposal	$200,000,000
Messina's 2025 Budget Proposal	$20,000,000
Degree to which Messina's Plan is Better	Completely *and* Utterly
Should a Federal DOJ exist?	No

Is this a standalone proper use of the taxpayers' limited resources?*	Yes
Does this expenditure unfairly benefit one American over another one?*	No
Does the expenditure meet the "Is this logical?" standard of fiduciary responsibility?	Yes
Can the goals be achieved by *not* spending the dollar more effectively than by spending it?	Yes

It is a crying shame that I need to even write anything for this section. Here is clearly a useful function of the Federal Government. There are boundless numbers of corrupt public officials that require punishment and the occasional (justifiably) Federal crime that requires prosecution. The American taxpayer is well served whenever a corrupt, thieving politician or public sector employee is discovered and then prosecuted to the fullest extent of the law.

Some parts of the rampant overreach and misapplication of scarce resources will "take care of themselves" when we shrink the government, end drug prohibition and take a massive scalpel to the Federal Register. But other issues are cultural and require our focus to address. Foremost among those issues is one that a normal person doesn't quite believe exists – until it happens to them.

"When the law becomes a trap for the unwary, it becomes an engine of oppression rather than a statement of the moral and ethical requirements of a society's citizens."[149] So writes Harvey Silverglate, who describes in terrifying detail how *any* American unlucky enough to be caught in a zealous DOJ employee's crosshairs can find himself wishing that he were living in a Kafka[150] novel instead. Every time the government implements some new law or rule, the citizens are forced to change our behavior to not suddenly discover that something we all did as part of our daily lives yesterday is now a Class C Felony. The litany of examples is long, and while an encyclopedic recitation of the insanity of both intended and

---

[149] Harvey A. Silverglate, *Three Felonies a Day: How the Feds Target the Innocent,* Encounter Books, NY, 2009, p.166

[150] For my younger readers who have had this brilliant Bohemian author's work hidden from them, lest they begin to understand the evils of uncontrolled government, Franz Kafka (1883-1924) wrote *The Judgment, The Metamorphosis, The Trial* and numerous other works. Go read them all and be thereby enriched.

unintended results from the lips and pens of bureaucrats has a certain artistic attraction, getting buried in details doesn't move my plot forward.

One cannot change the past, only modify future decisions. The best thing we can do is to drastically prune this bureaucratic beast back to a very bare stub. From there, we can decide how or if to build some of it back.

Applied correctly, the powers granted to a "department of justice" can be used as a force for great societal good. When pursuing and locking up career criminals who exploit the weak – whether through human trafficking or governmental corruption – the DOJ is one of the shining examples of the application of the force of Law for social good. There are numerous instances of cases investigated by the FBI and prosecuted by the US Attorneys which are sterling examples of fine public service, integrity and all the things one would want from a system of laws.

None of the changes I suggest here would change any of that ability of the Executive Branch to do an excellent service on behalf of us all. US Attorneys can be appointed on an *ad hoc* basis, kind of like jury duty.

One of the finest programs I've seen in years is the DOJ's emphasis on prosecuting and preventing financial fraud against the elderly. This is an excellent example of what the government *should* be using its disproportionate weight for (www.justice.gov/elderjustice) – using the collective power of the American taxpayer to bang hard hammers on the heads of dirtbags who target lonely elderly people to scam them out of their life savings.[151]

I state unequivocally that *most* of what I have encountered from the modern day DOJ has been an excellent track record of dedicated, intelligent and capable professionals trying their hardest to make the law a positive instrument in society. By the very nature of this work dedicated to improving our governmental functions, I must highlight the problem areas in need of attention. No one gets excited or moved to action to applaud a job well done.

We need to trim the way the DOJ operates to bring its overall incentive structure in line with what we the American people rightly want our Justice Department to spend its time on. Unfortunately, it has been so abusive in recent years, that the best way forward is to dissolve the DOJ entirely and work without it for awhile. All of the workaday things a federal pack of lawyers does is overshadowed by the abuses, real or apparent.

The glaring exceptions to that fine track record include the FBI's becoming a weapon of the Democrat Party in its insane persecution of Donald Trump and its appalling protection of Hunter Biden *who videotaped himself committing drug felonies with prostitutes while waving around a handgun whose application for purchase he had to have lied on.* I touch on the specifics of the FBI below, which has deserved its dissolution since J. Edgar Hoover roamed the halls dressed in women's clothes while destroying with the able help of Roy Cohn thousands of American lives for his own petty agenda.

When applied incorrectly or applied with an unreasonable or political filter the DOJ can just as readily be a source of tremendous social disruption.

---

[151] Other resources include: www.member.aarp.org/money/scams-fraud, www.consumerfinance.gov/older-americans, www.stopfraud.gov/report.html, www.napsa-now.org/get-help/help-in-your-area, www.ncea.aoa.gov, www.aging.senate.gov/fraud-hotline.

A random sampling of Justice's "achievements" over the last two decades:

- In December 2001, acting on orders from Attorney General John Ashcroft, FBI and DEA swooped down on California marijuana producers *who operated legally under California law* while the World Trade Center fires were still burning from the terrorist attacks of September 11, 2001.
- Under Eric Holder, taxpayers funded the transfer of 2,000 assault rifles to Mexican drug gangs in a ridiculous operation dreamed up by heaven only knows which idiotic armchair warriors who'd seen one too many Bruce Willis movies. The *intent* of "Fast and Furious" – itself the name of a Hollywood movie of hyper cool criminals headed by Vin Diesel who somehow commit all their crimes in souped-up, Japanese mid-market family sedans, kitted out with nitrous boosters, neon underlighting and spinning chrome rims – was to somehow lead to convictions of gun smugglers. Instead, the savvy gun smugglers who are criminals professionally rather than theoretically, delivered the guns successfully and a large number of those guns have been used in murders on both sides of the US-Mexican border, in one case killing an American Border Patrol Agent.
- Zealous DOJ attorneys moonlighting as Buzzkills Against a Good Time decided to prosecute and incarcerate Tommy Chong for his comedic performances under the thin guise of convicting him *for selling glass smoking pipes* which *could or could not* be used for smoking tobacco or marijuana.
- DOJ attorneys were rebuked in a scathing ruling by Federal Judge Hanen on 19 May 2016 for repeatedly and deliberately *lying to multiple courts* about their covering up illegal, unilateral changes to immigration law by (former Constitutional Law Adjunct Instructor) Barack Obama in 2014.
- [trillions of dollars] wasted on chasing ghosts that don't exist. Massive swathes of the DOJ's time has been chewed up to grave societal destruction on the basis of pure ideological lies. The particular lie which has wrought so much havoc goes back to the Original Justice Sin of replacing individual responsibility and individual action with the very blurry, ill-defined and therefore *unjust* idea of collective responsibility and collective action. The same idiotic and totalitarian thinking which has brought us so much else that is wrong, bad and cancerous in American society brought you the stupid idea of "disparate impact."
- Protecting the Democrat Party from prosecution of obvious crimes – from Hillary Clinton's maintenance of private server in her basement for hiding emails from the public while she was Secretary of State, to *not* investigating Hunter Biden's obvious – *and self recorded!* – criminal behavior.
- Attacking concerned parents as "terrorists" under the PATRIOT ACT when those parents objected to public sector teachers unions spewing radical leftwing indoctrination about a dozen genders and related nonsense, or when those same idiots *kept children out of school from 2020-2022 and would have tried for longer* all based on utter nonsense and hysteria about the Wuhan Panic.

The *incentives* for personal performance at the DOJ need to be brought in line with society's reasonable expectations for the department. Society wants good things like corrupt politicians locked into small cages and poked with sharp sticks. Society doesn't want the bizarrely Orwellian, "whoops-you-committed-a-crime-without-knowing-it" jackpot anti-lottery "justice" system we currently have.

While I lay out my prescription for curing the root cause of this massive social illness in my suggested Constitutional Amendments, described further later in the book, I have kept some of the reasoning and discussion in this section. I have drawn heavily from two absolutely wonderful books on the topic of Justice. There are, I am sure, a few others, but these two should suffice to make my point.

In the first book, *Three Felonies a Day,* Harvey Silverglate writes chillingly:

> Today, in spite of Jackson's warning, it is only a slight exaggeration to say that the average busy professional in this country wakes up in the morning, goes to work, comes home, takes care of personal and family obligations, and then goes to sleep, unaware that he or she likely committed several federal crimes that day. Why? The answer lies in the very nature of modern federal criminal laws, which have become not only exceedingly numerous (Jackson's main fear at the time of his admonition to his prosecutors) and broad, but also, since Jackson's day, impossibly vague. As the Morissette scenario indicated, federal criminal laws have become dangerously disconnected from the English common law tradition and its insistence on fair notice, so prosecutors can find some arguable federal crime to apply to just about any one of us, even for the most seemingly innocuous conduct (and since the mid1980s have done so increasingly).
>
> A study by the Federalist Society reported that, by the year 2007, the U.S. Code (listing all statutes enacted by Congress) contained more than 4,450 criminal offenses,[152] up from 3,000 in 1980. Even this figure understates the challenge facing honest, law-abiding citizens. Since the New Deal era, Congress has delegated to various administrative agencies the task of writing the regulations that implement many congressional statutes. The volume of federal crimes in recent decades has exploded well beyond the statute books and into the morass of the Code of Federal Regulations, handing federal prosecutors an additional trove of often vague and exceedingly complex and technical prohibitions, one degree removed from congressional authority, on which to hang their hapless targets.
>
> This development may sound esoteric to some -- until they find themselves at the wrong end of an FBI investigation into, or indictment for, practices they deem perfectly acceptable. It is then that citizens begin to understand the danger posed to civil liberties when our normal daily activities expose us to potential prosecution at the whim of a government official.
>
> How these prosecutions work and what we can do about this perilous state of affairs is the subject of this book. The dangers spelled out here do not apply only to "white collar criminals," state and local politicians, and myriad professionals, though their stories will predominate in the chapters that follow. No field of work nor social class is safe from this troubling form of executive branch overreaching and social control, and nothing less than the integrity of our constitutional democracy hangs in the balance. After all, when every citizen is vulnerable to

---

[152] John S. Baker, Jr., *Measuring the Explosive Growth of Federal Crime Legislation,* Federalist Society for Law and Public Policy Studies White Paper, May 2004, updated 16 June 2008. http://www.heritage.org/Research/LegalIssues/lm26.cfm.

prosecution and prison, then there is no effective counterweight to reign in government overreaching in every sphere. The hallowed notion of "a government of laws" becomes a cruel and cynical joke.[153]

Even leaving aside the more fundamental changes required to roll back the machinery of oppression our government has become, the Department of Justice needs a serious overhaul. Its operating principles and the incentives for individual action and advancement almost guarantee perverse outcomes. One can see how it happens. All systems of incentives reward Results and Action; to ensure a good and just society, it is crucial to think about *which* Actions lead to *which* Rewards. Most people place no value on the choice to do nothing, which, arguably is the best choice we can ask of our public servants. Also the system currently fails to weigh *which kind* of action is being taken, so long as it's active and it costs lots of money and some people as a result end up having their lives damaged.

"Our" federal government put the comedian and actor Tommy Chong in jail *for being a wiseass*, basically. We the taxpayers wrote a check for this piece of DOJ farce to the tune of **$12 million** including "investigation," trial, imprisonment and post-release parole. In keeping with their frustrated penchant for ever-elusive coolness, the folks in charge of this insane abuse of power and egregious waste of money called the effort to entrap, arrest and imprison Tommy "Operation Pipe Dream."

Watching Josh Gilbert's documentary about his prosecution and imprisonment, *a/k/a Tommy Chong,* is terrifying. There are clips showing Mary Beth Buchanan, U.S. Attorney for the Western District of Pennsylvania, holding press conferences about the case, citing Tommy Chong and his comedic collaborator Cheech Marin for the horrible "crimes" of daring to be funny stoners and counter-culture heroes from a bygone age. In the film, we are treated to courtroom "evidence" about his "crimes" which consisted of... *clips from his publicly released movies!*

The *entire case* against Tommy Chong was based on elaborate government entrapment in the first place. All history is gossip, so here is some for the ages: Two states at the time had laws on their books against shipping drug paraphernalia across state lines, Pennsylvania being one of them. A man in Beaver Falls, PA called Chong's Glass/Nice Dreams – the glass pipe business run by Tommy's son, Paris Chong – at least 20 times trying to order pipes from them in California. The company declined every time, citing the Pennsylvania law.

Then the man traveled to California to place a large order in person. As the company was filling the order, the man from Beaver Falls flew back to Pennsylvania, called Chong's and said "Oh, sorry, but I had to head home. Look, can you just mail them to me?"

Sadly for Tommy, for America and for the Rule of Law, the fine folks at Chong's Dreams decided after all this hassle to just ship the already-packed boxes to Beaver Falls. In a rational nation, that decision would be called good customer service.

Bad Move.

---

[153] Harvey A. Silverglate, *Three Felonies a Day: How the Feds Target the Innocent,* Encounter Books, New York, 2009

The Feds swooped in decked out in riot gear in the early morning hours and the insane persecution – yes, it's not a typo and my editor did not miss this when it should have been "prosecution" – of Tommy Chong commenced.

Did you call your Congressional Representatives or The White House at any time in 2003 saying, "Hey, with all the massive problems the country faces, could you please authorize a U.S. Attorney in Pennsylvania to blow $12,000,000 on investigating an old comedian for selling glass pipes? That'd be a great use of my tax dollars." Because if you did, then you got what you wanted. The rest of us, not so much.

Lest you think – or wish – that this kind of thing can only happen to celebrities who draw the unjustifiable ire of a politically-aspirant U.S. Attorney looking for headlines, think again. The DOJ randomly chooses to attack some citizens out of dozens or hundreds of others who have done the exact same thing.[154]

The second book I've turned to for help in sorting out my thoughts on how the US Department of Justice has deviated from the application of truly just actions is actually a collection of books. If you've traveled at all in the United States and are the sort of person who pokes around opening drawers in hotel rooms, you may have encountered it. In English, it's called *The Bible.*[155] Most Americans until the Vietnam Draft Dodger Generation seized the reins of the "Education System" were very familiar with this collection of ancient wisdom and guide to morality and justice. While the Draft Dodger Generation were busy fulfilling their smug, selfish roles as the Useful Idiots destroying society for the godless heathen Communist Party, part of their mandate included removing understanding and analysis of *The Bible* from the common public canon based on a woefully ignorant misunderstanding of the clause in the US Constitution about the separation of Church and State.

I need to modify that. Some of them may have been woefully ignorant, but the most persistent and pernicious among them were completely aware of how crucial a common morality or even "just" common stories are to societal cohesion, so have done their all to sever those threads of common understanding, all the better to increase "group" identity and cross-group hatred amongst Americans.

What good is "identity politics," after all, if 100% of Americans believe that we are Americans first and any other affiliation is at best a secondary affectation or culturally enriching historical family remnant? The destruction of a sense of common history – by replacing "history" in schools with meaningless nonsense like "social studies" – was just one part of the plan to destroy American social cohesion, the better to enable an Omnipotent State to arise like Marshal Tito in Yugoslavia to hold together splintered groups with nothing in common except The Iron Fist of the State.

Watch that trend, carefully, kids, because these ideological enemies of freedom do not suffer from logical consistency. Nope. The same chuckleheads who bow down to the Constitution when they claim it demands the complete removal of religion from the public

---

[154] Harvey A. Silverglate, *Three Felonies a Day: How the Feds Target the Innocent,* Encounter Books, New York, 2009

[155] G-d, *The Bible*, written through human agents, circa 3200 BCE – 220 CE, multiple publishers

299

square don't care in the slightest about the same Constitution that does less important things – from a collectivist, totalitarian, centralized power perspective – like guaranteeing little things like the freedom of speech or the freedom to defend yourself and your family.

True Justice in a Free Society is Individual

If you take *nothing* at all away from this book, please let it be this timeless truth. The only true justice in any society is rooted in the rights and responsibilities of each individual. There is no communal guilt, no hereditary guilt. The entire apparatus of identity politics, racist groupthink and everything that comes with those evils which attempt to remove the individual from the heart of our sense of Justice does nothing but destroy any real sense or system of Justice.

I told you at the outset that everything I write here can be boiled down to a few very simple, clear truths.

If you are the kind of person who finds yourself tearing your hair out when reading about some governmental bully abusing her power to force a citizen to do anything at all the citizen does not want to do, and the description of the legal cudgel being used to enforce bad ideas and bad laws makes your blood boil but you're not quite sure why, I hope this section proves useful.

A tremendous way to force change in the DOJ is to hew to the formative principles I laid out in my introduction. Term limits and pre-hiring, real-world work requirements would go a long way to mitigating the negative effects of an entitled bureaucratic mindset. By ensuring that the lawyers who now and again get called to public service have nothing but a good sense of civic zeal to gain by so doing, the American people will get a truer application of federal justice than we do now.

Even better would be to craft a system of "U.S. Attorney Duty" which mirrors every citizen's obligation *and* privilege to perform jury duty. Imagine what a great system we would get if prosecutors were called to service for a period of time, which would be just part of one's societal responsibilities if one is granted the privilege of being an officer of the court.

The other major thing that needs to change is the whole mess of federal laws which have expanded like wildfire since the 1940s. A direct result of sloppy abdication of legislative responsibility is Congress's habit of tossing over the actual writing of the *details* of the laws they pass to unaccountable, unelected and – under current public sector union restraints – non-terminable bureaucrats. That, combined with excessive overreach into what should constitute a federal crime in the first place has wrought havoc with Americans' sense of fairness and due process.[156]

---

[156] *As Federal Crime List Grows, Threshold of Guilt Declines,* By GARY FIELDS And JOHN R. EMSHWILLER, Wall Street Journal, Sept. 27, 2011

As of this writing – and for years before – no one in the Federal Government can even tell you how many laws exist. That's right – from Ten Commandments which covered arguably the range of crimes a human could commit, we now have a cancerous mass of laws and rules in the tens of thousands and growing. Rules may as well be laws, because if you violate one – even unknowingly – the Government can steal your property and put you in prison.

More Americans are being prosecuted for unwitting violations of surprisingly abrasive laws with ridiculously drastic penalties attached to them. One of the longest-running bedrock principles of criminal law is *mens rea* – "guilty mind" in Latin. It is one of the strongest defenses a citizen has against abusive government. If the police and prosecutors need to prove *not only* that you, say, caught a certain species of fish and ate it, *but also* as part of that prosecution, that you *knew* it was illegal to catch that fish, then the government has to be really clear not only about the laws, but about a citizen's awareness of the laws.

If Federal prosecutors – or *any* part of the bureaucracy – were hampered by basic logic and consistency, they would *of course* support *mens rea.* After all, an entirely unconstitutional and insane apparatus of punishment has been developed to prosecute "hate crimes" as distinct, apparently, from "regular crimes." What on earth could possibly differentiate a "hate murder" from a "regular, friendly murder" than *the intent of the person committing the crime?* All "hate crime" legislation and prosecution *depend on* the government "knowing" what was in a person's mind when that person committed a crime. So if the government "knows" the *mens rea* of a person they want to accuse of a crime which is trending on social media, then why are they not required to have the same omniscient comprehension of the *mens rea* of someone who happened to catch the wrong fish out of season?

Pay attention. This kind of thing always happens to someone else.

Until it happens to *you.*

$5.5 million *and Threats of Criminal Prosecution* to Prevent Anthropologists from Examining 9,000-year-old skeleton of Kennewick Man

I don't have to be paranoid to hate what has become of what should be "our" government. I just need to read *Smithsonian,* the monthly magazine published by that most hallowed of American scientific bodies – the Smithsonian Institute. In September 2014, the magazine recounted both the fascinating scientific investigation into the ancient human prehistory of North America *and* the insane lengths to which the US Army Corps of Engineers and the Department of Justice went to prevent that scientific investigation from occurring.[157]

In 1996, two college students in Kennewick, Washington, stumbled on a human skull while wading in the Columbia River. They called the police and a local archaeologist named James Chatters got called in to examine the oddly shaped skull, which resulted in his finding a complete skeleton which he removed to his lab.[158] That next step in the investigation of a potentially very exciting archaeological discovery kicked off the fiasco that followed.

To be fair, there is quite a bit of historical context around the proper treatment of human remains in North America when it comes to anthropological investigation. I am striving in this book to avoid the sort of strident jingoism that some authors – are you listening, Joe Stiglitz? – bake into their works on public policy. I support wholeheartedly the laws that preserve Native Americans' cultural rights to their heritage and ancestors' remains. Grave robbery is theft, whether done in 1855 by archaeologists unearthing 4,000-year-old burial complexes or tomorrow night by thieves who know your grandmother was buried with her favorite diamond brooch.

Changing times lead to changing interpretations of historic or cultural rights, and the evolving process keeps developing. In 1990 the US passed the Native American Graves Protection and Repatriation Act, which – rightly, in my opinion – requires human remains and certain cultural artifacts to be returned to tribes who can prove descent.

All that said, in this instance, there were sound scientific reasons to show there were no valid claims to be made and therefore the law would not apply. The article describes $5,500,000 of *your* tax dollars spent persecuting the scientists who were trying to analyze some very exciting and rare prehistoric remains.

The US Army Corps of Engineers *seized* the remains from the local coroner and his archaeologist collaborator, Douglas Owsley who had in fact been a leading champion of repatriating remains from Smithsonian collections to Native American tribes. He called the Army Corps repeatedly and in true bureaucratic fashion, they simply ignored him. The Corps had determined the remains were to be "returned" to the Umatilla tribe for burial and that was that.

The irony in all of this is that the 1990 NAGPRA law *requires* scientific study to determine whether discovered remains are affiliated with the tribe claiming the bones.

---

[157] "The 9,000-Year-Old Man Speaks," by Douglas Preston, *Smithsonian,* September 2014
[158] Results of the eventual analysis can be found in *Kennewick Man: The Scientific Investigation of an Ancient American Skeleton,* Douglas Owsley, editor, 680 pages, Texas A&M Press, 2014.

Owsley was asking for a day *at his own expense* to study the remains, at the very least to learn something about them and *in keeping with the law's requirements* to determine if possible their relation to the current claimants.

When the scientists decided to sue the Feds to stop the bones from being buried and lost to science forever, the ever-value-additive Department of Justice stepped in. DOJ lawyers called the Smithsonian Institution and *threatened them*, saying that Owsley and his colleague Stanford might be violating criminal conflict of interest statues which prohibit employees of the United States from making claims against the government.

In the interests of time, space and my sanity, I urge you to go read both the Smithsonian article and the book detailing the eventual scientific findings. For our purposes here, I want you to ponder DOJ lawyers – with all the wide sweep of things to prosecute and deal with across this crime-ridden land of ours – spending their time and $5,500,000 of your money[159] threatening esteemed scientists who wanted to pursue scientific investigations of some of the oldest human remains on this continent.

How About a Victim Protection Program Instead?

I sat on a jury trial in New York City during June 2008. The "key witness" in this particular case was a non-ethnic-Italian knucklehead who got involved with one of the Mafia families in New York and when things went sideways, cried like a little baby and decided to snitch on his former associates, some of whom if I recall correctly, he was related to by marriage.

It got me thinking. Why on earth are the taxpayers footing the bill for keeping the evil, confessed career criminal alive? Wasn't the rationale behind a Witness Protection Program to *protect innocent people* who witnessed a crime that organized criminals would execute before testimony, or afterwards as punishment? How did this become a way to protect professional sleazebags - often murderers - who decided to testify against their former colleagues?

Space restricts my comments here, but this is the kind of thing we the taxpayers need to have open debates about. The prosecutor can say, "Yes, Mr. Scumbag is a career criminal, but unless he gives testimony about his bosses, who are guilty of murder and multiple other felonies, those bosses will remain unprosecuted, so we want to pay for Mr. Scumbag to hide his identity and live a life somewhere else."

Then, maybe, we have a grand jury type of entity which debates whether to spend money protecting Mr. Scumbag or not. But just covering this guy's costs without anyone having a say on behalf of the check writers is just one more example of wasteful spending.

------

[159] To keep beating this drum until the rhythm never leaves your mind: As the $5,500,000 the "Justice" Department spent on this fiasco is actually *borrowed,* the real cost assuming 20-year debt is more than $6,800,000. That's a lot of school lunches or potholes filled in, or *real criminals* prosecuted.

In relation to protecting victims of crime who come forward, as ever, when left to its own devices, the private or civil sector steps in to provide solutions. One of the greatest all-volunteer organizations I've ever come across is Bikers Against Child Abuse.

I have no space left to expand on their mission, but I urge you to look into them as well as any other civil-society, voluntary groups focused on protecting the innocent from predatory criminals. Sadly, human nature will always mean some very dangerous, mean and violent people will try to prey on others.

It is in the nature of such predators that they never try to attack someone stronger than they are. All evil people understand is countervailing force, applied as needed.

Abolish the FBI

Year Founded:	July 26, 1908
Founded by President	Lyndon Johnson
Funding Budget 2023	$10,800,000,000
Messina's 2023 Budget Proposal	$2,500,000,000
Messina's 2024 Budget Proposal	$1,000,000,000*
Degree to which Messina's Plan is Better	Completely *and* Utterly
Should a Federal Bureau of Investigation exist?	Yes**

Is this a standalone proper use of the taxpayers' limited resources?*	Yes
Does this expenditure unfairly benefit one American over another one?*	No
Does the expenditure meet the "Is this logical?" standard of fiduciary responsibility?	Yes
Can the goals be achieved by *not* spending the dollar more effectively than by spending it?	Yes

* Under my plan, the standing force of a permanent FBI is to be replaced by *ad hoc* task forces contributed by State law enforcement personnel. Some dollar budget is required to cover those costs that go along with investigations. Currently the FBI does unfairly benefit some Americans over others; that must stop for people to regain faith in our governing authorities.

** Some kind of Federal investigative authority is desirable. I suggest that rather than maintain a "standing force" like the FBI, that instead we have a sort of "Federal police investigative duty" like jury duty, whereby States contribute law enforcement personnel on an ad hoc basis when Federal crimes are alleged. The FBI in its current form has lost the faith of the American people in its unbiased fairness; that loss of faith is sufficient for scrubbing this and starting afresh.

One of the most chilling ironies of recent years (writing in May 2022) has been the resurgence of all the horrible abuses the nation witnessed under J. Edgar Hoover. I will leave that date of May 2022 in the text because as I thought this book was *finally* nearing completion in August 2022, the FBI handed the nation the best reason for their abolition ever on 8 August 2022. On 10 August 2022, I changed the title of this section from "Reform the FBI" to "Abolish the FBI." At some point, when you are pruning a rotting tree, you discover the rot is not cosmetic and only affecting some of the limbs but has penetrated to the heartwood.

The fact that more than *thirty* FBI agents spent more than nine hours rifling through *anyone's* private residence *while banning the residence owner's lawyers from observing their search* is enough to fire all the agents involved immediately and have a court toss out anything they might have "discovered" during that search. As Senator Rand Paul put it on an interview on 10 August 2022, the FBI's actions have eroded even further any trust Americans may have had in them, after the litany of abuses from James Comey and Peter Strozk during the 2006 election cycle. It is logical to ask why Trump's lawyers were banned from observing the search, *as is the right of every American.*

How can we believe it's true if in a week after such an event Attorney Merrick Garland holds a press conference, holding up, say, a Russian-made grenade and says, "This was among the items the FBI found during our search of Mar-A-Lago," when the only witnesses to that "discovery" were comprised of the very people persecuting this man? Our *entire* system of justice relies upon the checks and balances afforded by shining bright lights on evidence and all proceedings. Secret, one-sided "courts" like the FISA Court or the kangaroo show hearings that I call *January 6th: The Musical!* do not provide justice, because no one rational and impartial can trust that *the process* is fair.

The FBI must be shut down, with everyone laid off. The FBI building in Washington should be turned into condos or offices for *private sector* businesses. A plaque explaining how an organ of blind justice destroyed itself through picking a political side can be mounted in the lobby.

Once the desks are cleared out, *Congress* can debate fully with all members present and cameras rolling whether a process should be put in place to examine what kind of federal investigative body – if any – the taxpayers should set up going forward.

In the interim

While we sort out the abolition or reform of the FBI, we the people need to ensure that the FBI is required to start digitally recording its interviews. Few things fly in the face of fair play, justice and protection of the civil rights of Americans than the farce of the "302" report. This is the FBI's primitive method of memorializing what was said in an interview, based on handwritten notes and post-hoc editing. Sunlight is the best disinfectant; the credibility of the FBI has been eroded significantly by the behavior of its agents and attorneys in cases like Mike Flynn, Donald Trump and Tommy Chong. There is no good reason for the FBI to refuse to allow people to record their interviews, nor is there any good reason to maintain these 302 reports, which can basically say whatever the agents writing it after the interview is long over want it to say.

It just looks like a way for the FBI to avoid accountability. The appearance of actions which a reasonable person would find suspicious is more than enough to avoid the government taking those actions. One of my favorite American lawyers is Harvey Silverglate. I cite his excellent writing elsewhere in this book. On the topic of the 302 Report, I had the joy and privilege to host Harvey as a guest on my podcast Messy Times. He is eloquent in explaining how he never lets his clients be interviewed by the FBI without making a recording. As the FBI will not allow recording, the interviews therefore never take place.

Have a listen to the discussion: https://youtu.be/0LpsNRLug9M

End Privatized Prisons

The US prison system requires radical reform from top to bottom.

I can recall one of our American history lessons in *primary school* where the teacher noted that judges in the pre-Civil War border states who ruled on whether a given person was a slave or free had distorted incentives. Were a judge to find a man "free," he got paid $3 for the ruling. Should the person in front of the bench turn out to be a "runaway slave," to be returned to his or her master, the judge got paid $10, the difference being made up from the pocket of the slave's owner.

Well before my voice broke and I started noticing girls, I learned that providing perverse (or any) economic incentives to participants in the "justice" system was to invite abuse. Any system that provides personal economic incentives to imprison people guarantees certain destruction of the blindness Lady Justice is supposed to have.

This is a very serious issue Americans need to face squarely. Are we willing to bear the costs of incarceration for all the people we continue to lock up? There can be no skirting of this, no moral ambiguity. If we want to put people in little boxes for, say, selling a bag full of a weed that G-d Himself felt fit to germinate, then we as a nation need to bear the costs of that decision. Turning prisoners into a profit center is plain wrong, full stop.

We need to abolish all for-profit prisons immediately.

Beyond that, Americans have "lawyered" ourselves into a bizarre situation. Prior to 1790, imprisoning someone was a prelude to a trial and possible punishment. Gaols were run by gaolers who charged their prisoners for "room" and board, while possibly receiving a stipend from the local government for maintaining a place of confinement.

Imprisonment itself *as* a punishment only came into being beginning that year in Philadelphia, when Quaker-led governments decided that confinement to workhouses would henceforth become the punishment and hopefully rehabilitation of convicted criminals.

When all you've got is a hammer, everything looks like a nail. When putting someone in a cage is the only punishment available, then logically every crime is defined in terms of the amount of time one should be boxed up. But for many crimes, society's interests are not served by spending huge amounts of money to prevent a convicted criminal from roaming freely across the land. When the convict is a violent offender prone to shooting, raping or stabbing the innocent citizenry, incarceration is a wise choice and money well spent, at least until such time as we can make capital punishment effective and immediate. But for a range of other offenses against civilized norms, surely we can rifle through the historical playbook for a fresh approach to punishment, one that metes out justice but gives us the taxpayer value for money in the process.

In early 2019, a delightful scandal erupted which the media loved. In the midst of Harvard having to pretend its exclusion of high test-scoring Asians was different than its exclusion of high test scoring Jews sixty years' previously, came a different tale involving rich folks paying "consultants" who photoshopped the faces of high schoolers onto athletes' action shots, all the get their little precious darlings into the university of their choice. This one featured famous people and not just nerds of a certain ethnicity, so it sold more papers or – in the currency of 2019 – provided better clickbait to monetize views.

Hollywood denizens Lori Loughlin and her designer husband Mossimo Giannulli were charged with paying $500,000 to have Olivia Jade and her sister, Isabella Rose Giannulli, 20, admitted into the University of Southern California as fake crew recruits. If convicted, they could have faced 40 years in prison.[160] In the end, Lori sat in Federal prison for two months. Why? How were the American taxpayers benefited by this absurdity? Have

---

[160] https://pagesix.com/2019/04/20/tensions-rise-in-lori-loughlins-marriage-after-admissions-scandal/

her pay a fine. Give her work-release jobs to pick up litter on the highways wearing a "I bribed college admissions" t-shirt. But we shelled out cash to lock her up for 60 days. Gosh, that'll change the college admissions process, as if *that* is a matter of urgent concern to all Americans in the first place.

There are a dozen things wrong with this picture. The insanity of the US university system and the erroneous belief – one might call it marketing – that says a piece of paper from a certain school means a better life certainly contributed to this particular "scandal." But for the purposes of the proper use of American taxpayer funds, the very idea that two Hollywood flakes spending a half million dollars to pretend their pretty daughters are athletes means that we the taxpayer will then spend millions to cover their room and board in prison for 40 years apiece is ridiculous. Not only will we write a check for their jail time, but we'll also forego the income tax revenue they would have paid had they *not* gone to prison in the first place. All for what? "Justice" because *their* pretty girls got to (potentially) take another pretty girl's place at the University of Spoiled Children?

Trust me, pretty girls of pleasant disposition coming from Hollywood parents are likely to enjoy good lives, whichever college they decide to spend four years playing at.

Here's a fine instance of the hammer of imprisonment as the sole punishment our society recognizes leading to a ludicrous outcome. These chuckleheads are no danger to society, certainly not in the way the prosecutors assert. Whether the vapid hours of brain-numbing "content" they produce has the potential to weaken the logical faculties and moral acuity of the population subject to it is another story. Producing and acting in stupid shows is not – yet – a prosecutable offense. Don't tempt me.

Arguably, every idiot parent who paid into the millions of dollars to fake their darling offspring's resumes for a college application should be pitied and tested for mental adequacy to handle their own affairs. Had these idiots truly understood the money machine that is Higher Indoctrination in the United States as of 2015 or further back, they would have known that they could have simply stroked a check for the same amount *or less* as a donation to the schools, and their darling kids would have been admitted readily. It all would have been perfectly legal and – here's the kicker – would have been *tax deductible* as a donation to a not-for-profit college! It would have been a *better deal* and have come with the added benefit of immunity from prosecution for the *exact same quid pro quo*.

Sweet, sweet irony.

Long Past Time to Transform Our Prison System

> The degree of civilization in a society can be judged by entering its prisons.
> -   Fyodor Dostoevsky

Two types of prisons arguably work "best" in dealing with criminals. The first kind of prison should be so insanely awful that is a bone-chilling deterrent. Think of the Turkish prison depicted in *Midnight Express*.[161] The goal of course with that approach is to scare people so insanely that they will do anything other than commit a crime. The other kind is the complete opposite – a place to rehabilitate or help a person stop being a criminal. Endless debates take place about the merits of each approach.

What does *not* work is what we have now in America. A harsh place that is a total bummer and would drive any normal person crazy, but comfy enough with laws and guards and rules to in theory make time alone be the punishment, with some efforts at classes and group therapy.

This is an enormous topic which I am only touching on here as a launch pad for you to do your own research.

Resources abound. One talk which was concise and thoughtful was given by District Attorney Jeff Rosen on 30 January 2017, which was about his experience touring German prisons with a group of Americans.

Also, a very interesting documentary was done as part of a series called *Inside the World's Toughest Prisons*. One episode was about the new prison built in Nuuk, Greenland. Scandinavian prisons tend to focus on rehabilitation over punishment, so the prison looks more like a hostel or low-key hotel than a prison. No bars, windows looking out at the gorgeous scenery, a fully stocked kitchen complete with knives for cooking. All designed to prepare prisoners for reentry to society.

Again, a complicated topic which each community, city, state should decide for themselves, balancing punishment for criminal transgressions with the overall good of society. For example, if a repeat car thief just isn't getting the message, do we want to pay to lock him up for a year, so he can ponder the error of his ways? Let's say yes. Do we also want to punish his two kids, aged 4 and 6, and his wife, assuming they have a happy marriage? No, those three people don't need to be punished because Dad just can't stop hotwiring German cars to sell to drug cartels for fast cash. We have to decide how to balance those things – beyond nasty, hostile "visiting" rooms where guards stare balefully at you and his kids are terrified to visit.

Then at the other end of the spectrum are completely evil sociopaths who like rape, murder and generally inflicting misery on others. I myself have no problem flipping a switch on those scum and adjusting the phrase "cruel and unusual punishment" to fit the benchmark *they* applied to their victims. I'd have public auctions to raise money for victim compensation – let's let billionaires bid for the right to cut a murderer's head off, with the cash going to support the family of the murderer's victim. That's my opinion. Others have different ones. Fine, let's have the debate and decide how best to deal with penal policy.

What I state categorically next is what I think should require no argument. To the extend it does require argument, then I am happy to have that fight all day long.

End Privatized Prisons and Alien Processing Facilities

There are private prison camps dotted throughout the country where random employees get to act as totalitarian overlords to detainees. There have been numerous

---

161 1978 American film about a dumbass who tried to smuggle hashish out of Turkey in 1971.

studies and documentaries made about these facilities; the reader is free to seek those out. My argument is simple and clear. **However we decide to treat prisoners, it is incumbent upon us to bear the costs of that incarceration.**

Anything else is cheating. If society wants to mete out punishment society must pay the bill for that punishment. While the idea behind for-profit businesses running prisoners can on the surface seem rational, in practice it is a terrible misapplication of resources and creates a set of conditions that almost guarantee torture, bribery and bad outcomes.

If it is 100% bad to have a for-profit prison industry, it is 100000% worse to allow private companies to operate detainment camps for illegal aliens.

It is utterly horrifying to see that our government has put in place a set of conditions and laws that means any unemployed buffoon who'd like to exercise the kind of absolute tyranny feudal lords were accustomed to in the 1600s can rock up, fill out a job application and pretty soon be pushing around defenseless, scared foreigners. And if the creep is lucky enough, he can find time in his schedule of pestering immigrants to have sex (forced, coerced or maybe sometimes willing) with numerous inmates under his control.

Seal the borders. Eject lawbreakers who enter our nation illegally. Maintain efficient courts to decide who goes and who stays. By bearing the objective, transparent costs of this process, the American taxpayer can decide whether to spend dollars on permitting Chinese triads, Mexican cartels and coyotes to make hundreds of millions on smuggling people across our southern border.

Right now, the Biden Administration has chosen to just lie to the American people as millions of illegal border violators enter our nation unhindered. The best of those are just immigrants looking for a better life. The worst of them are murderers and fentanyl smugglers killing thousands of Americans every year.

A nation without borders is not a nation. Either way, the public must bear the costs of dealing with these issues.

End Civil Forfeiture

It is hard to believe that this practice exists in the United States. Police departments across the nation seize the property and assets of people *who have never been convicted* of a crime and in some cases *have not and will never be indicted* for any crime. You're reading that right. If you're one of the many Americans who will be as astonished as I was when I first heard about this insanely unconstitutional, immoral and downright ridiculous legalized theft of Americans' property, please feel free to put a bookmark here and go spent some time researching "civil forfeiture" on the Interwebs. The class will wait for you. Hint: start with the Institute for Justice's website.[162]

There. You're back after screaming in astonishment at what your quick research uncovered. Now that you've calmed down enough to keep reading and we're all on the

---

[162] https://ij.org/issues/private-property/civil-forfeiture/

same page, let's address how this craziness began and what we need to do to end it now, once and for all.

This legislation was created in 1984. Current President Joe Biden was one of the co-authors of this insane law.

As of October 2021, Representative Tim Walberg (R – Michigan) has introduced legislation called the FAIR ACT[163] to end this insane practice. Amazingly Congress still has not bothered to stop cops stealing innocent people's cash and property.

Across the nation, police departments and sheriff's departments steal money and valuable property from people using the twists and turns of this terrible Federal law. It must end immediately. The Institute for Justice estimates that the various levels of US government have stolen $68,000,000,000 from honest Americans who have committed no crimes.[164]

I urge you to read their report, but this is from the Executive Summary:

Many jurisdictions fail to provide a full accounting of forfeiture activity, so any estimate of forfeiture's scope will undercount. Still, by any measure, forfeiture activity is extensive nationwide, sending billions of dollars to government coffers.

- In 2018 alone, 42 states, the District of Columbia, and the U.S. departments of Justice and the Treasury forfeited over $3 billion. This is the year for which we have data from the largest number of states.
- Looking at a longer time period, 2002 to 2018, 20 states and the federal government forfeited over $63 billion. The remaining states did not provide data for those 17 years.
- Since 2000, states and the federal government forfeited a combined total of at least $68.8 billion. And because not all states provided full data, this figure drastically underestimates forfeiture's true scope.
- Among the states with 2018 data, Florida, Texas, Illinois, California and New York took in the most forfeiture revenue. But once state populations are factored in, Florida, Illinois, Tennessee, Rhode Island and Nebraska used forfeiture most extensively.

It is madness. It is unjust, unfair, unevenly applied and is simply theft. Period. Whatever screaming arguments the police will make about this being about "drug cartels" is hogwash of the first degree. No American should ever have their property taken without being convicted of a crime *and* after due process.

As for the proceeds of any property forfeiture, the cash should most certainly *not* be handed to the very police departments and district attorneys' offices who stole, er, confiscated the property. If after all those very real Constitutional hurdles, property is still confiscated, the law must be amended so the proceeds go directly to the charity specified by the underlying crime's victims.

---

163 Text - H.R.1525 - 118th Congress (2023-2024): FAIR Act of 2023 | Congress.gov | Library of Congress
164 Policing for Profit - Institute for Justice (ij.org)

This is so painfully obvious it is emblematic of why the nation is in the troubled state it is. People who used to rant about the government spying on them and stealing their stuff used to be labeled crazy. Now they're just observant. This must end.

Figure 26: The DOJ staffer who came up with the idea of spending $6,000,000,000 of taxpayer money to hire corporate privateers to steal more money from innocent Americans being feted by his colleagues.

In 2023, a horrible practice in brazen disregard of the Constitution, due process and basic fairness got kicked up a notch.

The Institute for Justice continues their wildly valuable work in holding the metastasizing cancer of the Federal Government to some form of account.

As highlighted in a recent video[165], the IJ exposes the fact that we US taxpayers are being forced to borrow $6,000,000,000 so the Department of "Justice" can pay private sector companies to steal property from our fellow citizens.[166]

---

[165] https://youtube.com/shorts/KnDd-qyMveA?feature=share

Whilst the Constitution prohibits individual States from issuing Letters of Marque - incidentally, my third favorite kind of Letter - apparently an unelected organ of government has decided it can issue land-based Letters of Marque to modern privateers so long as they do their theft via paperwork and without rippling broadsides on the high seas.

This is so painfully obvious that no matter what else you think of this book, put it down to call your Congressional Representative's and Senators' offices to demand they ban civil forfeiture at once. There is no reason this horrible abuse of the citizens should have lasted this long, never mind one more day.

The Institute's wonderful book, _Policing For Profit_, is in its 3rd edition and should enjoy pride of place on every American's bookshelf right next to the family Bible, Koran, Torah or sacred scripture of choice. To give you a sense of its paramount import:

In 2019, nursing student and single mother Stephanie Wilson had not one, but two cars seized by the Detroit Police Department, losing the first one forever. That same year, the U.S. Drug Enforcement Administration and the Transportation Security Administration seized retiree Terry Rolin's life savings of $82,373 from his daughter as she passed through Pittsburgh International Airport on her way to open a joint bank account for him. Three years earlier and about 1,000 miles away, a sheriff's deputy in rural Muskogee, Oklahoma, seized more than $53,000 from Eh Wah, the tour manager for a Burmese Christian musical act, during a routine traffic stop; the funds were concert proceeds and donations intended to support Burmese Christian refugees and Thai orphans. None of these victims were convicted of any crime.

Their stories illustrate a nationwide problem: civil forfeiture. Civil forfeiture allows police to seize property on the mere suspicion that it is involved in criminal activity. Prosecutors can then forfeit, or permanently keep, the property without ever charging its owner with a crime. By contrast, criminal forfeiture requires prosecutors to prove beyond a reasonable doubt that an owner is guilty of a crime and then, in the same proceeding, prove the property is connected to the crime.

Does this sound like the America you believe you live in? Me, neither. **From 2000 to 2019, the Federal government stole, er "compelled civil forfeiture" of property valued at $45,700,000,000.** Not content with fleecing innocent Americans of that property, the bright sparks at "Justice" are now going to spend $6 billion on private contractors to help them steal more from us.

I love it when the media calls anyone a "right wing paranoid conspiracy theorist" for merely quoting government agencies. Over at the Asset Forfeiture Slush Fund Office, it's a non-stop party:

---

166   https://open.substack.com/pub/christophermessina/p/department-of-justice-spending-6?r=erlb4&utm_campaign=post&utm_medium=web&showWelcomeOnShare=true

Figure 27: DOJ Asset Forfeiture Dance Crew

I would love to be a fly on the wall for the staff meetings. How does one encourage American civil servants to head out on a theft rampage targeting innocent people? Is that covered in *How to Win Friends and Influence People?*

Figure 28: The DOJ Deputy Director of Civil Forfeiture exhorting her troops to cross the next pass into a valley full of innocent Americans who have not even been charged with a crime, so those Americans' assets may be seized for no reason.

Given that the United States and Eritrea are the only two nations which tax their citizens' income no matter where a person lives, one can only assume there are fat expatriate postings for diligent asset thieves baked into this $6 billion privateer fund. A Kiwi friend took a picture of the DOJ team appropriating Maori war dance traditions ahead of stripping unsuspecting Americans of their rightfully owned property.

Figure 29: The DOJ's New Zealand expatriate team culturally appropriating the Haka ahead of a North Island raid on Americans' lawfully owned property.

I await news of their gargantuan haul. It is sure to snag some choice *pounamu* carvings which I bet mysteriously disappear from the DOJ warehouse before being logged for sale at auction.

What can you do? Well, amazingly enough in the House of Representatives, there is some motion on stopping this appalling madness.

In March, Congress reintroduced an enhanced version of the bipartisan Fifth Amendment Integrity Restoration (FAIR) Act, H.R. 1525, which would enact a sweeping overhaul of federal civil forfeiture laws. The bill would remove the profit incentive that drives so many federal forfeitures, end the federal "equitable sharing" program that is used to circumvent state law protections for property rights, and eliminate the unfair administrative forfeiture process.

The vast majority of federal forfeitures are civil in nature, meaning that the government is not required to charge the owner with a crime, let alone secure a conviction, in order to permanently keep their property. From 2000 to 2019, 84% of DOJ forfeitures were civil forfeitures, while from 2000 to 2016, 98% of Treasury forfeitures were civil forfeitures. The vast majority of those civil forfeitures—93% of DOJ's and 98% of Treasury's—were processed administratively, meaning property owners never got their day in court.

While forfeiture is a multibillion-dollar business for law enforcement, most seizures and forfeitures are quite small. From 2015 to 2019, half of all DOJ currency forfeitures were worth less than $12,090. From 2015 to 2016, half of Treasury's currency forfeitures were worth less than $7,320. Those figures show how ordinary Americans—not drug lords or mafia kingpins—bear the brunt of federal forfeiture abuses.

Figure 30: Congressional staffers, caught in the middle of drafting important legislation.

The Institute for Justice advocates to end forfeiture through litigation, strategic research, and legislation. IJ has class action lawsuits aimed at stopping seizures of cash at airports, roadside seizures on highways, and the FBI's unconstitutional forfeiture notices. IJ's landmark study looking at state and federal forfeiture, Policing for Profit, is now in its third edition. IJ's advocacy has led to Maine, Nebraska, and New Mexico ending civil forfeiture and replacing it with criminal forfeiture.

Find your Representative with this helpful link:

https://www.congress.gov/members/find-your-member

After your obligatory chuckle about using a governmental website to find your member, call him or her to express your deep anger at this awful practice and demand they vote to end civil forfeiture. Presumably, if enough people demand the abolition of civil forfeiture, the gremlins and goblins who do the actual bill drafting will get down to work making America a better, freer place.

God Bless America, whose citizens may one day live lives free of Overweening Administrative State Oppression as their Creator and Founding Fathers intended.

Drug Enforcement Agency

Year Founded:	1973
Founded by President	Richard Nixon
Funding Budget 2023	$3,100,000,000
Messina's 2024 Budget Proposal	$120,000,000
Messina's 2025 Budget Proposal	$0
Degree to which Messina's Plan is Better	Completely
Should a Federal DEA exist?	No

"Let's face it, the war on drugs was a disaster."
- Colorado Governor John Hickenlooper

"Let's face it, Denver was a lot more pleasant before hundreds of stoners were wandering around downtown spaced out beyond belief when they're not harassing passersby."
- Me

I must admit I struggle mightily with this topic. Logic dictates that criminalizing the human desire to get wiggly of an evening is absurd. Most people who smoke a joint or have a beer or even drop some acid on a Friday night are back at work on Monday with few side effects, unless you call impulse late night TV shopping sprees, babies conceived and marriage proposals side effects. There is even abundant evidence to support the idea that psychoactive mushrooms were instrumental in helping proto simians evolve into human beings.

The massive damage done to our society from making some drugs illegal, while some others are not, is empirically true and devastating. However, I look at the panoply of intoxicants and I do believe some things should never be available for consumption. Synthetic fentanyl cooked in Mexican jungle labs in rusty oil barrels, then formed into brightly colored pills that look like candy, or *any* methamphetamine are seriously horrendous killers of thousands of Americans every year. That is where the complexity comes into play – but I am not sure criminal prosecution is the answer to fentanyl and crystal meth.

It is not illegal to drink raw bleach or chemicals used to drain hair clogs, and I can assume that one would experience some kind of mind-altering experience (on the way to death) from either of those. Yet people are not clamoring for a bleach fix. No DEA bust is on for bleach dealers.

By reversing the complete failure of the "war on drugs," we would *instantly* as in this coming fiscal year swap $41,000,000,000 in *spending* on arresting, trying and jailing drug users and sellers, for *tax receipts* of $46,700,000,000.[167] Those tax receipts could be deployed more productively on drug regulation, quality enforcement and treatment programs for those who want treatment. (Those specific numbers may be a few years out of date, but you get the point.)

Collateral benefits include the reduction of social damage to the tune of thousands of murders *not* happening in the States, Mexico and Latin America as a result of decriminalization.

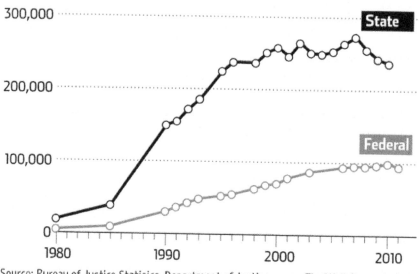

Inmates in Ever-Growing Numbers
Prisoners incarcerated for drug offenses

Source: Bureau of Justice Statisics, Department of Justice   The Wall Street Journal

Further, eliminating the prohibition on *some* mind-altering substances would have the benefit of strengthening the rule of law and reduce the costs associated with hewing to the Constitution's requirement in the Sixth Amendment for the right to a speedy trial. By removing a sea of court cases related to "this guy we found with 6 crack rocks in his pocket," the courts and police will be able to focus on the dirtbags we *all* want shoved into dank dark holes: child molesters, rapists, ballot stuffers and squeegee guys.

I find utterly fascinating the continuing kabuki theatre of American politics that insists despite all proof to the contrary that (a) drug Prohibition is desirable socially and (b) that spending billions of dollars "fighting" the propensity of *Homo sapiens* to get tipsy is practicable.

This ties in with my comments regarding the Department of Justice above. Here I cite two forms of fiscal balancing: (1) releasing immediately *every* inmate in jail for non-violent drug offenses and (2) taxing drugs to raise revenue the way we tax alcohol and cigarettes.

---

[167] CATO Foundation study Hari cites in *Chasing the Scream.*

While the roots of this pointless "war on drugs" go back to Harry Anslinger, in at the least the semi-modern context of the Vietnam Draft Dodger Generation, it surpasseth all understanding how a policy begun by Richard Nixon cannot have been overturned during periods of Democratic dominance of White Houses and Congress. How has this bizarre fantasy remained yet another third rail of American politics?

The true craziness of this "global war on drugs" is that the insanity *began* in the United States. "Our" government's power was seized by a guy named Harry Anslinger, who *insisted despite all scientific and medical evidence to the contrary,* that *his* particular fantasies about "true" drug addiction become law of the land. That one man and his insane abuse of power *in direct contravention of Congressional law and Supreme Court rulings* set in motion the millions of wasted lives and trillions of wasted dollars over the last century.

Surprised? Why? Karl Marx was responsible for just that kind of damage, if not more.

Never underestimate the power of an idea. This entire book was written with that in mind. We can only hope that my words prove more persuasive than Karl's.

Making drugs illegal has magnified the damage caused by almost incalculable degrees. Instead of one idiot overdosing or wasting his life and maybe ruining his family's life – which he is still free to do now via alcohol – entire nations are convulsed in drug cartel violence, gangs proliferate on our nation's streets and police officers are detracted from real crimes.

The damage to people far, far away from the US shores continues to the present day. In Myanmar, in 2016, a country emerging from decades of oppressive control by a military junta, a country which presumably has really pressing problems to address, the legacy of Anslinger is busy causing violence and likely to continue eating up scarce government resources in a project that would make Don Quixote blush for its absurdity:

> Christian antidrug vigilantes are asking Ms. Suu Kyi's party, set to take power in a week, to intervene in a clash with villagers who don't want to see their undulating hillsides of opium poppies destroyed.
>
> Violence between the two groups in recent weeks, ahead of Myanmar's harvest season, has injured dozens and underscored the difficulty of controlling the rugged borderlands, where rival factions and business interests thrive.
>
> "I thought I was going to die, I was so afraid, I just kept praying to God," said Mon Aung, a 42-year-old volunteer with the mostly Baptist Pat Jasan group. He was shot on a recent poppy-clearing mission and was recuperating on a shabby hospital bed[.]
>
> "But even if I died, I would have died for my people and my country," he said.
>
> It was Mr. Mon Aung's first poppy-clearing mission, and though he was afraid, he says he was motivated after watching his "brothers, neighbors and friends turning into thieves and murderers because of drugs."
>
> ....Most drug experts, including the U.N.'s drug agency, don't support eradication or Pat Jasan's hard-line tactics, which include beatings to cure drug users or their addiction. They say the solution must include a broad development plan for the area and a cessation of ethnic conflicts.
>
> ...Eliminating drugs and the conflicts they fuel will be a test of how well a civilian NLD government can work together with the military.

...Lt. Col. Myint Hoo, who heads the police here in Kachin state, said authorities have been trying to crack down on opium poppy but "nothing has changed or been reduced." He blames the conflict.

One farmer said he earns about 9,000 kyats, or about $7, a day selling the yield from his poppy plants to traders from China, just minutes away.

Here in these mountains, he says, there isn't any other viable way to make a living.[168]

To be clear, "drugs" did not turn Mon Aung's friends and neighbors into murderers and thieves; *drug prohibition* did that. To be even clearer, he was shot because instead of leaving a farmer alone to make the only $7 per day available to feed his family he went into someone else's agricultural fields to destroy that person's livelihood. I, too, would shoot someone who trespassed on my property with the intent of taking away my ability to feed my family.

Enter the "experts" at the U.N. who are talking their book. From their privileged, first world, protected lives, they are lying to justify their fat, tax-free salaries which so far as they are concerned, are conjured magically from thin air with *no* reference to practical, real economic activity anywhere – with continuing empty bromides about "a broad development plan for the area" as if a U.N. "drug expert" bureaucrat knows anything about generating business activity. To complete the C.Y.A., complete non-accountability charade, he made sure to throw in a few choice words about "ethnic conflict" fueling the drug trade. As if people living in peace and tolerating cultural or religious differences will suddenly mean that opium is no longer fun to smoke and attractive to sell at the inflated price caused by prohibition.

Lastly, the same laughable kabuki theatre is employed to talk about "eliminating drugs" being a test of the new government. If a hard-headed military junta that was free to kill, torture and arbitrarily imprison anyone who looked sideways at them could not stamp out drugs, how is a democratically elected government which allows freedom of movement to pesky Western journalists with video cameras going to do so?

Alternatives to drug prohibition abound, beginning with, uh, non-prohibition in its simplest form. As 100+ years of heavy-handed Nanny State involvement in your personal biochemistry have made it unlikely that the US can jump to that immediately, we can look at models of drug delivery which have done a whole lot to basically make heroin injection as boring as taking statins on a daily regimen. The news from Switzerland is informative.

Users can stay on this program for as long as they want, but the average patient will come here for three years, and at the end of that time, only 15 percent are still using every day.

Before, being a heroin addict was violent and thrilling – you were chasing and charging around. In Switzerland today, it is rather dull. It involves sitting in clinics, and being offered cups of tea. The subculture is gone.

---

[168] "Drug War to Test Suu Kyi's Government," Shibani Mahtani & Myo Myo, *Wall Street Journal,* 26 March 2016

After the clinics opened, the people of Switzerland started to notice something. The parks and railway stations that were filled with addicts emptied. Today, children play there once again. The streets became safer. The people on heroin prescriptions carry out 55 percent fewer vehicle thefts and 80 percent fewer muggings and burglaries. This fall in crime was "almost immediate," the most detailed academic study found. The HIV epidemic among drug users stopped. In 1985, some 68 percent of new HIV infections in Switzerland were caused by injection drug use, but by 2009, it was down to approximately 5 percent.

...

The program costs thirty-five Swiss francs per patient per day, but it spares the taxpayer from having to spend forty-four francs a day on arresting, trying and convicting the drug user. So when people ask: "Why should I pay for this?" the pragmatic Swiss answer is: This doesn't cost you money. It saves you money. [169]

So once more we find that something which is really, really complex in terms of human behavior — how a society organizes itself one person at a time under free choice — has been distorted and tortured by the heavy hand of a government which would do better to go mind its own — more narrowly defined — business.

Once more, it appears that humans left to themselves to sort out each of their own lives on their own terms is exactly what the best-intentioned government should be doing if said government *really* cared about its people as opposed to just being a self-promoting platform for narcissists to preen themselves in public about *appearing* to care about the individuals they claim to be in "public service" to. It turns out that an individual's propensity to use drugs in a damaging way is linked intimately to his or her relationships to others — something no legislation can mandate.

The opposite of addiction isn't sobriety. It's connection. It's all I can offer. It's all that will help [my addict friend] in the end. If you are alone, you cannot escape addiction. If you are loved, you have a chance. For a hundred years we have been singing war songs about addicts. All along, we should have been singing love songs to them.

One thing has the potential — more than any other — to kill this attempt at healing. It is the drug war. If these [drug using] people are picked up by the police during a relapse, and given a criminal record, and rendered unemployable, then it will be even harder for them to build connections with the world.[170]

Government and social structures *emerge* from individual human interactions. Those interactions can be distorted by social engineering or left where they belong — to the people. Individually. As governmental structures have inevitable impacts on people, let's all try to agree as a matter of principle that the structures we accept are ones that limit government taxation and regulatory interference so that a culture — not just an economy — of opportunity and pursuit of *productive* happiness may flourish.

----

[169] Hari, Johann, Chasing the Scream; the First and Last Days of the War on Drugs, Bloomsbury 2015, p220
[170] Hari, Johann, ibid, pp.293-4

As we cannot micromanage each of 300,000,000 lives, let's set conditions so that it is optimally likely for a given statistical individual to be able to live a life as free from economic worry as possible and therefore as open as possible to choosing paths which lead to positive social relationships.

Happy individuals don't want to radically dissociate themselves from their normal perceptions of reality. Even if they occasionally do, it's no reason for us to have conjured from thin social air a century's worth of massive violence and social disruption.

We got to legalize it. Unfortunately, at the same time, we got to figure out a better way to solve non-economic societal goals without using the same old blunt hammer of economic means. It is an inescapable dilemma known personally at the individual bar owner's level who has to decide between making money on his "best" customer, when that customer happens to be the town's raging alcoholic. A drug company makes more profits when addicts convince doctors to write more prescriptions.

How do we square the stock market's demand for quarterly financial *growth* returns from pharmaceutical companies with the broader society's *larger* demand (or desire) for a healthier population which will need *fewer* drugs, not more? In mining and oil & gas, the historical, huge external costs imposed on the public for land remediation have been moved legislatively onto the actual companies' balance sheets as liabilities. In all developed and many emerging market mining jurisdictions, before extracting a single pound of material, mining companies need to post money in the form of a remediation bond to be held by a third party, to cover the costs of post-mine-exhaustion closure and land rehabilitation.

Perhaps the same logic should apply in pharmaceuticals. In return for access to the most lucrative market in the world, Big Pharma needs to post annual Rehab Bonds to a third party, which funds are then deployed to clean up the addictive messes their drugs create. That would create properly aligned incentives. This quick example demonstrates my reasoning.

Table 7: Pharma profits with and without Rehab Fund social insurance payouts

Annual Net Revenues	Taxes	Rehab Fund Payouts	Profits
$10,000,000,000	($2,000,000,000)		$8,000,000,000
$10,000,000,000	($2,000,000,000)	($6,000,000,000)	$2,000,000,000

In line one of the first table, we can see that the drug company ends up with $8 billion in profits. That represents the conditions today. In the second line, we see the impact of having a "Rehab Fund" set aside which, if it paid out nothing, would mean the drug's company keeps its whole $8 billion.

In line two, however, we see what I call "the Sacklers' Nightmare,' which is a $6 billion payout to cities impacted by addiction and death from their drug sales. My oh my, that is a $2 billion profit instead. What if in response to the analysis showing *how* drug prescribing leads to rehab fund liabilities, the drug company then rationally restricts drug sales? The impact is seen below.

Table 7: Pharma profits with and without Rehab Fund social insurance payouts

Annual Net Revenues	Taxes	Rehab Fund Payouts	Profits

$3,000,000,000	($600,000,000)		$2,400,000,000
$3,000,000,000	($600,000,000)	(0)	$2,400,000,000

While net revenues are $7 billion lower than the first scenario, end profits are $400 million *higher* than before, because their highly addictive product has been deployed *very carefully* with doctors controlling the care of their patients instead of just writing a higher dose for more pills.

It is obviously a simplified model but bear in mind my never-ending guidelines that *the closer personal responsibility comes to dealing with an issue, the better are the outcomes.* In the fully developed "Rehab Fund" model, all who are involved would pay into the Rehab Fund. Done right, meaning no payouts for rehab care, medical care of penalty fees for overdoses, those who put money *into* the Rehab fund should get a dividend from profits at the end of the year. Again, let's align incentives in support of the results we want.

There is right now a very inefficient version called the "class action lawsuit" which can strip drug companies of billions of dollars, but it is not working to actually *fix* drug addiction because years and decades can separate, say, a high school student overdosing on Oxycontin and a drug company writhing a check, 33% of which goes immediately to the law firm bringing the suit.

The *best* idea I've yet heard to counter the demand side of drug use in this country is a *marketing* message. Howard Buffett cites a young man from Mexico,[171] Mario Berlanga, who gives a talk to American "recreational" drug users, and the impact of their choices to get high at a rave on the people in his village. There are likely dozens or thousands of ideas to counter the drug abuse in our nation – all the best ones come from the same place, building community and personal connections.

There are many things that cannot be legislated into or out of existence. Personal choices around drug use are included in those things. Strengthening community is personal, local and has nothing to do with the Federal Government, if that government does the right thing and gets out of people's lives.

My suggested budget is for the next year, the DEA budget is slashed to $120,000,000 – all of that to be used to shut down operations, hand off law enforcement to States and localities and sell off real estate. Every single employee of the DEA should be offered the chance to interview for a useful job in the private sector, or for reassignment to a (thoroughly revamped) USDA or FDA. Despite all the hard work and dedication, the DEA certainly after 40+ years of effort has not stopped middle class kids from getting stoned on their way to college and a bright, white-collar future, nor poor kids from getting stoned and shot at on their way to an early grave or a prison cell with a dim, criminal future.

By every single metric, the DEA is an abject failure, except one: the long line of hundreds of thousands of people who've made careers out of the kabuki theatre of trying to hold back the tide on a 50-mile beach using an inflatable toy ducky and five hundred crazy

---

[171] Buffett, Howard G., pp. 288-289

straws. Even worse, the "tide" in this instance being crime related to drug abuse was *created by the very drug war itself*. Quite literally, the DEA's very existence as the enforcement arm of drug prohibition is its own self-perpetuating problem-creation engine.

I am quite sure that most of the folks who signed up to become DEA agents did so in an effort to improve our country. Their concerns are to be applauded and are very real: misuse of recreational drugs can most assuredly lead to antisocial behavior, poor health outcomes and criminal stupidity. But so, one could reasonably argue, does overeating, lack of exercise, choosing TV over book learning and voting morons into office. We don't have entire Federal bureaucracies dedicated to preventing people from doing any of those suboptimal things.

Trust me – they are going to roll out horrifying video footage of kids addicted to heroin and all kinds of other images showing the real damage that drug addiction can do. When they show you this heartstring-tugging propaganda, just remember that the plural of "anecdote" is not "data," and that no matter how well we run a society, bad things will always happen to good people.

Those same sad stories about alcoholics freezing to death in the snow stumbling home from the local bar are also true, and also sad, but we tried making alcohol illegal. All that did was give us Teddy Kennedy as a Senator.

A proper role for Justice

I am potentially open to the idea that a distant, non-local oversight function for police, judiciary and prisons is in order. Unfortunately, nothing in this world is perfect, including my guiding assumption that "local is better." "Local is better" gave us the Jim Crow laws, a range of localized abuses like for-profit work farms and the 21-year corruption horror show known as Sheldon Silver in the New York State Legislature. Granted, we still have for-profit businesses employing slave, er, prison labor, often in such startling roles as call-center professionals interacting with an unsuspecting public.

It would also be marvelous if the Department of Justice, a *Federal* entity, mind you, would enforce the text of the Constitution, starting with violations of said Constitution by people who went out of their way to swear obedience and adherence to the terms of that wonderful, if highly-abused and increasingly-ignored social contract.

Harry Reid for *six years* was *required* as the head of the Senate to deliver a written budget for deliberation. He simply just did not do so for the entire term of the Obama Presidency. You will have heard about his protests from his prison cell.

Oh, wait, no you would not have, because far from being arrested and prosecuted for his *failure to comply with his Constitutional obligations,* nothing at all has happened to him as a consequence.

You just try, say, not paying your property taxes, or failing to appear in court for a minor traffic summons. You see how quickly the bills mount up and how swiftly you are arrested once found by one or other arm of the "Law" in this once-great nation of ours. The only way you're going to get away with just not doing what you're legally required to do is to become an elected member of government.

Then you're above it all, you see, you're special, you're *a public servant*. How sweet can it get?

There may be a role for a Department of Justice in our Federal Government. When we have trimmed its mandate, purged it of its authoritarian, meddling political personnel and restructured the *personal* incentives people have for serving the DOJ for a period of time, we the American people with constant oversight and keen attention can enjoy the benefits of an effective DOJ paying attention to a much narrower list of things than is currently their remit.

So what should they be doing, if in fact we don't just can the whole rotten experiment? Arguably, the most important change would be to end the idea of working at the DOJ as a career. US Attorneys should be a rotating role kind of like jury duty. If one cannot build a career on being a lawyer at Justice, then Americans will be far better served by having officers of the court rotate through prosecutorial roles are required. Humans respond to incentives, and I am going to be of expansive generosity to include lawyers in that statement.

We've already seen how bad incentives empowered US Attorneys to waste millions of dollars on entrapping, prosecuting and imprisoning an ageing Canadian comedian for selling glass pipes across state lines. The same kind of dynamic occurred during the Enron collapse in 2007.

Sidney Powell wrote a book[172] which shines brightly amongst the constellation of brilliant works penned by professionals with firsthand experience wrestling the Swamp Beast. The US Attorneys involved in the Enron case *so desperately wanted to find scalps to display* that they wasted huge amounts of time and money going after a trader and a banker based on the flimsiest of "evidence" about their supposed wrongdoing. There was never any substantial reason to believe the people they chased down had done anything wrong. The Enron CEO Skilling and CFO Fastow had certainly committed all kinds of crazy fraud, but most of the people around them, including bankers who were duped into setting up deals which *the bankers had no way of knowing were fraudulent*, had nothing to do with the criminal fraud which brought down Enron.

The Department of "Justice" went after them anyway *because locking people up in high-profile cases is good for your career,* whether any illegal activity had occurred in the first place.

For wasting tens of millions of dollars of taxpayer funds and, along the way, doing their very best to destroy the professional and family lives of innocent people, these corrupt hucksters were not fired for their unethical and likely evil abuse of power. Nope! President Obama promoted them to star positions in his Administration. Heck, when a totalitarian Progressive finds capable people willing to attack and destroy innocent Americans to advance a political agenda about "evil corporations," that power grasping progressive feels a deep, gut-level urge to polish those rough cudgels into finer weapons to be used against good people.

---

[172] Licensed to Lie: Exposing Corruption in the Department of Justice

Proper Funding for Public Defenders and Allocation of Costs

In a book awash in strong recommendations to *cut* spending, there are a few areas of government which all Americans – if they take time to think about the issue carefully – should be in unanimous support.

"I want a lawyer." That should be the *only* sentence *any* American utters if they find themselves in handcuffs. Period. Don't even give them your name. Your lawyer can give that to them when she arrives. The Innocence Project[173] found that 25% of people who were innocent but ended up convicted spoke to the police, and those statements were indeed used against them in a court of law.

The Miranda rights are read to every person arrested. The statements are clear, and *you* should read them closely and take time to understand them.

"You have the right to remain silent. Anything you say can and will be used against you in a court of law. You have a right to an attorney. If you cannot afford an attorney, one will be appointed for you."

Note that it does *not* say that anything you say *may* be used against you in a court of law. Nope. Straight up, it says that you're an idiot for saying a damned word. If in the course of human events, you, as an honest citizen innocent of wrongdoing, happen to be arrested, *shut up.* Think about it if you want and then, after you have thought about it some more, *continue to shut up.*

The time for someone to speak is not during your arrest and the person to do the speaking is your attorney, not you. If you keep your wits about you, the only four words you should say from the time a cop stops you to the time hopefully just before you are free are "Not guilty, your honor." That's if you go to trial. If you don't get that far, the only words you should say are, "I want a lawyer."

Like it or not, the justice system is not about justice. It's full of people with personal and professional incentives. Very few of those incentives remotely approach caring about whether a person arrested is guilty or innocent. All humanity likes the easiest path forward in life. Same goes for cops – if there is a crime committed and they nab someone who flaps his gums after being arrested, it'd make everyone's life – except the accused – a whole lot easier to wrap this up quick and send his ass to prison.

Whilst this book is about the Federal Government, more broadly it is about honesty and clarity in public funding of communal resources. One issue which matters to all Americans equally – even if some do not know it yet and may never encounter it personally

---

[173] www.innocenceproject.org

– is how the costs of trials are incurred in each State. True Justice requires that a defendant in any trial has the best possible legal representation.

Relatedly, no matter the outcome of the trial, we must change the law so that the defendant does *not* have to pay anything for legal services rendered. It is a travesty that someone, say, can be arrested at 18 for a misdemeanor, serve four years or more in jail and then when he gets out, he is unable to put together a functional life on the right side of the law because his jail time was not his whole punishment. Nope – he was also saddled with "court costs" often including a bill for his supposedly "public" legal representation. If that bill comes to $5,000 or more, for someone with no high school diploma, it may as well be $5 million in terms of his ability to get an hourly job, pay taxes on income, find a place to live and eat and all those things. If he cannot vote or get a driver's license until his court costs debts are paid, it makes it even harder to overcome that debt mountain.

The system in this instance almost *requires* an ex-con to dabble in some crime just to pay off his legal court fees, from a proceeding he did not want to be part of, the sole goal of which was to cut him off from society and which now demands he pay for with money the same system makes it almost impossible for him to earn legally. It would be hard to come up with a dumber system.

As a matter of creating a real Justice System fair to all, I propose a variant on Road Trip Rules: *Gas, Grass or Ass.* Everybody pays; nobody rides for free. The corollary to that is that each person only must pay once. Free people able to contract freely in a free society – albeit a mobile one – long ago came up with a completely fair allocation of costs. We could do worse than emulate that simple, clear and just system of cost-sharing towards a common goal.

Using that simple rubric, a person who has served physical jail time has paid with his or her ass. No other costs may thereafter be allocated to the ex-con. I am simplifying, of course; in cases of theft, sentences often include restitution to victims, where that is possible. What we should all object to is unreasonable and unpayable "court fees" being slapped onto someone who has already had his or her freedom denied.

Secondly, public defenders must be able to bill for their hours in a manner comparable to their private sector counterparts. I've earlier suggested a form of "jury duty" for private sector attorneys, and this is where it comes into play. Obviously, we're not going to pay for six defense attorneys billing $1,000 per hour, but if we as a society want quality justice delivered – and believe me, you do – then we need to remunerate people well. Right now, we get very junior attorneys who cannot wait to move on to a job which pays more. Because we are trying to "save money" by paying very little, we're getting the worst of both worlds: inexperienced or just plain indifferent attorneys doing a mediocre job *and* higher costs because the stated annual salary is just one component of how much it costs to run a department of, say, twenty attorneys. High staff turnover creates its own costs as money is spent on recruiting and hiring new, junior attorneys who are desperate for work and therefore cannot wait to be walking back out that rotating door themselves.

Thirdly, judges need to get paid more. I remember clearly an old Wall Street colleague of mine who said that when graduated from law school and got his first job as an associate at a Wall Street law firm, his father who was a Federal judge instantly quit his job saying, "I'm a damned Federal *judge* with 30 years of experience and first year legal associates are making *double* my salary!" Market forces have the virtue of valuing goods and services. You get what you pay for in this world. You pay peanuts, you get monkeys. Or –

and this is what we oddly depend on – you get idealists who toil hard, long hours as a *personal sacrifice* that their families endure out of some starry-eyed set of ideals not shared by the entire population.

Once again, we have this weird situation of some individuals willing to be paid far less than they are worth to do a job that is in all our interests be done well. Let's remove that bizarre uncertainty from our system. Let's set reasonable salaries for experienced professionals.

If we adhere to this plan of proper court funding, aside from better justice for all, it brings a few wonderful fiscal and societal benefits:

➢ People will have more clarity and faith in the justice system. Deep cynicism and distrust about who gets locked up and why abounds in this country. I am not going to wade into the dozens of possible factors which contribute to calls to defund the police and the like, beyond stating the obvious. Something is wrong with our system and it is worth overhauling. Starting with what we can do – costs and processes – let's make sure that we insist our courts live up to our shared values of fairness and due process.

➢ When taxpayers understand their personal share of paying for the true costs of trying people, those same taxpayers will ask more searching questions, such as "why are 90% of these insane laws in existence in the first place, when the country got along just fine without them for our first 200 years of existence?"

➢ Those convicted of crimes will actually be able to repent of their societal transgressions, pay for their crimes and hopefully emerge back into society one day to become productive members of society, rather than being almost literally forced into a career as a criminal.

Executing Pimps and Slave Owners

The DOJ and law enforcement do focus on some very important things. In conjunction with volunteer, civic entities like the Polaris Project,[174] our tax dollars are very well spent chasing down the lowest of the low: people who make a living exploiting other people's vulnerabilities. Everyone in government and civil society that can assist in finding these evil people should be encouraged in the hunt.

This is the kind of thing Americans of all stripes – barring, of course, sex traffickers and the creepy sleazebags who show up at hotels to have forced sex with imprisoned women and children – are happy to see tax dollars spent on.

The only changes I would make to the pursuit of these evil sleaze is more money for people and technology to find the exploited, and a fast track execution process for those

---

[174] www.polarisproject.org

convicted of such heinous crimes. Anyone remember what a positive civic combination can be fashioned from a good length of rope and a stout tree branch on the town common, after a duly administered court of law rendered judgment on child molesters and murderers?

Sometimes you just can't improve on old-fashioned, time-tested judicial traditions.

Chapter 21: Department of State

Year Founded:	1789
Founded by President	George Washington
Funding Budget 2023	$60,400,000,000
Messina's 2024 Budget Proposal	$50,000,000,000
Messina's 2025 Budget Proposal	$45,000,000,000
Degree to which Messina's Plan is Better	8.5%
Should a Federal State Dept exist?	Yes

Is this a standalone proper use of the taxpayers' limited resources?	Yes
Does this expenditure unfairly benefit one American over another one?	No
Does the expenditure meet the "Is this logical?" standard of fiduciary responsibility?	Yes
Can the goals be achieved by *not* spending the dollar more effectively than by spending it?	No

Thomas Jefferson was our first Secretary of State. It's been a bumpy road since then. Lots of highs and lows, which is to be expected, though I am betting that many things I consider deep lows other Americans would consider political triumphs. Such is life in a democracy.

The idea of a group of people in the governmental apparatus paying close attention to international issues that do and could potentially impact the US or US interests is a solid one. What *should* be debated with greater honesty and clarity is the extent to which any *actions* should be allowed to be taken by any given individual in any given administration. Less discretion given to the permanent bureaucracy is better than more, if only because for all its flaws, a representative republic guided by civic participation has turned out to be less completely awful than every other type of government structure.

Changing the direction of national foreign policy is like steering an aircraft carrier with one rudder in heaving seas. Having spent many years pondering this, and in working with some very excellent people who serve as professional staff in the State Department and related agencies, my main critiques are the strong potential for groupthink and the disbursement of cash to foreign governments.

The State Department website has a good overview and history:[175]

The Department of State has grown significantly over the years. The first Secretary of State, Thomas Jefferson, oversaw a small staff of one chief clerk, three other clerks, a translator, and a messenger and only maintained two diplomatic posts, in London and Paris, as well as 10 consular posts.

World War I (1914–1918) and World War II (1939–1945) brought vastly increased global responsibilities to the United States as it emerged as a preeminent

---

[175] https://history.state.gov/departmenthistory

power. New challenges after the end of the Cold War and the fall of the Soviet Union, included:

- the newly independent states,
- the global economy,
- terrorism, and
- the security of the American overseas presence.

To address these changing global circumstances, the number of domestic and overseas employees (not counting local employees) grew to:

- 1,228 in 1900,
- 1,968 in 1940,
- 13,294 in 1960,
- and 15,751 in the year 2000.

The number of diplomatic posts increased from 41 in 1900 to 168 in 2004 and continues to grow.

It is an important entity, with thousands of dedicated civil servants, both full-time professionals as well as political appointees who come and go with each Administration. Are there improvements to be made and criticisms to be leveled? Sure, as there are with any complex organization. My only comments here relate to making sure that there is accountability to the American people and – as ever – to keep things are simple as possible, but no simpler.

The more the State Department's actions are directly related to national security and support of our global allies, the better off we are. As I am mostly in favor of the State Department as a viable department necessary for effective Federal Government operation, I will leave it to the reader to go down the various rabbit holes available which describe its funding details. The Office of the Historian is a great place to start.

Some representative highlights over the years from a budgetary perspective include:

From Obama 2012 Budget:

Funding Highlights:

- Provides $47 billion for the Department of State and the U.S. Agency for International Development, a 1 percent increase from 2010, when costs for Overseas Contingency Operations are excluded. Significant levels of funding are continued for operations and assistance in Iraq, Afghanistan, and Pakistan. Increases are made in the areas of food security and global health. Savings have been created through foreign assistance reductions in several countries.

- Makes strategic investments essential for U.S. national security in a time of constrained resources, and strengthens core diplomatic and development activities essential for U.S. global leadership.

- Promotes U.S. exports and economic growth by supporting the President's National Export Initiative through increased resources for the Export-Import Bank.

- Supports implementation of the Presidential Policy Directive on Global Development by targeting investments that will support economic growth, democratic governance, game-changing innovations, sustainable capacity, and mutual accountability, especially through initiatives in global health, climate change, and food security.

- Invests in multilateral institutions, including the multilateral development banks, leveraging resources from other donor partners and supporting key countries and Administration priorities.

- Reduces bilateral programs and the Assistance for Europe, Eurasia and Central Asia account to focus funding on regions with the greatest assistance needs.

- Reduces funding for the African Development and Inter-American Foundations by nearly 20 percent and directs the organizations to seek partnerships to leverage and maximize remaining funding.

- Continues a multi-year initiative to strengthen U.S. diplomatic and development expertise in countries of the greatest strategic importance.

- Advances efforts to address national security challenges through a cooperative approach that includes funding to support a Global Security Contingency Fund that integrates Defense and State resources to address security crises involving both agencies.

- Supports U.S. Agency for International Development operational and programmatic improvements, including reforms to procurement systems and investments in science and technology, innovation, and monitoring and evaluation.

If you want to dive into the functions of the State Department, having read such a summary, the logical question is where to begin? First and foremost, any organization is a living, organic being whose efficacy, quality and return on investment will vary over time. As the popular saying in business goes, "culture eats planning for breakfast."

Very patriotic Americans who choose to serve in the State Department are striving to advance American interests in myriad ways, often through individual focus on a given nation's government, or through focus on an industry or issue that crosses borders. For example, some professionals at State focus on mining and mineral supply chain issues that are important to American economic and national security. They aim to support investments and operations to benefit – ultimately – American national interest while boosting economic outcomes for allies.

Others work to stem the scourge of child trafficking or indeed any kind of slavery, by coordinating with multinational law enforcement and military teams in support of governments trying to stamp out this evil. I am not spending a lot of time on those types of efforts except to say I for one wholeheartedly support important work that makes the world a better place.

It is in the nature of things – or at least in the nature of the spirit that animates this book – to dwell on the causes for significant change, rather than spend a large amount of time explaining the positive aspects of those governmental functions that I believe should be maintained.

Americans are well served by the range of tasks performed by foreign service officers at US Embassies and Consulates around the world. It is an excellent idea for more Americans to experience directly and for prolonged periods living in foreign countries. There are many seasoned State Department employees and veterans who will likely have far more insight into different details of the service and what could be improved. So I will not wade into that here.

I will opine from the interactions I have had both here and abroad with the State Department that the mantra threading through this book applies to the State Department as well as any other branch. Less is more. By all means, let's cultivate a diverse work force composed of the full panoply of linguistic skills required to at the very minimum understand the nations of the world and their relationship to ours.

Here is the summary for the Biden Administration's proposed 2023 budget, quoted here:

> President Biden believes deeply in the ability of U.S. global leadership to solve challenges, and the Administration recognizes that diplomacy and development are vital tools for advancing U.S. interests and values. That is why the Fiscal Year 2023 President's Budget requests $60.4 billion for the Department of State and the U.S. Agency for International Development (USAID), $1.9 billion, or 3 percent, above the Fiscal Year 2022 Request, and $7.4 billion, or 14 percent, above FY 2021 enacted levels. With these resources, we can advance our foreign policy agenda and deliver for the American people.
>
> The Budget will fund a range of Department of State and USAID priorities, including:

Support for Ukraine and Our Allies and Partners in the Region: The Request includes $1.6 billion to support Ukraine against Russia's premeditated, unprovoked, and unjustified invasion and assist other countries across Europe and Central Asia threatened by regional insecurity. The Request provides significant assistance to our allies and partners while building their capacity to counter actions from malign actors.	I'd like to see the audited books for where all that money is going. Russians are pricks for invading Ukraine. I feel sorry for bombed civilians, but Ukraine is a wildly corrupt government and country.
Affirming U.S. Alliances and Renewing U.S. International Leadership: The Request maintains longstanding commitments to key partners; advances peace, prosperity, and security across the Indo-Pacific and Europe; expands diplomatic and development initiatives in Africa and Asia; and positions us to effectively compete with the People's Republic of China (PRC) and Russia. This Request includes $4 billion to support U.S. commitments to international organizations and affirms U.S. leadership at a moment when our competitors are seeking to expand their influence.	This is the kind of meat and potatoes work State should be doing. Great. Go get it done. Beat back the Communists in China focused on being the dominant world force.
Addressing the Climate Crisis: The Request has $2.3 billion to support U.S. leadership in addressing the existential climate crisis through diplomacy; scaled-up international climate programs that accelerate the global energy transition to net zero by 2050;	There is no "crisis." A crisis by definition is something urgent in nature bounded by

support to developing countries to enhance climate resilience; and the prioritization of climate adaptation and sustainability principles in Department and USAID domestic and overseas facilities.	immediacy in time. John Kerry's private jet is paid for by the taxpayers while he spews CO2 across the world. Hypocrisy is a bad look.
Strengthening Global Health Systems: The United States is the international leader in advancing global health outcomes that benefit the American people and millions of others around the world. The Budget requests $10.6 billion in Department and USAID funding to continue to collaborate with international partners to invest in cross-cutting health systems to prevent child and maternal deaths, combat infectious diseases, and control HIV/AIDS.	Insanity. The American healthcare system does not help our own citizens. Fix that first.
Revitalizing Alliances and Partnerships in the Indo-Pacific: To strengthen and modernize America's alliances and partnerships in a vital global region and affirm U.S. leadership in strategic competition, the Request includes $1.8 billion to implement the Indo-Pacific Strategy to support a free, open, connected, secure, and resilient Indo-Pacific Region, and an additional $400 million for the Countering PRC Malign Influence Fund (CPMIF).	Sounds great in theory. I look forward to seeing it in practice.
Defending Democracy Globally: In response to increasing authoritarianism around the world, the Request has more than $3.2 billion to advance democratization, protect universal human rights, bolster anti-corruption work, and increase programming that builds inclusive, legitimate, and effective governance – consistent with the commitments made during the President's Summit for Democracy.	Sounds great, but what on earth can it possibly mean in practice? Other nations organize themselves the way they want to.
Promoting Gender Equity and Equality Worldwide: The Request includes $2.6 billion to advance gender equity and equality across a broad range of sectors, more than doubling such funding over the FY 2022 Budget. This entails $200 million for the Gender Equity and Equality Action (GEEA) Fund to advance the economic security of women and girls.	A laudatory goal, no doubt but color me skeptical that these billions of dollars will do anything at all to achieve such a vague target.
Revitalizing and Expanding the Diplomatic and Development Workforce: This Request would equip the Department and USAID to continue to recruit, retain, and develop a diverse, dynamic, and highly capable workforce to tackle 21st century challenges. It advances diversity, equity, inclusion, and accessibility; supports professional development opportunities; and builds capacity in critical new areas such as cyberspace and emerging technology.	Generic H.R. talk for hiring good people and training them well. Sure, OK, please do that.

When one gets into the particulars, that is where the problems arise. A general mission for the State Department to gather data, draw conclusions and provide advice to our diplomatic corps and the Administration is a benefit to the nation. But $200 million of taxpayer money "for the Gender Equity and Equality Action (GEEA) Fund to advance the economic security of women and girls" is nonsense of the highest order. What the heck can that possibly mean in practice aside from highly inflated salaries paid to NGO employees who travel business class to stay in lovely hotels while attending conferences about "gender equity?"

If we're going to spend that money, I'd rather pick 100,000 broke women per year and give each of them $2,000. In nations with per capita annual incomes between $700 - $10,000 per year, that would be a significant investment in those women's futures and would do wonders to advance their equality in economic terms. Kind of like a public sector "angel investor" round – don't try to spend hours agonizing; just allocate the cash to 100,000 women randomly selected from applications across, say 50 qualifying low-income nations. The private market demonstrates that over time, a distribution of outcomes will be achieved, but their economies will grow and the women who get the check will have life-altering opportunities which middle-class Americans grew up blessed with.

You want to see opinions about America turn for the better over time? Do more stuff like that, if we're going to spend the cash to begin with.

I highlight the bullet points and add my comments to show that robust debate about our funding choices should be core to American civic participation. The winner gets to choose how to set policy, so will there be more yowling about a supposed "climate emergency" that never actually manifests itself under a Democrat Administration than under a Republican? Sure, and that's how our system functions.

Bureau of Intelligence and Research (INR)

INR is the direct successor to the OSS and is one of the 16 intelligence agencies in the Federal Government.

I touch elsewhere on the multifaceted redundancy of what can collectively be labeled "the IC or Intelligence Community." To examine how tax dollars are spent, it makes a great deal of sense to operate this group within the State Department.

As the intelligence agency "closest to the coal face," being tied to the US Embassies around the world and supporting diplomatic efforts, INR is arguably one of the intelligence divisions which should remain in place. With thousands of State personnel across 170 or so diplomatic posts around the world, INR has a rich and wide pool of perspectives to draw on to manage information flows relating to the varying conditions in the nations we deal with.

One of the most important and hard to manage factors of value across any government agency is personal dedication to service. Just as one cannot legislate morality, one cannot force people to perform at their peak all the time by drowning them in detailed rules. I raise and emphasize that point, because I drafted this budget as a way to more closely align incentives across the government with the interests of American citizens as a whole.

That can never be a perfect fit, because you can never please everyone at the same time. Some Americans see a role for a more muscular, interventionist approach to world problems, while others lean towards pacifism. Working within the always fuzzy boundaries raised by that lack of 100% agreement in the voting public, the best government can do is to *minimize* the things it attempts to do, to then *excel* at performing the few tasks remaining and thereby – hopefully – delivering positive results at home and abroad.

That will always be cultural and driven by individual initiative. We the taxpaying people should expect that those who are honored to do this work on our behalf, do so wholeheartedly and with our nation's best interests at heart.

I suggest trimming the budget for State considerably, both because we *need* to cut out of control spending *for real this time* and because most of the programs which would be cut will be extraneous to data gathering and analysis for policymakers. State spends a lot of money on projects in other countries – well-intentioned, to be sure – that would be best left to those countries to fund, if they find them so valuable. The American enterprise is flat damned broke – we don't need to pay Deloitte or Booz Allen or any other consultants to advise other nations' government departments on the right way to do things. All that information is freely available on the Internet.

Now we come to the nasty, cancerous blight within State which must be excised immediately. The nasty censorship crap we have grown inured to in the DC Swamp has infected the State Department as well. Nothing drives politicians crazier than Free Speech. They all hate it. Period.

The State Department is so unhappy a newspaper published details about where it's been spending your taxes, it's threatened to only show a congressional committee its records *in camera* until it gets a "better understanding of how the Committee will utilize this sensitive information." Essentially, Tony Blinken is threatening to take his transparency ball home unless details about what censorship programs he's sponsoring stop appearing in papers like the *Washington Examiner*.

A year ago the *Examiner* published "Disinformation, Inc.," a series by investigative reporter Gabe Kaminsky describing how the State Department was backing a UK-based agency that creates digital blacklists for disfavored media outlets. Your taxes helped fund the Global Disinformation Index, or GDI, which proudly touts among its services an Orwellian horror called the Dynamic Exclusion List, a digital time-out corner where at least 2,000 websites were put on blast as unsuitable for advertising, "thus disrupting the ad-funded disinformation business model."

The culprit was the Global Engagement Center, a little-known State Department entity created in Barack Obama's last year in office and a surprise focus of Twitter Files reporting. The GEC grew out of a counter-terrorism agency called the CSCC and has a mission to "counter" any messaging, foreign or domestic as it turns out, that they see as "undermining or influencing the policies, security, or stability of the United States." The GEC-funded GDI rated ten conservative sites as most "risky" and put the *Examiner* on its "exclusion" list, while its ten sites rated at the "lowest level of disinformation" included *Buzzfeed*, which famously published the Steele Dossier knowing it contained errors and is now out of business.[176]

338

Americans need to demand the State Department stick to its knitting. That knitting being – since many of their staff don't seem to know this – having *experienced*, capable Americans gathering data about nations and political movements abroad, then conveying that information is an unfiltered a form as possible back to the President so he or she can make sound decisions about American foreign relations.

Period.

No more taxpayers paying hundreds of millions of dollars to consultants like Booz Allen Hamilton and Deloitte for "advice." When we restructure how we pay civil servants, we will get highly qualified people to work *for* the government – for awhile – to lend their skills to their fellow Americans. No more underpaid bureaucrats engaging consulting firms whose partners make millions for the work that should be done by the actual government employees.

Chapter 22: Department of the Treasury

Year Founded:	September 2, 1789
Founded by President	George Washington
Funding Budget 2023	$20,530,00,0000
Messina's 2024 Budget Proposal	$10,000,000,000
Messina's 2025 Budget Proposal	$10,000,000,000
Degree to which Messina's Plan is Better	Completely
Should a Federal Treasury Dept exist?	Yes

Is this a standalone proper use of the taxpayers' limited resources?	Yes
Does this expenditure unfairly benefit one American over another one?	No
Does the expenditure meet the "Is this logical?" standard of fiduciary responsibility?	Yes
Can the goals be achieved by *not* spending the dollar more effectively than by spending it?	No

Our national bank account, it is a core and crucial department of the government. Its efficacy and service to the American people depends in large part by the people who staff the department.

As the nation is flat broke, it is important that the national cash register be maintained in proper working order so that as we correct the horrendous course we are on, there is a functional body able to be worthy of the title of United States Treasury.

One of the glaring issues I touch on in this book is the mismatch between tasks and experience that happen throughout government. It should be an *earned* privilege to work in the Federal government, with fierce competition for the roles available. Cutting numbers of staff, banning unions while raising compensation and putting in place stricter testing requirements will improve the quality, focus and dedication of the Federal workforce.

This excerpt is from Tim Geithner's book, straight out of the gate in chapter two, titled "An Education in Crisis:"

> The Constitution didn't grant the executive branch much direct power over the domestic economy. But the Treasury has more influence in foreign economic affairs, and its international division, a group of about two hundred civil servants when I joined, was known as a great place to work on issues that mattered. My first assignment was to write an analysis of what European financial integration could mean for the United States, a topic I knew nothing about at the time, though I would grapple with its consequences two decades later. It was interesting stuff for a twenty-seven-year-old kid.[177]

---

[177] Geithner, Timothy, Stress Test: Reflections on Financial Crises, Crown, 2014, p.36

While I am excited to read that the US taxpayer is funding the educational fascination of twenty-somethings, it strikes me that there is not a whole lot of value *to the American people* in having someone "write an analysis" about something incredibly complex, a topic which that person "knows nothing about." This busywork generated by eager youngsters in DC is tragically the norm. While there is a wonderful role for young Tims to play in providing *research support* to an experienced professional writing analyses of various issues of import to the American people, that role should *always* be subordinate and directed.

My intent is *not* to create a snarky book sniping at people with selective quotes. While I disagree mightily with many of the missteps of the Bush and Obama Administrations during the 2007-2009 crisis, including much of what Geithner championed, his book is fairly presented and confirms many of the things I am asserting here. For example, later in that same chapter, in relating his posting to Tokyo, he describes how he was responsible for producing Treasury's quarterly forecast for the Japanese economy.

> This was a useful education, mostly in making me skeptical of forecasting. I talked to economists and executives. I studied the data. But how on earth were we supposed to predict Japan's growth rate over the next two years? Even the best forecasts, I learned, were just educated guesses. They could tell a story about how the economy might evolve, but they couldn't predict the future.[178]

So once again, the American taxpayers – if you ask them, which I have – believe comfortably that our government only hires experienced subject matter experts to drive policy decisions. Unfortunately, it is actually paying for the fun overseas post-graduate education of kids who know next to nothing about what they are supposedly "analyzing." All of which confirms my assertion that the *only* proper way to drive national policy is from *a priori* first principles. As politicians and bureaucrats allow themselves to be swayed this way and that in reaction to predictions of dubious value, the uncertainty inherent in an unstable government restricts economic activity and suppresses opportunity.

One thing which I touch on in the section on the Federal Reserve is the need for market-driven interest rates. Not only is it better from a long-term economic growth perspective to have hundreds of millions of people create the true market rate for interest on loans, but it also saves us from the current insanity of insulated bureaucrats trying to forecast the future for years to come, from which forecast the Federal Reserve then "sets" interest rates for us all.

Bureaucrats with no personal money at stake playing with fancy models is a terrible way to set monetary policy when the data collection, observation and analytical tools exist for us to see the price of money (interest rates) fluctuate in real time across the real economy.

Those considerations should guide *all* hiring decisions in the government, including Treasury.

---

[178] Ibid, p.39

Below find a summary table from the President's budgetary request.[179] It breaks down the $20,530,000,000 requested to run the Treasury Department. It is a helpful breakdown, because we can judge what we think is worthwhile going forward and what can be chopped immediately. My budget and comments assume the new simplified tax structure I propose. A few big items leap out at me which I highlight here.

Line Item	Biden's Budget	Messina's Budget	Comments
Management	$2.05 B	$1.0 B	Slim it down to match upcoming changes
IRS Taxpayer Services	$3.68 B	$4.0 B	Better customer service; help Americans navigate the new, simplified tax code
IRS Enforcement	$6.3 B	$1.2 B	The new code will be really easy; less temptation to cheat
IRS Ops & Systems	$4.2 B	$1.0 B	Simplicity of new tax code will make operations leaner
Multilateral Development Banks	$1.9 B	0	Enough nonsense; stick to basic functions, please

For things like "Business Systems Modernization" which has eaten up $250-330 million per year for the last four years at least, we need to get a swift public-private steering committee in place to fix that immediately.

---

[179] 02-05.-Executive-Summary-FY-2023-BIB.pdf (treasury.gov)

President's Budget Discretionary Appropriation Request

Dollars in Thousands

	FY 2021 Enacted (post IRS transfer)[2]	FY 2022 Annualized CR	FY 2022 Enacted	FY 2023 President's Budget	FY 2023 President's Budget (with IRS Technical Adjustments)[3]
Management & Financial	**$1,554,281**	**$1,554,281**	**$1,704,947**	**$2,056,804**	**$2,056,804**
Departmental Offices Salaries and Expenses	$233,000	$233,000	$243,109	$293,242	$293,242
Committee on Foreign Investment in the United States (CFIUS)	$20,000	$20,000	$20,000	$20,000	$20,000
CFIUS Fees	($20,000)	($20,000)	($20,000)	($20,000)	($20,000)
Subtotal CFIUS Fund (non add)	**$20,000**	**$20,000**	**$20,000**	**$20,000**	**$20,000**
Office of Terrorism and Financial Intelligence	$175,000	$175,000	$195,192	$212,059	$212,059
Cybersecurity Enhancement Account	$18,000	$18,000	$80,000	$215,000	$215,000
Department-wide Systems and Capital Investments Program	$6,118	$6,118	$6,118	$11,118	$11,118
Office of Inspector General	$41,044	$41,044	$42,275	$43,878	$43,878
Treasury Inspector General for Tax Administration	$170,250	$170,250	$174,250	$182,409	$182,409
Special Inspector General for TARP	$19,000	$19,000	$16,000	$9,000	$9,000
Special Inspector Pandemic Recovery	$0	$0	$8,000	$25,000	$25,000
Community Development Financial Institutions Fund	$270,000	$270,000	$295,000	$331,420	$331,420
Financial Crimes Enforcement Network	$126,963	$126,963	$161,000	$210,330	$210,330
Alcohol and Tobacco Tax and Trade Bureau	$124,337	$124,337	$128,067	$150,863	$150,863
Bureau of the Fiscal Service	$345,569	$345,569	$355,936	$372,485	$372,485
Digitization of Unredeemed Matured Savings Bonds Records	$25,000	$25,000	$0	$0	$0
Tax Administration[1]					
Internal Revenue Service Total	**$11,919,054**	**$11,919,054**	**$12,594,054**	**$14,100,667**	**$14,100,667**
Taxpayer Services	$2,587,606	$2,763,606	$2,780,606	$3,385,723	$3,684,593
Enforcement	$5,004,622	$5,004,622	$5,437,622	$5,861,649	$6,272,313
Operations Support	$4,104,102	$3,928,102	$4,100,826	$4,543,268	$3,833,734
Business Systems Modernization	$222,724	$222,724	$275,000	$310,027	$310,027
Subtotal, Treasury Appropriations excluding TEOAF	**$13,473,335**	**$13,473,335**	**$14,299,001**	**$16,157,471**	**$16,157,471**
Treasury Forfeiture Fund Total	**($75,000)**	**($75,000)**	**($175,000)**	**$0**	**$0**
Permanent Rescission	($75,000)	($75,000)	($175,000)	$0	$0
Subtotal, Treasury Appropriation including TEOAF	**$13,398,335**	**$13,398,335**	**$14,124,001**	**$16,157,471**	**$16,157,471**
Treasury International Programs	**$1,890,319**	**$1,942,319**	**$2,056,460**	**$4,374,515**	**$4,374,515**
Multilateral Development Banks	$1,481,244	$1,481,244	$1,527,172	$1,906,315	$1,906,315
Food Security	$32,500	$32,500	$48,000	$43,000	$43,000
IMF PRGT Grant	$0	$0	$102,000	$0	$0
IMF Resilience and Sustainability Trust Subsidy Cost	$0	$0	$0	$20,000	$20,000
Environmental Trust Funds	$139,575	$139,575	$274,288	$2,300,200	$2,300,200
Office of Technical Assistance	$33,000	$33,000	$38,000	$38,000	$38,000
Debt Restructuring	$297,000	$401,000	$134,000	$134,000	$134,000
Total, Treasury Appropriations excluding TEOAF	**$15,363,654**	**$15,415,654**	**$16,355,461**	**$20,531,986**	**$20,531,986**
Total, Treasury	**$15,288,654**	**$15,340,654**	**$16,180,461**	**$20,531,986**	**$20,531,986**

[1] FY 2021 Enacted (post IRS transfer) includes a transfer of $208 million from Enforcement to Taxpayer Services ($32 million) and Operations Support ($176 million).

[2] Excludes funding provided for COVID-19 Pandemic response.

[3] The 2023 Budget includes changes to IRS appropriation language that allow the IRS to move certain support activities from the Operations Support appropriation to charge the full cost of mission activities to the Taxpayer Services and Enforcement appropriations. In the 2023 budget, the IRS proposes to move Rent and CFO expenses. These proposed changes are reflected here.

[4] In FY 2021, Congress also appropriated $120 million to Treasury's debt restructuring account for clearing Sudan's arrears with the IMF on an emergency basis.

What Treasury *Should* be Doing

Let's peruse the Constitution to see what it says about the division of labor between the Treasury and the Federal Reserve. Oh, look, there is no provision in that organizational document for the Federal Reserve. Well, that's a relief, because we'll be consigning *that* stupid experiment to the dustbin of history shortly. So the Treasury can get back to managing the monetary supply.

Many of the wise changes I propose in this budget plan can be effected immediately – like defunding the Department of Education which can happen with the stroke of a pen. The complexity of transitioning to a post-Federal Reserve world will take some management. Great news for us all! The US is the center of the global capital markets, so we are chock full of the expertise relevant to managing the transition from our current fiscal mess to a simpler, clearer and more honest state of affairs.

The Treasury will take on those data collection and reporting tasks relating to the price of money, capital flows and a simplified, clarified taxation function. The beautiful thing from an operational and cultural perspective is that the Treasury Department in any private sector company does those things on a regular basis. The more the government adopts best practices from the private sector, the better off we all are.

Internal Revenue Service

The IRS does a largely admirable job. Respected and loved by all in the land, its officers tend to be diligent, intelligent, sweet-natured, handsome of mien and dignified of deportment. It is clear their staff are not hired from the muddy pool of genetic mortals that you and I spring from. No! Their divine bearing and ridiculous physical, moral and intellectual perfection would lead one to believe that IRS agents are formed whole in magical vats filled with angel's breath and unicorn sparkles.

The very fact that such divine beings deign to sully themselves with implementing the overly complex set of institutionalized abuse that is filling out tax forms aside, there are some small issues around the edges that need to be addressed to make their lives easier and to – incidentally – improve American society by also easing the administrative burden on hardworking taxpayers.

The IRS officials have done a wonderful job on the whole. Let's reward them by making their lives easier.

First off, how did we get here? When did the Swamp Beast begin feeding itself *directly* off the lifeblood of every single citizen? Don't take my narration for it – let's go right to the National Archives.

Passed by Congress on July 2, 1909, and ratified February 3, 1913, the 16th amendment established Congress's right to impose a Federal income tax.

Far-reaching in its social as well as its economic impact, the income tax amendment became part of the Constitution by a curious series of events culminating in a bit of political maneuvering that went awry.

The financial requirements of the Civil War prompted the first American income tax in 1861. At first, Congress placed a flat 3-percent tax on all incomes over $800 and later modified this principle to include a graduated tax. Congress repealed the income tax in 1872, but the concept did not disappear.

After the Civil War, the growing industrial and financial markets of the eastern United States generally prospered. But the farmers of the south and west suffered from low prices for their farm products, while they were forced to pay high prices for manufactured goods. Throughout the 1860s, 1870s, and 1880s, farmers formed such political organizations as the Grange, the Greenback Party, the National Farmers' Alliance, and the People's (Populist) Party. All of these groups advocated many reforms (see the Interstate Commerce Act) considered radical for the times, including a graduated income tax.

In 1894, as part of a high tariff bill, Congress enacted a 2-percent tax on income over $4,000. The tax was almost immediately struck down by a five-to-four decision of the Supreme Court, even though the Court had upheld the constitutionality of the Civil War tax as recently as 1881. Although farm organizations denounced the Court's decision as a prime example of the alliance of government and business against the farmer, a general return of prosperity around the turn of the century softened the demand for reform. Democratic Party Platforms under the leadership of three-time Presidential candidate William Jennings Bryan, however, consistently included an income tax plank, and the progressive wing of the Republican Party also espoused the concept.

In 1909, progressives in Congress again attached a provision for an income tax to a tariff bill. Conservatives, hoping to kill the idea for good, proposed a constitutional amendment enacting such a tax; they believed an amendment would never receive ratification by three-fourths of the states. Much to their surprise, the amendment was ratified by one state legislature after another, and on February 25, 1913, with the certification by Secretary of State Philander C. Knox, the 16th amendment took effect.

Yet in 1913, due to generous exemptions and deductions, less than 1 percent of the population paid income taxes at the rate of only 1 percent of net income.

This document settled the constitutional question of how to tax income and, by so doing, effected dramatic changes in the American way of life.[180]

There you have it – some tax-loathing politicians gambled that the people would not vote themselves into federal taxation. Amazingly, they failed to consider that 99% of people would *not* be taxed, so the Ever-Present Politics of Jealousy would make lots of people vote to tax *"the rich,"* never considering that if you give government an inch, they take a thousand miles. Much as happened in the United Kingdom with the Brexit vote on 23 June 2016, some politicians decided to put a very bad idea to popular vote, confident that the measure would not pass. Do people ever learn?

If this were 1914, if you were among the 99% of income earners, you wouldn't send a plug nickel to Washington, DC. If you earned in the top 1% of annual incomes, you would have to cough up 1% of your earnings to Uncle Sam. How did that already confiscatory, abusive rate of governmental theft turn into the Life Sucking Permanent Parasite we all deal with today?

---

[180] https://www.archives.gov/milestone-documents/16th-amendment

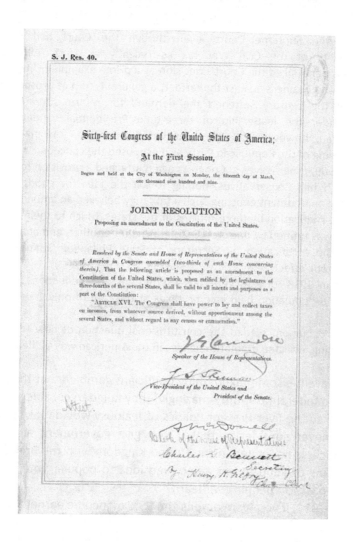

S. J. Res. 40.

Sixty-first Congress of the United States of America;

At the First Session,

Begun and held at the City of Washington on Monday, the fifteenth day of March, one thousand nine hundred and nine.

JOINT RESOLUTION

Proposing an amendment to the Constitution of the United States.

Resolved by the Senate and House of Representatives of the United States of America in Congress assembled (two-thirds of each House concurring therein), That the following article is proposed as an amendment to the Constitution of the United States, which, when ratified by the legislatures of three-fourths of the several States, shall be valid to all intents and purposes as a part of the Constitution:

"ARTICLE XVI. The Congress shall have power to lay and collect taxes on incomes, from whatever source derived, without apportionment among the several States, and without regard to any census or enumeration."

Speaker of the House of Representatives.

Vice-President of the United States and President of the Senate.

Attest.

Short of rescinding the 16th Amendment – a stunningly good idea – we need to just clean up around the edges to make the current system of income taxation work to the benefit of the American people instead of its current role of fattening the wallets of politicians while bankrupting the nation.

The issues we need to address include:

1. IRS enforcement and audit powers have been used for political ends, to squash speech inimical both to the current administration *as well as* dangerous to the perpetuation of the IRS itself.
2. Serious conflicts of interest exist in having the employees of the taxing arm of the government be able to form a union.
3. A lack of both personal and institutional accountability which would have made George Orwell blush with embarrassment beneath the withering gaze and red pen of his editors had he proposed them as a storyline.

Since access to money is the ultimate end of all power-hungry sociopaths – more commonly known as "politicians" – it is of crucial importance for free people to maintain *strict* control over the taxing power of government. Sadly, over the years, we the people have most assuredly lost all oversight, never mind control, over the taxing power of the Federal and State governments.

Fortunately, there is a very *simple* way to fix this particular situation with one sweep of the metaphorical arm across the (still metaphorical) desk of government.

Proposal to improve our tax collection system:

1. Scrap the entire Federal Tax Code. Whew, that was a relief.
2. Implement a simple flat tax, payable by residents of the United States.
3. To the extent any staff remain, those staff will be trained *to help taxpayers fill out* the simple 3-line annual tax form, with a few to perform audits on those few people who will still try to cheat.

Simplicity is the people's friend. Complexity is the weapon of oppressors.

To take one issue somewhat at random, of grave concern to our freedoms, the IRS has become divorced from its Constitutional master, the Executive Branch. A fine man named Mick Mulvaney joined the Trump Administration in the Office of Management and Budget. One of his priorities was to make sure the IRS submits its rulemakings to the White House before those rules are implemented. *That had never before been required.* That idea of course died with the Biden Administration.

Ponder that. One of the most invasive and pervasive arms of the Federal Government – the one that *every* American must deal with – was in November 2019 fighting to keep from having to submit for review rules to its boss, you know, the one elected by American voters. One would reasonably ask why that is, and certainly ask even more forcefully how that came to be the case in the first place.

Another, even worse idea, which is kind of amazing, was put forth in May 2021 by the Biden Administration in its first proposed budget.[181] This insane idea if adopted will take the IRS's freedom from its supposed boss – the Executive Branch – and add to that complete freedom from accountability to Congress, formerly known as the Legislative Branch. It would insulate the IRS from having to answer *any questions* from Congress. That's right – by putting their budget on autopilot, Congress would have *zero ability* to influence anything being done by supposed employees of the taxpayer.

Given how little regard some IRS functionaries already have for Congress – witness Lois Lerner's smirking non-testimony when it was *demonstrated clearly* that she had abused her power to restrict freedom of speech of Republican-leaning non-profits – it seems amazing that "our" representatives would want to have *less* authority over what can easily become one of the worst tools of oppression in any government. By the way, after abusing her position, damaging potentially thousands of careers and doing her best to limit free

---

[181] https://www.whitehouse.gov/wp-content/uploads/2021/05/appendix_fy22.pdf

speech, Lois got to retire *and keep all of her benefits and pension payments* for the rest of her useless life.[182]

Chew on that, American taxpayer, while you research the abuses of power and sheer incompetence at the IRS, which, I need remind you, is *not* at all a reflection of the vast majority of current IRS employees who appear as angels descended from Heaven, trying mightily to be a shining, guiding light to us mere mortals.

All my suggestions for improving the functioning of the IRS are in line with the ages-old dictum that pretty people should be rewarded for the pleasant way their appearance makes others feel. To steal from those awesome road works signs, let's give 'em a break.

AMT is an embarrassing admission of Congressional incompetence – and that's what's *good* about it

In the preamble to all the numbers in the 2012 budget, there is a piece about the "AMT fix." This is one of the numerous absurdities of the US government, even aside from the linguistic fun of trying to figure out what is meant by an "Alternative Minimum Tax." The AMT was implemented in 1969 to "get" something like 30 millionaires *who by following the IRS's rules* did not have any tax liability. That's right: thirty people were the target of legislation which now ensnares tens of millions of taxpayers every year. Those 30 people were *not* breaking the law – nope, they were *following the laws* with all their deductions and special interest carveouts.

This prime piece of politically jealous fury was concocted to say, *"OK, smarty pants who actually read what we voted on and then made it work for you despite our intending it not to, we're going to write a special law targeted at you to take more of your stuff."* Rather than just simplify the tax code in 1969 to remove the loopholes and carveouts, the clowns in Congress decided to add another layer of complex idiocy to the tax code.

The AMT at its heart is a bald-faced admission of Congressional incompetence turned into bureaucratic small-minded bullying. It's the pimply junior class president who cites an obscure student constitution rule to make sure the star football player does two hours of community service before he can play in the homecoming game, all for violating some strange technicality about on-time attendance. That would be bad enough from a public policy and national pride perspective, but those jealous pimply Congressional asshats of yesteryear neglected to index to inflation the income level at which the AMT kicks in. As of 2020, about 25% of taxpayers now pay the AMT.

It is firmly in the American interest to delete this whole pack of nonsense immediately, which luckily will just happen when we scrap the entire current tax code.

---

[182] Remember the IRS targeting scandal? No one ever got punished for it | Washington Examiner 18 January 2018

FATCA – Why the Administrative State Flourishes on Your Indifference

One thing I try to drive home *repeatedly* is that the Administrative State *relies* upon each American thinking about *only* his or her own, personal, narrow interests. That indifference to the general principles of Universal Objective Justice means that if the government is "only" abusing those 230 people over there, then, well, we 300,000,000 other people not being screwed by *this* particular issue can ignore it.

I hope by now you are beginning to see the pattern and the problem. When it comes *your turn* on the torture rack of governmental abuse, and *you* start screaming about how unjust it is, say, to have *your home and bank accounts seized* under "civil forfeiture" *without your having even been arrested for a crime,* you're left wondering how this insane injustice can occur in a supposedly "free" country under the "rule of law."

The answer is that the government makes sure to only attack a tiny percentage of people at one time on one issue, trusting – and it has proven true so far! – that Americans' rampant indifference to the suffering of their neighbors and good public policy will mean that not a single bureaucrat is fired nor a single politician is voted out of office due to any one particular outrageous, illegal and just plain nasty abuse of a given taxpayer.

Every abuse of an American citizen by "our" government must be seen as an assault on every American. Labor union organizers in the 19th and 20th centuries understood this perfectly. When it comes to the Federal Leviathan, I urge every American to pay close attention to every abuse of any citizen. If you don't speak out about the injustice heaped on the family across town, why do you think anyone will speak out for you?

This idea of how crucial it is to call out injustice and governmental abuse is not a new one. Applying it and bearing the consequences of doing so requires fresh courage against every new outrage that governments come up with. There is a seeming inexhaustible supply of bad ideas in the minds of governmental types – if only we could harness that energy to transform it into electricity, we'd have solved any foreseeable "energy crisis." The hard choice to speak out against governmental abuse is nothing new; that does not make it any harder to live it in practice.

> First they came for the Communists, and I did not speak out –
> Because I was not a Communist.
> Next they came for the Socialists, and I did not speak out—
> Because I was not a Socialist.
> Then they came for the Trade Unionists, and I did not speak out—
> Because I was not a Trade Unionist.
> Then they came for the Jews, and I did not speak out—
> Because I was not a Jew.
> Then they came for me—
> and there was no one left to speak for me.
>
> — Martin Niemöller[183]

---

[183] Lutheran pastor and theologian born in Germany in 1892, who wrote this in 1946 about the

Granted, throughout this book I suggest that we go after the Communists and Socialists to ensure they do not control the American government, and a clear part of my program is to rid the nation of *public sector* Unionists, but the lovely intent of the poem remains. Speak up for your fellow Americans who are being abused; the simplest way to do that is to demand the starvation of the Swamp Beast whose selfish thrashings destroy lives without any hesitancy.

Fix Obvious Things Immediately

In the immediate here and now, while the reforms I've proposed get churned through the body politic on their way to implementation, there are some things that the IRS should do in terms of streamlining and making processes logical while taking efforts *not* to assist criminal enterprises. For example, there is a Death Master File that is released publicly. The original reason for that file being prepared is so that banks or others who have a legitimate need to review information on SSNs can check on the accuracy of records, look for potential fraud, etc.

As reported by *Bloomberg Businessweek* in May 2012,[184] bereaved parents of children who had died found out their dead children's SSNs had been stolen by others who used the data fraudulently in filing tax returns. What a horror. I imagine all honest Americans would favor changing the rules so that this file of dead names is *not* posted publicly. It should only be available via a legitimate needs request from a legitimate entity, such as a Federally-regulated bank or securities firm. This would seem to be one clear example of the "Duh" factor in decision-making.

The fine folks at the IRS are surely aware of myriad issues like that which they have come across while performing their jobs; perhaps we have a popular ballot initiative to create mini-bounty bonuses for each such mistaken rule discovered and eliminated? Tech firms pay "bug bounties" all the time to hackers who find flaws in software. Why not set up a similar "bad rule bounty" program that all Americans can participate in? You want participatory citizenship? I sure do – and this would be one driver of that civic zeal.

Lawmakers must take time from other things to write, introduce and vote on a new bill to stop this misuse of personal data. On the other hand, lawmakers taking time to vote on laws simplifying the government over small issues of practical use rather than meddling in big things like ObamaCare is a win-win for us all. We'd all be better off if they spent their time ferreting out goofy laws to repeal and stupid rules to kill. How great would those Congressional campaigns be every two years? *"Me? I've spent the last 18 months repealing*

---

cowardice of German clergy and intellectuals in not speaking out against Hitler and Nazism leading into WW2.

[184] "Grave Robbing for a Refund," Bloomberg Businessweek, May 14-20, 2012, p35

no fewer than seventy-three pieces of insane legislation, making the country and this district a better place. How many pieces of bad law has my opponent repealed in all that time???"

Granted, under my proposed system, you'd only get to make that pitch once for your one shot at reelection, but what a fine example of civic zeal and personal values that would set for our youth. Imagine if the citizens who stepped forward to *serve* our country were all fired up with the desire to leave the government a better, more honest, more efficient thing than they found it, that when their term of service was over, they laid aside the trappings of rule and headed back to their families, as did Cincinnatus in 439 BCE.

As our reformed tax system will be one based on electronic postcard-sized filings from the citizenry, along with slightly-larger ones from corporations, we can begin to right-size the IRS. Given the funding trajectory it has been on, it may well be possible to allow natural attrition to take care of the staff size.

We are still going to need auditors – just as any corporation of reasonable size maintains internal audit staff to ensure everyone is doing the right thing – so the bulk of IRS employees in future years should be mainly technical / IT experts and forensic accounting auditors. We all need the national books to be in good order, and no one should evade the taxes to be paid as part of the privilege of being an American.

Right now, the IRS is put into the unenviable position of behaving like the Berlin Wall. As Ronald Reagan said outside the Brandenburg Gate in 1987, "Isn't it strange that there's only one part of the world and one philosophy where they have to build walls to keep their people in?"

Well, the US uses the IRS as a far more effective wall than the bricks in Berlin ever were. We are the only nation on earth that taxes a person's income no matter where that income was earned or where that person lives. Further, if an American citizen makes a balanced decision to renounce her citizenship in favor of another nation, the IRS levies insane financial penalties. Kind of like a wall built to keep one in, isn't it? If this place is so great, why is "our" government penalizing people who want to leave?

The IRS can be shaped into an organization of helpful experts that exist to pick up the phone and help Americans perform one of the greatest acts of a participatory democratic republic – contributing to the funding operations of the important but very few things government does for us all.

It is an honor and a responsibility to be an American citizen. It is proper for us all to fund the *correct* amount of government we need. Let's make it really use for everyone to do that by fixing the tax code and helping the IRS employees make sure the national cash register stays filled.

Bureau of Alcohol, Tobacco, Firearms and Explosives (ATF)

Year Founded:	1972 (precursors to 1886)
Founded by President	Lyndon Johnson
Funding Budget 2023*	$1,700,000,000
Messina's 2024 Budget Proposal	$30,000,000
Messina's 2025 Budget Proposal	$0
Degree to which Messina's Plan is Better	Completely
Should a Federal ATF exist?	No

* Their website only has data current to 2019. Enacted budget was $1.4 billion in 2020 for 5,082 employees. Other sources cite Biden allocating $1.7 billion to the ATF to pester honest American gun owners. (I may be glossing that a bit.)

I'll just get it out of the way immediately: "Gee, I'd love to work *there.* Those are four of my favorite things!" Or: "Who says guns and booze don't mix?!" And "It was *already* a cool place to work in the 1990s, but *then* they gave them stuff that goes *'BOOM!'* as well??!! C'mon! Sweet gig."

On the plus side, these guys do sometimes investigate really bad people and take dangerous weapons from them. But so do local cops and the FBI. While some kind of "weights and measures" standards and safety organization — like old gun proofing houses that tested firearms for safety standards — is certainly of benefit to society, the ATF in its current incarnation is a fountain of abuse of the rights of Americans. There is a never-ending stream of videos on YouTube made about ATF agents abusing Americans' rights with little to no recourse.[185]

Under the anti-gun animus of the Biden Administration, the ATF has been showing up at Americans' doors, often two or three ATF agents accompanied by one or two local law enforcement. Why are they doing that? They claim to be checking for "straw purchasers" who are buying guns to transfer illegally to people who are not legally able to buy firearms.

"Do they have a warrant for this?" a rational person would ask. No, no they do not. Fully armed and scarily equipped ATF Agents are showing up to harass people who committed the crazy sin of buying more than one firearm at a time. The videos I have seen of this strongly suggest this is about state-sponsored intimidation of law-abiding Americans for their political views.

Everything in the ATF's institutional DNA points to abusive tactics against American citizens. When their predecessor agency was created in 1886 it was called the Revenue

---

[185] ATF Agents Handcuff US Navy Sailor & Rob Him At Gunpoint - YouTube A 20 year veteran of the Navy, with no criminal record at all, happens to be at a gun store when the ATF swoops in, handcuffs him, steals $20,000 of his legally owned firearms and accessories and as of 26 November 2022 weeks after the event, just refuses to return them to him, with agents *on tape* threatening him that if he "dares" to keep calling them for the return of his lawfully-owned property, they will arbitrarily issue charges against him.

Laboratory as part of the Treasury Department. It morphed and metastasized over the years until its placement back with Treasury in 1972.

On their website,[186] they've got a Strategic Plan for 2017-2022. Here it is:

Strategic Goal Statements

Deter Illegal Firearms Trafficking and Violent Gun Crime
Utilize effective firearms enforcement techniques to reduce violent firearm-related crimes in the United States and abroad, thereby enhancing public safety.

Research Fire and Investigate Arson
Advance the science of fire investigation globally, by setting and delivering the highest standards in response, research, information sharing, and training.

Combat Criminal Organizations
Make our communities safer by identifying, targeting, and dismantling those criminal organizations that utilize firearms, arson, explosives, and alcohol or tobacco diversion in furtherance of violent criminal activity.

Modernize Our Processes and Systems
Modernize business processes and systems for improved information sharing and knowledge management. Use innovative technologies to support ATF's mission.

Deter Misuse of Explosives, Bombs, and Bombings
Advance domestic and international explosives expertise to prevent, detect, and investigate acts of violent crime, terrorism, and enhance public safety.

Manage Our Workforce
Attract, develop, and retain a diverse, expert, and high-performing workforce to execute the ATF mission and administrative responsibilities in the current and emerging business environment.

Strategic Plan Fiscal Years 2017 – 2022
www.atf.gov

They should be embarrassed by this. Not just a little, but a whole lot. None of what they write there requires an ATF to exist. Each of the first four things is already handled capably by police and fire departments. The last two are super embarrassing. After 150+ years of existence, *"Managing Our Workforce" and "Modernizing Processes"* are strategic goals? A reasonable taxpayer might ask what the hell have they been doing if their workforce has heretofore been unmanageable and their systems antiquated?

The entire origin of the ATF lies in – of course – taxation. Not safety or "regulation" or "pointless interference in Americans' Constitutional rights." Their website has a very helpful timeline.[187]

Creation of the Office of Internal Revenue – 1862

In 1862, Congress creates the Office of Internal Revenue within the Department of the Treasury specifically to collect taxes, including highly lucrative tariffs on imported distilled spirits and tobacco products. By 1863, tax evasion and organized crime activities have become so widespread that Congress authorizes the hiring of three detectives to investigate alcohol tax evaders. This act is the first coordinated effort between tax collection and law enforcement; the three detectives are the forerunners to today's ATF Agent.

---

[186] https://www.atf.gov/about-atf/budget-performance
[187] https://www.att.gov/our-history/atf-history-timeline

What they call "organized crime" in 1862 most normal Americans would call "American farmers and merchants involved in producing booze and tobacco for their customers who resent having huge chunks of their income stolen by a Federal Government that thinks it's got better uses for the money than the people who earned it." But I guess that's too wordy.

The ostensible "justification" for wasting tax dollars to bully political opponents at the grassroots level is trying to root out criminal activity. The absurd pretext for this targeted harassment is that the government believes career criminals get their guns from otherwise law-abiding citizens who fill out background checks at Bass Pro Shops to treat themselves before hunting season starts to a new shotgun and a new bolt action rifle. It's an appalling abuse *and* pointless waste of tax dollars.

The rational Americans so bullied mostly ask the agents for a warrant and then tell them to f*$% off because they're trespassing on private property. Good for those fine Americans. Unfortunately, most normal, law-abiding people tend to trust government officials, so they agree to illegal searches.

Let's see what other treasures lurk in their historical record, shall we?

March 1927

Bureau of Prohibition Act, March 3, 1927 (44 Stats. 1381)

The Prohibition Unit is reorganized into the Bureau of Prohibition.

General Lincoln C. Andrews, of World War I fame is appointed to the Assistant Secretary of the Treasury in charge of Prohibition in May of 1925. He assesses the current capabilities of the Prohibition Unit and in a 1927 Letter to the President of the Senate, states, "...This is a fair picture of the conditions today facing the executive department charged with the enforcement of the prohibition laws. Conspiracies are nationwide in extent, in great numbers, organized, well financed, and cleverly conducted. No parallel of this situation exists in normal times. It is similar, rather, to war. Our efforts must be nationwide and as thoroughly organized. We are in particular need of a highly developed department of intelligence to keep the forces of society informed as to the personnel and methods used by the law breakers..."

He reorganized the Prohibition Unit into the Bureau of Prohibition and begins to professionalize the service, building a veritable army to fight organized crime.[188]

Have you ever had a beer? Maybe at a bar, or a restaurant or in your own backyard on Independence Day weekend?

Then *you*, dear citizen, are the "law breaker" referred to in the ATF's proud historical record. During Prohibition, you would have been targeted by the gun-toting thugs of the Bureau of Prohibition, a precursor to the ATF.

Much nearer to the present time, in September 2023, two men were sentenced to *prison* for making and selling novelty bottle openers.

---

[188] https://www.atf.gov/our-history/atf-history-timeline

Matt Hoover got 60 months in prison and Justin Irving got 68 months in prison[189] *for selling a novelty item that did not work* to make a semi-automatic gun into an automatic gun. You read that right.

AutoKey Card: Matthew Hoover & Kristopher Justin Ervin Sentenced to 5 Years in Federal Prison

Ammoland Inc. Posted on September 7, 2023 by John Crump

Autokeycard.com Seized By the ATF, Owner Arrested For Selling A Drawing

Jacksonville FL – Judge Marcia Morales Howard has sentenced Matthew Hoover of CRS Firearms and Kristopher Justin Ervin, the defendants in the AutoKey Card case. Ervin and Hoover were convicted in a Florida Federal Court in April 2023 for transferring machinegun conversion devices, known as Autokey Cards.

The AutoKey Card is a slim metal card that has etched markings that resemble a lightning link. A lightning link allows users to modify certain AR-15-style rifles and convert them into machine guns. As per the National Firearms Act of 1936 (NFA), any device that can change a gun into a machine gun is regulated as a machine gun itself.

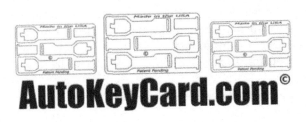

Ervin considered the card as a conversation starter. He intended it to spark a discussion about gun rights and the foolishness of gun laws. During the trial, it was disclosed that Ervin did not want a deep etching on the card, in order to prevent buyers from cutting out the lightning link. It was also revealed that the lightning link etching was not the correct size to function as a lightning link, even if someone could cut it out from the card.

Even the ATF itself couldn't get the lightning link to function by cutting out an AutoKey Card along the lines. The only way the ATF could get a firearm equipped with a lightning link made from the AutoKey Card to fire automatically was by jamming the fire control group and causing hammer follow. The ATF lawyers argued that the men believed the device would work, so it didn't matter that the AutoKey Card wasn't functional.

Hoover was convicted of conspiracy. However, he neither sold the card nor owned any part of the company. His role was advertising the item on his popular YouTube channel, CRS Firearms. According to the government, the majority of the company's sales were directly attributed to its advertisement campaign.

---

[189] https://youtu.be/sirlkckRyIc?si=gaJwYmUIzBScYKJZ

The court recommended a sentence of 22 to 34 months in prison or supervised release for Hoover based on the pre-sentencing report (PSR). Meanwhile, the PSR suggested time served and a three-year probation for Ervin, who has been in jail for nearly three years. Our reporter and Richard Hughes from the YouTube channel FlyingRich were given access to the PSR, which prompted the government to attempt and fail to obtain gag orders against our reporting.

The Department of Justice disagreed with the pre-sentencing report (PSR) and urged the judge to impose a harsher sentence on two men. The Assistant US Attorney (AUSA) leading the case, Laura Cofer Taylor, requested the judge punish the defendants severely.

The DOJ recommended a sentence of *19 1/2 to 24 1/2 years* in federal prison despite the fact that the men had no prior felony convictions.

During the trial, the judge acknowledged that the Pre-Sentence Report (PSR) failed to consider that the ATF considers the AutoKey Card to be machine guns. However, the judge also stated that she would never sentence the accused men to the minimum punishment that the government wanted. Furthermore, the judge questioned why the ATF is not proactively recovering the AutoKey Cards from people's houses if they pose such a great danger.

The judge handed down the sentences on the second day of the sentencing hearing. Kristopher Justin Ervin and Matthew Hoover were both sentenced to five years in prison. Although the sentence is not what the government had hoped for, it still seems excessively harsh for a crime with no victims.

Both men are expected to appeal the verdict.[190]

The fact that this indictment went to trial in the first place has only emboldened an unaccountable Administrative State. The Department of "Justice" suggested each man be taken from his family and put in prison for up to 25 *years* for selling a novelty item designed to highlight the absurdity of the ATF and idiotic laws drawn up by evil or ignorant people.

I cannot even wrap my head around the idea of twelve jurors in Florida voting to convict these two men on such absurd charges.

At least those two guys can eventually leave prison. Not so fortunate is Bryan Malinowski who was killed by the ATF on Tuesday, 19 March 2024, when they invaded his home at 6 am in Little Rock, AR using a no-knock warrant.[191] The American people need to demand some or all of the agents involved be arrested and tried for murder.

There was *no* reason for them to bust down the door of a 53-year-old executive director of the Bill and Hillary Clinton National Airport over some potential paperwork discrepancies they were investigating. They could have swung by his office at the airport in the middle of the day to question him. It is *natural* for someone whose home is being violently invaded to grab a firearm to defend his family. Of course, Mr. Malinowski probably

---

[190] AutoKey Card: Hoover & Justin Ervin Sentenced to 5 Years in Federal Prison (ammoland.com)
[191] Brother of airport director shot by ATF agents speaks out about shooting | AP News

shot at the violent men bursting through his front door. The surest way to not defend yourself and your family is to *wait* to shoot at someone breaking down your door without announcing themselves as law enforcement loudly and clearly.

This is not the first example of a no-knock warrant leading to an innocent American's death. Breonna Taylor was murdered by police on 13 March 2020 in Louisville, KY after her boyfriend shot at the men performing a violent home invasion in the middle of the night.

We know they are lying,
they know they are lying,
they know we know they are lying,
we know they know we know they are lying,
but they are still lying.
Aleksandr Isayevich Solzhenitsyn

I could go on, but you get the point.

There is no need for the ATF's police state antics.

The purely administrative parts of their jobs – like the background check system for firearms purchases – can be turned over to the Commerce Department. The bits to do with alcohol stamp taxes and tobacco can be turned over to the USDA or its State-level equivalents.

The ATF's string of senseless homicides and other egregious abuses of American citizens must end now.

Chapter 23: Federal Deposit Insurance Corporation (FDIC)

Year Founded:	June 16, 1933
Founded under President	Franklin Delano Roosevelt
Funding Budget 2023	$2,400,000,000
Messina's 2024 Budget Proposal	$2,000,000,000
Messina's 2025 Budget Proposal	$1,900,000,000
Degree to which Messina's Plan is Better	Debatable Robustly
Should a Federal FDIC exist?	Yes

Is this a standalone proper use of the taxpayers' limited resources?	Yes
Does this expenditure unfairly benefit one American over another one?	No
Does the expenditure meet the "Is this logical?" standard of fiduciary responsibility?	Yes
Can the goals be achieved by *not* spending the dollar more effectively than by spending it?	No

A creature of and reaction to the Great Depression, the FDIC serves as a prime example both of what can go right with governmental intervention and what can go very, very wrong. I suggest we keep the oversight and auditing functions, while modifying the engagement process and invoke the sort of temporary expertise rotating door model to ensure up to date knowledge that does not grow stale.

Bank examiners are an invaluable tool. Sunlight is always the best disinfectant, so it is in the nation's collective interest that there is an oversight body with the ability on sudden or no warning to plunge into a bank's books. I am a huge fan of free enterprise and free capital markets. So I would *love* to believe that everyone of their own volition will act appropriately and honestly in their commercial dealings.

Because I have also had a front-row seat to sleaze weasels who found the temptation of "cutting corners" to be irresistible, I like that we have sterling civil servants who can peer into the heart of our banking system. Sadly, too many people have failed to absorb the clear moral lessons baked into our religious systems and our secular philosophical systems, all of which emphasize the necessity for observing some common rules of behavior in commercial matters.

Straight from their website is a description of their mission:

Mission, Vision, and Values

The Federal Deposit Insurance Corporation (FDIC) is an independent agency created by the Congress to maintain stability and public confidence in the nation's financial system by:

- Insuring deposits,
- Examining and supervising financial institutions for safety and soundness and consumer protection,
- Making large and complex financial institutions resolvable, and
- Managing receiverships.

This sounds like a valuable task of government, but I'm not so sure.

Despite this fine-sounding mission, there have been banking scandals and problems with honest accounting since the FDIC was created.

Prior to the creation of the FDIC and its partner agency, people were *very careful* about where they put their hard-earned money. If you entrusted your money to a sound, well-run bank which made prudent loans to people with good credit, you were likely to enjoy a level of security that your money would be available to you in the future, and it might even grow a bit. Conversely, if you entrusted your cash to a pack of drunken fools who made huge loans to deadbeats, then you lost your cash because the bank had given it away to people who either could not repay the bank or never had any intention of paying it back in the first place.

A strict market purist would say, "Let people bear the consequences of their choices, including losing everything if the bank they entrust their money to goes bust." Another, equally concerned, equally thoughtful person would say, "It is nearly impossible for the average person to examine the balance sheets, profit-and-loss statements and risk assessments of any given bank. Most retail clients need basic services like checking, payment deposits and a safe place to park their cash that avoids total loss if a house is burned down or robbed. Those folks should not have to worry about the risk of a given retail bank being run by people who make loans that turn out badly."

I really don't have a concrete, black-and-white answer for this conundrum. When banks go bust now, the taxpayers repay the depositors, at most up to a retail level of $250,000 per account. That hardly seems fair; if I put my money in a well-run bank and earn 0.5% per annum for 20 years, while you put your money into Go-Go Good Times Savings & Loan Baby Loan Bank at 15% interest, when your pack of liars goes bust, why am I making you whole for the Ponzi returns you got for 10 years?

The FDIC is a gray area for me, balancing market purist ideals against the overall social good of retail customers having a payments and savings mechanism. Given the other, larger swamp beasts that *require* slaying, this is not the hill I'm going to die on.

My main recommendation here is consonant with the rest of my suggestions for those lucky enough to enjoy a higher-paying, skills-based, non-unionized job with the Federal Government. The FDIC should be staffed on a rotating basis by skilled bankers, accountants and risk managers who serve in their roles for 2-6 years on a staggered basis. It should be an honor to spend some time serving the nation by applying one's financial markets skills to an institution dedicated to maintaining trust in our financial system.

The major *flaws* in a busybody organization like the FDIC became apparent after the government-caused financial meltdown of 2007-08, which the folks in DC went on to make worse through the devastating, pointless and idiotic Dodd-Frank Act, which I touch on elsewhere. For purely FDIC-focused idiocy, know-nothing bureaucrats decided to attack a small Texas bank *with a loan default rate below the national average*. Why, one might ask, would a bank examiner who should be focused on the soundness of a given bank's management attack a bank and its President for running a successful bank, especially when so many others were failing?[192]

We come back to the old Sorcerer's Apprentice problem. The clowns who wrote the Dodd-Frank Act knew *just enough* about banking to convince people like Chris Dodd and Barney Frank that they could craft intelligent legislation to prevent any further "banking crises."

Of course, the rampant stupidity of this approach began with the fact that the entire 2007-08 crash was *caused* by stupid Federal housing policy and had *nothing* to do with banking policy or "deregulation." Because of the half-experienced people charged with writing horribly damaging legislation, we got the worst of both worlds – rampant interference in capital markets *and* taxpayer bailouts.

Thomas Depping in 2011 was running Main Street Bank in Kingwood, Texas, when the FDIC began to torture him and his team. From the 10 August 2011 article:

> Mr. Depping has been on a collision course with regulators since 2009, when FDIC examiners began questioning the bank's large concentration of small-business loans. Nearly all of Main Street's $175 million loan portfolio has gone to customers like dentists, owners of fast-food franchises and delivery-truck drivers, who use the loans to purchase equipment. The bank's average loan size is $100,000 to customers who have less than $1 million in annual revenue, Mr. Depping says.
>
> Mr. Depping says that Main Street's focus on small-business lending has sheltered the bank from much of the devastation that has swept the industry, including 385 bank failures since the start of 2008.
>
> Main Street had profits of $1 million in the second quarter and wrote off 1.25% of its loans as uncollectible. That is below the industry's charge-off rate of 1.82% in the FDIC's data for the first quarter, the latest available. The bank has earned nearly $11 million in the past year.
>
> In July 2010, the FDIC slapped Main Street with a 25-page order to boost its capital, strengthen its controls and bring in a new top executive. Regulators also said the bank was putting too many eggs in one basket. Mr. Depping says regulators wanted the bank to shrink its small-business lending to about 25% of the total loan portfolio, down from about 90%.
>
> Mr. Depping says he explained to regulators that Main Street has focused on small-business lending since he bought the bank in 2004 with a group of investors. He says the bank makes credit decisions based on a combination of the borrower's personal-credit and business-credit histories, among other factors.
>
> "We felt that servicing small business is something the country needs and that we're really good at it. I thought the model was working just fine," Mr. Depping says.

---

[192] Fed Up: A Texas Bank Calls It Quits - WSJ August 10, 2011, *Wall Street Journal*

This is almost the perfect example of the damage the unthinking (at best) and deliberately malicious (all too often) unaccountable drones inflict on us all every day. Here is a bank operating profitably while providing loans to small borrowers and because of a financial crash brought on by mortgage banking stupidity *created by the Federal Government,* FDIC bureaucrats are pestering a successful business to change its operating model to lend to *other*-sized customers just, well, because I guess some busybody tool felt like flexing arbitrary authority over an uppity bank president. I can never prove it, but I bet that somewhere in this story was Mr. Depping telling an FDIC official that the official was an idiot.

The American taxpayer does not write checks to the Treasury Department every year so some petty bureaucrat can get his or her revenge on someone in the private sector who treated them dismissively. Well, let me amend that. Currently, *we do* write those checks and they do hire petty bureaucrats to screw with people for no reason. This book is written to change that negative state of affairs to a positive one where we are all pulling in the same direction for the good of the nation.

Again, when dealing with complexity and people's livelihoods, having a rotating cast of temporary officials dealing with a bank's problems, potentially with a private-sector "grand jury" type of body by whom enforcement actions must be approved, we can improve our system's overall health while removing damaging officials who currently can run roughshod over any private business without risk of personal harm.

We need to fix the operational culture of the FDIC, but I do not recommend getting rid of it wholesale at this point. Maybe next year.

Privatize the FDIC Fund

Currently, all member banks pay into the FDIC Insurance Fund. This is supposed to be the pool of capital to cover any losses a depositor may experience. That nonsense must be phased out as quickly as practicable. Whether or not it made sense in the 1930s to have government-priced risk models, advances in markets, in big data analytics and financial technology have bounded ahead to the point that the best way to price risk is via the free market.

If societally we value sound banks, then the best way to price the risk associated with banking activities is through private market underwriting. We do this all the time – car insurance, flood insurance and all kinds of insurance are priced by actuaries using objective data, with final pricing determined by insurance executives who examine the risk model output from their actuaries and then decide how much risk they'd like to take for their own risk balance sheet.

It's not a huge operational change. To maintain an FDIC membership, a bank must buy insurance in the private market. Anyone with an adequate balance sheet can take the data provided by the bank, analyze it, play with historical data – you know, do what professional asset managers do all day long. If a bank is operating soundly, with good risk controls and the like, it will have multiple bidders for its risk paper. Much like the CDS (Credit Default Swap) market, the more analysts playing with rich data, the more accurately will the market price the risk associated with bank operations. The FDIC website already has searchable bank data that anyone can log in and play around with.

The Nanny State Administrative Totalitarians will whine that there will not be a single, unanimous view of what the risk in a given bank "is." The attentive reader by now knows with certainty that *anything* Administrative State Swamp Beasts see as a flaw is really a positive feature of a functioning market. With hundreds if not thousands of potential insurers, reinsurers and portfolio managers bidding to guarantee bank risk, we'll get a more objective view of the market's perception of risk *and* have a far more robust and elastic safety net for average retail bank customers.

And because risk will be privatized, some banks could, say, offer deposit insurance above the $250,000 per account limit – professional risk traders, actuaries and insurers could price that risk and decide whether to insure against multimillion dollar losses. All of this would happen in transparent markets, instead of the opaque ways private banks "guarantee" the assets of their largest clients. The most resilient markets have the largest possible number of buyers and sellers and most transparent sources of rich data. The same things that make liquid markets resilient can be used to make US commercial retail banking far less prone to taxpayer bailouts.

Let a thousand risk models bloom.

Figure 31: Proposed new facade for the revised FDIC; risk management is serious business with existential consequences.

Chapter 24: United Nations, IMF and Other Fictions

There is a whole passel of insane claims on the US taxpayer that need to be unraveled post-haste. These figures do not appear in the Federal Budget as "budgeted" line items, another function of the fantasy of government "accounting," which appears to be defined as "how we move numbers around with no other guiding principle than how effectively we can lie to the American people who *legally* are our employers, but who *actually* have become our slaves."

The United States has the maximum assessed contribution to the UN regular budget of 22%. In 2009 the assessed amount was $598,292,101. The minimum assessed contribution is 0.001%. The scale of assessments for each UN member for the required contributions to the regular budget is determined every 3 years on the basis of Gross National Product (GNP).

Only nine countries (starting with the largest contributor: United States, Japan, Germany, United Kingdom, France, Italy, Canada, Spain, China) contribute 75% of the entire regular budget. Cuba contributes .043% of the regular budget. Oil-rich Saudi Arabia contributes .713%.

There are some arguments in favor of having a collective, convening forum for nations to speak amongst themselves. In theory, such a thing was created after WW2 on the idea that wars arise from a lack of communication. Well, it is not clear that that hypothesis has been proven true. Both Ukraine and Russia are members of the United Nations. That has not stopped Russia from invading Ukraine twice in a decade.

In reality, in 2022 the United States kicked in about $18 billion to the United Nations when spread across lots of programs.

The experiment had failed even before October 7th, when United Nations employees were filmed murdering and abducting Israelis with the Gazan Government. Your tax dollars employed evil men who raped, killed and abducted innocent, unarmed people.

Enough is enough.

It is just one of many claims on your tax dollars which need to be identified and ended.

International Development Finance Corporation

Year Founded:	2019
Founded by President	Donald J. Trump
Funding Budget 2023 (Operations)	220,000,000
Funding Budget 2023 (Investment Funding Allocated)	780,000,000
Messina's 2024 Budget Proposal	5,000,000
Messina's 2025 Budget Proposal	1,000,000
Degree to which Messina's Plan is Better	Completely
Should a government-funded investment company exist?	No*

* Potentially yes, if its significant current structural flaws can be fixed.

Is this a standalone proper use of the taxpayers' limited resources?	No
Does this expenditure unfairly benefit one American over another one?	Yes
Does the expenditure meet the "Is this logical?" standard of fiduciary responsibility?	No
Can the goals be achieved by *not* spending the dollar more effectively than by spending it?	Yes

Here is another organization which could *in theory* be a tremendous tool of American foreign policy. In a world in which first the Soviets and now the Chinese Communists throw cash around to poorer nations to buy allegiance – which rarely works empirically – one could see how great it would be for the US Government to be able to offer financing for dams, roads and whatnot. So that *we* could then be the object of foreign gratitude, adoration and allegiance. Except for the centuries of evidence that that has not happened, but you know, details....

The *idea* behind the DFC and its predecessor (OPIC) is, well, let's take their words for it[193]:

What is U.S. International Development Finance Corporation?

U.S. International Development Finance Corporation (DFC) is the U.S. Government's developing finance institution. DFC partners with the private sector to finance solutions to the most critical challenges facing the developing world today. We invest across sectors including energy, healthcare, critical infrastructure, and technology. DFC also provides financing for small businesses and women entrepreneurs in order to create jobs in emerging markets. DFC investments adhere to high standards and respect the environment, human rights, and worker rights.

Sounds great, huh? The problem as always is that one must hire *people* to implement the goals adumbrated and that's where the whole thing falls over.

---

[193] https://www.dfc.gov/who-we-are/overview

Having had direct interactions with "development finance" bureaucrats over the years, I can assert with confidence that the only bureaucrats involved with investment decisions should be low-level analysts playing with spreadsheets at the request of a rotating cast of private-sector volunteers. Since bureaucrats are humans and since there is nothing stranger than a fixed-salary civil servant claiming to make investment decisions when their take home pay does not change one dime whether or not the projects or companies they invest in succeed or fail, the tendency is once again for a cozy, cossetted, closed club of Washington insiders to get their pet projects funded with taxpayer money, while really valuable projects which would aid national security get ignored.

There is one example fresh in my mind. As someone who has worked in the global capital markets and mining finance for years, I became aware of a project in critical minerals development which needed financing. The company's owners and promoters were hard-driving, brilliant, proven entrepreneurs who had found the *perfect* set of mining and metals-processing assets. Those assets would largely *fix* America's profound problem that meant (and means, because this is still not fixed) an antagonistic Chinese regime controls the supply of dozens of really important materials that the American private sector (cellphone, windmills) and military (jets, ships) depend on.

These entrepreneurs failed to cough up huge checks for nonsensical noise like $5,000 per plate dinners for home-state Senators, mainly because like all *real* entrepreneurs, they were busy creating value out of nothing and didn't have hundreds of thousands of dollars of bribery, er, lobbying dollars to spend. These same entrepreneurs initiated discussions with OPIC, which then became DFC. *On paper* the deal was perfectly in line with *publicly stated* American public policy interests. The Trump Administration was loudly vocal about the pressing need to finally fix this major gap in American supply chains.

By chance, I spoke with a member of the Administration who left to enter private practice in January 2021. We were discussing the ongoing problem of critical materials to the US economy. I asked him if he had any insights to share about why the awesome project presented for funding by those brilliant entrepreneurs had gone nowhere, while DFC was busy scattering cash to lots of other, highly inferior projects. His answer was simple and terrifying for every American taxpayer.

The project was awesome, all right, everyone agreed. But the private sector guys who were driving the project and promoting it failed to "kiss the ring" and bow and scrape to the DFC bureaucrats, indeed had the "temerity" to suggest that the paper pushing bureaucrats might not be very good at their jobs, and further that the bureaucrats were not advancing the US national interest. In short, the DFC bureaucrats "didn't like" the entrepreneurs.

As Milton Friedman observed, Hell hath no fury like a bureaucrat scorned. Ponder that. You, the taxpayer, cough up your hard-won earnings *and* are forced to borrow money for decades, all because you've been told it's in your interest to fund the vast Federal bureaucracy. Here's how that worked in practice:

1. US Government interns write multiple white papers and studies decrying our dependence on foreign supplies of things like rare earths and other critical materials that we *need* to operate our economy.
2. You the taxpayer pay dozens of bureaucrats at the DFC to look for investments to advance the national interest.

3. Those bureaucrats do nothing at all to find good deals to invest in. Entrepreneurs bring them the best deal in the world for them to fund, which will fix the problem of *most* of the critical materials on the list of concern.[194]
4. From the US taxpayers' perspective *as well as the Trump Administration's perspective,* investing in this company would be the best use of the funds entrusted to the DFC.
5. The US State Department weighs in, saying they support the company's goals as it fits neatly with the nation's foreign policy goals. Heck, the company's principals are invited to the White House to discuss the project with the National Security Council.
6. The DFC staff review the materials presented and get very excited, making very promising noises to the entrepreneurs, who – being rational risk seeking businesspeople – think that the promising noises will lead to cash investment.
7. Weeks turn into months and nothing happens.
8. When the entrepreneurs keep asking the DFC staff – who by the way, keep changing, so it's never the same person twice – when they can begin the process of taking investor funds to, you know, *solve* the critical minerals problem for the US taxpayer, the DFC staff decide they'd rather *not* be asked to do their jobs, take a dislike to the American patriot entrepreneurs and simply stop responding to their calls. Yep – like jealous kids on the junior high school playground, they decided they weren't going to invest in a really important company in the American interest – which is *their entire job description* – because the cool kids who owned the company didn't bow down to them with sufficiently groveling "respect."

Huge amounts of money wasted, an increasing problem *still* threatening American national security, and all of that happened while the spoiled brat bureaucrats kept collecting their salaries and benefits, while the American patriotic entrepreneurs who *risked their own capital and time* to fix this problem lost everything they invested.

That *exact* set of events transpired. Should I be contacted with threat of lawsuit from DFC's attorneys, I stand prepared to testify to that in elaborated detail in open court. Bring it on, boys. I can guarantee I'm going to like my answers splashed across the front pages of the *Washington Post* a whole lot more than you will.

Multiply those petty actions – or inactions – a hundredfold and you get the picture. Even when these bureaucrats *do* deign to get out their special bejeweled pen to allocate investment capital into a company that is important to national security, it happens on a timeline that is so divorced from commercial reality that they may as well not bother. As I was ranting about the appallingly glacial approach the DFC took with a friend in government, he laughed and related how a few years back, he'd been part of an interagency effort to improve relations with a country in central Africa. The DFC team took *more than*

---

[194] Interior Releases 2018's Final List of 35 Minerals Deemed Critical to U.S. National Security and the Economy (usgs.gov). There are lots of lists like this. Go search for them.

two years to make a loan decision. It's absurdity – neither politics nor commercial reality has room for anything that takes two years to get done. Literally by the time these unaccountable bureaucrats reached their decision, the entire set of reasons why the investment was good for America had disappeared.

Given how parasitic entities like the DFC act, it needs to be either thoroughly reformed or – more intelligently – dissolved. The world is awash in investment capital. The justification for something like the DFC – or any "development bank" – is that somehow there are awesome investments to be made that private investors will not make – usually because of political risk (meaning a Third World government might just take your company from you), and therefore we need the DFC.

But we don't need it. Because the DFC will only invest in projects *that already have private capital invested.* That's right – if you're wondering why the US taxpayers should invest in something that *already has attracted private capital,* then you're on the right track! This is just one more slush fund for crony capitalists to take money from hardworking Americans.

To make it really clear to those readers who do not work in the capital markets, it's as if you want to buy a successful restaurant business to run it. The owner wants you to buy it for $1,000,000. You have $100,000 in cash and go to the bank for a loan. The bank says they'll give you a $900,000, 10-year loan at the cost of 7% per year, fixed rate. The DFC pops up and says "A brew pub like this one down the street from our offices is definitely in the national interest. Here's the $900,000 on a 20-year basis for 5.5%. You have the thanks of a grateful nation and a thirsty bureaucracy."

Dissolve it. The bureaucrats blowing $140,000,000 per year on salaries, really nice offices and lots of comfy travel and snacks will have to find something more productive to do with their lives, while the $700,000,000 they were dispensing to crony capitalists who are already rich and can therefore afford to spend millions of lobbyists, will just have to find investment capital from private investors.

Better for everyone involved, unless of course you count the folks who like getting richer by taking money from the American taxpayer.

Inter-American Development Bank

This beast was founded in 1959. Headquartered in New York, its stated purpose is to provide "development financing" for Latin America and the Caribbean. One wonders why such a beast if it must be on US soil is not in Miami.

When someone tells you that they are "in development," you need to understand that what they are saying is "I spend a lot of other people's money on ill-defined projects wrapped in Good Intentions, with no accountability and without any discernible way of determining a Return on Investment of the dollars spent. Oh, and I get paid handsomely to do so."

Someone in the field of economic value creation is called a venture capitalist, a private equity investor, an entrepreneur or a worker.

I am not going to peer back into history and debate whether there was a real need in 1959 best filled by this IADB. Now I do know that in a world awash in excess capital, much of it housed in sovereign wealth funds and public pensions, there is no need whatsoever for any of these "development" banks.

Here's the perfect test of whether any of these ridiculous entities are actually valuable: let's start a privatization auction process for them all, beginning perhaps with the IABD. If sophisticated investors see value in it, they'll buy shares. If not, they won't. In any case, once we the American people draw a line through any continuing taxpayer contributions, it's up to the rest of the world's governments to decide if they'll pick up a (far larger) tab going forward.

International Monetary Fund

This internationalist behemoth takes up a lovely block in DC. Created in 1945 as part of a package of postwar reforms designed at Bretton Woods hopefully to stave off the conditions which were perceived to lead to cycles of war, it has long since outstripped its original mandate. It is a tremendous example of how biological systems will adapt to change in order to perpetuate their survival.

After Nixon closed the gold window in 1971, every other vestige of the Bretton Woods system should have disappeared. But wily bureaucrats flush with – mainly – US taxpayer money reinvented themselves as "development experts" to keep the funding coming. They've been pestering people around the world ever since, with absolutely zero evidence that the mandarins at the IMF know a single thing about true business development.

While examples of the IMF's ongoing folly can – and do – fill volumes, I've chosen one example at somewhat random regarding the insane "advice" the IMF doles out.

Japan's VAT Blunder
A consumption-tax increase hits growth as the coronavirus looms.
Opinion By The Wall Street Journal Editorial Board
Feb. 17, 2020 11:23 am ET

The third time wasn't the charm for Tokyo's long-running attempt to increase its consumption tax. Data released Monday show Japan's economy contracted in the last three months of 2019 as the tax hike hammered growth—as many warned and like the previous two times the tax has been raised since its 1989 introduction, in 1997 and 2014.

Japan's economy contracted by 6.3% on an annual basis from October to December. Plummeting consumer spending, which fell by 11.5%, is the main culprit. No wonder since Prime Minister Shinzo Abe raised the consumption-tax rate to 10% from 8% on October 1.

Some of the drop-off is a result of consumers trying to front-run the tax hike by ramping up consumption earlier in the year. Don't expect a major reprieve once the VAT shock wears off. Wage growth is anemic despite a tight labor market, and the Labor Ministry calculates that inflation-adjusted pay fell 3.5% from 2012-2018. The tax rise creates a new and higher squeeze on household incomes.

The timing of the increase couldn't be worse coming before the coronavirus outbreak in China, which depressed tourism and consumption during the lunar new year in January. Mr. Abe has managed to throttle Japan's economy at precisely the moment it most needs resilience. Some analysts fear Japan is already in a consumption-tax-and-coronavirus recession, which is defined by two quarters in a row of negative growth.

The usual suspects are now calling for more Keynesian spending on public works and social spending. Three decades of similar blowouts have created the fiscal mess that always becomes justification for more consumption-tax hikes. Japan's government debt is now about 240% of GDP.

The International Monetary Fund thinks the consumption-tax rate will have to rise to 15% over the next decade, and to 20% by 2050. But first the fund's wizards say Tokyo must expand its Keynesian spending to make the economy "strong" enough to bear the tax hikes to pay for the spending. Got that?

Mr. Abe started out with better ideas, riding back into office in 2012 with a promise to press ahead with major policy reforms to unleash the Japanese economy. Had he done so, perhaps wage growth would be peppier now, the economy would be better able to endure shocks such as a Chinese epidemic, and economic growth would be boosting revenue.

It's too late for Japan to avoid the costs of Mr. Abe's economic failures. But other governments can learn the lessons that Japan's leaders refuse to heed.

This whole package of pointlessness – IMF, World Bank and the like – must be tossed to the roadside. They have proven to be nothing but negative influences.

Chapter 25: Government *can* be great

"The true object of propaganda is neither to convince nor even to persuade, but to produce a uniform pattern of public utterance in which the first trace of unorthodox thought reveals itself as a jarring dissonance."
- Leonard Shapiro, writing on Stalin

"The Nation that makes a great distinction between its scholars and its warriors will have its thinking done by cowards and its fighting done by fools."
- Lieutenant-General Sir William Francis Butler

Unfortunately, most people in government seem to view the private sector as some mysterious enemy. At best they view it as a Perpetual Piggybank that exists solely as a source of funds for the things they feel like spending Other People's Money on. This disease is *not* limited to any one segment of the population or members of any specific "party."

A main reason for this problem is that we the American citizenry *allow* people with no private sector experience to join the government in the first place. Absent any real-world experience, they are bound by suspicion coupled with lack of knowledge to believe that the form of legal compliance is somehow a replacement for actual compliance. In addition, human nature recoils from self-criticism. The hardest thing psychologically for a person to admit is that they are objectively lacking in qualifications, skills or aptitude.

Of course, this are no fool-proof methods of preventing ideologues hostile to personal freedom from entering government, any more than there are any 100%-successful methods of managing anything as diverse and crazy as a group of people numbering from two people to 360 million.

Further, given their vast lack of experience with reality, they have a sneaking suspicion that perhaps they are not asking the right questions, so the best CYA they can come up with is to load more nonsensical paperwork onto people. The premise of all these regulations and forms and bureaucrats is that honest Americans are guilty until they prove their innocence somehow through reams of paperwork.

I've got a zany idea. How about we presume that we are innocent of wrongdoing? And then have a much smaller army of surprise auditors to wander from valley to dell, popping in on people spending federal dollars to see how they are doing so.

One of the most damaging developments to occur to the US has been the growth of the public sector, both absolutely and relative to the private sector. What used to be held up as a joke regarding other, inferiorly run countries, is now the norm in America: a bloated civil service.

It is bloated in size and its horrendous deadweight incompetence. There are valuable things for good Americans to do in government, and I've weighed in here on my vision of what those things are. There are also lots of redundant jobs, pointless agencies and bored people riding their time to retirement. From a human capital and social happiness perspective alone, I hate to see sad people trudging sadly through meaningless lives.

Let' put some zip into the step of our fellow Americans who have been trapped by golden benefits and cossetted by public sector unions. Let's set them free! Let millions of people become acquainted with the exciting vigor and friction of the private sector. It's the humanitarian and loving thing to do.

Those who demonstrate aptitude and fitness for a role in the new, improved, union-free, accountable and dynamic Federal Government will deliver exciting results to a nation grown cynical. Imagine how awesome it will be to have competitive, driven people filling *all* the roles in government, not just a few.

This is very much our circus and it is up to us to choose the performers.

Government Supremacy as Religious Belief

With some very rare exceptions, I do not believe any Americans – whether normal, healthy people or diseased, distortions infected with politicianitis – wake up every morning and say "I know! I'm going to destroy the country so it sucks for everyone." That is the magic of unintended consequences. You can wake up, do your exercises, have your granola and berry breakfast with coffee and go perform a series of well-meaning tasks that result in horrendous impacts on people.

I wrote that paragraph before the Wuhan Panic Hysteria of March 2020, when hundreds of politicians, thousands of stuffed shirt, teeth whitened teleprompter jockeys playing dress up as journalists and a truly horrifying number of Americans decided to destroy the economy and ruin society because of a thoroughly irrational fear of a virus from China. The events of the Wuhan Virus Panic Depression and the completely insane 2020 Summer of Marxist Destructions have changed my mind about how willing some Americans are to destroy the nation, whether they understand they are doing so or not.

The period from March 2020 until December 2022 has been a dystopian atrocity, with government destroying lives on a daily basis, all over a manufactured panic about a seasonal flu which kills old people who are already sick, old people who statistically would not even have been alive to catch the Wuhan Virus if it has come along in 1960. Morons atop government simply *shut down* the economy, locked kids out of schools and demanded people stay imprisoned in their homes.

This was done illegally and for no good reason. No data ever existed to support this descent into madness. The fact that Americans outside of Florida and Texas *permitted* this evil nonsense still makes my head throb in rage and astonishment.

The engine of economic growth is the private sector. Period. Government is *not* the source of "investment" and most assuredly not the source of innovation. Government is a highly necessary *cost center* that we require to keep order. If, for example, individual humans lacked the urge or inclination to commit crimes, we would not need to pay for police. But the criminal urge refuses to leave the human animal, so we are willing to pay taxes to field police forces to smack dirtbags in the head with nightsticks on the way to the gray bar hotel. A scumbag who has undergone a wood shampooing and been locked in a cage is a scumbag who will *not* be holding you and your loved ones up at gunpoint on a breezy summer evening. Perhaps with time galore to reflect on the error of his ways (and a bump on his skull to remind him lest he forget), he may emerge from prison a finer human, ready to contribute to society.

That is just one example of the very few things a self-governing people should expect from government.

There is a delicate balance of expenditure versus the "return" we the people get on our funding government. No system will ever be perfect, but I suggest strongly that we start viewing government in and of itself as a positive force; let's all view it as warily as the Founding Fathers did. They rebelled against an arbitrary government embodied in a monarchy. The Leviathan we have allowed to grow in the Swamps of DC is no different in kind than any monarchy ever was.

The economy has migrated and grown from a postwar manufacturing engine to a more diversified economy with increased services. On a manufacturing level, in 1960 there were 15,000,000 Americans employed in manufacturing jobs, with 8,700,000 people employed by the government. By early 2011, there were 22,500,000 people working on the government payroll, with only 11,500,000 working in manufacturing.

That economic bounty if it is not guarded can become the power source to run a despotic, centralizing regime that only cares about its own power, not the people from whom it derives its financial strength.

For your own research, go find examples just in the last 30 years of appalling wastes of money by unaccountable politicians and bureaucrats, united in their smug, erroneous belief that government somehow sits "above" we poor unwashed masses still yearning to breathe free.

Christina Romer who was a chairman of the Council of Economic Advisers (2009-2010) in the Obama Administration staked her career on the idea that borrowing money from my grandchildren in order to expand unemployment benefits to people today will somehow contribute to economic growth, rather than the so-obvious-it-hurts reality that it will do just the opposite.

The ridiculousness is bipartisan. Bush II decided to send everyone a $300 check in 2004 to "stimulate" the economy. Trump and Biden printed trillions of dollars to "give" to people after destroying the country for no reason during the Wuhan Hysteria. For those people (I'm writing this on 1 January 2023) who will wonder what I am talking about, trust me, a nation with accumulated unfunded liabilities nearing $200 trillion is destroyed – we just haven't noticed it yet. For further color on this phenomenon, go read Isaac Asimov's *Foundation* series about the slow collapse of the Galactic Empire.

In every age, there are people who misread the current state of affairs and take it to be a constant. One of the most fascinating things I have ever read was in the *Journals of David E. Lilienthal,* an enthusiastic New Dealer that FDR put in charge of all kinds of things, including the Tennessee Valley Authority. Lilienthal's journal entry of 3 June 1933 contained this about his discussions with Supreme Court Justice Louis Brandeis:

> During the past year I have had an opportunity of visiting several times with Mr. Justice Brandeis, once at his summer home at Chatham on Cape Cod about a year ago, and the other times at his home in Washington. One point which he has made consistently in these conferences has special timeliness right now. He pointed out that we can't have a democracy and at the same time have great fortunes, nor great disparities in wealth and power derived from wealth. Accordingly, he would tax great wealth out of existence through income and inheritance taxes. This would produce tremendous revenues for the government, which he would use for a

program of social service which would have the effect of rendering useful service and still providing employment.

The importance of this latter part of his thesis is emphasized by his insistence that we are through increasing our productive machinery as a part of private business. In support of this point he referred to the experience in the razor blade industry, with which he is familiar as a former counsel for the Gillette people of Boston. He had just heard that the Gillette people had purchased the plant and property of certain other razor blade companies, not for the purpose of using those plants to produce razor blades, but for the avowed purpose of scrapping them, since the existing facilities owned by the Gillette people and operated by them were adequate to supply all the need for razor blades which it might have. The same with many other industries where existing facilities were more than adequate for any possible need, and duplication of facilities was maintained for private competitive reasons.

Accordingly, he said, we must look around for enterprises which private business cannot go into because there is no profit in them and because of the public nature of the enterprises, which will render service to the community and at the same time furnish necessary employment to the millions of men who will otherwise be permanently unemployed because of the technological developments of which the razor blade instance is an illustration.

When I asked him concretely what he had in mind, he referred as an instance to the control of soil erosion. He had some figures on the enormous extent to which the rich topsoil of the country was being washed off and carried out to sea by surface waters, with the consequent irreparable loss in value to the country's agriculture, a process which if indefinitely continued might eventually threaten the country's capacity to produce food. Here, he said, is a project calling for billions of dollars of expenditure which no private agency could possibly undertake and which would call for the employment of millions of men, as with forestation, reforestation, slum clearance and other similar enterprises.

All of this (which he talked to me first about on January 4, 1933) is particularly interesting in view of President Roosevelt's comments at the time he announced the Tennessee Valley project. The President had there I mind the employment of men to improve the economic and social conditions of that valley, irrespective of whether the improvement would pay in dollars and cents. He apparently had in mind two things – the necessity for employing men rather than keeping them on some form of dole for which no useful work was performed, and second, the necessity of enriching the community life of that part of the country. This sounds very much like Brandeis' [sic] ideas applied to a particular area.[195]

That is quite simply a breathtaking passage for a range of reasons, not least of which is the solid evidence that bad ideas persist no matter how many times they are thoroughly disproven with concrete evidence.

Note the eternal *a priori* faith of The Government Overlord Class: that the government (in this case Brandeis in a capacity that he as Justice most assuredly was not

---

[195] The Journals of David E. Lilienthal, Volume I: The TVA Years 1939-1945, Harper & Row, New York, 1964

granted by the Constitution) would in some magical way better use *your* money for a "program of social service" than you would do in keeping your hard-earned money in the first place. Further, that this "program of social service" would in some mysterious way be a better system of social organization than a free-market economy populated by educated, driven individuals.

What exact "services" would be provided that a free-market economy would not provide? Those pesky details are never divulged, of course. Otherwise, rational citizens may start to question why a pack of lawyers sitting in Washington, DC should rake in trillions of tax dollars from hard-working citizens.

And all this from a man who *knew* – not believed or opined, mind you – that "we were [in 1933] through increasing our productive machinery as a part of private business." I am typing this book on a PC with word processing software – both of which technologies were invented and produced by companies that did not exist in 1933. I am sitting on a bouncy, mesh-backed chair of eminent breathability with up-down controls, adjustable lumbar support all of which is made of a material which likely had not been invented in 1933.

It's just stunning that Brandeis and Lilienthal, both cozily cossetted in plush government jobs, would sit and chatter smugly to one another that all this private activity pursued by supposedly "free" American citizens was somehow *wrong* and – crucially for the continuing damage pesky "public sector" parasites continue to inflict on us all – that *they have the right* to eliminate what *they* see as "unnecessary" duplication of manufacturing facilities *because* those facilities are maintained for – THE HORROR – "private competitive reasons."

Nowhere in this type of thinking is the restraining idea of: "Oh, well, I may not know all there is to know about another person's life work and specialization in an area of manufacturing. Perhaps what I see as a static snapshot of 'unnecessary' duplication of capacity is really an industry betting on growth and building capacity ahead of time. Or perhaps there are swings in demand seasonally or otherwise that necessitate additional capacity in the market, lest prices in some periods peak so high that average working stiffs cannot keep their faces or legs shaven. Perhaps one factory just built is 57% more efficient than the others, and so its investors over time believe they will take business away from their competitors. Perhaps – just perhaps – there could be *improvement* in types of razor blades, so that what I am really seeing is industrial evolution and – THE HORROR again – private competition working their creative destruction to improve razor blades overall."

And even if *that* humbling idea never crossed their minds, let's keep it really simple to this one: "In a supposedly free country, *who am I to tell another private citizen how to invest his or her money?*" Basically, where do people like Lilienthal, FDR, Brandeis, Barry Hussein Soetoro, Governor Eliot "Client Number Nine" Spitzer, Comrade-Mayor Bill de Blasio, Elizabeth Warren and Joe Biden get the idea that they have *the right* to usurp public office for their own petty jealousies and vengeances? If I have the money to invest in a new razor blade factory and I survey a field of what Brandeis would call "unnecessary capacity" and yet I choose to go ahead and build another one, *who told him that it was any of his business what I do with my investment capital?*

How about this, Mr. Justice? I don't think in a country full of poor people who have been made unemployed – perhaps in part due to *your* work as a counsel to "the Gillette people" – that it is right that you have two homes, one on Cape Cod and one in Washington.

One of those needs to be taxed away from you, and given to a poor family, preferably one laid off because of automation in the razor blade industry, so that democracy will not be harmed by your having a summer home to go to when DC gets a wee bit hot in the summer months. Ninety years later, the quaint notion of only two homes seems downright Spartan when one looks at the four homes owned by the millionaire Communist from Vermont Bernie Sanders, whose wife destroyed a college through financial mismanagement and who spends all his time screaming about how everyone else should pay more taxes.

Every single one of these hypocritical, sanctimonious meddlers in *your personal affairs* ought to make you really angry, angry enough to throw these bums out of office and demand immediate governmental operational change and – as soon as practicable – lasting Constitutional change; I've provided a helpful blueprint in Chapter 32.

When pressed for an example of what he could possibly mean by a good enterprise that private capital won't touch, Brandeis talks about soil erosion on the grandest of collectivist scales, mistaking along the way the *actual, individual, voluntary, local* and *private-sector* cooperative ways in which agricultural communities address soil erosion, water rights, etc. None of which required or require any monolithic "agency" to deploy any "dollars," never mind the impressive-sounding figure of "billions" the two-home-owning lawyer somehow knows is "required." I'd love to review his (paper) spreadsheets and the objective data he undoubtedly marshaled before providing an estimate of the dollar amounts required per centimeter-acre of soil retained for farming purposes.

If any of this sweeping social engineering and *spending your money* sounds familiar to your 21st century ears, it's because it's the same shallow, mistaken, egotistical, condescending, centralization-of-power, ignorant nonsense you heard from the Obama Campaign and Administration for eight long, bleak years. You can still hear it from the crowd controlling the White House in 2024, and you've never stopped hearing it from the media's babbling heads, though to be fair, their strident faith in centralized government control is a bit drowned out by their perpetual hair-on-fire shrieking about President Trump, even three years after he left office.

What is most impressive is the *consistency* with which The Left's true believers have maintained adherence to the religious belief in their own superiority. You can hear it today in the ponderings of self-described liberals who say things like "Well, of course most college-educated people are liberals – they're smarter so it makes sense." Without wasting ink on refuting the absurdity of that proposition, I refer you back to Burton on cowards and fools. His words were so brilliant that people have tried to attribute them to Thucydides.

Once again, Mr. Lilienthal provides a valuable window into the core, left-leaning mindset, so much of which was forged during the New Deal battles, when every policy setback or political opposition they faced did *not* cause FDR and his fellow travelers to stop and consider that maybe, just maybe, they were on the wrong track. Oh no, you see, it's that the *lumpen proletariat* were just too dumb to understand how much smarter their overlords, er, public servants were.

> I have sometimes thought that the futility of certain kinds of liberals and liberalism is due to an unwillingness to be realistic in this sense. The phrase "tired liberal" is a common one, and the number of "tired liberals" makes you tired. You never hear of a "tired conservative" unless "tired businessman" is a synonym, which it isn't. Liberals get tired, disillusioned and bitter, partly because they refuse to accept that

we are dealing with human beings who are subject to certain mass diseases of the emotions. The emotional ups and downs of ordinary intelligent people are very great, as we all know, and beyond rational explanation at times. How much greater is the instability of masses of men under the lash of fear and worry![196]

There you have in a few sentences the succinct vision of the "I'm-smarter-and-better-than-you Progressive." Do you see Obama, Clinton(s), Pelosi, Lenin, Biden, Warren, Harris and Castro in there? Rational, intelligent people are one thing, the great masses of men who need the guidance of their cooler-headed betters are quite another. Candidate Obama explained away the objection to his ideas by the fine people of Pennsylvania in terms that Lilienthal would have been right in line with: "And it's not surprising then that they get bitter, they cling to guns or religion or antipathy to people who aren't like them or anti-immigrant sentiment or anti-trade sentiment as a way to explain their frustrations."[197]

My only great sadness in reading this passage is that unfortunately for the nation, there are no more "tired liberals." Quite the contrary: they are all fired up after eight years of the utter disaster of the Obama Presidency, and now the utter disaster of the Biden Presidency which insanely enough they have been taught to believe were successes in some weird way imperceptible to those of us constrained by logic and objectivity. Come the ridiculous summer of 2020 with mobs rampaging in the streets howling inchoate Marxist nonsense, pulling down statues and demanding the ruination of everyone who fails to affirmatively support a list of insane propositions which grow by the day, The Left finally found the crowds to give physical expression to their four-year tantrum. The American people have had to endure 24/7 screaming from the deranged lunatics who blew hundreds of millions of dollars on a range of fairy tales relating to President Trump, including a bizarre cheapening of the impeachment power which will I assume make it *de rigueur* to start impeachment proceedings every time the House of Representatives is controlled by a party other than the President's.

By November 2016 there were plenty of "tired businesspeople" across the nation after 8+ years of politicians vilifying the people who with their own capital, sweat and ingenuity create value, jobs and wealth in this nation. The vast administrative law apparatus acting as a lead pipe enforcer for the dictates of the regulatory nanny state had indeed left the entrepreneurs and business investors of this once-great nation tired and angry at the government which does nothing but criticize them in the press and tax them by day while picking their pockets by night via hundreds of obscure fines, fees and findings.

In his Introduction to Lilienthal's *Journals* Henry Steele Commager put forth an analysis which captures some correct conclusions, along with a slew of incorrect ones. As a fellow alumnus of The College at the University of Chicago, I am quite sure he intended his writing to be an accurate and objective reflection of the circumstances under examination.

---

[196] Lilienthal, vol. 1, p173.
[197] Fowler, Mayhill, blog on The Huffington Post, April 6, 2008

[T]he depression dealt a mortal blow to the ideas and practices of laissez-faire. The death was a lingering one, to be sure, and in the next generation nothing was more astonishing than to see men in high political life solemnly intoning the old litanies against governmental intervention and as solemnly voting for Federal subsidies to agriculture, calling for Federal intervention in labor disputes, and insisting on Federal supervision of what was taught in colleges, displayed in museums, or circulated in libraries. This was the negative side of the shield. On the positive side was the firm establishment of the principle of political responsibility for the well-being of the economy and society. The degree of responsibility, and the form it should take, remained matters of dispute all through the next generation, but no realistic politician denied the fact.

Implicit in this were two far-reaching developments. First, the coming of the welfare state, so long delayed; second, the rapid growth of Federal centralization. Both of these developments were greeted with the gravest misgivings not only by outraged conservatives but by worried liberals as well. As it turned out, none of the malign consequences so confidently predicted materialized. The welfare state did not, in fact, regiment the economy or society; it did not create a giant governmental bureaucracy that interfered with the private affairs of men; it did not dry up initiative, sap energies or create a nation of dependents. If the average American came to enjoy less freedom from governmental control that in the past, he enjoyed greater freedom from the vagaries of the economic order. Nor did Federal centralization create a monolithic government, or seriously impair the powers of the states or the liberties of the citizen.[198]

Ah, what a difference a few years will make! The horrible consequences of the "coming of the welfare state" and "the rapid growth of Federal centralization" did not occur by 1964 when Commager was writing, therefore he concluded *ipso facto* the conservatives and worried liberals were wrong in their predictions of doom.

Add 40-60 years to the time series and – whoops! – *precisely all* the "malign consequences so confidently predicted" have come to pass! Let's take it point by point, shall we?

Malign Consequence Dismissed by Commager	Current State of Affairs in the United States (1Q24)
The welfare state did not, in fact, regiment the economy or society.	49% of Federal Budget is devoted to the Entitlement State
[It] did not create a giant governmental bureaucracy that interfered with the private affairs of men	OMG Squared! There is not a single aspect of life in America which is not drowning under a morass of red tape.
[It] did not dry up initiative, sap energies or create a nation of dependents.	The expansion of government and the regulatory state enforced by unaccountable administrative law has

---

[198] Henry Steele Commager, Introduction, The Journals of David E. Lilienthal, pp. xxiv-xxv

	done nothing but that.
Federal centralization created a monolithic government.	Check.
Federal centralization seriously impaired the powers of the states.	Check.
Federal centralization seriously impaired the liberties of the citizen.	Check.

What Commager *did* perceive correctly was the hypocrisy of "men in high political life." Laurence Lindsay wrote a trenchant book in 2016, *Conspiracies of the Ruling Class, How to Break Their Grip Forever.* In it, he describes the process by which the self-described "progressives" grabbed control of the universities and the media. In his examination, he wondered why – objectively measured- people of lower IQ manage to slither themselves into powerful positions. Read the book for its brilliance, but in summary, he attributes the rise of The Progressive Left's power to their sense of "class cohesion" or what I'd call religious affiliation.

People focused on personal liberty do not group together to promote each other. It's kind of baked into the philosophical conviction of the value of personal independence. The rise of the stifling Administrative State staffed by people who have conspired to give themselves lifelong immunity from firing leads to a self-perpetuating Control Class. Washington, DC votes Democrat by more than 92%.

This is all the result of *decades* of commitment by a core of Americans to change the shape of American society.

When I read what Bill Ayers and Saul Alinsky have written or said, I am quite literally at a loss to understand how a rational, mature adult with the best interests of our society at heart could *perceive* the world the way they clearly do. I have explanations which *fit* objectively their utterances.

The first fits perfectly with my observation of the Perpetual Adolescence of the Draft Dodger Generation. Put simply, those people of that generation who dodged their responsibilities never actually matured in a societal sense, no matter how gray and thinning their ponytails have become. My semi-completed training in Anthropology provided me with dozens of examples from around the world of the critical importance to individual identity in a society from structured adulthood rituals.

The second comes from a thoughtful monologue performed by Michael Cain, playing the role of Alfred in *The Dark Knight,* the 538th movie in the Batman franchise. It the monologue, he was trying to explain the sociopathic actions of The Joker (played by tragically subsequently overdosed thespian Heath Ledger):

Alfred: A long time ago, I was in Burma. My friends and I were working for the local government. They were trying to buy the loyalty of local leaders with precious stones. But their caravans were being raided north of Rangoon by a bandit. So, we went looking for the stones. But in six months, we never met anyone who had traded with him. One day I saw a child playing with a ruby the size of a tangerine. The bandit had been throwing them away.

Bruce Wayne: So why steal them?

379

Alfred: Because he thought it was good sport. Because some men aren't looking for anything logical, like money. They can't be bought, bullied or reasoned with. Some men just want to watch the world burn.

Keynes was a Drunken Dilettante

No greater fantasy was ever promulgated than the suite of damaging policies associated with the phrase "Keynesian." To be fair to Lord Keynes himself, he pushed for government-spending stimulus *under very specific circumstances.* He never claimed that rampant money printing was always and everywhere the "solution" to an economic slowdown. I find myself in a weird position, defending Keynes, but I am consistent. I will give you a dozen reasons why the man was an idiot in his conclusions, but I don't need to say there is a thirteenth reason based on something he never said.

What the fans of "Keynesian" money printing will never tell you, because it would blow away a whole host of sacred paper cows, is that their Patron Saint, the Socialist in a Wheelchair who originated vote buying in between bouts of incestuous infidelity thought Keynes himself was an idiot after the one meeting they had.

That's right. Even FDR – a major fan of every bad economic idea he ever heard – thought Keynes was a moron and demanded he never be allowed back into the White House again.

The sickness is universal

On the state level, things are not much better. What began as a post-war exercise to give civil service workers wages on par with the mighty private sector blue collar workforce has turned into a vicious – and I choose that word carefully – cycle in which public sector union workers promise votes to politicians in return for richer and richer goodies.

This tight-knit cabal of unaccountable politicians stealing money from the smaller and smaller *productive* section of the economy to give to their voting-machine union pals is not content with mere unproductive rent-seeking. Oh no, they want to ensure that the Poverty Industry keeps a steady supply of held-down malcontents to feed their public-sector, wealth-distribution-and-destruction machine. To take one massive blue state fiasco at random, in New York City alone, three massive private sector investment projects were not permitted to occur.

The Bronx Armory which had been vacant for decades, was not allowed to become a shopping mall and office complex and Wal-Mart was not allowed to build a store in an economically-depressed area of Brooklyn. The massive granddaddy of all economic development – Amazon choosing to locate 25,000 people in offices in Queens – was stopped by a popular young Communist elected by 152,661 voters in what's got to be the funniest Congressional district in America.

Why, you ask, should government *stop* private money from making capital investments into areas of the city that need it? Because politicians didn't like the wages that some of the potential business will pay some of their potential employees. Never mind that unemployment ranges from 10%-35% or more in some of these areas and that *any job* is better *for the individual worker* than no job. No – that is of no concern to those who make their living by building a career on "helping" the poor.

The colossally evil clowns destroyed tens of thousands of jobs because doing so was – oddly – popular with the people who voted for them. No one asked the potential employees of these never-created businesses.

"Zoning" or how the loser you pitied (or tortured) in 4th grade can tell you whether you can build an addition to "your" home

Houston, Texas is a splendid place to live for a range of reasons from fun gun laws to BBQ beef ribs to healthy, spirited young people unafraid of a second helping of potato salad. It's also a dynamic jewel of economic development and urban growth *because* of its complete lack of zoning regulations. If you can buy a piece of property and get the funding to build something on it, you are free to do so. Have at it. Rational town governments hope you are successful so they can tax you on your success.

In my hometown of New York, one of my favorite businesses is The Strand bookstore. Sitting on the corner of Broadway and 12th Street, it was once part of Booksellers Row. All the other booksellers are gone. In 2018, a sweepingly incompetent and brazenly corrupt Comrade Mayor De Blasio – an embarrassment and blight to the good name of all Italian-Americans everywhere – took a payoff from some real estate developers and got it designated as a Landmark Building.

Why, one might ask, would someone lobby to get *someone else's* property designed a "landmark?" Simple. Money. "Landmark" status is a massive pain in the ass to the property owner – it often requires all kinds of elaborate and expensive forms of maintenance and renovation, which mere "buildings" are not. It could force the property owner to suddenly spend millions of dollars to be "in compliance" with the enhanced "landmark" building ordinances.

So cynical real estate developers who would *love* to take possession of that building were hoping to use the force of city government to make the building owner sell because of the sudden and potentially financially ruinous new costs. As the owner said at a Landmarks Preservation Commission meeting, this could "destroy her business." What honest purpose could there be in saddling a property owner with a slew of new taxes? This kind of sleaze happens daily *because the average American is not paying attention to the nonstop sleaze professional politicians engage in daily.*

And it goes both ways....

Lest we think that the only people dipping into others' pockets are in the public sector, let's be clear about the horrendous emergence of people *pretending* to be risk-taking entrepreneurs, who are just very clever rent-seekers with their eyes on your bank account. They're just asking their political pals to raise taxes and fees to drain that bank account so it can be put into their hands instead.

Why are American taxpayers giving millions of dollars to Elon Musk to build $250,000 electric sports cars? Isn't Elon already a billionaire? If he cannot put up or raise the capital required for Tesla Motors, then perhaps he should work harder on his pitch or not build the damned things in the first place.

Elon has benefited from multiple taxpayer-funded giveaways including giving high income earners free cash off their income taxes if they buy a Tesla instead of a gas-powered car. I don't mean to pick on him – he's just a high-profile example of the kind of crony capitalism that distorts markets and lets government pick economic winners and losers. Far outnumbering him are the thousands of real estate managers throughout the country who score sweetheart rental deals at above market rates, for long periods, from governmental bodies. This is not the place to come up with an encyclopedic list of graft – perhaps someone reading this will be inspired to compile that massive compendium.

Mortgage Meltdown

The largest example of the damage government can do to society comes from the market for housing. The federal government in one form or another subsidizes 90% of the housing market. That complete shifting of equity risk of homeownership away from individuals onto the Socialist Collective is the *precise cause* of the major distortion in this most fundamental of markets.

This is a bipartisan problem.[199] Both parties supported idiotic policies which *sounded great* on the surface, but ended up causing massive damage to markets and people.

I have been engaged over the last few years with talking to a lot of people from different backgrounds and in reading what I can lay my hands on about the housing markets. Unsurprisingly, when we're talking about two intimately related and independently important things (money and the shelter in which people live), there are not very many calm, collected and wholly-objective opinions to be found.

Generally speaking, for finance and business types, including me, the initial and natural way of looking at mortgage markets is through the lens of property rights, contract responsibilities and a sound system of credit. Other people, and I will not even try to label them, get outraged by "predatory lenders" as they bear witness to the individual, family and community devastation that can come from people entering into mortgage relationships that they did not understand and feel victimized by when prices fall rather than rise. I have come to see that which view is "correct" in a given situation all comes down to context.

There are no easy answers here. If Guy #4 took out an adjustable-rate mortgage (ARM) from Countrywide for $50,000 on a $55,000 house in 2002, then sold the house in 2003 for $100,000, thereby making a profit of $45,000 on an initial $5,000 equity

---

[199] "The Fannie Mae Republicans," WSJ Editorial Board, 16 November 2010

investment (less interest, of course, but I'm keeping it simple), then Guy #4 pocketed his cash with happiness and believed he was smart in the real estate market.

Guy #4 certainly did not go complain to any politician or regulator that a predatory lender forced me to buy a house I couldn't afford on my $17,000 per year salary.

But if the same Guy #4 took out the same mortgage in 2006, and then the house when he tried to sell it in 2008 was worth $30,000 (meaning after selling the house he would still *owe* Countrywide $25,000 + interest), well, then, he called Elizabeth Warren, his mayor, his local senator, the ACLU and all kinds of people to complain that *a predatory lender forced me to buy a house I couldn't afford on my $17,000 per year salary.* People only cry about the housing market when they lose money; rationality would dictate that people be upset about *all* government decisions that move property markets, but human nature is not rational.

The very real personal tragedies that came from bad housing policy are why I took the time to quote this book so extensively. Here is one such story of how bad government policy ruins lives.

Ohio had some of the weakest lending laws in the nation. Slavic Village [in Cleveland], a neighborhood full of unwanted dwellings, was ground zero for exploitation. Between 2000 and 2010, Slavic Village's population dropped 27 percent, on its way down from its all-time high of seventy thousand to twenty thousand. During a time when banks were willing to write mortgages to *anyone*, for any amount of money, there was cash to be squeezed out of empty houses. Here's how one scam worked, according to Tony Zajac, an aide to Slavic Village's city councilman Anthony Brancatelli. When Zajac's aunt was eighty-nine, her son moved her into a nursing home. He put a "PRIVATE SALE" sign on her ten-room house, offering it for $40,000. The buyer took out a $90,000 mortgage, stating on the purchase agreement that she intended to use the balance for rehab. Instead, she split the money with the mortgage broker and the appraiser who had conspired to falsify the home's value.

"They took the fifty thousand dollars and split it to line their pockets with gold," Zajac said. "Three years ago, Aunt Mary and her son were sued by the lender, Deutsche Bank. They falsify the income of the purchase and they fly. They leave the house once they got the money."

Then there were the flippers. They paid old women $40,000 for their houses, then turned around and sold them for $60,000 to suckers whose greed was inflamed by "Get Rich Quick in Real Estate!" infomercials, and by the inflated real estate market of the late 1990s, when properties were doubling and tripling in value. Hapless bargain hunters purchased houses on the Internet, only to find them boarded up and stripped of every metal fixture. A California artist looking for a cheap home/studio bought a Slavic Village house that turned out to be condemned. (After many trips to housing court, he brought it back up to code.)

The lenders were so aggressive they went door-to-door on the East Side of Cleveland, pointing out loose shingles, collapsing chimneys, or sagging porches. Money from a second mortgage could repair any of those defects, the door-to-door brokers told the homeowners. They never mentioned the adjustable rate.

Anita Buckner's sons[200] fell for that scam. Buckner, who worked thirty-one years as a heavy-duty machinist and welder at TRW Automotive, bought a two-story house on the East Side for $21,000 back in the early 1970s. It was almost paid off when she was diagnosed with Chiari malformation, a brain disorder that left her too ill to work or even walk up the stairs to her bedroom. So she bought a one-story home, a converted liquor store, and signed the old house – "My Buckingham Palace, a place where I could cover the walls with my paintings and close off the world" – over to her two thirtysomething sons. When Buckner had moved in, every house was owned by an autoworker or a steelworker with a wife, four or five children, and a new car. Then J&L Steel, the neighborhood's largest employer, closed in 1999. The blue-collar workers moved out, and the mortgage brokers began moving in, attracted by the remaining residents' financial desperation. Having lost their paychecks, these dispossessed factory rats were told they still had a source of income, in the houses they'd bought cheap and paid off with union wages and frugality.

"This couldn't have happened if people had good jobs," Buckner said. "Or why would they change their mortgage? They were desperate for money. It was targeted. It was definitely targeted. Mortgage agents were going door-to-door, calling on the phone. It was in the air: 'You don't have to have credit. You can have nice things.'"

Buckner's sons fell for the pitch. Neither had ever been able to afford nice things. The elder brother had served eleven years on a drug charge. When he got out of prison, the only job he could find was delivering furniture for Sears. The younger brother worked as a restaurant supply salesman. When an agent from Countrywide Financial[201] offered them a $70,000 mortgage on their mom's almost-paid-off house, they signed. Buckner suspects the agent falsely inflated the home's value in order to write a bigger mortgage. Agents received bigger commissions for adjustable-rate mortgages. The boys used the second mortgage for a shopping spree. A black Hyundai Tiburon sports car. A new couch. A big-screen TV. A refrigerator in the garage, full of beer.

The monthly payments began at $436 a month, but as the boys missed payments, it more than doubled to $950, far more than they could pay on their small-time jobs. When the past-due amount reached $4,000, Buckner's sons appealed to Mom for a bailout.

Buckner paid the arrears, plus an $800 transaction fee, plus a series of six $1,000 "good-faith payments" to return the note to its original payment plan. A Realtor friend negotiated with Countrywide to buy the house back for $25,000 – which Buckner raised by borrowing on her new house. The mortgage lending crisis ate up her life savings.

"I'm out of money," she said. "This is all my retirement money. I have enough to live on, but all the money I had stuffed under the mattress, it's gone. Meanwhile, my mortgage on the new house jumps from six hundred dollars to nine hundred dollars."

---

[200] Buckner is a pseudonym. While the real names are used in the book from which I quote, my point is *not* to single out random citizens by name, but to highlight a phenomenon and shoddy reporting. If you really care what Anita's surname is, go read the book.

[201] Please, please, *please,* Dear Reader, never lose sight of Chris Dodd's deep pocket-lining relationship with Countrywide... While not strictly a footnote, I cannot let that slide...

Buckner evicted her sons – "they don't deserve this, they don't understand what the palace is" – but two months after buying back her house from Countrywide, she was informed that the employee with whom she'd negotiated had no authority to cut a deal.

"Why should we take twenty-five thousand dollars when we can get seventy thousand dollars?" a Countrywide agent told Buckner. "We will get the money from your son. We will prosecute him."

Countrywide sued Buckner's sons and began foreclosure proceedings on the house. Desperate, she applied to an organization called ESOP – Empowering and Strengthening Ohio's People. As a social service agency in the nation's foreclosure capital, ESOP was devoting a large part of its resources to mortgage counseling. Having lived a middle-class life, Buckner was a little put off by ESOP's office. A room in the back of a church, with two or three people working on mismatched furniture, it reminded her of a sweatshop or a numbers runner's den. But Buckner joined ESOP's campaign against Countrywide, which had been writing shady mortgages all over northeastern Ohio. Wearing a shark's head, Buckner joined a picket of Countrywide's headquarters, where ESOP members passed out the personal cell phone number of CEO Angelo Mozilo. Busloads of protesters picketed Mozilo's country club. (They were followed, needless to say, by vanloads of TV cameras.) ESOP blew up the company's fax machine with photographs of foreclosed homes. Finally, Countrywide settled with Buckner for another $6,000. Buckingham Palace was hers again, but the rest of her street was a cemetery.

"There was seventy-six houses on the street, and now only eleven are occupied," she said.

This raises a question. Which is the greater social ill: allowing people who can no longer afford their mortgages to stay in their houses, thus undermining the credit system by letting people skip out on their payments, or evicting people from houses for which there is no buyer, thus undermining the property itself and the surrounding neighborhood? Ted Michols and Anita Buckner would say let the poor folks stay and look after their houses. Vacant houses attract criminals. Michols called the cops on a stripper trying to tear the aluminum drainpipe off a house at eleven o'clock in the morning. In a 150-foot radius around a vacant house, property values go down at least $7,000. A vacant house reduces its *own* value even more, since it's usually denuded of plumbing fixtures, boilers, carpeting, sinks, toilets, heating pipes, and any architectural sconces that can be peddled in a secondhand shop. Yellow foreclosure stickers and plywood windows are not warnings, they're invitations. After homeowners exhaust the equity, inner-city scavengers salvage the last pennies of value out of a house, until the mortgage lender ends up paying the city for demolition.[202]

There is a great deal to be appalled and dismayed at in that excerpt. The main thing which jumps out at *me* from all this is that there are no easy solutions to the myriad personal failings and plain old slings and arrows of Fate demonstrated here. To choose a point at random: If each person in America were better educated – or just more sensible –

---

[202] Edward McClelland, Nothin' but Blue Skies: The Heyday, Hard Times, and Hopes of America's Industrial Heartland, Bloomsbury Press, 2013, pp..232-235

there would be no "suckers" dumb enough to buy a house sight unseen due to late-night TV infomercial flimflam. As they are not and there are, it falls to us as a society to create rules that protect people from their own idiocy whenever possible.

Actually, it doesn't. Freedom is freedom – including the freedom to be an idiot. If you are an idiot, it would be nice if friends and family, recognizing your idiocy, would provide you with advice and help on such issues.

I would take issue as well with the presentation of Anita Buckner's sons as victims who "fell for [a] scam" perpetrated on them by a mortgage salesman. Those guys made a choice as timeless as it was before Faust struck his deal with Mephistopheles: Give me goodies for a brief period now, and then destroy my life down into Hell in return. Had I been an unmarried ex-con living in my Mom's house in Cleveland, I personally would have gone for the one-year, knee-buckling love of a hot, elegant and busty 18-year-old German girl over a Hyundai and flat-screen TV, but to each his own. To be fair, the mortgage brokers weren't offering Goethe's Gretchen, and given the choice between a new car and fun toys versus a few pointless nights at a Cleveland jiggle joint (whose pole dancers double as scrap metal thieves), I'm saying the Buckner boys went the right way... But I digress.

The fact that one of the Buckner boys had been a guest of the state for 11 years I touch on elsewhere in regards to the massive social damage caused by The Drug Wars.

And – at least according to this rendition of her story – Mrs. Buckner is as much at fault as her sons. She signed the house over to them, and when they screwed the pooch with their profligate borrowing, she should most certainly *not* have burned through her own nest egg to buy back the house that Countrywide owned.

A trail of tears all the way 'round, mostly for Mrs. Buckner, I'm assuming. With all due respect to the personal pain this episode surely caused her, we must all realize objectively that contrary to McClelland's assertion, "[t]he mortgage lending crisis" most assuredly *did not* "[eat] up her life savings." The poor choices she made after discovering the bad contracts her sons had entered into did that for her. She should have let Buckingham Palace go – it was a bad financial choice in a decaying neighborhood and absent a cure for Chiari's she was never going to live there again anyway.

The likely-valid assertion by Buckner that the Countrywide agent – whose *personal* incentives were focused on making a large dollar-volume of loans, with *no* personal accountability should the loans go unpaid – inflated the house's value does not change her responsibility for her own choices, although it is a fine example of why I elsewhere argue for very simple, strict and "non-game-able" rules for debt underwriting. If Angelo Mozilo and Countrywide were actually *on the hook* for the loans they were writing, their entire behavior sets would have differed, as would the incentive structures they created for their sales teams.

As for the unmitigated scumbaggery that was Countrywide – the description of their treatment of Mrs. Buckner *after* selling her back her house *is precisely why we as a society need to fund properly a sound and swiftly-functioning Justice system.* When those sleaze weasels tried to abrogate a contract one of *their* employees signed, Mrs. Buckner should have been able to stroll right down to the local courthouse, present the case (possibly with a sound civil servant drafting the memorandum in proper order), and have a judge within 48 hours not only tell Countrywide to get stuffed, but also levy fines and send a sheriff to arrest the dirtbag who started the process to extort her for more money *on a transaction which was already settled.*

Another point worth dwelling on is tied to the plight the J&L Steel "factory rats" found themselves in when the company shut its doors. Their plight gives one reason to ponder the never-ending drumbeat of "homeownership is always a good thing" on which so much flawed American housing policy rests. A steelworker who was renting a home in 1999 could have left once his or her lease ran out. A steelworker who was also a homeowner was doubly screwed if no other comparable employment was available in the area.

The *deeper* questions are also all tied up in what constitutes an average American citizen's sense of self-worth, responsibility, dignity, etc. I do not shy away from such questions, as there is ongoing and broad historical and current evidence for Americans' serious preoccupation with all manner of self-help, self-improvement and religious interest.

It's important to note that lots of "professionally smart" people also got hosed by the collapse of the mortgage market brought on by bad government policy. As I argue elsewhere – and as I said to surprised FINRA and SEC examiners when I was Chief Compliance Officer of a broker/dealer – I am a *fan* of *good* regulation, meaning regulation which provides for orderly markets, punishes corner-cutting scumbags and is simple to both understand and abide by.

It's easy to judge situations in hindsight, but there is a great description of the ramifications of poor policy by Charles Gasparino in his book *The Sellout* which speaks directly to a simple proposal I submitted for consideration to the Federal Reserve in 2008 and which – so far as I know – got no further than someone's circular file.

> [David] Einhorn [of Greenlight Capital], meanwhile was losing his shirt on M.D.C., but that was nothing compared to his investment in New Century Financial, one of the era's success stories. Its loan origination jumped to $60 billion in 2006 from just $5 billion in 2001, the result of its automated loan system, which, through algorithmic modeling, allowed the company to grant a mortgage in as little as 12 seconds.
>
> New Century may have been fast, but that didn't translate into quality. Brokers figured out how to manipulate the system by tweaking credit scores and pushing loans on people without the means to repay them, because as long as there was a demand for product from Wall Street, the mortgages were no longer the bank's problem. New Century issued most of its mortgages through independent brokers, who had no stake in making sure the borrowers were creditworthy, and neither did New Century for that matter, because of Wall Street's voracious appetite for packing its mortgages into bonds.
>
> But as Wall Street underwriting slowed, New Century was forced to hold more and more subprime debt on its own books. Unlike First Franklin, New Century didn't have a big new corporate parent to shield it from the losses. As subprime defaults picked up steam into 2007, New Century found itself the first casualty of the now-expanding mortgage crisis. Einhorn wasn't singing the mortgage business'[s] praises now; he resigned from the board just before New Century filed for Chapter 11 bankruptcy protection in early March 2007.[203]

---

[203] Charles Gasparino, The Sellout: How Three Decades of Wall Street Greed and

The simple proposal I had submitted for consideration by the Fed and FDIC while they were in a flurry of desperation to throw new rules at the wall? It fit on an index card:

Rule 1: Every mortgage must remain on the originating bank's books for at least one year from issuance.

Rule 2: When the originating bank wants to push a mortgage into a structured product or in any other way sell it to another party, there is a random lottery process run whereby some fraction of mortgages – between, say, 1/8th and 1/12th of originated mortgages – are required to remain on the books of the originating bank *forever.*

Dodd-Frank's behemoth was 2,400+ legislative pages and God only knows how many tens of thousands of pages of often-contradictory and certainly pointlessly-burdensome regulatory rules. They tried to "fix" problems like New Century through those millions and millions of words and billions of dollars of economic drag on the economy – and I can assure you all that work did not have the same powerful, *positive* impact as my proposed two rules would have done in creating safer mortgage markets.

Deep questions aside, the Dodd-Frank Act rested in part on a massive fantasy called "predatory lending." Now, as we have seen, bad incentives mixed with stupidity and cupidity led to sleazy mortgage brokers selling worthless loans to people. But the free market is a place for people to make mistakes, so while putting some guidelines in place as I suggest above is a healthy way to restrict overly-stupid behavior, the government always tends towards massive overkill. The government doesn't like simple. Simple doesn't generate thousands of patronage jobs, is easy to understand and therefore useless as a tool of societal control.

> FCIC's investigation of predatory lending was never able to demonstrate with data that it was a significant factor in the financial crisis. There were plenty of anecdotes and much testimony, but never any numbers to suggest that predatory lending was so widespread as to require a whole new regulatory scheme at the federal level or the new rules for mortgage lending that imposed heavy penalties for making a loan that a borrower ultimately could not afford. It was clear that large numbers of mortgages went to people who ultimately could not meet their obligations, but it is far more likely that borrowers were taking advantage of the reduced underwriting standards produced by government policies that that originators were taking advantage of ignorant borrowers. [204]

The Glass-Steagall Act itself was a total of 34 pages and managed to restructure commercial banking and securities dealing effectively after the Great Depression. My proposal is shorter by 33.75 pages, but then again, politicians always like to pad their work;

Government Mismanagement Destroyed the Global Financial System, HarperCollins, 2009
[204] Peter Wallison, Bad History, Worse Policy; How a False Narrative about the Financial Crisis Led to the Dodd-Frank Act, American Enterprise Institute, 2013, p.22

back in the day before word processors, a Senator might well find himself getting the cold shoulder from the typing pool should he suggest a piece of legislation much longer than 50 pages...

There are lots of currents underlying the story of a New Century: the sometimes-correct belief that massive data analysis and speed can be a benefit in a competitive business, the desire to deploy capital in a market demanding it, the judgment of investors and executives that their scenarios of possible losses are accurate. In and of themselves, these are market decisions which can bring one profits or losses, and do not require regulation.

But had my simple 2-rule regulatory law been in place, a New Century would *not* have been able to do what it did in allowing brokers to game a 12-second-analysis system, as New Century would have been wearing real risk from crappy mortgage underwriting. A *proper* and *simple* regulatory structure would have prevented New Century's runaway growth and subsequent spectacular crash. Who knows? It may well have been an excellent service and profitable company under more rational conditions. Or maybe not. That's not the point I'm making here.

It's not a point you, dear reader, should ignore. The fiasco of decades of Federal housing policy wiped out $14,000,000,000 of national wealth in one big fart. That is $46,000 *per person* in America. It does not include the additional $36,000+ per person of additional national debt the fools in Washington threw at not just the *wrong* problem, but a *false* problem they made up entirely to suit their fantasies of how the world *should* work, not how it actually functions.

Don't beat yourself up about it. They've been telling this lie repeatedly since 1929 and their entire *careers* and indeed sense of self-worth – hah! – are tied up in believing this illusory, shifting mirage that is always just a bit out of reach, but *attainable* if only they just add some more regulations, laws and social engineering.

Mistakes were made...

On 27 January 2009, the brand-new Treasury Secretary Tim Geithner – whose qualifications for the job of being the head of the IRS included not knowing he had to pay taxes – met with President Obama and others in the Oval Office. Obama wanted to "fix" the financial crisis. Geithner presumably agreed that was a good idea, but in his book he recounts, "I agreed, but with a qualification. There was intense pressure on us to punish the Wall Street gamblers who had gotten us into this mess." He was right about the judgment inasmuch as the vast public did then and continues to blame "Wall Street" for Washington's crimes, aided of course by the support for that narrative from the financially ignorant media and deeply-self-interested politicians looking to deflect blame at all costs.

But Geithner's problem – or one of them – is that he fails to refute that nonsense to begin with.

One point he makes over and over again is the quasi-religious belief about centralizing Statists that panics require governmental interference to calm. Interestingly he writes, "Uncertainty is at the heart of all financial crises. They simply don't end without governments assuming risks that private investors won't, taking catastrophe off the table."[205]

That is one heavy set of ideas captured in two sentences. The first contention and uncertainty being at the heard of all financial crises I'd agree with, but I have many problems with the assertion that only a government intervention can stop a crisis.

I must admit it took me a lot to read *Stress Test.* I lived my career on Wall Street during this turbulent period, and I laid a lot of the blame for bad decisions at the feet of Geithner and his cohorts. I was correct in those assessments. At the time, I wrote an extremely accurate forecast of what all the stupid policy choices would result in. Life is short and while it may be clear from this book that I read a great deal, reading is like any other area of knowledge: there will always be more available than one can access. So spending a half-day reading *Stress Test* meant not reading something else. I am glad I read the book – it confirmed for me what an incompetent, pretentious fool he is. That does not excuse many of the horrendous choices his cabal foisted on the nation, but it did make reading his book really annoying.

As Geithner writes about those choices and policies, "Conventional wisdom still holds that we abandoned Main Street to protect Wall Street – except on Wall Street, where conventional wisdom still holds that President Obama is a radical socialist consumed with hatred for moneymakers. The financial reform law that *we wrote and pushed through* [italics mine] a bitterly divided Congress after the crisis, the most sweeping overhaul of financial rules since the Depression, is widely viewed as too weak, except in the financial sector, where it is described as an existential threat."[206]

I have always wanted to ask Geithner, *"Why do you think we on Wall Street see Obama that way? Are financial professionals particularly stupid people?"* Maybe he'll be forced to answer that question if this book gets sufficient popularity.

Reading Geithner's book reinforced many of the concerns I attempt to address in this book. His recounting of his early years working for the Treasury Department, living in Japan where despite his limited knowledge of the language and zero knowledge of business had to perform acts of almost absurd diplomatic and economic importance, reinforces my suggestion for reform of the civil service. Reading his accounts of his early years in Japan, when he was thrilled to be suddenly the "knowledgeable insider" the US Ambassador relied on, should make every taxpayer seethe with anger.

Given what an outsized role his terrible decisions had on my life and more importantly when magnified hundreds of thousands of times across the financial markets, I took some notes about his work to highlight just why and how he and people trained to think like him are so utterly wrong. Geithner's heady mix of arrogance and incompetence stand as a wonderful example for us all about why we so very much need to crush the government we have in order to create the government we *should* have.

Many people believe that bailing out indebted nations caused moral hazard and therefore the Asian contagion was a result of bailing out Thailand and Indonesia, rather than letting them burn. I agree, but Tim does not.

He writes,

---

[205] Geither, Timothy F., Stress Test; Reflections on Financial Crises, p.8
[206] Ibid, p.18

It is possible that at the margin, the success of the Mexico program made investors somewhat more confident about financing the Asian boom, not because they thought it marked the end of crises o they expected protection from losses, but because we had demonstrated a way to reduce the depth of the crisis – the extent and duration of the decline in economic activity. But there is no way to solve a financial crisis without creating some moral hazard, without protecting investors and institutions from some of the consequences of excessive risk taking. They were, in Ted Truman's phrase, collateral beneficiaries of than effective emergency program. It was impossible to design an effective rescue for the intended beneficiaries – the people who lived and worked in those countries – without some collateral beneficiaries.

But the success in Mexico did not produce Asia's boom or the willingness of investors to help finance it. During one meeting in Manila early in the Asian crisis, when some of Europe's finance bureaucrats were invoking Mexico and moral hazard to argue against a generous financial response, Stan Fischer, the excellent American economist who was the IMF's deputy director – I would later recommend him to Obama as a potential Fed chair as well – passed me a note pointing out that condoms don't cause sex. Stan's point was that the IMP loan program didn't cause financial crises. It's hard to believe that the existence of firehouses causes fires.

I clearly have many issues with this. Firstly, who says that a "financial crisis" needs to be "solved" in the first place? Excessive risk-taking should be punished, pure and simple. Rewarding really bad behavior while punishing just slightly bad behavior tells people to never risk borrowing $1,000 as you'll be screwed to the wall for failure to repay. No – you need to borrow $10 billion, as your inability to repay magically becomes someone else's (i.e., the American taxpayer's) "problem" to "solve."

Secondly while the note is cute and everyone loves to sound clever, the analogies about condoms and firehouses are telling in their inaccurate understanding about the range of risks and rewards in this world. In a world without condoms, of course "sex" won't cease to exist. But sexual activity may be expressed – ahem – in ways less likely to lead to pregnancy. In a world without firehouses, people will be more likely to build with fire-retardant materials and keep open flames to a minimum.

Fairly early in his book around page 70 he opines that there are all kinds of deep lessons he learned during that crisis which informed what he did in 2007.

"We learned it could be costlier to offer too little money than too much; as President Zedillo put it, when markets overreact, policy should overreact, too. We also learned that while no one wants to hand out money without strings attached, too many strings could strangle."

Of course, a politician said that to save his useless ass. Firstly, markets cannot by definition "overreact," people can. One person's perceived crazy risk and willingness to sell is someone else's chance to buy value cheaply. Secondly, policy should be unwavering and based on sound principles.

Later, on pp.120-121 he talks about the start of the 2007-08 crisis. He sees the European Central Bank pump cash into Europe in response to BNP Paribas suspending redemptions on products related to the US mortgage market, which they had to do because those markets had become so illiquid, they couldn't even price the assets in their portfolios.

The situation in August 2007 seemed more dangerous and more systemic. We quickly pumped $62 billion into the U.S. financial system – not as much as the ECB poured into Europe, but enough to send a message that we were on the case. It was a fairly modest and completely conventional early-stage escalation by a central bank, injecting some liquidity into markets. Yet some of our colleagues on the FOMC already thought we were being too aggressive, prompting a debate reminiscent of the discussions we used to have about moral hazard during the Asian crises. On a conference call the morning of the 10th, Dallas Fed President Richard Fisher suggested we were helping banks without getting anything in return, "putting our finger in the dike" without extracting promises of more lending now or more responsible behavior in the future. He said he wanted to make sure "we don't send any signal that we're just going to be... indiscriminate."

"I don't think that's the way to think about it," I said. We needed to signal that cash was available, to help thaw what Ben called "a general freeze-up" in mortgage markets, so that liquidity shortages didn't create a vicious spiral of forced asset sales and falling asset prices. That meant committing to provide the liquidity that markets needed to function, without condition, even if it did make us look indiscriminate. "You can't condition that statement without undermining its basic power," I said.

Fisher's discomfort foreshadowed what we were up against. Even inside the Fed, we were susceptible to Old Testament and moral hazard critiques. One day into the crisis, some already thought we were coddling the perpetrators. That's the way it always is in a crisis. And I felt that familiar nausea of foreboding.[207]

Oh, how prescient was Richard Fisher

The massive spiral occurred *anyway* because the regulators demanded that firms and their prime brokers mark every position to market. This is a little esoteric, and the kind of thing experts in a specialized field shy away from explaining to a broad audience. But this is really important for voters and taxpayers to understand.

"Marking to market" simply means that it is *usually* best practice to let normally functioning markets determine "the" current price for a given asset, say a stock or a bond. In order to keep everyone in a market honest, it makes sense for the price at which, say, a stockbroker tells her client the stock in his portfolio is trading at, is determined by a disinterested third party, rather than the broker being able to say "Hey, 40 shares of IBM are worth 70 gazillion dollars."

For example, stocks traded on, say, the New York Stock Exchange, are automatically "marked to market" because their price changes are publicly available information. More technically, when hundreds of thousands of individuals place orders to buy or sell a share of stock, the price at which it is bought or sold at any given millisecond *is* "the market" for that stock at that point in time. The law of large numbers makes it more likely that the given

---

[207] Geithner, pp120-121

price at that moment is "market consensus" of its value. That does *not* mean that everyone believes that is what it "should" be now or six minutes or five years from now.

But when it comes to things like bond markets or cross-currency OTC swaps, those prices are determined with far fewer bids and offers from many fewer market participants. When a crisis is not present, those markets work pretty well. But when a crisis occurs, liquidity can evaporate. That lack of bids and offers for a given security *does not necessarily mean anything about the security.*

Here is an example. You own a 20-year mortgage-backed security which is a kind of mutual fund containing commercial mortgages on 20 Class A office buildings in Chicago and Cleveland. All of those buildings are in fine shape, and the building owners are paying their monthly mortgage payments on time. Let's say you've owned it for 5 years, so there are 15 years to go on the monthly stream of mortgage payments. The security has a market value of $100 per share.

Suddenly the "financial crisis" hits. As you hear the panicked news every day, you call the custodial bank who "services" the mortgage pool. The agent tells you everything is fine with these buildings and the mortgages. Nothing anticipates any impairment, so the exact same cashflow is coming to you next month as last month. For whatever reason, you decide just for peace of mind to see what you can sell your shares for. Because the world is on fire, the best bid you can get is $20 per share, which is $80 *less* than it was on your last brokerage statement.

Now, "mark to market" rules demand that you value that position at $20 per share. But you're wondering why that should be true. *Nothing* about the fundamental cashflows coming from that security have changed. All that has changed is the external market environment. *If* you are forced to sell it, apparently you would have to take a massive loss. But that is only *if* you must sell. If not, you don't have to worry about anything – it has 15 more years to go and the crisis panic will be over within a few months. In fact, if you have spare cash on hand, you could try to *buy* more shares at the $20 the market says it can be bought for.

That is just you, the person. But if "you" are a massive pension fund or mutual fund or hedge fund, your prime broker who lends you money for trading operations will say to you, "Sorry, this position is no longer worth $100 per share, it's $20 per share on the open market (which actually has no trading at all – just one stale bid) and so you now owe us additional margin money against this position." Spluttering with astonishment, you've got to go find cash to post to your broker, which leads you to sell other things at fire sale prices, which only adds to market pressure on prices for all kinds of assets in the market.

You get the picture – nothing changed about the underlying reality of the financial structure of the mortgage backed security, but because of "mark to market" rules, you suddenly had to sell something you didn't otherwise want or need to. Multiple that by thousands of market participants and *that* is what drove the market crisis to such depths.

With that dynamic in mind, let's continue to browse Geithner's musings, shall we?

Page 158-159 contain a tremendous case study in *why* their ham-handed approach was wrong. Geithner claims that the buyout of Bear Stearns and taxpayer support was "necessary" to avert a crisis. If that were true, then the 90 days it took to close the deal should have seen the universe implode. But it didn't. Markets don't care about promises – they care about reality.

On page 160, he makes a statement which has deep philosophical implications. "Crisis responders who get obsessed with moral hazard and Old Testament justice make crises worse."

Well, maybe. In Geithner's personal experience with an n=3 of crises, that is his interpretation. For people like me, this was not halakhic justice, but letting markets discipline those who took bad risks and lost. Every time a government steps in to "save" someone, they are choosing to protect that person or firm from economic reality. That protection is not free – it is paid for by taxpayers who would not have benefited had the trade gone the right way and therefore should not be left to pick up the pieces just because the trade went wrong.

But many empirical realities flow from a point-in-time decision hinging on decisions made. For example, assume his assertion is correct, and Old Testament justice means that no lifeline is thrown to reward people for bad decisions. If you believe – as I do – that the clearest path to progress is absolute acceptance of reality, then whether or not a "crisis" gets "worse" or not is utterly beside the point. Many CEOs and boards of public companies when faced with a bad situation, decide to completely clean house and air out *all* the company's dirty laundry, take all the write downs, cut to the bone at once, rather than limp along with a market wondering whether a new piece of bad news is coming. The benefit to adding *all* the bad news at once – even when only half of it may be required to acknowledge – is that once the wound is fully cleansed, there is nothing left to fester and rot away at the healthy flesh.

So in that case, "making the crisis worse" may be just the right thing to do.

Geithner also provides totally clear evidence as to why rational private sector actors should *always* view the public sector with suspicion.

> Bank of America had agreed to give Lehman another look, but it hadn't even sent a due diligence team. Ken Lewis was in a dispute with the Fed related to his Countrywide purchase, and even after Ben promised to deal with it, Lewis told me he wouldn't even look at Lehman without assurances in writing. "If you don't believe the word of the chairman of the Fed, we have a larger problem," I told him. Lewis agreed to send his team.[208]

Lo and behold, eight years later, the evidence of the political witch hunt and extortion of bounty from Bank of America shareholders provides the most complete conclusion ever: Ken Lewis was right not to trust "the word" of the chairman of the Fed. He should have gotten written, legally binding indemnification from the Federal government for the risks he put Bank of America's shareholders on the hook for.

Geithner also – unwittingly – provides strong support for my thesis about the lack of accountability of government officials. When discussing the risks that financial firm executives take, he makes an interesting point about personal risk:

---

[208] Geithner, p177

I used to joke that there would be less moral hazard in the Fed liquidity facilities if financial executives had to put up their own homes as collateral, ahead of the assets of their firms. That would be real skin in the game. When I was visiting my former Treasury colleague Lee Sachs on Martha's Vineyard that summer, we saw a graceful oceanfront mansion during a walk on the beach. Lee, who had worked at Bear Stearns in happier times, told me it belonged to the firm's former president.

"That one right there should've been the first loss," I said.[209]

Classic unaccountable government bureaucrat. Markets and legal systems had developed property right and rules around segregated assets and risk over centuries. But Tim here, strolling on the beach, felt *entitled* to wipe away the entire structure of risk management, law and equity because, well, I don't know why. He certainly was not qualified – and no one had asked him – to rewrite centuries of settled bankruptcy law and property rights. Is he really stupid enough to believe that the entire financial system we have would have been just the way it was, *but* the entire edifice of mutualized risk and segregated property titles would be different?

Let's fast forward just a few weeks to a decision that Geithner played a leading role in, namely quarterbacking governmentally mandated control over supposedly private capital decisions.

.... I believed that if we could find a buyer to play the JPMorgan role and buy Lehman, and we had to take some risk to close the deal, it would be in the best interests of the country for us to do so, whether we liked it or not.[210]

Notice you don't see Geithner putting forward the idea of putting his and his wife Carole's home and their children's college funds up as "first loss" in front of the "some risk to close the deal" he was so sure the American taxpayer – without being consulted – should be saddled with.

His hubris about the importance – or indeed, valid role *at all* – of the American taxpayers' representatives and checkbook, er, limitless credit card, in dealing with this mess is at least consistent. When Hank Paulson's team leaked to the press the talking points about why Lehman would not be bailed out, Geithner "told Hank this was a huge mistake, irresponsibly damaging to confidence. This was not the time to tell the markets they were on their own. By committing to do nothing now, we'd end up having to do more and put more taxpayer money at risk later."[211]

We all know how that worked out. The federal government *never* "had" to put taxpayer money at risk. That was the political choice made by people currently in office at the time. Every American's liar radar should ping loudly every time a politician says that the government "has" to do something. In very few instances is that true.

---

[209] Geithner, pp167-8
[210] Geithner, pp178-9
[211] Geithner, p180

That left the Fed as the only realistic option. Lending to an insurer still felt like a serious Rubicon to cross, but we had crossed plenty of Rubicons. As Ben pointed out, the troublesome parts of AIG behaved more like an investment bank than an insurer, and we were already lending to investment banks. Ben and Hank both recognized before I did that we had to do something about AIG.

It was hard to feel light while the world burned, but the acerbic Barney Frank, who shared my aversion to moral hazard fundamentalism, made me smile on a call that Monday. If nothing else, he mused, the terror of the free fall could dampen enthusiasm for government inaction and shock the political world into taking the crisis seriously.

"Maybe this will shut up the crazies," he said.

Yup, that Barney Frank, the career parasite who voted to "roll the dice" longer with Fannie and Freddie lending to deadbeats who couldn't repay their mortgages, the prostitute-frequenting john and then landlord to a pimp, calling people who understand markets "crazies." Our nation would be a finer place with more of those "crazies" and far fewer Barney Franks.

Crucially, fifteen years after "the crisis," the decisions made then were still impacting America's ability to function properly and sharply restricting our growth. With the lending to insurers' Rubicon crossed, the Fed plunged wholeheartedly into monetizing the national debt. Add the bizarre monkeying around with fiscal policy during the Wuhan Hysteria, and there is no end in sight to this madness, or at least under current policies and conditions there aren't.

Fifteen years after government housing policy wreaked havoc in financial and commercial markets, the fools who did this to us have still not admitted fault, and nothing bad has happened to them.

This entire fiasco was not theoretically harmful. For my investors and me, this colossal fool's actions were actively detrimental. The Dodd-Frank Act and its thousands of pages of idiotic rulemaking destroyed my commodities asset management business. Dozens of very smart, very experienced market professionals from places like Prudential were all willing to commit capital to our business, but the idiots who wrote Dodd-Frank caused the Federal Reserve to label Prudential a SIFI (a "systemically important financial institution") and the Feds demanded Prudential not invest in our firm.

We had nothing to do with mortgage markets, nothing to do with government-backed leverage – in fact our lack of correlation to those markets was part of why Prudential's brilliant team was drawn to us. Reality does not matter to ideologues, so my firm was one of hundreds if not thousands that got "Dodd-Franked" for zero rational reason. The value destruction caused by that stupid law runs into the hundreds of billions of dollars.

After all that madness, I did what real adults do. I stood myself back up and moved on to other ventures. As it so happened, I was engaged by the exchange group NYSE Euronext at the time to advise the Qatar Investment Authority on the restructuring and business development of the Doha Securities Market. That work resulted in the launch of the Qatar Exchange. During that process, I put my name forward to run the disastrous TARP program. I was prompted to do so by reading in the *Wall Street Journal* that the guy in charge named Neel Kashkari admitted no one on their team knew a thing about securities valuation, derivatives pricing or fair value analysis.

I relate the story of my flirtation with running TARP later on when discussing monetary police. Suffice it to say, I did not fit the profile they were looking for, even though someone with my background and experience was *exactly* what was required to deal with pricing, negotiating and buying distressed assets from wily bankers on Wall Street.

Ultimately, Geithner and the crowd – lacking my expertise or the expertise of anyone with my skillset – decided that instead of doing what TARP legislation said – buy up toxic assets from banks – the Treasury would instead buy up to $250 billion worth of preferred stock from financial institutions.

They should have just done nothing, but sadly that is the only thing Swamp bureaucrats find themselves unable to do. In the course of this madness, they shoveled money at *all banks,* even those who were run well.

"Stigma was a real danger," he writes, so these geniuses decided they would force banks to borrow money they did not want. "Recapitalizing the entire system would benefit everyone, so allowing firms to opt out and still enjoy those benefits would have been truly unfair.[212]

That is almost a poetic masterpiece in Collectivist Progressive "logic."

Let's go on a fun, hypothetical journey back to the real world of free markets where decisions have consequences. Geithner is up front about the fact that the federal government used *your* money to reward firms that should have gone bankrupt, while *demanding* that well-run firms take a punitive loan they did not need and did not want.

I love the twisted logic. We in the free markets always want to *avoid* free-riders who take advantage of others' hard work and risk. Here, you've got the unelected-to-any-political-position head of the New York Fed saying that because he and his pals decided to shovel taxpayer cash at firms who deserved to go bankrupt, it "wouldn't be fair" to "allow" well-run firms to avoid taking punitive-rate loans they had no use for, as this big money blizzard from heaven would "systemically" benefit them.

Wow. Only in the fevered dreams of bureaucrats could that sentiment not only be created, but also subsequently put down on paper and passed through an editorial process on the way to being published. Let me provide you with one real-world impact of this horrendous line of Centralizing Bureaucrat Logic:

> Nevertheless, our failure to impose haircuts on AIG's counterparties would become Exhibit A for the populist outrage and criticism. They didn't have better solutions; they just didn't like ours.

Um, no, I *did* have a better solution, as did many rational market actors who were *not* career bureaucrats being manipulated by savvy traders. And my outrage was not "populist," it was practical.

The high drama never ends. In defending the "need" for American taxpayers to reward Citi for being an out-of-control mess, Geithner claims "[t]he system couldn't have

---

[212] Geithner, p.235

handled the sudden collapse of a $2 trillion institution that provided much of the world's financial plumbing."[213]

He conflates two separate but related things: the operational continuity of the *functions* Citi provides and the retention of equity value for the shareholders of Citi. Those are *not* the same thing at all. The employees who handled all of that work could easily have been told "You keep on showing up here. Your paychecks are guaranteed by the government. When we unwind this holy mess, you'll all be in line for a performance bonus, provided you show up on time and do your job diligently. Feel free to forget the names of all the people who until 5 minutes ago constituted 'Citi's upper management.' They're gone and are not coming back. You perform a critical role in the nation's financial infrastructure and nothing is going to stand in the way of your doing your job properly."

Sheila Bair, the head of the FDIC knew this distinction well. She understood that there was no reason whatsoever that the people doing the actual work of the "world's financial plumbing" would stop showing up to work should the shareholders of Citi lose everything. "On a conference call Sunday morning, Hank [Paulson] nearly had a fit when Sheila suggested the FDIC could force Citi into receivership without melting down the system. 'If Citi isn't systemic, I don't know what is!' he replied."

Now, in the heat of a crisis with passions running high, I can forgive a few things. Mr. Paulson by all accounts is an effective leader and very competent investment banker. That does not mean necessarily that he was able to make the proper distinction between market operations functions *in the moment* and the really terrible ongoing distortion of incentives for everyone when the Feds decided to bail out the managers and shareholders who pushed Citi into its mess. I am not driving in the rear-view mirror. I had this very debate with many experienced Wall Street colleagues as it was all unfolding.

In so many ways, I want our nation to function better, so from a public policy perspective, the following passage is enraging. But from the perspective of its providing robust proof for my entire book, it's absolute gold.

Subjecting our plan to criticism – you could call it stress testing the stress test – helped make the President somewhat more confident in our approach. On April 27, for instance, he hosted a White House dinner for some of America's leading economists, including critics such as Paul Krugman, Jeff Sachs, and Joseph Stiglitz. The President began with a pointed reminder that our strategy was my baby. "I'd like to hear your views," he told the group. "You already know what Tim thinks." The President invited each of them to speak, and most of what he heard was the familiar complaints that our plan was limp and unambitious, a recipe for zombie banks, too generous to the financial system. When the President asked each of them what they would suggest we do instead, he was exposed to an outside version of what he had inside the White House: more concerns and critiques, a few ideas, but nothing that sounded achievable, nothing that didn't bring problems of its own.[214]

---

[213] Geithner, pp.252-3
[214] Geithner, pp343-4

How magic is that? Three completely wrong-about-everything Leftist flakes masquerading as "economists" (whose collective forays into the real-world private sector were mainly advising Enron) had nothing substantive to offer. Wow, no kidding. Geithner of course doesn't mean it the way I mean it; his whole book is peppered with false humility about how he's valiantly trying to save a world – which by the way existed mainly in his mind – and everyone else is carping from the sidelines, with nothing of substance to offer in place of Tim's Grand Ideas. Did he mention he'd lived through other crises before?

His snide comments about how other people's ideas brought "problems of their own" are meaningless. If we are to take him at his word, he thought that his own plans brought plenty of problems in their wake, so as a criticism of others' ideas, that rings petty and hollow.

Never mind the meta-hilarity of dubbing these three perpetually-wrong-about-everything-upon-which-they-opine academics as among "America's leading economists," as if that is even a thing.

It makes me disappointed that the Acting Head of TARP was afraid of me and didn't hire me to run TARP. The outcomes would have been really different, not because I am a unique genius, but because there were then and are now plenty of models for dealing with liquidity or confidence crises in markets without doing the rampant damage Dodd-Frank and the misapplication of TARP ended up doing. Having someone at the helm who trusted markets more than "experts" would have shifted the emphasis from DC types who think they should "do something" to market types who would have addressed each piece of the puzzle as it came along, calmly and rationally.

Framing a narrative is everything. In this instance, Geithner uses the phrase "Old Testament" a dozen or more times, always to link a market-based view of consequences *not* with rational economic action, but rather a befuddled "religious" inclination to scorched earth Justice, the economic fallout be damned. I don't know the man, so I don't know if he actually believed that or it's a convenient falsehood to hide behind.

Given that fact that he *never* had to balance a P&L in the private sector, and always had a free hand with other people's money, for which he was never accountable in any real way, I am betting that he doesn't understand why his assertions were wrong. He oddly mistook people who were clamoring for the risk side of risk-reward to earn the downside of their poor actions for irrational humans who wanted to destroy the entire socio-economic fabric of America, if only they could squat atop the ruins muttering smugly to themselves that "they" got what was coming to them.

Some of the *best* parts of reading Geithner's book come from his unintended exposure of the *true* problems besetting the economy and country under Obama and still under Trump and now Biden because decades of terrible decisions are really hard to unwind swiftly. While lamenting the problem of "housing" – as if the Federal Government should have a damned thing to do with *individual* homeowners' choices, and as if fifty years of *bad* governmental "housing policy" hadn't driven the nation to the crisis in the first place, a *fact* not mentioned *once* in Geithner's telling – Geithner treats us to this gold-dusted, chocolate-coated, diamond-centered nugget: "If there had been a game-changing housing plan that could have provided more relief, we would have embraced it. *We had some of the nation's best progressive talent working on housing.*" [italics mine]

399

There. That magical sentence was almost worth the time I spent on his book. It is almost too delicious to be true. If this were a work of fiction, and I had my main protagonist utter those words, any editor worth her salt would put an angry red line through it, with some cutting marginalia about its lacking plausibility. It's like a gift from Heaven for anyone who has a clear view of the fact that *the nation's best progressive talent* **caused** "the housing crisis" in the first place. Barney Frank – when he took time away from renting his apartment out to a pimp he used to pay for sex – was "rolling the dice" a little more on the Left's grand experiment to subsidize housing. His actions and those traveling along with him *caused* housing prices to inflate and therefore gallop ever further out of reach of low-income workers, who then got *more* cheap credit which caused house prices to rise *even more*. It's so insane that it's hard to believe it happened.

Earlier in the book, Geithner expresses how angry he got when people criticized him. Not to be petty, but given the fact that policies he championed bankrupted my business and forced me to lay off people before Christmas 2012, I've got to say I was not sorry to read that he, too, was angry and losing sleep and family time during that period. I sure was.

Schadenfreude aside, his entire manifesto is a complete documentation of the Left's incorrect set of beliefs about how the world should work. He himself *never* took private sector risk, yet there he was, sitting atop the New York Fed and then the Treasury, wasting my grandchildren's tax receipts by borrowing frantically to feed his delusions of market-influencing grandeur.

He continues about how he was "saving housing," as if preventing price drops towards a market-clearing level was a good thing. Oh, wait, isn't that what caused this problem in the first place, government artificially inflating house prices???

Details….

He writes *approvingly* about continuing the flow of cheap credit to Fannie and Freddie so "homeowners" could continue to buy property with artificially cheap money. He erroneously believes that subsidizing credit is *good* for lower-income people, despite the – never-addressed by Geithner and his fellow travelers – fact that a wall of cheap borrowing is precisely what causes asset prices (houses) to *rise* out of the reach of the very people he's claiming to help!

He demonstrates sweeping ignorance of capital markets. As he puts it, he and the Obama Administration "were at war with the banks and other special interests that were trying to water down our reforms."[215]

Geithner of course believes that an entire career spent as a parasite, er, public servant that "dealt" with financial issues makes him an "expert." His arrogance is sweeping. As he relates, "I remember Boeing's CEO came to tell me that the status quo was better for Boeing because they could get better terms through private arrangements with their derivatives dealers. 'Look, if everyone is coming in and telling me they're getting special deals from their dealers, maybe nobody is getting a good deal," I told him.[216]

---

[215] Geithner, p412

400

The fact that the CEO did not literally punch Geithner in his smug face after that puerile comment is rock solid testimony to the restraint he had to muster in order to realize that while that was the *only appropriate* response to such an offensive comment, it would not further Boeing's corporate interests.

Could that be any more obnoxious, condescending *and* ignorant, all wrapped up in one heady package? What an offensive, arrogant, hubristic man one must be to believe that entire corporate treasury departments, CFOs, CEOs and experienced bankers are just plain stupid, that they don't all have access to market data on prices from Bloomberg terminals, Reuters, Dow Jones and the derivatives exchanges against which they compare the *multiple* bids from dealers. No – those people are just stupid and Supreme Lord Geithner knows better. He "knows" for some bizarre reason which is completely incomprehensible to those of us who actually transact in derivatives markets, that "everyone" is getting a bad deal, they're too dumb to know it, and by the way, they're definitely going to get "better" deals when pricing is posted on a futures exchange.

You'll note, also, his arrogance in ignoring something very crucial that these very same dumb corporate drones – including Boeing's CEO – are telling him when they said they're getting *"better terms"* from their banks. The professionals did *not* tell him they're getting "special deals" as if this were some late-night infomercial about classified ads and real estate dreams. No, they said they were – due to their balance sheets, multifaceted banking relationships and customized risk trades – getting *better deals* than they would get by "dealing on an exchange." This would be common knowledge to Geithner and his ilk if they had ever had to work in the private sector.

A little bit of knowledge is a dangerous thing, as he exhibits here. What is amazing is that a number of years passed between his talking to the Boeing CEO and writing his memoirs. The amazing part is that *he didn't bother to find out what he didn't understand then*. He had the chance to revise history – no one would have known. Instead, thankfully for those of us looking for honest, first-person explanations of bad decisions made, he went ahead and wrote those words condemning him for all time.

Had he bothered to *listen* to people who know better, he would have understood *why* huge corporations get better terms when creating bespoke interest rate swaps rather than buying bulk futures contracts. I wonder if now that someone gave him a job in the private sector, he is embarrassed by having written any of this.

There are plenty of resources available for anyone who wants to dive into the details of corporate treasury departments and their myriad complex relationships with banks and the capital markets. If you want confirmation of the validity of my sweeping condemnation of Geithner's ignorant comments, just bear in mind that a Fortune 100 corporation could well do business in 70+ countries, using 25+ different local currencies, whose operations are funded using all the options at their disposal, including bank loans, supply chain financing and the bond markets – all of which can mean interest rate exposure in terms of fluctuating, unpredictable debt service schedules. The US corporation reports its earnings in USD, which opens it up to a whole range of headaches relating to fluctuating

---

[216] Geithner, P412

foreign exchange rates and volatility. Those two complexities are often intertwined, as when a Belgian subsidiary is borrowing in euros. To manage all this complexity, corporate treasurers rely on a range of derivatives to transfer some of that interest rate and foreign exchange rate risk to the capital markets. That treasurer cannot manage those risks effectively or efficiently by buying futures contracts which have to be managed for margin calls and eventually "rolled over" when they expire, and whose standardized terms will definitely not match in time or size the actual exposures the corporation faces.

Which is *why* the Boeing CEO was trying to teach Geithner something basic about modern finance. Geithner of course ignored the opportunity to learn something and instead continued in the smug fashion of all consequence-free politicians and bureaucrats to jam his stupid "solutions" down the throat of corporate America because the public hysteria *caused* by politicians in the housing finance market had now – insanely and ironically – given them *even more power* to screw up the financial system. Geithner rode the nonsensical "Greedy Wall Street Bankers did this!" train the politicians probably couldn't believe the American people were stupid enough to believe.

My unrevised analysis of the unfolding idiocy in September 2008

When I make a prediction, I am willing to have its accuracy judged as events unfold. I sent this email to family and friends while I was on Doha restructuring their stock exchange. It was Ramadan so I was eating in my hotel room and watching the Congressional circus on television while trying not to scream at the morons on the screen.

Here is the unedited email I sent. You judge whether I was accurate in my diagnoses and comments.

From: Christopher Messina
Sent: Sunday, September 21, 2008 9:44 AM
To: [Long list of friends and family]
Subject: Markets and politicians - ruminations from Doha....

If any of you are watching $700 billion of our taxpayer money go to some process you don't wholly understand and would like some color on why all this craziness is happening in the first place, I offer the following bijou.

Firstly, before I begin, this whole noise in the press about which talking head blabbermouth (of the two poor choices we've been handed yet again) has the better sound bite about wholly unprecedented financial issues currently to hand is just boring, pointless chatter that gives TV "journalists" something to do so people don't realize they're really only (barely) qualified to act as parking meter attendants in minor cities. Hank Paulson is one of the most seasoned, competent, cool-thinking financiers in 100 years and he and his team are facing complicated decisions whose outcomes are not pre-determined. So to expect either Obama or McCain to have anything intelligent to parrot from their advisors (who themselves are playing out scenarios in their heads as I and my team are every day) is just plain stupid.

Allow me to share briefly with you the view from the *inside* of the global financial meltdown. Many of us in the financial community have known of these problems and potential flaws for years, but the main headache *originates with the U.S. Congress*. Had Congress not 25+ years ago defined rational credit scoring as the basis for lending as "discriminatory," bankers wouldn't have been *forced* to lend to people who they knew couldn't pay back the loan.

Ignore the sideshow distractions about "derivatives" – those valuation and systemic counterparty problems only exist because of the mortgage crisis. None of this would be a dangerous "house of cards" had the real economy been allowed to work as it was supposed to without – gasp! – the meddling of incompetent, ignorant buffoons (otherwise known as your elected officials).

Once Congress defined proper banking practice (i.e. the prudent lending to borrowers of the banks' *customers'* – that is yours and my – deposits) as "discriminatory" against the poor, they forced banks to lend to those who couldn't pay it back (thereafter fancifully named in PoliticSpeke as "subprime" borrowers getting a shot at the American Dream).

In strict terms, absent the FDIC, we depositors should have been deathly worried by this development, and the only prudent thing to do as a depositor would have been to run to the bank to put your money somewhere safer than a prone-to-default mortgage – say, your mattress. But since the same Congress was willing to backstop depositors' losses on bum loans, hell, we stopped paying attention (if we ever had been) to this whole mess and stopped pondering the logic of Congress's unsubstantiated assertion that there was a link between "social lending justice" and our own hard-earned cash.

Mortgage bankers without a catchy Populist slogan of their own ("Hard work is rewarded, so tighten your belt and afford a mortgage some other day" just didn't have the same zip as Congress's pitch) sighed and viewed this as another implicit tax on their shareholders (who would be forced to bear the brunt of write-downs associated with loaning to people who can't pay back the loan), but then some clever ducks said, "Hey, let's package this crap and sell it! Then it's off our balance sheets and someone else can deal with it."

Individual banks' problem solved! But only at the cost of shifting the final day of reckoning out in to the indeterminate – and hopefully distant – future. Doesn't look so distant or indeterminate from being inside it right now, does it?

Fannie and Freddie loved this as it became a great way to reward people with insanely-high-paying jobs (to pay off politicians' debts to their pals), wholly decoupled from their actual abilities, because these were people who couldn't survive in the real Wall Street competitive <u>market</u> environment, but who did extremely well in the Washington <u>political</u> environment. As the beasts overseen by this set of stuffed-shirt clowns churned out mortgage-backed paper to feed their growing appetite for patronage cash to ill-qualified political appointments, they increased exponentially the amount of cash available for lending.

Buyers of this paper (including all public and private pension funds) loved it because they were getting a yield above Treasurys but carrying an implicit (now explicit) US Govt guarantee – which is risk-free arbitrage which in Economics 101 CANNOT EXIST EXCEPT FOR GOVERNMENTAL DISTORTIONS TO THE MARKET. You are all familiar with this principle in the old wisdom of the adage, *There ain't no such thing as a free lunch.*

There is NO risk-free arbitrage (where you can make a certain profit on a trade with no chance of loss) in free markets, only in distorted markets such as the one handed us by the Federal Monkeys in Washington. Who distorted the true economic realities of market growth all for personal political gain about which they may frankly have been most too stupid to realize and are now of course blaming all this rampantly expanding mess not on themselves for their own ill-conceived legislation, but on the supposed "greed" of those evil Wall Streeters...

So mortgage bankers post-Congressional diktat made money on the FEES associated with writing the mortgage and began to care little for the underlying credit of the borrower. The mortgage brokers who sprang up like weeds in communities across America really didn't care about whether these loans would get paid – at least a bank had the loan sitting on its books for a week or month or so until it could be sold on to Freddie or Fannie. A storefront mortgage broker was just a go-between – if that loan went into default the millisecond after he/she pocketed his origination fee, it was immaterial to his/her success as a broker.

And, to make it even better, when the Mortgage Bankers' Association suggested to Congress the responsible idea that mortgage brokers be regulated and that certain minimum standards of fiduciary duty (similar to a stockbroker) be enforced, howls of Populist protest rang from Capitol Hill to the Pacific and the Atlantic and the Gulf of Mexico! Those bankers were discriminating again! Yup, this time they were discriminating against minority (sometimes) entrepreneurs who were building a business sourcing loans from the poor to commercial banks. Congress – and this is one for the record books, perhaps a unique event – refused to regulate mortgage brokers.

Here is the insanity: If I as a Series 7 registered financial representative am sitting at Goldman Sachs, I cannot sell a single share of $20 stock to, say, a professional fund manager at IBM Pension Fund without being a regulated person. But any fool who can open a storefront in a poor neighborhood can sell an intensely complicated multi-year balloon mortgage with complex rate-reset provisions for $200,000 to someone who – in theory and often in practice – has never graduated from high school. How is that for crazy?

For quite a long time, asset prices kept inflating in a game of hot potato: because ready money was available from Fannie and Freddie, banks and brokers raked in fees, fund managers stuffed funds with artificially-inflated returns and there was no loss because as prices rose, house buyers became house sellers and the inflated asset price meant the original shaky loan got paid off, so not many of us outside Wall Street noticed the problem.

Anytime we did mention the problem, we were told we were "against the little guy," whoever that may be, and wanted to restrict wealth creation to some vaguely-defined "elite," presumably our customers. Since most Americans' wealth has historically been tied to real estate, anything that smacked of "holding back the market" could only be discriminatory against the majority of Americans. So went the Populist logic – it's not looking so logical now, is it?

All asset prices revert back to the mean long-term growth of a given area (or nation), so any divergence from that average growth line either represents an artificial inflation of prices (a bubble) or deflation of prices (great buying opportunity). Learn this equation by heart, and when asset prices (houses) around you go up faster per year than this percentage, it's a bubble.

Population growth (x%) + GDP growth (y%) + inflation(z%) = mean line asset growth over time (x+y+z%).

So when people got rich on real estate, they were getting rich on artificially-inflated prices CAUSED by the same Federal Government who is now asking you and me to bail this out with our tax dollars. Any finance professional could have told you 18, 24 or 200 months ago (and would have) that artificial asset-price growth will ALWAYS end in a burst bubble and misery for the community. But while the sun is shining, people like to make hay...

Make no mistake: Congress and the Federal Government created this problem by setting the rules of the game improperly, for their own political ends. And now that it has gone tits up in the water, they are blaming Wall Street for this mess. We would never have suggested this stupid set of conditions, in fact tried to kill Fannie and Freddie or at least regulate and manage them properly, but you can't fight City Hall and after awhile, we just kept our heads down and dealt with non-market interventionary distortions with the best tools we had to manage the risk associated with the stupidity Washington gave us.

No one in Washington will ever admit that. Terrifyingly, 95% of them are probably too dumb to know it's true and the other 5% who aren't already out of office or dead sure ain't gonna stand up to tell America they knew but didn't bother to say anything.

Happy Election, everyone.

Chapter 26: Financial Regulation – Purpose and Staffing Need to Change

Securities and Exchange Commission

Founded	June 6, 1934
Founded under President	Franklin D. Roosevelt
Funding Budget 2023	$2,150,000,000
Messina's 2024 Budget Proposal	$2,400,000,000
Messina's 2025 Budget Proposal (combined)	$5,000,000,000
Degree to which Messina's Plan is Better	Completely
Should a separate SEC exist?	No

Commodities Futures Trading Commission

Founded	April 1975
Founded under President	Gerald Ford
Funding Budget 2023	$365,000,000
Messina's 2024 Budget Proposal	$450,000,000
~~Messina's 2025 Budget Proposal~~	~~[merged with SEC]~~
Degree to which Messina's Plan is Better	Completely
Should a separate CFTC exist?	No

Is this a standalone proper use of the taxpayers' limited resources?	Yes
Does this expenditure unfairly benefit one American over another one?	No
Does the expenditure meet the "Is this logical?" standard of fiduciary responsibility?	Yes
Can the goals be achieved by *not* spending the dollar more effectively than by spending it?	Maybe

Free markets require excellent supervision and enforcement. Too many sleaze weasels try to steal from honest people. If people in general come to distrust the honesty of financial markets, society crumbles. So I am a major fan of *properly applied* regulation, not the mishmash of approaches we have today. Firstly, we need to merge the SEC and CFTC into one thing. Secondly, we need to make sure that the combined agency *can pay market rates* for relevant trading and capital markets expertise.

The Securities and Exchange Commission (SEC) and the Commodity Futures Trading Commission (CFTC) regulate the financial activities of brokers, dealers, investment bankers and futures commission merchants. Unlike in the United Kingdom, Australia, Germany and other mature financial markets, the SEC and CFTC are *two separate* regulatory entities. There are some historical reasons for that division of oversight, but modern markets make no distinction between a portfolio composed of listed stocks and one composed of stocks, bonds and futures contracts. It would be better for all concerned to have a single financial regulator.

Basic logic dictates the two be merged into one. It would be less expensive for the taxpayer to fund one agency and for those paranoid conspiracy theorists out there, it would be impossible for financial wizards to engage in "regulatory arbitrage," which is a fancy way of saying "I'm going to choose an activity according to the regulator in charge of that activity in the hopes of slipping something by one that I am afraid I could not slip by the other."

Why don't we get it? Because politicians love money, and millions of dollars are committed to election funds every year by market participants. If the Congress voted to merge the SEC and CFTC, by definition there would be fewer Congresspeople to bribe, er, influence, er, commit reelection funds to. "In 1950 senators could get elected by spending $100,000 on their campaigns; by 1980 that number was typically several million dollars; by 2010 many Senate candidates spent $20-$30 million to win or retain their seats. Multimillion-dollar races became common in the House as well."[217]

So once again, you've got the Members of Congress *acting together in their own interests* that have nothing to do with the overall interests of the country at large or even particularly with the interests of their own constituents, if you would prefer a narrower interpretation of their fiduciary duty to the American taxpayers.

To be fair, the existence of the two entities also has a lot to do with institutional inertia and the self-interest of the people who staff each regulatory agency. We've also got FERC pestering energy market traders about trades that for often very hazy reasons irritate energy regulators.

Even with a superfluity of regulatory entities, that burden on markets was not enough for the ideologues staffing the Obama regime. On 17 June 2009, the Obama Administration released a white paper called *Financial Regulatory Reform – A New Foundation: Rebuilding Financial Supervision and Regulation.*[218] In the History of Bad Ideas, this white paper contained one of the all-time worst, which is the idea for a "systemic risk regulator."

Robert Kaiser in his beautifully-titled book *Act of Congress* pointed out how stupid this was. Even with his limited understanding of financial markets knew that this big, crazy idea was swept into legislation with *no* examination of its merits. "Authors of the white paper hoped the use of this power would enable regulators to limit or terminate risky behavior by financial institutions before it posed a risk to the system. This was a radical idea, new in the history of American capitalism. It survived the legislative process, and became part of Dodd-Frank, without ever being debated or much discussed in the House or Senate."[219]

There is *only* one critique of this insanity required to prove what a phenomenal waste of money is the FSOB – Financial Stability Oversight Board. By definition, anyone who can read the various tea leaves in the economy and *accurately predict* systemic risks would already be 100x times richer than Bill Gates, Warren Buffett, Elon Musk and the Google founders combined.

------

[217] Kaiser, Robert, *Act of Congress*, p.88
[218] http://www.financialstability.gov/docs/FinalReport_web.pdf
[219] Kaiser, Robert, *Act of Congress*, p.92

So, that's simple. For the FSOB to exist – even as a one-person shop – please step up and provide to the American people the proof that your net worth is 100x that of that group, and you get the job. No one else can pretend to be qualified.

No one is qualified or capable of performing these absurd acts of prediction, but that never stopped a bureaucrat from drawing a salary and building an empire! The ridiculous, parasitic Board exists and churns out a forest of printed paper every year to no productive purpose anyone rational can discern.

One of the *biggest* causes of distortions in the market for information is a guild, cartel or union system. That is as true in financial markets as in any other market. Every new business that has an innovation in, say, how to let investors participate directly in commodity or shipping markets, must waste a year and spend tens if not hundreds of thousands of dollars asking permission to be in business – from their future competitors. FINRA must license a business to be a "broker-dealer." Every member of FINRA understand competition very well – they would prefer a tiny club of big dealers control all financing activity at nice, fat profit margins.

This same group LOVED it when Congress fixed brokerage rates and got hopping mad when the market – GASP! – was allowed to set brokerage rates, which spawned whole new online brokerages like E*TRADE to appear. Guild members loathe competition. They like fat profits protected by legal bans on faster, cheaper competitors entering their markets.

Whenever the idea to "protect" consenting adults in the marketplace from financial decisions is floated, it always *seems* so reasonable. Obama himself made it a mainstay of his chorus to intone about "simple, commonsense rules of the road," which in fact means nothing at all other than "Let's have more unaccountable bureaucrats with no financial experience and probably a law degree rather than a quantitative skill set pester largely-honorable, intelligent and creative people on Wall Street for years on end without having a clue as to what they are asking or why, the only result of which will be increased costs for the financial sector, which *will* be passed on to consumers in one way or another."

The most amazing part of this whole fiasco has been to watch the process by which *no one in power seems to want to understand what really happened.* Just as the "investigative report"[220] on the 2009 Fort Hood shootings when an Army Major (and psychiatrist) named Nidal Hasan killed 13 people and wounded 43 while shouting "Allahu Akbar!" *does not mention once in 53 pages* (and another 4 appendices) the terms "Islam" or "Muslim," so too was the Dodd-Frank Act passed *before Obama's commission delivered its results.*

And even if the Obama Administration was not intent on proving that George Orwell was a starry-eyed optimist, it would not have mattered, because there are maybe 30 people in a Congress of 535 people who even vaguely understand how financial markets work.

As Chris Dodd himself said, cited in Kaiser's book, "'[W]e didn't need a Pecora Commission to find out what was going wrong. We had mortgages being sold in this country

---

[220] *Protecting the Force: Lessons from Fort Hood,* report of the DoD Independent Review, January 2010

to people who couldn't afford them, marketing them in a way that guaranteed failure, securitizing them so [their creators] could be paid and then skipping town in a sense. I didn't need to have hours of hearing to found out what was the cause of it.'"[221]

To which I – and many others – say heartily, "Amen, brother! Amen! But what on earth does this wholesale overregulation of the entire financial system do about that particular problem?" Lost in this entire insanity is that the root cause of the economic collapse of 2007-2009 was created by Federal and State Governmental decisions about housing. Absent the 30-odd years of insane policy which was the main cause of the real estate bubble, this collapse would never have happened.

Dodd-Frank did many damaging things, but it did not address the main problem which set this whole headache off. Robert Kaiser himself shows his biases and ignorance of the real financial world as he chooses to confuse ill-informed opinion with fact in his oh-so-sophisticated brushing-aside of the *main* intelligent critique of this whole charade. Kaiser's writing is so engaging because he is dragging me along towards what I think is going to be a refreshing respite from the usual parroting noise from the Beltway Echo Chamber... and then he reverts to form:

The historical context made Dodd-Frank possible. In 2008 and 2009 the country suffered a catastrophe, in part because of Congress's own negligence – its eager complicity over nearly three decades in the systemic deregulation of the American financial system. In the 1980s, 1990s, and 2000s, deregulation became the consensus position in Washington.[222]

You see what he did there? You're reading along with delighted surprise about *Congress's own negligence* ... and then he screws the pooch by being *precisely wrong* about what those buffoons had been negligent *about.* They'd been negligent all right – they had been negligently empowering a raft of crony capitalists at Fannie Mae and Freddie Mac to pump overwhelming oceans of taxpayer cash into the home-ownership market, arm-in-arm gleefully with the other buffoons careening through the White House and plush offices in entities like HUD. They'd neglected to force mortgage brokers to be registered and regulated the way stockbrokers are. They'd neglected to do the only thing that a crowd of people with no financial expertise *should have done* which was to keep their fingers off the scales of the private economy.

Absent those wild pools of Federal dollars, this party could never have gone to the dizzying heights that it had, and therefore could never have crashed to earth as resoundingly as it eventually did.

Could there have been and should there still be better regulation? Sure, of course, but that also has eluded the vast dragnet of Dodd-Frank. The *simplest* – from a boring, logical, make-the-world-a-better-place standpoint – would be to have *one* regulatory body overseeing financial services firms. Dodd-Frank for all its original 2,000 pages and the subsequent tsunami of regulatory verbiage did not merge the SEC and CFTC into one body.

---

[221] Kaiser, Robert, p. 367
[222] Kaiser, Robert, p. 370

409

Nope!

Wanna know why? *Because those are things the politicians in Washington use to reward their friends and to raise money about.* So if you, dear reader, choose to ignore any of the rest of what I have written here, ponder that one, and perhaps lay my book aside for awhile until you think you may want to look at it with fresh eyes.

While you're at it, don't forget to ponder their concomitant unwillingness to deal with the big chocolate mess that is Fannie Mae and Freddie Mac, *taxpayer-backed* quasi-private companies where Jamie Gorelick, a lawyer, not a banker, whose only qualification was working for the Clinton Administration could earn $26,466,834 from 1998 - 2003 in a Vice Chairman role in the mortgage market, the same years in which a 48-year-old mortgage investment banker with 25 years of experience would be lucky to earn half of that.

Kaiser's bought the happy Kool-Aid on that main problem, as well, hook, line and pimp-landlord sinker.

Another popular Republican talking point was the failure of Dodd-Frank to deal with Fannie Mae and Freddie Mac. Roy Blunt of Missouri, a member of the Republican leadership, used this one: "The root cause of the problem we have in the economy today was caused by these entities," Blunt asserted, a proposition no serious economist would endorse. "They are not addressed" by Dodd-Frank, he continued, proof of the bill's inadequacy. [223]

This from the man who quoted Senator Moynihan to the effect that while you're allowed to have your own opinion, you're not entitled to your own facts.

It is worth recalling the dangers of illogic and propaganda. As chess legend Garry Kasparov noted in 2016, "The point of modern propaganda isn't only to misinform or push an agenda. It is to exhaust your critical thinking, to annihilate truth." I'm not accusing Kaiser of pushing propaganda; my point is more subtle, that the mental shortcuts we *all* take in our daily lives to cope with an incredibly complex world often lead us to the sort of sloppy thinking demonstrated in Kaiser's work.

The massive boondoggle of the GSEs causing the housing and then financial catastrophe was not "a Republican talking point." It was, is and will forever *be* the main cause of the entire financial collapse. It may *also* be a talking point – that does not make it wrong; it's like saying the phrase "Hitler was an evil, genocidal monster" was an Allied talking point in 1945. So? Perhaps it's a "talking point" because it's true.

Even for a Washington journalist like Kaiser, I'd expected more than him assuring us that "no serious economist would endorse" this idea, *when every single person I know on Wall Street and in the private sector* will laugh at the idea that the Crash was at the root caused by anything *other* than a sea of politically driven "Housing Is An Unqualified *Right*" taxpayer cash.

Given my general disdain for "economists," I'm perhaps willing to believe some of them – like Austen Goolsbee or Paul Krugman who long ago sold their souls and intellectual

---

[223] Kaiser, Robert, p.363

integrity for a taste of fame – might contend that Fannie and Freddie were but parts of larger movements,[224] but Kaiser's silly statement undoes quite a lot of credibility that he built up spottily elsewhere in the book. I know from reading his book that he does not understand financial markets in the slightest, but I'd been taking his word for his understanding the legislative process sufficiently to explain it to those of us with better things to do. But sweeping errors like this make me wonder. If he's totally wrong about things I know about, how can I be sure that he's not totally wrong about things I don't know about?

For more color on the details behind all the greedy pocket liners on both the governmental and private sector side of this sleazy collaboration, I urge you to read Charles Gasparino's wonderful work, *Sellout: How Three Decades of Wall Street Greed and Government Mismanagement Destroyed the Global Financial System,* published in 2009. If I tried to quote everything relevant from all the smart folks who've examined this nightmare objectively, this book would be 3,000 pages long; suffice it to say that I urge you to find out for yourself just how many "serious economics" *knew* the real cause of this disaster was Federal housing policy. Misery, I've heard tell, loves company. In the muddy-headed thinking surrounding the "crisis" of 2007-08, American politicians were by no means alone in doing everything they could to *avoid* finding the true, objective causes of the misery inflicted on millions of their own citizens. Beyond that, every politician exists because of the pronounced size of their lizard brain, which demands placing personal survival above all other considerations, including such paltry issues as personal honor, integrity, decency, honesty and true civic duty.

Bipartisan consensus – with a few noted outliers – was that "greedy bankers" had done this to America. Anything Congress or Fannie and Freddie had done was out of a pure desire to help average Americans attain the American Dream. Conveniently lost in that fantastic retelling were all the grimy, sleazy details of grift and rent-seeking by those pushing this new set of lies about immediate past history.

The housing boom had done many things, including papering over the accounting scandals that hit both agencies. During this time, the top executives at both agencies earned salaries that could be found only on Wall Street. Fannie Mae chief Franklin Raines earned a whopping $90 million between 1998 and 2004, when he was forced to leave amid an accounting scandal not much different from what had occurred at Enron or WorldCom.

There was just one difference: Fannie and Freddie were doling out the American Dream to the poor, and consequently the outcry, particularly from the press, was muted.[225]

When this bill became law, the chorus of derisive incredulity that arose from the people I know best was focused squarely on the insanity of using "the Crisis" as an excuse for "financial reform," which has turned out to be nothing more than a sea of legislative

---

[224] For example, both Fannie and Freddie made contributions to ACORN, the sleazy Leftwing outfit whose operatives were caught *on camera* offering advice on how to lie to get a mortgage to people posing as a pimp and his underage prostitute.

[225] Gasparino, *Sellout,* p.233

garbage fulfilling the fevered dreams of generations of Leftists *while doing nothing to address the main cause of that Crisis*. Watching this craziness unfold has been by turns horrifying and comical in a gallows-humor kind of way.

Don't get me wrong – there was plenty of legislative and regulatory stupidity *before* Chris Dodd put down the bottle and Barney Frank took a break from harboring pimps so they could join hands to take time to screw up America. One of the dumbest decisions – made in the context of a sweeping string of breathtakingly stupid initiatives – was to *legislatively mandate* the stamp of approval from one of three ratings agencies. This rubber-stamping exercise was either gasoline or the oxygen thrown into the Fannie- and Freddie-kindled overheated mortgage bonfire.

I don't have time or space to expand on this but very briefly the idea was to have "third party ratings agencies" analyze bonds and structured products like mortgage backed securities, so that investors could "know" which were relatively riskier than others. The problem was that the ratings agencies were for-profit ventures that had to win business from the creators of the securities, who paid for the ratings. Even a four-year-old can see the problems inherent in that approach. How could anyone expect an objective analysis of risk when there were two competitors ready to tell a bond issuer that "Meh, it's not as bad as Ranging Agency A says it is...."?

Dodd and Frank, who in the aftermath of the mortgage bubble, pointedly have ignored their *personal* roles as big cheerleaders for the increase of Fannie and Freddie, did actually – accidentally, likely – have their minions include something about removing the cartel status of the ratings agencies. They did nothing to address the other value-subtractive headaches various regulatory strangles place on *you,* the retail investor, which regulations may sound abstract, but reduce *your* portfolio's value in death by a thousand cuts.

As the Chief Compliance Officer and CEO of a broker/dealer, I have had ample opportunity to deal with FINRA, the regulatory organization that oversees investment banking and securities businesses in the United States. I have my fair share of insane stories of absurdity emanating from FINRA, but on the whole, each individual with whom I have dealt has appeared to want to do a good job. That said, the *organization* and its Supreme-Court-approved unaccountability is a serious breach of the principles of the rule of law.

High Court Declines to Weigh In on Finra's Immunity
Wall Street Journal MARKETS
JANUARY 17, 2012, 1:51 P.M. ET
By ANDREW ACKERMAN

WASHINGTON—The Supreme Court on Tuesday refused to consider an appeal that questioned whether the Financial Industry Regulatory Authority and other so-called self-regulatory organizations are immune from private lawsuits.

Self-regulatory organizations carry responsibilities for supervising market activity at a more granular level than the Securities and Exchange Commission, which oversees them.

Critics have warned these quasi-government agencies have become abusive and unaccountable to the public. Though the self-regulators are private organizations, they generally enjoy absolute legal immunity for activities related to their government-delegated regulatory authority.

The high court rejected a challenge brought by Standard Investment Chartered Inc., a small California broker-dealer. Standard Investment was challenging the legality of a 2007 merger that created Finra, when the National Association of Securities Dealers purchased the regulatory arm of the New York Stock Exchange.

Lower courts dismissed the case, ruling that Finra, which oversees nearly 4,600 brokerage firms, has broad immunity against lawsuits. Standard, however, argued that Finra shouldn't have absolute protection from lawsuits, particularly for alleged conduct that isn't directly related to its regulatory functions.

In its own defense, Finra said that every court to review the issue has agreed that self-regulators are "absolutely immune from private lawsuits for money damages attacking conduct that falls within the scope of their regulatory functions."

Standard Investment argued that NASD, one of the two Finra predecessor firms, wasn't acting in a regulatory capacity when it sought to merge with NYSE-Regulation. Instead, the firm said NASD was acting in a "proprietary" capacity, driven to increase its revenue base from membership dues and to eliminate a competing regulator.

Standard Investment objected to the merger in part because it involved changes to the self-regulator's bylaws in a way that diluted the power of smaller member firms. It also contended that NASD officers failed to indicate in proxy statements that they would benefit financially if the merger went through.

The Second U.S. Circuit Court of Appeals ruled against Standard Investment last year, finding that NASD's proxy statements and merger were shielded from liability because they were "incident" to its regulatory functions.

The Supreme Court let that ruling stand without comment.

This is completely contrary to the Rule of Law. The idea that one private citizen — who happens to have a job at a "regulator" — could potentially make decisions that arbitrarily harm another private citizen *without the danger of suffering damage for so doing* is precisely how totalitarian systems operate. At the very least, this is a debate that should be had in the open light of day; granting someone utter immunity from the consequences of their actions is inimical to any fair system of justice.

Politics by *ad hoc* Criminalization

There are a number of issues with our current regulatory approach which need to be subject to the bright sunshine of transparency. I raise a few of them here to give my fellow Americans not versed in such minutiae just how much work remains to be done.

One of the most ridiculous bits of political retribution, er kabuki theatre, er financial regulation was a multi-year storm of Congressional and regulatory "outrage" about American banks doing business in China hiring employees who could generate business for them. For those readers who have never worked in the investment banking industry and/or been involved with the global capital markets, the core of almost all business done is based on strong relationships.

All investment banking hires are made based on skills and relationships. Any idiot can play with Excel sheets and copy PowerPoint presentation slides — the reason some people are good investment bankers is because they can cultivate new business relationships as well as leverage existing ones.

Yet, if JP Morgan Chase hires, say, a daughter of a connected Chinese Communist Party official, for some reason the US Congress wants to waste *your* tax dollars on hearings into this supposedly "corrupt" arrangement. Never mind that during said hearings the young man or woman handing notes to the thundering Congressional Representative behind the podium is often a child of privilege, and has gotten his or her internship through a mix of hard work and family connections...

Or never mind that Chelsea Clinton – whom I have never met – was hired at 24 years old at $600,000 per year by NBC to be a reporter, with no experience that would justify such a handsome pay packet for anyone else doing that job at that age. I don't care about this use of private funds if NBC's shareholders don't care. What I find appalling and what I would like *all* my fellow taxpayers to ponder is why it's OK for NBC to curry influence with Bill and Hillary Clinton by hiring their daughter, at the *same exact time* Congress was busy raking Chase Bank over the coals for hiring as *qualified* investment bankers offspring of political figures in China.

It's all just one more example of the sleazy tit-for-tat politics that consumes millions of tax dollars for no justifiable public purpose whatsoever. Remove the cheddar and the rats will go somewhere else.

Dodd-Frank Financial "Reform"

When the prospect of this sweeping set of rules for financial markets first raised its head, I said, "OK, here's a bit of hysteria coming on the back of public outrage regarding the financial meltdown and the utterly pointless bailout of Wall Street. I mean, come on! Obama's much-touted *bipartisan* investigative panel into the *causes* of the financial crisis is still months away from publishing any conclusions. Chris Dodd and Barney Frank were some of the loudest cheerleaders for Fannie Mae, Freddie Mac and the ridiculous Federal distortion of mortgage markets that *got the country into this mess.* Surely, wiser heads will prevail, and there's no way this nonsense will actually go into effect."

It's not the first time I've been wrong.

The named cosponsors of this atrocity are a caricature of everything wrong with Washington, DC as currently constituted.

This is the Barney Frank who in 1987 hired a prostitute named Frank Gobie first for sex, then for potentially other tasks, who then let that prostitute *run a prostitution ring from his (Congressman Frank's) apartment.* You will doubtless recall the jail time Congressman Frank served for running a bordello with his pimp partner/lover/paid sex worker/mentee? Oh, no you won't, because for a *crime* that any American who is *not* a Member of Congress would get jail time for, Barney Frank got a "Congressional reprimand" voted on 408-18. Wow, that's some disparity in fair sentencing laws. I guess New York State Governor Eliot Spitzer knew his case law when wondering whether he'd go to jail in later years for trafficking hookers across State lines and then paying with a check for services rendered.

Again, it's so hard not to digress when writing about the moral sinkhole that is our government. How about the next time you, dear citizen, are convicted, say, for soliciting a

414

prostitute and then – having entrepreneurially permitted that prostitute to turn your home into a brothel – instead of jail time, a fine, 100 hours of "pervert reeducation classes," an expensive divorce, limited and monitored visitation rights with your kids and your name in the paper, you say to the judge, "I'd prefer it, Your Honor, if 408 friends of mine tell me that I was a naughty boy, while 18 other friends stand around saying *'meh, it's not so bad.'* After which, I go on with my life and have the power to impact hundreds of millions of lives in ways that hundreds of millions of people clearly never actually requested I be empowered for. Can I have that punishment instead?"

Barney Frank, partner, john and landlord of pimps chose to shove his oar into the financial markets because, well, because he saw himself – and the nation allowed him this vanity – as an important guy *sui generis*. Barney and every clown in Congress like him saw himself as being perfectly entitled to wreck millions of lives through some 21st-century variant of divine right, not because of a confluence of historical accidents allows someone *with no real-world private sector experience* to be in charge of trillions of dollars of taxpayer expenditure.

Ditto for all that with the added cherry topping on this turd sundae of the astonishingly arrogant and utterly unrepentant (at least as of January 2017 when I had a chance to ask him about it at a conference in New York) Chris Dodd.

Robert Kaiser – a long-time Washington reporter – has written a compelling narrative about the genesis and path to reality of the Dodd-Frank Act. He wins major style points for titling his opus *Act of Congress*. His work, while illuminating and entertaining, is in many places shockingly wrong. In many instances in which he purports to "discuss" financial markets, products and reform, he exhibits the by-now traditional biases of the left-leaning, liberal-arts graduate terrified either overtly or in the closet by numbers.

Early in his work, Kaiser already makes the case that Barney Frank *alone unto himself* decided with Tim Geithner and Larry Summers in late 2008 that "financial reform" had to be undertaken. He then goes on to show how shocking events can derail or catalyze plans in Washington. AIG got into trouble, posted a $100 billion loss. But, tragically for the strength of his arguments, Kaiser weakens his trustworthiness by either extremely shoddy fact-checking or willful ignorance when it comes to the very financial markets that lie at the heart of the legislative process he is narrating.

In trying to describe what AIG Financial Products division did, Kaiser treats us to this:

> Its (AIGFP's) primary business was "derivatives," the exotic financial instruments that played a big role in the Great Crash, and would come to bedevil members of the House and Senate. Derivatives trading was not regulated by the federal government, so the operations of AIGFP, as it was known, were mostly hidden from public view. During the housing bubble, AIG offered "credit default swaps," a type of derivative that amounted to insurance on the securities that Wall Street created from subprime mortgages.[226]

---

[226] Kaiser, Robert G., *Act of Congress,* Alfred A. Knopf, New York, 2013, p40

Firstly, I address the outright lies or mistakes that collectively Kaiser, his reviewers or editors never bothered to catch or correct:

1. "Derivatives trading" was most assuredly a highly regulated activity well before 2008. The CFTC oversaw and continues to oversee all listed derivatives trading, exchanges and markets. Market participants who traded their own capital had to manage risk on their own to avoid bankruptcy, while regulated firms managing other people's money most assuredly were bound by rules relating to what could or could not be done with that money.

2. Most of the people warning about a "housing bubble" for *years* were private sector players concerned about governmental distortions of what should be private financial matters. Barney Frank *was one of the biggest cheerleaders* for the massive government-backed behemoths who did more to shovel cash at people unable to repay loans. This sly assertion by Kaiser (who because he *knew* back then that there was a "housing bubble" I presume made billions of dollars shorting the mortgage market alongside John Paulson) connects the normal course of a derivatives sales desk with the utterly unsubtle assertion that there was some nefarious intent at AIGFP to *lose* money. It's ridiculous.

3. "Credit default swaps" are *not* "insurance on the securities that Wall Street created from subprime mortgages." CDS *are* a type of insurance on *any kind of debt*, as the name clearly states. An investor who owns, say, a bond issued by General Motors or IBM or even New York State, can choose to protect her potential losses arising from the debtor's failure to pay by entering into a swap agreement with a big company like AIG. Kaiser's phrasing once again is chockfull of the bias of *how to phrase* a simple sentence to make your subject appear dishonest in some way.

Secondly, the not-so-subtle conspiracy theory accusations: AIGFP's business was "hidden from public view," as if the normal course of business operations of, say, the local McDonalds or regional auto parts warehouse are on public display to anyone who wants to, you know, come in and have a look around.

Would Kaiser like me to be able to stroll into his home office and poke through his notes and computer files? Why not? I think it's mighty suspicious that he does not want me and 300,000,000 of his fellow Americans to see what he's doing when researching and preparing a story. That's downright sneaky, if you ask me. Barney Frank should have hearings. The Attorney General should look into that – oh, wait, Eric Holder *did* authorize wiretaps on journalists in the name of national security.[227] Did the press applaud him for exposing the dastardly and sneaky out-of-the-public-view doings of crafty journalists?

Lastly, for some bizarre reason, I have watched with bemusement a parade of journalists and politicians automatically link the adjective "exotic" to the noun "derivatives" without ever explaining why. What is "exotic" about something people do all day long, and even little children handle with ease?

---

[227] Sheryl Attkisson

A perfect example of a kind of derivative called a "forward swap" is when Sally, aged 6, says to Bobby, aged 7, "Bobby, if your mother puts those cookies in your lunchbox tomorrow, I promise that tomorrow at lunch if you give me your chocolate chip cookie, I'll give you my two peanut butter crunch bars." Sally can enter into this transaction on equal terms with Bobby, as everyone knows girls develop sooner than boys.

There. Little Sally and Bobby have just entered into an "exotic derivative transaction." They have agreed to a cross-commodity forward swap! Call the SEC and the White House and maybe the CFTC! These children pose systemic risk to lunchroom harmony and need to be regulated. At the very least, their cookie-for-crunch-bar evil swap transaction needs to be recorded, identified, reported to three regulatory bodies, with a third-party banking custodian posting collateral against the potential failure of the trade due, say, to either Bobby or Sally developing sniffles overnight, missing tomorrow's lunch time trade fulfillment. Surely, some clearinghouse needs to guarantee performance of this bilateral trade.

Good heavens! We're just getting started on the parade of work that needs to be done as a result of this wildly dangerous, *exotic* forward swap agreement. Someone needs to provide a marking-to-the-market for the forward swap. A data aggregator – perhaps Bloomberg – needs to poll dozens, preferably hundreds of other first graders to get pricing on similar trades. Ideally, hundreds of kids will have agreed the rate of one-cookie-for-one-crunch bar. But what if 20% of the kids agreed *two* cookies for one crunch bar? OMG! *What is* "the right price" for Sally and Bobby's swap? To be sure, their respective banks should demand double collateral against counterparty delivery!

And what about the *systemic risk*?! What if Bobby was only agreeing to tomorrow's trade with Sally because five minutes before speaking to Sally, he had somewhat irresponsibly agreed with Arjun, aged 8, that he would trade a peanut butter crunch bar for Arjun's Milky Way bar at after-school soccer. But Bobby had no prior assurance of *having* a crunch bar when he agreed the trade with Arjun!

OMG-squared! Bobby was entering into a *naked short* position with respect to his Milky Way transaction! Call the police! Arrest him for proprietary trading! Let that former Fed Chairman well past his sell-by-date Volcker opine on the nature of his trading activity!

But wait. Bobby is not dumb – his knowledge of the market told him that Sally had a serious craving for chocolate chips, *and* he knew Arjun's mother would not allow peanut butter crunch in their house because of his sister Priya's nut allergy. To Bobby's thinking, a Milky Way was equal in value to *at least* three peanut butter crunch bars, and he had been willing to trade his book all the way to that risk limit, but when Arjun jumped at the one-for-one trade, Bobby coolly booked the transaction and wandered off to find Sally. Not only did he have his Milky Way locked in, he was long an extra crunch bar he could trade for something else he might want. Or eat.

That is what politicians and regulators want to control and make predictable: the vibrant price discovery and *individual* meeting-of-needs in the free market. It drives social-engineering control-freaks absolutely crazy that they cannot predict what will happen five minutes from now, never mind in some fantasy land where regulators are going to peer months and years into the future and strip away the risk of bad things happening.

Their utter, objective inability to make those predictions does not of course prevent them from making laws that rest on their *belief* that they can make those predictions. Make no mistake: whenever someone intones about "managing" something called "systemic risk," they are utterly and completely lying to you, whether they know it or not.

And when the functions of this "systemic risk management" are to be entrusted to some "committee" or "oversight board," you may as well assume that whatever these megalomaniacal, deluded, parasitic nut jobs are doing will result in the deformation and likely destruction of the "system" whose "risks" are being so "managed."

I'm talking to you, Elizabeth Warren.

Practical Damage in the Real World

There is a gallows humor phrase market participants who lived through the early days of implementation of this stupid law. More than half of the entrepreneurs and finance professionals who developed products or services around the 2008-2010 time frame have a story of "getting Dodd-Franked," which means royally screwed and often bankrupted by this idiotic law and its myriad destructive tentacles.

Even when there were a few legislative turds that could be polished into mildly-useful or at least not utterly-destructive market fetters, Americans should still be enraged by the insane waste of time, money and brainpower required to *force* some market-friendly results out of a Socialist-driven ideological hatred of free markets. Chris Giancarlo in his excellent book *CryptoDad* describes his efforts as a CFTC Commissioner under Obama in fighting off Dodd-Frank inspired stupid rules about how swaps "should" trade in the United States. After the CFTC had issued rules that paid no attention to how the swaps market actually, functioned, Giancarlo and his staff did a huge amount of work to make sure US markets and market participants were not harmed, especially in relation to financial market participants around the world who were *not* shackled by stupid US regulatory nonsense.

As he writes, he won this battle in terms of allowing US markets to function, but lost the larger war because the battle was only won "temporarily," without the dumb rules being removed. In practice that means that it is rational to distrust American regulators – at any moment, the regulator can act like a whimsical king and just decide to put back in place the dumb rules. It is an unstable and uncertain way to run a government, makes a mockery of the rule of law and makes America more and more a banana republic.

In this extract from his book, a "SEF" is a Swap Execution Facility, the formal name for an electronic platform authorized by the CFTC to do business.

> Though delighted with the result, I was disappointed by the elaborate, administrative procedure that produced it. That result was a fair amount of circumvention of the ill- conceived SEF rules. Those peculiar rules, by their terms, required SEFs to restrict their business models to just two means of interstate commerce: "request for quote" and "central limit order books." CFTC staff were now recommending, however, approval of SEF registrations that allowed a broad set of trading methods. In my view, that was exactly the right outcome, because that was what Congress had always envisioned and specified in the language of the Act. But what a ridiculous, roundabout way to do the right thing. The guts of the workaround hinged on conditioning SEF approvals on applicants' compliance with five staff letters, called "no-action letters." Each letter effectively waived flawed swaps trading rules that I had identified in my white paper. This was bad administrative law on several levels. First, rather than the CFTC lifting the

inappropriate limits on SEF business models, the CFTC was just ignoring those limits. Second, the opaque mechanisms being used would make it very hard for other market participants to understand what modes of swap execution the CFTC was really permitting. Observers would have to pore over the fine print of each and every SEF registration that was approved and then extrapolate the unstated rules that were quietly being applied. Third, relying on a hodgepodge of "no action" letters would force market participants to jump through pointless hoops of make-work.[228]

That is an example of Dodd-Frank *working well*. In a practice I cover elsewhere in this book, Congress abdicated its Constitutional responsibility to, you know, actually *write or understand* the law they created. The folks in Congress are too important, you see, to bother to do their six-figure job of crafting legislation. Nope! They wave their hands over 3,000 page monstrosities and say "Unelected bureaucrats will create the rules by which Americans can be fined or imprisoned." A horrible Supreme Court idea called *Chevron deference* has allowed them to get away with this awfulness for decades.

The implementation of this terrible law then fell to hundreds if not thousands of staff members in various departments and agencies. In sharp contradistinction to how I wrote this book, each of those people worked in a silo, without bothering to even inquire how other parts of the law's rules were being written. No one sat atop the massive wasteful exercise to make sure all the rules so promulgated fit into a cohesive whole, whether any of those rules contradicted one another, how many were redundant and how many – Hint: LOTS! – were just plain stupidly destructive of economic value and innovation.

The book you're holding started out from the premise that if one does not keep the whole picture in mind, addressing or fixing one component is pointless. For truly useful and effective reform to happen, each detail must make sense on its own *and* must fit logically with every other detail. Otherwise, one gets a massive mess. In this instance, that is known as the US regulatory state.

I hope by now you're already sending outrage emails to your Senators and Congressional Representatives. For more ammunition, read on, read on.

Consumer Financial Protection Bureau

Created by Dodd-Frank, whose main underpinning assumptions are that fifty-eight pre-crisis regulators were unable to prevent a financial crisis, so therefore *fifty-nine* would clearly make sure everything is fine going forward, the CFPB is rooted in a perhaps admirable idea, but its form and function are ridiculous abuses of non-accountable technocratic absolute power divorced from the rule of law.

It has always reminded me of the office of an "Ombudsman" in New York City government. The Ombudsman exists to look after the interests of the citizens, which is a blatant, in your face admission that the *rest* of the people in government most certainly *do not* work in the interests of the citizens. If *all* civil servants were focused on helping

---

[228] Giancarlo, J. Christopher, *CryptoDad,* Wiley Books, 2021

taxpayers in need, then you the taxpayer would just call the relevant office for help. Whether fixing the pothole in front of your hours, or raising an issue about unresponsive DMV staff, you'd just call them. The entire concept of the Ombudsman is that the edifice of government is set *against* you, so the Ombudsman is the sole official in government fighting for you.

Same thing here. One might wonder what dozens of Federal and State regulatory agencies are doing all day if they are *not* "protecting consumers." Quite reasonable, in fact. As it turns out, by design and implementation by a pack of mostly left-leaning life bureaucrats, the CFPB has chosen to wade into issues in banking via a board seat on the FDIC

In a massive middle finger to the Constitution, all of it operations and annual funding are set on autopilot. This invasive abomination gets its money from the Federal Reserve, absent Congressional approval in violation of the clear Constitutional role Congress plays as the holder of the nation's purse strings.

End it immediately.

Jealous Looky-Loos with Undies-All-A-Bunched, er, "Say on Pay"

One of the massive problems with the whole Dodd-Frank exercise is that a laundry list of pent-up Leftist wishes was chucked into the sausage as it was being made. One section of the law requires companies to first *calculate* the "median pay" of its workforce and then compare that calculated middle-of-the-pay-pack remuneration to the CEO's remuneration. Supposedly, this intensive burden of accounting and regulatory filing is supposed to inform investors of something or other, of what I am not quite sure, with the result of investors then using this ostensibly crucial metric to then... I dunno, tell the Board that a CEO should be punished on the basis of this metric, absent any other considerations. You can bet your bottom dollar the drafters of this silly provision never considered that the "information" this ratio provides could be used to *reward* a CEO.

All this despite the fact that *investors* both individual and institutional have not asked for this particular ratio be calculated. Mainly because it means nothing – nothing real related to economic value, that is. For jealous whiners who specialize in telling *you* how to spend *"your"* money (the money they allow you to keep back from the paying-your-fair-share taxes, that is), it's apparently a powerful thing to screech about. It must be loud in the echo chamber these people share, because I can assure you that their screeches only reach rational people when translated into onerous laws and regulations which strangle the private sector and restrain growth.

This *one* ratio has been calculated to cost American business $1,300,000,000 per year to report. Yup, one billion dollars plus another 300 million dollars, *just to calculate and present a meaningless statistic.*

At an average wage in the US of $52,000, that means 25,000 jobs were *not* created, so that this politically driven, economically-value-destroying *line item in a regulatory filing* could be presented to complete yawns from investors. You want to know *how* you can know for sure that this is an insane waste of money? Michael Bloomberg is a billionaire because he created a more efficient way to collect and distribute financial markets data to professional investors, *who pay thousands of dollars per person per month* to receive. If there were real demand for this particular statistic, Mike's minions would long ago have calculated and sold it for a profit, without any prompting from the Jealousy Police.

Sarbanes-Oxley was already killing American stock markets

I highlight the silly CEO-to-median worker pay ratio to give you a deeper sense of just how badly "our" government treats us. The vast proliferation of millions of little rules here and there adds up to death by a thousand paper cuts. And yes, a rule that costs $1.3 billion per year *is* a "little rule" that the Administrative State has chosen to impose on us all.

Prior to Dodd-Frank, the Congress created a ridiculously stupid and damaging law called Sarbanes-Oxley, itself a nonsensical reaction to a "problem" that didn't exist in securities laws. Back in 2001, Houston-based energy trading company Enron collapsed in spectacular fashion.

Enron – the *only* private sector company that ever hired Paul Krugman for his esteemed advice – was so rife with fraudulent behavior that its financial filings were complete fabrications by the time of its collapse.

As you, dear reader, have better things to do with your life than dive into the intricacies of Enron's bad behavior, let me summarize:

1. Enron's CFO and other executives committed serious fraud.

2. The Justice Department correctly indicted Enron officers, notably the CEO and CFO under laws on the books at the time.

3. The government also indicted Price Waterhouse Coopers, the accounting firm, which effectively destroyed the firm.

4. Not to let a (manufactured) "crisis" go to waste, Congress created this stupid law, based on the fantasy that somehow *this* new law would have made them into honest people. The dumb idea at the core of Sarbanes-Oxley is this: Jeff Skilling and Andy Fastow after signing dozens of completely fraudulent documents could come to this brand new document defined by Sarbanes-Oxley which in effect says *"We, the CEO and CFO hereby certify that the reported financial accounts of the firm are accurate,"* and suddenly stop and say *"Wow! We've been creating false documents and fake cash flows all year long without losing any sleep, but now we have to sign one more piece of paper and we won't! We'll turn ourselves in to the authorities! Drat you, Sarbanes and Oxley!"*

5. In subsequent years, because all this pointless paperwork is just one more tax on a business in the form of cash it pays out with no chance of earning a return, many companies decided *not* to go public on American stock exchanges and many smaller companies decided to de-list, meaning any growth in profitability

of those now-private companies could no longer be enjoyed by the average retail American investor.

Congress creates nothing useful. It can either impose financially destructive rules or sets clear, reasonable limits against fraudulent behavior so free people can make free decisions about their economic lives. If Dodd-Frank and Sarbanes-Oxley have had *any* positive impact on the capital markets or the American economy more broadly, it happened by pure accident. If you identify such a regulatory unicorn, by all means keep it to yourself so they don't set about "fixing" the loophole.

Regulators should regulate the rules, not the outcomes

There are always "political entrepreneurs" who will try to alter the rules of the market, or to game those rules that are already in place.

There has been a lot of kabuki theatre on a range of topics in the financial markets in the recent years, as every cynical politician or grasping fool who is too incompetent to actually *earn* a living trots out another "class action" lawsuit alleging evil, fraud and just downright badness on behalf of Wall Street. My recent favorite – so hard to choose! – is regarding algorithmic trading firms. For those who are unfamiliar with how these stock-trading firms operate, instead of a row of people sitting on a trading desk telling their brokers to buy or sell given amounts of stock on a given day, there are rows of people programming computers to issue buy or sell orders for given amounts of stock on a given day. For some reason, this telling a computer how to place stock orders causes outrage (or the media pretends it causes outrage) in a country in which tens of millions of retail investors submit stock market orders through Ameritrade, Schwab, E*TRADE or other online brokers.

The "logic" behind this assault on these high-tech, "quantitative" firms is that it is somehow "unfair" to other market participants that with millions of dollars in technology expenditure and tens of millions in human capital that a firm could enter a stock order a wee bit faster than Joe Public hitting "buy" on his retail brokerage account. Of course, it helps the cause of politically-motivated lawyer-types that these trading strategies are "quantitative" which is a word guaranteed to scare all liberal arts majors, dredging up subconscious revulsion rooted in their night sweat fears of their C- performance on high school physics and calculus tests, and leading them therefore to instantly lash out at their mathematical demons.

But all Joe Public wants is deep, liquid markets[229] in which to buy or sell at a price he wants. Whether that liquidity comes from a market-making floor local on the New York Stock Exchange willing to stand behind a price one trade at a time or from millions of micro-

---

[229] For those unfamiliar with the terminology describing how markets work, "liquidity" means how easy it is to buy or sell something at the price you want. If you want to sell 10 shares of Apple stock "at the market price," you will sell it the millisecond after you place the order. If you want to sell your house, it can take days, weeks or months. Apple's stock is very liquid. Real estate is not.

second buy-sell orders emanating from computers *programmed by people* makes no difference to him. Or doesn't, until someone gets on MSNBC and intones with brows furrowed that there is something "unfair" about the particular *way* in which the market liquidity that is good for *everyone* is brought about.

This is nothing new. This mental illness and crazed obsession with "too much" trading in stocks goes back – as so many bad ideas do – to John Maynard Keynes. Keynes - himself a major punter on the stock exchange - keeps true to authoritarian character in deciding that what's fine for him ought to be restricted for others. No wonder Krugman and Stiglitz get all warm and fuzzy when they talk about being "Keynesian."

If you have paid *any* attention to the droolings and thunderings of our chattering classes over the last few years, you would doubtless have heard that while "investment" is a great and noble thing, one that ideally results in lots of jobs and then punitive taxes on "the rich" who made the investment, "speculation" by contrast is an evil thing, devoid of societal benefit and based solely in a nasty, shadowy intent to somehow defraud honest, hardworking Americans.

Never you mind that each activity requires putting down a dollar right now in anticipation of getting more dollars from that first dollar later. Please be sure to leave to one side the inconvenient fact *there is no empirical way* to say "that dollar put there into investment X is invested responsibly for the future growth of the economy versus that dollar put there into investment Y is an evil, parasitic attempt to earn free money for no societal benefit." Any statement of Obama, Pelosi or Krugman (who, let's not forget, advised Enron, the *only* time a private sector company requested his esteemed advice) to the contrary notwithstanding, *there is simply no difference between risking the dollar on investment X and investment Y.*

I raise this point because in Book IV, Section VI of Keynes's *General Theory of Employment, Interest, and Money,* he expressly lays out *his* distinction between the two.

> "If I may be allowed to appropriate the term *speculation* for the activity of forecasting the psychology of the market, and the term *enterprise* for the activity of forecasting the prospective yield of assets over their whole life, it is by no means the always the case that speculation predominates over enterprise. As the organisation of investment markets improves, the risk of the predominance of speculation does, however, increase."[230]

While his artificial distinction between *speculation* and *enterprise* (what we would now call *investment*) does not bear any real force of logic, it has become for many the ideological rule of the land when it comes to investment markets in the United States. If that were not terrifying enough, part of *why* his distinction is pure nonsense lies in how he defines investment. The idea that "forecasting the prospective yield of assets over their whole life" is *even remotely possible* in a deterministic, definitive way is complete insanity and Grade-A horse manure. *No one* can predict with any accuracy what will happen with a

---

[230] Keynes, John Maynard, General Theory of Employment, Interest, and Money, p.149

given investment in one year's time, five years' time and certainly not "their whole life," which in the case of an equity investment is quite literally impossibly to determine.

For a loan or a bond of a fixed term, say, 10 years, you can make *some* predictions about the range of likely outcomes, but for an equity investment in, say, the next Google or the next Enron, it is *impossible to predict* the financial outcome. That is why the first dollar invested in a new company is subject to the highest risk of loss - and therefore the highest chance of gain, while a dollar loaned for 30 days to General Electric faces a very low risk of loss and therefore a very low chance of gain.

So Keynes's conceit - for conceit it is, and nothing more - that he or anyone else can buy a share of stock based on "forecasting the prospective yield of assets over their whole life" is utter noise and nonsense and therefore in no way to be distinguished from buying a share of stock based on "forecasting the psychology of the market." For those of you playing the home game, that is otherwise known as the great evil, *speculation.* At the end of the day, no matter which approach the buyer of stock took in picking which share to buy, *the only price at which he can sell it in ten minutes, five days or twenty years* is the price at which someone else at that point in time is willing to buy it. Period. Plain and simple. All the fancy forecasting means *nothing* if the seller of the share and the buyer of the share cannot agree on a price at which to exchange dollars for stock.

Actually, it means nothing at all. The price in a free market is the price *at a given moment* that a willing buyer and willing seller agree freely to exchange. How each of them came to their conclusions about price is irrelevant to the transaction. That is the power and socially beneficial beauty of the free system we used to enjoy, before the politicians shoved their hands in for personal gain.

Which is why you, the American citizen, should be completely and utterly outraged at unelected bureaucrats like Steven Chu shoveling over $743,000,000 (including interest) of *your (borrowed) money* to Solyndra without any market determining whether that was a good idea.

As an important aside, I ask you to notice the creepy similarity of Keynes's definition of "speculation" to all the subsequent "thought police" ideologies which surround us in the age of "political correctness," "hate crimes" and other thought crimes, *the actions of which are utterly impossibly to distinguish* from the exact same actions taken with a possibly different set of intentions held in the mind. This pretension to mind-reading is *not* an accidental coincidence. Its pervasive destructiveness lies at the heart of almost every single bad idea emanating from the halls of government.

Back to Keynes. Let's go to the source, now that we have a clearer picture of what he means by speculation:

> This is only another way of saying that, when he purchases an investment, the American is attaching his hopes, not so much to its prospective yield, as to a favourable change in the conventional basis of valuation, *i.e.* that he is, in the above sense, a speculator. Speculators may do no harm as bubbles on a steady stream of enterprise. But the position is serious when enterprise becomes the bubble on a whirlpool of speculation. When the capital development of a country becomes a by-product of the activities of a casino, the job is likely to be ill-done. The measure of success attained by Wall Street, regarded as an institution of which the proper social purpose is to direct new investment into the most profitable channels in

terms of future yield, cannot be claimed as one of the outstanding triumphs of *laissez-faire* capitalism - which is not surprising, if I am right in thinking that the best brains of Wall Street have been in fact directed towards a different object.

These tendencies are a scarcely avoidable outcome of our having successfully organised "liquid" investment markets. It is usually agreed that casinos should, in the public interest, be inaccessible and expensive. And perhaps the same is true of Stock Exchanges. That the sins of the London Stock Exchange are less than those of Wall Street may be due, not so much to differences in national character, as to the fact that to the average Englishman Throgmorton Street is, compared with Wall Street to the average American, inaccessible and very expensive. The jobber's "turn", the high brokerage charges and the heavy transfer tax payable to the Exchequer, which attend dealings on the London Stock Exchange, sufficiently diminish the liquidity of the market (although the practice of fortnightly accounts operates the other way) to rule out a large proportion of the transactions characteristic of Wall Street. The introduction of a substantial Government transfer tax on all the transactions might prove the most serviceable reform available, with a view to mitigating the predominance of speculation over enterprise in the United States.

Well, that's a mouthful. There's a whole lot of opining going on there, with a marked absence of what I would call robust critical analysis. Not surprising, if you've ever had the fun of being in a university debate society, which is the kind of environment Keynes was most at home in.

What I hope is refreshing and fun for the reader is to realize that there is nothing new in the pronouncements of Barney Frank, Chris Dodd, Paul Krugman, Barry Hussein Soetoro Obama, Liz Warren, Bernie Sanders, Joe Biden, Joseph Stiglitz and the rest of this army of People Who Know So Much Better Than Everyone Else What *Should* Be Done By Private Individuals In Ostensibly Private Sector Markets. All they've ever done is parrot the drunken British dilettante whose ideas sucked so badly that even the New Deal Socialist-in-a-Wheelchair thought he was a flake the one and only time he met him.

Of course, to a certain type of hanger-on, the fact that Keynes was a *homosexual* with a pukka British accent just adds a certain *frisson* of thrill to his worship.

How often have you heard this "casino" analogy made about the stock market? It's one of those little phrases that liberal arts majors like to say smugly to one another at cocktail parties, surrounded by like-minded spirits. It's also utter nonsense. When you buy a share of stock, you own something. Its value may change, upwards or downwards, but buying a share of stock and holding it for 20 years or 5 minutes before selling it, has nothing to do with putting a dollar down to bet black on roulette and finding out in a minute or two whether you get your dollar back plus some of the house's dollars, or just lose your dollar.

Ironically, there *is* a sense in which gambling is a positive part of investing risk capital in markets. It is ironic, because in very fundamental and interesting ways, the human urge to put money down against a future event lies behind both investing in financial markets and betting in games of chance. Moreover, the mathematics which describe the odds of a distributed range of outcomes are *also* very similar. In some instances, the mathematics that describes probability was developed for one activity and transported successfully to the other.

Don't get me wrong. I am a big fan of the rule of law and correctly structured markets. Plenty of the abuses and outright fraud that prevailed in the securities markets in the late 19th and early 20th century served *no social purpose* as a place for the formation of capital investment, precisely because those practices were not *clearly* presented as having the characteristics of a rigged game of chance. But as of Keynes's writing, all those abuses had been outlawed. He characterized liquidity itself as some kind of *a priori* social evil.

In the fine tradition of Progressive Authoritarians everywhere, he knows better than dozens, hundreds and thousands of "best brains" actually putting their capital at risk. I repeat here, over the protests of my editor who loves trees overmuch and moreover believes you, dear reader, can flip back a page, the words of Keynes:

> The measure of success attained by Wall Street, regarded as an institution of which the proper social purpose is to direct new investment into the most profitable channels in terms of future yield, cannot be claimed as one of the outstanding triumphs of *laissez-faire* capitalism - which is not surprising, if I am right in thinking that the best brains of Wall Street have been in fact directed towards a different object.

Left out of this massive conceit, of course, is the fact the Keynes himself was a stock market punter – who eventually lost. Imagine how different his comments on Wall Street may have been had he been lolling in hot tubs guzzling Champagne amidst fields of high cotton on the vast estates his profitable speculations would have earned him. Or ponder if you will the considerable likelihood that he would never have bothered to spend time penning such a ponderous work of fiction at all, had he not been animated by the kind of sordid pecuniary motivations which afflict those who have lost their little all on the exchange.

No politician ever went bust beating up on Wall Street. Bill Clinton thundered during his campaign about the supposed "evils" of "excessive" executive compensation.

You'll note Bill and Hillary have themselves never met a speaking fee they declined or asked to have reduced because it was "excessive." Hillary Clinton during her campaign for President hammered on the "unfairness" of executive pay. And yet – she gladly took $600,000 in speaking fees *from the shareholders of Goldman Sachs.* As she spoke for a total of 2 hours, if you turned that hourly rate into a yearly pay package – as if she were a Goldman Sachs executive who average 60-hour work weeks (on the low side) – that would mean she got paid $936,000,000 per annum for her work there. As the CEO Lloyd Blankfein only made $41,000,000 in 2015, that would make her the highest paid Goldman Sachs employee ever. If Candidate Hillary believes that CEO pay is "excessive" and ripping off shareholders, I am curious to understand why she believes she is of such insane value to shareholders to warrant that executive compensation.

If Goldman Sachs executive management valued her at 22.8x their own CEO, one has to wonder what exactly Goldman thought they were buying for that outrageous sum?

All that fun still to come in the future, back in 1993, Bill Clinton forced through a bunch of tax-related laws that made it effectively "illegal" for a company to pay an executive more than $1,000,000 per year. Never mind if that particular executive happened to do a massively great job, generating perhaps billions of dollars in shareholder value. Nope – while not actually making it illegal for a company to strike of its own free will a deal with an executive, what Clinton had Congress and the Internal Revenue Service do was to make any cash payments above $1 million *not deductible* as an expense when computing corporate income taxes to be paid.

Since the value of effective senior management did not magically by Progressive Legal Stick suddenly plummet, the result was that companies started to make up what they *would* have paid in cash to the executive by much-increased grants of equity – stocks, options, warrants. As the stock markets then for a range of reasons went on a huge tear, what ended up happening was the Left's detested – and *meaningless* from an economic standpoint – ratio of CEO pay to median worker pay went in 1995 from being 122.6 times what their average worker made to 231 times in 2011. There are lots of reasons for this, but even the SEC Commissioner Christopher Cox who oversaw this at the time lays the blame for this increased "unfairness" at the feet of Clinton as social justice warrior meddling with the tax code and therefore the incentives for companies to attract talent via greater equity components to pay packages.

You're once more sitting there, thinking that I must be making this up, that this kind of chicanery *can't* go on in our fine nation. I am sorry that you bought the lies your grammar school teacher told you about this being a "free" country. *Surely,* you say, *you can't be telling me that under a Constitution which specifically prohibits bills of attainder to avoid the law being used to revenge petty jealousies, "our" government didn't actually pass a law saying that!*

Oh, yes, yes it did. And as with almost every – if not every – attempt of the champions of the Politics of Jealousy to try to change *outcomes* they don't like, it not only created market distortions but ended up *increasing* the very symptom they hate. Alternative Minimum Tax, anyone?

> One of the most significant reasons that non-salary forms of compensation have ballooned since the early 1990s is the $1 million legislative cap on salaries for certain top public company executives that was added to the Internal Revenue Code in 1993. As a member of Congress at the time, I will remember that the stated purpose was to control the rate of growth in CEO pay.[231] With complete hindsight, we now all agree that this purpose was not achieved. Indeed, this tax law change deserves pride of place in the Museum of Unintended Consequences.
> -Testimony of Former SEC Chairman Christopher Cox

I happened to be writing this particular section on the first Sunday of the 2016 Rio de Janeiro Summer Olympics. One of the ads I couldn't avoid because the remote was too far away to bother reaching for was an ad by Presidential Candidate *Hillary* Clinton featuring her doing a voiceover while the camera shows a picture of Lower Manhattan (Wall Street,

---

[231] Ponder, my fellow citizen, how on earth it could possibly be in the US public's interest to have Congress *legislate* how much a private company can pay its own employees. Never mind where one would find In the Constitution the "right" for Congress to so meddle in *what once were and should be again* private affairs.

get it?), with graphic overlays saying how she's going to pay for *her* Class Warrior Jealousy Taxes by making "the rich" and "corporations" pay their "fair share."

History not only repeats itself. It rhymes.

Chapter 27: NASA

Founded	July 29, 1958
Founded under President	Dwight D. Eisenhower
Funding Budget 2024	$27,400,000,000
Messina's 2024 Budget Proposal	$27,400,000,000*
Messina's 20225 Budget Proposal	$35,000,000,000*
Degree to which Messina's Plan is Better	Debatable; this is a team effort
Should NASA exist?	Absolutely; I need an escape plan.

* A severe reorganization needs to be done, eliminating any non-spaceport or fundamental research functions.

Is this a standalone proper use of the taxpayers' limited resources?	Yes
Does this expenditure *unfairly* benefit one American over another one?	Yes
Does the expenditure meet the "Is this logical?" standard of fiduciary responsibility?	Yes
Can the goals be achieved by *not* spending the dollar more effectively than by spending it?	Maybe

Here is something that we must fund to the hilt, *but* that hilt must be far more carefully defined *by the services demanded of NASA by the private sector.* I live on the Space Coast in Florida and as with anything, familiarity can breed contempt. For example, as SpaceX and other private companies are dominating all launches, the revenues paid to Cape Canaveral for operating a spaceport are analogous to paying the FAA and local airports for safe air travel.

So having NASA operate some spaceports and perhaps doing some R&D is a great idea. But right here on the Space Coast, there is a "business development office" at NASA which is supposed to, er, develop private business. Sounds good, but it has long outstripped its original purpose; effective managers close operational groups that are no longer needed. Elon Musk at SpaceX and Jeff Bezos at Blue Origin are not listening to NASA's business development office, nor is anyone else in the private sector. The group used to be a couple of people who could pretend to have once touched the private sector. Last I checked there are more than 30 people drawing government salaries, none of whom have done or will do one thing to change how many rockets get launched or how many private satellite companies pay for launch services.

There is *plenty* of fat to be cut from the NASA budget that the taxpayer covers. Frankly, much like Amtrak, if NASA is not running at a profit every year, with the exception of *some* R&D, the solution is to examine it like the private sector. Maybe running at a loss for a few years is OK if by doing so we are building capacity for more spaceports and increased commercial activity which will within a few years turn it profitable. Or maybe it's time to start slashing staff until commercial revenues rise.

Go check out www.nasa.gov for the cool range of things NASA scientists and engineers do. Lots to learn and massive fun for kids of all ages. *This* is money well spent.

NASA brings together brilliant, hardworking minds from both the public and private sectors to work on some of the most complicated problems in engineering, physics and math. The work done at NASA provides hugely important advances in science and engineering, technological development and social evolution. As we spread out from this planet, humanity will look back and praise the massive national – and now international – work that was supported by taxpayers of all walks of life, whose pooled capital did so much to discover and invent so many brilliant things to benefit our future and the here and now.

Humanity will become for better or worse a spacefaring species. Americans should lead the way in that endeavor, so that we may plant our culture on the planets we colonize. The Universe will become a better place if its original citizens arrive full of the ideals of a nation conceived as a project of independence, which nation has done its best to overcome the vagaries of human nature to more consistently strive for a perfected vision of self-governance. Anything can happen, but I'd like to think that off-world colonies composed of free people who've volunteered to contribute their skills to building brave new worlds will be superior and more satisfying places to live down the generations than colonies founded by repressive totalitarian regimes.

Or maybe it won't matter. Perhaps cosmic geography will prove to be destiny. Perhaps modern Australians would be the exact same people if their ancestors hadn't been chucked out of England for failing to get away with stealing a loaf of bread or a pair of shoes, but had been free Poles fleeing the Hapsburgs. The Kiwis are convinced of their superiority because of their (supposed) lack of convict ancestry, but I'm not sure it's not all down to the geographical differences between New Zealand and Australia *and* the relative ease with which Aboriginals were pushed around versus the marked lack of ease one experiences in trying to force the Maori to do things they're uninterested in doing.

Kurt Vonnegut said in *The Sirens of Titan* "The idea that humans should inhabit every planet in the universe is akin to saying everyone should have athlete's foot." Kurt lived through the firebombing of Dresden. As eyewitness to some of the worst the human species has ever behaved, he took a dim view of human nature. A more optimistic man who embraced the limitless promise of science and human creativity, Isaac Asimov, drew sweeping pictures for us of humanity's future as a Universal species, so far removed from our home planet that Earth itself is viewed as a mythical place, a bizarre idea of a single planet Eden whence human life spread.

In the here and now, the various facilities around the country that NASA operates are crucial scientific research, development and testing facilities for aerospace applications both publicly and privately funded. This kind of demand-driven public funding is a great use of taxpayer dollars; when private aerospace companies want to test how their people movers and other equipment operate in the vacuum of space, they pay good money to rent NASA facilities for those tests. Everyone wins.

The next order of business is to convene a sort of Private Sector Grand Jury to examine every role and job at NASA. Many of the paper pushing bureaucrats on fat salaries who add nothing to the productivity or safety of the space industry need to find something else to do. My budgetary slash is designed to create the framework to make that judgement process both easier and urgent.

Figure 32: Proposed Sculpture for NASA Headquarters Courtyard

Chapter 28: Money in Politics

Surely, you're thinking, the preceding 27 chapters were about money in politics. Are you losing your touch, Mr. Messina? Perhaps you should have taken the advice of friends and family and gotten a more detail-oriented editor to help you out on this project.

You, dear, patient reader, would be right in wondering what this exciting new chapter could be about. Bear with me, because while the entirety of how the petty despots who've seized control of our wallets and nation are in a large sense about money in politics, the topic has a particular meaning which is worth focusing on.

For years, both sides of the aisle – depending largely on who is out of power at the moment – have been yammering on about "campaign finance reform." Much like the War on Drugs, it is pointless and impossible to enforce limits on speech in relation to elections without significant collateral damage to both society and individuals caught up in crazy laws gone wild. Moreover, *unlike* the War on Drugs *there is no public interest whatsoever* in restricting political speech. Quite the contrary; it is usually politicians who want to tell the electorate to shut up about what a lousy job they're doing.

The best analogy to understand *why* government should have *no* ability to tell anyone how to or if they can spend money on telling other Americans about their political views is to look at politics like business. Politicians – believe you me – are well aware they are onto a sweet train of never-ending gravy and have *no* desire to be ejected from that awesome train ride. Imagine if there were only two tech companies, Apple and Microsoft. Then imagine that Apple and Microsoft *together, mind you, in bipartisan fashion* made it illegal for any tech startup to receive more than $1,000 in venture capital funding to create tech products that offer better value to consumers.

Such a law – let's call it "McApple-Feinsoft" after the real-world collusion of John McCain and Russ Feingold, two Senators who wanted the government to be able to *put you in jail* for expressing political views they may not like – would have prevented Google or Facebook from being created, or thousands of tech startups including video game producers, all because McApple Feinsoft was "protecting" you, the American consumer, from content that might distort your appreciation of the wonders of either Apple or Microsoft. Google would have been prohibited from creating a third party operating system called Android, because the wonderful "innovation finance reform" McApple-Feinsoft Law would have prohibited free people in a free country from investing in a company which created a third option for an operating system.

The idea that government officials should be able to tell an American citizen what he or she cannot say is *precisely* the way Hugo Chavez, Vladimir Putin, Barack Obama, the Chinese Communist Party, the US Democrats 2020-24 version and the entire howling horde of "woke social justice warriors" operate. (I put that phrase in quotes, because I hope subsequent generations reading the 33rd annotated version of this book will need to research that phrase to discover the terrifying mob-driven insanity behind such an apparently benign string of four words.) The whole point of freedom of the press and freedom of speech is that *the people* in the USA are the foundation and source of governmental authority, not the other way around. For me, barring some loony crackpots, I want to listen *more closely* to the speech of people the government doesn't like.

I take that back. I am always happy to get a fine, fresh helping of loony crackpot, so they should be free to blather away like everyone else. And not only because if someone somewhere is given the right to define "loony crackpot" and therefore silence that voice, that there is a large chance yours truly would find himself so labeled.

This is not an angels-on-pinheads theoretical issue. In August 2020, Florida's 11th Congressional District Primary was won by Laura Loomer, a fascinating and provocative investigative journalist who with true bravery uncovered some appalling abuses of power. Because the Left-leaning Big Tech companies and media chattering classes *did not like* what she was uncovering, they did something to her called "de-platforming." A woman who had millions of followers on her Twitter, Instagram, YouTube and Facebook accounts was suddenly and effectively silenced.

What I find absolutely fascinating is the extent to which politicians of all stripes but most especially in recent history those who self-identify as being on the Left will go to quash free speech. Despite my usual policy of restricting my mental intake of goofiness, I was drawn to watching a talk show by Bill Maher on HBO on 24 May 2012. I stopped channel surfing when I saw he was "interviewing" — more like giving an on-air verbal, ahem, "massage" to — Dan Rather, a retired Angry Lefty "journalist" who'd spent his career spewing lies on air about Republicans, liberty and anything Karl Marx would have taken issue with. After the plethora of gratuitous, groveling praise, Bill abandoned Dan to take his seat at the head of the panel of "experts", including a former basketball player turned Senator turned.... dunno what to call him, Lefty Shill?, and two other people.

During the segment, Maher started out by naming billionaires who were supposedly "distorting the national conversation" on politics by daring to spend money telling Americans why Barack Obama is such a horrible President. Maher hammered on and on about this, claiming that *Citizens United* is a stake in the heart of democracy.[232]

He neglected to say that *other* billionaires, like Steve Schwartzman of Blackstone, George Soros, or Haim Saban were "distorting" democracy by spending money to *support* Obama. Never mind the over-the-top meta-hilarity of a mere multimillionaire spending an *entire TV show* discussing political topics, cheering for one candidate over another. Apparently, Bill Maher's hour-long hammering on about how great is The One[233] and how sordid and petty is the Private Equity Mormon With The Magic Underwear[234] is perfectly OK, and in no way a "distortion" of "the national conversation" about our elected officials.

Why is Bill Maher's blatantly political speech not subject to the Federal Electoral Commission rules? I don't think there should be any restraint on "political speech," but he clearly does, so it seems fair to ask why he's exempt. Guys like this seem utterly terrified that anyone should have an opinion other than theirs — the absolute definition of the totalitarian mindset described so beautifully by Hayek and put into action so brutally in North Korea, China, Cuba, Venezuela, Russia, New York City and every university in the United States that gets a single dollar from the Federal Government.

I've got a good heads up tip for anyone listening to a politician talk about the "secret" elements and "dark money" undermining their elections. Watch events in China, Russia, Syria, Iran, Venezuela or Argentina — places where dictators have a firm grasp on the levers of power and feel free to imprison, beat, gas and otherwise torment their populations. When confronted by public demonstrations of people who have taken so much abuse they are willing to risk death to get freedom, the *first* thing any one of these thugs will say when the people hit the streets in protest is *not* "well, apparently, my decades of brutal

---

[232] The Supreme Court ruled in 2010 in *Citizens United v. Federal Election Commission 558 US 310* that the Federal Government cannot restrict Americans' First Amendment rights, including those exercised by voluntary organizations like corporations or unions.

[233] Barry Hussein Soetoro Obama

[234] Mitt Romney

repression have finally pushed my people to the breaking point." Quite the contrary. They *always claim* that these protests are not homegrown at all – *why no, the people here are very happy laboring under my jackboot. No, no – these "protestors" in the streets are the result of foreign, secret providers of funds, here for their own shadowy agendas, stirring up trouble amongst an otherwise happy populace.*

Now do an Internet search for any of the press statements by Nancy Pelosi, Barack Obama, Joe Biden or Chuck Schumer or *the entire Democratic Party during the Mueller Investigations.*[235] Time after time, they make *explicit* statements about this supposed wall of "secret money" which is hell-bent on lying to otherwise happy Americans. Americans under Obama who were living through 20% unemployment while being told that it's actually 7.5% because the other 12.5% have "stopped looking for work," watching government employees live large on the backs of taxpayers were *not upset* about the myriad failures and corruption and government. Oh no, they were totally content with everything until those suspicious "outside dollars" paid for ads and articles to tell them "lies" about how high national debt, high gas prices and high unemployment are *not* actually the great gifts from Washington, but are in fact somehow bad things that politicians should be fired for providing.

For a refresher on those insane parade of Obama Administration lies, you need look no further than Obama 2.0 as Biden's Administration spews the same ridiculous lies in even *worse* social and economic conditions.

If it were not so terrifying, it would be funny.

I had an absolutely fascinating conversation with a professional colleague on this topic. He seemed adamantly convinced that somehow "money in politics" is "destructive of democracy." His argument boiled down to "but if someone spends more money on advertising than their opponent, that additional airtime will correlate exactly with the greater airtime winning any argument."

To his credit, he seemed genuinely astonished by my counterargument that – even if I were to agree with his equation of more minutes heard translating directly into winning elections – the problem is that *currently elected politicians* are exempted from being considered when they are speaking to the public. So an incumbent can suck up all the airtime she likes, without penalty, but if someone who wants to *change* the current government wants to broadcast her message, that contender for office is suddenly under the thumb of dozens of laws restricting her ability to let you know just how awful a job the current officeholder is doing.

One of our nation's finest politicians was Matthew Lyon (July 14, 1749 – August 1, 1822), who among other things, holds the distinction of being the only person ever elected

---

[235] An appalling waste of at least $30 million, all based on a ridiculous throwaway comment made on Election Night by John Podesta, the Chairman of Hillary Clinton's failed Presidential bid, that "the Russians" "colluded" with the Trump 2016 Campaign. It was all nonsense and the final Report found zero evidence of any such collusion, but it remained (as of April 2024) an Article of Core Faith among some Democrats that the wily Vladimir Putin who as recently as 2015 hosted Americans from the Obama Administration had turned suddenly into the Puppet Master of American Elections via 56 well timed Tweets.

to Congress while incarcerated – thereby bringing a refreshing truth to politics which has been lacking ever since. The *reason* he was in jail is illuminating.

He was convicted on 10 October 1789 under the Alien and Sedition Acts which made it illegal to criticize the government or any official thereof. Being a printer, Lyon founded and published his own newspaper, one not only replete with excellent content but one with the best title for a periodical this nation has ever enjoyed, *The Scourge Of Aristocracy and Repository of Important Political Truth.* During the Quasi War with France, on October 1st Lyon printed an editorial which stated among other things that President John Adams had an "unbounded thirst for ridiculous pomp, foolish adulation, and selfish avarice."

For printing what even from a distance sounds like a fair assessment of any sitting American President, Lyon got four months in prison in a tiny cell and was fined $1,000, which took his descendants until 1840 to get refunded with interest from Congress. Lyon's argument which many at the time disagreed with was that he was free under the First Amendment to say whatever he damned well chose to say about anything he damned well wanted to opine on, especially when it came to something as important as the people who are controlling the purse strings and – in time of war – the very blood in our soldiers' veins.

To this day, every politician in power desperately conflates *his or her* own position in office with the far vaguer "respect" for the government and law overall. Nothing could be sillier – many Americans revere the office of the President while simultaneously wander the streets of DC wearing goofy pink hats symbolizing something or other relating to President Trump's alleged offenses against women or while snorting into their cocktails whenever Barry Hussein Soetoro Obama's name(s) come(s) up.

I was very hopeful that the complete failure in 2019-2020 of billionaires Tom Steyer (a hedge fund manager who made his money investing in oil and gas companies before turning into a deacon of the Climate Hysteria Apocalypse Alarmist Church) and Mike Bloomberg (a Wall Street entrepreneur who made a fortune off of collecting, packaging and disseminating price information on bonds and related financial instruments) to get *a single vote* as they ran for President in the Democrat primary would put the final nail in the coffin of this unconstitutional desire to restrict speech. But of course it has done no such thing. "Campaign finance reform" was never about logically leveling a playing field of voices. It was always about thought control and using the mailed fist of the State to squelch free speech.

Those are just some of the philosophical reasons why any restriction on political speech is a violation of the First Amendment. The *practical* reasons include the fact that when the stakes are high, people will game any set of rules provided to them.

In the Obama 2012 campaign, an army of tech talent including billionaires and mere millionaires from Google set up a technical infrastructure that managed to eke out every vote possible, wherever it may have lurked. In the Clinton 2016 campaign, a for-profit company The Groundwork did a huge amount of big data and communications effectiveness testing, email outreach and so on. This is all fine, and the FEC rules say that campaigns must pay "market rates" for these services. So far, so good.

But with politically motivated billionaire investors, that does *not* mean that the amount the campaign spends relates to what the campaign *gets*. "Campaign finance reform" always focuses on the amount of cash that can be donated to a certain political candidate, with different amounts defined for giving to things like "political action committees," all of which comes with an insane bureaucracy to prevent "coordination" or direct advocacy of a given candidate, which can be – and has, just ask Wisconsin residents – abused mightily for political purposes. But there is *nothing* – and rightly so – to prevent an individual or company from investing capital in a for-profit business, one possible customer of which could be political campaigns.

All tech startups require equity investment and usually operate at a loss until they gain market traction. In practical terms, that means that Eric Schmidt of Alphabet/Google and his pals could invest $100 million into a great new *for-profit* data analytics company, build $90 million worth of cutting-edge technology with applications helpful to a political campaign and offer those services for $500,000 to each customer, in this case, the Clinton Campaign.

There is nothing illegal about this. Companies can price their services however they like. Microsoft offers you an annual subscription to Office for $99 to cover five machines. Microsoft has spent billions on developing Office – no one ever said each customer must pay to cover the overall product development costs.

So in this case, a not-so-hypothetical company called, say, The Groundwork, could raise unlimited money to build a huge technical infrastructure, and then sell their services to a politician's campaign for 0.05% of what the equity capital paid to build. After the election is over, they could get other customers or possibly go out of business, because unfortunately, after Clinton won or lost, it turns out that they failed to get any other customers. Most tech startups fail, so whatever the investors' intentions were, they'll even have empirical evidence on their side to defend themselves against someone claiming the whole thing was designed to get around campaign finance laws.

The point is that much like a good first grade teacher knows to never issue a rule you can't enforce, all the laws created to hold back free speech certainly do personal damage to the individuals ensnared in the unconstitutional assault on the First Amendment, but the greater damage done to the society overall is chilling. Not only should the American people reject any attempt to control "political speech," but as history shows us time and again, it can't be done.

Federal Election Commission

Founded	April 1975
Founded under President	Gerald Ford
Funding Budget 2023	$81,700,000
Messina's 2024 Budget Proposal	ZERO
Messina's 2025 Budget Proposal	ZERO
Degree to which Messina's Plan is Better	Completely
Should a Federal Election Commission exist?	No

We elected Presidents, Senators and Congressional Representatives *before* 1975, so clearly this bureaucratic beast is not required for politicians to be elected to positions in our federal government. Most of the departments my budget eliminates have *some* money allocated to its final year to wind it down. In this case, zero – just flat out zero. Can it. Turn off the computers and power and tell everyone they're out of a job the Constitution says they should never have had in the first place. The world is full of businesses who do wind down fire sales and the like.

This appalling abuse of freedom and Americans' rights to free speech must be abolished immediately. Elections to political office are affairs of individual States. Not only is there no compelling interest for Federal intervention in elections, quite the contrary. We the people have a strong, compelling interest in ensuring that Federal politicians and bureaucrats are *banned* from affecting anything to do with the electoral process.

The www.fec.gov website is a clearinghouse of information, of a sort, but there is no particular reason that a federally funded entity must exist to collect and display it. Arguably, once Americans have shaken off the sloppy thinking and bad ideas which led to its creation, and therefore have destroyed all the insanely unconstitutional violations of free speech and privacy which is all the FEC *does*, then there will be far less data to collect in the first place.

If there was not already no logical connection between "dollars spent" and "elections won" or "bought" as the screeching chattering classes like to say, then the tumbling, *expensive* demise of Mike Bloomberg's $1,000,000,000 bid for the Democrat Party nomination in 2019-20 should be it. Mike spent all that cash – and did not get a single electoral vote for his efforts.

There is *no* valid reason to restrict political speech in this country. None. Zero. Zip. Nada. Let hundreds of millions of voices ring out. Ignore some, like some, argue with some, whatever you do don't let the government tell you that the government is here to "protect" you against "misinformation" or whatever their latest term is for "truths about politicians they don't want you to hear."

Citizens United and the Desperate Lies of the Political Class

It is worth reiterating this book's central idea: Since market forces will *always* make people crave money and power, no matter the obstacles and laws placed in the way of getting those heady rushes of adrenaline, the *only* real solution that will make people stop fighting to attain political power in the United States is to take away all the money and power that one gets by joining government. No one competes if there is no prize at the end of the contest.

The fight over a *movie* made it all the way to the Supreme Court. Most Americans who have even heard of "Citizens United" can't tell you what the movie was about. In the Democrats' fevered imaginations – expressed daily on all media whenever the phrase "Citizens United" appears – the Supreme Court made a *horrible* decision to permit corporations to buy elections.

Here I am, in the odd position of praising the Court. In *Citizens United v. Federal Election Commission,* what the Court was *actually* ruling on was the Federal Election Commission suppressing *any* American's First Amendment free speech rights, particularly when those rights matter most, within 30 – 60 days of an election. A non-profit group called Citizens United made a movie in 2008 called, simply enough, *Hillary: The Movie.*

Citizens United wanted to release the movie 30 days before the Democrat Party primary. It was – rightly – concerned that *federal election laws made it a felony crime for them to do so.* You read that correctly. Congress drafted and passed a law and a numbskull President Nixon signed it (on 7 February 1972) that *prohibits the release of any material endorsing or criticizing* a candidate for public office leading up to that election. How on earth any *one* of the cotton-wool-between-their-ears idiots in *either* chamber of Congress thought restriction of First Amendment political speech was fine, when any 7th grader would realize such prohibition of speech is in violation of the Constitution is also why I took the time to write this book.

Really. How did *any* of the fools who voted for this stupid law think it was OK in any way, shape or form? Back to the Supremes who saw through this illegal, unconstitutional and downright nasty attempt to control Americans by *throwing anyone in jail who dares criticize a politician running for office:*

> The law before us is an outright ban, backed by criminal sanctions. Section 441b makes it a felony for all corporations—including nonprofit advocacy corporations—either to expressly advocate the election or defeat of candidates or to broadcast electioneering communications within 30 days of a primary election and 60 days of a general election. Thus, the following acts would all be felonies under §441b: The Sierra Club runs an ad, within the crucial phase of 60 days before the general election, that exhorts the public to disapprove of a Congressman who favors logging in national forests; the National Rifle Association publishes a book urging the public to vote for the challenger because the incumbent U. S. Senator supports a handgun ban; and the American Civil Liberties Union creates a Web site telling the public to vote for a Presidential candidate in light of that candidate's defense of free speech. These prohibitions are classic examples of censorship.
>
> Modern day movies, television comedies, or skits on Youtube.com might portray public officials or public policies in unflattering ways. Yet if a covered transmission during the blackout period creates the background for candidate

endorsement or opposition, a felony occurs solely because a corporation, other than an exempt media corporation, has made the "purchase, payment, distribution, loan, advance, deposit, or gift of money or anything of value" in order to engage in political speech. 2 U. S. C. §431(9)(A)(i). Speech would be suppressed in the realm where its necessity is most evident: in the public dialogue preceding a real election. Governments are often hostile to speech, but under our law and our tradition it seems stranger than fiction for our Government to make this political speech a crime. Yet this is the statute's purpose and design.[236]

Get it clear, kids, whether you're a Republican, Democrat or neither. The federal government created a law that enables the Federal Election Commission to put you in federal prison for a felony, that "felony" consisting of your exercising your First Amendment rights by, say, making a video or a podcast expressing to your fellow Americans why you think your choice of candidate is awesome and why the other candidate is a stinking, lying thief.

That is what the Supreme Court had to step in to correct. No noise about "corporations buying elections," but the rights of every single American to express his or her opinion, including silly opinions about whether "his and her" don't adequately convey a person's options for gender identity.

It's just plain exhausting trying to keep up with these lying, evil clowns who spend every waking moment trying to take away our personal freedom.

Similar "logic" was put on ugly display in Wisconsin in 2014, when *a heavily armed SWAT team at 5am broke down the door* of a woman[237] who was employed as an executive assistant in the Governor's office. What horrendous crime was she reasonably suspected of committing that justified such a psychotically heavy-handed show of armed force via a no-knock warrant? Cocaine smuggling? Running a child sex trafficking ring, perhaps? Serial murders spanning a decade and seven states of which she'd finally been identified as the perpetrator?

Nope. She might have sent some emails from her office computer, rather than a home computer, in contravention of *Federal Election Commission rules* regarding the use of public sector offices or office equipment for conducting political campaigns.

Under a ridiculous, totalitarian theory called "coordination," government prosecutors claim to be able to discern when separate groups acting on their own are "*actually*" secretly coordinating. What, one might ask, are they coordinating about and what makes this coordination worthy of heavily armed men breaking down the doors of middle-aged female office workers and their families? Those diabolic destroyers of democracy are – gasp! – *coordinating* the messages being delivered to the public about their clearly stated political views! Of all the dastardly distortions of the public square!

---

[236] Citizens United v. Federal Election Commission
[237] The interested reader can find out her name easily enough without my causing her a flurry of unwanted attention. Her identity is unimportant beyond being an American citizen whose rights were trampled unjustly.

For a clear analogue of this insanity, let's put it this way. The Roman Catholic Church, the Greek Orthodox Church, the Church of England, Presbyterians, Episcopalians, Pentecostals and Baptists are not formally grouped into one, formal organization. They don't even have – in most cases post the Great Schism of 1054 and then Martin Luther's 95 Theses nailed to the church door in Wittenberg on All Hallow's Eve 1517 – written agreements between them. But all these supposedly "independent groups" are *coordinating* – those clever hierophantic ducks! – their message to the world that Jesus Christ is the only begotten Son of Almighty God and is commensal in authority with Him and the Sacred Ghost, whose name later got watered down to Holy Spirit so as not to scare sensitive American children post Vatican Council II, silly hippies. They are *illegally coordinating* the message of Christianity, you see!

A reasonable person reading that hogwash would respond, *Well, did it ever occur to you that all these organizations are saying pretty much the same thing because, well, they all believe the same thing, i.e. Christianity?*

It truly is a case of prosecutors "reading between the lines" to determine that two or more separate people or organizations "really" have a secret club, a cabal, if you will, complete with a hidden, mood-lit underground lair in which they meet to plot their nefarious schemes on red leather banquettes, cocooned in cigar smoke. *Bwahahahah!*

Remember that the *very same people* who claim to be able to read minds and determine which crime is a "hate crime" versus, I don't know, a "poorly expressed affection crime," also can read minds to determine when a few very clever people are hiding their "coordination" from the rest of the world, versus political allies whom one would logically *expect* to express the same kind of political views and policy preferences. These powerful mind readers ruling over us are *also* the people who want to strip the requirement of *mens rea* from prosecuting normal citizens who are likely completely unaware which of the 80,000+ laws they may have broken, 78,000+ or so of which have been created out of thin air by regulatory fiat in the last forty years.

Are you sensing a pattern here? Hint: Start with the result of complete totalitarian control over every aspect of your life and then work backwards to create a chain of "logic" – no matter how torturous or implausible – until you can fit the facts to the theory that gets *you,* the supposedly free American citizen, stripped of all your rights, subject to an Almighty Federal Government that tells you what kinds of car you're allowed to drive, what kinds of *laundry machine* or *light bulb* you're allowed to buy and when you can show up for jail, thank you very much, for daring to express an opinion during an election season that the Government didn't allow you to express.

Back to Wisconsin. Not only were armed governmental stooges terrorizing people in their homes *for political speech* the government didn't like. Under a law so insanely unconstitutional it's amazing it even needs to be said, **they were banned from speaking to anyone about their ordeal** *under the "John Doe" provisions of the appalling, unjust laws they were being abused by.*

You read that right. In the United States, where children are – or were – taught in grammar school that the Constitution gives you the right to a fair trial and to face your accuser, apparently in Wisconsin when you say things the government doesn't like, all your "rights" are optional. The mailed fist of the Wisconsin State threatened these people with jail time and insane, bankruptcy-inducing fines *if they dared tell anyone the State was holding them for trial in secret kangaroo courts* as if this were already the Venezuela or Cuba

440

that Biden, Obama, Sanders, Harris and that cute dingbat who auditioned to become a Congresswoman from the Bronx are all so very much longing for us to become.

Labor unions have been lied to all right, but not by the people they think

I watched with disgust and horror the film footage from 11 December 2012 in Michigan, where big, brawny teamsters assaulted a tent full of protestors who were assembled to express an opinion on public policy. These scumbags pulled down a tent on women, elderly and disabled people – all because these thugs could not stand that someone had a different opinion about the proper way to structure the rights of free men and women to associate in the ways each individual thinks best. One particular man is caught on video screaming that he'll "kill 20 people with guns!" and is wearing a hardhat with what I assume is his surname on the back of it. Go do your own research if you care; I am not going to grant Tough Guy immortality by naming him here.

Tough Guy and his pals were beating up old people and women to *prevent* free speech. It's not quite the same thing as brave men facing off against armed Pinkerton guards in the steel patch in the 1930s, is it? If as his union avers "workers" are "better off" when the State *restricts* a person's choice about whether to pay union dues, then why on earth would he even be off his couch in the first place, never mind assaulting people in front of television cameras?

Did Obama's Attorney General Eric Holder prosecute any of these men? Not that I know of, though he certainly felt fit to shove his oar in on plenty of other matters best left to the States.

In any event, the major problem here is *not* that some greedy mean people – to hear the media tell it, "Republicans" – want to take away money and things from the working class. No, unfortunately, the major problem is that the lie *started* from the time a politician said "Hey, if you work for 20 years and pay fifteen cents a day towards your retirement, from the day of your retirement onwards for maybe 60 years, we'll give you 85% of your last year's salary. With Cost-of-Living Adjustments. And health insurance. And free lawn bowling kit."

Pardon the redundancy, but that politician was a lying sleazebag of the first water. He duped the workers into believing that the government could put them on easy street by waving a wand saying so, knowing full well that the small minority of financially literate taxpayers who *knew then* that this was impossible would be ignored by the vast majority who like to believe in unicorns until it's too late.

The other major, and related, problem is that of entitlements granted to public sector employees by the irresponsible clowns they helped put in office in the first place. There are myriad examples of this headache, but I have grabbed this one at random from 2010 as illustrative of the problem.

States Skip Pension Payments, Delay Day of Reckoning
By GINA CHON

WSJ POLITICS AND POLICY APRIL 9, 2010

State governments from New Jersey to California that are struggling to close budget deficits are skipping or deferring payments to already underfunded public-employee pension plans. The moves could help ease today's budget pressures, but will make tomorrow's worse.

New Jersey's governor, a fiscal conservative, has proposed not making the state's entire $3 billion contribution to its pension funds because of the state's $11 billion budget deficit. Virginia has proposed paying only $1.5 billion of the $2.2 billion required pension contribution. Connecticut Republican Gov. M. Jodi Rell is deferring $100 million in payments this year to the pension fund for state employees to help close a $518 million budget gap

"Yes it's wrong," said New Jersey Republican State Sen. Robert Singer. "But the governor "has no other choice."

The deferrals come as pension experts say the funds need the money more than ever, after losses during the financial crisis. Before the 2008 market collapse, 54% of public pensions for states and local governments had assets totaling at least 80% of their liabilities. Last year, only 33% of plans met that criterion, according to a study released Thursday by the Center for State and Local Government Excellence and the Center for Retirement Research, both nonpartisan groups.

The issue of the contributions is heating up right now with legislatures in the thick of budget season. The recession has left states with less means to make their pension payments just as they are rising.

Now or Later

Annual required contribution to one major pension system in the state and what governments actually paid in, in billions.

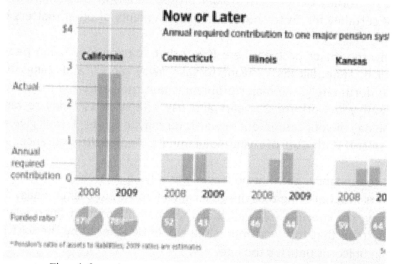

The deferred payments are particularly irksome to some public union employees who say they have been unfairly blamed for the fiscal burden of public pensions on taxpayers.

"The state has kicked the can and now the can has become a 55-gallon drum," said Anthony Wieners, president of the New Jersey State Policemen's Benevolent Association. "But our members have sacrificed, some with their lives, and they deserve and expect to have their full pension."

Of 71 pension plans that submitted 2009 contribution figures so far, the Center for Retirement Research found that more than 50%, or 39, reported not paying their full pension bill.

The "kick the can" approach has surfaced before in times of trouble, for example in years after the Sept. 11 attacks. Sometimes the pain gets alleviated if markets improve and pension funds' assets rise.

But this time funds are expected to face pressure because accounting practices are pushing out some of the pain of 2008's market declines into later years, leading to a jump in pension contributions next year.

The delays mean higher bills in the future, because pension payments—the funds' liabilities—are guaranteed to the government workers whose money the pension funds manage. With 401(k) plans, by contrast, employees can enjoy more upside if markets rise but also stand to lose savings if they decline.

In a worst-case scenario, in which a public pension fund was so underfunded that there were concerns it wouldn't be able to pay benefits, a state could resort to taking funding away from schools, social-service programs or other services to fully pay the pension bill.

While funds on average remain close to the recommended 80% funding level, the ratio is expected to decline further unless contribution levels increase, Thursday's study concludes.

(State public pensions are generally viewed as adequately funded at the 80% level because, unlike private corporate pensions with stricter standards, governments generally don't face the same risks of bankruptcy that companies do.)

In New Jersey, Republican Gov. Chris Christie followed steps of his predecessor to address a budget gap for the coming fiscal year by proposing last month to skip a $3 billion payment to the retirement systems for teachers, state employees and other public employees, valued at $66 billion as of June 30.

New Jersey's prior governor, Democrat Jon Corzine, mostly missed a $2.5 billion payment to the pension system and allowed cities and other local governments to pay only 50% of their share of the pension contribution. The fund is one of the most underfunded in the country.

Illinois, with the worst unfunded pension liability in the country, has failed to pay its full annual contribution for its five retirement systems in the past few years. Democratic Gov. Pat Quinn had proposed that the state pay $300 million less than the total $4.5 billion estimated contribution to the state's pension systems for the next fiscal year. The state last month passed bills to scale back pension benefits; the measures are expected to save $100 billion over several decades, according to legislators.

Even states that had been making their full annual contributions have fallen short this year because of budget issues. Connecticut previously had paid all or a big chunk of its annual required contribution for the state employee fund, but this year it paid less.

"Connecticut has only reduced the contribution as a result of the extraordinary financial situation facing the state," said Jeffrey Beckham, undersecretary for legislative affairs.

Some states, like Kansas, have legal limits on their contributions that prevent them from paying the full amount. That has helped reduce costs for those governments but also hurt the funding status of pensions. Some legislators in Kansas have recently contended that was a dangerous course. A bill currently in the state Senate would gradually increase the employer contributions until it reaches the annual required contribution.

Even states that have traditionally met their full contributions have seen funding levels decrease, largely because of the decline in their pension fund's assets because of investment losses. The $113 billion Florida Retirement System, with strict funding payment policies, had been overfunded since 1997 but dropped last year to 88.5%. The state made more than 100% of its annual pension payment to the system from 2007 to 2009.

A few states have tried to mitigate the impact of their delay. Because Virginia recently decided not to pay $620 million of its annual pension-fund payment for the next fiscal year to help balance the budget, the state legislature approved a repayment measure earlier this year.

"We understand this is money that has to be replenished," said Republican State Sen. Walter Stosch, an accountant.

In writing this book, the urge has been strong to dive deep into the statistics surrounding politicians promising money to people they have no way of paying. But I have remained strong. In a weird way, if politicians gave *any* thought to my writing this book, they would *want* me to throw more piles of numbers at you so the sea of statistics and figures would make your eyes cross, so you would stop paying attention. Gina Chon wrote a fairly concise version of the story and it got to be a slog halfway through. What she is writing about is wildly important, so don't let the particular figures get in the way of your comprehension.

That is their plan – to make it all boring and horrible and quantitatively numbing for the majority of people who are not numerate to begin with. I will keep it simple: No politician or government agency should ever be allowed to make the future promise of a single dollar in payment to anyone.

Period.

Defined contribution funds, 401(k) plans, IRAs – whatever the form of retirement savings, the cash must be placed directly in the employee's personally-controlled accounts. No more grubby politicians' paws on funds – whether real or illusory – that will have to be paid out later.

Ethanol

Every interventionist nightmare begins with someone somewhere having a positive desire to socially-engineer their particular outcome, er, make America more betterer for everyone else who lacks enlightenment. Ethanol is one of the finest boondoggle dollar-transfer mechanisms ever created.[238] In 1978, Congress kicked off this idiocy with the Energy Policy Act. I will leave it to you do dive down the complex rabbit hole of blowing taxpayer dollars to shove food into your gas tank.[239]

---

[238] "Al Gore's Ethanol Epiphany" *Wall Street Journal* Op-Ed, NOVEMBER 27, 2010 He concedes the industry he promoted serves no useful purpose.

[239] TCS-Biofuels-Subsidies-Report.pdf (taxpayer.net) - as good a place to start as any.

End it. Now. Tell the Iowan, Nebraskan and Minnesotan Senators (not an exhaustive list, but chief culprits) who keep this alive to go into private business making and selling ethanol if it is such a great deal. The American people would be *happy* to give them any and all Intellectual Property that has been developed over the years, if they promise to quit sucking at the taxpayer teat for this nonsense.

I only call out the specifics of some of the swirling idiocy to illustrate for you, my dear reader and (maybe) fellow citizen, how this cancer has grown upon us and is smothering the nation. All of these things will be swept away during the Great Budgetary Restructuring coming to a Swamp near you. These tales of madness are designed to stiffen your resolve when they plead with you that *"I agree! So much of DC is pure waste! But **this particular** bit of wasteful crap is actually really important and will probably save the children in some way I cannot define right now."*

A Fine for Not Using a Biofuel that Doesn't Exist

Some of the most sweeping injustices created by Congress are captured in quite literally impossible situations. Because of the way this law and its set of rules were written, it *assumes* the existence of something to be regulated. In a way, it's a perfect summation of how disconnected from reality politicians are – it would never occur to a private sector attorney drafting a contract to not insert language asserting the possibility of fulfilment. A futures contract for oil contains the condition that the oil be available for delivery.

In this instance, the law *demands* that some people use a product that *cannot be bought because it does not exist* and then the law *fines* those people for not using the nonexistent thing. Imagine if you were told by "your" government, *Starting Monday, if you don't use 2 rolls of fooberdydubintallinfest every evening, you'll be fined $25. But don't worry, 200 rolls of fooberdydubintallinfest only cost 10 cents.*

While you're irritated by this, you have sadly been worn into submission by thousands of pointless rules and regulations designed to destroy your will, so you shrug, sigh mightily and say, *OK, terrific, I give up. Where do I buy these rolls of fooberdydubintallinfest?*

To which reasonable question, the government responds, You can't buy them anywhere. The rolls don't exist, nor do we expect them to ever exist. So please write us a check for $25 x 365 days per year = $9,125.

Matthew Wald covers this madness perfectly:

> When the companies that supply motor fuel close the books on 2011, they will have to pay substantial penalties to the Treasury because they failed to mix a special type of biofuel into their gasoline and diesel. While this may seem like a cut-and-dried violation of regulations, the difficulty here is that compliance was literally impossible, as the required biofuels have not been produced in large enough quantities, says the New York Times.

- The original goal set by the Energy Independence and Security Act for vehicle fuel from cellulose was 250 million gallons for 2011 and 500 million gallons for 2012.

445

- These minimum quotas were reduced by the Environmental Protection Agency (EPA) to 6.6 million gallons in 2011 and 8.65 million gallons for 2012 when the agency realized how little biofuel was available to be bought.
- The standards for cellulosic fuel are part of an overall goal of having 36 billion gallons of biofuels incorporated annually by 2022.
- Failure to reach the quota in 2011 will end up costing refiners approximately $6.8 million for 2011, and this figure could rise for 2012 as the quota increases.

The federal government's regulations are aimed at reducing the nation's greenhouse gas emissions, its reliance on oil imported from hostile places and the export of dollars to pay for it. Despite these intentions, however, the creators of the regulations simply failed to account for the fact that the technology does not exist to produce cellulosic ethanol at the required capacity.

Plants are being built that will attempt to produce the fuel in large quantities, including a site in Emmetsburg, Iowa, owned by the company Poet, and a plant in Kinross, Michigan (partly owned by General Motors) that received $80 million from the Energy Department. However, neither project offers much hope to refiners in the immediate future, as they are both slated to begin producing in 2013. Until then, refiners will likely be unable to meet their EPA-mandated quotas.[240]

Lawrence Lessig touches – or rather, beats on – the insanity of ethanol in his erudite work on government distortions. In a chapter titled *Why Don't We Have Free Markets?* he discusses the interactions between American obesity due in part to the inclusion of corn byproducts as sweeteners in all our packaged foods, the crazy quilt of subsidies provided to make sugar artificially expensive, which makes food companies buy high fructose corn syrup as opposed to sugar, which then made the corn lobby get in on the game of subsidies.

Once the corn lobby was onto a good thing in creating artificial demand for corn, they seized on another opportunity to yank cash from the unsuspecting American taxpayer.

The strategy of the concentrated corn industry is not just to protect HFC. It is also to increase the demand for corn generally. Enter ethanol – perhaps the dumbest "green" energy program ever launched by government. Whole forests have been felled pointing out the stupidity of a subsidy to produce a fuel that is neither a good fuel (as in, it packs a good punch) nor, when you consider the cost of refining it, a green fuel. As libertarian author James Bovard puts it, ethanol is "a political concoction – a product that is exists and is used solely because of the interference of politicians with the workings of the marketplace." One 2008 report estimated that the biofuel mandates of Congress would cost the economy more than $100 billion from 2005 to 2010. That's sixty-five times the total amount spent on renewable energy research and development programs during the same period.[241]

---

[240] Matthew L. Wald, "A Fine for Not Using a Biofuel That Doesn't Exist," *New York Times*, January 9, 2012.
[241] Lessig, Lawrence, Republic, Lost; How Money Corrupts Congress – and a Plan to Stop It, 2011, p.50

The result of all this insanity is the taxpayer pays and pays and pays some more – all to line a few pockets and add needless fines and regulatory constrictions to the economy. Not only that, but corn derivatives make everyone fat, fatter and obese which is *a priori* a bad thing, but also means fatties are unhealthy, so medical costs skyrocket and drug companies create more drugs to help people mitigate the impacts being obese brings.

All because powerful Senators (under our current system, the one I am urging you demand be replaced with a good one) demand taxpayers foot the bill for turning corn to unnatural uses. Do you recall asking the government to do any of that?

Congressional Research Service

Another way for the government that *we the people* pay for to be of better use to *us* is for the kind of real transparency that Obama – along with so many other lying politicians – promised us while he was running for office the first time around, and that as soon as he got *into* office became far less a priority. A fine example of the self-serving hypocrisy of "our" elected officials is the Congressional Research Service.

Since the CRS does not deign to share its research with the people who pay for its operations, a private group called Open CRS was created to share publicly the research generated by the CRS. As described on their webpage (http://opencrs.com/about/), Open CRS quite literally depends on a private citizen noting the random releases of CRS reports by any particular member of Congress, and then reporting that release to Open CRS. How much simpler would it be for the CRS to just publish its findings as they are generated?

As they note:
About Open CRS

American taxpayers spend over $100 million a year to fund the Congressional Research Service, a "think tank" that provides reports to members of Congress on a variety of topics relevant to current political events. Yet, these reports are not made available to the public in a way that they can be easily obtained. Open CRS provides citizens access to CRS Reports that are already in the public domain.

CRS Reports do not become public until a member of Congress releases the report. A number of libraries and non-profit organizations have sought to collect as many of the released reports as possible. Open CRS is a centralized utility that brings together these reports.

Unfortunately, there is no systematic way to obtain all CRS reports. Because of this, not all reports appear on the Open CRS web site. We believe that it would be far preferable for Congress to make available to the public all CRS Reports.

So deeply ensconced are the crucial flaws in the Beltway belief system that the April 2011 CRS report entitled "Reducing the Budget Deficit: The President's Fiscal Commission and Other Initiatives" has a section titled "Social Effects" [of the Federal Government] whose first sentence is: "Certain federal programs are specifically aimed at reducing income inequality."[242]

Without harping too much on what could simply be poor phrasing, I think it important to highlight to the author, Ms. Levit, and other readers that *no* Federal programs should be aimed at "income inequality." Any social goals advanced by use of the taxpayer dollars should be aimed solely at ensuring a level playing field for all Americans to be able to pursue life, liberty and the pursuit of happiness without being unfairly hindered by arbitrary restraints.

"Income" is not something that is *a priori* subject to "equality" or lack thereof. Income is a function of effort, risk, timing and luck and therefore is not something the Federal government should have anything whatsoever to do with. The resultant statistical distribution describing over, say, the previous year how much each person earned in dollar terms is a pure description of an emergent property of a vastly complex system. Trying to manage "income inequality" is like trying to manage "weight inequality" in the population. It's meaningless.

Public Sector Unions Should Never Have Been Allowed

The public expenditure sphere is a constant push-and-pull between payers and payees, much like the rest of life. Wisconsin learned a very hard and useful lesson in 2011.[243] The money to pay for all the goodies showered on public sector employees must come *from* someone else – someone productive, generating economic value in the private sector. There is nothing *a priori* wrong with that – we all pay for services constantly with hard-earned dollars, and public education is one of the *very few* public goods that we should all be burdened with paying for. Investing in the future of the country, providing opportunity for every child born and living here legally, is a definite communal benefit.

That said, *how* citizens are taxed for that specific public good and *how* teachers are paid to deliver that good is subject to a wide range of arrangements.

Even the Progressive Left's favorite Socialist-in-a-Wheelchair FDR thought it ridiculous to allow public sector employees to unionize.

Keeping government small and simple benefits us all. Playing politics with parts of the law *always* ends in disaster. In 1962 President Kennedy signed Executive Order 10988. It seemed fairly benign but it set in motion the entire apparatus of public sector unions which led to trillions of dollars in pension benefits that taxpayers are being saddled with.

------

[242] Levit, Mindy R., "Reducing the Budget Deficit: The President's Fiscal Commission and Other Initiatives," April 2011, p.8

[243] *Union curbs rescue a Wisconsin school district*, Byron York, WSJ.com *Chief Political Correspondent* *@ByronYork* | 06/30/11 http://washingtonexaminer.com/politics/2011/06/union-curbs-rescue-wisconsin-school-district#ixzz1QsOyT7Hm

Beyond the long-term deleterious effects of public sector unions, they damage American interests in the here and now. Unions control hiring, prevent firing and make entire departments literally unmanageable by their Constitutionally-appointed leaders. I touch elsewhere on the insane frustrations faced by the incoming ninth Secretary of Veterans Affairs,[244] stymied in the *most basic* task of any boss – finding and hiring competent leaders to execute his or her managerial goals.

Whatever one thinks about a given politician or a given set of policy goals, the entire point of public service is to drive the agenda of the President who has been elected by the people because of his campaign promises and vision for the nation. A *decent* human being when faced with a CEO with whom they disagree, would tender his or her resignation rather than serve such a leader. Alas, that is not how Washington, DC works. As Mike Pompeo described his tenure as Secretary of State under President Trump, with a hostile bureaucracy:

> Let's start with the unions – principally, the American Federation of Government Employees and the American Foreign Service Association. You, the American taxpayer, provide office space and full-time staff for union bosses to do their work. They specialize in creating inefficiencies. They draft work rules that make fast processes and teamwork very difficult. They file grievances on behalf of workers who were harmed by paper cuts and cold coffee. They leak. They complain. And then they cash their paychecks, underwritten by citizens with real jobs. Among the reasons government fails so epically is because incentivizing high performers, and the inverse of that proposition, is nearly impossible. A good start for fixing the State Department, and much of our federal government, is simple: at-will employment and no unions. This is what millions and millions of us outside of government sign up for. What makes federal service so different as to deserve protection of your job for nearly a lifetime? My answer: nothing.[245]

Funny, that's my answer, too.

To pick another example at random, here is a *New York Post* Editorial from March 2016. In it, the fine reporters at the *Post* did some digging into *where* all the massive seas of cash from bridge and tunnel tolls – as well as "airport fees" – go. You don't have to be a native New Yorker to be caught in this insanity. If you flew through or into a NY/NJ metro area airport, the Port Authority skimmed some cash from your wallet for quite literally *no* value to you in return.

Obscene salaries at the Port Authority explains those soaring tolls
> By Post Editorial Board
> March 22, 2016 | 9:10pm
> Ever wonder how the Port Authority spends its take from soaring tolls? Promise not to jump off a PA bridge, then take a peek at some crazy new data on what the authority's paying employees.

---

[244] Shulkin, David, *It Shouldn't Be This Hard to Serve Your Country*, 2019
[245] Pompeo, Mike, *Never Give an Inch: Fighting for the America I Love*, Broadside Books, 2023

One PA cop, Joseph Macaluso, pulled down a whopping $348,095 last year. That's right: $348,095 for a cop. A chief maintenance supervisor, Stephen Olmo, raked in $325,880, including $186,846 in overtime.

It sounds surreal. But data just released by the Empire Center show that the average PA employee got $100,253 last year, up from $97,673 in 2014.

An executive, Michael Francois, topped the list at $366,698. But three dozen employees took in $250,000 each, including 25 PA cops. And 170 PAPD officers pulled down $200,000-plus, again thanks to juicy OT.

Why does the PA even need its own cops?

To be fair, not all the cash from PA tolls, which have shot up five straight years now, goes to outrageous pay; some also covers outrageous pensions.

Last year, 44 retirees got more than $150,000 each in pensions. A stunning 437 got six-figures-plus.

Is anyone watching the till? Motorists — and passengers who pay added fees at PA-run airports — are paying through the nose to prop up obscene PA pay and pensions.

That's hardly the only big waste: The agency just spent $4 billion, or $80,000 per daily rider, for a gaudy PATH station.

OK, part of the problem is that this $8 billion-a-year agency is run by two states, New York and New Jersey. Its board and top officers answer to two governors. And no one's accountable to the public.

But if Govs. Cuomo and Chris Christie can't stop the hemorrhage of PA money, maybe they should move to scrap the whole agency and start from scratch.

Before people start jumping off bridges.

Abolish Public Sector Taxpayer-Guaranteed Defined Benefit Pensions

By making public sector workers as concerned with their individual futures as those of us in the wild private sector are, those public sector workers will stop acting like perpetual infants and will have to (wo)man up to face the harsh reality they have been cocooned from for so long. The best way to keep all citizens' interests aligned is while we're tossing the insanity of public sector unions on the bonfire of history, along with them go any arrangement which forces future taxpayers to pay for promises made by politicians today.

You'll notice that I have no objection to defined benefit plans *per se*. A "defined benefit" plan simply says that the recipient will get X dollars per month over the course of his or her retirement. The problem comes from the underfunding of such plans, meaning not enough dollars are set aside to make sure there is adequate cash on hand every month to pay all the retirees. That underfunding is usually matched by a taxpayer guarantee – meaning that even if the plan manager loses all the capital in the fund, the retiree doesn't care, because the taxpayers then need to make up the balance.

An annuity can be a defined benefit plan. So long as some future pack of fools, er, Congress or State Legislature, does not step in to set up *another* Pension Benefit Guaranty Corporation for taxpayers to once again guarantee the performance of the annuity, then private companies should be free to offer defined benefit contracts to individuals or companies.

Far better from a personal moral development standpoint as well as a sound fiscal standpoint, any and all retirement plans need to be defined contribution. Meaning if you

450

want to save for retirement, the more you save and invest now, the more you'll have to spend in your retirement.

What a radical idea for the public sector unions – it's what workers in the productive private sector call "reality."

Infrastructure

This is often one of the biggest boondoggles, although when infrastructure spending is done correctly, meaning with a minimum of pork project mutual back scratching, everyone can benefit. The nation's roads, bridges, tunnels and the range of water and electricity utilities all require constant maintenance and a huge amount of new capital investment to bring them up to speed.

The problem with roads, bridges and the like is that politicians *love* announcing new ones, and smashing bottles of sparkling wine at their openings – you get great photo ops from that and the lovely new bridge always comes across nicely in press shots. But gosh, who knew that cleaning and painting and checking for cracks and rust was so darned *expensive?* There are no excellent photo opportunities for politicians unless they want to get into the muck and grime on *Dirty Jobs with Mike Rowe.*

So while we need the arteries of commerce, and maintenance of these public assets actually is one of the few things government should be doing, we the American people need to trim down the extraneous mound of things government shouldn't be doing and insisting that care and maintenance of our built environment is done responsibly and is well-funded.

Isaac Asimov in his brilliant *Foundation and Empire* had infrastructural neglect play a starring role in Hari Seldon's perception that the Galactic Empire had reached its zenith and was beginning a descent into decay, chaos and dissolution.

Back in the here and now of the early 21st century, a non-founder of the discipline of psychohistory with some experience in investment made a few points in favor of a reinvigorated American focus on infrastructure. Barton Biggs was chief investment strategist and in July 2011 as partner at hedge fund Traxis Partners, he made some comments in support of a new WPA.[246] The Works Progress Administration at least was created during a time when hard work, discipline and living an upright life were if anything more important than the roads built or tunnels dug. People got kicked out of WPA work camps all the time for drinking or other bad behavior. Can you imagine trying to enforce public morality when giving handouts to the unemployed today?

Apparently, when old Morgan Stanley hands age, they become deluded Socialists. While I entirely agree with him – and many others – that the nation's ageing infrastructure can be one of the fonts of future prosperity in the nation, I disagree *in toto* that all infrastructure spending must be publicly-financed and forced to bear the unsustainable burden of a neo-Keynesian objective. He pointed to a belief common in the Obama years that American economic growth would "never" get above 1.5% again or so, and therefore –

---

[246] Simon Constable, *"Barton Biggs: U.S. Needs a Massive Public Works Program,"* WSJ JULY 1, 2011

logic I still find impossible to apprehend – the "solution" was for more government cash to be shoveled at things.

Or, if infrastructure is to be financed publicly, let the decision to do so be made as locally as possible. If a small county bridge is of vital import to the local economy, let the county pay for its creation and upkeep. If it is a regional or state-wide fixture, then let a larger municipal or state pay for it. Only clearly national infrastructure, such as bridges for interstates or interstate railways should be handled at the federal level. And, importantly, tolls ought to be levied *in a clear and transparent manner* to support their upkeep. No money shifting around in the shadows: clear data regarding traffic and per-vehicle fees on a monthly basis for any interested party to review.

Infrastructure financing is one of the few things government should have a hand in. I will leave this dangling, that others may pick up the torch to find better ways to select relevant projects, finance relevant projects and provide robust governance to ensure tax dollars are used wisely.

Figure 33: Spy Cam capturing the budgeting process for infrastructure bills

Chapter 29: The Political Class Must Be Destroyed

The *major* problem which trickles through to all the others is that we have permitted the creation of a Political Class which lives in a bubble protected from the vicissitudes of Fate, unlike the rest of Americans. Restoration of a prosperous potential future for the US rests solidly on *We the People* ridding ourselves of this ridiculous, self-appointed aristocracy.

How can an institution whose public approval ratings hover near 11% have an aggregate reelection rate of 97%? Simple: the members of Congress are not *really* competing with one another. Heck, no, that would be a bummer. No, they *ensure* that they keep each other in office via gerrymandering election districts.

Luckily for us all, the solution to this massive headache is simple:

1. term limits of four (4) terms for one's entire life *for every single elected and appointed position in the government*,
2. term limits of two (2) terms for any one of those positions,
3. an objective, analytic geometrical formula for evenly and with the simplest shape (meaning fewest vertices) possible for dividing a State into even voting districts,
4. a set of prerequisites regarding sufficient private sector experience prior to being allowed to attain office,
5. a Constitutional Amendment that requires Congress to sit *in camera* the way the British, South African, Canadian and Australian Parliaments do, and
6. a Constitutional Amendment that requires Congressional Representatives and Senators to *personally write* the laws and regulations they vote on, rather than passing that awesome responsibility to unelected and unaccountable faceless bureaucracies.

While not nearly as important, I would add:

7. a law that mimics the US Postal Service's rules about putting someone on a postage stamp: you are not allowed to have a building or swimming pool or park or anything else named after you while you are still alive, if that structure has been paid for in whole or in part with taxpayer dollars. This rule shall include dedicatory plaques saying "you" did this or that, *unless* you paid for the entirety of the project, building or park out of your own, post-tax personal dollars.

When we make a political office a true civic duty and take away the goody bag of prizes and ego-boosting perks, that will suck the money out of politics far more effectively than rafts of laws which trample the Constitutional rights of Americans to free speech. When people of true civic zeal, personal conviction and proven merit congregate to make reasoned decisions in a spirit and framework of fairness and equality, we just *might* get some good work product from the fetid swamp on the Potomac.

Robert Kaiser described Chris Dodd's decision to forsake his onerous duties of Congressman, taking just enough time out from chasing young women around Washington to run for Senate:

> Reelection was never difficult. Dodd cruised to victory in 1976 and again in 1978. "I might have stayed in the House" for many years, Dodd said, "had I not been sentenced to Rules." When Abraham Ribicoff, a three-term senator, announced his intention to retire – "it was May 3, 1979," Dodd recalled more than thirty years later – "at that point this was not a hard choice. I was six years in the House [it was actually four years and four months]. I was not going to sit there for the next twenty years waiting to climb up to be chairman of the Rules Committee at age eighty."[247]

How magic is that? The man who helped oversee the destruction of the mortgage market and the co-architect of America's demise as a financial center, would have *stayed put in the House* had he been on a more exciting committee. Not a word about the important legislative work that needed (and still needs) to be done to strip further power from the Federal Government, or for careful debate of infrastructure spending bills or better laws to protect people's rights from an already-overzealous public sector union movement – nope, he was convinced that ten reelections *were a given* but, geez, what a bummer of a committee to be stuck on...

Wow. Breathtaking. The civic zeal and passion for hard work for the public good just ooze from his pores. Oh, wait, no, that's the whiskey fumes. The lush couldn't even remember the time he'd spent in office. I won't even touch the fact that the man who presumed to tell *me* and my fellow numerate finance professionals how finance ought to work thought in 1979 that he'd be eighty years old after twenty more years in the House, which is tricky math, as he was thirty-five years old at the time he ran for the Senate.

Multiply his self-serving parasitic worldview and you've got most of Congress. Political office needs to become simultaneously a privilege and a true civic duty. By taking away the possibility of decades in office, we're taking a firm step in the right direction.

Securities Laws Would Send You to Prison for Years – but not Nancy Pelosi!

Even during a severe economic crisis, with howls of anger from every stripe of the political spectrum, Congress repeatedly declined to – in the felicitous and in this case ironic phrasing of Obama – "play by the rules" that every other American has to play by. Here are a few choice snippets from the Swamp.

Panel Cancels Vote on Insider Ban
Wall Street Journal DECEMBER 8, 2011
By Brody Mullins

---

[247] Kaiser, R. p63

WASHINGTON—One day after scheduling a vote on legislation banning insider trading in Congress, a House committee canceled the vote, saying there isn't enough agreement to proceed.

Rep. Spencer Bachus (R., Ala.), chairman of the House Financial Services Committee, postponed the vote after meeting with senior House Republicans. "A significant number of members of the committee on both sides of the aisle have indicated a desire for additional time to study this issue before the committee moves forward with the markup that was announced for Dec. 14," Mr. Bachus said in a statement Wednesday evening.

The move is a blow to the legislation, which had been rapidly gaining momentum in recent weeks. The bill, sponsored by Rep. Louis Slaughter (D., N.Y.), had garnered the support of more than 180 lawmakers.

Mr. Bachus didn't identify the specific issues that remain to be resolved. At a committee hearing Tuesday, several Republicans and Democrats criticized the bill for being too broad—and for being too narrow. Rep. Judy Biggert (R., Ill.) said the legislation could lead to a "witch hunt" for lawmakers improperly trading stocks. Others, including Rep. Sean Duffy (R., Wis.), said the bill should go further by requiring lawmakers to put all their investments in blind trusts.

Mr. Bachus said he would consult with other committee chairmen who have authority over the legislation before rescheduling a committee vote.

It is truly breathtaking. Of course, in some ways, their flouting the law out in the open for all to see is their best defense. If they *hid* their corruption, it could be exposed. By breaking laws and the oath of office right out in public for all to see, on the rare occasion a reporter or citizen dares to say something, they can say, *"What? I told you repeatedly I'm trading stocks with inside information or using tax dollars to ferry my mistresses hither and yon, while getting them green cards. Why are you moaning about it now?"*

One of the hallmarks of an aristocratic class is their willingness when pressed to give a very publicly raised middle finger to the rest of the country. Your self-appointed "betters" in Washington, DC have only gotten more brazen in their lies and their arrogation of power with each passing year. There are so many examples to choose from, and to update with each passing month; I'm just grabbing a few to get you started.

Rangel Blamed for Ethics Offense
FEBRUARY 26, 2010, 12:12 A.M. ET

By GREG HITT and BRODY MULLINS

WASHINGTON—The House ethics committee has found Ways and Means Chairman Charles Rangel, a New York Democrat, violated House rules by failing to properly disclose financial details of trips to the Caribbean, senior congressional officials said Thursday.

After several months of investigation, the ethics panel determined Mr. Rangel didn't inform the ethics committee of the corporate source of funds for trips that took place in 2007 and 2008. The panel determined his staff knew the trips were paid for by corporations, and found that Mr. Rangel—who says he didn't know—should still be held accountable, officials said.

Charles Rangel

Mr. Rangel, central player in Congress on tax and health care legislation, called a news conference late Thursday and said there is "nothing in the record" to indicate he knew the source of funding for the trips, and questioned whether members of Congress should be held accountable for errors by their staff, the Associated Press reported.

Mr. Rangel is being admonished by the panel, known formally as the Committee on Standards of Official Conduct, and likely will be asked to repay the value of the trips, officials said. A handful of other lawmakers who also took part in the trips are also expected to be asked to repay the value of the trips.

In a statement expected to be released as soon as Friday, the ethics panel wrote that it didn't find sufficient evidence to conclude that Mr. Rangel knew that misleading information was provided to the ethics committee before the trips were approved.

A statement released by Mr. Rangel's office stressed the ethics committee "found that the chairman himself had no actual knowledge that the trip in fact violated House rules" and added that "Congressman Rangel will of course refund the funds in question."

The House ethics panel has been investigating several trips taken by Mr. Rangel and several other Democratic lawmakers in 2007 and 2008.

The investigation looked at travel by Mr. Rangel to conferences in 2007 and 2008. At issue is whether companies that employ lobbyists sponsored the conferences and whether Mr. Rangel properly disclosed the names of the sponsors on travel disclosure forms filed with the House.

The ethics panel in June said a November 2008 conference in St. Maarten was arranged by "an organization known as Carib News or Carib News Foundation." Travel forms filed by some of the lawmakers on the trip listed the New York Carib News as the sponsor of the event.

But Peter Flaherty, the president of the conservative National Legal and Policy Center, provided the committee with evidence suggesting that several companies that employ lobbyists may have underwritten at least a portion of the event. Ethics rules approved by Democrats severely restrict lawmakers from travel funded by companies that employ lobbyists.

Mr. Flaherty snapped pictures of lawmakers in front of signs that thanked corporate sponsors. He also provided The Wall Street Journal with a copy of the event's program, which included the names of corporate sponsors.

The ethics investigation is one of several targeting the activities of Mr. Rangel. The committee is also looking at whether Mr. Rangel filed inaccurate forms with Congress disclosing his personal assets. Last summer, Mr. Rangel updated his personal-financial-disclosure forms for the past few years, revealing more than $500,000 in assets he hadn't before made public.

The new committee action is sure to increase pressure on Mr. Rangel to give up his chairmanship. Republicans have staged several House votes calling on Mr. Rangel to step aside. Each has failed on fairly party-line votes.[248]

Eventually, the Congress made Rangel stand on the floor while they censured him. Wow. What a penalty. Gee, where do I sign up for that trade? I'd like to fail to declare income, use my power *over other people's checkbooks* to win sweetheart rental deals for myself and then... when it's all discovered, I don't face jail time or financial penalties; I get to listen to some people scold me, while I pretend to look contrite, while laughing on the inside. Sounds awesome. And I can probably be stone drunk for the scolding, so long as I manage to walk shakily to my place on the floor and wobble accommodatingly.

I had the pleasure in mid-2008 of watching Charlie Rangel perform on NY1 (the New York City news station) during his "trial" in Congress. The young kid who'd been recently hired to host the nightly political talk show (because the previous, more experienced host had finally been canned after a pattern of brutal spousal abuse could no longer be ignored by his producers) looked literally scared witless, but he went ahead and asked probing questions of the wily old Congressman. Rangel was in fine form, dismissive of this young punk's pertinacity in daring to question this glittering war hero who'd been sucking from the public teat for decades.

What was most telling (to me) about Rangel's attitude and his responses was how utterly and completely clear it was that he believed he was above all this. The look on Charlie's face seemed to say that this kid who is a taxpayer in New York and therefore right to question Rangel about the serious allegations of impropriety, had in fact no right whatsoever to question his betters.

The "betters" in this case being the untouchable solons of Congress. So what if Rangel used taxpayer dollars to splash his name across various publicly-funded entities across New York City? So what if Nancy Pelosi got access to personally buy shares in the Visa IPO *while she was handling legislation relating to credit card companies?* So what if Chris Dodd got handsome bribes in the form of discounted mortgage rates from Countrywide while driving Fannie and Freddie to loan more taxpayer-backed dollars to deadbeats who could never pay back their loans, and then instead of going to jail, got to "reform" the financial sector and then retire with the taxpayers still paying an annual pension to his useless ass? So what?

As David Mamet says in his wonderful book *The Secret Knowledge,* it astonishes him that some portions of the public are surprised to find that politicians get into politics mainly if not solely to fatten their wallets. Mamet writes with all the fervor of the convert – in this

---

[248] *Wall Street Journal*, February 2010

instance, his conversion from being a vapid dimwit Lefty to becoming a rational, thoughtful citizen.

A wonderful man I've not yet had the chance to meet named Hembree Brandon penned this opinion piece in *The Farm Press*.

At $5 billion yearly, the public may wonder: Is Congress worth the cost?
by Hembree Brandon in Farm Press Blog
Sep. 2, 2011 12:00am

    In 2010, the cost to support a Congress of 535 people was budgeted at almost $5 billion (up nearly 6 percent from the previous year, and likely up more this year). More and more, taxpayers are wondering if it's worth the cost to support a group that seems less and less able to solve problems, work together, and take care of business.

    So, OK, we all know that used car salespeople and lobbyists have always been at the bottom of the totem pole in terms of how the public views professions.

    In last December's annual Gallup Poll, sure enough, used car salespersons were ranked second from the bottom in perceived honesty and ethics. Lobbyists came in dead last.

    But, guess which group was third from bottom — those ranked down there with the dregs of public disfavor?

    You probably didn't have to think hard about that one: Congress.

    Fifty-seven percent of those polled had a very low or low opinion of the honorables, 32 percent only average, and a piddly 9 percent high/very high.

    Geez, even we wretched newspaper folk ranked six notches higher, at 22 percent very high/high (but one percentage point behind TV reporters — go figure).

    In a more recent CNN poll, only 14 percent of respondents approved of how Congress has been doing its job.

    It would be interesting to conduct a poll of the public's opinion of Congress after those being polled had been briefed beforehand as to how much money they and other taxpayers spend each year to support their chosen representatives and senators, their staffs, their numerous facilities, the Capitol police, visitor centers, travel, meals, health care, retirement, and on and on and on.

    In 2010, the cost to support a Congress of *535 people* was budgeted at almost $5 billion (up nearly 6 percent from the previous year, and likely up more this year).

    Given that members of Congress spend more and more time figuring ways to enhance their images and in raising money to perpetuate themselves in office, one might find it difficult not to wonder if it's worth the cost to support a group that seems less and less able to solve problems, work together, and take care of business.

    Now, it seems it's more about which party can be the most obstructionist, or which ideologies can be the most hyped, or who can best play the game of brinksmanship.

    David Walker, CEO of the Comeback America Initiative and a former Comptroller of the U.S., said at a University of Arizona town hall forum earlier this year that "the last 10 years have been the most fiscally irresponsible years in the history of the U.S., with spending completely out of control — and both parties are to blame for it. *Every day, we're spending $4 billion more than we take in.*"

If the government just prints more money, Walker said, "You're devaluing the currency. That creates pressures for inflation over time, and with inflation, arguably the cruelest tax of all, you can't manage, can't make decisions."

A tax-and-spend fiscal policy and a too loose monetary policy need to be brought under control "if we want to fight inflation and be able to fight the U.S. debt crisis," he said.

"The American people "are a lot smarter than their elected officials give them credit for," Walker said. "They get it — they understand that both parties are responsible."

Robert Bixby, executive director of the Concord Coalition, participating in the same forum, said that just eliminating waste in federal government, as many suggest, would be "nowhere near enough to plug the deficit hole we're going to face in the future ... and we can't possibly hope to grow our way out of it or cover the cost just by trimming some waste."

In a recent NPR interview, Bixby said: "There is a broad, bipartisan agreement that a lot of the things that would make the budget look a lot better aren't going to happen ... If Congress just went home, the budget would be in a lot better shape ... If they'd make no further decisions, the budget would be in pretty good shape by the end of the decade."

We could only wish...

That's $9.3 million *per parasite*, er, honorable Congressional legislator. *And they don't even do their Constitutionally mandated jobs much of the time.* If you or I – or any other "normal" person – so much as lie under oath in a civil trial, we can face time in jail. But the Leader of the Senate, Harry Reid had as of January 2012 gone 925 days without submitting a budget *as required by the Constitution*. The caesura in his official obligations may well have lasted longer; someone else can go research the appalling details.

He simply did not do his job. At all. He completely flouted the Rule of Law. And one of the "checks and balances" that we as naïve schoolchildren learned about in grammar school was run by a *former Constitutional Law School Adjunct Instructor* who in his entire eight years in office did *nothing* to force Reid to do *what the Constitution required him to do*.

It's amazing to me that even some of my intelligent friends believe that the various angry Americans calling themselves Tea Party members were all just some fiction dreamt up by Fox News. As if the facts of what all these people in Washington do are not sufficiently appalling to warrant true grass roots outrage. Written during the Obama years, the catchy terminology changed a bit, but the substance remained the same.

Current Biden Administration labels for "Tea Party members" is "white supremacist MAGA Republicans." I wonder what they'll be in a couple of more years.

I left that paragraph in place for my dear readers, because as the ascension of Trump proved, the outrage to which I referred was indeed very real and is only growing.

Beware a Politician Claiming Transparency

At one time or another, all politicians are pushed to intone sonorously about greater transparency in government and more thoughtfulness in public affairs. First Time

Presidential Candidate Obama said on multiple occasions that *all legislation including health care reform* would be subject to open, fully transparent debate, live on C-SPAN. Hah!

There is nothing new in politicos trying to ram through their pet projects, knowing full well what a damned hard sell it would be to marshal arguments and *convince* rational people of their point of view. Why bother? That sounds like work. That's the kind of hard yards efforts entrepreneurs and finance guys like me go through in pitching investors and clients to buy what we are selling. How awesome would it be if we could just *slip money from people's pockets* without having to actually prove we are providing real value?

As my go-to guy on such matters, I quote from David Lilienthal's journal entry dated 4 October 1939, written on the plane heading home from Washington. He had earlier in the day been meeting in the Oval Office with Tom Corcoran, Ben Cohen and FDR.

> What a curious kind of government it all is. Tom [Corcoran] doesn't seem to realize that the method of which he is so extensive a practitioner of trying to slip things through, without adequate consideration and discussion, may have a good deal to do with the growth of that practice among others. It never seems to occur to him that he could be of greater help to the President if he would help in setting up adequate machinery to insure *study* and all-round *consideration* of such problems as the War Resources Board or the power coordination idea, than in fostering the practice of avoiding such consideration by slipping things through, as they tried to slip the TVA matter through this time.[249]

Do you recall Nancy Pelosi trying to pass ObamaCare *without subjecting it to a Congressional vote at all* through an arcane process by which the legislation would be "deemed" passed? It was the ultimate conclusion to the Progressive Collectivist Dream: to pass massive, socially disruptive, economically transformative legislation without a single Democrat having to affirmatively go on record as voting for it.

It would appear she had a copy of Tom Corcoran's playbook as her bedside reading.

There are thousands of examples which would kill too many trees and try too much patience to cite here. Enjoy yourself finding them on your own or – better yet – demand the change required in "our" government so true transparency is attained. Once we fix the budget, all of these headaches fall away. Human nature means someone will try to re-sleaze the Swamp, but hopefully the next generation of free people will remember the Great Reorganization of 2024-2026 and cut those new sleaze weasels off at the knees before they gain any traction.

Eliminate Taxpayer-Guaranteed Perks and Pensions

The biggest single thumb in the face to the American people whom they ostensibly "serve" is the lavish benefits and "retirement" packages politicians have voted *for* themselves. How great is that?

---

[249] Lilienthal's Journals, Vol 1, p135

Imagine walking into your boss's office and saying to her, *"Hey, I was thinking that I do such a great job for you and the shareholders – despite being on vacation for 20 weeks a year, dating my subordinates in contravention of company policy and making decisions that others need to bear the costs of while I swan about the country and planet on an unlimited expense account – that I slid down to H.R. while you were away last week and got the H.R. Director to guarantee me a salary and benefits for life totaling at least $1 million. Why are looking so surprised? I've been working at this company for 3.5 years now, and this whole thing where every two years I need to go through a huge exercise manufacturing "achievements" to keep my job another two years is taking a toll on my health and marriage. Which is why I send rude pictures to college girls. I wasn't intending on telling you about my new retirement package, but since H.R. was indiscreet enough to alert you to the cash I just granted myself, I thought I'd swing by to stick my finger in your eye a bit before I took off for a week at the Cape with my girlfriend. I've been planning this vacation for months, as it's the only week this year my wife is taking the kids to see her family."*

While you and I were busily studying, working hard, saving and trying to make a better life for ourselves and our families, when we were, to borrow Obama's favorite phrase and this time *using it accurately* "playing by the rules," it turns out the whole mass of elected officials got there by promising to take our stuff and give it to other people, with little rhyme nor reason to the whole exercise beyond the unions and elected officials keeping themselves in gravy.

One of the thoroughly-consistent themes I have discovered in the course of sixteen years of research – aside from the massive ulcers these parasites give a thinking person – is that *without fail* politicians and their public-sector union allies will do *anything* to keep stealing cash from you, the taxpayer, *even after they have been convicted of corrupt crimes directly related to their "civil service" jobs.*

To take one example – at random, really at random, there are too many to even put in the footnotes – from New York State in April 2016, while 90% of New Yorkers polled agree with the totally-reasonable assertion that a "public servant" convicted of crimes should not receive a pension from the State, New York's politicians *have done nothing* to pass a very simple bill which would save taxpayers from sending monthly checks to felons convicted of crimes committed in violation of the public trust.[250]

This should not be a surprise. The same folks who look serious and intone about "the public trust" and "public service" whenever a camera is rolling, are focused wholly on lining their own pockets by stealing the cash in yours. They sure aren't going to pass legislation that would strip the pension from a politician convicted of corruption – heck, that could easily be any one of them any day now!

This organized theft of your hard-earned dollars is so obnoxious and glaringly against the public interest that even a news network whose opinions veer sharply leftward felt the need to shine a light into the darkness of the Beltway Grift Machine.

---

[250] "Pensions for felonious pols: An outrage NY lawmakers refuse to fix," *NY Post* Editorial Board, 30 April 2016

CNN Exposes 'Lavish' Government Pensions despite Economic Crisis
OPINION: FEDERATION FEATURE
FEBRUARY 26, 2010, 4:02 P.M. ET

Government employees can draw on their pension beginning at age 50; depending on the years of service they can get as much as 80 percent of their final salary.

By ANTHONY KANG
From the Media Research Center

All this week CNN has been taking a look at "Broken Government" and in some cases the cable channel deviated from the mainstream media norm by providing a critical view of government.

That was the case on Feb. 23 when Wolf Blitzer and Lisa Sylvester scrutinized lavish pension-plan and retirement-packages for government officials during "The Situation Room."

"Many Americans will spend half a lifetime or more working for the same company only to find little or no safety-net when that job ends," Blitzer said to begin the report. "Others, especially those on Capitol Hill don't have that problem."

"This is certainly nice work if you can get it," reporter Lisa Sylvester noted, alluding to the troubling disparity. "Lawmakers on Capitol Hill get automatic pay-raises and they never have to worry about their retirement, but that's not the case for many middle-class Americans."

How to get by after retirement is a question that weighs on many citizens. CNN found a former auto parts worker who had his pension cut 30 percent by the federal Pension Benefit Guaranty Corporation after his company Delphi went bankrupt and his pension was taken over by the government.

While the economy and many Americans struggle to find or keep jobs and pay their bills, the public-sector has been rapidly expanding. The U.S. is also facing a fiscal crisis with the national debt currently above $12.4 trillion, but that hasn't stopped "generous" pensions for former government officials.

"They can draw on their pension beginning at age 50; depending on the years of service they can get as much as 80 percent of their final salary, there are cost-of-living-adjustments added on, and they're still eligible to receive Social Security."

Citing the analysis of the National Taxpayers Union (NTU), Sylvester used Sen. Chris Dodd, D-Conn., as an example of broken government. NTU, a nonpartisan taxpayer group that has worked under the guiding principle "This is your money and the government should return it to you" since its inception, found that Dodd will have a starting annual pension of $125,500 when he retires next year.

Sylvester interviewed NTU's vice president for policy and communications Pete Sepp about what he considers the root of the broken system.

"Unlike even the state and local pension plans, the federal Congressional pension system is simply a direct line into the taxpayer's wallet," Sepp told CNN. "There's no investments that need to be made, no fund balances they get worried about – whatever the liability is for a given year – taxpayers cough up the money for it."

CNN even found one rare politician who has fought for pension-reform. Rep. Howard Coble, R-N.C., told CNN: "I elected to refuse the pension, on the ground that taxpayers are subsidizing my salary now. I figure when I leave they've taken good care of me – but let me do the best I can once I leave after the service in Congress has been accomplished."

The Congressional pension system is not alone in its excess. The state of California also promised lavish pensions for other public employees. Currently the state is on the hook for $100 billion to $300 billion in unfunded pension and health care liabilities on top of its projected $25 billion budget deficit.

Lisa Sylvester closed her "Broken Government" piece with a story about Rep. William Jefferson, D-La., who was found with $90,000 stashed in his freezer.

"And amazingly, up until recently, even if a Congressional member committed for a crime, they could still get their full pension. But a 2007 law barred members convicted of felonies from receiving their pensions. Still, there are a number of members of Congress like Congressman William Jefferson – his corruption offenses took place before that year – so he will still receive a pension paid for by the taxpayer."

Throughout the CNN series "Broken Government" has examined ballooning cost overruns, blocked confirmations, gerrymandering, Obama's broken quid-pro-quo promise regarding lobbyists, federal inefficiencies and state budget gaps just to name a few.

But some in the series have hypocritically called for a government solution to the problem being discussed as Kyra Phillips did on Feb. 25. The first segment of the series longed for the return of better days when unions were in power and a call for economic security.

It's breathtaking, isn't it? Hypocritical "public servants" smoking pot and drinking whiskey in hot tubs with prostitutes at IMF parties the night before they vote on increasing "three strikes" laws that will land poor city kids in jail for decades… It's all so ridiculously horrible on a grand scale, it's proof positive of Goebbels's contention that people only get caught in minor lies. Keep repeating the Big Lie[251] – that government in its present form is anything but a fetid pool of steaming, self-interested kleptomaniacal narcissists like Chuck Schumer and Jerry Nadler – long enough, and the vast bulk of people will be unable to believe it's a lie in the first place.

(Through this book, I tend to pick on New York politicians as I am most familiar with them or was until I escaped to the Last Free State in America, Florida. I don't mean to imply other States have more honorable or honest Senators and Representatives.)

Peter Schweizer puts it very well in *Throw Them All Out: How Politicians and their Friends get Rich off Insider Stock Tips, Land Deals, and Cronyism that Would Send the Rest of us to Prison.*

At the root of the Permanent Political Class is a profound sense of arrogance. A good military commander should never consider himself to be

---

[251] "If you tell a lie big enough and keep repeating it, people will eventually come to believe it. The lie can be maintained only for such time as the State can shield the people from the political, economic and/or military consequences of the lie. It thus becomes vitally important for the State to use all of its powers to repress dissent, for the truth is the mortal enemy of the lie, and thus by extension, the truth is the greatest enemy of the State."

irreplaceable, but many politicians in Washington believe precisely that of themselves. It is an ugly form of elitism, less overt than what we would see from the royalty of Europe in the seventeenth and eighteenth centuries, when the Sun King could proclaim, "I am the state." The modern, subtler version of this arrogance is the politician's belief that if we restrict his ability to engage in legal graft, the nation will suffer, because we won't be able to attract bright people (like them!) to run the country.

Over the past forty years we have been governed by the best educated political class in our history. Today, debts mount, the financial markets are in turmoil, the economy is in terrible shape – and the Washington games continue. The problem is not a lack of smart people in Washington. There is no "smart gap." There is, however, a "character gap." Like the financial crisis on Wall Street, the root of the problem is not ignorance but arrogance.

The Permanent Political Class tell us: We need them. Only they can dissect the entrails of the latest bill or understand the complexities of financial reform. They are making so many sacrifices on our behalf, they say. They are smart and well educated and could be making a lot more money somewhere else, they claim. We should tolerate a little honest graft on the side, or the occasional financial indiscretion, like failing to report income on their tax returns.

Yet, of course, the political class is hardly the only group of people in the country making a sacrifice for public service. Our soldiers are underpaid. Those who enter West Point, the Air Force Academy, or Annapolis, or those who go through ROTC at a rigorous school, are just as smart. They certainly could be doing something else with their time. They choose the armed forces as an act of service; they are not looking to get rich as officers. Enlisted soldiers are not looking to cash in by joining the infantry. In the military they will never earn anything close to what they might earn in the private sector. And many of our best leaders over the last century or more have come out of our armed services. These are individuals who could have been running large corporations or institutions for far more money. Two-, three-, and four-star generals make less than a freshman member of Congress, even though they may be responsible for the safety and operation of more than 100,000 troops. If today we had a five-star general like Dwight Eisenhower—and we don't—he would still be paid less than a freshman congressman.[2] And yet it is impossible to imagine that the military brass would ever argue that they deserve to make a little "on the side" as indirect compensation for their service.

Indeed, in the early 1980s, when the United States was in the midst of another (smaller) budgetary crisis, President Ronald Reagan released to the public letters he had received from American soldiers serving in Europe. They weren't griping about possible cuts. Just the opposite: they offered to take a pay cut if it would help the country. When was the last time you heard a member of the Permanent Political Class offer to do that?

When Gordon England was appointed to become deputy secretary of defense in 2006, members of the Senate committee that would hold hearings and vote on his confirmation had a simple and blunt request: You must give up the lucrative stocks and options you have in companies that do business with the Pentagon. Such divestment had been a requirement of the Senate Armed Services Committee of senior Pentagon appointees for decades, designed to eliminate any "military-industrial complex" conflict-of-interest concerns that might arise. The restriction was not limited to just missile manufacturers or companies that made bullets. "We're not allowed to buy Coca-Cola stock because military guys drink Coke," said England, "and we couldn't have stock in cereal companies because military guys eat cereal."

And who were the senators sitting across from England at those hearings? The same senators who wrote the defense bills, added earmarks, determined which military systems were bought or rejected. The same senators who were privy to private conversations with contractors and Pentagon officials, and received classified briefings on defense contracts, military systems, and Pentagon strategy. In other words, the very people who controlled the federal budget. They were free to buy and sell as many shares of defense stocks as they wanted to. Indeed, 19 of the 28 senators on that committee at the time held stock in companies that do business with the Pentagon.

The Permanent Political Class tells us they are concerned about financial corruption and financial crimes. They applaud legal crackdowns on corporate criminals and berate corporate executives for their huge salaries and tax shelters. The Permanent Political Class believes that everyone needs to be policed on this front. Everyone, that is, except for themselves. Why did the Tammany Hall political machine gain so much power in New York City? Why was it a dominant force for more than a century? You could point to the patronage system, or the payoffs. But in the end the machine survived *because the public came to accept it*. New Yorkers came to tolerate the idea that you could use "legal graft" to get rich from "public service" because that was just the way things were done. Sadly, the same attitude holds true today when it comes to crony capitalism. We get outraged when members of Congress or the President breaks the law, but we ignore the legal graft that is far more prevalent.

Unfunded liabilities, government promises made by self-interested individuals who never have to deal with the negative consequences, literal double standards when it comes to conflicts of interest: All these must end, starting with starving the beast at the heart of all these problems.

When it comes to retirement funding, there can be a defined contribution along the same lines as in the private sector, but that's it. Why are we the American taxpayers paying for Chris Dodd's "retirement," after he has decided that it's not as much fun as it used to be actively messing things up for my family and the rest of the nation? His old running buddy Teddy died and – sheesh! – the populace just doesn't understand why he's such a great guy and the pesky press (for a while, anyway) kept hammering him on sweetheart mortgage deals from Angelo Mozilo at Countrywide. Old Dodd must have been thinking, *"Who needs this crap? I can get out of here, go on the lecture circuit at $50,000 a pop and sleep even later than I did when I was 'working' three hard days a week in the Senate. I've already as my swan song delivered a massively-destructive and without-merit 'financial reform bill' – which I made sure had nothing inconvenient in there about independent investigators looking into political payoffs that occurred before I left office – so it's time to get on with the next phase of my parasitic life."*

Luckily for Chris Dodd, the Motion Picture Association of America hired him to be sure that billionaires in Hollywood *were specifically carved out of* Obama's post-reelection "tax fairness" initiatives. Whew! That's a relief. I was worried about how he was going to get along on the $120,000 annual pension we're on the hook for until he croaks.

There's one unnamed hero I want to meet and buy a beer: the guy at a University of Connecticut basketball game who gave Dodd the finger as a fine expression of the rank disgust Dodd's "constituents" felt for his bloated backside as a result of all the sweetheart mortgage deals and decades of self-serving that Connecticut papers were finally unearthing. Robert Kaiser tells that anecdote along with a broader picture of how Congress had evolved during Dodd's time of direct parasite sucking off the taxpayer teat:

> Much else had changed in Dodd's world over those thirty-five years. He entered one kind of Congress, and now served in something very different. He had a longer view than most others, because he could remember his father's Congress of the 1950s, and the cross-party fraternizing of that era. As recently as the 1960s, members of the House and Senate got just three paid trips home per year. Soon after Dodd arrived in the House in 1975, that number was raised to forty, an early warning of what was to come. Today there are no limits on the number of paid trips home that a member can take.
>
> Ed Silverman had been Dodd's chief of staff in the late 1980s. He recalled that Dodd in those days often ate lunch in the senators' dining room in the Capitol where only members were welcome. "Many days sixty senators had lunch there," socialized with one another, talked frankly without any staff in the room, Silverman recalled. "Now, I don't think anyone eats lunch there."[252]

Dodd was right that things had changed. He pointed to the rise of the Reagan Republicans who believed that government was the problem, and to the Democratic Party's partisan warfare which took the form of aggressively redistricting House seats to ensure they maintained control. To Dodd's credit – and believe me, coming from a man whose company was destroyed by this parasite, it hurts to write that but unlike him and his cronies, I'm honest – he's on record as having said "If I could change one thing, it would be how districts are drawn." He rightly saw that the insanity of gerrymandering House districts into homogenous areas far less diverse than many states has been a detriment to good, trustworthy governance.

In an era when NASA has *an undercover police force running sting operations on American citizens hawking moon rocks*, I am not alone among the Americans who want the people elected to Congress to actually *do something to fix our system*. We are not remotely concerned about whether they all get chummy with each other while learning to scratch each other's backs at the wider nation's expense.

A family member who lives in Washington, D.C. told me in August 2013 that some of her friends who are lobbyists were then starving for business. Ironically, even in an era of insane public sector bloat, the grinding stalemate deadlock in Washington means that no one who usually pays for lobbyists sees a point in paying a lawyer $750 per hour to talk to Congressional members. Why should they? No matter how much cash one spends, there's no chance of legislation happening – so why not keep the cash for something else like, uh, payroll or business growth?

Progress of a sort.

---

[252] Kaiser, page 231

Included in the Political Class are Unaccountable, Empirically Tested and Wholly Disproven Court Astrologers, er, Economists

There is nothing new under the sun. Ecclesiastes urged us to ponder this thousands of years ago, and I echo him today. To what end, I don't know. One of my favorite writers (and fellow Chicago anthropologist) Kurt Vonnegut once had a character of his gloss Santayana by saying, "You know, we'd better write all these events down, so no one makes these mistakes again...." Untold millions of personal relationships have ended with the lie, "It's not you. It's me."

Appended to and dependent on the Political Class is a vast apparatus of scraping toadies whose very livelihoods are derived *not* from creating any wealth or value in society but in extracting cash payments from *you*, the taxpayer, via the helpful mechanism of Congress. This has long been the traditional role of Court Astrologers throughout history – the wizards who cut open goats and chickens while mumbling arcane formulations, casting the entrails dramatically upon the royal floor and then "reading" those entrails for portents about the future.

I take but one example at random, because to perform even a moderately-exhaustive citation and critique of this kind of gibberish would require 500,000 pages of tiny print. I don't have time to write it and you most assuredly don't (or shouldn't) have the time or inclination to read it.

Joseph Stiglitz is not alone nor original in criticizing the *absolute* or "strong form" of the Efficient Markets Hypothesis. He is correct in writing that "[t]he theoretical arguments are complex," but he is either dishonest or too stupid to know better to then go on to posit some simplistic "examples" of why the "market for information" is actually efficient without specifying *which form* of the Efficient Markets Hypothesis he is supposedly "proving."

As vast human experience with totalitarian collectivist thinking and propaganda has shown us, he is probably not stupid.

> I explain the problem to my students in another way. Assume that while you're listening to my lecture, a $100 note falls by each of you. You can go on listening to my lecture, learning the important principles of economics. At the end of the lecture, each of you bends down to pick up the $100 bill next to you. That's the efficient solution. But it's not a market equilibrium. One of you, noticing that your neighbors are not bending down, will quickly do so, not only to pick up the $100 that's by you but also to get the $100 that's by your neighbor. As each of you realize what your neighbor is going to do, you too will instantaneously bend down. Each wants to get there before the others. In the end, you each get the $100 bill that you would have had you waited, but the lecture has been interrupted and your education shortchanged. [253]

I am going to leave aside the fruit hanging so low that the slightest breeze will make it brush the ground, jokes like *you can't pay for drinks and movie tickets with three seconds of a Stiglitz lecture, but you sure can with $100.*

I am not going to leave aside pointing out the sweeping hubris in the idea that pausing to pick up a slip of paper or two rather than remain riveted to the words of the Great And Mighty Stiglitz would result in one's "education" being "shortchanged," rather than one being given a brief albeit delightful reprieve from the bloviation to be endured on the way to earning a degree to maybe go out and earn a real living.

I pick on him because he has more than earned it. One more Court Astrologer mumbling holy gibberish, begging for table scraps and tenure from actual wealth creators or – in this case – public sector wealth controllers.

Economics is not a scientific discipline

More people would live happier lives knowing that economics is a branch of politics and rhetoric. It is *not* a scientific or quantitative discipline. While it takes in – when it suits its practitioners – objective data, it is in no way an objective science striving to uncover or discover core truths about reality. If "Economics" were a scientific, objective discipline, there would be no such thing as "a left-wing economist" or a "conservative economist."

There aren't any "left wing" mathematicians or biologists, nor are there any "right wing" physicists or chemists. Those adjectives have no meaning in the true sciences, where the only "truths" or working hypotheses are determined in the case of the sciences by the ongoing application of The Scientific Process which used to be taught in schools, or developed from pure logical rigor in the case of mathematics.

Of course, in the Soviet Union, science was heavily politicized, with people being imprisoned and executed for having the "wrong" scientific theory. That was unique to the Soviets until the Wuhan Virus Hysteria swept America starting in 2020, when the gigantic idiots atop the government led by Anthony Fauci criminalized scientific rationality. They chanted "I follow the science!" at us which was a mantra that meant, "I am a Democrat who hates Donald Trump, knows nothing about science, less about statistics and demands that anyone unafraid of a slightly bad influenza season must be shut up, banned from social media and fired from their job."

Anthony Fauci, Deborah Birx and thousands of others should stand trial for crimes against humanity. The fact that they have not been arrested and still have their jobs tell you all you need to know about the politically motivated disregard for rationality that has consumed some scary percentage of Americas as of early 2024.

Anyway. Economics is not a science. Economists who make noise in public are shills paid to argue a political point. Feel free to listen, if you'd like, but know they are no more prescient about economic matters than any other politician.

---

[253] Stiglitz, page 269

If they knew the future, they'd all be richer than Bill Gates and Jeff Bezos combined.

Culture Eats Planning for Breakfast

That's a fun old chestnut from the management consultancy world. But it's true here as well. Much as when you are mountain biking, what you focus on is what becomes your future. If you see a rock in the middle of your path, the surest way to hit that rock — and possibly go flying over your handlebars — is to stare at that rock, trying to be sure to miss it. The best way to miss the rock is to focus your attention *somewhere else.*

If everyone keeps focusing on the rocks in their individual paths — the snarky "fact checking" websites which confirm that your political opponents are not only possessed of a different philosophy but are actually *wrong!* — then the only thing we'll get is an increasingly hate filled nation falling apart at the seams.

Your best bet is to follow my every word religiously.

Your second best bet is to examine everything — including this book — with deep skepticism. Go back to original principles and right and wrong. Have a gander at the Ten Commandments. Read, re-read and memorize the Constitution, the Declaration of Independence and both the *Federalist Papers* and the *Anti-Federalist Papers.* Check out the authors who influenced our Founding Fathers.

Read whatever you like. I ask you to think about framing your view of the USA in a positive light — as an ongoing experiment in self-government, assuming the *best* of your fellow citizens and the *worst* of your elected officials.

There are solid reasons to provide constructive criticism about *how* we govern ourselves, and also right now as I am asserting, *whether* we govern ourselves, or have been hijacked by a sliver of self-interested people who have rigged the system in their favor.

This entire book is a refutation of *Whataboutism.*

Let's get back to basics — imperfect humans striving to attain a perfect operating system under which we can all get along.

Figure 34: The Republic is beset on all sides by dangers and difficulties to overcome

Chapter 30: Tax Policy for a Just and Prosperous Society

Perhaps the only thing Americans of all political flavors can agree on is that general prosperity for all people is a desired outcome of economic activity. Some want to get to that widespread prosperity through a bewildering array of "government programs" based on taxing the stuffing out of everyone who performs actual value-added work and some want to achieve prosperity through much greater personal freedom, minimal government employment and low, low taxes. But even the most ardent "Democratic Socialist" at heart believes that "more stuff" lies at the heart of "social justice."

Aristotle might disapprove of my laying out the *dénoument* of my tax argument straight out of the gate, rather than building up to a dramatic catharsis, but time is short, so here's my suggestion for our nation's tax policy going forward:

1. Elimination of the entirety of the current Federal tax code, including the insanity of taxing citizens working outside of the US
2. Corporate tax rate = 5%
3. Individual federal tax rate = 15%
4. No double taxation of corporate dividends.
5. Capital gains tax rate = 5%, with one's asset cost basis indexed to inflation, so a long-term investor is not penalized for "gains" which are not real. Period. With unlimited carryforwards from capital losses.
6. Wind down Social Security, replacing all transfer payments directly to an IRA or 401(k) controlled by individual workers *or* the minimum of mandatory Superannuation-type structures, which are fully funded by defined contributions.
7. Abolition of *all* non-value-creating taxes, e.g. payroll taxes. Medicare and Medicaid will sunset along with government-managed Social Security.
8. No more taxation of inheritance within families.
9. Abolition of all Federal transfer block payments to States.

There have been lots of ideas floated about tax reform, many of which contain seeds of useful ideas, and many of which are just awful. Laurence Kotlikoff ran for President as a write-in candidate in 2016, which I think is delightful. I've read his 66-page book in which he lays out the case for his Presidency, based in hard facts about many of the same headaches which prompted me to write this book.

Kotlikoff and I part ways over taxation, and I think it's because he's spent so much time doing very real work with very real governments, that he's lost sight of some of the critical behavioral aspects to taxation systems based on consumption and wealth taxes, versus our current focus on income taxation.

I urge you to read his book to compare his thoughts to mine. I have two main concerns about his tax plan – one, a VAT-style taxation structure violates one of the best single principles about *just* taxation I've ever heard. Ronald Reagan – despite the caricatures promulgated incessantly by a non-reflective, knee-jerk, groupthink press corps and whiny college professors – was a man of deep thought and firmly-held convictions. Reagan's conviction was that whatever level of taxation we as a political body come to, what should be *inviolable* is that the level of taxation *is perfectly clear and simple to understand.*

A VAT ("value added tax," because there is no end to the linguistic irony in the tax code) hides multiple layers of taxation in a daisy chain of continually additive costs. That lack of clarity hinders people from understanding where and when taxes are being extracted from them. In addition, that lack of clarity is an invitation to political mischief down the road; 'tis easier by far to add 0.25% to a hidden VAT tax, which could get "buried" in general cost of living price rises, than to state the case clearly to the public that an income tax raise of 0.25% is required of *everyone.*

Second, Kotlikoff wants to replace the income tax and capital gains tax structures now with a consumption tax and a non-avoidable inheritance tax. The idea of a tax on assets is a terrible one – if you think income tax reporting is invasive, just wait for the IRS to have the authority to peer literally into every crevice of your property and personal life, searching for property you own. The invasiveness does not end with the *detection* of your assets – it then relies on non-market-based "appraisals" of your assets, which as billions of examples across America in relation to housing prices has shown, is an invitation to massive fraud, corruption and breakdown of social trust.

I have so many favorite tax-related one-liners emanating like swamp gas from the Beltway, that I am hard pressed to choose an absolute winner. But if I *had* to do so, it would be the repetitive, intentionally-hypnotic way in which Biden, Harris, Obama, Reid, Schumer et alia keep saying how "we" – meaning your Political Overlords – are going to *"ask"* the "rich" – which rapidly becomes "everyone" as the AMT showed – to "pay a little more" in income taxes. When you "ask" something of someone, it is within their set of choices *not* to give you what you ask for. Therefore, this incessant, Orwellian phrasing does not even approach being the truth which is: "We are going to put you in jail and fine you into bankruptcy if you fail to pay the extra amounts we claim we are 'asking' you to pay."

And even that is only true if you happen to disagree with the Party currently in power politically. If you are, say, oh, I don't know, the *Ultimate Boss of the IRS,* Timothy Geithner or, I don't know, a racist parasite *and MSNBC "reporter"* Al Sharpton, they can let your tax foibles slide. The Biden Presidency gave us the spectacle of the President's son failing to report millions of dollars in income; as of this writing (March 2024), the Department of "Justice" was still trying to give him a slap on the wrist for an amount of back taxes that sent the actor Wesley Snipes to prison.

The years since Eisenhower have been chock full of value-subtracting, fiscally irresponsible and wildly immoral parasites who have driven our nation into absolute bankruptcy. They have been lying to us for so long that their biggest desire has come true; the people have tuned out, leaving the Political Class to steal more and more with ultimate impunity.

For a painfully irritating period during the Obama Years, the media and politicians kept waving around the "Buffett Rule" named after one of the most hypocritical cynics ever to pay money for political favors. In return for Obama (eventually Biden) canceling the Keystone Pipeline which was designed to bring thousands of jobs and millions of barrels of oil from Canada to the US Gulf Coast, all of which benefited Buffet's holdings in BNSF Railroad,[254] the *prime beneficiary* of the canceled pipeline, Warren pulled his disinterested

American grandpa act, wagging a finger at how rich folks like himself pay a lower effective rate in taxes than his secretary.

Well, there are many responses that spring to mind, but the first is, since Obama and everyone is just "asking" people to pay more taxes, why cannot the Sage of Omaha *choose* to pay a higher rate? After all, he thinks it is more socially just that the government spend his money the way bureaucrats and politicians believe best, so why wait for something as slow-moving as Congress to "ask" for the cash from his wallet? There is nothing stopping him, or Barbara Streisand or Nancy Pelosi or anyone else for that matter, from whipping out a checkbook and sending a big whack of dollars to the US Treasury.

They'll cash the checks.

But Warren has not done that and will not do that. Quite the contrary – he has donated vast chunks of his wealth to his pal Bill Gates's Foundation. I've got no problem with that – Warren is probably right that the Gates Foundation will put his money to better use than the Federal government. What I've got a problem with is his vast, sweeping, immoral hypocrisy in encouraging the government to gouge more cash from my income at the same time as he is making sure that his does not receive the same treatment. Let's fix this all at once by implementing my suggestions or others in a similar, simplifying structure.

GAAP Accounting and Transparent, Rules-Based Budgeting

The best way to put constraints on government spending is to make government live by the rules most Americans (except those who've learnt to game the taxpayer-funded system) live by. There is a *great* model in use successfully by the Chilean government, at the behest of *Los Chicago Boys,* the fine, upstanding economic advisers that provided various Latin American governments the fiscal tools required to rein in their own unsustainable, runaway spending orgies. Using the Chilean government model and a robust form of transparent GAAP, that means this is the amount of cash the government has to blow in a given year is capped. Period. Capped for real, not as in *"oh, we're hitting the debt ceiling, so now we've got to vote to raise it."*

There is an intimate relationship between taxation, sound money, true fiscal restrictions on government spending and the Just Society. Your American family must live within your means or suffer terribly. I suggest one of the firmest, non-negotiable points of the proper relationship of the government to the people is a no-exceptions rule that *everything* in the public sector must be *at least* as restrictive as what the private sector lives with.

---

[254] Disclaimer: Warren is a very clever man, with a slew of aggressive lawyers. I infer this "exchange" of political favors by examining the economics of moving crude by his BNSF rail instead of a pipeline, which President Biden finally deliver on his first day in office in 2021.

Throughout the 1990s and 2000s, the US Federal Government spent not like drunken sailors – who after all eventually cannot drink any more whiskey or bed any more whores before their ship leaves port – but rather like, er, the Federal Government. In essence, they party like rock stars on *your* dime – to keep the analogy going, as the sailors were getting herded (broke and syphilitic) back onto their ships, the rock stars had their managers call the hotel desk to say they're keeping the Emperor Suite and could they please send up another case of Champagne and a kilo of blow to go with the fresh round of call girls? These chuckleheads spent and spent and continue to spend and whenever they run into the "legal debt ceiling," which would mean they would have to live within their means... they vote to raise the ceiling.[255]

Wow. How much fun would it be to call Visa from the Ferrari dealership where your card had just been declined to say "Hey, raise my limit so I can drain the rest of this bottle of tequila and then take this hot red Quattro out for a spin in the desert!"

That spending was just a precursor to the *insanity* of devaluing the dollar and forcing hundreds of millions of people to be imprisoned in their homes and thrown out of work, all in the name of a non-existent threat called the Wuhan Virus in the first few months of 2020.

Hypocrisy in politics is nothing new, but what I love from a zaniness standpoint is the 1:1 correlation between folks who claim to adhere to "Keynesian" principles by shoveling "public stimulus" cash at the nation in hopes of stimulating economic activity, but who actively oppose leaving the cash in individuals' hands in the first place. If a healthy economy is created by – in their own words – driving demand in the form of individual spending, then it would follow logically that people having more cash to spend would be a good thing. Therefore, lower taxes which result in people having more cash to spend would be a "Keynesian stimulus."

Yet... they never seem to want that, because that takes away their true intention, which is centralizing control, which thrives when individuals suffer and "need" the government to "help" them. They don't want you to have more money in your pocket; they want to dictate everything you do, say and increasingly, think.

Super Committee – Oh boy! – on mass privatization asset sales

As part of right-sizing the government, we need to pay off accrued debts. This is a very complex topic which will require some devoted public-private partnership work in the near term. We need to sell off all the assets directly related to the Departments we are defunding – HUD, Education, Labor, et alia. We also need to start privatization processes for the vast Federal holdings in each State, something on the order of $4+ trillion or so, all of

---

[255] On occasion, politicians even have tried to rein in spending. It has not worked. We need to demand real change or this will just go on in perpetuity until we are destroyed, impoverished nation with rich people living behind high walls with private armies with which to fend off the desperate masses.

which needs to be sold to American private investors or turned over to the States in which those assets sit.

The proceeds from all those asset sales must be committed to paying down the national debt – not "earmarked" so the funds can be diverted to some politician's pet project at 5pm on a sleepy summer Friday when no one is watching. After debt retirement to a certain level – to be determined as some leverage is a good thing – the proceeds from asset sales will be distributed pro rata as required to top up individual retirement funds created from the mess of the Social Security Administration.

There is not likely to be anything left over from those two commitments, but if there are funds, they are to go into a special reserve account against emergencies which are sure to arise.

Capital gains are the reward for prudence in life and saving

Class Warriors adept in the Politics of Jealousy *love* to attack capital gains. They do so for the same reason Willie Horton robbed banks – that's where the money is.

Biden's Jealousy Brigades propose a massive *doubling* of the capital gains tax rate! Since many States also steal from hard working investors by dipping their hands into what should be *your* profits, here's a summary map of how much theft you can expect if the Biden Jealousy Tax Proposals go through:

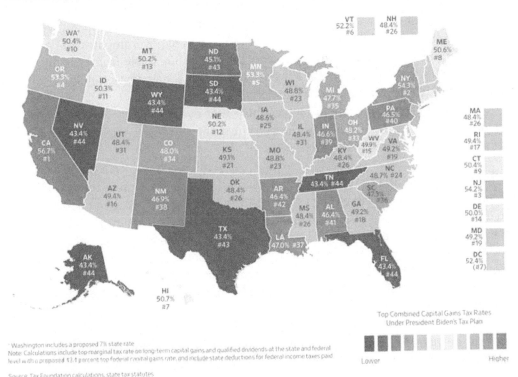

Confiscatory Taxes on Capital Gains
The combined state-federal tax rate on gains by state under Biden's proposal

475

To make clear what is meant by indexing your cost basis to inflation, consider the following example. Let's say your grandparents were immigrant factory workers who scrimped and saved to accumulate enough money to buy a two-family house in a tough area of a small city. Let's say it cost them $10,000 in 1970. Now it is mid-2022 and they want to sell it to provide educational funds for you. They are able to sell the building for $250,000 in today's dollars. Here are the different amounts of tax the government will confiscate from them, depriving you of funds for your education:

	Obama's Rate	Biden's Rate	Messina's Rate
Capital Gains Tax	23.80%	43.80%	5%
Tax Levied	$57,120	$105,120	
Inflation Adjusted*	$43,391	$79,854	$9,116

* To be clear, only Messina's tax proposal takes inflation into account; I provide the other two to show the mitigating impact on tax theft for Biden and Obama's rates if they accounted for inflation.

Remember, this was a building your grandparents owned for 52 years. This simplistic model does not take into account the annual property taxes and costs of maintenance, which if added to the inflation adjustment would definitely mean they *lost money* by owning this building, so their real capital gain would be zero. *And* this assumes they live in Florida, Texas or a tiny number of other States that don't grab their own chunk of your grandparents' investment as part of the "privilege" in living in such a wonderful place.

Whilst my proposal is eminently better for society than the wild levels of theft our various Political Overlords put into law, I am torn on *any* capital gains tax. From an overall societal view it is better to have an increasing capital stock, meaning investable funds available to pay for education or new ventures. Therefore an ideal rate might well be zero. But I balance that against the need to pay for the tiny bits of government we'll have left and there are lots of people who don't get paid via a salary but solely from investing. They're taking risk with their capital to make a living, so the capital gains rate should be lower than the riskless salary rate, but for now, it shouldn't be at zero.

May we get to an economy so booming that everyone wants it to be switched to zero. My plan gets us there, whereas the current trajectory guarantees never-ending cycles of misery and authoritarian overreach.

Rather than do the right thing and have a *truly fair* tax system that provides *equal treatment for all citizens* rather than stealing from hard workers to give goodies to people who didn't earn them, the Biden Administration wants to steal from thrifty savers who if left alone could pay for their grandchildren's college costs. Instead of that nation full of self-sufficient families building a strong, resilient and free society, he'd rather have the Federal Government blow $1,800,000,000,000 on his ridiculous "American Families Plan."

Never mind the irony that decades of leftwing policies and propaganda demonstrate nothing but *hatred* for the traditional family. "Families" are evil propagators of traditional values which include strong religious bonds inimical to centralized State control, therefore they must be vilified and destroyed. Until it's public relations messaging time and suddenly they slap the label "Families" on one more piece of societally destructive Socialist insanity.

Breathtaking, isn't it? *Go big or go home* is the motto they're living by, I suppose. Wouldn't it be great when all these destroyers of value and political thieves just go home and leave us all alone? Tell your Congressional Representatives and Senators that if they fail to vote to enact Messina's Budget, you'll vote them out in the next cycle.

Remove the distortions created by the mortgage interest deduction

On your federal income tax form, you pay taxes on the interest you earn and get to deduct taxes on the interest you pay. The government constantly forces people who choose to rent the place they live in to subsidize the people who choose to borrow money via a mortgage to buy the place they live in. It's ridiculous and aside from once more benefiting one persistent lobbying group, it places appalling costs on citizens for no reason at all.

My wife and I discovered the sharp limits to one consistent story spun by the Federal Government (with the full support of the residential brokerage lobby), to wit that home ownership is an unqualified good. We had bought a lovely duplex in Brooklyn Heights and then as the economy went downhill (not to mention the debris from the World Trade Center snowing onto our balcony and into our home), we decided we wanted to sell, so we could move to Australia while I went to graduate school.

We delayed our trip to Sydney by a full year because we couldn't find a buyer. That's a year of our lives we'll never get back. Had we been renters, we could have let the lease run out and gotten on that flight twelve months sooner.

This is just one example of behavioral and economic distortions baked into the tax code. Strip them all away. No more deductions.

True Costs of Government

For a time, I sat on a volunteer, private-sector committee whose sole purpose was to assist one portion of the military procurement process become more efficient. The details of that panel – while not overly exciting – *are* subject to an NDA I signed, but luckily, the point I'm making applies universally to government finances. One of our committee members was the CEO of a large public company, prior to which he'd been a general in the Air Force. After one particularly exasperating conference call, he and I had lunch. He made the robust point that all the fiddling around the edges we could do would be meaningless if government agencies were immune to the real costs of doing their jobs.

The example he gave was one of the meetings we had at some truly glorious office space in a suburb of DC. Palatial lobby, spacious offices, cubicles scattered liberally through airy floor plans... All because the bureau inhabiting this lovely space *was not charged out of their own budget for its use.* The United Kingdom – not a bastion of robust, free market thought since, oh, maybe 1939 – realized the massive costs this sort of thing imposed on the taxpayer and changed their rules to make every government department pay *all* their costs.

Amazingly, the offices of UK bureaucracies overnight become far more efficient in use of space. It's just one more example of how unfettered, unaccountable government bureaucrats steal benefits and perquisites for themselves *from you, the American taxpayer,* benefits that they'd never get in the private sector and wouldn't be willing to pay for their employees if they happened to invest their own money into a business.

So please bear in mind that if we adopt the blueprint I am proposing, we'll be forcing GAAP accounting and fully-allocated costs on the few remaining bits of Leviathan that survive the coming Great Shrinkage. Imagine that! The government living within the same constraints – or tighter – than American families live within.

Simpson-Bowles 2010 National Commission

The opening lines set the stage right out of the gate. The first heading for the report headlined *The Looming Fiscal Crisis* begins thusly. "Our nation is on an unsustainable path. Spending is rising and revenues are falling short, requiring the government to borrow huge sums each year to make up the difference."[256] If I had a magical time machine to bring us back to the fiscal reality that prevailed back then, in December 2010, I would do so in an instant as the nation was in a far better place fiscally than it is today.

This commission was set up by Congress and the President to examine many of the precise issues I have chosen to focus on here all on my own.

Its recommendations were pretty clear. Cut spending drastically. Balance the budget. Marvelously enough, upon receiving these recommendations, Obama declined to follow the advice of the commission he set up. In true Stalinist or Chavismo style, the apparatchik gets to decide what conclusions he'll listen to.

Of all the myriad ways the government finds to waste our money, my personal favorites all tend to come with a heavy spoonful of irony mixed in, for example when the money and time being spent is specifically being spent to "fix" a problem, usually a problem that politicians don't think is a problem until enough of the disgruntled masses dare to complain pointedly.

To that end, I need to highlight one of my favorite parts of the 2010 budget supplementary tables, page 2, Table S-1:

FISCAL COMMISSION
The Administration supports the creation of a Fiscal Commission. The Fiscal Commission is charged with identifying policies to improve the fiscal situation in the medium term and to achieve fiscal sustainability over the long run. Specifically, the Commission is charged with balancing the budget excluding interest payments on the debt by 2015. The result is projected to stabilize the debt-to-GDP ratio at an acceptable level once the economy recovers. The magnitude and timing of the policy measures necessary to achieve this goal are subject to considerable uncertainty and will depend on the evolution of the economy. In addition, the Commission will examine policies to meaningfully improve the long-run fiscal

---

[256] The Moment of Truth. Final Report on the National Commission on Fiscal Responsibility and Reform, chaired by Alan Simpson and Erskine Bowles, December 2010

outlook, including changes to address the growth of entitlement spending and the gap between the projected revenues and expenditures of the Federal Government.

I have underlined the clause that makes this such a succulent citation. As any overstretched credit card user knows full well, one's annual budget is not balanced if one just chooses to ignore the costs of financing one's overspending ways. If you have post-tax, take-home income of $1,000 per month and your rent is $750 and food budget is $250 *and* the interest due on your ridiculous credit card balance is $250, then you're in serious trouble. You cannot wish away $250 of that $1,250 you owe... unless of course you're the Federal Government with a handy dollar printing press in your basement. The fact of indebtedness and the real costs associated with paying interest on previous expenses do not go away just by shoving fingers in one's ears and chanting "LA LA LA LA LA!" at the top of one's lungs.

Douglas Adams, the supreme documentarian who created the five-book trilogy *The Hitchhikers' Guide to the Galaxy* once said of deadlines that he very much liked them because he loved the wonderful swooshing noise they made as they flew by. Similarly, we've now blown right by 2015 and the "Fiscal Commission" of 2010 budget lore – if it ever existed, which I frankly lack the calming medicine to even investigate – clearly did not balance our budget, with or without taking into account debt service.

Swoosh.

Joint Select Committee on Deficit Reduction

The political theatre of The Deficit is fueled by committees and hearings and all sorts of things. You know that politicians are looking for extra juice when they have to call a committee a supercommittee. The in-hindsight hilariously misnamed Budget Control Act of 2011 created this wonderful SuperCommittee which was supposed to end in an agreement about how to reduce spending.

Much commentary on all sides was spent on lobbing ideological grenades at one another. The saddest part of this waste of taxpayer money is that *most of the politicians involved with this effort had no desire to see it succeed.* I mean, if the deficit magically were to disappear on its own, they'd certainly claim that their "work" had made it happen and now that we the sheeple have seen how they can make deficits disappear, we should be happy to let them print us back into a sea of red ink again.

The bipartisan Committee failed to reach any agreement by its November 2011 deadline, so the Disaster Train kept trundling towards national bankruptcy. If we could have the fiscal condition of late 2011 instead of the nightmare we have in late 2023, we'd all vote strongly hard "yes, please" to that proposal.

Plain Old Boring Regular Committee to End our Fiscal Mess

I am open to suggestion if someone has a better name for this. Rather than give it a grand title, let's keep it simple. For those in the corporate world, this will be familiar. It's a workout. We're taking a bankrupt organization which would not get an auditor's positive "going concern" opinion and we're going to restore the national corporation to fiscal health.

We will have to develop a process to pull together private sector (mainly) executives and a few (so they can tell us how stupid decisions got made) experienced folks from the public sector to form the Board.

That Board will be tasked with:

1. Making sure the wonderful folks at the IRS take full opportunity to relax because of their implementation of the wonderful new "Three Line Uniform Tax" process.
2. Overseeing in a transparent manner all the real estate and capital assets being sold off by the slew of departments being closed or resized.
3. Ensuring as part of that asset sale process that every single dollar of gross proceeds goes directly to paying off the national debt.
4. Evaluating all new proposed lease and other long-term agreements struck between the government and the private sector. No more sweetheart rental agreements 200% above market for decades. This last function smells like it could become a permanent bureaucracy, so it will perform this task for a set period, then shut down, leaving behind a set of best practices standards for future stewards of our fiscal health to be guided by.

A grateful nation will not begrudge the Board Members commemorative plaques as part of their service. Proud citizens should clamor to line up for the Solve The Problem Committee.

States have rights, including the right to self-sufficiency

At the start of this chapter, I laid out seven rules for improving the taxation system. Number 7 is the Abolition of all Federal transfer block payments to States.

Nothing could be more insane and pointless than the Federal government reaching into the pockets of individual taxpayers in each of the 50 States, and then turning around to send chunks of that cash *back* to the governments of those States. Sorry – it is insane from a public interest perspective, but the politicians in charge of handing you the holiday turkey they bought with *your* money love to play the role of smiling benefactor. Quit buying their act; none of them are giving you anything but *your* money.

Ofttimes, the only good to come out of any crisis is a heightened awareness amongst more of the citizenry of the glaring problems that in times of general prosperity and peace go unnoticed except by policy wonks and cranky critics like yours truly. During the wholly government-caused Wuhan Flu Panic Depression of 2020, governors of "blue states" – those mainly run by Democrats who have racked up truly startling amounts of debt on runaway deficit spending and unfunded pension liabilities to public sector unions – who during a booming economy *in December 2019 were facing financial ruin* suddenly saw light at the end of the tunnel. They could claim the Wuhan Shutdowns were the cause of their crazy debt loads, and therefore ask the Federal Government (that would be *you*, dear taxpayer, if you've not been paying attention thus far) to bail them out of decades of horrific overspending that had nothing to do with any economic destruction wrought politically using the fig leaf of a Chinese-lab-related coronavirus.

One colossal, lifelong professional parasite even wrote an opinion piece[257] in the *Wall Street Journal* claiming that because States and Cities cannot print their own money, "[e]very respected economist has made clear there is no alternative to further federal aid" to fix the budget problems in the States which overspent on their credit cards for decades.

Once again, I am forced to leave aside plucking low-hanging fruit like "Well, if every respected economist believes something, then we know with certainty that the exact opposite is true." Of course, all the economists *I respect* share my view that more destruction of the value of the US dollar is *a priori* a bad idea, so they would suggest States live with the consequences of their actions, in the same way, say, American families are forced to live with their decisions. What a radical idea I'm proposing in this book, that the government lives within its means. Crazy, I know.

Ravitch sings the same old boring song about "Well, blue states pay more in Federal taxes than they get back from Washington, so blue states have been 'subsidizing' red states for years, so now it's time to repay the favor." There are numerous problems with that, starting with those who whine about this particular state of affairs *are focusing on the wrong problem.* If in fact New York taxpayers sent $100 to the IRS and New York State only "got back" $50 of those dollars, then you'd expect New York politicians to be firmly in support of my Principle #7, so that the circular flow of cash stops. They have not of course, so one has to wonder why.

But the really fun part is that this particular Big Lie – there are so many! – is just that. A lie.

Let's start with how individuals calculate their Federal tax burden. Until President Trump fixed this problem, there was a weird part of the Federal taxation which meant fiscally prudent, low- or no-income-tax States were in fact already subsidizing profligate, high-income-tax States. It was called the SALT deduction for "State and Local Taxes." It worked like this:

In Florida, Citizen A makes $100,000 of taxable income. She pays $30,000 in income tax to the IRS. She writes that check and sends it off. Florida has no State income tax.

In California, Citizen B makes $100,000 of taxable income. Her calculated liability to the IRS is also $30,000, but wait, there's more! In California, she has to pay the State and, say, City of San Francisco $12,000 and $3,000 respectively. Under the SALT deduction, she only sends the IRS a check for ($30,000 - $12,000 - $3,000) = $15,000. So her total tax burden was still $30,000 even though she lives in a State with an income tax, whereas her Floridian counterpart earning the same does not.

---

[257] Ravitch, Richard, "Blue States Deserve Money From Washington," WSJ 19 July 2020. Mr. Ravitch served as chairman of the Empire State Development Corp. (1975-77), chairman of the Metropolitan Transportation Authority (1979-83) and lieutenant governor of New York (2009-10).

How, one might wonder, is that fair? Why is Citizen A contributing $30,000 to the functions of the Federal Government, national defense, bloated salaries for Congressional Parasites, et alia, while Citizen B only has to kick in half of her obligation as a United States citizen? Instead of having $60,000 with which to pay for office space, air conditioning and the legal racketeering of defined benefit pensions, the Treasury only has $45,000 when one of those two citizens does not pay her fair share.

Not only is it not fair, but it empowers the politicians ruining, er, running, high-tax States to avoid the political reckoning that comes from being – GASP! – *honest* with their citizens about the true costs of government.

When President Trump finally rectified this gross injustice, it had the salutary benefit of making high-income-tax States have open and honest discussions about the relative benefits and trade-offs to living in States with massive public sector budgets.

When SALT was removed, suddenly Citizen B in California had an income tax bill of $45,000, instead of $30,000. Now she has to pay her fair share of the costs of running the Federal Government *and* because she likes living in San Francisco, she has the added privilege of kicking in another $15,000 to finance her city and state budgets. She is delighted by this as she has (statistically) been voting for higher taxes and more spending her entire adult life, and now she's finally been empowered by Donald Trump's correction of tax policy to live her convictions.

I'm just kidding. It made Citizen B scream in outrage and the politicians in those States instantly try everything possible to keep the gravy flowing. They sued the IRS. I believe they tried suing the President. They came up with crazy ideas to suddenly recharacterize state income taxes as "charitable contributions" to the State, so that the former SALT deduction could magically reappear as a charitable deduction instead.

Once President Biden took the reins, the Democrats from solid blue states immediately started trying to reinstate the SALT deduction. One particularly appalling example – from an intellectual consistency standpoint, not from a self-interested political standpoint – are a Democrat from New York, Tom Suozzi and a Democrat from New Jersey, Josh Gottheimer, who are both pitching for a reinstatement of the SALT deduction.[258] The reason I point them out is not because they are any better or worse than their colleagues but because they belong to a party that constantly insists that government should have more money to spend. So why would they oppose their constituents paying their – accurately defined – fair share?

Enough. You get the point. Slash the size of government. Quit cycling money from citizens to The Swamp and (some portion) back to the States.

We'll have a stronger society.

---

[258] As of 5 May 2021

Chapter 31: Monetary Policy in Support of a Strong Economy and Nation

Oscar Wilde said that bad artists borrow and good artists steal. In that spirit, rather than craft my own introductory condemnation of the US Federal Reserve, I will quote wholly from James Rickards in his illuminating and well-reasoned *Currency Wars*, written in 2011:

> Ed Koch, the popular mayor of New York in the 1980s, was famous for walking around the city and asking passersby, in his distinctive New York accent, "How'm I doin'?" as a way to get feedback on his administration. If the Fed were to ask, "How'm I doin'?" the answer would be that since its formation in 1913 it has failed to maintain price stability, failed as a lender of last resort, failed to maintain full employment, failed as a bank regulator and failed to preserve the integrity of its balance sheet. The Fed's one notable success has been that, under its custody, the Treasury's gold hoard has increased in value from about $11 billion at the time of the Nixon Shock in 1971 to over $400 billion today. Of course, this increase in the value of gold is just the flip side of the Fed's demolition of the dollar. On the whole, it is difficult to think of another government agency that has failed more consistently on more of its key missions than the Fed. [259]

Aside from my taking issue with his assertion that it would be difficult to find other organs of government equal in its failure to produce positive outcomes for the American taxpayer, I agree with Rickards. He's a bright, thoughtful guy who has done quite a lot to attempt to educate public officials – among others – on the national security and indeed existential implications of poor monetary and fiscal policy decision making. He is not always right – none of us are – but on the big picture view of the colossal failure of the Federal Reserve model of central banking, he's spot on.

Rickards's most glaring error is his startling misunderstanding of the derivatives markets. In the midst of a rational essay about the benefits of breaking up large banks to avoid over-concentration of lending risks, he asserts that syndicates of smaller banks instead of massive monolithic banks mean that bank failure "would no longer be a threat. The costs of failure would become containable and would not be permitted to metastasize so as to threaten the system. The case for banning most derivatives is even more straightforward. Derivatives serve practically no purpose except to enrich bankers through opaque pricing and to deceive investors through off-the-balance-sheet accounting." [260]

Rickards is outright wrong about derivatives. I raise that issue here because it's critical to understand that global derivatives markets – from futures markets for wheat and oil, to interest rate and cross-currency swaps traded bilaterally between banks and

---

[259] Rickards, James, *Currency Wars*, 2011, Penguin USA, p176
[260] Rickards, James, *The Death of Money: The Coming Collapse of the International Monetary System*, Penguin 2014, p11

corporations – are the *richest* source of information regarding the *true* perception of the risks present in the economy at any point in time. Live, real-time derivatives markets tell both traders, corporate executives, investors and policy makers (if they are paying attention and understand what they are seeing) *precisely* the health of the economy both right now and its perceived future state of health from the point of view of the present.

As money *should* be the reflection of true value in the economy, the best possible data one can have to judge the true price of money (whether expressed in terms of ounces of gold or any intelligent indexed basket of broadly-used commercial goods) comes from the trillions of dollars of derivatives transactions entered into, traded, unwound or extended each and every day. What *should* a central bank if it is to exist at all be concerned with? The true value of money. Rickards is by no means alone in this weird sweeping condemnation of the greatest invention for risk pricing and transfer ever invented by mankind, as I touch on throughout this book.

Aside from that one blind spot about the proper role various kinds of derivatives transactions play in the capital markets – which I hope to help him rectify as soon as practicable, and which to be fair he may already have rectified in the intervening thirteen years – he is spot on right about the rampant abuses wrought by central banks manipulating fiat currencies.

Kings, potentates and now perpetually-elected-via-gerrymandering "democratic" governments have always been drawn to buying their way out of trouble with someone else's money. That includes creating and encouraging inflation, which is nothing more than a stealth tax on the wealth you worked hard to build, or manipulating interest rates to artificially raise or lower the return you earn on savings. The best defense against all this chicanery is to (a) put all levels of government on a strict and permanent spending diet and (b) to restrict sharply the functions of our monetary authority.

There is a critical relationship in the maintenance of a sound money supply between *objective* collection, collation and presentation of data in conjunction with a firm conviction that *predictability* and *freedom from political interference or social engineering fantasies* are the requirements for a dollar a person can trust.

The Federal government and the Federal Reserve have wandered through a glitteringly barren land of fantasy and figure-flattering mirror houses for so long that the inhabitants of Fedlandia no longer have any clue as to which false door leads back into reality. They play with numbers, issue and re-issue and revise and re-define things like "core inflation," "seasonally-adjusted employment," "unemployment" and "stimulus." None of this activity is tied to reality any more firmly than would a policy of reading slaughtered pigs' guts by moonlight on the National Mall every third New Moon.

There is a great saying that most economic decisions made today are the result of stale lessons received in classrooms thirty years prior.

Too many central bankers mistake the unit of account for the actual thing of value. Sir Mervyn King, former head of the Bank of England, wrote an interesting book[261] published in the summer of 2016. As I knew I'd have time on my hands between taking hikes in the

---

[261] King, Mervyn, *The End of Alchemy; Money, Banking, and the Future of the Global Economy,* 2016

clean mountain air and feeding expensive bait to wily lake trout and Northern pike, I took Sir Mervyn's effort with me to the Adirondacks. I am glad I was able to read his book in such soothing surroundings.

To his credit, I believe he tried hard in his career to make sense of the world around him and to work assiduously first as an academic then a central banker. He had the unenviable position of leading the Old Lady of Threadneedle Street during a tumultuous time in the markets. He had the further misfortune of living an intellectual life based on shaky assumptions, which led him and his ilk to attempt a skirting of financial disaster by colluding in the massive asset bloat of 2009-2024 (and counting).

I urge you to read his book. His comments are illuminating inasmuch as he was a direct eyewitness to and an active participant in many of the decisions made about the money supply and an increasingly activist role for central bankers during the 2007-08 Financial Crisis Caused by Decades of US Government Fair Lending Law and Related Stupid Policy. He makes some good points sprinkled in amongst others that I disagree with. One thing that he and I are squarely in lockstep about is the quasi-religious faith that many people place in central banks. This is nothing new and indeed forms the basic organizing principle of a great book targeted at a non-specialist audience, *Secrets of the Temple* written by William Greider in 1989. Monetary value like political authority is often enhanced by reference to divine sponsorship; arguably why the actual Federal Reserve building in the DC Swamp is built to resemble a Classical Greek temple.

Another problem with the Fed is – again – repeated throughout the public sector bureaucracy. You'll no doubt have heard the phrase that "Nature abhors a vacuum." In biological systems, that means that where life can exist, it will – you will not find a random patch of desert of 144 square feet smack dab in the middle of a rain forest. That patch of ground 12 feet on a side might be cleared by a forester, but it will not remain barren; Nature will recolonize it.

In places like the Fed, if a job opening is created, *it will be filled.* Whether or not there exists a person capable of doing that job properly for the benefit of the US taxpayer is not even a consideration. Neel Kashkari is a phenomenal example of this issue. I feel free to pick on him because our career trajectories crossed and bumped into each other back during the value-destructive TARP episode. As of 4Q20, he was the President of the Minneapolis Federal Reserve. Back in 2008, he had been selected by then-Secretary of the Treasury Hank Paulson to run the TARP program.

We crossed paths because he commented to a reporter in 4Q08 than no one at the Treasury Department had the requisite skills to value and then negotiate the purchase of the "Troubled Assets" that were to be purchased to "Relieve" pain at the banks who owned those assets. As I *do have* the requisite skills to value and risk-assess a portfolio, I reached out to the Treasury Department to help my country in its hour of need.

I will summarize a three-month long saga to say that after a few rounds of interviews, I was the top candidate chosen by the Treasury staff to run the TARP program, with my final interview held in early January 2009. The Treasury Director who had been championing my candidacy said, "We're policy wonks. If we're going to be sitting across the table from a$$&*%s from Goldman Sachs negotiating purchase prices, we'd prefer to have our own a$$&*% doing the negotiating. No offense."

I said, "No offense taken. It's why I called."

My final interview was with a guy who was "Acting Chief Operating Officer" of the TARP program. He was on loan from his day job as the General Counsel of another Federal department. His identity is unimportant; his role as a public sector *lawyer* and bureaucrat are critical to what happened next. We were scheduled to speak at 4pm. I waited until 4:20 for the phone to ring, then called his office to follow up. His assistant picked up the phone and when I explained why I was calling, she said in a tone that I *wish* I could convey in writing, "Well, *he's a very important man.*"

Nonplussed by a response I would never have received from the CEO's office at a major private corporation, I said, "Well, if the very important man would like to call me within the next ten minutes, I'll be here. After that, I won't." He did call me back and the discussion went off the rails rapidly. I was calling to take a serious pay cut to help my country execute a plan which was stupid on its face, but which I could at least help get taxpayers the best possible result from. The "very important man" who knew nothing about finance thought he was interviewing an underling begging for a job. After five minutes, I was interviewing him, asking what the team was doing as every day of the crisis mattered. To each of a series of six or seven questions, he responded, "We're waiting to see what the incoming (Obama) Administration wants to do."

I was probably intemperate in my response, asking pointedly what on earth they were all busy *doing*, since every question was met with the response they were waiting on Obama's guidance. I expressed my frustration at that non-answer, saying "I doubt very much the community organizer is going to have any practical insights into pricing shonky debt portfolios," and he snapped at me, "Everyone here is working really hard!"

My response: "So is a gerbil on a wheel."

That answer combined with the very important man's assertion that I'd probably have to liquidate all my private investments for the privilege of getting underpaid to attempt to put a Band-Aid on the gory gash Congress had ripped into the financial system, pretty much killed the interview right there.

I didn't get the job and apparently Neel had the foresight to get out of the building as fast as he could.

Clearly no one else qualified showed up, as they instantly abandoned TARP as written into law – which was based on buying securities from banks that didn't want them – and just decided on no legal basis I can discern to shovel billions of dollars onto banks and insurance companies' balance sheets instead.

From his office atop the Minneapolis Fed, Mr. Kashkari has done *nothing* but spout utter nonsense. His latest and greatest ridiculous "achievement" – *so far* – has been to jump on the idiotic Democrat bandwagon about shutting down the entire US economy in hyper overreaction to the spread of the Wuhan Virus.

"The problem with the March-to-May lockdown was that it was not uniformly stringent across the country. For example, Minnesota deemed 78 percent of its workers essential," Kashkari and his co-author Michael Osterholm wrote in – of course – an August 2020 opinion piece in *New York Pravda*.[262]

---

[262] Should the reader wish to get a refresher on fact-free, irrational propaganda posing as "news," she

486

No, Neel and Mike. The problem with the 2020 March-to-May lockdown is that it was complete and total nonsense in the first place, should never have been forced upon the American people and should result in armed rebellion should these clowns try it again. Of course, with the perspective granted by living until the *following May* 2021, with the insanity of California, New York, Michigan and other states mismanaged by tinpot dictator fools, whose States had by that point been shut down going on 14 months, the opinion piece's words were even dumber.

What is it about Minneapolis? Perhaps we should form a commission to test the groundwater.

In any event, all that fun diversion into Neel Kashkari's career aside, why is a central bank officer opining on draconian social controls instead of paying close attention to the value of the dollar? I am always willing to let slide mistakes made in good faith, but the moment he chose to shove his oar into advocating for utterly destructive and insane – not to mention illegal – home imprisonment and closing of schools, that makes his terrible judgment fair game. He's not remotely alone in promulgating these awful policies, but this is the section on the Fed, so he gets some immortality in these pages.

The Fed Needs to Focus on Monetary Policy Exclusively

We need to repeal the Humphrey-Hawkins Full Employment Act signed by Jimmy Carter in 1978. (Lest I digress, I would assume that the country would be better off if we were to repeal *all* legislation signed by Carter, but I'll leave that fun project to someone else to put data behind...)

Considerations extraneous to a sound money supply should play *no role* at all in what a central bank does. All the stuff the Fed staffers busy their heads with they should quit fretting about. Employment levels in particular *have nothing to do with monetary value and therefore should have no bearing on monetary policy*. It was one more holdover from Keynes's error-filled analysis of a particular state of affairs that he and others mistakenly broadened into universal principles.

---

should feel free to check *New York Pravda* out at www.nytimes.com.

487

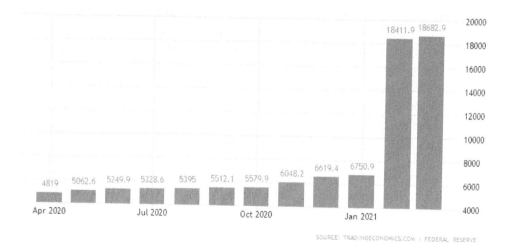

SOURCE: TRADINGECONOMICS.COM | FEDERAL RESERVE

Coming into the Government-Caused, Unnecessary, Totally Optional Wuhan Virus Hysterical Panic Depression of 2020, the US money supply and fiscal condition were already totally awful. They took that awful set of conditions and went hog wild on a path towards complete monetary and societal collapse.

The chart above shows the increase of the M1 money supply pumped out to the US economy, on the idiotic belief that (a) any shutdowns due to a seasonal virus were a good idea and (b) that once said shutdowns were put in place that necessitated 14+ months and counting of shoveling free cash at people.

Since the Government-Caused Through Decades of Stupid Housing Law Financial Crisis of 2007-08, the Fed spent years monetizing the debt, and *shoveling* free revenue at the banks, all of this done, mind you, under the Obama Administration whose droning mantra was about how they were trying to help the little people and make everyone adhere to "common sense rules of the road." The Trump Administration *should have* demanded the immediate unwinding of "quantitative easing," but they also failed to do so, even though Treasury Secretary Steve Mnuchin *should* have learned better at Goldman Sachs.

Given how much those smelly losers made life in downtown Manhattan unpleasant for my family and neighbors, it's miraculous that on this issue, Occupy Wall Street and I are on the same page about the Fed bailing out failed big institutions.

The previous paragraph reminds me of why I've written this book and why I'm doing my best to make highly complex, often mind-numbingly boring processes crystal clear to my fellow citizens. It is *not* because I am "looking down" on anyone – quite the contrary. It's because I know that *the Political Class* is doing the condescension, and is doing so with focused, self-interested purpose. Biden, Harris, Obama, the Clintons, Pelosi and all the rest of them are *relying* upon what they do to be so boring and complex that everyone's eyes will just glaze over, so the Politicians can get back to lining their own pockets and sticking the rest of us with the bill. Those few politicians who *do* actually want to right the monetary ship – Ron Paul, Rand Paul, Josh Hawley and Donald Trump among them – are so busy fighting other, ancillary and – dare I say it? – *derivative* issues that this one, core issue keeps getting punted down field for "someone else" to deal with.

"Monetizing the debt" means that the Federal Reserve is showing up to Treasury auctions and buying huge chunks of the Treasury bonds being sold. That means that the government is buying debt from itself. How good would it be if you were able to print your own money to pay off your credit card bill? It's even better, because to keep the analogy real, once you printed your own money to pay MasterCard, *you then stuck your neighbors with the bill.*

George Shultz and some of his pals wrote a succinct little essay in September 2012.[263] During the 2011 fiscal year, 75% of the debt issued by the Treasury was bought by the Federal Reserve. That's like saying, "My company is doing really well. I sold products for $100 in revenue out of my left hand and my right hand paid $75 of that, so I'm doing great!"

Bill Gross of PIMCO wrote a piece[264] in October 2012 trying to give some color to the investor universe about just how awful the US's fiscal position is.

> America's abusive tendencies can be described in more ways than an 11% fiscal gap and a $1.6 trillion current dollar hole which needs to be filled. It's well publicized that the U.S. has $16 trillion of outstanding debt, but its future liabilities in terms of Social Security, Medicare, and Medicaid are less tangible and therefore more difficult to comprehend. Suppose, though, that when paying payroll or income taxes for any of the above benefits, American citizens were issued a bond that they could cash in when required to pay those future bills. The bond would be worth more than the taxes paid because the benefits are increasing faster than inflation. The fact is that those bonds today would total nearly $60 trillion, a disparity that is four times our publicized number of outstanding debt. We owe, in other words, not only $16 trillion in outstanding, Treasury bonds and bills, but $60 trillion more. In my example, it just so happens that the $60 trillion comes not in the form of promises to pay bonds or bills at maturity, but the present value of future Social Security benefits, Medicaid expenses and expected costs for Medicare. Altogether, that's a whopping total of 500% of GDP, dear reader, and I'm not making it up. Kindly consult the IMF[265] and the CBO[266] for verification. Kindly wonder, as well, how we're going to get out of this mess.

So... the Draft Dodger Generation managed to take the sacrifice and hard work of the arguably-accurately-described Greatest Generation and the generations before them and drove the country literally into insolvency. Now these whiny brats are retiring in droves and think that *we* – all the post-Baby Boomers – are going to keep shoveling cash at them *and* pay off all their debts.

The Greatest Generation was indeed that in an overall sense, because for all his zany Socialist leanings, FDR – or at least his Treasury Secretary Morgenthau – insisted on paying for WWII through increased taxation and quasi-compulsory personal savings via the war bond program. They did *not* a la Bush II *cut taxes* during wartime and crank up the monetary printing presses to pay for their foreign-soil-liberation adventures.

-----

[263] Shultz, George et alia, "The Magnitude of the Mess We're In," *Wall Street Journal*, 16 September 2012

[264] Gross, Bill, "The U.S. debt damage," 9 Oct. 2012, originally published on PIMCO website

[265] International Monetary Fund

[266] Congressional Budget Office

When the Fed buys Treasury debt, it depresses the yield on the bonds and notes issued by the Treasury Department. Indeed, Fed Governor Marriner Eccles in the early 1950s was insistent upon ending the WWII wartime interest-rate peg, because in a world of fiat currency: "As long as the Federal Reserve is required to buy government securities at the will of the market for the purpose of defending a fixed pattern of interest rates established by the Treasury, it must stand ready to create new bank reserves in an unlimited amount. This policy makes the entire banking system, through the action of the Federal Reserve System, an engine of inflation."[267]

The "good" news in all of this is that misery loves company, whether or not it is actually *useful* to be miserable with others. The European Central Bank also has been chasing down the rabbit hole of wishful thinking with their own quantitative easing. The *fabulous* part of the ECB's decision in Spring 2015 was to combine flooding easy (cheap) money into the banking sector *while simultaneously* raising capital requirements on those same banks! That ensures that the flood of money will stay trapped on bank balance sheets, rather than performing the reserve-based intent of driving additional loan generation. There are three ways to boost capital reserves in a bank: sell more equity in the bank, cut dividends and make fewer loans. Those are the choices, all of which result in lower valuation for the bank and fewer business-supporting loans being made.

The same people who claim to want job creation do almost everything in their power to ensure that no economic growth has a chance of happening.

As I tell every employee I hire and every client I advise: there are a few areas of human existence in which *acceptance* of reality is the requisite first step on the path to positive progress. Those three areas are alcoholism, Buddhism and finance. There are likely to be others, but the point is that unless one accepts objective reality, one is always going to be *fixing the wrong problem*.

The first major thing we need to accept, and the Fed needs to acknowledge is that money in and of itself *is nothing*. Money is a unit of account describing transactions in the underlying real economy. Its role as a "store of value" evaporated with the abandonment of the gold standard. Its true role as a "medium of exchange" is metadata referring to deeper underlying economic value.

Lastly, money is international, but currency is national. However one conceives of "money" – and Lord Rothschild famously said that very few people understand the true nature of money, and none of those people have much of it – it is vital to understand that true money is accepted everywhere; currency is bound by borders.

Whatever final form our new US Central Bank is to have, we must insist that it hews to the following clear, simple principles so Americans can once more have a currency that serves society rather than the other way around.

Principle 1: Interest rates are to be observed, not manipulated.

---

[267] Marine Eccles quote

This is core to a true reform of the Fed. We don't allow the government to set the price of a share of Microsoft, Ford Motors or any other equity price. There is no "reference equity price" below or above which other shares of stock are to trade. So why do we allow the Fed to sit amongst themselves, pondering spreadsheets and – to a greater or lesser extent, depending on Fed Governor – the political desires of the folks on The Hill or in the Oval Office to determine in hieratic fashion what "the price" of lent capital is to be?

It's madness.

As if being insanely illogical wasn't reason enough to abolish a governmental policy – as thousands of years of governmental history proves – how about the fact that this ridiculous ability of a few boring folks sitting around a private table get to set the price of capital and therefore value for not just Americans but the whole world?

> Trading on Christmas Eve was thin and markets closed early, but maybe bank liquidity isn't what investors are worried about. Stocks have fallen four straight trading days since the Federal Reserve again raised its benchmark interest rate and signaled no change in the pace of its quantitative tightening. Since the Fed's announcement at 2pm Wednesday, the S&P 500 had fallen 8.2% and the Dow Jones average by 8.1% through Monday.[268]

The editors are pointing out the impacts of unwinding the unprecedented interference in free markets that Ben Bernanke euphemistically called "quantitative easing," but my broader point is that if the Fed did not have the authority to *set interest rates,* then none of the paragraph above would mean anything. It could well have aggregated data across the private markets regarding the cost of debt capital and *reported* a change in interest rates and could even have opined on the future course of interest rates. But that's not the same as setting those rates.

It is remarkably simple to *report* an observed cost of debt capital across the credit spectrum, from which an index could be published which would serve as the basis for a range of credit prices, including a desired range of the federal funds rate. The federal funds rate is the price at which banks will willingly lend one another their reserves and is an underpinning of contemporary monetary policy. There are many other rates that matter to markets – prime rates, intraday repo, cross-currency swaps pairs – that are all deeply informative about the market's perception of risk and the cost of capital. The data gathering, cleansing, aggregating, reporting and analytics capabilities are all well within our reach. Frankly, it's all Bloomberg does all day long, along with Dow Jones, Reuters, Markit and myriad other data analytics companies.

If they are not observing millions of educated market professionals deciding the cost of capital all day long, what does the Fed currently do in order to arrive at the interest rates they then force on the world? The modeling gnomes at the Fed try to manufacture a sighting of three theoretical and unobservable phenomena and one quasi-measurable phenomenon: (T1) the "potential" output of the economy, which is then compared to (QM1) the "actual" output of the economy to determine the (T2) difference between the

---

[268] Editorial Board, "Overconfidence at the Fed," *Wall Street Journal,* 24 December 2018

actual and potential output of the economy, to then set the (T3) natural/neutral rate of interest which would make QM1=T1.

They pin this calculated difference between one really-hard-to-measure thing (actual economic output/QM1) and one nonexistent thing (potential economic output/T1) on a culprit, which is another theoretical and unobservable (whether it exists or not I'd be happy to discuss over a drink in front of a fire on a long winter night) thing called the neutral real rate of interest (T3). After performing this crazy, religious operation, the Fed then sets a target range for the federal funds rate, which is supposed to nudge the economy in the direction of the theoretical potential economic output.

Oh, and since Carter, that nudging is also supposed to result in "full employment," though of course they fudge that number away from the only *empirically-observable* measure (quite simply: Actual Unemployment = (# of people employed)/(# of people of employment age)) to another wholly fantastical figure with no grounding in real reality as understood by your basic, educated human

Wow.

Put that way – and I am proud of having distilled down thousands of pages into two paragraphs – it's crackerjack nutty.

In August of 2016, the Federal Reserve Bank of Kansas hosted the world's central bankers in Jackson Hole, Wyoming. Leaving aside the idea that perhaps even non-Keynesians would think that hosting thousands of bigwigs and their staff in an economically-struggling area would be better for Americans than enriching the hotel owners in One-Percenter-Land, let's focus on what the hierophantic priesthood and its academic acolytes were attempting to "do" at this Rocky Mountain Love-In.

One strong faction in the economics academic community was pushing for a revision of the inflation target from 2% to 3-4%. That's right, kids, rather than pondering how – or indeed *if* – central banks can do *anything positive* to impact economic growth, having taken interest rates to zero, having flirted with negative interest rates *to charge "savers" for the privilege of storing their cash in a bank*, those who believe money itself it a real thing versus the measure of an actual real thing now want to make goods and services *more expensive* for people suffering under low wage growth. Making already expensive, stress-filled lives more expensive is somehow magically supposed to grow the economy.

Wow.

Put that way – and I am proud of having distilled down thousands of pages and hundreds of hours of on-the-taxpayer open-bar cocktail chatter at $900-a-night Wyoming resort hotels into one paragraph, albeit with one really long sentence – it's crackerjack nutty.

Basically, I'm looking for a way to explain the Fed's actions which is *not* crackerjack nutty.

Stepping away from polemic and back to clear analysis, I am helped by Kevin Warsh, a former member of the Federal Reserve board, as of August 2016 a distinguished visiting fellow in economics at Stanford University's Hoover Institution.

> A change in inflation targets would also add to the growing list of excuses
> that rationalize the economic malaise: the persistent headwinds from the crisis of

the prior decade, the high-sounding slogan of "secular stagnation," and the convenient recent alibi of Brexit.

A numeric change in the inflation target isn't real reform. It serves more as subterfuge to distract from monetary, regulatory and fiscal errors. A robust reform agenda requires more rigorous review of recent policy choices and significant changes in the Fed's tools, strategies, communications and governance.

Two major obstacles must be overcome: groupthink within the academic economics guild, and the reluctance of central bankers to cede their new power.

First, the economics guild pushed ill-considered new dogmas into the mainstream of monetary policy. The Fed's mantra of data-dependence causes erratic policy lurches in response to noisy data. Its medium-term policy objectives are at odds with its compulsion to keep asset prices elevated. Its inflation objectives are far more precise than the residual measurement error. Its output-gap economic models are troublingly unreliable.[269]

Can I get an AMEN?

As the Treasury will set auctions in line with Fed recommendations, it's actually quite simple to turn that information-discovery mechanism 180 degrees around. Treasury auctions of all tenors should be open to all qualified bidders. No more special Primary Dealers – what was once needed is no longer, and only acts as a cartel system to ensure some banks make profits out of an intermediation function that most if not all market participants do not require. I myself have a couple of pieces of advanced exchange software sitting in my portfolio we could deploy inside of six months to bring the wonders of crowdfunding to Treasury auctions.

Principle 2: The Fed may not monetize the national debt

This is fancy talk for saying the Central Bank can play a role in smoothing capital flows among market participants, but it has no business owning a balance sheet chock full of the US Government's own bonds. If private entities or other sovereign nations choose to judge the US Government a good credit risk, they will show up and bid at Treasury auctions. If the cost of that borrowing rises too high, they'll – gasp! – not be able to steal any more money from future generations to fund their keep-me-elected-goody-grab-bag sleaze anymore.

Again, this is one more simple change which would fuel a virtuous cycle where *truly* civic-minded individuals choose to enter government service as a *duty* performed willingly for their community.

The Fed's unprecedented balance sheet containing US obligations is a result of decisions taken during the 2007-2009 crisis. Tim Geithner describes discovering in 2004 the – to him – surprising limitations on what the Fed could so "in a crisis" when he peered into the New York Fed binder known internally as "the Doomsday Book:"

---

[269] Warsh, Kevin, "The Federal Reserve Needs New Thinking; Its models are unreliable, its policies erratic and its guidance confusing. It Is also politically vulnerable," Wall Street Journal Opinion, 24 August 2016

In addition to its monetary policy instruments, the Fed could lend to institutions that needed cash in a crisis — but only if we thought they were fundamentally solvent, with their assets worth more than their liabilities. We did have additional authority in "unusual and exigent circumstances" through Section 13(3) of the Federal Reserve Act, but the Fed hadn't invoked it since the Great Depression, and even that break-the-glass, only-in-extremis power was severely constrained. Under 13(3), the Fed could conceivably lend to a non-bank we deemed solvent, but only if it was in such deep trouble that no one else would lend to it, and even then only if we could secure collateral that could plausibly cover our exposure. So we wouldn't be able to take much risk, and we wouldn't have much preemptive power to help firms before they were past the point of no return, *even if we thought the financial system depended on it.* [emphasis mine] That struck me as a problem, too.[270]

Frankly, had the Fed stuck to those pre-crisis limitations, we'd all be better off. These core banking principles predated Geithner's grandparents' conception and were described clearly by Walter Bagehot[271] in 1873 with the publication of his brilliant work *Lombard Street – A Description of the Money Market.* Country banks would sell discounted notes to the big banks in London, getting liquidity to smooth the engines of agricultural trade. All central bank liquidity provision had to be done on the basis of real economic activity. The further away from real assets (real collateral) a banking system strays, the greater the chance for explosive disaster becomes.

The very fact that Geithner thought problematic all these rational controls on risk-taking by the taxpayers' central bank goes a long way to explaining the insane expansion of Fed powers that took place when a Federal-government-caused crisis reared its head. I emphasized his comment about the financial system "depending" on a bailout of some kind, as a reminder that not thirty pages earlier in the very same book, he described the limitations of ever trying to predict the future.

Any claim about sudden new policy changes being what's "absolutely necessary" for the "financial system" should be greeted with the deepest skepticism, and this is no exception.

Unsurprisingly, these principles reinforce one another. For example, the massive buying of Treasury securities by the Fed directly impacts the level of interest rates. FDR back in 12 May 1933 signed into law the utterly G-d-awful Agricultural Adjustment Act, which contained in it Title III, known as the Thomas Amendment drafted by Oklahoma Senator Elmer Thomas.

Senator Thomas and his enabling Socialist-in-a-Wheelchair with the Mighty Pen tried to fight the very real causes of farm state economic collapse — the sharply declining prices of agricultural commodities and therefore farmland after the Great War ended and European farms began producing again in 1920 which meant an 80% reduction in US

---

[270] Geithner, p.82
[271] Walter Bagehot (born February 3, 1826, Langport, Somerset, England—died March 24, 1877, Langport)

agricultural exports from its 1918 peak – with complete nonsense about price supports and government rationing boards. The Thomas Amendment was the third bullet shot into the corpse of the American economy, as it provided FDR the ability to fiddle with the monetary supply as capriciously as he fiddled with his mistresses. (Lest you be confused, if you're reading the likes of Bernanke, Stieglitz or Krugman, this third bullet in their mistaken telling was actually the *beneficial* third supporting leg of wonderful New Deal agricultural policy.)

One of the intellectual viruses behind so much awfulness in American policy was Professor Irving Fisher, whose counsel to Sen. Thomas led to the creation of such stupid policies. Fisher thought private businessmen were too stupid to be allowed to let the market set prices for commodities and interest rates and things, and therefore a governmental board of wise men like him should "manage" commodity prices and the overall economy, thereby removing the ups and downs of economic cycles. He could do that, you see, because of how smart he was. He was so smart that 10 days before the October 1929 Stock Market Crash he declared publicly that the stock market had reached a "permanently high plateau" and had invested his and his wife's money fully into that market.

He lost the fortune he'd made by inventing the Rolodex, right along with his wife's inherited fortune.

Oh, the AAA was declared unconstitutional.[272]

One of the core tenets of the Thomas Amendment was to allow the Treasury to just print out of thin air up to $3,000,000,000 of completely unfounded greenbacks, should the Fed decline to print the money to buy bonds. How good is that? FDR couldn't get the Fed to do his ridiculous bidding, so he signed a law to let a Cabinet Secretary create money instead. Kind of sounds like Obama frustrated that Congress wouldn't do his goofy bidding, so he'd just in fine authoritarian fashion do so with his phone and his pen.[273]

Fast forward to the Obama Administration and Bernanke Fed, and the government was doing exactly what the Thomas Amendment envisaged. There is no substantive difference between Treasury printing physical greenbacks and the kabuki theatre of Treasury issuing 3-year notes at 0.35%, the only reason those yields staying so low is because the Federal Reserve is the dominant buyer at the issuing auction. If the Fed did not stand ready to buy such low-yielding paper, then the clearing price for the debt would be a lot higher. That is currency printing.

It's a wonder to me that half the country does not understand why a good chunk of *rational* Americans chose to elect a boorish real estate developer named Donald Trump to be President, given the utterly awful alternative. On Election Day 2016, the nation decided that while Trump *might* be crazy, it was an absolute certainty that he was better than the proven corrupt Hillary with her clear track record of bad decisions, stupid political views and scores of failed initiatives.

Come April 2020, and the fools atop the Federal Government were at it again, this time in response to economic problems completely and utterly caused by human panic in the face of a viral infection.[274] The fools in Washington, hand-in-hand with (mostly) fools in

---

[272] United States v. Butler, 1936

[273] On 14 January 2014, Obama gave a speech in the Cabinet Room expressing his frustration with a Congress who wouldn't do his bidding, stating he'd just decree new rules by personal dictate.

State Capitols across our fair land, *destroyed* the most prosperous economy in global history, and ruined children's normal development, all because of a fear that already-sick, already-old Baby Boomers *may have died* a little earlier than had been anticipated a couple of months before.

Selfish beyond belief.

A very bright man and experienced investor, Paul Singer of Elliott Management wrote a letter in mid-April 2020 to his investors in which he warned about the idiocy of watering down the value of the US dollar.

> In the play "Waiting for Godot" by Samuel Beckett, which premiered in 1953, two characters wait for the arrival of someone named Godot, who never arrives. In our version, Good-Dough is sound money, and its chance of arriving is just about as slim...
>
> Too much debt, unsound financial institutions, oblivious corporate executives, and arrogant and clueless central bankers brought the world to the brink of financial extinction in 2008. Then, so the story goes, these same central bankers morphed into heroes and saved the world with their monetary fire hose on "full crowd control" and "confetti" settings. That tsunami of newly printed free money lifted securities prices, deepened inequality and unleashed the political testiness that comes along with such a novel and distorted recovery, and it tested and kept testing the willingness of people to accept cotton-candy money at full value.
>
> Sadly, when people (including those who should know better) do something stupid and reckless and are not punished, it is human nature that, far from thinking that they were lucky to have gotten away with something, they are encouraged to keep doing the stupid thing, keep believing the unbelievable and keep assuming that they were just plain wrong to be concerned about "old-fashioned" restraints (like sound money: Good-Dough). As we have pointed out ad nauseam et beyondum, doubling down on unsound policy just raises the stakes and the intensity of the future "payback."
>
> As of May 2021, the Fed is on its continued rampage of monetary debasement and unjustified interference in Americans' lives. The entire Board of Governors now votes in unison for this insanity; not a dissenting voice to be heard! Chairman Powell refusing to listen to the clear market signals about impending inflation insists that the Fed will "be patient" in keeping interest rates artificially low – near zero – through at least 2023, and also promises that the central bank will continue to buy *at least* $1,440,000,000,000 of Treasury bonds and mortgage-backed securities per year until "we've made substantial further progress towards our goals."[275]

---

[274] The Wuhan Flu Panic Depression of 2020. See other sections in this book on the cumulative idiocy that not only meant a lack of preparedness, but also a lack of rational response; Education, CDC, Defense...

[275] Central Bank Will Begin Reducing Bond Purchases 'Well Before' Raising Interest Rates, Powell Says - WSJ

A rational citizen might well ask what on earth these goals are? They certainly have nothing to do with sound money and a stable currency. This madness of the Fed buying Treasury obligations was *sold to us* as a "temporary but necessary" outrage during the Government-Caused Financial Crisis of 2007-08. Amazingly, one more "temporary" government intervention has turned into a perpetual stone around our collective necks.

None of this craziness is required. The Constitution itself only provides for silver as the basis for our national currency.

Let's immediately demand this massive amount of debt securities be sold off from the Fed's balance sheet. I know a few firms who can handle the requisite liquidation planning and execution.

Principle 3: The Fed may operate as a lender of last resort

Like it or not, there occur occasional convulsive panics of confidence in free markets. That is part of the reality and nothing to be shunned. Such moments are above all instances of excellent, strong market information for everyone to see.

In such times, what I *do* believe is of positive marginal utility to society is to have a central bank able to provide *liquidity* in those instances and to those entities that are credit-rich and momentarily cash-poor. All of that liquidity, however, must be conducted on the basis of the real bills doctrine, meaning the central bank can advance financing against real commercially-incurred notes stemming from actual economic activity. There is *always* real economic activity – what a lender of last resort does is to cut the Gordian Knot when market conditions freeze. "Well, my receivable is outstanding from my battery pack buyer, so I cannot remit payment I owe to the firm that sold me the nickel, who therefore cannot pay its monthly debt service to its bank...." That kind of thing is a momentary freeze to smooth payment flows; a lender of last resort can step in and say, "Right – nothing has changed about your relative creditworthiness. You're all just a bit panicked about cash flows right now, so we're going to remit payment throughout that supply chain and everyone can calm down and continue operations."

Note how different that is from "Let's print trillions of dollars!" which is what central banks have been doing since 2008 to wildly deleterious impact.

Under this new, excellent plan, we will no longer permit our central bank – whatever final form it takes – to embark on the insanity of "Quantitative Easing" which is just damned money printing.

Principle 4: The Fed will cease to be a "Regulator"

As an adult who has dealt with financial regulators, let me tell you if you're one of those people who believe the economy works better and that some all-seeing "adult" is keeping those squirrelly bankers and broker in line, you're not getting your money's worth. Worse than that, pretty much everything the regulators do is a drag on the economy and destructive of economic growth, innovation and salutary benefits of all kinds that should be heading your way and *not* into the pockets of bureaucrats.

Any central bank should focus on the soundness of money and currency. Period.

As Hall McAdams said succinctly: "For the well-run bank any reserve requirement is too high, but for a poorly run bank no reserve requirement is high enough."[276] We can as a society certainly require certain operational guidelines for banks which are chartered within our nation's borders, but we've already got an FDIC which pokes its nose into commercial banks' books and operations whenever it sees fit.

The Bottomless Font of Myriad Awful Ideas – the Dodd-Frank Act – slapped the Fed with additional regulatory duties in relation to banks. Ditch that idiocy *in toto* along with pretty much every other regulatory role overseeing banks.

Principle 5: The Fed is a Central Bank, not a tool of totalitarian control

Sitting as it does at the nexus of every single transaction in the nation, the Fed is a highly tempting tool for any politician bent on mischief. There are so many ways in which people aiming for totalitarian social control try to bend the Fed to their means that there's room for an entire 3-book compendium on the topic. I will stick to just a couple here, to give my readers a spine-chilling flavor of what some people want to do to your vanishing freedoms. None of this social manipulation has – ready to be surprised? – *anything* to do with monetary soundness.

First up is the demand from some people that we abolish cash. No longer will you be able to carry physical dollars to pay for anything. Nope! Everyone must be forced to carry around electronic devices to make sure that every single thing you buy is recorded and watched by the government. Among my most favorite – meaning utterly terrifying – rationales for "getting rid of cash" is the frank acknowledgment by many of the Political Class that doing so is a tool for universal surveillance of the population. The mandarins have so completely convinced themselves how important they all are, that they've come to believe that the State and its bureaucracy has the *a priori* right to know everything about what an individual citizen does in what used to be her "private" life.

Many people have written on the supposed "desirability" of eliminating cash from the system, that only purely electronic methods of payment should be "allowed" by, of course, The All-Seeing Government. Kenneth Rogoff, who has done some interesting empirical work around financial crises, has strayed far into this totalitarian fantasy land. He advocates for the abolition of cash, with one of his primary arguments being that "we" should "know" what people are spending their money on.

The almost magical part of the fallout from their going ahead with their plan is that *maybe, just maybe* they would have to face that money is not a thing in and of itself, merely an easy way of accounting for the real credit created by human action and hard assets. Because if these Statist totalitarians get to have Rogoff's damp dream, they'll find out that more and more Americans start transacting with one another using Bitcoin, or in local areas, locally agreed tender chits. In a word, the US would go *back* to a time of locally agreed monetary units. Your Newport Dollars would work in Newport, but by the time you got to

---

[276] Tamny, John, *Who Needs the Fed?*, p104

Boston, perhaps you'd be forced to swap your NDs for Boston Shillings in order to buy a beer at a brew pub.

It'd be awesome watching their frantic efforts to then identify, locate, arrest and prosecute people who used alt-cash money. I have no doubt they would do so – failure of a policy in government does *not* mean it is reversed and abandoned. Nope! Rank failure means they throw more resources at it. Take a look at HUD, Fannie Mae, the Drug War or any of the other myriad delusions of the utterly misnamed Great Society.

A second excellent example of how far from its core task the Fed has strayed is its wading into "climate change." At least they are *au courant*; they're not concerned with "Global Warming," which some of you may recall was "an emergency" pretty recently until the data showed, well, no warming that is statistically valid. As of November 2019, the Fed declared itself a paid-in member of the Climate Hysteria Apocalypse Church.

I've already touched on some stupidity emanating from the Minneapolis Fed. Guess whence this new – utterly manufactured from thin air as Congress certainly has not passed any laws about this new Fed "mandate" – preoccupation with "climate change" emanates? If you guessed the San Francisco Fed, you get a cannabis green sticker!

> "Climate change is an economic issue we can't afford to ignore," Federal Reserve Bank of San Francisco President Mary Daly said in a speech Friday [8 November 2019] at the start of a conference at her bank about the issue, in a first-ever event for the central bank.
>
> "Early research suggests that increased warming has already started to reduce average output growth in the United States. And future growth may be curtailed even further as temperatures rise," Ms. Daly said. "There's little doubt that we need to recognize, examine, and prepare for these risks in order to fulfill our core responsibilities," she said.[277]

I am not even going to comment on the ridiculousness of the "early research" that suggests "increased warming" is already reducing output growth. These people have no shame. Climate changes. Duh. It always has. Whatever temperatures do, they do on a global scale and the hubristic concept that Fed modeling gnomes are going to determine in any statistically viable way what specific impacts it may have on the US productivity growth is simple absurdity. It's so dumb it hurts. How is the Fed going to "prepare for these risks?" It's just make-work and virtue signaling. Enough of this nonsense already.

Beyond the *a priori* absurdity of the exercise, how, many rational people have asked, is the Fed authorized to start fretting about temperatures? Good question. Excellent question, in fact. In one of the most serious efforts to stretch a mandate well past its most tenuous breaking point, the "entry point" for this new meddling in the economy is Chairman Powell's statement that the Fed as a bank regulator has to be "sure" that the banks it regulates are "able to withstand the impact of severe weather events."

The arrogance coupled with sheer insanity is breathtaking.

---

[277] Fed's Daly: Fed Cannot Ignore What Climate Change Is Doing to Economy, Michael Derby, WSJ, 8 Nov 2019

You can wait for my upcoming 3,000-word summary of Fed Errors or do your own research on the ridiculous non-monetary-policy mischief they get up to.

End the Fed.

Figure 35: The Revamped Central Bank Memorial Frieze to the F.O.M.C., R.I.P.

Chapter 32: Constitutional Amendments

There is nothing new to the idea that amendments to our operating system agreement should be made with strong consensus of the people. The 55 "Founding Fathers" who gathered in Philadelphia to sweat through a summer were themselves really "Amending Fathers" who'd come together to remedy stark defects in the original operating system, the Articles of Confederation. It's why our current OS doc refers to forming a *more perfect* union," not "a union." We already had a union. What was needed in 1787 was to take the lessons of the first experimental OS and tweak its core code to improve its functionality.

My proposed amendments below are designed to bolster the principles laid out above. What could be more fun than proposing real editorial changes to the Constitution, rather than taking the lazy "Living Constitution" fake way out of the hard work required to *actually* change our legal system?

Amendment XXVIII

Section 1. The people's Representatives in the Legislature shall be required to sit physically in camera for either or both Houses of the Congress to be deemed in session.

Section 2. As stated clearly in Article I, Section 1, all legislative Powers herein granted shall be vested in a Congress of the United States. Further, to ensure equitable representation for all Americans, no Representative or Senator shall be restricted from full participation in any and all legislative processes performed by the Congress.

Section 3. Congress shall pass no law without the Representatives and Senators constructing the law in its final, full form. No law, portion thereof or rules shall be enforceable unless they shall have been written and voted on in their entirety by the Representatives and Senators. Lest time and fading memory change anyone's sense of the intent of this section, Representatives and Senators herein are defined as the actual persons elected to represent their Congressional district or State, not unelected persons to whom elected Representatives or Senators delegate their legislative responsibilities.

Section 4. Prior to any proposed legislation in its final form being presented to the President for signature or veto, that final form legislation needs to be presented to the public in as many ways as possible to ensure every voting citizen can review and comment on it. This period of public examination shall in no case be fewer than ten (10) full business days.

Section 5. In relation to all prior laws, rules, regulations based in administrative law and Federal mandates that have been drafted and created regarding legislation drafted in processes contrary to Section 3, prior to adoption of this Amendment, all shall be deemed null and void. Should the Congress wish to reenact specific laws, rules or mandates, they shall be entitled to do so in accordance with this Amendment.

Section 6. Congress shall pass no law that does not apply equally to all U.S. citizens. If any law passed or regulation created prior to the adoption of this Amendment, every such violation of equal treatment shall be deemed null and void, along with the law, rule, regulation which creates that unequal condition.

Section 7. No person shall hold elected office in the U.S. Government for more than four terms during the course of his or her life, further that for any particular elected office, the limit shall be for two terms.

Section 8. No person shall be permitted to hold an appointed position with the U.S. Government in any capacity until that person has had a minimum of ten years work experience in the private sector.
(a) Maximum 12 years in government service
(b) For Supreme Court Justices, the term of an incoming Justice shall be twenty years.

Section 9. No U.S. Government employee, whether elected or appointed, shall be a member of a union.

Section 10. No U.S. Government employee, whether elected or appointed, shall be entitled to a defined benefit pension or other guaranteed future payments or emoluments of any kind.

Section 11. As it appears the meaning of Amendment I has been lost and confused over the intervening years, we the people reiterate that Congress shall make no law that in any way infringes any person's freedom of expression as regards the composition, comportment or disposition of any and all aspects, employees and/or elected and appointed officials of any and all of the Legislative, Judicial and Executive branches of the Government. Any and all laws, regulations or rulings of courts of law or equity restricting any aspect of freedom of speech shall by this Amendment be nullified.

Section 12. No person shall hold elected or appointed office past the natural age of 75 years of age. Further, any person in elected or appointed office who is 55 years or older is barred from voting on or implementing financial projects, taxes, or any other claims on the public fisc whose fiscal impact is longer than 5 years. To account for changes in life expectancy over time, those age limits shall be adjusted one year for every five year change in population mean life expectancy.

Section 13. Within each State, the electoral Districts to determine representation in the House of Representatives shall be drawn by objective application of analytical geometry, such that each district's boundary lines shall meet the following criteria:
(a) the least possible number of sides to the resultant geometrical shape,

(b) the most numerically equitable population distribution across each Congressional District, and

(c) drawn in such a way that the State as a whole is divided using the fewest possible vertices to define the Districts.

Section 14. In order to more closely align our elected legislators' interests with the interests of the citizenry as a whole, Congressional base salaries shall be determined by the following formula: [mean private sector salaries in Congressional district less net taxes paid in Congressional district less federal tax dollars sent to Congressional district with appropriate modifiers to be agreed upon by the citizens every ten years, with initial formula laid out below.]

The inputs to the formula describe the intent of this Section to keep legislators' interests as nearly completely aligned with their constituents as possible. Over time, humans try to manipulate rules to distort the original intent, so in much the same way the US Census happens decennially, there will be a XVIII.15 Constitutional Convention every ten years following the date of this Amendment's ratification, the sole purpose of which will be to examine the Congressional compensation formula applied during the prior ten years to see whether there are any improvements to be made to more perfectly ensure that Congressional compensation is aligned with the source of all economic wealth, the private sector.

Input variables relate directly to the economic productivity of a given Representative's Congressional District or for Senators, one's State.

1. Mean salary in district
2. Median salary in district
3. [test between mean and median; tossing out outliers on distributions]

Base Salary = _____

Modifiers which apply equally to all of Congress, on a quarterly basis:

The First Modifier relates to national economic productivity.

Real Net Domestic Product Annualized Growth > 5.0%, Base times 2
Real Net Domestic Product Annualized Growth = 4.5%, Base times 1.75
Real Net Domestic Product Annualized Growth = 4.0%, Base times 1.5
Real Net Domestic Product Annualized Growth = 3.5%, Base times 1.25
Real Net Domestic Product Annualized Growth = 3.0%, Base times 1
Real Net Domestic Product Annualized Growth = 2.5%, Base times 0.75
Real Net Domestic Product Annualized Growth = 2.0%, Base times 0.50
Real Net Domestic Product Annualized Growth = 1.5%, Base times 0.25
Real Net Domestic Product Annualized Growth = 1.0%, Base times 0
Real Net Domestic Product Annualized Growth = 0.5%, Base times (-1.25)
Real Net Domestic Product Annualized Growth = 0%, Base times (-1.50)

Real Net Domestic Product Annualized Growth < 0%, Base times (-2)

All NDP figures rounded down to nearest 0.5%

The Second Modifiers relate to fiscal responsibility. The purpose of these incentives is to incentivize the government to reduce the nation's reliance on debt to its minimal level.

Outstanding Federal Debt as a Percentage of NDP over full year, weighted by day count, will impact a Representative's pay packet.

Debt as % NDP	Bonus
0 – 5%	5%
5.01 – 10%	4%
10.01 – 15%	3%
15.01 – 20%	2%
20.01 – 25%	0%
25.01 – 30%	-2%
30.01 – 35%	-8%
35.01 + %	-32%

Change in Outstanding Federal Debt as a Percentage of NDP may also be considered in the final version. Although after a base year, rewarding incremental change for its own sake may becomes self-defeating once an improved baseline is achieved.

Weighted Duration of Federal Debt under 5 years can also be added as a consideration, with bonuses or penalties applied for keeping debt as short-term as possible. The close to spot cash payments the government is in its current operations, the healthier is the public fisc.

Section 15. In order to form a more perfect union, and to discourage the resurgence of a political class operating under a different, privileged set of rules than the general public operates under, the Government shall be required to account for its activities in accordance with GAAP, IFRS or whatever other accounting standard applies to the rest of the nation's private sector businesses.

Section 16. In order for government to function smoothly, the authority granted to the Executive Branch shall be restored to the intention of the original meaning in the 18th century. All Presidential appointments are to be deemed as valid, with a strict 10-day nominee evaluation period for the "advice and consent" of the Senate. Nominees to be rejected must voted on by a two-thirds supermajority.

Discussion:

Section 1 is important to make sure that the people elected to Congress as Representatives are present and actively *representing* the citizenry for whom they work. Nothing is more absurd than the non-debates which don't occur on the floor of the House of Representatives. The people expect our representatives to be present for their jobs, and to listen to arguments, debate points and craft legislation when strictly necessary.

This section became even *more* urgent in May 2020 when House Speaker Nancy Pelosi (D-CA) issued a rule change that would overturn 230 years of precedent and permit votes to be cast without House Members being present. The excuse was the Wuhan Sniffle Panic which the Democrats seized upon as a last desperate measure to remove President Trump from office.

Section 2 is designed to restore true democratic representation to the American voter. By dint of historical accident and as an outcome of the very basest parts of our nature the Founders tried to guard against, there are numerous procedures created by tradition and then law which stymie full representative participation by the Members of Congress. As in *Animal Farm,* all are equal but some are more equal than others.

The inner workings of the United States Congress are difficult to explain, and difficult for citizens to grasp, which contributes to the gulf that historically has separated Congress from the people who choose its members. Like any legislative body, the House and Senate have had to develop rules and customs to enable them to function. Many are peculiar; some appear undemocratic. Sometimes it's easy to blame those rules and customs for the mess in Washington.

Every two years, new members are elected to the House and Senate who have promised to clean up that mess. Then they arrive in the Capitol and discover that the mess isn't exactly what they had imagined and campaigned against, and that cleaning it up won't be easy. There always is a mess, though the degree of messiness varies quite widely in different historical periods. A significant portion of the mess is deeply rooted in the histories of the House and Senate. Often there's a good explanation for why some unappealing traditions survive. The Committee on Rules of the House of Representatives exemplifies this phenomenon.

As the traffic cop for the House, the Rules Committee decides what bills will reach the floor for possible enactment; how long the debate will be on each bill that makes it to the floor; how the time for debate will be shared; and what amendments will get a vote. These powers have been exercised by Rules since 1890 when Thomas Brackett Reed of Maine, a progressive Republican and ally of Theodore Roosevelt's simultaneously held the jobs of speaker and chairman of the Rules Committee and used the combination to impose (with his colleagues' support) a new order – known as Reed's Rules – on the House.

The idea that the speaker, leader of the majority party, should control the flow of legislation to the floor and the terms of debate went out of fashion twenty years later. For most of the twentieth century, the Rules Committee exercised its vast power autonomously. For decades it was dominated by conservatives, particularly southerners who traditionally enjoyed long tenure – and thus acquired much seniority – in the House. But in 1975, the vast new Democratic majority elected in the Watergate landslide of 1974 restored control over Rules to the speaker, who was given the right to name all Democratic members of the committee, subject to the approval of the entire Democratic caucus. Republicans later adopted the same procedure. This meant that Rules was effectively controlled by the leadership, since the leaders could count on the loyalty of those they appointed to the committee – and could replace them if they slipped into disloyalty.

Control by leadership meant that even in a democracy, legislating was not an entirely democratic enterprise. Every member did not have an equal chance to pass or amend legislation; many in the minority had no chance at all once a bill got to the floor. Leaders, elected by their party caucus, could decide arbitrarily whose bill or whose amendment came to the floor, and under what circumstances. Both parties' leaders have taken full advantage of this power when they controlled the House.[278]

I personally don't blame "those rules and customs for the mess in Washington." I blame unrestrained human nature for that. The Rules Committee sounds like the shifting cliques in *Heathers*[279] or *Bring It On*[280] more than it does the controlling gate to what *Federal laws* are considered by "our" "elected" "Representatives."

Section 3 represents a very powerful tool to restrain runaway government. The delegation of work *they are elected to do* to non-elected staffs has eaten away at the dignity and *validity* of "our" laws.

Edward M. Kennedy slipped an important truth into the memoir he wrote just before he died: "Ninety-five percent of the nitty-gritty work of drafting [bills] and negotiating their final form is now done by staff. That... marks an enormous shift of responsibility over the past forty or fifty years." Could Kennedy really mean that staff took care of nearly all the important work? Yes, he could mean just that.

Perhaps the definitive demonstration of staff influence on hearings was provided by a fellow named Harley Dirks, the senior clerk in the 1970s of a subcommittee of the Senate Appropriations Committee. Dirks was known for scripting hearings so carefully that he knew in advance exactly how they would proceed. He demonstrated this talent in 1976 when half a dozen of his hearings where canceled to accommodate a tight legislative schedule. Nevertheless, the Government Printing Office produced thousands of pages of "transcripts" of those hearings that read as if the meetings had actually taken place. Dirks had embellished his scripts, which were based on statements provided by government agencies and senators' offices, to create this false impression, even including purported off-the-cuff remarks by senators and witnesses. When his maneuver was exposed in the press, Dirks had to resign.[281]

Note, please, that Dirks was not fired by his Senator bosses for faking records. No! Why would they do that? He had to resign only *after* a journalist had the temerity to

---

[278] Kaiser, Robert, pp104-105
[279] Michael Lehmann, director; Daniel Waters, screenplay; Denise Di Novi, producer; 1988
[280] Peyton Read, director; Jessica Bendinger, screenplay; Marc Abraham, producer; 2000
[281] Kaiser, Robert G., *Act of Congress,* Alfred A. Knopf, New York, 2013, p28

disclose his forgery to the public. There is a place in my heart for journalists who do their jobs properly.

American citizens who are called to jury duty get empaneled to a jury... and then they *do not* delegate to others the work of deciding on verdict to be delivered. So, too, should *all service* to one's country be performed.

Also, *crucially*, the runaway Administrative State cannot continue to churn out laws and violations literally without number, if Congressional representatives have to actually do the work of crafting legislation.

Section 4 is a wonderful tool for both empowering the citizenry and placing further restraints upon legislative excesses. I pulled this idea straight from the playbook of the anti-gun-ownership lobby. They're very much in favor of waiting periods between the time one buys a gun and the actual time one takes possession of it. The idea being that for something with a potential for great danger, it makes sense to enforce a fixed period between decision and possession. That wonderful show *The Simpsons* addressed this in an episode which saw Homer Simpson going into a gun store. When told that he would have to wait a mandatory period before taking possession of the gun of his choice, he exclaimed in dismay, "But I'm angry *now!*"

Whether or not I agree with that re: guns and the Second Amendment, the idea has a great deal to recommend it. I know that I personally have caused grave discomfiture to salespeople in various places when I tell them – in buying jewelry, or electronics or a car – that for any purchase over a certain amount, I at least sleep on it before handing over my hard-earned cash.

At least some portion of the electorate should be wildly in favor of this. If you are a person who thinks waiting 5 days to buy a handgun is wise, then you should be really excited by the idea of a 10-day waiting period for Federal legislation. After all, a gun while dangerous can only harm a few people in its use, but Federal legislation harms hundreds of millions.

Section 7 is a critical change that, taken with the other sections of this Amendment, will go a long way towards correcting the errors made in the original Constitution. There are times when long relationships are valuable things in society, but nothing is absolute. When it comes to performing a civic duty by *truly serving* one's country in elected office, a long-running set of cliques can do damage to the best outcomes for the American people as a whole. Funnily enough, a great description of the power of mutual backscratching comes from Robert Cialdini:

> The out-of-character vote of one of our elected representatives on a bill or measure can often be understood as a favor returned to the bill's sponsor.

While interesting from a sociological perspective, that very practical *current* way of getting legislation passed has not – I am sure we can all by now agree – resulted in very positive outcomes for the nation as a whole. The issue of back scratching will go away naturally with imposition of term limits, but it is best to solidify the principle.

Section 8 will from the moment of its adoption drive excellence in our civil service. There are already plenty of hardworking, mission-driven professionals working in our government. Just think of how much more value we the taxpayer will derive from making sure that those who serve in the Federal government come equipped to their roles with plenty of real world, private sector experience.

The adjustment of lifetime appointment to the Supreme Court is an important adjustment that I *believe* but don't know that the Founding Fathers would approve of. Life expectancy in late 1780s was about 38 years of age for a white male.

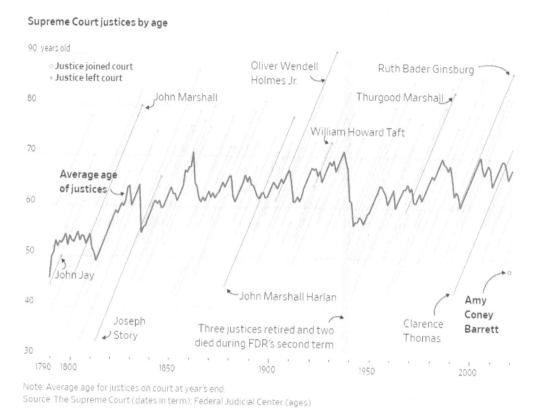

Supreme Court justices by age

Note: Average age for justices on court at year's end.
Source: The Supreme Court (dates in term); Federal Judicial Center (ages)

Section 13 is so important because as legislative Representatives from each of the several States impact the citizens not only of their State but those of other States, there is a compelling national interest in a fair and equitable electoral system. We need to address a very serious problem. How is it possible that when Congress enjoys a low approval rating 15% as of December 2023, the *reelection rate* for individual Members is 97%?

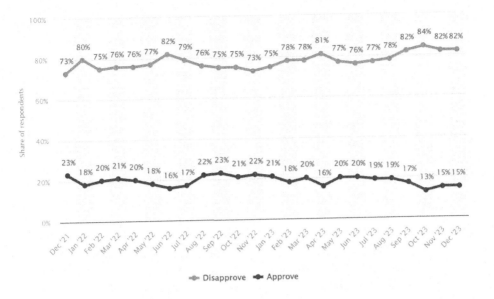

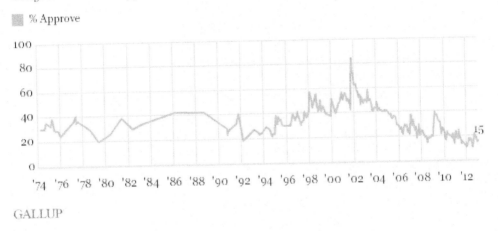

Congressional Job Approval Ratings Trend (1974-Present)

GALLUP

There are two answers here. The first is that, according to some commentators, voters tend to think that *all those other guys wasting our cash are a problem, but my Congressman is great.* The more compelling - because it's addressable in an actionable way - answer is gerrymandering, the process by which far from competing with one another, Members of Congress *help* each other stay on the public gravy train. They collude to ensure that they carve up Congressional districts in such a way that ousting a sitting Member is almost impossible. This process most assuredly does *not* serve "the public interest" at all – it serves the individual interest of the Congressman or Congresswoman.

And guess who often wades into this "States Rights" issue? The unelected bureaucrats in the Federal Government. The Department of Justice wielding the stick of the Voting Rights Act of 1965, continues to mangle and meddle in the affairs of States long after Jim Crow ended, and long after the nation elected a Black President. [282]

I think we can *all* agree that what the Civil War put into a coffin, the resulting growth of the nation has driven iron stakes through. States' Rights arguments are irrelevant because, e.g. a Barney Frank who "represents" one district in Massachusetts had the power to impact *every single American's* economic choices across the land and even beyond the physical barriers of the nation's geographic borders. Given the reality of the national government we have, this nonsense about a "Federal" government needs to be called what it is, and our Constitution amended appropriately.

Beyond the public interest reason, there is a *moral* reason to redraw these lines in this way: to finally and irrevocable remove the taint of racism, classism or all the other artificial lines which do *not* divide us anymore, except in the minds and actions of self-interested politicians and parasites like Al Sharpton who keep *themselves* in power by tell lies about how racist and/or otherwise self-dividing Americans are.

Section 14 is the tool by which the American people can *finally* make sure that Congressional Representatives and Senators actually care about the *real* wealth creators who are Congress's *real* bosses – the American worker and voter. For far too long, the preening narcissists in Washington, D.C. have been completely removed from the consequences of the decisions they make for everyone else.

The Wuhan Flu Panic of 2020 painted as glaring a picture as I hope to ever see in this nation again of just how much of a lordly, untouchable and princely class our elected officials and their public sector workers have become. As these colossal idiots plunged the nation into a Depression worse than the 1930s, they did so smugly secure in the continuation of *their* salaries and benefits, all while throwing *millions of Americans* out of work *every week* for six weeks.

I look forward to the pomp and celebration around the decennial "28-14" conventions, when each State chooses to send a splendid mix of old and young delegates, perhaps precocious young teen math whizzes deliberating with long haul truckers, ... It should become a wonderful badge of civic pride to be chosen as one of a State's delegates. What could be more important than analyzing how well our Constitution ensured that elected servants are actually that – servants – and not insulated overlords who do whatever they like while the stupid little people – that'd be you and me, currently – foot the bill.

It will be gratifying to see the annual Best XXVIII-14 Essays produced during competitions from grade schools to high schools to the few remaining colleges left across the land. I for one heartily look forward to the wonderful perspectives brought by children steeped in the civic virtue of holding Congress's feet to the fiscal fire. The genius of the nation's youth will pour forth discourses from the perspectives of classical philosophy, mathematics, systems theory, game theory, computer science, history, psychology, psychohistory, anthropology, biostatistics and for all I can predict, comparative critical ethnomusicology and applied poetry. I am sure there will be a pan-gendered critique of the notion of money as the appropriate remuneration for people called to – what will become – a higher devotion to country and cause than is currently the cesspool case.

---

[282] Silverglate, Harvey, *Three Felonies a Day*

I can see entrepreneurial kids silk-screening festive or caustic or daring T-shirts with "28-14 or Bust" placed strategically so as to enrage their stodgy, prudish elders. It's going to be wonderful. I can see their more pedantic contemporaries insisting stridently that it's actually "XXVIII-14," thank you very much – and can't they see how a willing renunciation of the legacy of Rome is eroding the moral and intellectual foundations of our Great Republic? Cannot they hear the earth rumbling as the Founding Fathers spin in their graves at the ignorance of Western Civilization's most unwieldy numerical system, yet one by which an enormous Empire was created and managed?

There will be black eyes aplenty arising from *those* disputes, I bet, which will make the Rock v. Disco schoolyard wars of the 1970s or the 1980s East Coast – West Coast fights seem quaint in comparison!

I invite you to you imagine the wild buildup starting in the year 2800, for the national celebrations that will happen on the night of 31 December 2813, and the *year* of wild partying and the pressure on the kids graduating in 2814 to produce *the greatest* XXVIII-14 Essays in the Great History of our Republic? Heady days, to be sure. I am sorry I won't be there to see the party.

Section 15 is required to make sure there is no more magical bookkeeping for the government, separate from how the private sector does its accounting.

Section 16 ensures that the Executive Branch can fulfil its obligation to the American people of staffing and operating the few things left that require the Federal Government to operate. The original intent of the Senate's "advise and consent" role was to provide a degree of deliberation between the two branches on appointments made by the President. Wisely, we as a republic still do not want a Caligula-like figure to become President and start appointing his horse to Cabinet positions, as tempting as that vision can be at times.

This minor modification to the advise and consent clause does at least two salutary things. Firstly, by removing the colossal waste of time and taxpayer money that go into televised show trials – just ask Supreme Court Justice Brett Kavanaugh – or arbitrarily holding up hearings on appointments, the American people get an empowered Executive who is able to hire and fire at will.

Secondly, by providing a 2/3rds majority provision, should the Senate opine strongly that a given candidate for appointed office is seriously unsuited to that role, the Senate gets a one-time chance to vote via supermajority to block that appointment.

Amendment XXIX

Section 1. [Go back to a variant of the original way of electing Pres and VP.]

Section 2. In every election for Federal office, each ballot presented for voting shall have an automatic line added to the list of candidates running for that office entitled "None of the Above." This Constitutional mandate is the sole Federal dictate to each State's balloting process. In any given election, if "None of the Above" gets more votes than any of the candidates for the position, then that position shall remain vacant until the next regularly scheduled election.

Discussion:

Section 1 once more forces Americans to come to reasonable, semi-consensus positions.

A serious added bonus is the sheer *fun* it would be to, say, watch an Administration composed of a President Trump and a Vice President Clinton, or, say President Biden and Vice President Trump. Talk about good times! I can smell the gridlock and frustration from here!

Section 2 solves a problem which the Founders could not see a solution for — the case in which the American people would be far better served by *not* having someone in office than by having someone in office. We can call it the Richard Pryor Amendment in honor of his stellar performance in *Brewster's Millions.*[283] For those silly people who have not yet seen the film, I ruin nothing by revealing that a key plot line in the film is that a man with sudden wealth thrust upon him funds a political campaign, the "candidate" of which is "None of the Above." So anyone voting for that "candidate" would be voting to leave the office vacant.

Every candidate should be running not only against the other candidate, but against the Ghost of Brewster. It will certainly make obscure "unopposed" single-candidate elections more exciting and dynamic. What a refreshing dose of clarity it will bring to elections when each candidate must articulate clearly "Why me." No more candidacies based purely on hatred of the other candidate(s). Whoever wins must prevail by articulating why having "my butt in that seat" is better than leaving the seat nice and empty. *Especially* since the default Ghost of Brewster position *costs the taxpayers nothing* at all, whereas electing someone to whatever position it is brings real costs with it.

To take current (2Q20 – 2Q24) events as an example of the Threat of Brewster to incumbent politicians: There was *never any reason* to destroy the economy to "fight" a virus which is about 50-70% more deadly than the seasonal flu. The idiotic decision to destroy hundreds of millions of lives in the face of a virus which statistically kills people 80+ years of age who have serious preexisting conditions is bipartisan madness which ought to be recognized and punished. Using the Richard Pryor Amendment, the citizenry would have the chance to, in theory, toss 33 or 34 Senators out of office along with all 435 Representatives, leaving one chamber completely dark and the other chamber without a quorum.

I am *not* a fan of the Federal Government having any say in business properly left to the States. I am therefore open to the idea that this modification should only be made at the State level. But I like it in the Constitution because it would be a fine reminder to not only

---

[283] Directed by Walter Hill, release date 22 May 1985, staring Richard Pryor, John Candy, Lonette McKee

people running for office but for every citizen that if we can't have a good person filling a role, we'd all be far better off leaving it empty for a term.

Amendment XXX

Section 1. From the date of ratification of this Amendment, all Federal Court and Supreme Court decisions must be made unanimously. A decision is only binding when each Judge or Justice has affirmed support for the decision.

Section 2. In the event that the Federal Government fails to remedy waterborne injury to one of the States, the State so impacted is hereby empowered to issue letters of marque.

Discussion:

Section 1 is necessary to correct a course of judicial action which has become an unaccountable and unbalanced power in "our" government.

The Constitution never says anywhere that a pack of unelected people – or even a simple majority of unelected people – can overturn legislation. As a Pulitzer Prize-winning scholar notes, "[t]he Framers made no general grant of a judicial power to invalidate laws passed by Congress and signed by the President. They made no grant to the Supreme Court of supremacy over the Constitution or the other branches of the federal government."[284]

The Supreme Court has evolved into a scary beast that does not meet even a schoolchild's understanding of the purported "checks and balances" we intone about respectfully when talking about the three branches of government.

Further, from a practical legal fairness standpoint, it makes no sense whatsoever that a divided bench of judges can impose a ruling on society by simple luck of the appointment draw. At the individual trial level, a jury of 12 people must come back with a unanimous verdict. That is for a case involving one person.

Finally, from a philosophical view, when looking to the judges we elevate to the highest court in the nation, we should expect those judges to have a beneficial effect on the nation, not a divisive one. Unanimous judgments, clearly explained, have a salutary effect on the nation. Unanimous judgments send the very clear statement that there is *one law* under which all are equal, not a "law of the moment" which happens to favor one political faction over others. Rational citizens are justified to question whether a ruling from the Supreme Court is "Constitutional" if the ruling comes without a unanimous endorsement. After all, if a ruling is "5 to 4," aren't the four Justices who *disagree* with the ruling just as smart, just as educated and just as experienced? So if those four people believe strongly that the *opinion* of the by-historical-change 5 Justice majority is *wrong,* why should a rational person accept that ruling?

---

[284] Burns, James MacGregor, *Packing the Court,* Penguin, New York, 2009, pp16-17

Right now, millions of people are justifiably skeptical of a government which appears never to have *all* Americans' best interests at heart. That view of government – as a separate powerful clique serving one special interest now, another one some other time – is reinforced by the practice of Supreme Court Justices voting on legal matters of national and often global importance.

Why should any citizen view as just or binding Supreme Court rulings which overturn a law passed by the Congress and (perhaps) signed by the President? That very intelligent question's existence poses a real danger to our society.

In practical commercial matters, people with differing views strive hard to accommodate positions they do not initially agree with, as the benefits of comity and unanimous support for a go-forward arrangement are superior to continued fragmentation. In commercial matters, however, there is a crucial difference from public policy: the alternative to a negotiated agreement is to simply do nothing. In critical legal affairs impacting the whole nation, that is a bad outcome.

How, then, do we as a society reconcile the correct view of the need for a unanimous verdict in a jury trial with the craziness of sweeping legislation-from-the-bench by five of nine folks who happened to be hit by the historical pitch when vacancies arose? Supreme Court decisions unfortunately have the power of law, delivered by unaccountable-to-any-electorate lifetime appointees. Kind of sounds like the monarchy our founding revolutionary generation fought to be free of, doesn't it?

The Supreme Court – and any other court – should not be in the position of legislating from the bench. In cases where the unanimous Court holds that a law is unconstitutional, a new step needs to be created to return power to the people. A Supreme Grand Jury will be convened, and arguments will be made before that Grandest of Juries, with the Supreme Court arguing the Justices' unanimous case for revocation or change of a law, and a Congressional representative arguing for the piece of legislation in question. We can model it on the process canon lawyers in the Vatican use for sainthood, perhaps.

Is any discussion needed of the merits of **Section 2**? Talk about reinvigorating the fighting spirit of our proud maritime traditions! States' Rights galore, complete with tales of derring-do, legalized piracy on the high seas and inland waterways! Who wouldn't spend a gap year as a crewmember on a floating, cannon-laden posse, avenging outrages visited upon one's sovereign State? The *NYS Hudson Avenger* could fire at will on fishing boats launched from the Jersey Shore to avenge overpriced NJ PATH commuter tickets imposed on New Yorkers, grabbing their morning haul of bonefish.

In return the *JS Gardener* could lob incendiary bombs into sailing boats leaving the Battery Park City Marina, boarding and pillaging them for their sunset wine and cheese platters.

What an exciting time that would be! For mating purposes, it'd be more exciting than sitting alone swiping right on a dating app.

I am open to the idea that many people might support only Section 1 of this Amendment, but I threw in Section 2 as a sweetener for those on the fence.

Chapter 33: Rational Patriotism

"Patriotism is supporting your country 100% of the time, and your government some of the time."
—   Mark Twain

"[Nations] are synthetic and imperfect creations and subject to change, and most have been the result of violent conflict at some stage... In order to persist and cohere, states usually require effective political institutions, a degree of materials well-being, efficient means of defense against external enemies, mechanisms for maintaining internal order and, very often, some kind of religious or ideological underpinning."
—   Linda Colley

"You're not to be so blind with patriotism that you can't face reality. Wrong is wrong, no matter who does it or says it."
—   Malcolm X

"Courage, then, my countrymen, our contest is not only whether we ourselves shall be free, but whether there shall be left to mankind an asylum on earth for civil and religious liberty."
–   Samuel Adams

"It is time to remember that old wisdom our soldiers will never forget: that whether we are black or brown or white, we all bleed the same red blood of patriots, we all enjoy the same glorious freedoms, and we all salute the same great American Flag."
–   Donald Trump

"We, the People, recognize that we have responsibilities as well as rights; that our destinies are bound together; that a freedom which only asks what's in it for me, a freedom without a commitment to others, a freedom without love or charity or duty or patriotism, is unworthy of our founding ideals, and those who died in their defense."
–   Barack Obama

"If the present tries to sit in judgment on the past, it will lose the future."
–   Winston Churchill

"If you don't have something nice to say, don't say it."
–   Everyone's Grandma

The summer of 2020 as I neared completion of this fine Collector's First Edition ended up worse for the nation than the summers of 1967 and 1968 combined. Myriad factors contributed to the fractured nation, factors many of which have been simmering for years and in many cases, decades. The catalyst for the rampant howling and destruction in the streets is of course the sudden, government-caused economic Depression that the nation was thrown into for no reason at all, or rather, because the eternally selfish Draft Dodger Generation decided to destroy America all because of a virus which *mainly* kills people over 75 *who were already sick with something else.*

Following the insane 2020 Summer of Leftist Destruction, we had a few more bumps along the road, including enough normal Americans infuriated by the out of touch ruling class *demanding* that normal people think 2020's riots were actually "free speech," that they showed up to demonstrate at the Capitol on 6 January 2021, to tell the Congress inside that they were unhappy with the results of the recent Presidential Election. Events got a bit out of hand, to be fair, but Americans are a passionate bunch.

As this book was going through final (so I thought, then) revisions, rabid partisans in Congress had once more tossed out due process and were treating the nation to a badly written, laboriously choreographed show trial I call *January 6th: The Musical!* Think 羅生門 *(Rashomon)*, but decidedly less artsy fartsy, and stripped of any other point of view. In Technicolor. So maybe nothing like *Rashomon.* At least *Rashomon* had katanas.

Then the FBI – who perhaps had read an earlier draft of this book and wanted to make sure I put them on the budgetary chopping block – sent 100 armed agents including dramatic helicopters and armed frogmen in the Intercoastal to raid an American citizen's home *without allowing his attorneys to observe their search.* The private citizen happened to be Donald Trump. For those Americans still naïve enough to believe they are living in a free republic, I ask them to ponder this. When a serial killer cannibal is arrested, his lawyers have the right to be present as police search his home and property for the remains of his victims. A serial rapist murderer has those rights, and no one blinks an eye.

Yet a billionaire former President had his lawyer shoved off the premises by the FBI while they wander around his home for six hours or more. Really ponder those two things, and you'll start to understand why we need to lance the boil of corruption that is the modern day FBI and DOJ.

All this dramatic nonsense is evidence to the rest of the world that the US is now a banana republic where those in power instantly arrest and imprison their political opponents. This is a symptom of things gone badly wrong.

So I am making a plea for *us all* to continue to keep our faith in the American Project, when right here and now, I am watching the very worst in American life – the older generation who I am sure were an eternal disappointment to their parents who fought the Nazis give us their last "gift" which consisted of for the first time in history closing the schools nationwide, *not* because the children are at risk of disease, but because the spoiled Boomer Brats *might be at risk* from the virus *maybe* transmitting between children. There is no other word for it; these selfish clowns had *already* run us into national bankruptcy through their creations of a psychotic, unsustainable entitlement state. That was back in the long-ago booming economy of January 2020.

We can take some excellent lessons from the societal destruction caused by a vicious, Maoist "cancel culture" that is seeing people *fired from their real world jobs* because of something they wrote or said decades earlier, or even because of something the fired person's *spouse* wrote on asocial media a couple of days back in response to one of the bizarre multitude of insane provocations that spew forth from the idiots and fools that inhabit those dark swamps. Tearing down statues in a mob rage, screaming from behind the anonymity of a keyboard for someone's job to be taken from them – these are just two excellent examples of destructive negativity.

Rational patriotism means *always* agitating for positive outcomes. It does not mean that one should never criticize the government – heck, 90% of this brilliant, engaging, life-changing book does that – but rather that when one criticizes, one does so only because one is proposing something positive to fix the problems identified.

I hope 100% of this book does that.

I don't know if there has ever been a sweet, mythical time when all Americans pulled together, rowing our Ship of Destiny in one direction in perfect harmony. Actually, I do know *that* has never been the case. It is quite possible that at those times in our history, when someone points to a decade or year that showed pronounced unity, that person's nostalgic view was entirely subjective and was not shared widely.

We don't need to pretend the past was perfect. We don't need to believe that we will not have disagreements amongst ourselves in the future. I am quite sure we will. There is nothing wrong with that. What would be productive would be for everyone to stop screaming past one another constantly. Surely my grandmother was not the only one who said *If you don't have something nice to say, don't say it.*

To those who are so in love with the drama of "Revolution," whatever they may think it means in theory, in reality, every true revolution is a period marked by violence, misery and suffering. The current (2018 - today) Great Awakening has delivered us such cultural delights as a former hooker who admitted to drugging her clients to steal their money and jewelry singing a "song" called "Wet Ass Pussy" to great acclaim *while the insane cancel culture cancer cult effectively banned six children's books by Dr. Seuss!*

The American Project can not only recover from this horrible period but can even once again thrive as a nation. I'll start respecting the Boomers when they retire and tell fun stories into their cocoa in the afternoons and stop plunging me and my children into bottomless debt.

It's a lot easier to scream and destroy than it is to build. There is individual and mutual benefit when each of us decides to take an optimistic view of our fellow Americans and the whole messy society we all contribute to. Negativity and group blame lead at best to fractured communities and more usually leads to physical violence.

What we call the Middle East today bears the scars of decades of incessant negativity and scapegoating. In 1200, if one wanted to find prosperous societies tolerant of differences, one would be a lot more likely to find happiness in Damascus, Baghdad, Cairo or Beirut than one would in Rome, London or Paris. It is very hard to project oneself into other cultures and especially other time periods, but if one were a Jew looking for a safe, clean city in which to conduct a business, study Torah and raise a family, Baghdad was a whole lot more congenial a spot than most of the smaller, dirtier European cities. If one were a Christian hoping to run a thriving commercial business, one would be far better off in Cairo than your Muslim counterpart would be in Vienna.

A Westerner dropped into those same cities today, unaware of that long, cosmopolitan history can be forgiven for believing the monolithic lie that today's sorry conditions are the inevitable result of how things "always were." Over the years, and largely since 1945, virulent strains of reactionary historicity gained currency in which Jews and Europeans play the role of oppressors and subversive destroyers of morality and society. The ejection of Jews from Iraq, Egypt, Syria, Jordan and other nations surrounding Israel was a precursor to the horrific genocidal attacks on Christian Copts in Egypt and Yazidis in Syria.

Those anti-Jewish ejections and all the never ending hatred coming from the Palestinians who have spent 75 years teaching their kids hate instead of productivity came right back around to Israel on 7 October 2023, when World War III began in earnest. Now that the Israelis are on the front lines not only for their nation's survival, but on behalf of Western Civilization against the forces of barbaric chaos, we are once more witnessing the evil Marxist Jew Hating Left growing bold enough on our university campuses and city streets to chant their evil, destructive hatred.

Part of today's fight is to rejuvenate a rational sense of patriotism, of realizing that no system is perfect, but the American Experiment is unique in trying to create a more perfect union from deeply imperfect individuals.

Rational patriotism is easy to distinguish from parasitic fake patriotism with a simple test. Is the idea proposed additive or negative? An example of positive community building would be "I know my neighbors down the road are struggling economically and they really need a new barn. I am going to offer my skills, time and muscle to help them build that barn and I am going to ask all of our other neighbors to similarly, *voluntarily* offer what they can to help build the barn. The materials cost will be around $5,000 but we're saving them $20,000 on labor, which is real savings for them in this difficult time. Since we all pitched in, we got the barn done over the course of two weekends." A real family in need gets a barn. A community has come together voluntarily to offer honorable assistance as the family getting the barn contributes to the cost and will always be around to offer help to those neighbors who helped them. Everyone involved is enriched by the experience, no one is treated like a charity case and the society and local economy are strengthened with personal dignity, hard work and practical neighborly love and respect.

An example of parasitic, centralizing government control would be "Hi, I am running for office in this State. I know some of the people in the State are struggling and could use new outbuildings on their farms. I am going to tax everyone in the State, then hire a pack of bureaucrats with swell salaries and long-term pensions who can never be fired. Those bureaucrats will then set up a bidding process that only big, connected, building contractors can afford to qualify for and if various lobbyists get their way, the bidding process will be laden with irrelevant nonsense about 'carbon neutrality' and 'prevailing wage' rules. Then another pack of bureaucrats will be assigned to take applications from poor farmers in need of new construction, because we want to avoid scamsters stealing from the taxpayers. After roughly 18 months and taking into account the costs of bureaucrats' salaries, we will have built a total of 10 barns at a cost per barn of $376,560. Whether or not another barn is needed, we now have an office full of civil servants dedicated to an ongoing annual cost of $4 million, not including my parasitic salary and benefits. As an added insult to the people I am stealing from via abusive tax legislation, for kicks and giggles, every time I do so, I am going to refer to that taxation as 'asking folks to pay their fair share.'"

Do you see the difference?

Fascinatingly, Raghuram Rajan uses the example of communal barn raising as an example of why the very existence of a distant, centralized government can be more harmful to communities than its absence. His generalized analysis rested in part on a social anthropological study of southern Italy in 1950, where community involvement was appallingly dismal. For example, nuns ran a charity for orphans out of a monastery crumbling into disrepair – this in a town full of underemployed stone masons who did not volunteer their ample free time towards repairing an historical building of current valuable use.

> The state, despite being recognizably apathetic, distant and nonfunctional itself, nevertheless dampened initiative. The faint hope that the government will dig a latrine, pave a road, or discipline school teachers can prevent the local population from organizing to do so. In frontier towns in the United States, the community raised a barn or built a road itself, knowing there was no one else who would do it. In dysfunctional communities where the government is closer, the misplaced expectation that the ghost of the inefficient government will eventually appear and do the job crowds out what little private initiative there is.[285]

So not only is it far less effective, efficient and timely for local people to depend on a centralized government for almost everything, the very existence of that far off government in and of itself can squash local initiative.

Nothing is ever perfect. I always tell students and employees that Probability happens in Heaven; Statistics happen here on earth. There is no set of conditions set in stone and frozen forever that make for a happy society. In the boisterous tumult of our daily lives, with all our positive impulses, disagreements, jealousies, misunderstandings, religious convictions, tribal needs and overwhelming desire to steal our neighbor's smoker while he's away, if we all (mostly) act in (mostly) good faith and a belief in our fellow's good will, things will turn out all right.

You should buy two copies of this book – one to markup extensively for further study and one to store in a hermetically-sealed, temperature and humidity-controlled container away from direct light, protected from drastic environmental change of any kind. Use, abuse and peruse the first copy. Handle the second one with cotton gloves and never touch it again; your grandchildren will sell it to buy a small island somewhere nice. Actually, buy a dozen and hand copies out to your fellow citizens in need.

As a brilliant man full of more love for his fellow man on a daily basis than I can claim to be always said, "If you don't start somewhere, you'll never get nowhere." In the course of this long journey, I've thought often of Bob Marley[286] and how much more fun it would have been to put in long hours playing music with friends in a holy cloud than reading thousands of pages of often mean-spirited discourses on petty political fights. But he had his path and I have mine.

When one is mountain biking and there is a rock in the path ahead, if one stares at the rock, the front tire will hit the rock. If one stares ahead and to the side of the rock, the bike will not flip over and the rider will have a safe, fun outing. What you focus on becomes your reality. If you focus on the rocks in the road and the negativity all around you, your

---

[285] Rajan, Raghuram, The Third Pillar; How Markets and the State Leave the Community Behind, Penguin 2019, p.15

[286] Robert Nesta Marley (born 6 February 1945, Nine Mile, Jamaica; died 11 May 1981, Miami, USA)

future will be negative. If you focus on getting to know your neighbors, commit even one day of your time every three months to work on a community volunteer project, take the time to understand who your elected and appointed representatives are and keep constant pressure on those people to spend precious resources wisely, then you'll be doing what you can to make your street, city, state and country a better place to live.

We the people of the United States of America can get all hopped up on rational, data- and love-based populist patriotism and do the great, hard, and rewarding work of perfecting this imperfect, precious Union.

You ready?

Selected Bibliography

Adams, John, *Defence of the Constitutions of Government of the United States*, 1787

Alba, Richard, *The Great Demographic Illusion*, 2020

Allawi, Ali, *The Occupation of Iraq; Winning the War, Losing the Peace*, 2007

Allen, Arthur, *Review of Leeway: Field Experiments and Implementation*, 1999

Amenta, Edwin, *When Movements Matter: The Townsend Plan and the Rise of Social Security*, 2008

Andonov, A., Bauer, R., Cremers, M., "Pension Fund Asset Allocation and Liability Discount Rates: Camouflage and Reckless Risk taking by U.S. Public Plans?," May 2012

Bagehot, Walter, *Lombard Street: A Description of the Money Market*, 1873

Bagehot, Walter, *The English Constitution*, 1867

Bahcall, Safi, *Loonshots: How to Nurture the Crazy Ideas That Win Wars, Cure Diseases, and Transform Industries*, 2019

Bailyn, Bernard, *The Ideological Origins of the American Revolution*, 1967

Bailyn, Bernard, *The Ordeal of Thomas Hutchinson*, 1974

Bell, Jeffrey, *Populism and Elitism: Politics in the Age of Equality*, 1992

Bell, Jeffrey, *The Case for Polarized Politics: Why America Needs Social Conservatism*, 2012

Biggs, Andrew, Hassett, Kevin, Jensen, Matthew, "A Guide for Deficit Reduction in the United States Based on Historical Consolidations That Worked," American Enterprise Institute for Policy Research, December 2010

Bongino, Dan, *Spygate: The Attempted Sabotage of Donald J. Trump*, 2018

Borjas, George, *We Wanted Workers: Unraveling the Immigration Narrative*, 2016

Brookhiser, Richard, *America's First Dynasty: The Adamses, 1735–1918*

Bruder, Jessica, *Nomadland*, 2017

Buckley, F.H., *The Republican Workers Party: How the Trump Victory Drove Everyone Crazy, And Why it Was Just What We Needed,* 2018

Buffett, Howard G., *Our 50-State Border Crisis; How the Mexican Border Fuels the Drug Epidemic Across America,* Hachette Books, 2018

Cassel, Gustav, *Money and Foreign Exchange After 1914,* 1922

Chancellor, Edward, *Devil Take the Hindmost: A History of Financial Speculation,* 1999

Chandler, David Leon, *Henry Flagler; the Astonishing Life and Times of the Visionary Robber Baron Who Founded Florida,* MacMillan Publishing New York, 1986

Cogan, John F., *The High Cost of Good Intentions: A History of Federal Entitlement Programs*

Darity Jr., William A., *From Here to Equality,* 2020

Darwall, Rupert, *Green Tyranny: Exposing the Totalitarian Roots of the Climate Industrial Complex*

Davis, Stephen; Lukomnik, Jon; Pitt-Watson, David, *What They Do With Your Money: How the Financial System Fails Us and How to Fix It,* Yale, 2016

Dutton, Kevin, "What Psychopaths and Politicians Have in Common," Sept-Oct issue *American Scientific Mind,* 2016

Electronic Privacy Information Center (https://epic.org)

Embery, Paul, *Despised: Why the Modern Left Loathes the Working Class,* 2021

Fergusson, Adam, *When Money Dies, the Nightmare of the Weimar Collapse,* 1975

Fingar, Thomas, *Reducing Uncertainty,* 2011

Forbes, Steve, *Flat Tax Revolution,* Regenery Publishing, 2005

Franken, Al, *Al Franken: Giant of the Senate,* Hachette Book Group, 2017

Friedman, Milton, *Free to Choose,* 1980

Geithner, Timothy F., *Stress Test: Reflections on Financial Crises,* Crown, 2014

Goetzmann, William H., *Money Changes Everything,* Princeton, 2016

Greenburg, Michael M., *The Court-Martial of Paul Revere,* University Press of New England, 2014

Haldane, Andy, *The Short Long,* Bank of England Speech, May 2011, http://www.bankofengland.co.uk/archive/Documents/historicpubs/speeches/2011/speech495.pdf

Hawes, Jim, *Cold War Navy SEAL: My Story of Che Guevara, War in the Congo, and the Communist Threat in Africa*, 2018

Hayek, Friedrich, *The Road to Serfdom,* 1943

Hayek, Friedrich, "The Use of Knowledge in Society," 1945

Hiaasen, Carl, *Bad Monkey,* Alfred A. Knopf, New York, 2013

Himmelfarb, Gertrude, *The De-Moralization of Society*, 1995

Hoffer, Eric, *The True Believer: Thoughts on the Nature of Mass Movements,* 1951

Husock, Howard, *America's Trillion-Dollar Housing Mistake*, Ivan R. Dee, 2003

Isenberg, Nancy and Andrew Burstein, *The Problem of Democracy: The Presidents Adams Confront the Cult of Personality,*   2019

Jauhar, Sandeep, *Doctored: The Disillusionment of an American Physician*, 2014

Johnson, KC & Taylor, Stuart, *The Campus Rape Frenzy: The Attack on Due Process at America's Universities*, 2017

Kaiser, Robert G., *Act of Congress; How America's Essential Institution Works, and how it Doesn't*, Knopf Borzoi, 2013

Keynes, John Maynard, *Indian Currency and Finance,* 1913

Keynes, John M., *The General Theory of Employment, Interest and Money,* 1936

Kurtz, Stanley, *Spreading the Wealth: How Obama is Robbing the Suburbs to Pay for the Cities*, 2012

Lambert, Andrew, *Seapower States*, Yale 2018

Lasch, Christopher, *The Revolt of the Elites,* 1994

Lyon, Matthew, *The Scourge of Aristocracy and Repository of Important Political Truth*, 1798

Magnet, Myron, *Clarence Thomas and the Lost Constitution*, Encounter Books, 2019

Mahar, Maggie, *Money-Driven Medicine; the Real Reason Healthcare Costs So Much*, HarperCollins, 2006

Markoe, Peter, The Algerine Spy in Pennsylvania, 1797

Mauss, Marcel, *The Gift: Form and Reason for Exchange in Archaic Societies,* trans. W.D. Halls, 1990, Norton, New York; original *Essai sur le Don,* 1950, Presses Universitaires de France

Mosher, Steven W, *Bully of Asia: Why China's Dream is the New Threat to World Order"*

Muir, Tamsyn, *Gideon the Ninth,* 2019

Muravchik, Joshua, *Liberal Oasis, the Truth about Israel*, 2014

Olson, Mancur, *The Rise and Decline of Nations,* 1982

Orwell, George, *The Road to Wigan Pier*, 1937

Pasquale, Frank, *The Black Box Society; the Secret Algorithms that Control Money and Information,* Harvard, 2015

Paul, Ron, *End the Fed,* 2009

Pillsbury, Michael, *The Hundred Year Marathon,* 2015

Powell, Sidney, *Licensed to Lie: Exposing Corruption in the Department of Justice, 2nd edition,* 2018.

Pfaff, John F., *Locked In: The True Causes of Mass Incarceration and How to Achieve Real Reform,* 2017

Philipsen, Dirk, *The Little Big Number; How GDP Came to Rule the World and What to do About it,* Princeton, 2015

Phillips, Andrew, and Sharman, J.C., *Outsourcing Empire: How Company-States Made the Modern World,"* Princeton University Press, 2020

Polybius, *The Histories,* 146 BC

Portes, Alejandro & Rumbaut, Ruben G., "Legacies: The Story of the Immigrant Second Generation," 2011

Potter, Wendell & Penniman, Nick, *Nation on the Take,* Bloomsbury Press, 2016

Putnam, Robert, *Bowling Alone,* 2000

Quinn, Sarah, American Bonds: How Credit Markets Shaped a Nation, Princeton 2019

Radosh, Ron, *Commies: A Journey Through the Old Left, the New Left, and the Leftover Left,* 2001

Ricardo, David, *The Principles of Political Economy and Taxation*, 1817

Rickards, James, *The Death of Money: The Coming Collapse of the International Monetary System*, Portfolio/Penguin, 2014

Rothstein, Richard, The Color of Law: A Forgotten History of How Our Government Segregated America, 2017

Rosett, Claudia, *What To Do About the UN,* Encounter Broadsides, 2017

Rothman, Noah*, Unjust: Social Justice and the Unmaking of America*, Regnery Publishing, 2019

Sanandaji, Nima, *Debunking Utopia: Exposing the Myth of Nordic Socialism*, 2016

Sasse, Ben, *Them: Why We Hate Each Other--and How to Heal*, 2018

Sasse, Ben, *The Vanishing American Adult: Our Coming-of-Age Crisis--and How to Rebuild a Culture of Self-Reliance*, 2017

Scalia, Antonin, *A Matter of Interpretation: Federal Courts and the Law*, 1997

Schlesinger Jr., Arthur, *The Disuniting of America, Reflections on a Multicultural Society*, 1991

Shellenberger, Michael, *Apocalypse Never: Why Environmental Alarmism Hurts Us*, 2020

Shelton, Judy, *Money Meltdown: Restoring Order to the Global Currency System,* Free Press, 1994

Shlaes, Amity, *Coolidge,* 2013

Shlaes, Amity, *Great Society: A New History*, 2020

Shlaes, Amity, *The Forgotten Man: A New History of the Great Depression*, 2007

Smith, Adam, *The Theory of Moral Sentiments*, 1759

Smith, Adam, *The Wealth of Nations*, 1776

Smith, David, *The Rise and Fall of Monetarism*, 1991

Somary, Felix, *The Raven of Zurich*, 1960

Sowell, Thomas, *Discrimination & Disparities*, 2018

Sprenger, Jacob, *Malleus Maleficarum,* 1486, Speyer

Starr, Paul, *The Social Transformation of American Medicine,* 1982

Stephens, Bret, *America in Retreat: The New Isolationism and the Coming Global Disorder,* 2015

Stevenson, Bryan, *Just Mercy,* 2015

Stockman, David A, *The Great Deformation: The Corruption of Capitalism in America, 2013*

Stringham, Edward P., *Private Governance: Creating Order in Economic and Social Life*, 2015

Sufi, Amir & Mian, Artif, *House of Debt: How They (and You) Caused the Great Recession and How We Can Prevent It from Happening Again*, University of Chicago Press, 2014

Tamny, John, *Who Needs the Fed? What Taylor Swift, Uber and Robots Tell Us about Money Credit and Why We Should Abolish America's Central Bank*, Encounter Books, 2016

Tartakovksy, Joseph, *The Lives of the Constitution: Ten Exceptional Minds that Shaped America's Supreme Law,* 2018

Thompson, C. Bradley, *America's Revolutionary Mind*, 2019

Tomasi, John, *Free Market Fairness*, 2012

Trammel, Joe, The CEO Tightrope: How to Master the Balancing Act of a Successful CEO

U.S. Commission on Civil Rights, "Peaceful Coexistence: Reconciling Nondiscrimination Principles with Civil Liberties," September 2016

Wasow, Omar, "Agenda Seeding: How 1960s Black Protests Moved Elites, Public Opinion and Voting," *American Political Science Review,* 13 February 2020

Weeden, Jason & Kurzban, Robert, The Hidden Agenda of the Political Mind: How Self-Interest Shapes Our Opinions and Why We Won't Admit It, Princeton, 2014

Wood, Peter W., *1620: A Critical Response to the 1619 Project*, 2020

Yang, Jia Lynn, *One Mighty and Irresistible Tide; The Epic Struggle Over American Immigration, 1924-1965,* Norton Books, 2020

Young, Patrick L., *Capital Markets Revolution: The Future of Markets in an Online World,* Financial Times / Prentice Hall, 1999

About the Author

Florida Man Christopher Messina loves living in the Last Free State in America, where he honed his skills wrangling Swamp Beasts. New York born, educated at the University of Chicago, University of Sydney and University of New South Wales, he is a markets-focused executive and entrepreneur with thirty years of deep, international experience in the global capital markets, commodities and advanced technology.

He is the host of the Messy Times podcast, a devoted father and husband and in the little spare time he has, a flyfishing fanatic and birder flirting with Big Lister status.

Made in the USA
Columbia, SC
27 October 2024

45139446R00291